T0280666

Expert MySQL

■ ■ ■

Charles A. Bell

Apress®

Expert MySQL

Copyright © 2007 by Charles A. Bell

All rights reserved. No part of this work may be reproduced or transmitted in any form or by any means, electronic or mechanical, including photocopying, recording, or by any information storage or retrieval system, without the prior written permission of the copyright owner and the publisher.

ISBN 978-1-59059-741-5

ISBN 978-1-4302-0346-9 (eBook)

Trademarked names, logos, and images may appear in this book. Rather than use a trademark symbol with every occurrence of a trademarked name, logo, or image we use the names, logos, and images only in an editorial fashion and to the benefit of the trademark owner, with no intention of infringement of the trademark.

The use in this publication of trade names, trademarks, service marks, and similar terms, even if they are not identified as such, is not to be taken as an expression of opinion as to whether or not they are subject to proprietary rights.

President and Publisher: Paul Manning
Lead Editor: Jason Gilmore
Technical Reviewers: Mike Kruckenberg, Lorraine Parker, Mikael Ronström
Editorial Board: Steve Anglin, Mark Beckner, Ewan Buckingham, Gary Cornell, Jonathan Gennick, Jonathan Hassell, Michelle Lowman, James Markham, Matthew Moodie, Jeff Olson, Jeffrey Pepper, Frank Pohlmann, Douglas Pundick, Ben Renow-Clarke, Dominic Shakeshaft, Matt Wade, Tom Welsh
Coordinating Editor: Tracy Brown Collins
Copy Editor: Liz Welch
Compositor: Susan Glinert
Indexer: Valerie Perry
Cover Designer: Anna Ishchenko

Distributed to the book trade worldwide by Springer Science+Business Media, LLC., 233 Spring Street, 6th Floor, New York, NY 10013. Phone 1-800-SPRINGER, fax (201) 348-4505, e-mail orders-ny@springer-sbm.com, or visit www.springeronline.com.

For information on translations, please e-mail rights@apress.com, or visit www.apress.com.

Apress and friends of ED books may be purchased in bulk for academic, corporate, or promotional use. eBook versions and licenses are also available for most titles. For more information, reference our Special Bulk Sales–eBook Licensing web page at www.apress.com/bulk-sales.

The information in this book is distributed on an "as is" basis, without warranty. Although every precaution has been taken in the preparation of this work, neither the author(s) nor Apress shall have any liability to any person or entity with respect to any loss or damage caused or alleged to be caused directly or indirectly by the information contained in this work.

The source code for this book is available to readers at www.apress.com. You will need to answer questions pertaining to this book in order to successfully download the code.

Contents at a Glance

PART 1 ■■■ Getting Started with MySQL Development

PART 2 ■■■ Extending MySQL

PART 3 ■■■ Advanced Database Internals

Contents

PART 1 ■■■ Getting Started with MySQL Development

PART 2 ▪▪▪ **Extending MySQL**

PART 3 ■■■ Advanced Database Internals

About the Author

CHARLES A. BELL conducts research in emerging technologies. He is an adjunct professor at Virginia Commonwealth University, where he teaches graduate-level computer science courses. He recently joined MySQL AB as a senior software developer. He lives in a small town in rural Virginia with his loving wife. Chuck received his Doctor of Philosophy in Engineering from Virginia Commonwealth University in 2005. His research interests include database systems, versioning systems, semantic web, and agile software development.

Chuck's research projects and development of an advanced database versioning system make him uniquely qualified to author this book. He is an expert in the database field and has extensive knowledge and experience in modifying the MySQL source code. With over 25 years' experience in enterprise development and systems architecture, Chuck is well qualified to create a book that gives excellent insight into developing and modifying open source systems.

Acknowledgments

I would like to thank all of the many talented and energetic professionals at Apress. My editor, Jason Gilmore, and project manager, Tracy Brown Collins, are wonderfully patient and insightful. Their efforts kept this book on track and me accountable. I also have to thank my production editor, Katie Stence, and copy editor, Liz Welch, for making me look so good in print. Thank you both very much!

I'd like to especially thank the technical reviewers: L. M. Parker and Mikael Ronström for their tireless commitment and for pushing me to the height of excellence, as well as Michael Kruckenberg for keeping my many programming examples on the right track and for his unique insight and experience with MySQL. I can now say I've worked with the best of the best.

Most importantly, I want to thank my wife Annette for her unending patience and understanding.

Introduction

MySQL has been identified as the world's most popular open source database and the fastest-growing database system in the industry. MySQL AB is reporting over 8 million active installations and nearly 50,000 downloads per day. MySQL is rapidly becoming the database system of choice for system integrators. According to an article in the *SD Times*, MySQL is now the number three "Top Deployed Database" in a recent survey of over 900 readers (www.mysql.com/why-mysql/marketshare/).

This book presents some advanced database system topics, examines the MySQL architecture, and provides an expert's workbook for examining, integrating, and modifying the MySQL source code for use in enterprise environments. The book provides insight into how to modify the MySQL system to meet the unique needs of system integrators and educators alike.

How This Book Is Organized

The material is divided into three parts. Each part is designed to present a set of topics ranging from introductory material on MySQL and the open source revolution to extending and customizing the MySQL system and even how to build an experimental query optimizer and execution engine as an alternative to the MySQL query engine.

Part 1

The first part of the book, "Getting Started with MySQL Development," is used to introduce concepts in developing and modifying open source systems. Part 1 provides you with the tools and resources necessary to begin exploring the more advanced database concepts presented in the rest of the book.

Chapter 1, "MySQL and the Open Source Revolution," is less technical and contains more narration than the rest of the book. It guides you through the benefits and responsibilities of an open source system integrator. It highlights the rapid growth of MySQL and its importance in the open source and database system markets. Additionally, it provides a clear perspective of the open source revolution.

Chapter 2, "The Anatomy of a Database System," covers the basics of what a database system is and how it is constructed. The anatomy of the MySQL system is used to illustrate the key components of modern relational database systems.

Chapter 3, "A Tour of the MySQL Source Code," presents a complete introduction to the MySQL source along with how to obtain and build the system. You are introduced to the mechanics of the source code along with coding guidelines and best practices for how the code is maintained.

Chapter 4, "Test-Driven MySQL Development," introduces a key element in generating high-quality extensions to the MySQL system. Software testing is presented along with the common practices of how to test large systems. Specific examples are used to illustrate the accepted practices of testing the MySQL system.

Part 2

Part 2, "Extending MySQL," uses a hands-on approach to investigate the MySQL system. It introduces you to how the MySQL code can be modified and how the system can be used as an embedded database system. Examples and projects are used to illustrate how to debug the source code, how to modify the SQL commands to extend the language, and how to build a custom storage engine.

Chapter 5, "Debugging," examines debugging skills and techniques that help make development easier and less prone to failure. Several debugging techniques are presented, along with the pros and cons of each.

Chapter 6, "Embedded MySQL," provides a tutorial on embedding the MySQL system in enterprise applications. Example projects assist you in applying the skills you'll learn to your own integration needs.

Chapter 7, "Building Your Own Storage Engine," is the first of the MySQL modification chapters. It demonstrates techniques that require the least amount of modifications to the MySQL code. The MySQL pluggable storage engine capability is explored, using examples and projects that permit you to build a sample storage engine.

Chapter 8, "Adding Functions and Commands to MySQL," presents the most popular modification to the MySQL code. You are shown how to modify the SQL commands and how to build custom SQL commands. The chapter includes examples of how to modify SQL commands to add new parameters, functions, and new commands.

Part 3

Part 3, "Advanced Database Internals," takes a deeper look into the MySQL system and provides you with an insider's look at what makes the system work. The part begins with an introduction to the advanced database technologies. Theory and practices are presented in a no-nonsense manner to enable you to apply the knowledge gained to tackle the more complex topics of database systems. This part also presents examples of how to implement an internal query representation, an alternative query optimizer, and an alternative query execution mechanism. Examples and projects are discussed in detail. Chapters 10 through 12 show you how to alter the internal structure of the MySQL system to implement an alternative query processing mechanism. These chapters provide you with a unique insight into how large systems can be built and modified.

Chapter 9, "Database Systems Internals," presents advanced database techniques and examines the MySQL architecture. Topics include query execution, multiuser concerns, and programmatic considerations.

Chapter 10, "Internal Query Representation," discusses the MySQL internal query representation. You are provided with an example alternative query representation. A discussion is included of how to alter the MySQL source code to implement an alternative query representation.

Chapter 11, "Query Optimization," presents the MySQL internal query optimizer. The chapter includes an example alternative query optimizer that uses the alternative query representation from the previous chapter. You'll learn how to alter the MySQL source code to implement the alternative query optimizer.

Chapter 12, "Query Execution," combines the techniques from the previous chapters to provide you with instructions on how to modify the MySQL system to implement alternative query processing engine techniques.

Appendix

The appendix provides a list of resources on MySQL, database systems, and open source software.

Using the Book for Teaching Database Systems Internals

Many excellent database texts are available that offer coverage of relational theory and practice. However, few offer material suitable for a classroom or lab environment. Even fewer resources are available for students to explore the inner workings of database systems. This book offers an opportunity for instructors to augment their database classes with hands-on labs. There are three ways that this text can be used in a classroom setting.

The text can be used to add depth to an introductory undergraduate or graduate database course. Parts 1 and 2 can be used to provide in-depth coverage of special topics in database systems. Suggested topics for lectures include those presented in Chapters 2, 3, 4, and 6. These topics can be used in addition to more traditional database theory or systems texts. Hands-on exercises or class projects can be drawn from Chapters 6 and 8.

An advanced database course for undergraduate or graduate students can be based on Parts 1 and 2, where each chapter can be presented over the course of 8 to 12 weeks. The remainder of the lectures can be spent on discussing the implementation of physical storage layers and the notion of storage engines. Semester projects can be based on Chapter 7 and allow students to build their own storage engines.

A special-topics course on database systems internals for the senior undergraduate or graduate students can be based on the entire text, with lectures based on the first nine chapters. Semester projects can be derived from Part 3 and allow students to implement the remaining features of the database experimental platform. These features include applications of language theory, query optimizers, and query execution algorithms.

Let's Get Started!

I have written this book with a wide variety of readers in mind. Whether you have been working in database systems for years, or maybe have taken an introductory database theory class, or even read a good Apress book on MySQL, you will get a lot out of this book. Best of all, if you ever wanted to know what makes a database system like MySQL tick, you can even get your hands on the source code!

PART 1

■■■
Getting Started with MySQL Development

This part introduces you to concepts in developing and modifying open source systems. Chapter 1 guides you through the benefits and responsibilities of an open source system integrator. It highlights the rapid growth of MySQL and its importance in the open source and database system markets. Chapter 2 covers the basics of what a database system is and how it is constructed. Chapter 3 provides a complete introduction to the MySQL source presented in this chapter along with how to obtain and build the system. Chapter 4 introduces a key element in generating high-quality extensions to the MySQL system. You'll learn about software testing as well as common practices for testing large systems.

CHAPTER 1

■ ■ ■

MySQL and the Open Source Revolution

Open source systems are rapidly becoming a force that is changing the software landscape. Information technology professionals everywhere are taking note of the high-quality, and in many cases world-class, development and support offered by open source software vendors. Corporations are paying attention because for the first time they have an alternative to the commercial proprietary software vendors. Small businesses are paying attention because open source software can significantly lower the cost of their information systems. Individuals are paying attention because they have more choices with more options than ever before. The majority of the underpinnings that make the Internet what it is today are based on open source software such as Linux, Apache HTTP server, BIND, Sendmail, OpenSSL, MySQL, and many others.

The most common business objective that drives the choice to use open source software is cost. Open source software, by its very nature, reduces the total cost of ownership (TCO) and provides a viable business model on which businesses can build or improve their markets. In the case of open source database systems, this is especially true. The cost of commercial proprietary database systems begins in the multiple thousands of dollars and, by the time you add support costs, can easily go into the tens or hundreds of thousands of dollars.

It used to be that open source software was considered by many to be limited to the hobbyist or hacker bent on subverting the market of large commercial software companies. Although it may be true that some developers feel they are playing the role of David to Microsoft's Goliath, the open source community is not about that at all. The open source community does not profess to be a replacement for commercial proprietary software, but rather they propose the open source philosophy as an alternative solution. As you will see in this chapter, not only is open source a viable alternative to commercial software, but it is also fueling a worldwide revolution of how software is developed and marketed.

■**Note** In this book, the term *hacker* refers to Richard Stallman's definition of hacker: "someone who loves to program and enjoys being clever about," and not the common perception of nefarious villain bent on stealing credit cards and damaging computer systems.

The following section is provided for those who may not be familiar with open source software or the philosophy of MySQL. If you are already familiar with open source software philosophy, you can skip to the section "Developing with MySQL."

What Is Open Source Software?

Open source software grew from a conscious resistance to the corporate property mind-set. While working for the Artificial Intelligence Lab at the Massachusetts Institute of Technology (MIT), Richard Stallman began a code-sharing movement in the 1970s. Fueled by the desire to make commonly used code available to all programmers, Stallman saw the need for a cooperating community of developers. This philosophy worked well for Stallman and his small community—that is, until the industry collectively decided software was property and not something that should be shared with potential competitors. This resulted in many of the MIT researchers being lured away from MIT to work for these corporations. Eventually, the cooperative community faded away.

Fortunately, Stallman resisted the trend and left MIT to start the GNU (GNU Not Unix) project and the Free Software Foundation (FSF). The goal of the GNU project was to produce a free Unix-like operating system. This system would be free (including access to the source code) and available to anyone. The concept of free was to not prohibit anyone from using and modifying the system.

Stallman's goal was to reestablish the cooperating community of developers that worked so well at MIT. However, Stallman had the foresight to realize the system needed a copyright license that guaranteed certain freedoms. (Some have coined Stallman's take on copyright as "copyleft" as it guarantees freedom rather than restricts it.) Stallman created the GNU Public License (GPL). The GPL is a clever work of legal permissions that permits the code to be copied and modified without restriction, and states that derivative works (the modified copies) must be distributed under the same license as the original version without any additional restrictions. Essentially, this uses the copyright laws against copyrights by removing the proprietary element altogether.

Unfortunately, Stallman's GNU project never fully materialized, but several portions have become essential elements of many open source systems. The most successful of these include the GNU compilers for the C programming language (GCC) and the GNU text editor (Emacs). Although the GNU operating system failed to be completed, the pioneering efforts of Stallman and his followers permitted Linus Torvalds to fill the gap with his then-infant Linux operating system in 1991. Linux has become the free Unix-like operating system that Stallman envisioned (see the sidebar "Why Is Linux So Popular?"). Today, Linux is the world's most popular and successful open source operating system.

WHY IS LINUX SO POPULAR?

Linux is a Unix-like operating system built on the open source model. It is therefore free for anyone to use, distribute, and modify. Linux is built using a conservative kernel design that has proven to be easy to evolve and improve. Since its release in 1991, Linux has gained a worldwide following of developers who seek to improve its performance and reliability. Some may even claim Linux is the most well developed of all operating systems. Since its release, Linux has gained a significant market share of the world's server and workstation installations. Linux is often cited as the most successful open source endeavor to date.

There was one problem with the free software movement. Free was intended to guarantee freedom to use, modify, and distribute, not free as in no cost or free-to-a-good home (often explained as "free" as free speech, not "free" as in free beer). To counter this misconception, the Open Source Initiative (OSI) was formed and later adopted and promoted the phrase "open source" to describe the freedoms guaranteed by the GPL; visit the web site at www.opensource.org.

The efforts of the OSI changed the free software movement. Software developers were given the opportunity to distinguish between free software that is truly no cost and open software that was part of the cooperative community. With the explosion of the Internet, the cooperative community has become a global community of developers. This global community of developers is what ensures the continuation of Stallman's vision.

Open source software therefore is software that is licensed to guarantee the rights of developers to use, copy, modify, and distribute their software while participating in a cooperative community whose natural goals are the growth and fostering of higher-quality software. Open source does not mean zero cost. It does mean anyone can participate in the development of the software and can, in turn, use the software without incurring a fee. On the other hand, many open source systems are hosted and distributed by organizations that sell support services for the software. This permits organizations that use the software to lower their information technology costs by eliminating startup costs and in many cases saving a great deal on maintenance.

All open source systems today draw their lineage from the foundations of the work that Stallman and others produced in an effort to create a software utopia in which Stallman believed organizations should generate revenue from selling services, not proprietary property rights. There are several examples of Stallman's vision becoming reality. The GNU/Linux (henceforth referred to as Linux) movement has spawned numerous successful (and profitable) companies, such as Red Hat and Slackware, that sell customized distributions and support for Linux. Another example is MySQL, which has become the most successful open source database system.

Although the concept of a software utopia is arguably not a reality today, it is possible to download an entire suite of systems and tools to power a personal or business computer without spending any money on the software itself. No-cost versions of software ranging from operating systems and server systems such as database and web servers to productivity software are available for anyone to download and use.

Why Use Open Source Software?

Sooner or later, someone is going to ask why using open source software is a good idea. To successfully fend off the ensuing challenges from proponents of commercial proprietary software, you should have a solid answer. The most important reasons for adopting open source software are

- Open source software costs little or nothing to use. This is especially important for nonprofits, universities, and community organizations whose budgets are constantly shrinking and that must do more with less every year.

- Open source software permits you to modify it to meet your specific needs.

- The licensing mechanisms available are more flexible than commercial licenses.

- Open source software is more robust (tested) than commercial proprietary software.

- Open source software is more reliable and secure than commercial proprietary software.

Although it is likely you won't be challenged or asked to demonstrate any of these reasons for adopting open source software, you are more likely to be challenged by contradiction. That is, proponents of commercial proprietary software (opponents of open source) will attempt to discredit these claims by making statements about why you shouldn't use open source software for development. Let's examine some of the more popular reasons not to use open source software from a commercial proprietary software viewpoint and refute them with the open source view.

Myth 1: Commercial Proprietary Software Fosters Greater Creativity

The argument goes: most enterprise-level commercial proprietary software provide application programming interfaces (API) that permit developers to extend their functionality, thus making them more flexible and ensuring greater creativity for developers.

Portions of this statement are true. APIs do permit developers to extend the software, but they often do so in a way that strictly prohibits developers from adding functionality to the base software. These APIs often force the developer into a sandbox, further restricting her creativity.

■**Note** Sandboxes are often created to limit the developer's ability to affect the core system. The main reason for doing this has to do with security. The more open the API is, the more likely it is for villainous developers to create malicious code to damage the system or its data.

Open source software may also support and provide APIs, but open source provides developers with the ability to see the actual source code of the core system. Not only can they see the source code, they are free (and encouraged) to modify it! Some of the reasons you may want to modify the core system are when a critical feature isn't available or you need the system to read or write a specific format. Therefore, open source software fosters greater creativity than commercial proprietary software.

Myth 2: Commercial Proprietary Software Is More Secure Than Open Source Software

The argument goes: organizations require their information systems in today's Internet-connected society to be more secure than ever before. Commercial proprietary software is inherently more secure because the company that sells the software has a greater stake in ensuring their products can stand against the onslaught of today's digital predators.

Although the goals of this statement are quite likely to appear on a boardroom wall as a mantra for any commercial software vendor, the realization of this goal, or in some cases marketing claim, is often misleading or unobtainable. Let's consider the Microsoft Windows server operating system. It can be shown that the Windows server operating system is less secure than Linux. While Microsoft has built in a successful and efficient patch system to ensure installations are kept free from exposed vulnerabilities, the fact that these mechanisms are part of everyday server maintenance is reason enough to consider that Microsoft hasn't obtained a level of security that is sufficient to ward off attacks. (Sadly, some would say as long as there is a Microsoft there will be digital predators.)

The main reason why Linux is more secure than Windows is because the global community of developers who have worked on Linux have worked together to ensure the system is protected against attacks (also called *hardening*). In the case of Linux, many developers throughout the world are working toward hardening the system. The more developers working on the problem, the more creative ways there are to solve it. When new vulnerabilities are discovered in Linux, they are fixed quickly and the door is slammed in the predator's face.

Microsoft, on the other hand, has far fewer developers to devote to hardening Windows and therefore fewer ideas on how to solve the problem. Thus, the hardening of Windows will be a much longer course than Linux. This argument probably isn't true for all open source software, but it does show that open source systems can adapt to threats and become more secure than commercial proprietary software.

Myth 3: Commercial Proprietary Software Is Tested More Than Open Source Software

The argument goes: software vendors sell software. The products they sell must maintain a standard of high quality or customers won't buy them. Open source software is not under any such pressure and therefore is not tested as stringently as commercial proprietary software.

This argument is very compelling. In fact, it sings to the hearts of all information technology acquisition agents. They are convinced paying for something means it is more reliable and freer of defects than software that can be acquired without a fee. Unfortunately, these individuals are overlooking one important concept of open source software.

Open source software is developed by a global community of developers, many of whom consider their role as defect detectives (testers). These individuals pride themselves on finding and reporting defects. In some cases, open source software companies have offered rewards for developers who find repeatable bugs. MySQL AB offers a significant reward for finding bugs in their MySQL database system. At the time of this writing, MySQL AB was offering a free Apple iPod nano to anyone who finds a repeatable bug in their software. Now, that's an incentive!

It is true that software vendors employ software testers (and no doubt they are the best in their field), but more often than not commercial software projects are pushed toward a specific deadline. These deadlines are put in place to ensure a strategic release date or competitive advantage. Many times these deadlines force software vendors to compromise on portions of their software development process—which is usually the later part: testing. As you can imagine, reducing a tester's access to the software (testing time) means they will find fewer defects.

Open source software companies, by enlisting the help and support of the global community of developers, ensure that their software is tested more often by more people. Therefore, open source software is tested more than commercial software.

Myth 4: Commercial Proprietary Systems Have More Complex Capabilities and More Complete Feature Sets Than Open Source Systems

The argument goes: commercial proprietary database systems are sophisticated and complex server systems. Open source systems are neither large nor complex enough to handle mission-critical enterprise data.

Although it is true that some open source systems are good imitations of the commercial systems they mimic, the same cannot be said for a database system such as MySQL. Earlier versions of MySQL did not have all of the features found in commercial proprietary database systems. However, with the release of version 5.0, MySQL has all of the advanced features of the commercial proprietary database systems.

Furthermore, MySQL has been shown to provide the reliability, performance, and scalability that large enterprises require for mission-critical data. Indeed, many well-known organizations use MySQL for mission-critical data. Therefore, MySQL is one example of an open source system that offers all of the features and capabilities of the best commercial proprietary database systems.

Myth 5: Commercial Proprietary Software Vendors Are More Responsive Because They Have a Dedicated Staff

The argument goes: when a software system is purchased, the software comes with the assurances that the company that produced the software is available for assistance or to help solve problems. Open source systems, by the very nature that no one "owns" it, means that it is far more difficult to contact anyone for assistance.

Most open source software is built by the global community of developers. However, the growing trend is to base a business model on the open source philosophy and build a company around it selling support and services for the software that they oversee. In fact, most of the major open source products are supported in this manner. For instance, MySQL AB owns the source code for their MySQL product. (For a complete description of MySQL's open source license, see `www.mysql.com/company/legal/licensing/opensource-license.htm`.) MySQL AB provides a wide range of support options, including 24×7 coverage and response times as low as 30 minutes.

Developers who develop open source software respond much more quickly to issues and problems than commercial developers. In fact, it can be nearly impossible to talk to a commercial software developer directly. Microsoft has a comprehensive support mechanism in place and can meet the needs of just about any organization. However, if you want to talk to a developer of a Microsoft product, you will have to go through proper channels. This requires talking to every stage of the support hierarchy—and even then are you not guaranteed contact with the developer.

Open source developers, on the other hand, use the Internet as their primary form of communication. Since they are already on the Internet, they are much more likely to see your question appear in a forum or news group. Additionally, open source companies like MySQL AB actively monitor their community and can respond quickly to their customers.

Therefore, it is not true that purchasing commercial proprietary software guarantees you quicker response times than open source software. It has been shown that in many cases open source software developers are more responsive (reachable) than commercial software developers.

What If They Want Proof?

I've listed just a few of the arguments that are likely to cause you grief as you attempt to adopt open source software in your organization. Several researchers have attempted to prove arguments such as these. One researcher, James W. Paulson, has conducted an empirical study of open source and commercial proprietary software (he calls it "closed"), which examines the preceding arguments and proves that open source software development can demonstrate measurable improvements over commercial proprietary software development. See Paulson's article, "An Empirical Study of Open-Source and Closed-Source Software Products," in the April 2004 issue of *IEEE Transactions on Software Engineering*.

Is Open Source Really a Threat to Commercial Software?

Until recently, open source software was not considered a threat to the commercial proprietary software giants. The two largest commercial competitors to MySQL AB are beginning to exhibit the classic signs of competitive threat. Microsoft continues to speak out against open source software, denouncing MySQL as a world-class database server while passively ignoring the threat. However, Oracle is taking a considerably different tactic.

Oracle has recently gone on a corporate spending spree, purchasing open source companies SleepyCat and Innobase. Both companies provide solutions that are part of the MySQL system. While support agreements are in place and no immediate consequences are expected from this maneuver, industry pundits agree that despite Oracle's claim of innocent diversification, the database giant is hedging its bets and staking a claim in the open source database segment. With an estimated $12 billion database server market projected for 2007 the stakes are clearly profit and market share.

Perhaps the most telling betrayal of Oracle's misdirected innocence is its recent attempt to purchase MySQL AB. What better example of a threat can one find than one's closest competitor desiring to own what you have? MySQL AB deserves great praise in standing their ground and refusing to sell their endeavors. Few would blame them for cashing in and enjoying their fortunes. However, the strength of the philosophy that is the open source world has prevailed and the CEOs of MySQL AB felt there is more to be gained by continuing their quest for becoming the world's best database system.

The pressure of competition isn't limited to MySQL versus proprietary database systems. At least one open source database system, Apache Derby, is touting itself as an alternative to MySQL and has recently tossed its hat into the ring as a replacement for the "M" in the LAMP stack (see the sidebar "What Is the LAMP Stack?"). Proponents for Apache Derby cite licensing issues with MySQL and feature limitations. Neither has deterred the MySQL install base, nor have these "issues" limited MySQL's increasing popularity.

WHAT IS THE LAMP STACK?

LAMP stands for Linux, Apache, MySQL, and PHP/Perl/Python. The LAMP stack is a set of open source servers, services, and programming languages that permit rapid development and deployment of high-quality web applications. The key components are

- *Linux*: A Unix-like operating system. Linux is known for its high degree of reliability and speed as well as its vast diversity of supported hardware platforms.

- *Apache*: A web application server known for its high reliability and ease of configuration. Apache runs on most Unix operating systems.

- *MySQL*: The database system of choice for many web application developers. MySQL is known for its speed and small execution footprint.

- *PHP/Perl/Python*: These are all scripting languages that can be embedded in HTML web pages for programmatic execution of events. These scripting languages represent the active programming element of the LAMP stack. They are used to interface with system resources and back-end database systems to provide active content to the user. While most LAMP developers prefer PHP over the other scripting languages, each can be used to successfully develop web applications.

There are many advantages to using the LAMP stack for development. The greatest advantage is cost. All of the LAMP components are available as no-cost open source licenses. Organizations can download, install, and develop web applications in a matter of hours with little or no initial cost for the software.

An interesting indicator of the benefits of offering an open source database system is the recent offering of "free" versions from some of the proprietary database vendors. Microsoft, which has been a vocal opponent of open source software, now offers a no-cost version of its SQL Server 2005 database system called SQL Server Express. Although there is no cost for downloading the software and you are permitted to distribute the software with your application, you are not permitted to see the source code or modify it in any way. Oracle also offers a "free" version of its database system called Oracle Database Express Edition. Like Microsoft, Oracle grants you a no-cost download and the right to distribute the server with your application, but does not permit modification or access to the source code. Both of these products have reduced features (Oracle more so) and are not scalable to a full enterprise-level database server without purchasing additional software and services.

Clearly, the path that MySQL AB is blazing with its MySQL server products demonstrates a threat to the proprietary database market—a threat that the commercial proprietary software industry is taking seriously. Whatever the facts concerning Oracle's recent open source spending spree (we may never know), it is clear they are reacting to the threat of MySQL AB. Although Microsoft continues to try to detract from the open source software market, they too are starting to see the wisdom of no-cost software.

Legal Issues and the GNU Manifesto

Commercial proprietary software licenses are designed to limit your freedoms and to restrict your use. Most commercial licenses state clearly that you, the purchaser of the software, do not own the software but are permitted to use the software under very specific conditions. In almost all cases, this means you cannot copy, distribute, or modify the system in any way. These licenses also make it clear that the source code is owned exclusively by the licenser and you, the licensee, are not permitted to see or reengineer it.

Open source systems are generally licensed using a GNU-based license agreement (GNU stands for GNU, not Unix). Most permit free use of the original source code with a restriction that all modifications be made public or returned to the originator as legal ownership. Furthermore, most open source systems use the GPL agreement, which states that it is intended to guarantee your rights to copy, distribute, and modify the software. It is interesting to note that the GPL does not limit your rights in how you use the software. In fact, the GPL specifically grants you the right to use the software however you want. The GPL also guarantees your right to have access to the source code. All of these rights are specified in the GNU Manifesto and the GPL agreement (`www.gnu.org/licenses/gpl.html`).

What is most interesting, the GPL specifically permits you to charge a distribution fee (or media fee) for distribution of the original source and provides you the right to use the system in whole or modified in order to create a derivative product, which is also protected under the same GPL. The only catch is you are required to make your modified source code available to anyone who wants it.

These limitations do not prohibit you from generating revenue from your hard work. On the contrary, as long as you turn over your source code by publishing it via the original owner, you can charge your customers for your derivative work. Some may argue that this means you can never gain a true competitive advantage because your source code is available to everyone. However, the opposite is true in practice. Vendors such as Red Hat and MySQL AB have profited from business models based on the GPL.

The only limitations of the GPL that may cause you pause is the limitation on warranties and the requirement to place a banner in your software stating the derivation (original and license) of the work.

A limitation on expressed warranties isn't that surprising if you consider that most commercial licenses include similar clauses. The part that makes the GPL unique is the concept of nonliable loss. The GPL specifically frees the originator and you, the modifier (or distributor), from loss or damage as a result of the installation or use of the software. Stallman did not want the legal industry to cash in should there ever be a question of liability of open source software. The logic is simple. You obtained the software for free and you did not get any assurances for its performance or protection from damages as a result of using the software. In this case, there is no quid pro quo and thus no warranty of any kind.

Opponents of the open source movement will cite this as a reason to avoid the use of open source software, stating that it is "use at your own risk" and therefore introduces too much risk. While that's true enough, the argument is weakened or invalidated when you purchase support from open source vendors. Support options from open source vendors often include certain liability rights and further protections. This is perhaps the most compelling reason to purchase support for open source software. In this case, there is quid pro quo and in many cases a reliable warranty.

The requirement to place a banner in a visible place in your software is not that onerous. The GPL simply requires a clear statement of the software's derivation and origination as well as marking the software as protected under the GPL. This informs anyone who uses this software of their rights (freedoms) to use, copy, distribute, and modify the software.

Perhaps the most important declaration contained in the GNU manifesto is the statements under the heading, "How GNU Will Be Available." In this section, the manifesto states that although everyone is permitted to modify and redistribute GNU, no one is permitted to restrict its redistribution further. This means no one can take an open source system based on the GNU manifesto and turn it into a proprietary system or make proprietary modifications.

Property

A discussion of open source software licensing would be incomplete if the subject of property were not included. Property is simply something that is owned. We often think of property as something tangible, something we can touch and see. In the case of software, the concept of property becomes problematic. What exactly do we mean when we say software is property? Does the concept of property apply to the source code, the binaries (executables), documentation, or all of them?

The concept of property is often a sticky subject when it comes to open source software. Who is the owner if the software is produced by the global community of developers? In most cases, open source software begins life as a project someone or some organization has developed. The project becomes open source when the software is mature enough to be useful to someone. Whether this is at an early stage when the software is unrefined or later when the software reaches a certain level of reliability is not important. What *is* important is the fact that someone started the project. That someone is considered the owner. In the case of MySQL, the company, MySQL AB, originated the project and therefore they are the owners of the MySQL system.

According to the GPL that MySQL adheres to, MySQL AB owns all the source code and any modifications made under the GPL. The GPL gives you the right to modify MySQL, but it does not give you the right to claim the source code as your property.

The Ethical Side

Everyone dreads the 12-headed dragon called ethics. Ethical dilemmas abound when you first start working with open source software. For example, open source software is free to download, but you have to turn over any improvements you make to the original owner. So how can you make any money off something you have to give away?

To understand this, you must consider the goals that Stallman had in mind when he developed the GNU license model. His goals were to make a community of cooperation and solidarity among developers throughout the world. He wanted source code to be publicly available and the software generated to be free for anyone to use. Your rights to earn (to be paid) for your work are not restricted. You can sell your derivative work. You just can't claim ownership of the source code. You are ethically (and legally!) bound to give back to the global community of developers.

Another ethical dilemma with open source software arises when you consider what should occur if you modify open source software for your own use. For example, you download the latest version of MySQL and add a feature that permits you to use your own abbreviated shortcuts for the SQL commands because you're tired of typing out long SQL statements (I am sure someone somewhere has already done this).

In this case, you aren't modifying the system in a way that could be beneficial to anyone but yourself. So why should you turn over your modifications? Although this dilemma is probably not an issue for most of us, it could be an issue for you if you persist in using the software with your personal modifications and eventually create a derivative work. Care must be taken whenever you modify the source code no matter what the reason. Basically, any productive and meaningful modification you make must be considered property of the originator regardless of its use or limits of its use.

However, if you are modifying the source code as an academic exercise (as I will show you how to do later in this book), the modifications should be discarded once you have completed your exercises or experiments. Some open source software makes provisions for these types of uses. Most consider the exploration and experimentation of the source code a "use" of the software and not a modification. It is therefore permissible to use the source code in academic pursuits.

Let the Revolution Continue!

Freedom is a right that many countries have based their government philosophies on. It is freedom that drove Richard Stallman to begin his quest to reform software development. Although freedom was the catalyst for the open source movement, it has become a revolution because organizations now have an opportunity to avoid obsolescence at the hands of their competitors by investing in lower-cost software systems while maintaining the revenue to compete in their markets.

Organizations that have adopted open source software as part of their own product lines are perhaps the most revolutionary of all. Most have adopted a business model based on the GPL that permits them to gain all of the experience and robustness that come with open source systems while still generating revenue for their own ideas and additions.

Open source software is both scorned and lauded by the software industry. Some despise open source because they see it as an attack against the commercial proprietary software industry. They also claim open source is a fad and will not last. They see organizations that produce, contribute to, or use open source software as being on borrowed time and that sooner rather than later the world will come to its senses and forget about open source software. Some don't despise open source as much as they see no possibility for profit and therefore dismiss the idea as fruitless. Others see open source software as the savior to rescue us all from the tyrants of commercial proprietary software and that sooner rather than later the giant software companies will be forced to change their property models to open source or some variant thereof. The truth is probably in the middle. I see the open source industry as a vibrant and growing industry of similar-minded individuals whose goals are to create safe, reliable, and robust software.

Whatever your perspective, you must conclude that the open source movement has caused a revolution among software developers everywhere. Now that you have had a sound introduction to the open source revolution, it is your turn to decide whether or not you agree to the philosophies. If you do (and I sincerely hope I have convinced you to), then welcome to the global community of developers. Viva le revolution!

Developing with MySQL

You've taken a look at what open source software is and the legal ramifications of using and developing with open source software. Now you'll learn how to develop products using MySQL. As you'll see, MySQL presents a unique opportunity for developers to exploit a major server software technology without the burden of conforming or limiting their development to a fixed set of rules or limited API suite.

MySQL is owned by MySQL AB. The "AB" is an acronym for the Swedish word "aktiebolag" or "stock company," which translates to the English (US) term "incorporated." What began as a capital venture to build an open source relational database system has become a credible alternative to the commercial database system market. MySQL AB generates revenue by selling commercial licenses, support, and professional development services, including consulting, training, and certification on their products.

MySQL is a relational database management system designed for use in client/server architectures. MySQL can also be used as an embedded database library. Of course, if you have used MySQL before, you are familiar with its capabilities and no doubt have decided to choose MySQL for some or all of your database needs.

MySQL has become the world's most popular and most successful open source database system. This popularity is due in large part to its reliability, performance, and ease of use. There are over 8 million installations of MySQL products worldwide. MySQL AB's success can be attributed to a sound core values statement: "To make superior data management software available and affordable to all." This core values statement is manifested by MySQL AB's key business objectives—to make its database system products

- The world's best and most widely used

- Affordable and available to everyone

- Easy to use

- Continuously improved while maintaining speed and data integrity

- Fun and easy to extend and evolve

- Free from defects

Clearly, MySQL AB has achieved all of these objectives and continues to surprise database professionals everywhere with the quality and performance of their products.

What you may not know is how MySQL came about and how it is constructed. At the lowest level of the system, the server is built using a multithreaded model written in a combination of C and C++. Much of this core functionality was built in the early 1980s and later modified with a Structured Query Language (SQL) layer in 1995. MySQL was built using the GNU C compiler (GCC), which provides a great deal of flexibility for target environments. This means MySQL can be compiled for use on just about any Linux operating systems. MySQL AB has also had considerable success in building variants for the Microsoft Windows and Macintosh operating systems. The client tools for MySQL are largely written in C for greater portability and speed. Client libraries and access mechanism are available for .NET, Java, ODBC, and several others.

MySQL is built using parallel development paths to ensure product lines continue to evolve while new versions of the software are planned and developed. Software development follows a staged development process where multiple releases are produced in each stage. The stages of a MySQL development process are as follows:

1. *Development*—New product or feature sets are planned and implemented as a new path of the development tree.

2. *Alpha*—Feature refinement and defect correction (bug fixes) are implemented.

3. *Beta*—The features are "frozen" (no new features can be added) and additional intensive testing and defect correction is implemented.

4. *Gamma*—Basically, this is a release candidate stage where the code is frozen and final rounds of testing are conducted.

5. *Stable*—If no major defects are found, the code is declared stable and ready for production release.

You'll often see various versions of the MySQL software offered in any of these stages. The parallel development strategy permits MySQL AB to maintain its current releases while working on new features. It is not uncommon to read about the new features in 5.1 while development is continuing in 4.0.10. This may seem confusing because we are used to commercial proprietary software vendors keeping their development strategies to themselves. MySQL version numbers are used to track the releases and contain a two-part number for the product series and a single number for the release. For example, version 5.0.12 is the 12th release of the 5.0 product line.

Tip Always be sure to include the complete version number when corresponding with MySQL AB. Simply stating the "alpha release" or "latest version" is not clear enough to properly address your needs.

This multiple-release philosophy has some interesting side effects. It is not uncommon to encounter organizations that are using older versions of MySQL. In fact, I have encountered several agencies that I work with who are still using the version 4.*x* product lines. This philosophy has virtually eliminated the upgrade shell game that commercial proprietary software undergoes. That is, every time the vendor releases a new version they cease development, and in many cases support, of the old version. With major architectural changes, customers are forced to alter their environments and development efforts accordingly. This adds a great deal of cost to maintaining product lines based on commercial proprietary software. The multiple-release philosophy frees organizations from this burden by permitting them to keep their own products in circulation much longer and with the assurance of continued support. Even when new architecture changes occur, as in the case of MySQL version 5.0, organizations have a much greater lead time and can therefore expend their resources in the most efficient manner allowed to them without rushing or altering their long-term plans.

While you are free to download any version of MySQL, you might want to first consider your use of the software. If you plan to use the software as an enterprise server in your own production environment, you may want to limit your download to the stable releases of the product line. On the other hand, if you are building a new system using the LAMP stack or another development environment, any of the other release stages would work for a development effort. Most will download the stable release of the latest version that they intend to use in their environment. For the purposes of the exercises and experiments in this book, any version (stage) of MySQL will work well.

MySQL AB recommends using the latest alpha series for any new development. What they mean is if you plan to add features to MySQL and you are participating in the global community of developers, you should add new features to the alpha stage. This permits the greatest opportunity (exposure) of your code to be tested prior to the last gamma stage (production release). You should also consider that while the stage of the version may indicate its state with respect to new features, you should not automatically associate instability with the early stages or stability with the later. Depending on your use of the software, the stability may be different. For example, if you are using MySQL in a development effort to build a new ecommerce site in the LAMP stack and you are not using any of the new features introduced during the development or alpha stage, the stability for your use is virtually the same as any other stage. The best rule of thumb is to select the version with the features that you need at latest stage of development.

Why Modify MySQL?

Modifying MySQL is not a trivial task. If you are an experienced C/C++ programmer and understand the construction of relational database systems, then you can probably jump right in. For the rest of us, we need take a moment to consider why we would want to modify a database server system and carefully plan our modifications.

There are many reasons why you would want to modify MySQL. Perhaps you require a database server or client feature that isn't available. Or maybe you have a custom application suite that requires a specific type of database behavior and rather than having to adapt to a commercial proprietary system, it is easier and cheaper for you to modify MySQL to meet your needs. It is most likely the case that your organization cannot afford to duplicate the sophistication and refinement of the MySQL database system, but you need something to base your solution on. What better way to make your application world-class than by basing it on a world-class database system?

■Note If a feature is really useful and someone considers it beneficial, the beauty of open source is that the feature will work its way into the product. Someone, somewhere will contribute and build the feature.

Like all effective software developers, you must first begin by planning what you are going to do. Start with the planning devices and materials that you are most comfortable with and make a list of all of the things you feel you need the database server (or client) to do. Spend some time evaluating MySQL to see if any of the features you want already exist and make notes concerning their behavior. After you've completed this research, you will have a better idea of where the gaps are. This "gap analysis" will provide you with a concentrated list of features and modifications needed. Once you have determined the features you need to add, you can begin to examine the MySQL source code and experiment with adding new features.

■Warning Always investigate the current MySQL features thoroughly when planning your modifications. You will want to examine and experiment with all of the SQL commands that are similar to your needs. Although you may not be able to use the current features, examining the existing capabilities will enable you to form a baseline or known behavior and performance that you can use to compare your new feature. You can be sure that the global community of developers will scrutinize any new feature and remove those they feel are best achieved using a current feature.

The best place to start learning the MySQL source code is to keep reading! This book will introduce you to the MySQL source code and provide you with knowledge of how to add new features as well as the best practices for what to change (and what not to change). Later chapters will also detail your options of how to get the source code and how to merge your changes into the appropriate code path (branch). You will also learn the details of MySQL AB's coding guidelines that specify how your code should look and what code constructs you should avoid.

What Can You Modify in MySQL? Are There Limits?

The beauty of open source software is that you have access to its source code for the software (as guaranteed by its respective open source license). This means you have access to all of the inner workings of the entire software. Have you ever wondered how the optimizer works in MySQL? You can find out simply by downloading the source code and working your way through it.

With MySQL, it isn't so simple. The source code in MySQL is often complex and difficult to read and understand. One could say the code has very low comprehensibility. Often regarded by the original developers as having a "genius factor," the source code can be a challenge for even the best C/C++ programmer.

While the challenges of complexities of the C/C++ code may be a concern, it in no way limits your ability or right to modify the software. Most developers modify the source code to add new SQL commands or alter existing SQL commands to get a better fit to their database needs. However, the opportunities are much broader than simply changing MySQL's SQL behavior. You can change the optimizer, the internal query representation, or even the query cache mechanism.

One of the challenges you are likely to encounter will not be from any of your developers. The challenge may come from your senior technical stakeholders. For example, my recent modifications to the MySQL source code were challenged by senior technical stakeholders because I was modifying foundations of the server code itself. One stakeholder was adamant that my changes "flew in the face of 30 years of database theory and tried and true implementation." I certainly hope you never encounter this type of behavior, but if you do and you've done your research as to what features are available and how they do not meet (or partially meet) your needs, your answer should consist of indisputable facts. If you do get this question or one like it, remind your senior technical stakeholder that the virtues of open source software is that it can be modified and that it frequently *is* modified. You may also want to consider explaining what your new feature does and how it will improve the system as a whole for everyone. If you can do that, you can weather the storm.

Another challenge you are likely to face with modifying MySQL is the question "Why MySQL?" Experts will be quick to point out that there are several open source database systems to choose from. The most popular are MySQL, Firebird, PostgreSQL, and Berkeley DB. The reasons that you would choose to use MySQL in your development projects over some of the other database systems include the following:

- MySQL is a relational database management system that supports a full set of SQL commands. Some open source database systems like PostgreSQL are object relational database systems that use an API or library for access rather than accepting SQL commands. Some open source systems are built using architectures that may not be suited for your environment. For example, Apache Derby is based in Java and may not offer the best performance for your embedded application.

- MySQL is built using C/C++, which can be built for nearly all Linux platforms as well as Microsoft Windows and Macintosh OS. Some open source systems may not be available for your choice of development language. This can be an issue if you must port the system to the version of Linux that you are running.

- MySQL is designed as client/server architecture. Some open source systems are not scalable beyond a client-based embedded system. For example, Berkeley DB is a set of client libraries and is not a stand-alone database system.

- MySQL is a mature database server with a proven track record of stability. Some open source database systems may not have the install base of MySQL or may not offer the features you need in an enterprise database server.

Clearly, the challenges are going to be unique to the development needs and the environment in which the modifications take place. Whatever your needs are, you can be sure that you have complete access to all of the source code and that your modifications are limited only by your imagination.

MySQL Licensing Explained

MySQL is licensed as open source software under the GPL. The server and client software as well as the tools and libraries are all covered by the GPL. MySQL AB has made the GPL a major focal point in their business model. They are firmly committed to the GNU open source community. Furthermore, all of the venture capitalists who sign on with MySQL AB are required to underwrite the same philosophy and license.

MySQL AB has gained many benefits by exposing their source code to the global community of developers. The source code is routinely evaluated by public scrutiny, third-party organizations regularly audit the source code, the development process fosters a forum of open communication and feedback, and the source code is compiled and tested in many different environments. No other database vendor can make these claims while maintaining world-class stability, reliability, and features.

MySQL is also licensed as a commercial product. A commercial license permits MySQL AB to own the source code (as described earlier) as well as own the copyright on the name, logo, and documentation (such as books). This is unique because most open source companies do not ascribe to owning anything; rather, their intellectual property is their experience and expertise. MySQL AB has retained the intellectual property of the software while leveraging the support of the global community of developers to expand and evolve the software. It should be noted that MySQL AB has its own full development team with over 100 employees worldwide. Although it is true that developers from around the world participate in the development of MySQL, MySQL AB employs many of them.

Some would consider this move by MySQL AB as a corruption of the original ideas of Stallman and the FSF. That isn't the case. MySQL AB has created an industry around open source database systems that is driven by the open source philosophy while retaining the ability to employ members of the same development industry. MySQL AB has shown it is possible to give away your ideas and still make money selling them.

This dual-license concept has created some confusion. Specifically, when should you use the GPL versus the commercial license? The GPL is best suited for general use of the software, participation in the global community of developers to add or refine features, and for conducting academic experiments. The commercial license is best suited to situations where you need warranties and assurances of capabilities (support) or when you use the software in mission-critical applications.

The subject of what license to use for modifications is also a source of some confusion. If you are planning features that are of interest to more than your own users, you should consider using the GPL and turn over your changes to MySQL AB. Although this means you are giving away your rights to own those changes, you are gaining the world-class support and all of the other benefits of the MySQL system. If you are making modifications that are of use to only you and your unique needs and you are not repackaging or distributing the changes (in any way), then you can use either license.

If you use the GPL and do not share your modifications, you will not get any support for the modifications and it will be your responsibility to maintain them. This could be a problem if you decide to upgrade to a new version of MySQL. You will have to make all of the modifications all over again. This may not be a difficult challenge, but it is something that will require careful planning. MySQL AB provides a number of support options for users of the GPL. The MySQL web site (www.mysql.com/support/community_support.html) has links for subscribing to a variety of free mailing lists, forums, and bug reporting. Consulting services and training are also available for a fee.

If you use the commercial license, you have the option of purchasing support from MySQL AB to assist you in making the modifications. You can even purchase rights that permit you to maintain ownership of the changes. This is especially important if you plan to repackage and redistribute the source code to your own customers. Table 1-1 summarizes the various support options currently available from MySQL AB. These support packages, called the MySQL Network, are available regardless of which license you choose to use, but may have certain restrictions associated with using the GPL.

Table 1-1. *MySQL Network Support Options*

Feature	Basic	Silver	Gold	Platinum
Software maintenance and upgrades	Yes	Yes	Yes	Yes
Service advisors available	Yes	Yes	Yes	Yes
Access to free knowledge base	Yes	Yes	Yes	Yes
Incident reports	2	unlimited	unlimited	unlimited
Phone support		8×5 (M–F)	24×7	24×7
Initial response time (max)	2 business days	4 hours	2 hours	30 minutes
Emergency response time (max)			30 minutes	30 minutes
Remote troubleshooting			Yes	Yes
Schema review				Yes
Query review				Yes
Performance tuning				Yes
Code reviews (client development)				Yes
Code reviews (user-defined functions)				Yes
Code reviews (server development)				Yes
Dedicated account manager				Option
Indemnification			Option	Option

■ **Note** MySQL has created the indemnification program to assist customers in copyright and patent infringement disputes.

So, Can You Modify MySQL or Not?

You may be wondering after a discussion of the limitations of using open source software under the GNU public license if you can actually modify it after all. The answer is simply, yes, you can!

You can modify MySQL under the GPL provided, of course, that if you intend to distribute your changes you surrender those changes to the owner of the project and thereby fulfill your obligation to participate in the global community of developers. If you are experimenting or using the modifications for educational purposes, you are not obligated to turn over your changes. Naturally, the truth of the matter comes down to the benefits of the modifications. If you're adding capabilities that can be of interest to someone other than yourself, you should share them.

You can also modify MySQL under the commercial license. In this case, either you're intending to use the modifications for your own internal development or you're bundling MySQL or embedding MySQL in your own commercial product.

Whatever licensing method you choose, the opportunity to modify the system is yours to take.

Guidelines for Modifying MySQL

Take care when approaching a task such as modifying a system like MySQL. A relational database system is a complex set of services layered in such a way as to provide fast, reliable access to data. You would not want to open the source code and start plugging in your own code to see what happens (but you're welcome to try). Instead, you should plan your changes and take careful aim at the portions of the source code that pertain to your needs.

Having modified large systems like MySQL, I want to impart a few simple guidelines that will make your experience with modifying MySQL a positive one.

The first thing you should do is decide which license you are going to use. If you are using MySQL under an open source license already and can implement the modifications yourself, you should continue to use the GPL. In this case, you are obligated to perpetuate the open source mantra and give back to the community in exchange for what was freely offered. Under the terms of the GPL, the developer is bound to make these changes available. If you are using MySQL under the commercial license or need support for the modifications, you should purchase the appropriate MySQL Network support and consult with MySQL AB on your modifications. However, if you are not going to distribute the modifications and can support them for future versions of MySQL, you do not need to change to the commercial license or change your commercial license to the GPL.

Another suggestion is to keep a developer's journal and keep notes of each change you make or each interesting discovery you find. Not only will you be able to record your work step by step, but you can also use the journal as a way to document what you are doing. You will be amazed at what you can discover about your research by going back and reading your past journal entries. I have found many golden nuggets of information scrawled within my engineering notebooks.

While experimenting with the source code, you should also make notes in the source code itself. You can annotate the source code with a comment line or comment block before and after your changes. This makes it easy to locate all of your changes using your favorite text parser or search program. The following demonstrates one method for commenting your changes:

```
/* BEGIN MY MODIFICATION */
/* Purpose of modification: experimentation. */
/* Modified by: Chuck */
/* Date modified: 3/19/2006 */
if (something_interesting_happens)
{
  do_something_cool;
}
/* END MY MODIFICATION */
```

Lastly, do not be afraid to explore the free knowledge base and forums on the MySQL web site or seek the assistance of the global community of developers. These are your greatest assets. However, be sure you have done your homework before you post to one of the forums. The fastest way to become discouraged is to post a message on one of the forums only to have someone reply with a curt (but polite) reference to the documentation. Make your posts succinct and to the point. You don't need to elaborate on the many reasons why you're doing what you're doing—just post your question and provide all pertinent information about the issue you're having. Also take care to make sure you are posting to the correct forum. Most forums are moderated and if you are ever in doubt, consult the moderator to ensure you are posting your topic in the correct forum.

A Real-World Example: TiVo

Have you ever wondered what makes your TiVo tick? Would you be surprised to know that it runs on a version of embedded Linux?

Jim Barton and Mike Ramsay designed the original TiVo product in 1997. It was pitched as a home network–based multimedia server serving streaming content to thin clients. Naturally, a device like this must be easy to learn and even easier to use, but most importantly it must operate error free and handle power interruptions (and user error) gracefully.

Barton was experimenting with several forms of Linux and while working at Silicon Graphics (SGI), sponsored a port of Linux to the SGI Indy platform. Due mainly to the stable file system, network, memory handling, and developer tool support, Barton believed it would be possible to port a version of Linux to the TiVo platform and that Linux could handle the real-time performance goals of the TiVo product.

However, Barton and Ramsay faced a challenge from their peers. Many at that time viewed open source with suspicion and scorn. Commercial software experts asserted that open source software would never be reliable in a real-time environment. Furthermore, they believed that basing a commercial proprietary product on the GPL would not permit modification and that if they proceeded, the project would become a nightmare of copyright suits and endless legal haranguing. Fortunately, Barton and Ramsay were not deterred and studied the GPL carefully. They concluded that not only was the GPL viable, it would permit them to protect their intellectual property.

Although the original TiVo product was intended to be a server, Barton and Ramsay decided that the bandwidth wasn't available to support such lofty goals. Instead, they redesigned their product to a client device, called the TiVo Client Device (TCD), which would act like a sophisticated video recorder. They wanted to provide a for-fee service to serve up the television guide and interface with the TCD. This would allow home users to select the shows they wanted in advance and program the TCD to record them. In effect, they created what is now known as a digital video recorder (DVR).

The TCD hardware included a small, embedded computer with a hard drive and memory. Hardware interfaces were created to read and write video (video in and video out) using a MPEG 2 encoder and decoder. Additional input/output (I/O) devices included audio and telecommunications (for accessing the TiVo service). The TCD also had to permit multiprocessing capabilities in order to permit the recording of one signal (channel) while playing back another (channel). These features required a good memory and disk management subsystem. Barton and Ramsay realized these goals would be a challenge for any control system. Furthermore, the video interface must never be interrupted or compromised in any way.

What Barton and Ramsay needed most was a system with a well-developed disk subsystem, supported multitasking, and the ability to optimize hardware (CPU, memory) usage. Linux therefore was the logical choice of operating systems for the TCD. Production goals and budget constraints limited the choice of CPU. The IBM PowerPC 403GCX processor was chosen for the TCD. Unfortunately, there were no ports of Linux that ran on the chosen processor. This meant Barton and Ramsay would have to port Linux to the processor platform.

While the port was successful, Barton and Ramsay discovered they needed some specialized customizations of the Linux kernel to meet the needs and limits of the hardware. For example, they bypassed the file system buffer cache in order to permit faster movement, or processing, of the video signals to and from user space. They also added extensive performance enhancements, logging, and recovery features to ensure that the TCD could recover quickly from power loss or user error.

The application that runs the TCD was built on Linux-based personal computers and ported to the modified Linux operating system with little drama—a testament to the stability and interoperability of the Linux operating system. When Barton and Ramsay completed their porting and application work, they conducted extensive testing and delivered the world's first DVR in March 1999.

The TCD is one of the most widely used consumer product running a customized embedded Linux operating system. Clearly, the TCD story is a shining example of what you can accomplish by modifying open source software. The story doesn't end here, though. Barton and Ramsay published their Linux kernel port complete with the source code. Their enhancements have found their way into the latest versions of the Linux kernel.

CONVINCING YOUR BOSS TO MODIFY OPEN SOURCE SOFTWARE

If you have an idea and a business model to base it on, going the open source route can result in a huge time savings in getting your product to market. In fact, your project may become one that can save a great deal of development revenue and permit you to get the product to market faster than your competition. This is especially true if you need to modify open source software—you have already done your homework and can show the cost benefits of using the open source software.

Unfortunately, many managers have been conditioned by the commercial proprietary software world to reject the notion of basing a product on open source software to generate a revenue case. So how do you change their minds? Use the TiVo story as ammunition. Present to your boss the knowledge you gained from the TiVo story and the rest of this chapter to dispel the myths concerning GPL and reliability of open source software. Be careful, though. If you are like most open source mavens, your enthusiasm can often be interpreted as a threat to the senior technical staff.

Make a list of the technical stakeholders who adhere to the commercial proprietary viewpoint. Engage these individuals in conversation about open source software and answer their questions. Most of all, be patient. These folks aren't as thick as you may think and will eventually come to share your enthusiasm.

Once you've got the senior technical staff educated and bought into the open source mind-set, reengage your management with a revised proposal. Be sure to take along a member of the senior technical staff as a shield (and a voice of reason). Winning in this case is turning the tide of commercial proprietary domination.

Summary

In this chapter, you explored the origins of open source software and the rise of MySQL to a world-class database management system. You learned what open source systems are and how they compare to commercial proprietary systems. You saw the underbelly of open source licensing and discovered the responsibilities of being a member of the global community of developers.

You also received an introduction to developing with MySQL and learned characteristics of the source code and guidelines for making modifications. You read about MySQL AB's dual-license practices and the implications of modifying MySQL to your needs. Finally, you saw an example of a successful integration of an open source system in a commercial product.

In the chapters ahead, you will learn more about the anatomy of a relational database system and how to get started customizing MySQL to your needs. Later in Parts 2 and 3 of this book, you will be introduced to the inner workings of MySQL and the exploration of the most intimate portions of the code.

CHAPTER 2

■ ■ ■

The Anatomy of a Database System

Have you ever wondered what goes on inside a database system? While you may know the basics of a relational database system (RDBS) and be an expert at administering the system, you may have never explored the inner workings of a database system. Most of us have been trained on and have experience with managing database systems, but neither academic nor professional training includes much about the way database systems are constructed. A database professional may never need this knowledge, but it is good to know how the system works so that you can understand how best to optimize your server and even how best to utilize its features.

This chapter covers the basics of the subsystems that RDBSs contain and how they are constructed. I use the anatomy of the MySQL system to illustrate the key components of modern RDBSs. For those of you who have studied the inner workings of such systems and want to jump ahead to a look at the architecture of MySQL, you can skip the next section.

Database System Architectures

Although understanding the inner workings of an RDBS isn't necessary for hosting databases or even maintaining the server or developing applications that use the system, knowing how the system is organized is essential to being able to modify and extend its features. It is also important to grasp the basic principles of the most popular database systems to understand how these systems compare to an RDBS.

Types of Database Systems

Most database professionals work with RDBSs, but several others are becoming popular. The following sections present a brief overview of the three most popular types of database systems: object-oriented, object-relational, and relational. It is important to understand the architectures and general features of these systems to fully appreciate the opportunity that MySQL AB has provided by developing MySQL as open source software and exposing the source code for the system to everyone. This permits me to show you what's going on inside the box.

If you are familiar with these types of database systems, you can skip to the "Relational Database System Architecture" section.

Object-Oriented Database Systems

Object-oriented database systems (OODBSs) are storage and retrieval mechanisms that support the object-oriented programming (OOP) paradigm through direct manipulation of the data as objects. They contain true object-oriented (OO) type systems that permit objects to persist between applications and usage. However, most lack a standard query language[1] (access to the data is typically via a programming interface) and therefore are not true database management systems.

OODBSs are an attractive alternative to RDBSs, especially in application areas where the modeling power or performance of RDBSs to store data as objects in tables is insufficient. These applications maintain large amounts of data that is never deleted, thereby managing the history of individual objects. The most unique feature of OODBSs is to provide support for complex objects by specifying both the structure and the operations that can be applied to these objects via an OOP interface.

OODBSs are particularly suitable for modeling the real world as closely as possible without forcing unnatural relationships between and within entities. The philosophy of object orientation offers a holistic as well as a modeling-oriented view of the real world. These views are necessary for dealing with an elusive subject like modeling temporal change, particularly in adding OO features to structured data. Despite the general availability of numerous open source OODBSs, most are based in part on relational systems that support query language interfaces and therefore are not truly OODBSs; rather, they operate more like relational databases with OO interfaces. A true OODBS requires access via a programming interface.

Application areas of OO database systems include geographical information systems (GISs), scientific and statistical databases, multimedia systems, picture archiving and communications systems, and XML warehouses.

The greatest adaptability of the OODBS is the tailoring of the data (or objects) and its behavior (or methods). Most OODBS system integrators rely on OO methods for describing data and build their solutions with that expressiveness in the design. Thus, object-oriented database systems are built with specific implementations and are not intended to be general purpose or generalized to have statement–response-type interfaces like RDBSs.

Object-Relational Database Systems

Object-relational database systems (ORDBSs) are an application of OO theory to RDBSs. ORDBSs provide a mechanism that permits database designers to implement a structured storage and retrieval mechanism for OO data concepts. ORDBSs provide the basis of the relational model—meaning, integrity, relationships, and so forth—while extending the model to store and retrieve data in an object-centric manner. Implementation is purely conceptual in many cases as the mapping of OO concepts to relational concepts is tentative at best. The modifications, or extensions, to the relational technologies include modifications to SQL that allow the representation of object types, identity, encapsulation of operations, and inheritance. However, these are often loosely mapped to relational theory as complex types. Although expressive, the SQL extensions do not permit the true object manipulation and level of control of OODBSs. The most popular ORDBS is ESRI's ArcGIS Geodatabase environment. Other examples include Oracle and Informix.

---

1. There are some notable exceptions, but this is generally true.

The technology used in ORDBSs uses the base relational model. Most ORDBSs are implemented using existing commercial relational database management systems (RDBMSs) such as Microsoft SQL Server and Oracle. Since these systems are based on the relational model, they suffer from a conversion problem of translating OO concepts to relational mechanisms. The following are some of the many problems with using relational databases for object-oriented applications:

- The OO conceptual model does not map easily to data tables.

- Complex mapping implies complex programs and queries.

- Complex programs imply maintenance problems.

- Complex programs imply reliability problems.

- Complex queries may not be optimized and result in slow performance.

- The mapping of object concepts to complex types[2] is more vulnerable to schema changes than relational systems.

- OO performance for `select all...where` queries is slower because it involves multiple joins and lookups.

Although these problems seem significant, they are easily mitigated by the application of an OO application layer that communicates between the underlying relational database and the OO application. These application layers permit the translation of objects into structured (or persistent) data stores. Interestingly, this practice violates the concept of an ORDBS in that you are now using an OO access mechanism to access the data, which is not why ORDBSs are created. They are created to permit the storage and retrieval of objects in an RDBS by providing extensions to the query language

Although ORDBSs are similar to OODBSs, OODBSs are very different in philosophy. OODBSs try to add database functionality to OO programming languages via a programming interface and platforms. By contrast, ORDBSs try to add rich data types to RDBSs using traditional query languages and extensions. OODBSs attempt to achieve a seamless integration with OOP languages. ORDBSs do not attempt this level of integration and often require an intermediate application layer to translate information from the OO application to the ORDBS or even the host RDBS. Similarly, OODBSs are aimed at applications that have as their central engineering perspective an OO viewpoint. ORDBSs are optimized for large data stores and object-based systems that support large volumes of data (e.g., GIS applications). Lastly, the query mechanisms of OODBSs are centered on object manipulation using specialized OO query languages. ORDBS query mechanisms are geared toward fast retrieval of volumes of data using extensions to the SQL standard. Unlike true OODBSs that have optimized query mechanisms, such as Object Description Language (ODL) and Object Query Language (OQL), ORDBSs use query mechanisms that are extensions of the SQL query language.

---

2. This is especially true when the object types are modified in a populated data store. Depending on the changes, the behavior of the objects may have been altered and thus may not have the same meaning. Despite the fact that this may be a deliberate change, the effects of the change are potentially more severe than in typical relational systems.

The ESRI product suite of GIS applications contains a product called the Geodatabase (shorthand for geographic database), which supports the storage and management of geographic data elements. The Geodatabase is an object-relational database that supports spatial data. It is an example of a spatial database that is implemented as an ORDBS.

Note There is no requirement that spatial database systems be implemented in ORDBSs or even OODBSs. ESRI has chosen to implement the Geodatabase as an ORDBS. More importantly, GIS data could be stored in an RDBS that has been extended to support spatial data. Behold! That is exactly what has happened with MySQL. MySQL AB has added a spatial data engine to their RDBS.

Although it is true that ORDBSs are based on relational database platforms, they also provide some layer of data encapsulation and behavior. Most ORDBSs are specialized forms of RDBSs. Those database vendors who provide ORDBSs often build extensions to the statement-response interfaces by modifying the SQL to contain object descriptors and spatial query mechanisms. These systems are generally built for a particular application and are, like OODBSs, limited in their general use.

Relational Database Systems

An RDBS is a data storage and retrieval service based on the Relational Model of Data as proposed by E. F. Codd in 1970. These systems are the standard storage mechanism for structured data. A great deal of research is devoted to refining the essential model proposed by Codd, as discussed by C. J. Date in *The Database Relational Model: A Retrospective Review and Analysis*.[3] This evolution of theory and practice is best documented in *The Third Manifesto*.[4]

The relational model is an intuitive concept of a storage repository (database) that can be easily queried by using a mechanism called a query language to retrieve, update, and insert data. The relational model has been implemented by many vendors because it has a sound systematic theory, a firm mathematical foundation, and a simple structure. The most commonly used query mechanism is Structured Query Language (SQL), which resembles natural language. Although SQL is not included in the relational model, SQL provides an integral part of the practical application of the relational model in RDBSs.

The data is represented as related pieces of information (attributes) about a certain entity. The set of values for the attribute is formed as a *tuple* (sometimes called a record). Tuples are then stored in tables containing tuples that have the same set of attributes. Tables can then be related to other tables through constraints on domains, keys, attributes, and tuples.

---

3. C. J. Date, *The Database Relational Model: A Retrospective Review and Analysis* (Reading, MA: Addison-Wesley, 2001).
4. C. J. Date and H. Darwen, *Foundation for Future Database Systems: The Third Manifesto* (Reading, MA: Addison-Wesley, 2000).

RECORD OR TUPLE: IS THERE A DIFFERENCE?

Many mistakenly consider a record as a colloquialism for tuple. One important distinction is that a tuple is a set of ordered elements whereas a record is a collection of related items without a sense of order. However, the order of the columns is important in the concept of a record. Interestingly, in SQL a result from a query can be a record whereas in relational theory each result is a tuple. Many texts use these terms interchangeably, creating a source of confusion for many.

The query language of choice for most implementations is Structured Query Language (SQL). SQL was proposed as a standard in the 1980s and is currently an industry standard. Unfortunately, many seem to believe SQL is based on relational theory and therefore is a sound theoretical concept. This misconception is perhaps fueled by a phenomenon brought on by industry. Almost all RDBSs implement some form of SQL. This popularity has mistakenly overlooked the many sins of SQL, including the following:

- SQL does not support domains as described by the relational model.

- In SQL, tables can have duplicate rows.

- Results (tables) can contain unnamed columns and duplicate columns.

- The implementation of nulls (missing values) by host database systems has been shown to be inconsistent and incomplete. Thus, many incorrectly associate the mishandling of nulls with SQL when in fact SQL merely returns the results as presented by the database system.[5]

The technologies used in RDBSs are many and varied. Some systems are designed to optimize some portion of the relational model or some application of the model to data. Applications of RDBSs range from simple data storage and retrieval to complex application suites with complex data, processes, and workflows. This could be as simple as a database that stores your compact disc or DVD collection, or a database designed to manage a hotel reservation system, or even a complex distributed system designed to manage information on the Web. As I mentioned in Chapter 1, many web applications (especially those that make up Web 2.0; see the accompanying sidebar) implement the LAMP stack whereby MySQL becomes the database for storage of the data hosted.

WEB 2.0

Web 2.0 is a buzzword coined to describe the dramatic change in the World Wide Web that permits people to share information and collaborate online. Web 2.0 applications therefore are applications that extend this concept of global electronic community. Examples include photo sharing, blogs, and information and audiovisual services. These applications typically implement many of the web advances of the last decade, such as LAMP. Most are built with open source solutions. While still being solidified, Web 2.0 is sure to change the landscape of the Internet in a profound way.

---

5. Some of the ways database systems handle nulls range from the absurd to the unintuitive.

Relational database systems provide the most robust data independence and data abstraction. By using the concept of relations, RDBS provide a truly generalized data storage and retrieval mechanism. The downside is, of course, that these systems are highly complex and require considerable expertise to build and modify.

In the next section, I'll present a typical RDBS architecture and examine each component of the architecture. Later, I'll examine a particular implementation of an RDBS (MySQL).

IS MYSQL A RELATIONAL DATABASE SYSTEM?

Many database theorists will tell you that there are very few true RDBSs in the world. They would also point out that what relational is and is not is largely driven by your definition of the features supported in the database system and not how well the system conforms to Codd's relational model.

From a pure marketing viewpoint, MySQL provides a great many of the features considered essential for RDBSs. These include the ability to relate tables to one another using foreign keys, the implementation of a relational algebra query mechanism, and the use of indexing and buffering mechanisms, to list a few. Clearly, MySQL offers all of these features and more.

So is MySQL an RDBS? That depends on your definition of relational. If you follow the user evolution of MySQL, then you should conclude that it is indeed an RDBS. However, if you adhere to the strict definition of Codd's relational model, then you will conclude that MySQL is lacking some of the features represented in the model. But then again so do many other RDBSs.

Relational Database System Architecture

An RDBS is a complex system composed of specialized mechanisms designed to handle all of the functions necessary to store and retrieve information. The architecture of an RDBS has often been compared to that of an operating system. If you consider the use of an RDBS, specifically as a server to a host of clients, you see that they have a lot in common with operating systems. For example, having multiple clients means the system will have to support many requests that may or may not read or write the same data or data from the same location (such as a table). Thus, RDBSs must handle concurrency in an efficient manner. Similarly, RDBSs must provide fast access to data for each client. This is usually accomplished using file buffering techniques that keep the most recently or frequently used data in memory for faster access. Concurrency requires memory management techniques that resemble virtual memory systems in operating systems. Other similarities with operating systems include network communication support and optimization algorithms designed to maximize performance of the execution of queries.

I'll begin our exploration of the architecture from the point of view of the user from the issuing of queries to the retrieval of data. The following sections are written so that you can skip the ones you are familiar with and read the ones that interest you. I encourage you to read all of the sections as they present a detailed look at how a typical RDBS is constructed.

Client Applications

Most RDBS client applications are developed as separate executable programs that connect to the database via a communications pathway (e.g., a network protocol like sockets or pipes). Some connect directly to the database system via programmatic interfaces, where the database system becomes part of the client application. In this case, we call the database an *embedded* system. For more information about embedded database systems, see Chapter 6.

For those systems that connect to the database via a communication pathway, most connect via a set of protocols called *database connectors*. Database connectors are most often based on the Open Database Connectivity (ODBC)[6] model. MySQL also supports connectors for Java (JDBC) and Microsoft .NET. Most implementations of ODBC connectors also support communication over network protocols.

WHAT IS ODBC?

ODBC is a specification for an application programming interface (API). ODBC is designed to transfer SQL commands to the database server, retrieve the information, and present it to the calling application. An ODBC implementation includes an application designed to use the API that acts as an intermediary with the ODBC library, a core ODBC library that supports the API, and a database driver designed for a specific database system. We typically refer to the set of client access, API, and driver as a *connector*. Thus, the ODBC connector acts as an "interpreter" between the client application and the database server. ODBC has become the standard for nearly every relational (and most object-relational) database systems. Hundreds of connectors and drivers are available for use in a wide variety of clients and database systems.

When we consider the client applications, we normally take into account the programs that send and retrieve information to and from the database server. However, even the applications we use to configure and maintain the database server are client applications. Most of these utilities connect to the server via the same network pathways as database applications. Some use the ODBC connectors or a variant like Java Database Connectivity (JDBC). A few use specialized protocols for managing the server for specific administrative purposes. And others, such as phpMyAdmin, use a port or socket.

Regardless of their implementation, client applications issue commands to the database system and retrieve the results of those commands, interpret and process the results, and present them to the user. The standard command language is SQL. Clients issue SQL commands to the server via the ODBC connector, which transmits the command to the database server using the defined network protocols as specified by the driver. A graphical description of this process is shown in Figure 2-1.

---

6. Sometimes defined as Object Database Connectivity or Online Database Connectivity, but the accepted definition is Open Database Connectivity.

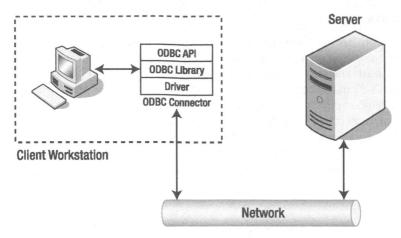

Figure 2-1. *Client application/database server communication*

Query Interface

A query language such as SQL is a language (it has a syntax and semantics) that can be used to represent a question posed to a database system. In fact, the use of SQL in database systems is considered one of the major reasons for their success. SQL provides several language groups that form a comprehensive foundation for using database systems. The *data definition language* (DDL) is used by database professionals to create and manage databases. Tasks include creating and altering tables, defining indexes, and managing constraints. The *data manipulation language* (DML) is used by database professionals to query and update the data in databases. Tasks include adding and updating data as well as querying the data. These two language groups form the majority of commands that database systems support.

SQL commands are formed using a specialized syntax. The following presents the syntax of a SELECT command in SQL. The notation depicts user-defined variables in italics and optional parameters in square brackets ([ ]).

```
SELECT [DISTINCT] listofcolumns
FROM listoftables
[WHERE expression (predicates in CNF)]
[GROUP BY listofcolumns]
[HAVING expression]
[ORDER BY listof columns];
```

The semantics of this command are as follows:[7]

1. Form the Cartesian product of the tables in the FROM clause, thus forming a projection of only those references that appear in other clauses.

2. If a WHERE clause exists, apply all expressions for the given tables referenced.

---

7. M. Stonebraker and J. L. Hellerstein, *Readings in Database Systems*, 3rd ed., edited by Michael Stone-braker (Morgan Kaufmann Publishers, 1998).

3. If a GROUP BY clause exists, form groups in the results on the attributes specified.

4. If a HAVING clause exists, apply a filter for the groups.

5. If an ORDER BY clause exists, sort the results in the manner specified.

6. If a DISTINCT keyword exists, remove the duplicate rows from the results.

The previous code example is representative of most SQL commands; all such commands have required portions, and most also have optional sections as well as keyword-based modifiers.

Once the query statements are transferred to the client via the network protocols (called *shipping*), the database server must then interpret and execute the command. A query statement from this point on is referred to simply as a *query* because it represents the question for which the database system must provide an answer. Furthermore, in the sections that follow I assume the query is of the SELECT variety, where the user has issued a request for data. However, all queries, regardless whether they are data manipulation or data definition, follow the same path through the system. It is also at this point that we consider the actions being performed within the database server itself. The first step in that process is to decipher what the client is asking for—that is, the query must be parsed and broken down into elements that can be executed upon.

Query Processing

In the context of a database system operating in a client/server model, the database server is responsible for processing the queries presented by the client and returning the results accordingly. This has been termed *query shipping*, where the query is shipped to the server and a payload (data) is returned. The benefits of query shipping are a reduction of communication time for queries and the ability to exploit server resources rather than using the more limited resources of the client to conduct the query. This model also permits a separation of how the data is stored and retrieved on the server from the way the data is used on the client. In other words, the client/server model supports data independence.

Data independence is one of the principal advantages of the relational model introduced by Codd in 1970: the separation of the *physical implementation* from the *logical model*. According to Codd,[8]

> Users of large data banks must be protected from having to know how the data is organized in the machine... Activities of users at terminals and most application programs should remain unaffected when the internal representation of data is changed.

This separation allows a powerful set of logical semantics to be developed, independent of a particular physical implementation. The goal of data independence (called physical data independence by Elmasri and Navathe[9]), is that each of the logical elements is independent of all of the physical elements (see Table 2-1). For example, the logical layout of the data into relations

---

8. C. J. Date, *The Database Relational Model: A Retrospective Review and Analysis* (Reading, MA: Addison-Wesley, 2001).

9. R. Elmasri and S. B. Navathe, *Fundamentals of Database Systems*, 4th ed. (Boston: Addison-Wesley, 2003).

(tables) with attributes (fields) arranged by tuples (rows) is completely independent of how the data is stored on the storage medium.

Table 2-1. *The Logical and Physical Models of Database Design*

Logical Model	Physical Model
Query language	Sorting algorithms
Relational Algebra	Storage mechanisms
Relational Calculus	Indexing mechanisms
Relvars	Data representation

One of the challenges of data independence is that database programming becomes a two-part process. First, there is the writing of the logical query—describing *what* the query is supposed to do. Second, there is the writing of the physical plan, which shows *how* to implement the logical query.

The logical query can be written, in general, in many different forms, such as a high-level language like SQL or as an algebraic query tree.[10] For example, in the traditional relational model a logical query can be described in relational calculus or relational algebra. The relational calculus is better in terms of focusing on *what* needs to be computed. The relational algebra is closer to providing an algorithm that lets you find what you are querying for, but still leaves out many details involved in the evaluation of a query.

The *physical plan* is a query tree implemented in a way that it can be understood and processed by the database system's query execution engine. A *query tree* is a tree structure in which each node contains a query operator and has a number of children that correspond to the number of tables involved in the operation. The query tree can be transformed via the optimizer into a plan for execution. This plan can be thought of as a program that the query execution engine can execute.

A query statement goes through several phases before it is executed; parsing, validation, optimization, plan generation/compilation, and execution. Figure 2-2 depicts the query processing steps that a typical database system would employ. Each query statement is parsed for validity and checked for correct syntax and for identification of the query operations. The parser then outputs the query in an intermediate form to allow the optimizer to form an efficient query execution plan. The execution engine then executes the query and the results are returned to the client. This progression is shown in Figure 2-2, where once parsing is completed the query is validated for errors, then optimized; a plan is chosen and compiled; and finally the query is executed.

---

10. A. B. Tucker, *Computer Science Handbook,* 2nd ed. (Boca Raton, FL: CRC Press, 2004).

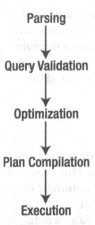

Figure 2-2. *Query processing steps*

The first step in this process is to translate the logical query from SQL into a query tree in relational algebra. This step is done by the parser and usually involves breaking the SQL statement into parts and then building the query tree from there. The next step is to translate the query tree in logical algebra into a physical plan. There are generally a large number of plans that could implement the query tree. The process of finding the best execution plan is called *query optimization*. That is, for some query execution performance measure (e.g., execution time), we want to find the plan with the *best* execution performance. The goal is that the plan be optimal or near optimal within the search space of the optimizer. The optimizer starts by copying the relational algebra query tree into its search space. The optimizer then expands the search space by forming alternative execution plans (to a finite iteration) and then searches for the best plan (the one that executes fastest).

At this level of generality, the optimizer can be viewed as the code generation part of a query compiler for the SQL language. In fact, in some database systems the compilation step translates the query into an executable program. However, most database systems translate the query into a form that can be executed using the internal library of execution steps. The code compilation in this case produces code to be interpreted by the query execution engine, except that the optimizer's emphasis is on producing "very efficient" code. For example, the optimizer uses the database system's catalog to get information (e.g., the number of tuples) about the stored relations referenced by the query, something traditional programming language compilers normally do not do. Finally, the optimizer copies the optimal physical plan out of its memory structure and sends it to the query execution engine. The query execution engine executes the plan using the relations in the stored database as input, and produces the table of rows that match the query criteria.

All of this activity requires additional processing time and places a greater burden on the process by forcing database implementers to consider the performance of the query optimizer and execution engine as a factor in their overall efficiency. This optimization is costly because of the number of alternative execution plans that use different access methods (ways of reading the data) and different execution orders. Thus it is possible to generate an infinite number of plans for a single query. However, database systems typically bound the problem to a few known best practices.

One of the primary reasons for the large number of query plans is that optimization will be required for many different values of important runtime parameters whose actual values are unknown at optimization time. Database systems make certain assumptions about the database contents (e.g., value distribution in relation attributes), the physical schema (e.g., index types), the values of the system parameters (e.g., the number of available buffers), and the values of the query constants.

Query Optimizer

Some mistakenly believe that the query optimizer performs all of the steps outlined in the query execution phases. As you will see, query optimization is just *one* of the steps that the query takes on the way to be executed. The following paragraphs describe the query optimizer in detail and illustrate the role of the optimizer in the course of the query execution.

Query optimization is the part of the query compilation process that translates a data manipulation statement in a high-level, nonprocedural language, such as SQL, into a more detailed, procedural sequence of operators, called a *query plan*. Query optimizers usually select a plan by estimating the cost of many alternative plans and then choosing the least expensive among them (the one that executes fastest).

Database systems that use a plan-based approach to query optimization assume that many plans can be used to produce any given query. Although this is true, not all plans are equivalent in the number of resources (or cost) needed to execute the query, nor are all plans executed in the same amount of time. The goal then is to discover the plan that has the least cost and/or runs in the least amount of time. The distinction of either resource usage or cost usage is a trade-off often encountered when designing systems for embedded integration or running on a small platform (with low resource availability) versus the need for higher throughput (or time).

Figure 2-3 depicts a plan-based query processing strategy where the query follows the path of the arrows. The SQL command is passed to the query parser, where it is parsed and validated and then translated into an internal representation, usually based on a relational algebra expression or a query tree as described earlier. The query is then passed to the query optimizer, which examines all of the algebraic expressions that are equivalent, generating a different plan for each combination. The optimizer then chooses the plan with the least cost and passes the query to the code generator, which translates the query into an executable form, either as directly executable or as interpretative code. The query processor then executes the query and returns a single row in the result set at a time.

This is a common implementation scheme and is typical of most database systems. However, the machines that the database system runs on have improved over time. It is no longer the case that the query plans have diverse execution costs. In fact, most query plans have been shown to execute with approximately the same cost. This realization has led some database system implementers to adopt a query optimizer that focuses on optimizing the query using some well-known good rules (called heuristics) or practices for query optimization. Some database systems use hybrids of optimization techniques that are based on one form while maintaining aspects of other techniques during execution.

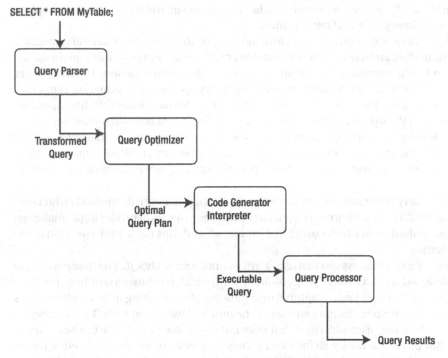

SELECT * FROM MyTable;

Query Parser

Transformed
Query

Query Optimizer

Optimal
Query Plan

Code Generator
Interpreter

Executable
Query

Query Processor

Query Results

Figure 2-3. *Plan-based query processing*

The four primary means of performing query optimization are

- Cost-based optimization
- Heuristic optimization
- Semantic optimization
- Parametric optimization

Though no optimization technique can guarantee the best execution plan, the goal of all these methods is to generate an efficient execution for the query that guarantees correct results.

A cost-based optimizer generates a range of query-evaluation plans from the given query by using the equivalence rules, and chooses the one with the least cost based on the metrics (or statistics) gathered about the relations and operations needed to execute the query. For a complex query, many equivalent plans are possible. The goal of cost-based optimization is to arrange the query execution and table access utilizing indexes and statistics gathered from past queries. Systems such as Microsoft SQL Server and Oracle use cost-based optimizers.

Heuristic optimizers use rules concerning how to shape the query into the most optimal form prior to choosing alternative implementations. The application of heuristics, or rules, can eliminate queries that are likely to be inefficient. Using heuristics as a basis to form the query plan ensures that the query plan is most likely (but not always) optimized prior to evaluation. The goal of heuristic optimization is to apply rules that ensure "good" practices for query execution. Systems that use heuristic optimizers include Ingres and various academic variants.

These systems typically use heuristic optimization as a means of avoiding the really bad plans rather than as a primary means of optimization.

The goal of semantic optimization is to form query execution plans that use the semantics, or topography, of the database and the relationships and indexes within to form queries that ensure the best practice available for executing a query in the given database. Though not yet implemented in commercial database systems as the primary optimization technique, semantic optimization is currently the focus of considerable research. Semantic optimization operates on the premise that the optimizer has a basic understanding of the actual database schema. When a query is submitted, the optimizer uses its knowledge of system constraints to simplify or to ignore a particular query if it is guaranteed to return an empty result set. This technique holds great promise for providing even more improvements to query processing efficiency in future RDBSs.

Parametric query optimization combines the application of heuristic methods with cost-based optimization. The resulting query optimizer provides a means of producing a smaller set of effective query plans from which cost can be estimated, and thus the lowest-cost plan of the set can be executed.

An example of a database system that uses a hybrid optimizer is MySQL. The query optimizer in MySQL is designed around a select-project-join strategy, which combines a cost-based and heuristic optimizer that uses known optimal mechanisms, thus resulting in fewer alternatives from which cost-based optimization can choose the minimal execution path. This strategy ensures an overall "good" execution plan, but does not guarantee to generate the best plan. This strategy has proven to work well for a vast variety of queries running in different environments. The internal representation of MySQL has been shown to perform well enough to rival the execution speeds of the largest of the production database systems.

An example of a database system that uses a cost-based optimizer is Microsoft's SQL Server. The query optimizer in SQL Server is designed around a classic cost-based optimizer that translates the query statement into a procedure that can execute efficiently and return the desired results. The optimizer uses information, or statistics,[11] collected from values recorded in past queries and the characteristics of the data in the database to create alternative procedures that represent the same query. The statistics are applied to each procedure to predict which one can be executed more efficiently. Once the most efficient procedure is identified, execution begins and results are returned to the client.

Optimization of queries can be complicated by using unbound parameters, such as a user predicate. For example, an unbound parameter is created when a query within a stored procedure accepts a parameter from the user when the stored procedure is executed. In this case, query optimization may not be possible, or it may not generate the lowest cost unless some knowledge of the predicate is obtained prior to execution. If very few records satisfy the predicate, even a basic index is far superior to the file scan. The opposite is true if many records qualify. If the selectivity is not known when optimization is performed because the predicate is unbound, the choice among these alternative plans should be delayed until execution.

The problem of selectivity can be overcome by building optimizers that can adopt the predicate as an open variable and perform query plan planning by generating all possible query plans that are likely to occur based on historical query execution and by utilizing the

---

11. The use of statistics in databases stems from the first cost-based optimizers. In fact, many utilities exist in commercial databases that permit the examination and generation of these statistics by database professionals to tune their databases for more efficient optimization of queries.

statistics from the cost-based optimizer. The statistics include the frequency distribution for the predicate's attribute.

Internal Representation of Queries

A query can be represented within a database system using several alternate forms of the original SQL command. These alternate forms exist due to redundancies in SQL, the equivalence of subqueries and joins under certain constraints, and logical inferences that can be drawn from predicates in the WHERE clause. Having alternate forms of the query poses a problem for database implementers because the query optimizer must choose the optimal access plan for a query regardless of how it was originally formed by the user.

Once the query optimizer has either formed an efficient execution plan (heuristic and hybrid optimizers) or has chosen the most efficient plan (cost-based optimizers), the query is then passed to the next phase of the process: execution.

Query Execution

Database systems can use several methods to execute queries. Most database systems use either an *iterative* or an *interpretative* execution strategy.

Iterative methods provide ways of producing a sequence of calls available for processing discrete operations (join, project, etc.), but are not designed to incorporate the features of the internal representation. Translation of queries into iterative methods uses techniques of functional programming and program transformation. Several algorithms are available that generate iterative programs from algebra-based query specifications. For example, some algorithms translate query specifications into recursive programs, which are simplified by sets of transformation rules before the algorithm generates an execution plan. Another algorithm uses a two-level translation. The first level uses a smaller set of transformation rules to simplify the internal representation, and the second level applies functional transformations prior to generating the execution plan.

The implementation of this mechanism creates a set of defined compiled functional primitives, formed using a high-level language, which are then linked together via a call stack, or procedural call sequence. When a query execution plan is created and selected for execution, a compiler (usually the same one used to create the database system) is used to compile the procedural calls into a binary executable. Due to the high cost of the iterative method, compiled execution plans are typically stored for reuse for similar or identical queries.

Interpretative methods, on the other hand, form query execution using existing compiled abstractions of basic operations. The query execution plan chosen is reconstructed as a queue of method calls, which are each taken off the queue and processed. The results are then placed in memory for use with the next or subsequent calls. Implementation of this strategy is often called *lazy evaluation* because the set of available compiled methods is not optimized for best performance; rather, the methods are optimized for generality. Most database systems use the interpretative method of query execution.

One area that is often confusing is the concept of *compiled*. Some database experts consider a compiled query to be an actual compilation of an iterative query execution plan, but in Date's work, a compiled query is simply one that has been optimized and stored for future execution. I won't use the word *compiled* because the MySQL query optimizer and execution engine do not store the query execution plan for later reuse (an exception is the MySQL query cache), nor does the query execution require any compilation or assembly to work. Interestingly, the concept of a stored procedure fits this second category; it is compiled (or optimized) for execution at a later date and can be run many times on data that meets its input parameters.

Query execution evaluates each part of the query tree (or query as represented by the internal structures) and executes methods for each part. The methods supported mirror those operations defined in relational algebra, project, restrict, union, intersect, and so on. For each of these operations, the query execution engine performs a method that evaluates the incoming data and passes the processed data along to the next step. For example, a project operation is where only some of the attributes (or columns) of data are returned. In this case, the query execution engine would strip the data for the attributes that do not meet the specification of the restriction and pass the remaining data to the next operation in the tree (or structure). Table 2-2 lists the most common operations supported and briefly describes each.

Table 2-2. *Query Operations*

Operation	Description
Restrict	Returns tuples that match the conditions (predicate) of the WHERE clause (some systems treat the HAVING clause in the same or similar manner). This operation is often defined as SELECT.
Project	Returns the attributes specified in the column list of the tuple evaluated.
Join	Returns tuples that match a special condition called the *join condition* (or *join predicate*). There are many forms of joins. See the accompanying sidebar for a description of each.

JOINS

The join operation can take many forms. These are often confused by database professionals and in some cases avoided at all costs. The expressiveness of SQL permits many joins to be written as simple expressions in the WHERE clause. While it is true that most database systems correctly transform these queries into joins, it is considered a lazy form. The following lists the types of joins you are likely to encounter in an RDBS and describes each. Join operations can have join conditions (theta joins), a matching of the attribute values being compared (equijoins), or no conditions (Cartesian products). The join operation is subdivided into the following operations:

- *Inner.* The join of two relations returning tuples where there is a match.

- *Outer (left, right, full):* Returns all rows from at least one of the tables or views mentioned in the FROM clause, as long as those rows meet any WHERE search conditions. All rows are retrieved from the left table referenced with a left outer join; all rows from the right table are referenced in a right outer join. All rows from both tables are returned in a full outer join. Values for attributes of nonmatching rows are returned as null values.

- *Right outer.* The join of two relations returning tuples where there is a match plus all tuples from the relation specified to the right, leaving nonmatching attributes specified from the other relation empty (null).

- *Full outer*: The join of two relations returning all tuples from both relations, leaving nonmatching attributes specified from the other relation empty (null).

- *Cross product*: The join of two relations mapping each tuple from the first relation to all tuples from the other relation.

- *Union*: The set operation where only matches from two relations with the same schema are returned.

- *Intersect*: The set operation where only the nonmatches from two relations with the same schema are returned.

Deciding how to execute the query (or the chosen query plan) is only half of the story. The other thing to consider is how to access the data itself. There are many ways to read and write data to and from disk (files), but choosing the optimal one depends on what the query is trying to do. File-access mechanisms are created to minimize the cost of access the data from disk and maximize the performance of query execution.

File Access

The *file-access mechanism*, also called the *physical database design*, has been important since the early days of database system development. However, the significance of file access has lessened due to the effectiveness and simplicity of common file systems supported by operating systems. Today, file access is merely the application of file storage and indexing best practices, such as separating the index file from the data file and placing each on a separate disk input/output (I/O) system to increase performance. Some database systems use different file organization techniques to enable the database to be tailored to specific application needs. MySQL is perhaps the most unique in this regard due to the numerous file-access mechanisms (called *storage engines*) it supports.

Clear goals exist that must be satisfied to minimize the I/O costs in a database system. These include utilizing disk data structures that permit efficient retrieval of only the relevant data through effective access paths, and organizing data on disk so that the I/O cost for retrieving relevant data is minimized. The overriding performance objective is thus to minimize the number of disk accesses (or disk I/Os).

Many techniques for approaching database design are available. Fewer are available for file-access mechanisms (the actual physical implementation of the data files). Furthermore, many researchers agree that the optimal database design (from the physical point of view) is not achievable in general and furthermore should not be pursued. Optimization is not achievable mainly due to the much improved efficiency of modern disk subsystems. Rather, it is the knowledge of these techniques and research that permit the database implementer to implement the database system in the best manner possible to satisfy the needs of those who will use the system.

To create a structure that performs well, you must consider many factors. Early researchers considered segmenting the data into subsets based on the content or the context of the data. For example, all data containing the same department number would be grouped together and stored with references to the related data. This process can be perpetuated in that sets can be grouped together to form supersets, thus forming a hierarchical file organization.

Accessing data in this configuration involves scanning the sets at the highest level to access and scan only those sets that are necessary to obtain the desired information. This process significantly reduces the number of elements to be scanned. Keeping the data items to be scanned close together minimizes search time. The arrangement of data on disk into structured files is called file organization. The goal is to design an access method that provides a way of immediately processing transactions one by one, thereby allowing us to keep an up-to-the-second stored picture of the real-world situation.

File-organization techniques were revised as operating systems evolved in order to ensure greater efficiency of storage and retrieval. Modern database systems create new challenges for which currently accepted methods may be inadequate. This is especially true for systems that execute on hardware with increased disk speeds with high data throughput. Additionally, understanding database design approaches, not only as they are described in textbooks but also in practice, will increase the requirements levied against database systems and thus increase the drive for further research. For example, the recent adoption of redundant and distributed systems by industry has given rise to additional research in these areas to make use of new hardware and/or the need to increase data availability, security, and recovery.

Since accessing data from disk is expensive, the use of a *cache mechanism*, sometimes called a *buffer*, can significantly improve read performance from disk, thus reducing the cost of storage and retrieval of data. The concept involves copying parts of the data either in anticipation of the next disk read or based on an algorithm designed to keep the most frequently used data in memory. The handling of the differences between disk and main memory effectively is at the heart of a good-quality database system. The trade-off between the database system using disk or using main memory should be understood. See Table 2-3 for a summary of the performance trade-offs between physical storage (disk) and secondary storage (memory).

Table 2-3. *Performance Trade-offs*

Issue	Main Memory vs. Disk
Speed	Main memory is at least 1,000 times faster than disk.
Storage space	Disk can hold hundreds of times more information than memory for the same cost.
Persistence	When the power is switched off, disk keeps the data, and main memory forgets everything.
Access time	Main memory starts sending data in nanoseconds, while disk takes milliseconds.
Block size	Main memory can be accessed one word at a time, and disk one block at a time.

Advances in database physical storage have seen much of the same improvements with regard to storage strategies and buffering mechanisms, but little in the way of exploratory examination of the fundamental elements of physical storage has occurred. Some have explored the topic from a hardware level and others from a more pragmatic level of what exactly it is we need to store. The subject of persistent storage is largely forgotten due to the capable and efficient mechanisms available in the host operating system.

File-access mechanisms are used to store and retrieve the data that is encompassed by the database system. Most file-access mechanisms have additional layers of functionality that permit locating data within the file more quickly. These layers are called *index mechanisms*. Index mechanisms provide access paths (the way data will be searched for and retrieved) designed to locate specific data based on a subpart of the data called a *key*. Index mechanisms range in complexity from simple lists of keys to complex data structures designed to maximize key searches.

The goal is to find the data we want quickly and efficiently, without having to request and read more disk blocks than absolutely necessary. This can be accomplished by saving values that identify the data (or keys) and the location on disk of the record to form an index of the data. Furthermore, reading the index data is faster than reading all of the data. The primary benefit of using an index is that it allows us to search through large amounts of data efficiently without having to examine or in many cases read every item until we find the one we are searching for. Indexing therefore is concerned with methods of searching large files containing data that is stored on disk. These methods are designed for fast random access of data as well as sequential access of the data.

There are many kinds of index mechanisms. Most involve a tree structure that stores the keys and the disk block addresses. Examples include B-trees, B+trees, and hash trees. The structures are normally traversed by one or more algorithms designed to minimize the time spent searching the structure for a key. Most database systems use one form or another of the B-tree in their indexing mechanisms. These tree algorithms provide very fast search speeds without requiring a large memory space.

During the execution of the query, interpretative query execution methods access the assigned index mechanism and request the data via the access method specified. The execution methods then read the data, typically a record at a time; analyze the query for a match to the predicate by evaluating the expressions; and then pass the data through any transformations and finally on to the transmission portion of the server to send the data back to the client.

Query Results

Once all of the tuples in the tables referenced in the query have been processed, the tuples are returned to the client following the same (although sometimes alternative) communication pathways. The tuples are then passed on to the ODBC connector for encapsulation and presentation to the client application.

Relational Database Architecture Summary

In this section, I've detailed the steps taken by a query for data through a typical relational database system architecture. As you'll see, the query begins with a SQL command issued by the client; then it is passed via the ODBC connector to the database system using a communications pathway (network). The query is parsed, transformed into an internal structure, optimized, and executed, and the results are returned to the client.

Now that I've given you a glimpse of all the steps involved in processing a query and you've seen the complexity of the database system subcomponents, it is time to take a look at a real-world example. In the following section I'll present an in-depth look at the MySQL database system architecture.

The MySQL Database System

While the MySQL source code is highly organized and built using many structured classes (some are complex data structures, some are objects, but most are structures), the system is not a true modular architecture. It is important to understand this as you explore the architecture and more important later when you explore the source code. What this means is you will sometimes find instances where no clear division of architecture elements exists in the source code. For more information about the MySQL source code, including how to obtain it, see Chapter 3.

Although some may present the MySQL architecture as a component-based system built from a set of modular subcomponents, the reality is that it is neither component based nor modular. It is true that the source code is built using a mixture of C and C++, and that a number of objects are being utilized in many of the functions of the system. It is not true that the system is object oriented in the true sense of object-oriented programming. Rather, the system is built on the basis of function libraries and data structures designed to optimize the organization of the source code around that of the architecture.

However, it is also true that the MySQL architecture is an intelligent design of highly organized subsystems working in harmony to form an effective and highly reliable database system. All of the technologies I described previously in this chapter are present in the system. The subsystems that implement these technologies are well designed and implemented with the same precision source code found throughout the system. It is interesting to note that many accomplished C and C++ programmers remark at the elegance and leanness of the source code. I've often found myself marveling at the serene complexity and yet elegance of the code. Indeed, even the code authors themselves admit that their code has a sort of genius intuition that is often not fully understood or appreciated until thoroughly analyzed. You too will find yourself amazed at how well some of the source code works and how simple it is once you figure it out.

■**Note** The MySQL system has proven to be difficult for some to learn and troublesome to diagnose when things go awry. However, it is clear that once one has mastered the intricacies of the MySQL architecture and source code, the system is very accommodating and has the promise of being perhaps the first and best platform for experimental database work.

What this means is that the MySQL architecture and source code is not for new C++ programmers. If you find yourself starting to reconsider taking on the source code, please keep reading; I will be your guide in navigating the source code. But let's first begin with a look at how the system is structured.

MySQL System Architecture

The MySQL architecture is best described as a layered system of subsystems. While the source code isn't compiled as individual components or modules, the source code for the subsystems is organized in a hierarchical manner that allows subsystems to be segregated (encapsulated) in the source code. Most subsystems rely on base libraries for lower-level functions (e.g., thread control, memory allocation, networking, logging and event handling, and access control). Together the base libraries, subsystems built on those libraries, and even subsystems built from other subsystems form the abstracted API that is known as the C client API. This powerful API is what permits the MySQL system to be used as either a stand-alone server or an embedded database system in a larger application.

The architecture provides encapsulation for a SQL interface, query parsing, query optimization and execution, caching and buffering, and a pluggable storage engine. Figure 2-4 depicts the MySQL architecture and its subsystems. At the top of the drawing are the database connectors that provide access to client applications. As you can see, a connector for just about any programming environment you could want exists. To the left of the drawing, the ancillary tools are listed grouped by administration and enterprise services. For a complete discussion of the administration and enterprise service tools, see Michael Kruckenberg and Jay Pipes's *Pro MySQL*.[12] It is an excellent reference for all things administrative for MySQL.

The next layer down in the architecture from the connectors is the connection pool layer. This layer handles all of the user access, thread processing, memory, and process cache needs of the client connection. Below that layer is the heart of the database system. Here is where the query is parsed and optimized, and file access is managed. The next layer down from there is the pluggable storage engine layer. It is at this layer that part of the brilliance of the MySQL architecture shines. The pluggable storage engine layer permits the system to be built to handle a wide range of diverse data or file storage and retrieval mechanisms. This flexibility is unique to MySQL. No other database system available today provides the ability to tune databases by providing several data storage mechanisms.

Note The pluggable storage engine feature is available beginning in version 5.1.

Below the pluggable storage engine is the lowest layer of the system, the file access layer. It is at this layer that the storage mechanisms read and write data, and the system reads and writes log and event information. This layer is also the one that is closest to the operating system, along with thread, process, and memory control.

Let's begin our discussion of the MySQL architecture with the flow through the system from the client application to the data and back. The first layer encountered once the client connector (ODBC, .NET, JDBC, C API, etc.) has transmitted the SQL statements to the server is the SQL interface.

---

12. M. Kruckenberg and J. Pipes. *Pro MySQL* (Berkeley, CA: Apress, 2005).

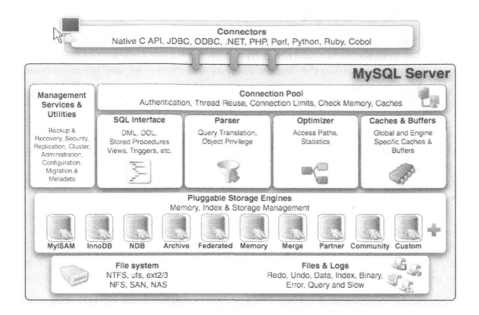

Figure 2-4. *MySQL server architecture (Copyright MySQL AB. Reprinted with kind permission.)*

SQL Interface

The SQL interface provides the mechanisms to receive commands and transmit results to the user. The MySQL SQL interface was built to the ANSI SQL standard and accepts the same basic SQL statements as most ANSI-compliant database servers. Although many of the SQL commands supported in MySQL have options that are not ANSI standard, the MySQL developers have stayed very close to the ANSI SQL standard.

Connections to the database server are received from the network communication pathways and a thread is created for each. The threaded process is the heart of the executable pathway in the MySQL server. MySQL is built as a true multithreaded application whereby each thread executes independently of the other threads (except for certain helper threads). The incoming SQL command is stored in a class structure and the results are transmitted to the client by writing the results out to the network communication protocols. Once a thread has been created, the MySQL server attempts to parse the SQL command and store the parts in the internal data structure.

Parser

When a client issues a query, a new thread is created and the SQL statement is forwarded to the parser for syntactic validation (or rejection due to errors). The MySQL parser is implemented using a large Lex-YACC script that is compiled with Bison. The parser constructs a query structure used to represent the query statement (SQL) in memory as a *tree structure* (also called an *abstract syntax tree*) that can be used to execute the query.

Considered by many to be the most complex part of the MySQL source code and the most elegant, the parser is implemented using Lex and YACC, which were originally built for compiler construction. These tools are used to build a lexical analyzer that reads a SQL statement and breaks the statement into parts, assigning the command portions, options, and parameters to a structure of variables and lists. This structure (named imaginatively Lex) is the internal representation of the SQL query. As a result, this structure is used by every other step in the query process. The Lex structure contains lists of tables being used, field names referenced, join conditions, expressions, and all the parts of the query stored in a separate space.

The parser works by reading the SQL statement and comparing the expressions (consisting of tokens and symbols) with rules defined in the source code. These rules are built into the code using Lex and YACC and later compiled with Bison to form the lexical analyzer. If you examine the parser in its C form (a file named /sql/sql_yacc.cc), you may become overwhelmed with the terseness and sheer enormity of the switch statement.[13] A better way to examine the parser is to look at the Lex and YACC form prior to compilation (a file named /sql/sql_yacc.yy). This file contains the rules as written for YACC and is much easier to decipher. The construction of the parser illustrates MySQL AB's open source philosophy at work: why create your own language handler when special compiler construction tools like Lex, YACC, and Bison are designed to do just that?

Once the parser identifies a regular expression and breaks the query statement into parts, it assigns the appropriate command type to the thread structure and returns control to the command processor (which is sometimes considered part of the parser, but more correctly is part of the main code). The command processor is implemented as a large switch statement with cases for every command supported. The query parser only checks the correctness of the SQL statement. It does not verify the existence of tables or attributes (fields) referenced, nor does it check for semantic errors such as an aggregate function used without a GROUP BY clause. Instead, the verification is left to the optimizer. Thus, the query structure from the parser is passed to the query processor. From there, control switches to the query optimizer.

LEX AND YACC

Lex stands for "lexical analyzer generator" and is used as a parser to identify tokens and literals as well as syntax of a language. YACC stands for "yet another compiler compiler" and is used to identify and act on the semantic definitions of the language. The use of these tools together with Bison (a YACC compiler) provides a rich mechanism of creating subsystems that can parse and process language commands. Indeed, that is exactly how MySQL uses these technologies.

■**Tip** The sql_yacc.yy, sql_lex.h, and lex.h files are where you would begin to construct your own SQL commands in MySQL. These files will be discussed in more detail in Chapter 8.

---

13. Kruckenberg and Pipes compare the experience to a mind melt. Levity aside, it can be a challenge for anyone who is unfamiliar with YACC.

Query Optimizer

The MySQL query optimizer subsystem is considered by some to be misnamed. The optimizer used is a SELECT-PROJECT-JOIN strategy that attempts to restructure the query by first doing any restrictions (SELECT) to narrow the number of tuples to work with, then performs the projections to reduce the number of attributes (fields) in the resulting tuples, and finally evaluates any join conditions. While not considered a member of the extremely complicated query optimizer category, the SELECT-PROJECT-JOIN strategy falls into the category of heuristic optimizers. In this case, the heuristics (rules) are simply

- Horizontally eliminate extra data by evaluating the expressions in the WHERE (HAVING) clause.

- Vertically eliminate extra data by limiting the data to the attributes specified in the attribute list. The exception is the storage of the attributes used in the join clause that may not be kept in the final query.

- Evaluate join expressions.

This results in a strategy that ensures a known-good access method to retrieve data in an efficient manner. Despite critical reviews, the SELECT-PROJECT-JOIN strategy has proven effective at executing the typical queries found in transaction processing. Figure 2-5 depicts a block diagram that describes the MySQL query processing methodology.

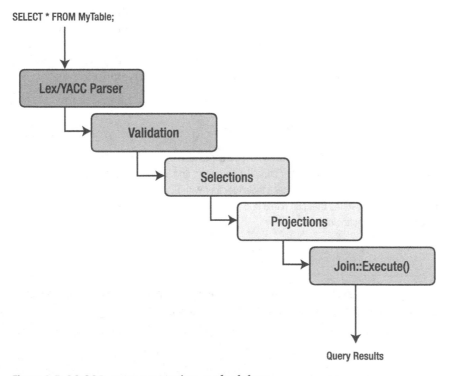

Figure 2-5. *MySQL query processing methodology*

■Note This is another tenet of MySQL AB: build features that optimize the current needs of the community.

The first step in the optimizer is to check for the existence of tables and access control by the user. If there are errors, the appropriate error message is returned and control returns to the thread manager, or listener. Once the correct tables have been identified, they are opened and the appropriate locks are applied for concurrency control.

Once all of the maintenance and setup tasks are complete, the optimizer uses the internal query structure (Lex) and evaluates the WHERE conditions (a restrict operation) of the query. Results are returned as temporary tables to prepare for the next step. If UNION operators are present, the optimizer executes the SELECT portions of all statements in a loop before continuing.

The next step in the optimizer is to execute the projections. These are executed in a similar manner as the restrict portions, again storing the intermediate results as temporary tables and saving only those attributes specified in the column specification in the SELECT statement. Lastly, the structure is analyzed for any JOIN conditions that are built using the join class, and then the join::optimize() method is called. At this stage the query is optimized by evaluating the expressions and eliminating any conditions that result in dead branches or always true or always false conditions (as well as many other similar optimizations). The optimizer is attempting to eliminate any known-bad conditions in the query before executing the join. This is done because joins are the most expensive and time consuming of all of the relational operators. It is also important to note that the join optimization step is performed for all queries that have a WHERE or HAVING clause regardless of whether there are any join conditions. This enables developers to concentrate all of the expression evaluation code in one place. Once the join optimization is complete, the optimizer uses a series of conditional statements to route the query to the appropriate library method for execution.

The query optimizer and execution engine is perhaps the second most difficult area to understand due to its SELECT-PROJECT-JOIN optimizer approach. Complicating matters is that this portion of the server is a mixture of C and C++ code, where the typical select execution is written as C methods while the join operation is written as a C++ object. In Chapter 11, I'll show you how to write your own query optimizer and use it instead of the MySQL optimizer.

Query Execution

Execution of the query is handled by a set of library methods designed to implement a particular query. For example, the mysql_insert() method is designed to insert data. Likewise, there is a mysql_select() method designed to find and return data matching the WHERE clause. This library of execution methods is located in a variety of source code files under a file of a similar name (e.g., sql_insert.cc or sql_select.cc). All of these methods have as a parameter a thread object that permits the method to access the internal query structure and eases execution. Results from each of the execution methods are returned using the network communication pathways library. The query execution library methods are clearly implemented using the interpretative model of query execution.

Query Cache

While not its own subsystem, the query cache should be considered a vital part of the query optimization and execution subsystem. The query cache is a marvelous invention that caches not only the query structure but also the query results themselves. This enables the system to check for frequently used queries and shortcut the entire query optimization and execution stages altogether. This is another of the technologies that is unique to MySQL. Other database system cache queries, but no others cache the actual results. As you can appreciate, the query cache must also allow for situations where the results are "dirty" in the sense that something has changed since the last time the query was run (e.g., an INSERT, UPDATE, or DELETE was run against the base table) and that the cached queries may need to be occasionally purged.

Tip The query cache is turned on by default. If you want to turn off the query cache, you can use the SQL_NO_CACHE SELECT option: SELECT SQL_NO_CACHE id, lname FROM myCustomer;.

If you are not familiar with this technology, try it out. Find a table that has a sufficient number of tuples and execute a query that has some complexity, such as a JOIN or complex WHERE clause. Record the time it took to execute, then execute the same query again. Note the time difference. This is the query cache in action. Listing 2-1 illustrates this exercise.

Listing 2-1. *The MySQL Query Cache in Action*

```
mysql> SELECT SQL_NO_CACHE professionals.last_name,
certifications.certificate_level
FROM professionals JOIN certifications
ON professionals.unique_no = certifications.unique_no
WHERE professionals.med_class > 1 AND certifications.last_name = 'Bell';
```

```
+-----------+-------------------+
| last_name | certificate_level |
+-----------+-------------------+
| BELL      | P                 |
| BELL      | S                 |
| BELL      | Y                 |
| BELL      | P                 |
| BELL      | S                 |
+-----------+-------------------+
5 rows in set (1.94 sec)
```

```
mysql> SELECT SQL_CACHE professionals.last_name,
certifications.certificate_level
FROM professionals JOIN certifications
ON professionals.unique_no = certifications.unique_no
WHERE professionals.med_class > 1 AND certifications.last_name = 'Bell';
```

```
+-----------+-------------------+
| last_name | certificate_level |
+-----------+-------------------+
| BELL      | P                 |
| BELL      | S                 |
| BELL      | Y                 |
| BELL      | P                 |
| BELL      | S                 |
+-----------+-------------------+
5 rows in set (0.61 sec)
```

```
mysql> SELECT SQL_CACHE professionals.last_name,
certifications.certificate_level FROM
professionals JOIN certifications
ON professionals.unique_no = certifications.unique_no
WHERE professionals.med_class > 1 AND certifications.last_name = 'Bell';
```

```
+-----------+-------------------+
| last_name | certificate_level |
+-----------+-------------------+
| BELL      | P                 |
| BELL      | S                 |
| BELL      | Y                 |
| BELL      | P                 |
| BELL      | S                 |
+-----------+-------------------+
5 rows in set (0.61 sec)

mysql>
```

Cache and Buffers

The caching and buffers subsystem is responsible for ensuring that the most frequently used data (or structures, as you will see) are available in the most efficient manner possible. In other words, the data must be resident or ready to read at all times. The caches dramatically increase the response time for requests for that data because the data is in memory and thus no additional disk access is necessary to retrieve it. The cache subsystem was created to encapsulate all of the caching and buffering into a loosely coupled set of library functions. Although you will find the caches implemented in several different source code files, they are considered part of the same subsystem.

A number of caches are implemented in this subsystem. Most of the cache mechanisms use the same or similar concept of storing data as structures in a linked list. The caches are implemented in different portions of the code to tailor the implementation to the type of data that is being cached. Let's look at each of the caches.

Table Cache

The *table cache* was created to minimize the overhead in opening, reading, and closing tables (the .FRM files on disk). For this reason, the table cache is designed to store metadata about the tables in memory. This makes it much faster for a thread to read the schema of the table without having to reopen the file every time. Each thread has its own list of table cache structures. This permits the threads to maintain their own views of the tables so that if one thread is altering the schema of a table (but has not committed the changes) another thread may use that table with the original schema. The structure used is a simple one that includes all of the metadata information for a table. The structures are stored in a linked list in memory and associated with each thread.

Record Cache

The *record cache* was created to enhance sequential reads from the storage engines. Thus the record cache is usually only used during table scans. It works like a read-ahead buffer by retrieving a block of data at a time, thus resulting in fewer disk accesses during the scan. Fewer disk accesses generally equates to improved performance. Interestingly, the record cache is also used in writing data sequentially by writing the new (or altered) data to the cache first and then writing the cache to disk when full. In this way write performance is improved as well. This sequential behavior (called *locality of reference*) is the main reason the record cache is most often used with the MyISAM storage engine, although it is not limited to MyISAM. The record cache is implemented in an agnostic manner that doesn't interfere with the code used to access the storage engine API. Developers don't have to do anything to take advantage of the record cache as it is implemented within the layers of the API.

Key Cache

The *key cache* is a buffer for frequently used index data. In this case, it is a block of data for the index file (B-tree) and is used exclusively for MyISAM tables (the .MYI files on disk). The indexes themselves are stored as linked lists within the key cache structure. A key cache is created when a MyISAM table is opened for the first time. The key cache is accessed on every index read. If an index is found in the cache, it is read from there; otherwise, a new index block must be read from disk and placed into the cache. However, the cache has a limited size and is tunable by changing the key_cache_block_size configuration variable. Thus not all blocks of the index file will fit into memory. So how does the system keep track of which blocks have been used?

   The cache implements a monitoring system to keep track of how frequent the index blocks are used. The key cache has been implemented to keep track of how "warm" the index blocks are. *Warm* in this case refers to how many times the index block has been accessed over time. Values for warm include BLOCK_COLD, BLOCK_WARM, and BLOCK_HOT. As the blocks cool off and new blocks become warm, the cold blocks are purged and the warm blocks added. This strategy is a least recently used (LRU) page-replacement strategy—the same algorithm used for virtual memory management and disk buffering in operating systems—that has been proven to be remarkably efficient even in the face of much more sophisticated page-replacement algorithms. In a similar way, the key cache keeps track of the index blocks that have changed (called getting "dirty"). When a dirty block is purged, its data is written back to the index file on disk before being replaced. Conversely, when a clean block is purged it is simply removed from memory.

Note Practice has shown that the LRU algorithm performs within 80 percent of the best algorithms. In a world where time is precious and simplicity ensures reliability, the 80 percent solution is a win-win.

Privilege Cache

The *privilege cache* is used to store grant data on a user account. This data is stored in the same manner as an access control list (ACL), which lists all of the privileges a user has for an object in the system. The privilege cache is implemented as a structure stored in a first in, last out (FILO) hash table. Data for the cache is gathered when the grant tables are read during user authentication and initialization. It is important to store this data in memory as it saves a lot of time reading the grant tables.

Hostname Cache

The *hostname cache* is another of the helper caches, like the privilege cache. It too is implemented as a stack of a structure. It contains the hostnames of all the connections to the server. It may seem surprising, but this data is frequently requested and therefore in high demand and a candidate for a dedicated cache.

Miscellaneous

A number of other small cache mechanisms are implemented throughout the MySQL source code. One example is the *join buffer cache* used during complex join operations. For example, some join operations require comparing one tuple to all the tuples in the second table. A cache in this case can store the tuples read so that the join can be implemented without having to reread the second table into memory multiple times.

File Access via Pluggable Storage Engines

One of the best features of MySQL is the ability to support different storage engines, or file types. This allows database professionals to tune their database performance by selecting the storage engine that best meets their application needs. Examples include using storage engines that provide transaction control for highly active databases where transaction processing is required or using the memory storage engine whenever a table is read many times but seldom updated (e.g., a lookup table).

MySQL AB added a new architectural design in version 5 that makes it easier to add new storage types. The new mechanism is called the MySQL pluggable storage engine. MySQL AB has worked hard to make the server extensible via the pluggable storage engine. The pluggable storage engine was created as an abstraction of the file access layer and built as an API that MySQL AB (or anyone) can use to build specialized file-access mechanisms called storage engines. The API provides a set of methods and access utilities for reading and writing data. These methods combine to form a standardized modular architecture that permits storage engines to use the same methods for every storage engine (this is the essence of why it is called pluggable—the storage engines all plug into the server using the same API).

What is perhaps most interesting of all is the fact that it is possible to assign a different storage engine to each table in a given database. It is even possible to change storage engines after a table is created. This flexibility and modularity permits database implementers (you!) to create new storage engines as the need arises. To change storage engines for a table, you can issue a command like the following:

```
ALTER TABLE MyTable
ENGINE = InnoDB;
```

The pluggable storage engine is perhaps the most unique feature of MySQL. No other database system comes close to having this level of flexibility and extensibility for the file access layer of the architecture. The following sections describe all of the storage engines available in the server and present a brief overview of how you can create your own storage engine. I'll show you how to create your own storage engine in Chapter 7.

The strengths and weaknesses of the storage engines are many and varied. For example, some of the storage engines offered in MySQL support concurrency. The default storage engine for MySQL is MyISAM. It supports table-level locking for concurrency control. That is, when an update is in progress no other processes can access any data from the same table until the operation is completed. The MyISAM storage engine is also the fastest of the available types due to optimizations made using indexed sequential access method (ISAM) principles. The Berkeley Database (BDB) tables support page-level locking for concurrency control; when an update is in progress, no other processes can access any data from the same page as that of the data being modified until the operation is complete. The InnoDB tables support record locking (sometimes called row-level locking) for concurrency control; when an update is in progress, no other processes can access that row in the table until the operation is complete. Thus, the InnoDB table type provides an advantage for use in situations where many concurrent updates are expected. However, any of these storage engines will perform well in read-only environments such as web servers or kiosk applications.

Concurrency operations like those we've discussed are implemented in database systems using specialized commands that form a transaction subsystem. Currently, only three of the storage engines listed support transactions: BDB, InnoDB, and NDB. Transactions provide a mechanism that permits a set of operations to execute as a single atomic operation. For example, if a database was built for a banking institution the macro operations of transferring money from one account to another would preferably be executed completely (money removed from one account and placed in another) without interruption. Transactions permit these operations to be encased in an atomic operation that will back out any changes should an error occur before all operations are complete, thus avoiding data being removed from one table and never making it to the next table. A sample set of operations in the form of SQL statements encased in transactional commands is shown here:

```
START TRANSACTION;
UPDATE SavingsAccount SET Balance = Balance - 100
WHERE AccountNum = 123;
UPDATE CheckingAccount SET Balance = Balance + 100
WHERE AccountNum = 345;
COMMIT;
```

In practice, most database professionals specify the MyISAM table type if they require faster access and InnoDB if they need transaction support. Fortunately, MySQL provides facilities to specify a table type for each table in a database. In fact, tables within a database do not have to be the same type. This variety of storage engines permits the tuning of databases for a wide range of applications.

Interestingly, it is possible to extend this list of storage engines by writing your own table handler. MySQL provides examples and code stubs to make this feature accessible to the system developer. The ability to extend this list of storage engines makes it possible to add support to MySQL for complex, proprietary data formats and access layers.

MyISAM

The MyISAM storage engine is the default file-access mechanism for all tables created without setting the ENGINE option on the CREATE statement. This storage engine is the one used by most LAMP stacks, data warehousing, e-commerce, and enterprise applications. MyISAM files are an extension of ISAM built with additional optimizations such as advanced caching and indexing mechanisms. These tables are built using compression features and index optimizations for speed. Additionally, the MyISAM storage engine provides for concurrent operations by providing table-level locking. The MyISAM storage mechanism offers reliable storage for a wide variety of applications while providing fast retrieval of data. MyISAM is the storage engine of choice where read performance is a concern.

Tip You can change the default storage engine by setting the STORAGE_ENGINE configuration server variable.

ISAM

The ISAM file-access method has been around a long time. ISAM was originally created by IBM and later used in System R. (System R was IBM's experimental RDBS that is considered by many to be the seminal work and the ancestor to all RDBSs today. Some have cited Ingres as the original RDBS.)

ISAM files store data by organizing them into tuples of fixed-length attributes. The tuples are stored in a given order. This was done to speed access from tape. Yes, back in the day that was a database implementer's only choice of storage except, of course, punch cards! It is usually at this point that I embarrass myself by showing my age. If you too remember punch cards, then you and I probably share an experience few will ever have again—dropping a deck of cards that hadn't been numbered or printed (printing the data on the top of the card used to take a lot longer and was often skipped).

The ISAM files also have an external indexing mechanism that was normally implemented as a hash table that contained pointers (tape block numbers and counts), allowing you to fast-forward the tape to the desired location. This permitted fast access to data stored on tape—well, as fast as the tape drive could fast-forward.

While created for tape, it is easy to see that the ISAM mechanism can be (and often is) used for disk file systems. The greatest asset of the ISAM mechanism is that the index is normally very small and can be searched quickly since it can be searched using an in-memory search mechanism. Some later versions of the ISAM mechanisms permitted the creation of alternative indexes, thus enabling the file (table) to be accessed via several search mechanisms. This external indexing mechanism has become the standard for all modern database storage engines.

MySQL included an ISAM storage engine (referred to then as a table type), but the ISAM storage engine has been replaced with the MyISAM storage engine. Future plans include replacing the MyISAM storage engine with a more modern transactional storage engine.

Note Older versions of MySQL supported an ISAM storage engine. With the introduction of MyISAM, MySQL AB has deprecated the ISAM storage engine.

InnoDB

InnoDB is a third-party storage engine licensed from Innobase (www.innodb.com) distributed under the GNU Public License (GPL) agreement. InnoDB is most often used when you need to use transactions. InnoDB supports traditional ACID transactions (see the accompanying sidebar) and foreign key constraints. All indexes in InnoDB are B-trees where the index records are stored in the leaf pages of the tree. InnoDB improves the concurrency control of MyISAM by providing row-level locking. InnoDB is the storage engine of choice for high reliability and transaction processing environments.

WHAT IS ACID?

ACID stands for atomicity, consistency, isolation, and durability. It is perhaps one of the most important concepts in database theory. It defines the behavior that database systems must exhibit to be considered reliable for transaction processing.

- *Atomicity* means the database must allow modifications of data on an "all or nothing" basis for transactions that contain multiple commands. That is, each transaction is atomic. If one of the commands fails, the entire transaction fails and all changes up to that point in the transaction are discarded. This is especially important for systems that operate in highly transactional environments such as the financial market. Consider for a moment the ramifications of a money transfer. Typically, multiple steps are involved in debiting one account and crediting another. If the transaction fails after the debit step and doesn't credit the money back to the first account, the owner of that account will be very angry. In this case, the entire transaction from debit to credit must succeed or none of it does.

- *Consistency* means only valid data will be stored in the database. That is, if a command in a transaction violates one of the consistency rules, the entire transaction is discarded and the data is returned to the state it was in before the transaction began. Conversely, if a transaction completes successfully, it will alter the data in a manner that obeys the database consistency rules.

- *Isolation* means that if there are multiple transactions executing at the same time, they will not interfere with one another. This is where the true challenge of concurrency is most evident. Database systems must be able to handle situations where transactions cannot violate the data (alter, delete, etc.) being used in another transaction. There are many ways to handle this. Most systems use a mechanism called locking that keeps the data from being used by another transaction until the first one is done. Although the isolation property does not dictate which transaction is executed first, it does ensure they will not interfere with one another.

- *Durability* means that no transaction will result in lost data nor will any data created or altered during the transaction be lost. Durability is usually provided by robust backup and restore maintenance functions. Some database systems use logging to ensure that any uncommitted data can be recovered on restart.

BDB

BDB stands for *Berkeley Database*. BDB is a third-party storage engine licensed from SleepyCat (www.sleepycat.com). The BDB storage engine is considered an alternative to InnoDB and also supports transactions along with additional transaction features such as COMMIT and ROLLBACK. BDB supports hash tables, B-trees, simple record number–based storage, and persistent queues.

■**Note** While Oracle now owns both InnoDB and BDB, agreements are in place to preserve the integration of both technologies for the next few years. However, BDB support may be dropped from the supported storage engines in the near future.

Memory

The *memory storage engine* (sometimes called *HEAP tables*) is an in-memory table that uses a hashing mechanism for fast retrieval of frequently used data. Thus, these tables are much faster than those that are stored and referenced from disk. They are accessed in the same manner as the other storage engines, but the data is stored in-memory and is valid only during the MySQL session. The data is flushed and deleted on shutdown (or a crash). Memory storage engines are typically used in situations where static data is accessed frequently and rarely ever altered. Examples of such situations include zip code, state, county, category, and other lookup tables. HEAP tables can also be used in databases that utilize snapshot techniques for distributed or historical data access.

■**Tip** A memory-based table is created under the /data_dir/database_name/table_name.frm directory. It is possible to automatically create memory-based tables using the --init-file=file startup option. In this case, the file specified should contain the SQL statements to re-create the table. Since the table was created once, you can omit the CREATE statement because the table definition is not deleted on system restart.

Merge

The *merge storage engine* is built using a set of MyISAM tables with the same structure (tuple layout or schema) that can be referenced as a single table. Thus, the tables are partitioned by the location of the individual tables, but no additional partitioning mechanisms are used. All tables must reside on the same machine (accessed by the same server). Data is accessed using singular operations or statements such as SELECT, UPDATE, INSERT, and DELETE. Fortunately, when a DROP is issued on a merge table, only the merge specification is removed. The original tables are not altered.

The biggest benefit of this table type is speed. It is possible to split a large table into several smaller tables on different disks, combine them using a merge table specification, and access them simultaneously. Searches and sorts will execute more quickly since there is less data in each table to manipulate. For example, if you divide the data by a predicate, you can search only those specific portions that contain the category you are searching for. Similarly, repairs on tables are more efficient because it is faster and easier to repair several smaller individual files than a single large table. Presumably, most errors will be localized to an area within one or two of the files and thus will not require rebuilding and repair of all the data. Unfortunately, this configuration has several disadvantages:

- You can only use identical MyISAM tables, or schemas, to form a single merge table. This limits the application of the merge storage engine to MyISAM tables. If the merge storage engine were to accept any storage engine, the merge storage engine would be more versatile.

- The replace operation is not permitted.

- Indexed access has been shown to be less efficient than for a single table.

Merge storage mechanisms are best used in very large database (VLDB) applications like data warehousing where data resides in more than one table in one or more databases.

Archive

The *archive storage engine* is designed for storing large amounts of data in a compressed format. The archive storage mechanism is best used for storing and retrieving large amounts of seldom-accessed archival or historical data. Such data includes security access data logs. While not something that you would want to search or even use daily, it is something a database professional who is concerned about security would want to have should a security incident occur.

No indexes are provided for the archive storage mechanism and the only access method is via a table scan. Thus, the archive storage engine should not be used for normal database storage and retrieval.

Federated

The *federated storage engine* is designed to create a single table reference from multiple database systems. The federated storage engine therefore works like the merge storage engine but allows you to link data (tables) together across database servers. This mechanism is similar in purpose to the linked data tables available in other database systems. The federated storage mechanism is best used in distributed or data mart environments.

The most interesting aspect of the federated storage engine is that it does not move data, nor does it require the remote tables to be the same storage engine. This illustrates the true power of the pluggable storage engine layer. Data is translated during storage and retrieval.

Cluster/NDB

The *cluster storage engine* (called NDB to distinguish it from the cluster product[14]) was created to handle the cluster server capabilities of MySQL. The cluster storage mechanism is used almost exclusively when clustering multiple MySQL servers in a high-availability and high-performance environment. The cluster storage engine does not store any data. Instead, it delegates the storage and retrieval of the data to the storage engines used in the databases in the cluster. It manages the control of distributing the data across the cluster, thus providing redundancy and

---

14. For more information about the NDB API, see http://dev.mysql.com/doc/ndbapi/en/overview-ndb-api.html.

performance enhancements. The NDB storage engine also provides an API for creating extensible cluster solutions.

CSV

The *CSV storage engine* is an engine designed to create, read, and write comma-separated value (CSV) files as tables. While the CSV storage engine does not copy the data into another format, the sheet layout, or metadata, is stored along with the filename specified on the server in the database folder. This permits database professionals to rapidly export structured business data that is stored in spreadsheets. The CSV storage engine does not provide any indexing mechanisms.

Blackhole

The *blackhole storage engine* is an interesting feature that has surprising utility. It is designed to permit the system to write data but the data is never saved. However, if binary logging is enabled, the SQL statements are written to the logs. This permits database professionals to temporarily disable data ingestion in the database by switching the table type. This can be handy in situations where you want to test an application to ensure it is writing data but you don't want to store it.

Custom

The *custom storage engine* represents any storage engine you create to enhance your database server. For example, you may want to create a storage engine that reads XML files. While you could convert the XML files into tables, you may not want to do that if you have a large number of files you need to access. The following is an overview of how you would create such an engine.

If you were considering using the XML storage engine to read a particular set of similar XML files, the first thing you would do is analyze the format, or schema, of your XML files and determine how you want to resolve the self-describing nature of XML files. Let's say that all of the files contain the same basic data types but have differing tags and ordering of the tags. In this case, you decide to use style sheets to transform the files to a consistent format.

Once you've decided on the format, you can begin developing your new storage engine by examining the example storage engine included with the MySQL source code in a folder named .\storage\example on the main source code tree. You'll find a makefile and two source code files (ha_example.h, ha_example.cc) with a stubbed-out set of code that permits the engine to work, but the code isn't really interesting because it doesn't do anything. However, you can read the comments that the programmers left describing the features you will need to implement for your own storage engine. For example, the method for opening the file is called ha_example::open. When you examine the example storage engine files, you find this method in the ha_example.cpp file. Listing 2-2 shows an example of the open method.

Listing 2-2. *Open Tables Method*

```
/*
  Used for opening tables. The name will be the name of the file.
  A table is opened when it needs to be opened. For instance
  when a request comes in for a select on the table (tables are not
  opened and closed for each request, they are cached).

  Called from handler.cc by handler::ha_open(). The server opens all tables by
  calling ha_open() which then calls the handler specific open().
*/
int ha_example::open(const char *name, int mode, uint test_if_locked)
{
  DBUG_ENTER("ha_example::open");

  if (!(share = get_share(name, table)))
    DBUG_RETURN(1);
  thr_lock_data_init(&share->lock,&lock,NULL);

  DBUG_RETURN(0);
}
```

Tip You can also create storage engines in the Microsoft Windows environment. In this case, the files are in a Visual Studio project.

The example in Listing 2-2 explains what the method ha_example::open does and gives you an idea of how it is called and what return to expect. Although the source code may look strange to you now, it will become clearer the more you read it and the more familiar you become with the MySQL coding style.

Note Previous versions of MySQL (prior to version 5.1) permit the creation of custom storage engines, but you were required to recompile the server executable in order to pick up the changes. With the new version 5.1 pluggable architecture, the modular API permits the storage engines to have diverse implementation and features and allows them to be built independently of the MySQL system code. Thus, you need not modify the MySQL source code directly. Your new storage engine project allows you to create your own custom engine and then compile and link it with an existing running server.

Once you are comfortable with the example storage engine and how it works, you can copy and rename the files to something more appropriate to your new engine and then begin modifying the files to read from XML files. Like all good programmers, you begin by implementing one method at a time and testing your code until you are satisfied it works properly. Once you have all of the functionality you want and you compile the storage engine and link it to your production server, your new storage engine becomes available for anyone to use.

Although this may sound like a difficult task, it isn't really and can be a good way to get started learning the MySQL source code. I'll return to creating a custom storage engine with detailed step-by-step instructions in Chapter 7.

Summary

In this chapter, I presented the architecture of a typical RDBS. While short of being a complete database theory lesson, this chapter gave you a look inside the relational database architecture and you should now have an idea of what goes on inside the box. I also examined the MySQL server architecture and explained where in the source code all of the parts that make up the MySQL server architecture reside.

The knowledge of how an RDBS works and the examination of the MySQL server architecture will prepare you for an intensive journey into extending the MySQL database system. With the knowledge of the MySQL architecture, you're now armed (but not very dangerous).

In the next chapter, I'll lead you on a tour of the MySQL source code that will enable you to begin your journey of extending the MySQL system for your own needs. So roll up your sleeves and get your geek on;[15] we're headed into the source code!

---

15. Known best by the characteristic reclined-computer-chair, caffeine-laden-beverage-at-the-ready, music-blasting, hands-on-keyboard pose many of us enter while coding.

CHAPTER 3

■ ■ ■

A Tour of the MySQL Source Code

This chapter presents a complete introduction to the MySQL source, along with an explanation of how to obtain and build the system. I'll introduce you to the mechanics of the source code as well as coding guidelines and best practices for how to maintain the code. I'll focus on the parts of the code that deal with processing queries; this will set the stage for topics introduced in Chapter 7 and beyond.

Getting Started

In this section, I examine the principles behind modifying the MySQL source code and how you can obtain the source code. Let's begin with a review of the available licensing options.

Understanding the Licensing Options

When planning your modifications to open source software, consider how you're going to use those modifications. More specifically, how are you going to acquire the source code and work with it? Depending on your intentions for the modifications, your choices will be very different from others. There are three principal ways you may want to modify the source code:

- You may be modifying the source code to gain insight on how MySQL is constructed and therefore you are following the examples in this book or working on your own experiments.

- You may want to develop a capability for you or your organization that will not be distributed outside your organization.

- You may be building an application or extension that you plan to share or market to others.

In the first chapter I discussed the responsibilities of an open source developer modifying software under an open source license. Since MySQL uses the GPL and a commercial license (called a *dual license*), we must consider these uses of the source code under *both* licenses. I'll begin our discussion with the GPL.

Modifying the source code in a purely academic session is permissible under the GPL. The GPL clearly gives you the freedom to change the source code and experiment with it. The value of your contribution may contribute to whether your code is released under the GPL. For example, if your code modifications are considered singular in focus (they only apply to a limited set of users for a special purpose), the code may not be included in the source code base. In a similar way, if your code was focused on the exploration of an academic exercise, the code may not be of value to anyone other than yourself. Few at MySQL AB would consider an academic exercise in which you test options and features implemented in the source code as adding value to the MySQL system. On the other hand, if your experiments lead to a successful and meaningful addition to the system, most would agree you're obligated to share your findings. For the purposes of this book, you'll proceed with modifying the source code as if you will not be sharing your modifications. Although I hope that you find the experiments in this book enlightening and entertaining, I don't think they would be considered for adoption into the MySQL system without further development. If you take these examples and make something wonderful out of them, you have my blessing. Just be sure to tell everyone where you got the idea.

If you're modifying the MySQL source code for use by you or your organization and you do not want to share your modifications, you should purchase the appropriate MySQL Network support package. MySQL's commercial licensing terms give you the option of making the modifications (and even getting MySQL AB to help you) and keeping them to yourself.

Similarly, if you're modifying the source code and intend to distribute the modifications, you're required by the GPL to distribute the modified source code free of charge (but you may charge a media fee). Furthermore, your changes cannot be made proprietary and you cannot own the rights to the modifications under the GPL. If you choose not to publish your changes yourself, you should contribute the code to MySQL for incorporation into their products, at which point that code becomes the property of MySQL AB. On the other hand, if you want to make proprietary changes to MySQL for use in an embedded system or similar installation, you should contact MySQL AB and discuss your plans prior to launching your project. MySQL AB will work with you to come up with a solution that meets your needs and protects their interests.

Getting the Source Code

You can obtain the MySQL source code in one of two ways. You could use the source control application that MySQL uses (BitKeeper) and get the latest version, or you can download the code without ties to the source control application and obtain a copy of a specific version release. You should use the source control application if you want to make modifications that will be candidates for inclusion into the MySQL system. If you're making academic changes or changes you're not going to share, you should download the source code directly from MySQL AB either through the MySQL Network site or via the developer pages on the MySQL AB site.

Tip I recommend downloading the source code from `http://dev.mysql.com` for all cases except when you either want the latest version of the source code or want to contribute to the MySQL project.

WHAT IS SOURCE CONTROL?

Source control (also known as version or revision control, code repository, or source tree) is a mechanism that stores documents in a central location and tracks changes to those documents. The version control technology is represented as a tree structure (or a similar hierarchical view) and was originally designed for engineering drawings and word processing files. The technology also works for source code. In this case, the technology allows developers to store and retrieve source code, modify it, and resave it to the repository. This process is called *checking in* and *checking out*.

    Not only does source control preserve the source code by managing the files, but it also allows tracking of changes to the files. Most source control applications allow diversions of the files to permit alternative modifications (called *branching*) and then resolve the conflicts at a later time (called *merging*). Source control therefore allows organizations to manage and track changes to the files in the repository. Source control is one of the many tools bundled in most configuration management tool suites. The source control used for the MySQL source code allows MySQL AB to permit many developers to work on the source code and make changes, then later manage which changes get placed in the final source build.

If you're using the MySQL Network licensing, you should contact a MySQL Network representative for assistance in choosing the correct version of the source code and location from which to download it. Your MySQL Network representative will also assign you a login and password for read-only access to the source code.

Using BitKeeper

Obtaining the source code from the source control application involves using a program called BitKeeper (see www.bitkeeper.com for more details). BitKeeper is a configuration management suite that permits developers to store and share source code and documents in a distributed environment (over the Internet).

■ **Caution** BitKeeper stores the very latest version, forks (branches), and all other development artifacts for the MySQL source code. It is what the MySQL AB developers use on a daily basis to store their revisions to the code. As such, it isn't always in the most stable of states. Use caution when choosing this method. Most of the new features will be incomplete or in some stage of refinement. If you have to have a stable build, use the code snapshots (described later in this chapter) or a release of the source code.

The first thing you need to do is remember the old adage about patience. This process can be a bit frustrating as it is very error prone. Although it seems to work well for most people, some users have had trouble getting and using the BitKeeper client. If you stick to my instructions, you shouldn't have any problems.

Installing BitKeeper

What you'll need to do is download the free BitKeeper client. This client is only available for POSIX-compatible Unix systems, but can be run from Windows clients if you use Cygwin. See the sidebar "Using BitKeeper on Windows Platforms" for information on obtaining and using Cygwin on Windows. Once the client is installed, you can point it to the MySQL repository and download the code. The entire process takes only a few minutes to complete on a broadband connection. Slower connection speeds will see significant delays as the entire source tree is downloaded. To download the BitKeeper client, open your browser and go to www.bitkeeper.com/Hosted.html.

On this page you'll find a link for downloading the client. Click on Download the client and save the bk-client.shar file in your home folder (or one of your choosing). The client is not built so you must make the executables. Do this using these commands:

```
%> /bin/sh bk-client.shar
%> cd bk_client-1.1
%> make
```

If your system is configured correctly and you have gcc and make installed, you should see a successful compilation of the BitKeeper client. Getting the source tree is easy. Just enter the following command:

```
sfioball -r+ bk://mysql.bkbits.net/mysql-5.1-new mysql-5.1
```

This command instructs the BitKeeper client to connect to the MySQL source tree named mysql-5.1-new and download the files into a new folder named mysq-5.1. You should see a long list of messages indicating that the source code is being transferred to your system. When the transfer is complete, you'll have the most recent copy of the MySQL source code. You're now ready to start exploring.

■Tip A list of all of the available MySQL source trees can be found at http://mysql.bkbits.net.

The instructions I have presented will only allow you to get a copy of the source tree; they don't permit you to update the repository with your changes. To do that, you must have a license key and permission to update the tree. If you want to pursue this option, you must download a copy of the commercial BitKeeper software. The process is detailed here:

1. Go to the BitKeeper site (www.bitkeeper.com) and click on Downloads.

2. Click on the link evaluation and download form.

3. Fill out the form with your request, checking the Eval Key and Download Instructions option. Be sure to include your justification for the request as well as a brief description of what you intend to do with the source code.

4. If your request is granted, you will receive an e-mail from BitKeeper detailing the steps for downloading and installing the commercial BitKeeper client.

Fortunately, the commercial BitKeeper client is available as a GUI on many platforms. They even offer a client that interfaces with Visual Studio. From here, you should use the client documentation to learn how to synchronize and update the source tree.

USING BITKEEPER ON WINDOWS PLATFORMS

Using the free BitKeeper client on Windows is a bit tricky. To do so, you must first download and install Cygwin. Cygwin is a Linux-like environment that permits you to compile and run Linux programs on Windows platforms (NT, XP, etc.). Once Cygwin is installed, you can download the free BitKeeper client using the instructions I gave you earlier and create your source tree copy. Follow these steps on Windows to download, install, and use the free BitKeeper client:

1. Download the Cygwin setup.exe executable from www.cygwin.com. You should see a link for Install or update now!.

2. Follow the onscreen instructions and leave the default installation folders (trust me, it's easier that way). Be sure to install gcc, make (located inside the Devel package on the Select Packages screen during setup), and all of the development install packages.

3. Download the BitKeeper client from www.bitkeeper.com/Hosted.Downloading.html.

4. Save the file in the c:\cygwin\home*username*\ folder (where *username* represents your home directory name).

5. Open a Cygwin command window (the installer placed a shortcut on your desktop).

6. Enter the command sh bk-client.shar.

7. Change the working directory using cd bk_client-1.1.

8. Use WordPad to open a file named makefile in the c:\cygwin\home*username*\bk_client-1.1 folder. Change the line that reads $(CC) $(CFLAGS) -o -sfio -lz -sfio.c to $(CC) $(CLFAGS) -o sfio sfio.c -lz. Note: do not remove the tab character before the $!

9. Compile the client using make all. Note: if this step fails, see the Caution on modifying the source to overcome an error with the getline function.

10. Change your path to the current folder (or use the referencing directives in the next steps) using PATH=$PWD:$PATH.

11. If you want to place the source tree somewhere other than the current directory, navigate there now.

12. Copy the source tree to your folder using sfioball -r+ bk://mysql.bkbits.net/mysql-5.1 / home/*username*/mysql-5.1.

You should now have a full copy of the source tree copied to your Windows client. Unfortunately, what you have is probably not going to be very Windows friendly. MySQL AB provides the Windows source code Visual Studio project files as a courtesy. As such, they are often not created until just before or soon after the source code build is released to the public (GA). However, you can still compile the code on Windows if you have a fully functional GNU development environment. I find it easier to use the GA source code whenever I explore the source code on Windows.

■**Caution** The BitKeeper client did not compile correctly on my Windows machine and it turns out to be a common problem for many. If this happens to you, you may have to modify the source code in a file named sfioball.c. The problem on my Windows client was that the function named getline was already defined in my copy of the stdio.h include file. Fixing this error is really easy. Simply do a search and replace getline with getline_fix. Then try the make all command again and you should have success. This and similar silly errors are the things that make life difficult for folks new to using BitKeeper, gcc, Cygwin, and the other tools necessary to get a copy of the source tree on Windows.

MySQL recommends that you update your copy of the source tree periodically. Once you have established a copy of the source tree, updating it is easy. Simply start your command window (or Cygwin command window on Windows), navigate to the BitKeeper folder, and enter the command

```
update bk://mysql.bkbits.net/mysql-5.1 mysql-5.1
```

■**Caution** This command may copy over any files you may have altered. See the BitKeeper web site for more details.

The free BitKeeper client permits you to examine the change log (what has changed since the last update) and the change history for any or all files in the source tree. You can open the file named BK/ChangeLog in the source tree and examine its contents for the history of the changes. Look for the section titled "ChangeSet." You'll find information on what file was changed when and the e-mail address of the person who changed it. This information is interesting as it gives you an opportunity to contact the developer who last worked on the file if you have any questions. MySQL AB is eager to hear from you, especially if you have suggestions for improvements or if you find new and better ways to code something.

■**Tip** If you use Windows, you may need to generate the Visual Studio project files and solution file. Check in the directory win and read the README file for the latest information about how to generate these files.

Downloading the Source

Obtaining the source code for download without using the source control application is easy. MySQL AB posts the latest source code for its products on their web site (http://dev.mysql.com/downloads).

When you go to that site, you'll see information about the two licenses of the MySQL products. The open source GPL products are called "MySQL Community Edition" and the commercial license products are called "MySQL Network." For use with this book, you need the MySQL

Community Edition. If you scroll down a bit, you'll see that MySQL AB offers three sets of links for the Community Edition:

- The current release (also called the generally available or GA) for production use

- Upcoming releases (e.g., alpha, beta—see Chapter 1 for more details on the types of releases MySQL AB offers)

- Older releases of the software

Also on this page are links to the many supporting applications, including the database connectors, administrative tools, and much more.

You can also download the source code using source code snapshots. The snapshots are usually alpha, development, or GA releases. The beta release is normally available on the main page. Use the source code snapshot if you want the latest look at a new feature or if you want to keep up to date by using the latest available stable release but don't want or need to use the code repository. (*Stable* in this case means the system has been tested and no extraordinary bugs have been found.)

For the purpose of following the examples in this book, you should download version 5.1.7 or higher from the web site. I provide instructions for installing MySQL in the next section. The site contains all of the binaries and source code for all of the environments supported. Notice that many different platforms are supported. You'll find the source code located near the bottom of the page. Be sure to download both the source code and the binaries (two downloads) for your platform. In this book, I'll use examples from both Red Hat Linux Fedora Core 5 and Microsoft Windows XP Professional.

Tip If you're using Windows, be sure to download the file containing all of the binaries or code, not the "essentials" packages. The smaller packages may not include some of the folders shown in the next section.

OS/2 SUPPORT

As of this writing, discussions were under way concerning removing OS/2 support from version 5.1. It is unlikely OS/2 will continue to be supported by MySQL AB. Various posts on the Planet MySQL blog (www.planetmysql.org) indicated that OS/2 support may be provided via variants of the source code contributed by the global community of developers.

Note Unless otherwise stated, the examples in this book are taken from the Linux source code distribution (mysql-5.1.7-beta.tar.gz). While most of the code is the same for Linux and Windows distributions, I will highlight differences as they occur. Most notably, the Windows platform has a slightly different vio implementation.

The MySQL Source Code

Once you have downloaded the source code, unpack the files into a folder on your system. You can unpack them into the same directory if you want. When you do this, notice that there are a lot of folders and many source files. The main folder you'll need to reference is the /sql folder. This folder contains the main source files for the server. Table 3-1 lists the most commonly accessed folders and their contents.

Table 3-1. *MySQL Source Folders*

Folder	Contents
/BUILD	The compilation configuration and make files for all platforms supported. Use this folder for compilation and linking.
/client	The MySQL command-line client tool.
/dbug	Utilities for use in debugging (see Chapter 5 for more details).
/Docs	Documentation for the current release. Linux users should use generate-text-files.pl in the support subfolder to generate the documentation. Windows users are provided with a manual.chm file.
/include	The base system include files and headers.
/libmysql	The C client API used for creating embedded systems. (See Chapter 6 for more details.)
/libmysqld	The core server API files. Also used in creating embedded systems. (See Chapter 6 for more details.)
/mysql-test	The MySQL system test suite. (See Chapter 4 for more details.)
/mysys	The majority of the core operating system API wrappers and helper functions.
/regex	A regular expression library. Used in the query optimizer and execution to resolve expressions.
/scripts	A set of shell script-based utilities.
/sql	The main system code. You should start your exploration from this folder.
/sql-bench	A set of benchmarking utilities.
/SSL	A set of Secure Socket Layer utilities and definitions.
/storage	The MySQL pluggable storage engine source code is located inside this folder. Also included is the storage engine example code. (See Chapter 7 for more details.)
/strings	The core string handling wrappers. Use these for all of your string handling needs.
/support-files	A set of preconfigured configuration files for compiling with different options.
/tests	A set of test programs and test files.
/vio	The network and socket layer code.
/zlib	Data compression tools.

I recommend taking some time now to dig your way through some of the folders and acquaint yourself with the location of the files. You will find many makefiles and a variety of Perl scripts dispersed among the folders. While not overly simplistic, the MySQL source code is logically organized around the functions of the source code rather than the subsystems. Some subsystems, like the storage engines, are located in a folder hierarchy, but most are located in several places in the folder structure. For each subsystem discussed while examining the source code, I will list the associated source files and their locations.

Getting Started

The best way to understand the flow and control of the MySQL system is to follow the source code along from the standpoint of a typical query. I presented a high-level view of each of the major MySQL subsystems in Chapter 2. I'll use the same subsystem view now as I show you how a typical SQL statement is executed. The following is the sample SQL statement I'll use:

```
SELECT lname, fname, DOB FROM Employees WHERE Employees.department = 'EGR';
```

This query selects the names and date of birth for everyone in the engineering department. While not very interesting, the query will be useful in demonstrating almost all of the subsystems in the MySQL system. Let's begin with the query arriving at the server for processing.

Figure 3-1 shows the path the example query would take through the MySQL source code. I have pulled out the major lines of code that you should associate with the subsystems identified in Chapter 2. Although not part of a specific subsystem, the main() function is responsible for initializing the server and setting up the connection listener. The main() function is in the file /sql/mysqld.cc.

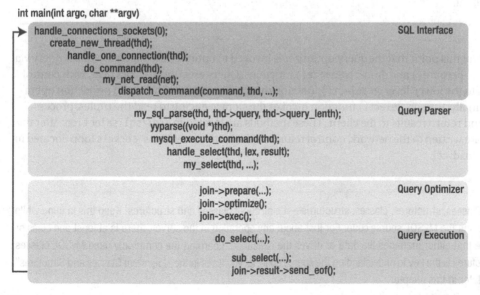

Figure 3-1. *Overview of the query path*

The path of the query begins in the SQL Interface subsystem (like most of the MySQL subsystems, the SQL Interface functions are distributed over a loosely associated set of source files). I'll tell you which files the methods are in as you go through this and the following sections. The handle_connections_socket() method (located in /sql/mysqld.cc) implements the listener loop, creating a thread for every connection detected. Once the thread is created, control flows to the handle_one_connection() function. The handle_one_connection() function identifies the command, then passes control to the do_command switch (located in /sql/sql_parse.cc). The do_command switch routes control to the proper network reading calls to read the query from the connection and passes the query to the parser via the dispatch_command() function (located in /sql/sql_parse.cc).

The query passes to the query parser subsystem, where the query is parsed and routed to the correct portion of the optimizer. The query parser is built in with Lex and YACC. Lex is used to identify tokens and literals as well as syntax of a language. YACC is used to build the code to interact with the MySQL source code. It captures the SQL commands storing the portions of the commands in an internal query representation and routes the command to a command processor called mysql_execute_command() (somewhat misnamed). This method then routes the query to the proper subfunction, in this case, my_select(). These methods are located in /sql/sql_parse.cc. This portion of the code enters the SELECT-PROJECT parts of the SELECT-PROJECT-JOIN query optimizer.

Tip A project is a relational database term describing the query operation that limits the result set to those columns defined in the column list on a SQL command. For example, the SQL command SELECT fname, lname FROM employee would "project" only the fname and lname columns from the employee table to the result set.

It is at this point that the query optimizer is invoked to optimize the execution of the query via the join->prepare() and join->optimize() functions. Query execution occurs next, with control passing to the lower-level do_select() function that carries out the restrict and projection operations. Finally, the sub_select() function invokes the storage engine to read the tuples, process them, and return results to the client. These methods are located in /sql/sql_select.cc. After the results are written to the network, control returns to the hand_connections_sockets loop (located in /sql/mysqld.cc).

Tip Classes, structures, classes, structures—it's all about classes and structures! Keep this in mind while you examine the MySQL source code. For just about any operation in the server, there is at least one class or structure that either manages the data or drives the execution. Learning the commonly used MySQL classes and structures is the key to understanding the source code, as you'll see in the "Important Classes and Structures" section later in this chapter.

You may be thinking that the code isn't as bad as you may have heard. That is largely true for simple SELECT statements like the example I am using, but as you'll soon see it can become more complicated than that. Now that you have seen this path and have had an introduction to where some of the major functions fall in the path of the query and the subsystems, you should open the source code and look for those functions. You can begin your search in /sql/mysqld.cc (/sql/mysqld.cpp for Windows source code).

Tip The Windows source code often has different file extensions for the source files. Most times you can simply substitute .cpp for .cc to find the equivalent Windows source code file. I'll point out any differences between the Linux and Windows files in cases where this rule does not hold.

OK, so that was a whirlwind introduction, yes? From this point on, I'll slow things down a bit (OK, a lot) and navigate the source code in more detail. I'll also list the specific source files where the examples reside in the form of a table at the end of each section. So tighten those safety belts, we're going in!

I'll leave out sections that are not relevant to our tour. These sections could include conditional compilation directives, ancillary code, and other system-level calls. I'll annotate the missing sections with the following: . . . . I have left many of the original comments in place as I believe they will help you follow the source code and offer you a glimpse into the world of developing a world-class database system. Finally, I'll highlight the important parts of the code in bold so you can find them more easily while reading.

The main() Function

The main() function is where the server begins execution. It is the first function called when the server executable is loaded into memory. Several hundred lines of code in this function are devoted to operating system–specific startup tasks, and there's a good amount of system-level initialization code. Listing 3-1 shows a condensed view of the code, with the essential points in bold.

Listing 3-1. *The main() Function*

```
int main(int argc, char **argv)
{
  ...

  if (init_common_variables(MYSQL_CONFIG_NAME,
        argc, argv, load_default_groups))

  ...

  if (init_server_components())

  ...
```

```
/*
 Initialize my_str_malloc() and my_str_free()
*/
my_str_malloc= &my_str_malloc_mysqld;
my_str_free= &my_str_free_mysqld;

...

if (acl_init(opt_noacl) ||
    my_tz_init((THD *)0, default_tz_name, opt_bootstrap))

...

create_shutdown_thread();
create_maintenance_thread();

...

handle_connections_sockets(0);

...

(void) pthread_mutex_lock(&LOCK_thread_count);

...

(void) pthread_mutex_unlock(&LOCK_thread_count);

...
}
```

The first interesting function is init_common_variables(). This function uses the command-line arguments to control how the server will perform. This is where the server interprets the arguments and starts the server in a variety of modes. This function takes care of setting up the system variables and places the server in the desired mode. The init_server_components() function initializes the database logs for use by any of the subsystems. These logs are the typical logs you see for events, statement execution, and so on.

I want to identify two of the most important my_ library functions: my_str_malloc() and my_str_free(). It is as this point in the server startup code (near the beginning) that these two function pointers are set. You should always use these functions in place of the traditional C/C++ malloc() functions because the MySQL functions have additional error handling and therefore are safer than the base methods. The acl_init() function's job is to start the authentication and access control subsystem. This is a key system and appears early in the server startup code.

Now you're getting to what makes MySQL tick: threads. Two important helper threads are created. The create_shutdown_thread() function creates a thread whose job is to shut down the server on signal, and the create_maintenance_thread() function creates a thread to handle any server-wide maintenance functions. I discuss threads in more detail in the "Process vs. Thread" sidebar.

At this point in the startup code, the system is just about ready to accept connections from clients. To do that, the handle_connections_sockets(0) function implements a listener that loops through the code waiting for connections. I'll discuss this function in more detail next.

The last thing I want to point out to you in the code is an example of the critical section protection code for mutually exclusive access during multithreading. A critical section is a block of code that must execute as a set and can only be accessed by a single thread at a time. Critical sections are usually areas that write to a shared memory variable and therefore must complete before another thread attempts to read the memory. MySQL AB has created an abstract of a common concurrency protection mechanism called a *mutex* (short for mutually exclusive). If you find an area in your code that you need to protect during concurrent execution, you can use the following functions to protect the code.

The first function you should call is pthread_mutex_lock([resource reference]). This function places a lock on the code execution at this point in the code. It will not permit another thread to access the memory location specified until your code calls the unlocking function pthread_mutex_unlock([resource reference]). In the example from the main() function, the mutex calls are locking the thread count global variable.

Well, that's your first dive under the hood. How did it feel? Do you want more? Keep reading—you've only just begun. In fact, you haven't seen where our example query enters the system. Let's do that next.

PROCESS VS. THREAD

The terms *process* and *thread* are often used interchangeably. This is incorrect as a *process* is an organized set of computer instructions that has its own memory and execution path. A *thread* is also a set of computer instructions, but threads execute in a host's execution path and do not have their own memory. (Some call threads lightweight processes. While a good description, calling them lightweight processes doesn't help the distinction.) They do store state (in MySQL, it is via the THD class). Thus, when talking about large systems that support processes, I mean systems that permit sections of the system to execute as a separate process and have their own memory. When talking about large systems that support threads, I mean systems that permit sections of the system to execute concurrently with other sections of the system and they all share the same memory space as the host.

Most database systems use the process model to manage concurrent connections and helper functions. MySQL uses the multithreaded model. There are a number of advantages to using threads over processes. Most notably, threads are easier to create and manage (no overhead for memory allocation and segregation). Threads also permit very fast switching because no context switching takes place. However, threads do have one severe drawback. If things go *wonky* (a highly technical term used to describe strange, unexplained behavior; in the case of threading, they are often very strange and harmful events) during a thread's execution, it is likely that if the trouble is severe, the entire system could be affected. Fortunately, MySQL AB and the global community of developers have worked very hard making MySQL's threading subsystem robust and reliable. This is why it is important for your modifications to be thread safe.

Handling Connections and Creating Threads

You saw in the previous section how the system is started and how the control flows to the listener loop that waits for user connections. The connections begin life at the client and are broken down into data packets, placed on the network by the client software, then flow across the network communications pathways where they are picked up by the server's network subsystems and reformed into data on the server. (A complete description of the communication packets is available in the MySQL Internals Manual.) This flow can be seen in Figure 3-2. I'll show you more details on the network communication methods in the next chapter. I'll also include examples of how to write code that returns results to the client using these functions.

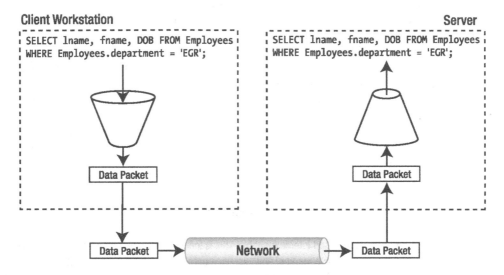

Figure 3-2. *Network communications from client to server*

At this point the system is in the SQL interface subsystem. That is, the data packets (containing the query) have arrived at the server and are detected via the handle_connections_sockets() function. This function enters a loop that waits until the variable abort_loop is set to TRUE. Table 3-2 shows the location of the files that manage the connection and threads.

Table 3-2. *Connections and Thread Management*

Source File	Description
/sql/net_serv.cc	Contains all of the network communications functions. Look here for information on how to communicate with the client or server via the network.
/include/mysql_com.h	Contains most of the structures used in communications.
/sql/sql_parse.cc	Contains the majority of the query routing and parsing functions except for the lexical parser.
/sql/mysqld.cc	Besides the main and server startup functions, this file also contains the methods for creating threads.

Listing 3-2 offers a condensed view of the connection-handling code. When a connection is detected (I've hidden that part of the code as it isn't helpful in learning how the system works), the function creates a new thread calling the aptly named create_new_thread() function. It is in this function that the first of the major structures is created. The THD class is responsible for maintaining all of the information for the thread. Although not allocated to the thread in a private memory space, the THD class allows the system to control the thread during execution. I'll expose some of the THD class in a later section.

Listing 3-2. *The Handle Connections Sockets Functions*

```
pthread_handler_t handle_connections_sockets(void *arg __attribute__((unused)))
{

  ...

  DBUG_PRINT("general",("Waiting for connections."));

  ...

  while (!abort_loop)
  {

  ...

    /*
    ** Don't allow too many connections
    */

    if (!(thd= new THD))

  ...

    if (sock == unix_sock)
      thd->security_ctx->host=(char*) my_localhost;

  ...

    create_new_thread(thd);
  }

  ...
}
```

OK, so now the client has connected to the server. What happens next? Let's see what happens inside the create_new_thread() function. Listing 3-3 shows a condensed view of the create_new_thread() function. The first thing you see is the mutex call to lock the thread count. As you saw in the main() function, this is necessary to keep other threads from potentially competing for write access to the variable. When the thread is created, the associated unlock mutex call is made to unlock the resource.

Listing 3-3. *The create_new_thread() Function*

```
static void create_new_thread(THD *thd)
{

  ...

  pthread_mutex_lock(&LOCK_thread_count);

  ...

    if (cached_thread_count > wake_thread)
    {
      start_cached_thread(thd);
    }
    else
    {
      int error;
      thread_count++;
      thread_created++;
      threads.append(thd);
      if (thread_count-delayed_insert_threads > max_used_connections)
        max_used_connections=thread_count-delayed_insert_threads;
      DBUG_PRINT("info",(("creating thread %d"), thd->thread_id));
      thd->connect_time = time(NULL);
      if ((error=pthread_create(&thd->real_id,&connection_attrib,
        handle_one_connection,
        (void*) thd)))
      {
        DBUG_PRINT("error",
          ("Can't create thread to handle request (error %d)",
          error));

  ...

      }
    }
    (void) pthread_mutex_unlock(&LOCK_thread_count);
  }
  DBUG_PRINT("info",("Thread created"));

  ...

}
```

A very interesting thing occurs early in the function. Notice the start_cached_thread() function call. That function is designed to reuse a thread that may be residing in the connection pool. This helps speed things up a bit as creating threads, while faster than creating processes, can take some time to complete. Having a thread ready to go is a sort of caching mechanism for connections. The saving of threads for later use is called a *connection pool*.

If there isn't a connection (thread) ready for to reuse, the system creates one with the pthread_create() function call. Something really strange happens here. Notice the third parameter for this function call. What seems like a variable is actually the starting address of a function (a function pointer). pthread_create() uses this function pointer to associate the location in the server where execution should begin for the thread.

Now that the query has been sent from the client to the server and a thread has been created to manage the execution, control passes to the handle_one_connection() function. Listing 3-4 shows a condensed view of the handle_one_connection() function. In this view, I have commented out a large section of the code that deals with initializing the THD class for use. If you're interested, I encourage you to take a look at the code more closely later (located in /sql/mysqld.cc). For now, let's look at the essential work that goes on inside this function.

Listing 3-4. *The handle_one_connection() Function*

```
pthread_handler_t handle_one_connection(void *arg)
{
  THD *thd=(THD*) arg;

  ...

    while (!net->error && net->vio != 0 &&
           !(thd->killed == THD::KILL_CONNECTION))
    {
      net->no_send_error= 0;
      if (do_command(thd))
        break;
    }

  ...

}
```

In this case, the only function call of interest for our exploration is the do_command(thd) function. It is inside a loop that is looping once for each command read from the networking communications code. Although somewhat of a mystery at this point, this is of interest to those of us who have entered stacked SQL commands (more than one command on the same line). As you see here, this is where MySQL handles that eventuality. For each command read, the function passes control to the function that begins reads in the query from the network.

It is at this point where the system reads the query from the network and places it in the THD class for parsing. This takes place in the do_command() function. Listing 3-5 shows a condensed view of the do_command() function. I have left some of the more interesting comments and code bits in to demonstrate the robustness of the MySQL source code.

Listing 3-5. *The do_command() Function*

```
bool do_command(THD *thd)
{
  char *packet;
  uint old_timeout;
  ulong packet_length;
  NET *net;
  enum enum_server_command command;

  ...

  packet=0;

  ...

  net_new_transaction(net);
  if ((packet_length=my_net_read(net)) == packet_error)
  {
    DBUG_PRINT("info",("Got error %d reading command from socket %s",
          net->error,
          vio_description(net->vio)));

    ...

  }
  else
  {
    packet=(char*) net->read_pos;
    command = (enum enum_server_command) (uchar) packet[0];
    if (command >= COM_END)
      command= COM_END;          // Wrong command

    ...

  }
  net->read_timeout=old_timeout;     // restore it
  /*
    packet_length contains length of data, as it was stored in packet
    header. In case of malformed header, packet_length can be zero.
    If packet_length is not zero, my_net_read ensures that this number
    of bytes was actually read from network. Additionally my_net_read
    sets packet[packet_length]= 0 (thus if packet_length == 0,
    command == packet[0] == COM_SLEEP).
    In dispatch_command packet[packet_length] points beyond the end of packet.
  */
  DBUG_RETURN(dispatch_command(command,thd, packet+1, (uint) packet_length));
}
```

The first thing to notice is the creation of a packet buffer and a NET structure. This packet buffer is a character array and stores the raw query string as it is read from the network and stored in the NET structure. The next item that is created is a command structure, which will be used to route control to the appropriate parser functions. The my_net_read() function reads the packets from the network and stores them in the NET structure. The length of the packet is also stored in the packet_length variable of the NET structure. The last thing you see occurring in this function is a call to dispatch_command(), the point at which you can begin to see how commands are routed through the server code.

OK, so now you're starting to get somewhere. The job of the dispatch_command() function is to route control to a portion of the server that can best process the incoming command. Since you have a normal SELECT query on the way, the system has identified it as a query by setting the command variable to COM_QUERY. Other command types are used to identify statements, change user, generate statistics, and many other server functions. For this chapter, I will only look at query commands (COM_QUERY). Listing 3-6 shows a condensed view of the function. I have omitted the code for all of the other commands in the switch for the sake of brevity (I'm omitting the comment break too) but I'm leaving in the case statements for most of the commands. Take a moment and scan through the list. Most of the names are self-explanatory. If you were to conduct this exploration for another type of query, you could find your way by looking in this function for the type identified and following the code along in that case statement. I have also included the large function comment block that appears before the function code. Take a moment to look at that. I'll be getting more into that later in this chapter.

Listing 3-6. *The dispatch_command() Function*

```
/*
   Perform one connection-level (COM_XXXX) command.

   SYNOPSIS
     dispatch_command()
     thd              connection handle
     command          type of command to perform
     packet           data for the command, packet is always null-terminated
     packet_length    length of packet + 1 (to show that data is
                      null-terminated) except for COM_SLEEP, where it
                      can be zero.
   RETURN VALUE
     0    ok
     1    request of thread shutdown, i. e. if command is
          COM_QUIT/COM_SHUTDOWN
*/

bool dispatch_command(enum enum_server_command command, THD *thd,
          char* packet, uint packet_length)
{

   ...
```

```
switch (command) {
case COM_INIT_DB:
...
case COM_REGISTER_SLAVE:
...
case COM_TABLE_DUMP:
...
case COM_CHANGE_USER:
...
case COM_STMT_EXECUTE:
...
case COM_STMT_FETCH:
...
case COM_STMT_SEND_LONG_DATA:
...
case COM_STMT_PREPARE:
...
case COM_STMT_CLOSE:
...
case COM_STMT_RESET:
...
case COM_QUERY:
{
  if (alloc_query(thd, packet, packet_length))
    break;          // fatal error is set

...

  general_log_print(thd, command, "%s", thd->query);

...

  mysql_parse(thd,thd->query, thd->query_length);

...
}
case COM_FIELD_LIST:        // This isn't actually needed
...
case COM_QUIT:
...
case COM_BINLOG_DUMP:
...
case COM_REFRESH:
...
```

```
case COM_STATISTICS:
...
case COM_PING:
...
case COM_PROCESS_INFO:
...
case COM_PROCESS_KILL:
...
case COM_SET_OPTION:
...
case COM_DEBUG:
...
case COM_SLEEP:
...
case COM_DELAYED_INSERT:
...
case COM_END:
...
default:
...
}
```

The first thing that happens when control passes to the COM_QUERY handler is the query is copied from the packet array to the thd->query member variable via the alloc_query() function. In this way, the thread now has a copy of the query, which will stay with it all through its execution. Notice also that the code writes the command to the general log. This will help with debugging system problems and query issues later on. The last function call of interest in Listing 3-6 is the mysql_parse() function call. It is at this point that the code can officially transfer from the SQL Interface subsystem to the Query Parser subsystem. As you can see, this distinction is one of semantics rather than syntax.

Parsing the Query

Finally, the parsing begins. This is the heart of what goes on inside the server when it processes a query. The parser code is located in a couple of places (like so much of the rest of the system). It isn't that hard to follow if you realize that while being highly organized, the code is not structured to match the architecture.

The function you're examining now is the mysql_parse() function (located in /sql/ sql_parse.cc). Its job is to check the query cache for the results of a previously executed query that has the same result set, then pass control to the lexical parser, and finally route the command to the query optimizer. Listing 3-7 shows a condensed view of the mysql_parse() function.

Listing 3-7. *The mysql_parse() Function*

```
void mysql_parse(THD *thd, char *inBuf, uint length)
{

  ...

  if (query_cache_send_result_to_client(thd, inBuf, length) <= 0)
  {
    LEX *lex= thd->lex;

  ...

    if (!yyparse((void *)thd) && ! thd->is_fatal_error)
    {

  ...

      mysql_execute_command(thd);
      query_cache_end_of_result(thd);

  ...
    }
  ...
}
```

The first thing to notice is the call to the query cache. The query cache stores all of the most frequently requested queries complete with the results. If the query is already in the query cache, you're done! All that is left is to return the results to the client. No parsing, optimizing, or even executing is necessary. How cool is that?

For the sake of our exploration, let's assume the query cache does not contain a copy of the example query. In this case, the function creates a new LEX structure to contain the internal representation of the query. This structure is filled out by the Lex/YACC parser, shown in Listing 3-8.

Listing 3-8. *The SELECT Lex/YACC Parsing Code Excerpt*

```
select:
  select_init
  {
    LEX *lex= Lex;
    lex->sql_command= SQLCOM_SELECT;
  }
  ;
```

```
/* Need select_init2 for subselects. */
select_init:
  SELECT_SYM select_init2
  |
  '(' select_paren ')' union_opt;

select_paren:
  SELECT_SYM select_part2
    {
      LEX *lex= Lex;
          SELECT_LEX * sel= lex->current_select;
      if (sel->set_braces(1))
      {
        yyerror(ER(ER_SYNTAX_ERROR));
        YYABORT;
      }
      if (sel->linkage == UNION_TYPE &&
        !sel->master_unit()->first_select()->braces)
      {
        yyerror(ER(ER_SYNTAX_ERROR));
        YYABORT;
      }
          /* select in braces, can't contain global parameters */
      if (sel->master_unit()->fake_select_lex)
          sel->master_unit()->global_parameters=
              sel->master_unit()->fake_select_lex;
  }
  | '(' select_paren ')';

select_init2:
  select_part2
    {
      LEX *lex= Lex;
      SELECT_LEX * sel= lex->current_select;
      if (lex->current_select->set_braces(0))
      {
        yyerror(ER(ER_SYNTAX_ERROR));
        YYABORT;
      }
      if (sel->linkage == UNION_TYPE &&
          sel->master_unit()->first_select()->braces)
      {
        yyerror(ER(ER_SYNTAX_ERROR));
        YYABORT;
      }
  }
```

```
    union_clause
    ;

select_part2:
  {
    LEX *lex= Lex;
    SELECT_LEX *sel= lex->current_select;
    if (sel->linkage != UNION_TYPE)
      mysql_init_select(lex);
    lex->current_select->parsing_place= SELECT_LIST;
  }
  select_options select_item_list
  {
    Select->parsing_place= NO_MATTER;
  }
  select_into select_lock_type;

select_into:
  opt_order_clause opt_limit_clause {}
        | into
  | select_from
  | into select_from
  | select_from into;

select_from:
    FROM join_table_list where_clause group_clause having_clause
        opt_order_clause opt_limit_clause procedure_clause
      | FROM DUAL_SYM where_clause opt_limit_clause
       /* oracle compatibility: oracle always requires FROM clause,
          and DUAL is system table without fields.
          Is "SELECT 1 FROM DUAL" any better than "SELECT 1" ?
        Hmmm :) */
  ;

select_options:
  /* empty*/
  | select_option_list
    {
      if (Select->options & SELECT_DISTINCT && Select->options & SELECT_ALL)
      {
        my_error(ER_WRONG_USAGE, MYF(0), "ALL", "DISTINCT");
            YYABORT;
      }
    }
    ;
```

```
select_option_list:
  select_option_list select_option
  | select_option;

select_option:
  STRAIGHT_JOIN { Select->options|= SELECT_STRAIGHT_JOIN; }
  | HIGH_PRIORITY
    {
      if (check_simple_select())
        YYABORT;
      Lex->lock_option= TL_READ_HIGH_PRIORITY;
    }
  | DISTINCT         { Select->options|= SELECT_DISTINCT; }
  | SQL_SMALL_RESULT { Select->options|= SELECT_SMALL_RESULT; }
  | SQL_BIG_RESULT { Select->options|= SELECT_BIG_RESULT; }
  | SQL_BUFFER_RESULT
    {
      if (check_simple_select())
        YYABORT;
      Select->options|= OPTION_BUFFER_RESULT;
    }
  | SQL_CALC_FOUND_ROWS
    {
      if (check_simple_select())
        YYABORT;
      Select->options|= OPTION_FOUND_ROWS;
    }
  | SQL_NO_CACHE_SYM { Lex->safe_to_cache_query=0; }
  | SQL_CACHE_SYM
    {
      Lex->select_lex.options|= OPTION_TO_QUERY_CACHE;
    }
  | ALL       { Select->options|= SELECT_ALL; }
  ;

select_lock_type:
  /* empty */
  | FOR_SYM UPDATE_SYM
    {
      LEX *lex=Lex;
      lex->current_select->set_lock_for_tables(TL_WRITE);
      lex->safe_to_cache_query=0;
    }
```

```
    | LOCK_SYM IN_SYM SHARE_SYM MODE_SYM
      {
        LEX *lex=Lex;
        lex->current_select->
          set_lock_for_tables(TL_READ_WITH_SHARED_LOCKS);
        lex->safe_to_cache_query=0;
      }
    ;


select_item_list:
      select_item_list ',' select_item
    | select_item
    | '*'
      {
        THD *thd= YYTHD;
        if (add_item_to_list(thd,
                                  new Item_field(&thd->lex->current_select->
                                                   context,
                                                   NULL, NULL, "*")))
          YYABORT;
        (thd->lex->current_select->with_wild)++;
      };



select_item:
      remember_name select_item2 remember_end select_alias
      {
        if (add_item_to_list(YYTHD, $2))
          YYABORT;
        if ($4.str)
        {
          $2->set_name($4.str, $4.length, system_charset_info);
                $2->is_autogenerated_name= FALSE;
        }
        else if (!$2->name) {
          char *str = $1;
          if (str[-1] == '`')
            str--;
          $2->set_name(str,(uint) ($3 - str), YYTHD->charset());
        }
      };
```

I have included an excerpt from the Lex/YACC parser that shows how the SELECT token is identified and passed through the YACC code to be parsed. The way you should read this code (in case you don't know Lex or YACC) is to watch for the keywords (or tokens) in the code (they are located flush left with a colon like `select:`). These keywords are used to direct flow of the parser. The placement of tokens to the right of these keywords defines the order of what must occur in order for the query to be parsed. For example, look at the `select:` keyword. To the right of that you will see a `select_init2` keyword, which isn't very informative. However, if you look down through the code you will see the `select_init:` keyword on the left. This allows the Lex/YACC author to specify certain behaviors in a sort of macro-like form. Also notice that there are curly braces under the `select_init` keyword. This is where the parser does its work of dividing the query into parts and placing the items in the `LEX` structure. Direct symbols such as `SELECT` are defined in a header file (`/sql/lex.h`) and appear in the parser as `SELECT_SYM`. Take a few moments now to skim through the code. You may want to run through this several times. It can be confusing if you haven't studied compiler construction or text parsing.

If you're thinking, "What a monster," then you can rest assured that you're normal. The Lex/YACC code is a challenge for most developers. I've highlighted a few of the important code statements that should help explain how the code works. Let's go through it. I've repeated the example `SELECT` statement again here for convenience:

```
SELECT lname, fname, DOB FROM Employees WHERE Employees.department = 'EGR';
```

Look at the first keyword again. Notice how the `select_init` code block sets the `LEX` structure's `sql_command` to `SQLCOM_SELECT`. This is important because the next function in the query path uses this in a large switch statement to further control the flow of the query through the server. The example `SELECT` statement has three fields in the field list. Let's try and find that in the parser code. Look for the `add_item_to_list()` function call. That is where the parser detects the fields and places them in the `LEX` structure. You will also see a few lines up from that call the parser code that identifies the * option for the field list. OK, now you've got the `sql_command` member variable set and the fields identified. So where does the `FROM` clause get detected? Look for the code statement that begins with `FROM join_table_list where_clause`. This code is the part of the parser that identifies the `FROM` and `WHERE` clause (and others). The code for the parser that processes these clauses is not included in Listing 3-8, but I think you get the idea. If you open the `sql_yacc.yy` source file (located in `/sql`), you should now be able to find all of those statements and see how the rest of the `LEX` structure is filled in with the table list in the `FROM` clause and the expression in the `WHERE` clause.

■ **Note** Some Windows distributions do not include the `sql_yacc.yy` file. If you use Windows and do not find this file in the `/sql` directory, you will need to download the Linux source code, extract the file, and place it in the `/sql` directory.

I hope that this tour of the parser code has helped mitigate the shock and horror that usually accompanies examining this part of the MySQL system. I will return to this part of the system later on when I demonstrate how to add your own commands the MySQL SQL lexicon (see Chapter 8 for more details). Table 3-3 lists the source files associated with the MySQL parser.

Table 3-3. *The MySQL Parser*

Source File	Description
/sql/lex.h	The symbol table for all of the keywords and tokens supported by the parser
/sql/lex_symbol.h	Type definitions for the symbol table
/sql/lex_hash.h	Mapping of symbols to functions used in the parser
/sql/sql_lex.h	Definition of LEX structure
/sql/sql_lex.cc	Definition of Lex class
/sql/sql_yacc.yy	The Lex/YACC parser code
/sql/sql_parse.cc	Contains the majority of the query routing and parsing functions except for the lexical parser

■**Caution** Do not edit the files sql_yacc.cc, sql_yacc.h, or lex_hash.h. These files are generated by other utilities. See Chapter 8 for more details.

Preparing the Query for Optimization

Although the boundary of where the parser ends and the optimizer begins is not clear from the MySQL documentation (there are contradictions), it is clear from the definition of the optimizer that the routing and control parts of the source code can be considered part of the optimizer. To avoid confusion, I am going to call the next set of functions the *preparatory* stage of the optimizer.

The first of these preparatory functions is the mysql_execute_command() function (located in /sql/sql_parse.cc). The name leads you to believe you are actually executing the query, but that isn't the case. This function performs much of the setup steps necessary to optimize the query. The LEX structure is copied and several variables are set to help the query optimization and later execution. You can see some of these operations in a condensed view of the function shown in Listing 3-9.

Listing 3-9. *The mysql_execute_command() Function*

```
bool mysql_execute_command(THD *thd)
{
  bool  res= FALSE;
  int result= 0;
  LEX  *lex= thd->lex;
  /* first SELECT_LEX (have special meaning for many of non-SELECTcommands) */
  SELECT_LEX *select_lex= &lex->select_lex;
  /* first table of first SELECT_LEX */
  TABLE_LIST *first_table= (TABLE_LIST*) select_lex->table_list.first;
```

```
    /* list of all tables in query */
    TABLE_LIST *all_tables;
    /* most outer SELECT_LEX_UNIT of query */
    SELECT_LEX_UNIT *unit= &lex->unit;
    /* Saved variable value */
    DBUG_ENTER("mysql_execute_command");
    thd->net.no_send_error= 0;

    ...

switch (lex->sql_command) {
  case SQLCOM_SELECT:
  {

    ...

    select_result *result=lex->result;

    ...

      res= check_access(thd,
      lex->exchange ? SELECT_ACL | FILE_ACL : SELECT_ACL,
      any_db, 0, 0, 0, 0);

    ...

    if (!(res= open_and_lock_tables(thd, all_tables)))
    {
      if (lex->describe)
      {
        /*
          We always use select_send for EXPLAIN, even if it's an EXPLAIN
          for SELECT ... INTO OUTFILE: a user application should be able
          to prepend EXPLAIN to any query and receive output for it,
          even if the query itself redirects the output.
        */

    ...

    query_cache_store_query(thd, all_tables);
    res= handle_select(thd, lex, result, 0);

    ...

}
```

There are a number of interesting things happening in this function. You will notice another switch statement that has as its cases the SQLCOM keywords. In the case of the example query, you saw the parser set the lex->sql_command member variable to SQLCOM_SELECT. I have included a condensed view of that case statement for you in Listing 3-9. What I did not include is the many other SQLCOM case statements. This function is a very large function. Since it is the central routing function for query processing, it contains a case for every possible command. Consequently, the source code is tens of pages long.

Let's see what this case statement does. Notice the statement select_result *result=➡ lex->result. This statement creates a result class that will be used to hold the results of the query for later transmission to the client. If you scan down, you will see the check_table_➡ access() function. This function is called to check the access control list for the resources used by the query. If access is granted, the function calls the open_and_lock_tables() function, which opens and locks the tables for the query. I left part of the code concerning the DESCRIBE (EXPLAIN) command for you to examine.

■ **Note** Once when I was modifying the code I needed to find all of the locations of the EXPLAIN calls so that I could alter them for a specific need. I looked everywhere until I found them in the parser. There in the middle of the Lex/YACC code was a comment that said something to the effect that DESCRIBE was left over from an earlier Oracle compatibility issue and that the correct term was EXPLAIN. Comments are useful. . . if you can find them.

The next function call is a call to the query cache. The query_cache_store_query() function stores the SQL statement in the query. As you will see later, when the results are ready they too are stored in the query cache. Finally you see that the function calls another function called handle_select(). You may be thinking, "Didn't we just do the handle thing?"

The handle_select() is a wrapper for another function named mysql_select(). Listing 3-10 shows the complete code for the handle_select() function. Near the top of the listing is the select_lex->next_select() operation, which is checking for the UNION command that appends multiple SELECT results into a single set of results. Other than that, the code just calls the next function in the chain, mysql_select(). It is at this point that you are finally close enough to transition to the query optimizer subsystem. Table 3-4 lists the source files associated with the query optimizer.

■ **Note** This is perhaps the part of the code that suffers most from ill-defined subsystems. While the code is still very organized, the boundaries of the subsystems are fuzzy at this point in the source code.

Listing 3-10. *The handle_select() Function*

```
bool handle_select(THD *thd, LEX *lex, select_result *result,
                   ulong setup_tables_done_option)
{
  bool res;
  register SELECT_LEX *select_lex = &lex->select_lex;
  DBUG_ENTER("handle_select");
```

```
if (select_lex->next_select())
  res= mysql_union(thd, lex, result, &lex->unit, setup_tables_done_option);
else
{
  SELECT_LEX_UNIT *unit= &lex->unit;
  unit->set_limit(unit->global_parameters);
  /*
    'options' of mysql_select will be set in JOIN, as far as JOIN for
    every PS/SP execution new, we will not need to reset this flag if
    setup_tables_done_option changed for next execution
  */
  res= mysql_select(thd, &select_lex->ref_pointer_array,
        (TABLE_LIST*) select_lex->table_list.first,
        select_lex->with_wild, select_lex->item_list,
        select_lex->where,
        select_lex->order_list.elements +
        select_lex->group_list.elements,
        (ORDER*) select_lex->order_list.first,
        (ORDER*) select_lex->group_list.first,
        select_lex->having,
        (ORDER*) lex->proc_list.first,
        select_lex->options | thd->options |
                    setup_tables_done_option,
        result, unit, select_lex);
}
DBUG_PRINT("info",("res: %d  report_error: %d", res,
        thd->net.report_error));
res|= thd->net.report_error;
if (unlikely(res))
{
  /* If we had another error reported earlier then this will be ignored */
  result->send_error(ER_UNKNOWN_ERROR, ER(ER_UNKNOWN_ERROR));
  result->abort();
}
DBUG_RETURN(res);
}
```

Table 3-4. *The Query Optimizer*

Source File	Description
/sql/sql_parse.cc	The majority of the parser code resides in this file
/sql/sql_select.cc	Contains some of the optimization functions and the implementation of the select functions
/sql/sql_parse.cc	Contains the majority of the query routing and parsing functions except for the lexical parser

Optimizing the Query

At last! You're at the optimizer. However, you won't find it if you go looking for a source file or class by that name. Although the JOIN class contains a method called optimize(), the optimizer is actually a collection of flow control and subfunctions designed to find the shortest path to executing the query. What happened to the fancy algorithms and query paths and compiled queries? Recall from our architecture discussion in Chapter 2 that the MySQL query optimizer is a nontraditional hybrid optimizer utilizing a combination of known best practices and cost-based path selection. It is at this point in the code that the best practices part kicks in.

An example of one of those best practices is standardizing the parameters in the WHERE clause expressions. The example query uses a WHERE clause with an expression, Employees.department = 'EGR', but the clause could have been written as 'EGR' = Employees.department and still be correct (it returns the same results). This is an example of where traditional cost-based optimizer could generate multiple plans—one for each of the expression variants. Just a few examples of the many best practices that MySQL uses follows:

- *Constant propagation*—The removal of transitive conjunctions using constants. For example, if you have a=b='c', the transitive law states that a='c'. This optimization removes those inner equalities, thereby reducing the number of evaluations. For example, the SQL command SELECT * FROM table1 WHERE column1 = 12 AND NOT (column3 = 17 OR column1 = column2) would be reduced to SELECT * FROM table1 WHERE column1 = 12 AND column3 <> 17 AND column2 <> 12.

- *Dead code elimination*—The removal of always true conditions. For example, if you have a=b AND 1=1, the AND 1=1 condition is removed. The same occurs for always false conditions where the false expression can be removed without affecting the rest of the clause. For example, the SQL command SELECT * FROM table1 WHERE column1 = 12 AND column2 = 13 AND column1 < column2 would be reduced to SELECT * FROM table1 WHERE column1 = 12 AND column2 = 13.

- *Range queries*—The transformation of the IN clause to a list of disjunctions. For example, if you have an IN (1,2,3), the transformation would be a = 1 or a = 2 or a = 3. This helps simplify the evaluation of the expressions. For example, the SQL command SELECT * FROM table1 WHERE column1 = 12 OR column1 = 17 OR column1 = 21 would be reduced to SELECT * FROM table1 WHERE column1 IN (12, 17, 21).

I hope this small set of examples has given you a glimpse into the inner workings of one of the world's most successful nontraditional query optimizers. In short, it works really well for a surprising amount of queries.

Well, I spoke too fast. There isn't much going on in the mysql_select() function in the area of optimization either. It seems the mysql_select() function just identifies joins and calls the join->optimize() function. Where are all of those best practices? They are in the JOIN class! A detailed examination of the optimizer source code in the JOIN class would take more pages than this entire book to present in any meaningful depth. Suffice to say that the optimizer is complex and also difficult to examine. Fortunately, few will ever need to venture that far down into the bowels of MySQL. However, you're welcome to! I will focus on a higher-level review of the optimize() function.

What you do see in the optimize() function is the definition of a local JOIN class with the code statement JOIN *join. The next thing you see is that the function checks to see if the

select_lex class already has a join class defined. Why? Because if you are executing another
SELECT statement in a UNION or perhaps a reused thread from the connection pool, the
select_lex class would already have been through this part of the code once and therefore we
do not need to create another JOIN class. If there is no JOIN class in the select_lex class, a new
one is created in the create statement join= new JOIN(). Finally, you see that the code calls the
join->optimize() method.

However, once again you are at another fuzzy boundary. This time, it occurs in the middle
of the mysql_select() function. The next major function call in this function is the join->exec()
method. But first, let's take a look at what happens in the mysql_select() method in Listing 3-11.
Table 3-5 lists the source files associated with query optimization.

Listing 3-11. *The mysql_select() Function*

```
bool mysql_select(THD *thd, Item ***rref_pointer_array,
    TABLE_LIST *tables, uint wild_num, List<Item> &fields,
    COND *conds, uint og_num,  ORDER *order, ORDER *group,
    Item *having, ORDER *proc_param, ulong select_options,
    select_result *result, SELECT_LEX_UNIT *unit,
    SELECT_LEX *select_lex)
{
  bool err;
  bool free_join= 1;
  DBUG_ENTER("mysql_select");

  select_lex->context.resolve_in_select_list= TRUE;
  JOIN *join;
  if (select_lex->join != 0)
  {
    join= select_lex->join;

    ...

    join->select_options= select_options;
  }
  else
  {
    if (!(join= new JOIN(thd, fields, select_options, result)))
  DBUG_RETURN(TRUE);

    ...

  }

  if ((err= join->optimize()))
  {
    goto err;
  }
```

```
...

join->exec();

...
}
```

Table 3-5. *Query Optimization*

Source File	Description
/sql/sql_select.h	The definitions for the structures used in the select functions to support the SELECT commands
/sql/sql_select.cc	Contains some of the optimization functions and the implementation of the select functions

Executing the Query

In the same way as the optimizer, the query execution uses a set of best practices for executing the query. For example, the query execution subsystem detects special clauses like ORDER BY and DISTINCT and routes control of these operations to methods designed for fast sorting and tuple elimination.

Most of this activity occurs in the methods of the JOIN class. Listing 3-12 presents a condensed view of the join::exec() method. Notice that there is yet another function call to a function called by some name that includes select. Sure enough, there is another call that needs to be made to a function called do_select(). Take a look at the parameters for this function call. You are now starting to see things like field lists. Does this mean you're getting close to reading data? Yes, it does. In fact, the do_select() function is a high-level wrapper for exactly that.

Listing 3-12. *The join::exec() Function*

```
void JOIN::exec()
{
  List<Item> *columns_list= &fields_list;
  int      tmp_error;
  DBUG_ENTER("JOIN::exec");

  ...

  result->send_fields((procedure ? curr_join->procedure_fields_list :
                      *curr_fields_list),
                    Protocol::SEND_NUM_ROWS | Protocol::SEND_EOF);
  error= do_select(curr_join, curr_fields_list, NULL, procedure);
  thd->limit_found_rows= curr_join->send_records;
  thd->examined_row_count= curr_join->examined_rows;
}
```

There is another function call that looks very interesting. Notice the code statement result->send_fields(). This function does what its name indicates. It is the function that sends the field headers to the client. As you can surmise, there are also methods to send the results to the client. I will look at these methods later in Chapter 4. Notice the thd->limit_found_rows= and thd->examined_row_count= assignments. These save record count values in the THD class. Let's take a look at that do_select() function.

You can see in the do_select() method shown in Listing 3-13 that something significant is happening. Notice the last highlighted code statement. The statement join->result->send_eof() looks like the code is sending an end-of-file flag somewhere. It is indeed sending an end-of-file signal to the client. So where are the results? They are generated in the sub_select() function. Let's look at that function next.

Listing 3-13. *The do_select() Function*

```
static int
do_select(JOIN *join,List<Item> *fields,TABLE *table,Procedure *procedure)
{
  int rc= 0;
  enum_nested_loop_state error= NESTED_LOOP_OK;
  JOIN_TAB *join_tab;
  DBUG_ENTER("do_select");

  ...

    error= sub_select(join,join_tab,0);

  ...

    if (join->result->send_eof())

  ...
}
```

Now you're getting somewhere! Take a moment to scan through Listing 3-14. This listing shows a condensed view of the sub_select() function. Notice that the code begins with an initialization of the JOIN class record. The join_init_read_record() function initializes any records available for reading in a structure named JOIN_TAB and populates the read_record member variable with another class named READ_RECORD. The READ_RECORD class contains the tuple read from the table. Inside this function are the abstraction layers to the storage engine subsystem. I will leave the discussion of the storage engine and how the system is used in a query until Chapter 7, where I present details on constructing your own storage engine. The system initializes the tables to begin reading records sequentially and then reads one record at a time until all of the records are read.

Listing 3-14. *The sub_select() Function*

```
enum_nested_loop_state
sub_select(JOIN *join,JOIN_TAB *join_tab,bool end_of_records)
{

  ...

  READ_RECORD *info= &join_tab->read_record;

  if (join->resume_nested_loop)
  {

  ...

  }
  else
  {

  ...

    join->thd->row_count= 0;

    error= (*join_tab->read_first_record)(join_tab);
    rc= evaluate_join_record(join, join_tab, error, report_error);
  }

  while (rc == NESTED_LOOP_OK)
  {
    error= info->read_record(info);
    rc= evaluate_join_record(join, join_tab, error, report_error);
  }

  ...
}
```

■**Note** The code presented in Listing 3-14 is more condensed than the other examples I have shown. The main reason is this code uses a fair number of advanced programming techniques, such as recursion and function pointer redirection. However, the concept as presented is accurate for the example query.

Control returns to the JOIN class for evaluation of the expressions and execution of the relational operators. After the results are processed, they are transmitted to the client and then control returns to the sub_select() function, where the end-of-file flag is sent to tell the client there are no more results. Table 3-6 lists the source file associated with query execution.

Table 3-6. *Query Execution*

Source File	Description
/sql/sql_select.cc	Contains some of the optimization functions and the implementation of the select functions

I hope that this tour has satisfied your curiosity and if nothing else boosted your appreciation for the complexities of a real-world database system. Feel free to go back through this tour again until you're comfortable with the basic flow. I will discuss a few of the more important classes and structures in the next section.

Supporting Libraries

There are many additional libraries in the MySQL source tree. MySQL AB has long worked diligently to encapsulate and optimize many of the common routines used to access the supported operating systems and hardware. Most of these libraries are designed to render the code both operating system and hardware agnostic. These libraries make it possible to write code so that specific platform characteristics do not force you to write specialized code. Among these libraries are libraries for managing efficient string handling, hash tables, linked lists, memory allocation, and many others. Table 3-7 lists the purpose and location of a few of the more common libraries.

■**Tip** The best way to discover if a library exists for a routine that you're trying to use is to look through the source code files in the /mysys directory using a text search tool. Most of the wrapper functions have a name similar to their original function. For example, my_alloc.c implements the malloc wrapper.

Table 3-7. *Supporting Libraries*

Source File	Utilities
/mysys/array.c	Array operations
/mysys/hash.h and /mysys/hash.c	Hash tables
/mysys/list.c	Linked lists
/mysys/my_alloc.c	Memory allocation
/strings/*.c	Base memory and string manipulation routines
/mysys/string.c	String operations
/mysys/my_pthread.c	Threading

Important Classes and Structures

Quite a few classes and structures in the MySQL source code can be considered key elements to the success of the system. To become fully knowledgeable about the MySQL source code, you should learn the basics of all of the key classes and structures used in the system. Knowing what is stored in which class or what the structures contain can help you make your modifications integrate well. The following sections describe these key classes and structures.

The ITEM_ Class

One class that permeates throughout the subsystems is the ITEM_ class. I called it ITEM_ because a number of classes are derived from the base ITEM class and even classes derived from those. These derivatives are used to store and manipulate a great many data (items) in the system. These include parameters (like in the WHERE clause), identifiers, time, fields, function, num, string, and many others. Listing 3-15 shows a condensed view of the ITEM base class. The structure is defined in the /sql/item.h source file and implemented in the /sql/item.cc source file. Additional subclasses are defined and implemented in files named after the data it encapsulates. For example, the function subclass is defined in /sql/item_func.h and implemented in /sql/item_func.cc.

Listing 3-15. *The ITEM_ Class*

```
class Item {
  Item(const Item &);        /* Prevent use of these */
  void operator=(Item &);
public:
  static void *operator new(size_t size)
  { return (void*) sql_alloc((uint) size); }
  static void *operator new(size_t size, MEM_ROOT *mem_root)
  { return (void*) alloc_root(mem_root, (uint) size); }
  static void operator delete(void *ptr,size_t size) { TRASH(ptr, size); }
  static void operator delete(void *ptr, MEM_ROOT *mem_root) {}

  enum Type {FIELD_ITEM= 0, FUNC_ITEM, SUM_FUNC_ITEM, STRING_ITEM,
      INT_ITEM, REAL_ITEM, NULL_ITEM, VARBIN_ITEM,
      COPY_STR_ITEM, FIELD_AVG_ITEM, DEFAULT_VALUE_ITEM,
      PROC_ITEM,COND_ITEM, REF_ITEM, FIELD_STD_ITEM,
      FIELD_VARIANCE_ITEM, INSERT_VALUE_ITEM,
          SUBSELECT_ITEM, ROW_ITEM, CACHE_ITEM, TYPE_HOLDER,
          PARAM_ITEM, TRIGGER_FIELD_ITEM, DECIMAL_ITEM,
          XPATH_NODESET, XPATH_NODESET_CMP,
          VIEW_FIXER_ITEM};

  ...
```

```
    /*
      str_values's main purpose is to be used to cache the value in
      save_in_field
    */
    String str_value;
    my_string name;         /* Name from select */
    /* Original item name (if it was renamed)*/
    my_string orig_name;
    Item *next;
    uint32 max_length;
    uint name_length;                       /* Length of name */
    uint8 marker, decimals;
    my_bool maybe_null;      /* If item may be null */
    my_bool null_value;      /* if item is null */
    my_bool unsigned_flag;
    my_bool with_sum_func;
    my_bool fixed;                         /* If item fixed with fix_fields */
    my_bool is_autogenerated_name;         /* indicate was name of this Item
                                              autogenerated or set by user */
    DTCollation collation;

    // alloc & destruct is done as start of select using sql_alloc
    Item();
    /*
       Constructor used by Item_field, Item_ref & aggregate (sum) functions.
       Used for duplicating lists in processing queries with temporary
       tables
       Also it used for Item_cond_and/Item_cond_or for creating
       top AND/OR structure of WHERE clause to protect it of
       optimisation changes in prepared statements
    */
    Item(THD *thd, Item *item);
    virtual ~Item()
    {
#ifdef EXTRA_DEBUG
      name=0;
#endif
    }    /*lint -e1509 */
    void set_name(const char *str, uint length, CHARSET_INFO *cs);
    void rename(char *new_name);
    void init_make_field(Send_field *tmp_field,enum enum_field_types type);
    virtual void cleanup();
    virtual void make_field(Send_field *field);
    Field *make_string_field(TABLE *table);

    ...
};
```

The LEX Structure

The LEX structure is responsible for being the internal representation (in-memory storage) of a query and its parts. It is more than that, though. The LEX structure is used to store all of the parts of a query in an organized manner. There are lists for fields, tables, expressions, and all of the parts that make up any query.

The LEX structure is filled in by the parser as it discovers the parts of the query. Thus, when the parser is done the LEX structure contains everything needed to optimize and execute the query. Listing 3-16 shows a condensed view of the LEX structure. The structure is defined in the /sql/lex.h source file.

Listing 3-16. *The LEX Structure*

```
typedef struct st_lex
{
  uint   yylineno,yytoklen;        /* Simulate lex */
  LEX_YYSTYPE yylval;
  SELECT_LEX_UNIT unit;                          /* most upper unit */
  SELECT_LEX select_lex;                         /* first SELECT_LEX */
  /* current SELECT_LEX in parsing */
  SELECT_LEX *current_select;
  /* list of all SELECT_LEX */
  SELECT_LEX *all_selects_list;
  const uchar *buf;     /* The beginning of string, used by SPs */
  const uchar *ptr,*tok_start,*tok_end,*end_of_query;

  /* The values of tok_start/tok_end as they were one call of yylex before */
  const uchar *tok_start_prev, *tok_end_prev;

  char *length,*dec,*change,*name;
  char *help_arg;
  char *backup_dir;        /* For RESTORE/BACKUP */
  char* to_log;                                /* For PURGE MASTER LOGS TO */
  char* x509_subject,*x509_issuer,*ssl_cipher;
  char* found_semicolon;                       /* For multi queries - next query */
  String *wild;
  sql_exchange *exchange;
  select_result *result;
  Item *default_value, *on_update_value;
  LEX_STRING comment, ident;
  LEX_USER *grant_user;
  XID *xid;
  gptr yacc_yyss,yacc_yyvs;
  THD *thd;
  CHARSET_INFO *charset;
  TABLE_LIST *query_tables;  /* global list of all tables in this query */

  ...
} LEX;
```

The NET Structure

The NET structure is responsible for storing all of the information concerning communication to and from a client. Listing 3-17 shows a condensed view of the NET structure. The buff member variable is used to store the raw communication packets (that when combined form the SQL statement). As you will see in later chapters, there are helper functions that fill in, read, and transmit the data packets to and from the client. Two examples are

- my_net_write(),which writes the data packets to the network protocol from the NET structure

- my_net_read(), which reads the data packets from the network protocol into the NET structure

You can find the complete set of network communication functions in /include/mysql_com.h.

Listing 3-17. *The NET Structure*

```
typedef struct st_net {
#if !defined(CHECK_EMBEDDED_DIFFERENCES) || !defined(EMBEDDED_LIBRARY)
  Vio* vio;
  unsigned char *buff,*buff_end,*write_pos,*read_pos;
  my_socket fd;          /* For Perl DBI/dbd */
  unsigned long max_packet,max_packet_size;
  unsigned int pkt_nr,compress_pkt_nr;
  unsigned int write_timeout, read_timeout, retry_count;
  int fcntl;
  my_bool compress;
  /*
    The following variable is set if we are doing several queries in one
    command ( as in LOAD TABLE ... FROM MASTER ),
    and do not want to confuse the client with OK at the wrong time
  */
  unsigned long remain_in_buf,length, buf_length, where_b;
  unsigned int *return_status;
  unsigned char reading_or_writing;
  char save_char;
  my_bool no_send_ok;  /* For SPs and other things that do multiple stmts */
  my_bool no_send_eof; /* For SPs' first version read-only cursors */
  /*
    Set if OK packet is already sent, and we do not need to send error
    messages
  */
  my_bool no_send_error;
  /*
    Pointer to query object in query cache, do not equal NULL (0) for
    queries in cache that have not stored its results yet
  */
#endif
```

```
    char last_error[MYSQL_ERRMSG_SIZE], sqlstate[SQLSTATE_LENGTH+1];
    unsigned int last_errno;
    unsigned char error;
    gptr query_cache_query;
    my_bool report_error; /* We should report error (we have unreported error) */
    my_bool return_errno;
} NET;
```

The THD Class

In the preceding tour of the source code, you saw many references to the THD class. In fact, there is exactly one THD object for every connection. The thread class is paramount to successful thread execution and is involved in every operation from implementing access control to returning results to the client. As a result, the THD class shows up in just about every subsystem or function that operates within the server. Listing 3-18 shows a condensed view of the THD class. Take a moment and browse through some of the member variables and methods. As you can see, this is a large class (I've omitted a great many of the methods). The class is defined in the /sql/sql_class.h source file and implemented in the /sql/sql_class.cc source file.

Listing 3-18. *The THD Class*

```
class THD :public Statement,
           public Open_tables_state
{
public:

  ...

  String   packet;      // dynamic buffer for network I/O
  String   convert_buffer;              // buffer for charset conversions
  struct   sockaddr_in remote;     // client socket address
  struct   rand_struct rand;     // used for authentication
  struct   system_variables variables;  // Changeable local variables
  struct   system_status_var status_var; // Per thread statistic vars
  THR_LOCK_INFO lock_info;              // Locking info of this thread
  THR_LOCK_OWNER main_lock_id;          // To use for conventional queries
  THR_LOCK_OWNER *lock_id;              // If not main_lock_id, points to
                                        // the lock_id of a cursor.
  pthread_mutex_t LOCK_delete;     // Locked before thd is deleted

  ...

  char   *db, *catalog;
  Security_context main_security_ctx;
  Security_context *security_ctx;

  ...
```

```
  enum enum_server_command command;
  uint32     server_id;
  uint32     file_id;      // for LOAD DATA INFILE
  ...

  const char *where;
  time_t     start_time,time_after_lock,user_time;
  time_t     connect_time,thr_create_time; // track down slow pthread_create
  thr_lock_type update_lock_default;
  delayed_insert *di;

  ...

  table_map  used_tables;

  ...

  ulong      thread_id, col_access;

  ...

  inline time_t query_start() { query_start_used=1; return start_time; }
  inline void  set_time()    { if (user_time) start_time=time_after_lock=user_time;
                                 else time_after_lock=time(&start_time); }
  inline void  end_time()    { time(&start_time); }
  inline void  set_time(time_t t) { time_after_lock=start_time=user_time=t; }

  ...
};
```

Now that you have had a tour of the source code and have examined some of the important classes and structures used in the system, I will shift the focus to items that will help you
implement your own modifications to the MySQL system. Let's take a break from the source
code and consider the coding guidelines and documentation aspects of software development.

Coding Guidelines

If the source code I've described seems to have a strange format, it may be because you have a
different style than the authors of the source code. Consider the case where there are many
developers writing a large software program like MySQL, each with their own style. As you can
imagine, the code would quickly begin to resemble a jumbled mass of statements. To avoid
this, MySQL AB has published coding guidelines in various forms. However, as you will see
when you begin exploring the code yourself, it seems there are a few developers who aren't
following the coding guidelines. The only plausible explanation is that the guidelines have
changed over time, which can happen over the lifetime of a large project. Regardless of the

reasons why the guidelines are not being followed, most developers do adhere to the guidelines. More importantly, MySQL AB expects you to follow them.

The coding guidelines are included in the MySQL Internals Manual available online at `http://dev.mysql.com/doc`. Chapter 2 of the internals document lists all of the coding guidelines as a huge bulleted list containing the do's and don'ts of writing C/C++ code for the MySQL server. I have captured the most important guidelines and summarized them for you in the following paragraphs.

General Guidelines

One of the most stressed aspects of the guidelines is that you should write code that is as optimized as possible. This goal is counter to agile development methodologies, where you code only what you need and leave refinement and optimization to refactoring. If you develop using agile methodologies, you may want to wait to check in your code until you have refactored it.

Another very important overall goal is to avoid the use of direct API or operating system calls. You should always look in the associated libraries for wrapper functions. Many of these functions are optimized for fast and safe execution. For example, you should never use the C `malloc()` function. Instead, use the `sql_alloc()` or `my_alloc()` function.

All lines of code must be fewer than 80 characters long. If you need to continue a line of code onto another line, you should align the code so that parameters are aligned vertically or the continuation code is aligned with the indention space count.

Comments are written using the standard C-style comments, for example, `/* this is a comment */`. You should use comments liberally through your code.

■**Tip** Resist the urge to use the C++ `//` `comment` option. The MySQL coding guidelines specifically discourage this technique.

Documentation

The language of choice for the source code is English. This includes all variables, function names, constants, and comments. The developers who write and maintain the MySQL source code are located throughout Europe and the United States. The choice of English as the default language in the source code is largely due to the influence of American computer science developments. English is also taught as a second language in many primary and secondary education programs in many European countries.

When writing functions, you should use a comment block that describes the function, its parameters, and the expected return values. The content of the comment block should be written in sections, with section names in all caps. You should include a short descriptive name of the function on the first line after the comment and, at a minimum, include the sections, synopsis, description, and return value. You may also include optional sections such as WARNING, NOTES, SEE ALSO, TODO, ERRORS, and REFERENCED_BY. The sections and content are described here:

- *SYNOPSIS* (required)—Presents a brief overview of the flow and control mechanisms in the function. It should permit the reader to understand the basic algorithm of the function. This helps readers understand the function and provide an at-a-glance glimpse of what it does. This section also includes a description of all of the parameters (indicated by IN for input, OUT for output, and IN/OUT for referenced parameters whose values may be changed).

- *DESCRIPTION* (required)—A narrative of the function. It should include the purpose of the function and a brief description of its use.

- *RETURN VALUE* (required)—Presents all of the possible return values and what they mean to the caller.

- *WARNING*—Include this section to describe any unusual side effects that the caller should be aware of.

- *NOTES*—Include this section to provide the reader with any information you feel is important.

- *SEE ALSO*—Include this section when you're writing a function that is associated with another function or requires specific outputs of another function or that is intended to be used by another function in a specific calling order.

- *TODO*—Include this section to communicate any unfinished features of the function. Be sure to remove the items from this section as you complete them. I tend to forget to do this and it often results in a bit of head scratching to figure out I've already completed the TODO item.

- *ERRORS*—Include this section to document any unusual error handling that your function has.

- *REFERENCED_BY*—Include this section to communicate specific aspects of the relationship this function has with other functions or objects—for example, whenever your function is called by another function, the function is a primitive of another function, or the function is a friend method or even a virtual method.

Tip MySQL AB suggests it isn't necessary to provide a comment block for short functions that have only a few lines of code, but I recommend writing a comment block for all of the functions you create. You will appreciate this advice as you explore the source code and encounter numerous small (and some large) functions with little or no documentation.

A sample of a function comment block is shown in Listing 3-19.

Listing 3-19. *Example Function Comment Block*

```
/*
  Find tuples by key.

  SYNOPSIS
    find_by_key()
    string key            IN      A string containing the key to find.
    Handler_class *handle IN      The class containing the table to be searched.
    Tuple *               OUT     The tuple class containing the key passed.

    Uses B Tree index contained in the Handler_class. Calls Index::find()
    method then returns a pointer to the tuple found.

  DESCRIPTION
    This function implements a search of the Handler_class index class to find
    a key passed.

  RETURN VALUE
    SUCCESS (TRUE)                Tuple found.
    != SUCCESS (FALES)            Tuple not found.

  WARNING
    Function can return an empty tuple when a key hit occurs on the index but
    the tuple has been marked for deletion.

  NOTES
    This method has been tested for empty keys and keys that are greater or
    less than the keys in the index.

  SEE ALSO
    Query:;execute(), Tuple.h

  TODO
    * Change code to include error handler to detect when key passed in exceeds
    the maximum length of the key in the index.

  ERRORS
    -1                            Table not found.
    1                             Table locked.

  REFERENCED_BY
    This function is called by the Query::execute() method.
*/
```

Functions and Parameters

I want to call these items out specifically because some inconsistencies exist in the source code. If you use the source code as a guide for formatting, you may wander astray of the coding guidelines. Functions and their parameters should be aligned so that the parameters are in vertical alignment. This applies to both defining the function and calling it from other code. In a similar way, variables should be aligned when you declare them. The spacing of the alignment isn't such an issue as the vertical appearance of these items. You should also add line comments about each of the variables. Line comments should begin in column 49 and not exceed the maximum 80-column rule. In the case where a comment for a variable exceeds 80 columns, you should place that comment on a separate line. Listing 3-20 shows examples of the type of alignment expected for functions, variables, and parameters.

Listing 3-20. *Variable, Function, and Parameter Alignment Examples*

```
int     var1;                              /* comment goes here */
long    var2;                              /* comment goes here too */
/* variable controls something of extreme interest and is documented well */
bool    var3;

return_value *classname::classmethod(int  var1,
                                     int  var2
                                     bool var3);

if (classname->classmethod(myreallylongvariablename1,
                           myreallylongvariablename2,
                           myreallylongvariablename3) == -1)
{
  /* do something */
}
```

Warning If you're developing on Windows, the line break feature of your editor may be set incorrectly. Most editors in Windows issue a CRLF (/r/n) when you place a line break in the file. MySQL AB requires you to use a single LF (/n), not a CRLF. This is a common incompatibility between files created on Windows versus files created in UNIX or Linux. If you're using Windows, check your editor and make the appropriate changes to its configuration.

Naming Conventions

MySQL AB prefers that you assign your variables meaningful names using all lowercase letters with underscores instead of initial caps. The exception is the use of class names, which are required to have initial caps. Enumerations should be prefixed with the phrase enum_. All structures and defines should be written with uppercase letters. Examples of the naming conventions are shown in Listing 3-21.

Listing 3-21. *Sample Naming Conventions*

```
class My_classname;
int   my_integer_counter;
bool  is_saved;

#define CONSTANT_NAME 12;

int my_function_name_goes_here(int variable1);
```

Spacing and Indenting

The MySQL coding guidelines state that spacing should always be two characters for each indention level. You should never use tabs. If your editor permits, you should change the default behavior of the editor to turn off automatic formatting and replace all tabs with two spaces. This is especially important when using documentation utilities like Doxygen (which I'll discuss in a moment) or line parsing tools to locate strings in the text.

When spacing between identifiers and operators, you should include no spaces between a variable and an operator and a single space between the operator and an operand (the right side of the operator). In a similar way, no space should follow the open parenthesis in functions, but include one space between parameters and no space between the last parameter name and the closing parenthesis. Lastly, you should include a single blank line to delineate variable declarations from control code, and control code from method calls, and block comments from other code, and functions from other declarations. Listing 3-22 depicts a properly formatted excerpt of code that contains an assignment statement, a function call, and a control statement.

Listing 3-22. *Spacing and Indention*

```
return_value= do_something_cool(i, max_limit, is_found);
if (return_value)
{
  int var1;
  int var2;

  var1= do_something_else(i);

  if (var1)
  {
    do_it_again();
  }
}
```

The alignment of the curly braces is also inconsistent in some parts of the source code. The MySQL coding guidelines state that the curly braces should align with the control code above it as I have shown in all of our examples. However, if you need to indent another level you should indent using the same column alignment as the code within the curly braces (two spaces). It is also not necessary to use curly braces if you're executing a single line of code in the code block.

An oddity of sorts in the curly braces area is the switch statement. A switch statement should be written to align the open curly brace after the switch condition and align the closing curly brace with the switch keyword. The case statements should be aligned in the same column as the switch keyword. Listing 3-23 illustrates this guideline.

Listing 3-23. *Switch Statement Example*

```
switch (some_var) {
case 1:
   do_something_here();
   do_something_else();
   break;
case 2:
   do_it_again();
   break;
}
```

■**Note** The last break in the previous code is not needed. I usually include it in my code for the sake of completeness.

Documentation Utilities

Another useful method of examining source code is to use an automated documentation generator that reads the source code and generates function- and class-based lists of methods. These programs list the structures used and provide clues as to how and where they are used in the source code. This is important for investigating MySQL because of the many critical structures that the source code relies on to operate and manipulate data.

One such program is called Doxygen. The nice thing about Doxygen is that it too is open source and governed by the GPL. When you invoke Doxygen, it reads the source code and produces a highly readable set of HTML files that pull the comments from the source code preceding the function and lists the function primitives. Doxygen can read programming languages such as C, C++, and Java, among several others. Doxygen can be a useful tool for investigating a complex system such as MySQL—especially when you consider that the base library functions are called from hundreds of locations throughout the code.

Doxygen is available for both UNIX and Windows platforms. To use the program on Linux, download the source code from the Doxygen web site at www.stack.nl/~dimitri/doxygen.

Once you have downloaded the installation, follow the installation instructions (also on the web site). Doxygen uses configuration files to generate the look and feel of the output as well as what gets included in the input. To generate a default configuration file, issue the following command:

```
doxygen -g -s /path_to_new_file/doxygen_config_filename
```

The path specified should be the path you want to store the documentation in. Once you have a default configuration file, you can edit the file and change the parameters to meet your specific needs. See the Doxygen documentation for more information on the options and their parameters. You would typically specify the folders to process, the project name, and other project-related settings. Once you have set the configurations you want, you can generate documentation for MySQL by issuing this command:

```
doxygen </path_to_new_file/Doxygen_config_filename>
```

Caution Depending on your settings, Doxygen could run for a long time. Avoid using advanced graphing commands if you want Doxygen to generate documentation in a reasonable time period.

The latest version of Doxygen can be run from Windows using a supplied GUI. The GUI allows you to use create the configuration file using a wizard that steps you through the process and creates a basic configuration file, an expert mode that allows you to set your own parameters, and the ability to load a config file. I found the output generated by using the wizard interface sufficient for casual to in-depth viewing.

I recommend spending some time running Doxygen and examining the output files prior to diving into the source code. It will save you tons of lookup time. The structures alone are worth tacking up on the wall next to your monitor or pasting into your engineering logbook. A sample of the type of documentation Doxygen can generate is shown in Figure 3-3.

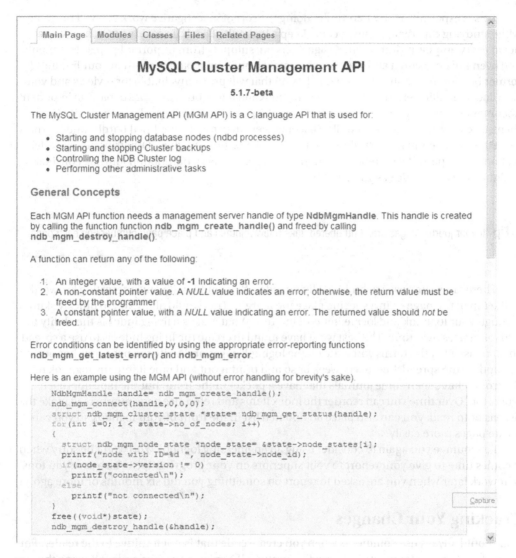

Figure 3-3. *Sample MySQL Doxygen output*

Keeping an Engineering Logbook

Many developers keep notes of their projects. Some are more detailed than others, but most take notes during meetings and phone conversations, thereby providing a written record for verbal communications. However, if you aren't in the habit of keeping an engineering logbook, you should consider doing so. I have found a logbook to be a vital tool in my work. Yes, it does require more effort to write things down and the log can get messy if you try to include all of the various drawings and e-mails you find important (mine are often bulging with clippings from important documents taped in place like some sort of engineer's scrapbook). However, the payoff is potentially huge.

This is especially true when you're doing the sort of investigative work you will be doing while studying the MySQL source code. Keep a logbook of each discovery you make. Write down every epiphany, important design decision, snippets from important paper documents, and even the occasional ah-ha! Over time you will build up a paper record of your findings (a former boss of mine called it her paper brain!) that will prove invaluable for reviews and your own documentation efforts. If you do use a logbook and make journal entries or paste in important document snippets, you will soon discover that logbooks of the journal variety do not lend themselves to being organized well. Most engineers (like me) prefer lined hardbound journals that cannot be reorganized (unless you use lots of scissors and glue). Others prefer loose-leaf logbooks that permit easy reorganization. If you plan to use a hardbound journal, consider building a "living" index as you go.

Tip If your journal pages aren't numbered, take a few minutes and place page numbers on each page.

There are many ways to build the living index. You could write any interesting keywords at the top of the page or in a specific place the margin. This would allow you to quickly skim through your logbook and locate items of interest. What makes a living index is the ability to add references over time. The best way I have found to create the living index is to use a spreadsheet to list all of the terms you write on the logbook pages and write the page number next to it. I update the spreadsheet every week or so and print it out and tape it into my logbook near the front. I have seen some journals that have a pocket in the front, but the tape approach works too. Over time you can reorder the index items and reference page numbers to make the list easier to read; you can also place an updated list in the front of your logbook so you can locate pages more easily.

I encourage you again to consider using an engineering logbook. You won't be sorry when it comes time to give your report to your superiors on your progress. It can also save you tons of rework later when you are asked to report on something you did six months or more ago.

Tracking Your Changes

You should always use comments when you create code that is not intuitive to the reader. For example, the code statement if (found) is pretty self-explanatory. The code following the control statement will be executed if the variable evaluates to TRUE. However, the code if (func_call_17(i, x, lp)) requires some explanation. Of course, you would want to write all of your code to be self-explanatory, but sometimes that isn't possible. This is particularly true when you're accessing supporting library functions. Some of the names are not intuitive and the parameter lists can be confusing. Document these situations as you code them, and your life will be enhanced.

When writing comments, you can choose to use inline comments, single-line comments, or multiline comments. Inline comments are written beginning in column 49 and cannot exceed 80 columns. A single-line comment should be aligned with the code it is referring to (the indention mark) and also should not exceed 80 columns. Likewise, multiline comments should align with the code they are explaining, should not exceed 80 columns, but should have the opening and closing comment markers placed on separate lines. Listing 3-24 illustrates these concepts.

Listing 3-24. *Comment Placement and Spacing Examples*

```
if (return_value)
{
  int     var1;                                /* comment goes here */
  long    var2;                                /* comment goes here too */

  /* this call does something else based on i */
  var1= do_something_else(i);

  if (var1)
  {
    /*
      This comment explains
      some really interesting thing
      about the following statement(s).
    */
    do_it_again();
  }
}
```

■**Tip** Never use repeating *s to emphasize portions of code. It distracts the reader from the code and makes for a cluttered look. Besides, it's too much work to get all those things to line up—especially when you edit your comments later.

If you are modifying the MySQL source code using the source control application BitKeeper, you don't have to worry about tracking your changes. BitKeeper provides several ways in which you can detect and report on which changes are yours versus others. However, if you are not using BitKeeper, you could lose track of which changes are yours, particularly if you make changes directly to existing system functions. In this case, it becomes difficult to distinguish what you wrote from what was already there. Keeping an engineering logbook helps immensely with this problem, but there is a better way.

You could add comments before and after your changes to indicate which lines of code are your modifications. For example, you could place a comment like /* BEGIN CAB MODIFICATION */ before the code and a comment like /* END CAB MODIFICATION */ after the code. This allows you to bracket your changes and helps you search for the changes easily using a number of text and line parsing utilities. An example of this technique is shown in Listing 3-25.

Listing 3-25. *Commenting Your Changes to the MySQL Source Code*

```
/* BEGIN CAB MODIFICATION */
/* Reason for Modification: */
/* This section adds my revision note to the MySQL version number. */
  /* original code:   */
  /*strmov(end, "."); */
  strmov(end, "-CAB Modifications");
/* END CAB MODIFICATION */
```

Notice I have also included the reason for the modification and the commented-out lines of the original code (the example is fictional). Using this technique will help you quickly access your changes and enhance your ability to diagnose problems later.

This technique can also be helpful if you make modifications for use in your organization and you are not going to share the changes with MySQL AB. If you do not share the changes, you will be forced to make the modifications to the source code every time MySQL AB releases a new build of the system you want to use. Having comment markers in the source code will help you quickly identify which files need changes and what those changes are. Chances are that if you create some new functionality you will eventually want to share that functionality if for no other reason than to avoid making the modifications every time a new version of MySQL is released.

■**Caution** Although this technique isn't prohibited when using source code under configuration control (BitKeeper), it is usually discouraged. In fact, developers may later remove your comments altogether. Use this technique when you make changes that you are not going to share with anyone.

Building the System for the First Time

Now that you've seen the inner workings of the MySQL source code and followed the path of a typical query through the source code, it is time for you to take a turn at the wheel. If you are already working with the MySQL source code and you are reading this book to learn more about the source code and how to modify it, you can skip this section.

I recommend, before you get started, that you download the source code if you haven't already and then download and install the executables for your chosen platform. It is important to have the compiled binaries handy in case things go wrong during your experiments. Attempting to diagnose a problem with a modified MySQL source code build without a reference point can be quite challenging. You will save yourself a lot of time if you can revert to the base compiled binary when you encounter a difficult debugging problem. I will cover debugging in more detail in Chapter 5. If you ever find yourself with that system problem, you can always reinstall the binaries and return your MySQL system to normal.

Compiling the source is easy. If you are using Linux, open a command shell, change to the root of your source tree, and run the `configure`, `make`, and `make install` commands.

Note If are using Linux and the configure file does not exist, you need to generate the file using one of the platform scripts in the BUILD directory. For example, to create the configure file for a Pentium-class machine using debug, run the command ./BUILD/compile-pentium-debug from the root of the source tree. Once the file is created, you can run the ./configure, make, and make install commands to build the server.

The configure script will check the system for dependencies and create the appropriate makefiles. The make and make install commands build the system for the first time and build the installation. Most developers run these commands when building the MySQL source code. If compiling for the first time, you may need to change the owner of the files (if you aren't using root) and make group adjustments (for more details see "Source Installation Overview" in the MySQL Reference Manual at http://dev.mysql.com/doc/refman/5.1/en/quick-install.html). The following outlines a typical build process for building the source code on Linux for the first time:

```
%> groupadd mysql
%> useradd -g mysql mysql
%> gunzip < mysql-VERSION.tar.gz | tar -xvf -
%> cd mysql-VERSION
%> ./configure --prefix=/usr/local/mysql
%> make
%> make install
%> cp support-files/my-medium.cnf /etc/my.cnf
%> cd /usr/local/mysql
%> bin/mysql_install_db --user=mysql
%> chown -R root  .
%> chown -R mysql var
%> chgrp -R mysql .
%> bin/mysqld_safe --user=mysql &
```

You can compile the Windows platform source code using Microsoft Visual Studio 2005 (some have had great success using Visual Studio 6.0 and 2005 Express Edition with the Microsoft platform development kit, but I have found Visual Studio 2005 to be more stable). To compile the system for the first time, open the mysql.dsw project workspace in the root of the source distribution tree and set the active project to mysqld classes and the project configuration to mysqld - Win32 nt. When you click Build mysqld, the project is designed to compile any necessary libraries and link them to the project you specified. Take along a fresh beverage to entertain yourself as it can take a while to build all of the libraries the first time. Regardless of which platform you use, your compiled executable will be placed in the client_release or client_debug folder depending on which compile option you chose. To run the new executable, simply stop the server service, copy the file to the bin folder under the MySQL installation, and restart the server service.

■**Caution** Most compilation problems can be traced to improperly configured development tools or missing libraries. Consult the MySQL forums for details on how to resolve the most common compilation problems.

The first thing you will notice about your newly compiled binary (unless there were problems) is that you cannot tell that the binary is the one you compiled! You could check the date of the file to see that the executable is the one you just created, but there isn't a way to know that from the client side. Although this approach is not recommended by MySQL AB and probably shunned by others as well, you could alter the version number of the MySQL compilation to indicate it is the one you compiled.

Let's assume you want to identify your modifications at a glance. For example, you want to see in the client window some indication that the server is your modified version. You could change the version number to show that. Figure 3-4 is an example of such a modification.

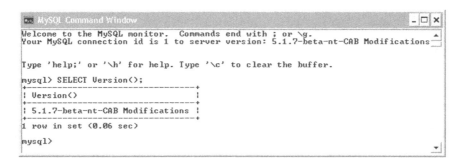

Figure 3-4. *Sample MySQL command cient with version modification*

Notice in both the header and the result of issuing the command, SELECT Version();, the version number returned is the same version number of the server you compiled plus an additional label I placed in the string. To make this change yourself, simply edit the set_server_version() function in the mysqld.cpp file, as shown in Listing 3-26. In the example, I have bolded the one line of code you can add to create this effect.

Listing 3-26. *Modified set_server_version Function*

```
static void set_server_version(void)
{
  char *end= strxmov(server_version, MYSQL_SERVER_VERSION,
                     MYSQL_SERVER_SUFFIX_STR, NullS);
#ifdef EMBEDDED_LIBRARY
  end= strmov(end, "-embedded");
#endif
#ifndef DBUG_OFF
  if (!strstr(MYSQL_SERVER_SUFFIX_STR, "-debug"))
      end= strmov(end, "-debug");
```

```
#endif
  if (opt_log || opt_update_log || opt_slow_log || opt_bin_log)
     strmov(end, "-log");                            // This may slow down system
  /* BEGIN CAB MODIFICATION */
  /* Reason for Modification: */
  /* This section adds my revision note to the MySQL version number. */
  strmov(end, "-CAB Modifications");
  /* END CAB MODIFICATION */
}
```

Note also that I have included the modification comments I referred to earlier. This will help you determine which lines of code you have changed. This change also has the benefit that the new version number will be shown in other MySQL tools such as the MySQL Administrator. Figure 3-5 shows the results of running the MySQL Administrator against the code compiled with this change.

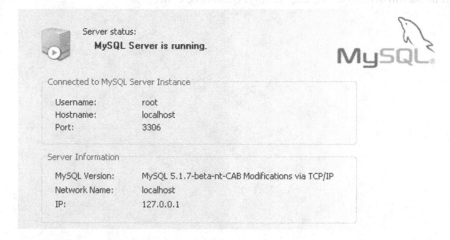

Figure 3-5. *Accessing the modified MySQL server using MySQL Administrator*

■**Caution** Did I mention this wasn't an approved method? If you are using MySQL to conduct your own experiments or you are modifying the source code for your own use, you can get away with doing what I have suggested. However, if you are using the code under source code control or you are creating modifications that will be added to the base source code at a later date, you should *not* implement this technique.

Summary

In this chapter, you have learned several methods to get the source code. Whether you choose to download a snapshot of the source tree, a copy of the GA release source code, or use the BitKeeper client software to gain access to the latest and greatest version, you can get and start using the source code. Now that is the beauty of open source!

Perhaps the most intriguing aspect of this chapter is your guided tour of the MySQL source code. I hope that by following a simple query all the way through the system and back, you gained a lot of ground on your quest to understanding the MySQL source code. I also hope that you haven't tossed the book down in frustration if you've encountered issues with compiling the source code. Much of what makes a good open source developer is her ability to systematically diagnose and adapt her environment to the needs of the current project. Do not despair if you had issues come up. Solving issues is a natural part of the learning cycle.

You also explored the major elements from the MySQL Coding Guidelines document and saw examples of some of the code formatting and documentation guidelines. While not complete, the coding guidelines I presented are enough to give you a feel for how MySQL AB wants you to write the source code for your modifications. If you follow these simple guidelines, you should not be asked to conform later.

In the next two chapters, I will take you through two very important concepts of software development that are often overlooked. The next chapter will show you how to apply a test-driven development methodology to exploring and extending the MySQL system, and the chapter that follows will discuss debugging the MySQL source code.

CHAPTER 4

▪ ▪ ▪

Test-Driven MySQL Development

Systems integrators must overcome limitations of the systems they are integrating. Sometimes the system lacks certain functions or commands that are needed for the integration. MySQL AB has recognized this need and includes flexible options in the MySQL server that add new functions and commands. This chapter introduces a key element in generating high-quality extensions to the MySQL system. I'll discuss software testing and explain some common practices for testing large systems. I'll use specific examples to illustrate the accepted practices of testing the MySQL system.

Background

Some of you may be wondering why I would include a chapter about testing so early in the book. I did so because I wanted to tell you about the testing capabilities available so that you can plan your own modifications by first planning how to test them. This is the premise of test-driven development: to develop and implement the tests from the requirements, write the code, and then immediately execute the tests. This may sound a tad counterintuitive to someone not familiar with this concept; after all, how do you write tests for code that hasn't been written? In the following sections, I'll clarify by providing some background information regarding this increasingly popular concept.

Why Test?

I often get asked this question whenever I lecture about software quality issues. Some students want to how much testing is enough. To those who feel testing is largely a waste of time or highly overrated, I offer them the opportunity to complete their software engineering class projects[1] using a minimal (or sometimes no) testing strategy. The results are often interesting and enlightening.

The students often speak of how well they code their modules and classes and how careful they are to use good modeling practices. Many use Unified Modeling Language (UML) diagrams to assist their development. While these are good practices, testing involves a lot more than making sure your source code matches your model. Students who insist that their highly honed coding

---

1. Which normally include large semester-long group projects beginning with requirements elicitation.

skills are sufficient often produce project deliverables that have feature and functionality issues. Although most do not suffer from fatal errors or crashes (which are often found during development), there are often issues with integration and how the software works. That is, students failed to ensure that their software worked the way the customer wanted.

If this scenario is all too familiar to you, then you know the value of software testing. There are many forms of software testing used to perform a variety of quality assurance and quality control. Choosing *which* technique to use *when* is the real nature of the science of software testing.

Tip If you have not had the opportunity to experience software testing firsthand or to work with a professional software tester, I recommend seeking one out. They often have incredible insight into how software works that few developers ever hone successfully. Don't be shy or embarrassed if they break your code—that's their job and most are very good at it!

Testing vs. Debugging

You may be tempted to conclude that debugging and testing are the same. Although they often have the same goal—identifying defects—they are not the same. Debugging is an interactive process designed to locate defects in the logic of the source code by exposing the internal workings of the source code. Testing, on the other hand, is used to identify defects in the execution of the source code without examining the inner workings of the source code.

Test-Driven Development

Test-driven development is often associated with agile programming. Indeed, test-driven development is often used by organizations that adopt extreme programming (XP) methods. While that may sound scary and could deter you from reading on, allow me to expose to you a secret about XP: you don't have to adopt XP to use agile practices!

I often find individuals who are deeply concerned about adopting agile practices because of all the negative hype tossed about in uninformed rants. I am often saddened to learn that those who view traditional software engineering processes as cast in stone think that agile practices are designed to do more with less and are therefore inferior. That is simply not the case.

Agile practices are designed to streamline software development, to reengage the customer, to produce only what is needed when it is needed, and to focus the job at hand on what the customer wants. It is the customer who is the focus of agile methods, not the process. Furthermore, agile practices are designed to be used either as a set or selectively in an application. That is, organizations are encouraged to adopt agile practices as they see fit rather than jumping in with both feet and turning their developers' world upside down. That is the true reason behind the negative hype—that and the resulting failures reported by organizations that tried to do too much too soon.[2] If you would like to learn more about the debate of agile versus traditional methods, direct your browser to the Agile Alliance web site, `www.agilealliance.org`.

One of the most profoundly useful agile practices is test-driven development. The philosophy of test-driven development is simple: start with a basic model of the solution, write the test, run the test, code the solution, and validate it with the test. While that sounds really intuitive, it is

---

2. Yes, this is a bit of a dichotomy considering agile practices are designed to reduce unnecessary work.

amazing how complicated it can become. Creating the test before the code sounds backward. You may be wondering how you can test something that doesn't exist. How can that help? Developing the test first allows you to focus on the design of your software rather than the code. I'll explain a typical test-driven agile development process so you can see how test-driven development complements the design and actually drives the source code. Yes, I know that sounds weird, but give it a chance and it will make sense.

Test-driven development begins with a simple model of the system. This is usually a simple class diagram of the basic classes within the system. The class diagram is set with just the empty class blocks annotated only with the *proposed* name of the class. I say proposed because this is usually the point at which developers used to traditional methods get stumped. In agile practices nothing is set in stone and anything can be a candidate for change. It just has to make sense to do so and to further the ultimate goal of producing the software that the customer wants.

Once an initial class diagram is created, it is copied, set aside, and referred to as the domain model because it depicts the initial layout of your classes. From there, use case diagrams and supplemental use case scenarios (textual descriptions of the use case and alternative execution sequences) are created. Each use case is then augmented by a single sequence diagram, which maps out the functions needed for the classes referenced.

As each class begins to take shape, you then begin writing the tests. Yes, even though the classes don't exist you still write the tests. The tests form a hybrid of integration, system, and interface testing (all white-box techniques) where each test exercises one of the classes in the domain model.

■**Note** *White-box testing* is testing without knowledge of how the system is constructed. *Black-box testing* is testing the behavior of the system given knowledge of its internal structures.

For most agile practices, it is at this point that the lessons learned from the first iteration of this sequence are incorporated into the appropriate parts of the design (use case, sequence diagram, etc.) and the appropriate changes are made.

■**Note** Some agile practitioners add another modeling step to the process by using robustness diagrams. This adaptation closely resembles the ICONIX process. For more information about the ICONIX process, see *Agile Development with ICONIX Process.*[3]

Sometimes these changes include the discovery of new classes, the reorganization of the existing class, and even the formulation of the methods and properties of the class. In other words, writing the test before the code helps validate the design. That is really cool because once you complete the level of design you want for your iteration and begin writing the source code, you already have your tests completed! You can simply run your tests and demonstrate

---

3. D. Rosenberg, M. Stephens, M. Collins-Cope. *Agile Development with ICONIX Process* (Berkeley, CA: Apress, 2005).

your code is working as designed. Of course, if you need to change the test and therefore the design, well, that's the beauty of agile development.

Benchmarking

Benchmarking is an activity designed to establish performance characteristics of software. You can use benchmarking to establish a known performance level (called a *baseline*) and then later run the benchmarks again after a change in environment to determine the effects of those changes. This is the most common use of benchmarking. Other uses include identification of performance limits under load, managing change to the system or environment, and identifying conditions that may be causing performance problems.

You perform benchmarking by running a set of tests that exercise the system and storing the performance counter results. These results are called benchmarks. They are typically stored or archived and annotated with a description of the system environment. For example, savvy database professionals often include the benchmarks and a dump of the system configuration and environment in their archive. This permits them to compare how the system performed in the past with how it is currently performing and identify any changes to the system or its environment.

The tests are normally of the functional variety and are targeted toward testing a particular feature or function of the system. Some benchmarking tools include a broad range of tests that examine everything about the system, from the mundane to the most complex operations, under light, medium, and heavy loads.

Although most developers would consider running benchmarks only when something odd happens, it can be useful to run the benchmarks at fixed intervals or even before and after major events, such as changes to the system or the environment. Just be sure to remember to run your benchmarks the first time to create a baseline. Benchmarks taken after an event without a baseline will not be very helpful!

Guidelines for Good Benchmarks

Many good practices are associated with benchmarking. In this section, I'll take you through a few that I've found to be helpful in getting the most out of the benchmarking experience.

First, you should always consider the concept of before-and-after snapshots. Don't wait until after you've made a change to the server to see how it compares to the baseline you took six months ago. A lot can happen in six months! Instead, measure the system before the change, make the change, and then measure the system again. This will give you three metrics to compare: how the system is expected to perform, how it performs before the change, and how it performs after the change. You may find that something has taken place that makes your change more or less significant. For example, let's say your benchmarks include a metric for query time. Your baseline established six months ago for a given test query was set at 4.25 seconds. You decide to modify the index of the table being tested. You run your before benchmark and get a value of 15.50, and your after benchmark produces a value of 4.5 seconds. If you had not taken the before picture, you wouldn't have known that your change increased performance dramatically. Instead, you might have concluded that the change caused the query to perform a bit slower—which might have led you to undo that change, thus resulting in a return to slower queries.

This fictional example exposes several aspects that I want to warn you about. If you are conducting benchmarks on the performance of data retrieval on systems that are expected to grow in the amount of data stored, you need to run your benchmarks more frequently so that you can map the effects of the growth of data with the performance of the system. In the previous example, you would have considered the before value to be "normal" for the conditions of the system, such as data load.

You should also be careful to ensure your tests are valid for what you are measuring. If you are benchmarking the performance of a query for a table, your benchmarks are targeted at the application level and are not useful for predicting the performance of the system in the general sense. Be sure to segregate application-level benchmarks from the more general metrics to be sure you don't skew your conclusions.

Another good practice that is related to the before and after concept is to run your benchmarks several times over a constrained period of activity (under a consistent load) to ensure your benchmarks are not affected by localized activity such as a rogue process or a resource-intensive task. I find running the benchmark up to several dozen times permits me to determine mean values for the results. You can create these aggregates using many techniques. You could use a statistic package to create the basic statistics or use your favorite statistical friendly spreadsheet application.[4]

Note Some benchmark tools provide this feature for you. Alas, the MySQL Benchmark Suite does not.

Perhaps the most useful practice to adopt is the idea of changing one thing at a time. Don't go through your server with a wide brush of changes and expect to conclude anything meaningful from the results. What often happens in this case is one of the six or so changes negatively affects the gains of several others and the remaining ones have little or no effect on performance. Unless you made one change at a time, you would have no idea which affected the system in a negative, positive, or neutral way.

You should also use real data whenever possible. Sometimes manufactured data contains data that falls neatly into the ranges of the fields specified and therefore never test certain features of the system (domain and range checking, etc.). If your data can change frequently, you may want to snapshot the data at some point and build your tests using the same set of data each time. While this will ensure you are testing the performance using real data, it may not test performance degradation over time with respect to growth.

Lastly, when interpreting the results of your benchmarks and managing your expectations, be sure to set realistic goals. If you are trying to improve the performance of the system under certain conditions, make sure you have a firm grasp of the known consequences before you set your goals. For example, if you are examining the effect of switching the network interface from a gigabit connection to an interface that performs network communication 100 times faster, your server will not perform its data transfer 100 times faster. In this case and ones similar to it, the value added by the hardware should be weighed against the cost of the hardware and the expected gains of using the new hardware. In other words, your server should perform some percentage faster, thereby saving you money (or increasing income).

---

4. Some statisticians consider the statistical engine in Microsoft Excel to be inaccurate. However, for the values you are likely to see, the inaccuracies are not a problem.

If you estimate that you need to increase your network performance by 10 percent in order to meet a quarterly expense and income goal that will lead to a savings, use that value as your goal. If your benchmarks show that you have achieved the desired improvements (or better yet surpassed them), go ask your boss for a raise. If the benchmarks show performance metrics that don't meet the goal, you can tell your boss you can save him money by returning the hardware (and then ask for a raise). Either way, you can back up your claims with empirical data: your benchmarks!

Benchmarking Database Systems

You would probably agree that benchmarking can be a very powerful tool in your arsenal. But what exactly do benchmarks have to do with database servers? The answer is a lot.

Benchmarking your database server can be accomplished on many levels. The most notable is benchmarking changes to your database schema. You would probably not create tests for a single table (although you can), but you are more likely to be interested in how the changes for a database schema affect performance.

This is especially true for new applications and databases. You can create several schemas and populate them with data, and write benchmark tests designed to mimic the proposed system. Hey, here's that test-driven thing again! By creating the alternative schemas and benchmarking them, and perhaps even making several iterations of changes, you can quickly determine which schemas are best for the application you are designing.

You can also benchmark database systems for specialized uses. For example, you may want to check the performance of your database system under various loads or in various environments. What better way to say for sure whether that new RAID device will improve performance than to run before-and-after benchmarks and know just how much of a difference the change to the environment makes? Yes, it is all about the cost. Benchmarking will give you the tool you need to help manage your database system cost.

Profiling

Sometimes a defect doesn't manifest unless the system is under load. In these cases, the system may slow down but not produce any errors. How do you find those types of problems? You need a way to examine the system while it is running. This process is called *profiling*. Some authors group profiling with debugging and while I would hesitate to say that profiling isn't a debugging tool, profiling is more than a debugging tool. Profiling allows you to identify performance bottlenecks and potential problems before they are detected in the benchmarks. However, profiling is usually done after a problem is detected and sometimes as a means to determine its origins. The types of things you can discover or monitor using profiling include memory and disk consumption, CPU usage, I/O usage, system response time, and many other system parameters.

The term *profile* (or *profiler*) is sometimes confused with performing the measurement of the targeted system parameters. The identification of the performance metric is called a diagnostic operation or technique (sometimes called a trace). A system that manages these diagnostic operations and permits you to run them against a system is called a profiler. Therefore, profiling is the application of diagnostic operations using a profiler.

Profilers typically produce reports that include machine-readable recordings of the system during a fixed period of time. These types of performance measurements are commonly called *traces* because they trace the path of the system over time. Other profilers are designed to produce human-readable printouts that detail specifics of what portion of the system executed the longest or, more commonly, where the system spent most of its time. This type of profiler is typically used to monitor resources such as I/O, memory, CPU, and threads or processes. For example, you can discover what commands or functions your threads and processes are performing. If your system records additional metadata in the thread or process headers, you may also discover performance issues with thread or process blocking and deadlocks.

Note An example of deadlocking is when a process has a lock (exclusive access) to one resource and is waiting on another that is locked in turn by another process that is waiting for the first resource. Deadlock detection is a key attribute of a finely designed database system.

You can also use profiling to determine which queries are performing the poorest and even which threads or processes are taking the longest to execute. In these situations, you may also discover that a certain thread or process is consuming a large number of resources (such as CPU or memory) and therefore take steps to correct the problem. This situation is not uncommon in environments with a large community of users accessing central resources.

Sometimes certain requests of the system result in situations where the actions of one user (legitimate or otherwise—let's hope the legitimate kind) may be affecting others. In this case, you can correctly identify the troublesome thread or process and its owner, and take steps to correct the problem.

Profiling can also be a powerful diagnostic aide when developing systems, hence the tendency to call them debugging tools. The types of reports you can obtain about your system can lead you to all manner of unexpected inefficiencies in your source code. However, take care not to overdo it. It is possible to spend a considerable amount of time profiling a piece of source code that takes a long time to execute such that you may never fully meet your expectations of identifying the bottleneck. The thing to remember is that some things take a while to execute. Such is the case for disk I/O or network latency. Usually you can't do a lot about it except redesign your architecture to become less dependent on slow resources. Of course, if you were designing an embedded real-time system this may indeed be a valid endeavor, but it generally isn't worth the effort to try to improve something you cannot control.

However, you should always strive to make your code run as efficiently as possible. If you find a condition where your code can be improved using profiling, then by all means do it. Just don't get carried away trying to identify or track the little things—go after the big-ticket items first.

BENCHMARKING OR PROFILING?

The differences between benchmarking and profiling are sometimes confused. *Benchmarking* is used to establish a performance rating or measurement. Profiling is used to identify the behavior of the system in terms of its performance.

While benchmarking is used to establish known performance characteristics under given configurations, profiling is used to identify where the system is spending most of its execution time. Benchmarking therefore is used to ensure the system is performing at or better than a given standard (baseline), whereas profiling is used to determine performance bottlenecks.

Introducing Software Testing

There is a field of study within computer science that concentrates on software testing. This field is viewed as increasingly vital to our industry because it's long been clear that a significant contributor to the failure of software systems is the lack of sufficient testing or time to conduct it.

However, the means by which the testing is conducted and the goals of testing itself are sometimes debated. For example, the goal of a well-designed test is to detect the presence of defects. That sounds right, doesn't it? Think about that a moment. That means a successful test is one that has found a defect! So what happens if the test doesn't find any defects? Did the test fail because it was incorrectly written, or did it just not produce any errors? These debates (and many others) are topics of interest for software-testing researchers.

I've found that some software testers (let's call them testers for short) consider a test successful if it doesn't find any defects, which isn't the same as stating that a successful test is one that finds defects. If you take the viewpoint of these testers, it is possible for a system to pass testing (all tests successful) and yet still have defects. In this case, the focus is on the software and not the tests. Furthermore, if defects are found after testing, it is seldom considered a failure of the tests. However, if you take the viewpoint that a successful test is one that finds defects, your tests fail only when the software has no defects. Thus, when no defects are found, the focus is making the tests more robust. There is a reason we have this dichotomy.

Functional Testing vs. Defect Testing

Testers are often focused on ensuring the system performs the way the specification (also known as a requirements document) dictates. They often conduct tests that verify the functionality of the specification and therefore are not attempting to find defects. This type of testing is called *functional testing* and sometimes *system testing*. Tests are created with no knowledge of the internal workings of the system (called *black-box testing*) and are often written as a user-centric stepwise exercise of a feature of the software. For example, if a system includes a print feature, functional tests can be written to execute the print feature using the preferred and alternate execution scenarios. A successful test in this case would show that the print feature works without errors and the correct output is given. Functional testing is just one of the many types of testing that software engineers and testers can use to ensure they produce a high-quality product.

The first viewpoint is called *defect testing*. Defect testing is the purposeful intent of causing the system to fail given a set of valid and invalid input data. These tests are often written with knowledge of the internal workings of the software (often referred to as *white-box testing*). Defect tests are constructed with the intent to exercise all of the possible execution scenarios (or paths) through the source code for a particular component of the software while testing all of its gate and threshold conditions. For instance, if you were to write defect tests for the print feature example, you would write tests that tested not only the correct operation of the feature but also every known error handler and exception trigger. That is, you would write the test to purposefully try to break the code. In this case, the defect test that completes without identifying defects can be considered a failed test (or simply negative—failed gives the impression that there is something wrong, but there isn't; simply put, no errors were found in this case).[5]

For the purposes of this book, I'll present a combination of the functional and defect testing viewpoints. That is, I'll show you how to conduct functional testing that has built-in features

---

5. For more information about software testing, see http://en.wikipedia.org/wiki/Software_testing.

for detecting defects. The testing mechanism we'll use allows you to conduct functional tests against the MySQL server using tests that execute SQL statements. Although it is possible to construct tests that simply test functionality, you can also construct tests to identify defects. Indeed, I recommend you write all of your tests to test the error handlers and exceptions. Should your test fail to identify a defect or a bug is reported to you later, I also recommend you create a test or modify an existing test to test for the presence of that bug. That way, you can be sure that you can repeat the bug before you fix it and later show that the bug has been fixed.

Types of Software Testing

Software testing is often conducted in a constrained process that begins with analyzing the system requirements and design. Tests are then created using the requirements and design to ensure the quality (correctness, robustness, usability, etc.) of the software. As I mentioned earlier, some tests are conducted to identify defects and others are used to verify functionality without errors (which is not the same as not having defects). The goal of some testing techniques is to establish a critique or assessment of the software. These tests are typically focused on qualitative factors rather than quantitative results.

Testing is part of a larger software engineering mantra that ensures the software meets its requirements and delivers the desired functionality. This process is sometimes referred to as *verification and validation*. It is easy to get these two confused. Validation simply means you are ensuring the software was built to its specifications. Verification simply means you followed the correct processes and methodologies to create it. In other words, validation asks the question, "Did we build the right product?" and verification asks the question, "Did we build the product right?"

While many software development processes include verification and validation activities, most developers refer to the portion of the process that validates the specifications are met as *software testing*. Moreover, the validation process is typically associated with testing the functions of the system and the absence of defects in the functionality rather than correctness of the software.

You can conduct many types of software testing. Indeed, there are often spirited discussions during early project planning about what type of testing should or should not be required. Fortunately, most developers agree testing is a vital component of software development. However, in my experience few understand the role of the different types of software testing. Only you can choose what is right for your project. My goal is to explain some of the more popular types of software testing so that you can apply the ones that make the most sense for your needs.

The following sections describe the popular software testing techniques, their goals and applications, and how they relate to continuous test-driven development. As you will see, the traditional stages of testing are milestones in the continuous testing effort.

Integration Testing

Integration testing is conducted as the system is assembled from its basic building blocks. Tests are usually written to test first a single component, then that component and another, and so on until the entire system is integrated. This form of testing is most often used in larger development projects that are built using semi-independent components.

Component Testing

Component testing is conducted on a semi-independent portion (or component) of the system in an isolated test run. That is, the component is exercised by calling all its methods and interrogating all its attributes. Component tests are usually constructed in the form of test harnesses that provide all the external communication necessary to test a component. This includes any dependent components, which are simulated using code scaffolding (sometimes called mock or stub components). These code scaffolds provide all of the input and output necessary to communicate and exercise the component being tested.

Interface Testing

Interface testing is conducted on the interface of the component itself rather than the component. That is, the purpose is to show that the interface provides all the functionality required. This type of testing is usually done in coordination with component testing.

Regression Testing

Regression testing is conducted to ensure any addition or correction of the software does not affect other portions of the software. In this case, tests that were run in the past are run again and the results compared to the previous run. If the results are the same, the change did not affect the functionality (insofar as the test is written). This type of testing is normally conducted using automated testing software that permits developers (or testers) to run the tests unattended. The results are then compared after the bulk of tests are completed. Automated testing is a popular concept in the agile development philosophy.

Path Testing

Path testing is conducted to ensure all possible paths of execution are exercised. Tests are written with full knowledge of the source code (white-box testing) and are generally not concerned with conformance to specifications but rather with the system's ability to accurately traverse all of its conditional paths. Many times, though, these tests are conducted with the functionality in mind.

Alpha Stage Testing

Traditionally, alpha stage testing begins once a stable development-quality system is ready. This is typically early in the process of producing software for production use. Testing at this stage is sometimes conducted to ensure the system has achieved a level of stability where most of the functionality can be used (possibly with minor defects). This may include running a partial set of tests that validate that the system works under guarded conditions. Systems deemed alpha are normally mostly complete and may include some known defect issues, ranging from minor to moderate. Typically passing alpha testing concludes the alpha stage and the project moves on to the beta stage.

When we consider what alpha stage testing means in a test-driven development environment, it is at this point that the system is complete enough so that all tests are running against actual code and no scaffolding (stubbed classes) are needed. When the test results satisfy the project parameters for what is considered a beta, the project moves on to the beta stage.

Beta Stage Testing

A project is typically considered a stable production-quality system when it boasts a complete set of functionality but may include some features that have yet to be made efficient or may require additional robustness work (hardening). Tests run at this stage are generally the complete set of tests for the features being delivered. If defects are found, they are usually minor. This type of testing can also include tests conducted by the target audience and the customer. These groups tend to be less scientific in their approach to testing, but they offer developers a chance to vet their system with the customer and make any minor course corrections to improve their product. Passing beta testing means the software is ready to be prepared for eventual release.

In a test-driven development environment, beta testing is another milestone in the continuing testing effort. A beta under a test-driven development is normally the point at which the majority of the features are performing well with respect to the test results. The level of stability of the system is usually judged as producing few defects.

Release, Functional, and Acceptance Testing

Release testing is usually functional testing where the system is validated that it meets its specifications, and is conducted prior to delivery of the system to the customer. Like the beta stage, some organizations choose to involve the customer in this stage of testing as well. In this case, the testing method is usually called *acceptance testing* as it is the customer who decides that the software is validated to meet their specifications. A test-driven development environment would consider these milestones as the completion of the tests.

Usability Testing

Testing is conducted after or near the completion of the system and is sometimes conducted in parallel to functional and release testing. The goal of usability testing is to determine how well a user can interact with the system. There is usually no pass or fail result but rather a list of likes and dislikes. Though very subjective and based solely on the users' preferences, usability testing can be helpful in creating software that can gain the loyalty of its users. Usability testing is sometimes completed in a laboratory designed to record the users' responses and suggestions for later review. However, most usability testing is done in an informal setting where the developer observes the user using the system or where the user is given the software to use for a period of time and then her comments are taken as part of a survey or interview.

Reliability Testing

Reliability tests are usually designed to vary the load on the system and to challenge the system with complex data and varying quantities of load (data), and are conducted in order to determine how well the system continues to run over a period of time. Reliability is typically measured in the number of hours the system continues to function and the number of defects per hour or per test.

Performance Testing

Performance testing is conducted either to establish performance behaviors (benchmarking) or to ensure the system performs within established guidelines. Aspects of the system being examined sometimes include reliability as well as performance. Performance under extreme loads (known as stress testing) is sometimes examined during this type of testing.

Note Usability, reliability, and performance testing are forms of testing that can be conducted in either a traditional testing or test-driven development environment.

Test Design

Now that you have had a brief introduction to software testing and the types of testing that you can conduct in your own projects, let's turn our attention to how tests are constructed. There are many different philosophies for constructing tests, all of which ultimately intend to exercise, validate, or verify a certain aspect of the software or its process. Let's look at three of the most prominent basic philosophies.

Specification-Based

Specification-based tests (sometimes called functional tests) are the type of tests that exercise the software requirements and design. The focus is to validate that the software meets its specification. These tests are usually constructed (and based on) a given requirement or group of requirements. Tests are organized into functional sets (sometimes called test suites). As a system is being built, the test sets can be run whenever the requirements are completed or at any time later in the process to validate continued compliance with the requirement (also known as regression testing).

Partition Tests

Partition tests focus on the input and output data characteristics of the system. Tests are created that test the outer, edge, and mean value ranges of the input or output data being tested. For example, suppose a system is designed to accept input of a positive integer value in the range of 1 to 10. You can form partitions (called equivalence partitions or domains) of this data by testing the values {0, 1, 5, 10, 11}. Some may take this further and include a negative value such as –1. The idea is that if the system does perform range checking, it is more likely that the boundary conditions will exhibit defects than will the valid, or even wildly invalid, data.

In our earlier example, there is no need to test values greater than 11 unless you want to test the internal data collection code (the part of the system that reads and interprets the input). However, most modern systems use system-level calls to manage the data entry and by their nature are very reliable (e.g., Microsoft Windows Forms). What is most interesting is you can form partitions for the output data as well. In this case, the tests are designed to exercise how the system takes in known data (good or bad) and produces results (good or bad). In this case, tests are attempting to validate the robustness aspect as well as accuracy of the processing the input data. Partition testing is useful in demonstrating the system meets performance and robustness aspects.

Structural Tests

Structural tests (sometimes called architectural tests) are constructed to ensure that the system is built according to the layout (or architecture) specified—that is, to verify that the system conforms to a prescribed construction. Tests of this nature are designed to ensure certain interfaces are available and are working and that components are working together properly. These categories of tests include all manner of white-box testing, where the goal is to exercise every path through the system (known as path testing). These tests can be considered of the verification variety because they establish whether the architecture was built correctly and that it followed the prescribed process.

MySQL Testing

There are a variety of ways to test the MySQL system. You can test the server connectivity and basic functionality using the `mysqlshow` command, run tests manually using the client tools, use the benchmarking tools to establish performance characteristics, and even conduct profiling on the server. The tools of choice for most database professionals are the MySQL Test Suite and the MySQL Benchmarking tool. The following sections describe each of these facilities and techniques.

Using the MySQL Test Suite

MySQL AB has provided the community with a capable testing facility called the MySQL Test Suite. The test suite is an executable named `mysqltest` (`mysql-test.exe` in Windows) and a collection of Perl modules and scripts designed to exercise the system and compare the results. Table 4-1 lists the directories and their contents. The test suite comes with the Unix/Linux binary and source distributions, although it is included in some Windows distributions.

■ **Note** The MySQL Test Suite does not currently run in the Windows environment. This would be an excellent project to take on if you wanted to contribute to the development of MySQL through the MySQL code contribution program. It can be run in the Cygwin environment if the Perl environment is set up and the Perl DBI modules are installed. See the "Perl Installation Notes" section in the MySQL Reference Manual for more details.

Table 4-1. *Directories under the mysql-test Directory*

Directory	Contents
/misc	Additional miscellaneous Perl scripts
/ndb	A complete set of cluster tests
/r	Result files of the tests run
/std_data	Test data for the test suite
/t	The tests

When MySQL is installed, you will find the `mysql-test-run.pl` Perl script in the `mysql-test` directory under the installation directory. Best of all, the test suite is extensible. You can write your own tests and conduct testing for your specific application or need. The tests are designed as regression tests in the sense that the tests are intended to be run to ensure all the functionality works as it has in the past.

The tests are located in a directory under the `mysql-test` directory named simply /t. This directory contains nearly 600 tests. While that may sound comprehensive, the MySQL documentation states that the test suite does not cover all the features of the system. The current set of tests is designed to detect bugs in most SQL commands, the operating system and library interactions, and cluster and replication functionality. MySQL AB hopes to ultimately accumulate enough tests to provide test coverage for the entire system. Indeed, MySQL AB has an open call for additional tests. The goal is to establish a set of tests that test 100 percent of the features of the MySQL system. If you create additional tests you feel cover a feature that isn't already covered by one of the tests in the `mysql-test/t` directory, feel free to submit your tests to MySQL AB.

■Tip You can find more information about the MySQL Test Suite by visiting the MySQL Internals mailing list (see `http://lists.mysql.com/` for more details and to see the available lists). You can also submit your tests for inclusion by sending an e-mail message to the list. You should upload your test files to the `ftp://ftp.mysql.com/pub/mysql/upload/` FTP site. If you decide to send your tests to MySQL AB for inclusion in the test suite, be sure you are using data that you can show the world. The tests are available to everyone. For example, I am sure your friends and relatives would not want their phone numbers showing up in every installation of MySQL!

For each test, a corresponding result file is stored in the `mysql-test/r` directory. The result file contains the output of the test run and is used to compare (using the `diff` command) the results of the test as it is run. In many ways, the result file is the benchmark for the output of the test. This enables you to create tests and save the expected results, then run the test later and ensure that the system is producing the same output.

However, you must use this premise with some caution. Data values that, by their nature, change between executions can be used but require additional commands to handle properly. Unfortunately, data values like these are ignored by the test suite rather than compared directly. Thus, time and date fields are data types that could cause some issues if used in a test. I'll discuss more on this topic and other commands in a moment.

Running Tests

Running tests using the test suite is easy. Simply navigate to the `mysql-test` directory and execute the command `./mysql-test-run.pl`. This will launch the test executable, connect to the server, and run all the tests in the /t directory. What, you don't want to run all 600 tests? Because running all the tests could take a while, MySQL AB has written the test suite to allow you to execute several tests in order. For example, the following command will run just the tests named t1, t2, and t3:

```
%> ./mysql-test-run.pl t1 t2 t3
```

The test suite will run each test in order but will stop if any test fails. To override this behavior, use the `--force` command-line parameter to force the test suite to continue.

The test suite is designed to execute its own instance of the `mysqld` executable. This may conflict with another instance of the server running on your machine. You may want to shut down other instances of the MySQL server before running the test suite. If you use the test suite from the source directory, you can create the mysqld executable by compiling the source code. This is especially handy if you want to test something you've changed in the server but do not or cannot take your existing server down to do so.

■**Caution** You can run the test suite alongside an existing server as long as the server is not using port 3306 or 3307. If it does, the test suite may not run correctly and you may need to stop the server or change it to use other ports.

If you want to connect to a specific server instance, you can use the --extern command-line parameter to tell the test suite to connect to the server. If you have additional startup commands or want to use a specific user to connect to the server, you can add those commands as well. For more information about the available command-line parameters to the mysql-test-run script, enter the following command:

```
%> ./mysql-test-run.pl --help
```

Also, visit http://dev.mysql.com/doc/mysql/en/mysql-test-suite.html for more details.

■**Note** Using the --extern command-line parameter requires that you also include the name of the tests you want to execute. Some tests require a local instance of the server to execute. For example, the following command connects to a running server and executes the alias and analyze tests: perl mysql-test-run.pl --extern alias analyze.

Creating a New Test

To create your own test, use a standard text editor to create the test in the /t directory in a file named mytestname.test. For example, I created a sample test named cab.test (see Listing 4-1).

Listing 4-1. *Sample Test*

```
#
# Sample test to demonstrate MySQL Test Suite
#
--disable_warnings
SHOW DATABASES;
--enable_warnings
CREATE TABLE characters (ID INTEGER PRIMARY KEY,
                    LastName varchar(40),
                    FirstName varchar(20),
                    Gender varchar(2)) TYPE = MYISAM;
EXPLAIN characters;
#
```

```
INSERT INTO characters (ID, LastName, FirstName, Gender)
            VALUES (3, 'Flintstone', 'Fred', 'M');
INSERT INTO characters (ID, LastName, FirstName, Gender)
            VALUES (5, 'Rubble', 'Barney', 'M');
INSERT INTO characters (ID, LastName, FirstName, Gender)
            VALUES (7, 'Flintstone', 'Wilma', 'F');
INSERT INTO characters (ID, LastName, FirstName, Gender)
            VALUES (9, 'Flintstone', 'Dino', 'M');
INSERT INTO characters (ID, LastName, FirstName, Gender)
            VALUES (4, 'Flintstone', 'Pebbles', 'F');
INSERT INTO characters (ID, LastName, FirstName, Gender)
            VALUES (1, 'Rubble', 'Betty', 'F');
INSERT INTO characters (ID, LastName, FirstName, Gender)
            VALUES (6, 'Rubble', 'Bam-Bam', 'M');
INSERT INTO characters (ID, LastName, FirstName, Gender)
            VALUES (8, 'Jetson', 'George', 'M');
#
SELECT * FROM characters;
#
EXPLAIN (SELECT DISTINCT LASTNAME from characters);
#
SELECT DISTINCT LASTNAME from characters;
#
# Cleanup
#
DROP TABLE characters;
# ...and we're done.
```

Notice that the contents of the test are simply SQL commands that create a table, insert some data, and then do a few simple selects. Most tests are a bit more complex than this, but you get the idea. You create your test to exercise some set of commands (or data handling). Notice the first six lines. The first three are comment lines and they begin with a # symbol. You should always document your tests with a minimal explanation at the top of the file to indicate what the test is doing. You should also use comments in the body of the test to explain any commands that aren't easily understood (e.g., complex joins or user-defined functions). The fourth and sixth lines are interesting because they are issuing commands to the test suite. Test suite commands always begin on a line with -- in front of them. These lines are directing the test suite to temporarily disable and then enable any warning messages from the server. This is necessary in case the table (characters) does not already exist. If I had left the warnings enabled, the test would have failed under this condition for one of two reasons:

- The server would have issued a warning.

- The output would not match the expected results.

The general layout of your tests should include a cleanup section at the beginning to remove any tables or views that may exist as a result of a failed test. The body of the test should include all the necessary statements to complete the test, and the end of the test should include cleanup statements to remove any tables or views you've created in the test.

Tip When writing your own tests, MySQL AB requests that you use table names such as t1, t2, t3, etc. and view names such as v1, v2, or v3, etc. so that your test tables do not conflict with any existing test tables.

Running the New Test

Once the test is created, you need to execute the test and create the baseline of expected results. Execute the following commands to run the newly created test named cab.test from the mysql-test directory:

```
%> touch r/cab.result
%> ./mysql-test-run.pl cab
%> cp r/cab.reject r/cab.result
%> ./mysql-test-run.pl cab
```

The first command creates an empty result file. This is necessary to ensure the test suite has something to compare to. The next command runs the test for the first time. Listing 4-2 depicts a typical first-run test result. Notice that the test suite indicated that the test failed. This is because there were no results to compare to. I have omitted a number of the more mundane statements for brevity.

Listing 4-2. *Running a New Test for the First Time*

```
Starting Tests

TEST                        RESULT
-------------------------------------------------------
cab                         [ fail ]

Errors are (from /home/Chuck/MySQL/mysql-5.1.9-beta/mysql-test/var/log
/mysqltest-time) :
mysqltest: Result length mismatch
(the last lines may be the most important ones)
Below are the diffs between actual and expected results:
-------------------------------------------------------
*** r/cab.result        2006-05-24 03:40:46.000000000 +0300
--- r/cab.reject        2006-05-24 03:42:50.000000000 +0300
**************

Ending Tests
Shutting-down MySQL daemon

Master shutdown finished
Slave shutdown finished
-------------------------------------------------------

Failed 1/1 tests, 00.0% were successful.
```

The next command copies the newest results from the `cab.reject` file over the `cab.result` file. You would only do this step once you are certain the test runs correctly and that there are no unexpected errors. One way to ensure this is to run the test statements manually and verify they work correctly. Only then should you copy the reject file to a result file. Listing 4-3 depicts the result file for the new test. Notice that the output is exactly what you would expect to see from a manual execution minus the usual pretty printout and column spacing.

Listing 4-3. *The Result File*

```
DROP TABLE if exists characters;
CREATE TABLE characters (ID INTEGER PRIMARY KEY,
LastName varchar(40),
FirstName varchar(20),
Gender varchar(2));
EXPLAIN characters;
Field Type Null Key Default Extra
ID int(11) NO PRI
LastName varchar(40) YES    NULL
FirstName varchar(20) YES    NULL
Gender varchar(2) YES    NULL
INSERT INTO characters (ID, LastName, FirstName, Gender)
VALUES (3, 'Flintstone', 'Fred', 'M');
INSERT INTO characters (ID, LastName, FirstName, Gender)
VALUES (5, 'Rubble', 'Barney', 'M');
INSERT INTO characters (ID, LastName, FirstName, Gender)
VALUES (7, 'Flintstone', 'Wilma', 'F');
INSERT INTO characters (ID, LastName, FirstName, Gender)
VALUES (9, 'Flintstone', 'Dino', 'M');
INSERT INTO characters (ID, LastName, FirstName, Gender)
VALUES (4, 'Flintstone', 'Pebbles', 'F');
INSERT INTO characters (ID, LastName, FirstName, Gender)
VALUES (1, 'Rubble', 'Betty', 'F');
INSERT INTO characters (ID, LastName, FirstName, Gender)
VALUES (6, 'Rubble', 'Bam-Bam', 'M');
INSERT INTO characters (ID, LastName, FirstName, Gender)
VALUES (8, 'Jetson', 'George', 'M');
SELECT * FROM characters;
ID LastName FirstName Gender
3 Flintstone Fred M
5 Rubble Barney M
7 Flintstone Wilma F
9 Flintstone Dino M
4 Flintstone Pebbles F
1 Rubble Betty F
6 Rubble Bam-Bam M
8 Jetson George M
```

```
EXPLAIN (SELECT DISTINCT LASTNAME from characters);
id select_type table type possible_keys key key_len ref rows Extra
1 SIMPLE characters ALL NULL NULL NULL NULL 8 Using temporary
SELECT DISTINCT LASTNAME from characters;
LASTNAME
Flintstone
Rubble
Jetson
DROP TABLE characters;
```

Lastly, we rerun the test using the expected results, and the test suite reports that the test passed. Listing 4-4 depicts a typical test result.

Listing 4-4. *A Successful Test Run*

```
Installing Test Databases
Removing Stale Files
Installing Master Databases
running  ../sql/mysqld --no-defaults --bootstrap --skip-grant-tables
    --basedir=. --datadir=./var/master-data --skip-innodb
    --skip-ndbcluster --skip-bdb
    --language=../sql/share/english/
    --character-sets-dir=../sql/share/charsets/
Installing Slave Databases
running  ../sql/mysqld --no-defaults --bootstrap --skip-grant-tables
    --basedir=. --datadir=./var/slave-data --skip-innodb
    --skip-ndbcluster --skip-bdb
    --language=../sql/share/english/
    --character-sets-dir=../sql/share/charsets/
Manager disabled, skipping manager start.
Loading Standard Test Databases
Starting Tests

TEST                         RESULT
--------------------------------------------------------
cab                          [ pass ]

--------------------------------------------------------

Ending Tests
Shutting-down MySQL daemon

Master shutdown finished
Slave shutdown finished
All 1 tests were successful.
```

Creating your own tests and running them is easy to do. You can repeat the process I just described as many times as you want for as many tests as you want. As you can see, this process follows the spirit of test-driven development by first creating the test, running it without proof of results, creating the solution (the expected results), and then executing the test and verifying successful test completion. I encourage you to adopt the same philosophy when creating your own MySQL applications and especially when extending the MySQL server.

For example, say you want to create a new SHOW command. In this case, you should create a new test to execute the new command, run it, and establish the test results. Naturally, the test will fail every time until you actually create the new command. The benefit of this philosophy is that it allows you to focus on the results of the command and how the command syntax should be prior to actually writing the code. If you adopt this philosophy for all your development, you won't regret it and will see dividends in the quality of your code. Once you have implemented the command and verified that it works by running the test again and examining the reject file (or running the command manually), you can copy the reject file to the result file, which the test suite will use for verification (pass/fail) in later test runs.

Advanced Tests

The MySQL Test Suite provides a rich set of commands you can use to create powerful tests. This section introduces some of the popular and useful commands. Unfortunately, no comprehensive document exists that explains all the available commands. The following are those that I found by exploring the supplied tests and online posts.

> **Tip** If you use the advanced test suite commands, you can create the result file using the `--record` command-line parameter to record the proper results. For example, you can run the command `./mysql-test-run.pl --record cab` to record the results of the cab test file.

If you're expecting a certain error to occur (say you're testing the presence of errors rather than the absence of detecting them), you can use the `--error num` command. This command tells the test suite that you expect the error specified and that it should not fail the test when that error occurs. This command is designed to precede the command that produces the error. You can also specify additional error numbers separated by commas. For example, `--error 1550, 1530` indicates these (fictional) errors are permitted for the command that follows.

You can also use flow of control code inside your test. For example, you can use a loop to execute something for a fixed number of times. The following code example executes a command 100 times:

```
let $1=100;
while ($1)
{
  # Insert your commands here
  dec($1)
}
```

Another useful command is sleep. The sleep command takes as a parameter the number of seconds to pause before executing the next command. For example, --sleep 3.5 tells the test suite to pause for 3.5 seconds before executing the next command. This command can help if there is unexpected latency in the network or if you're experiencing tests failing due to heavy traffic. Using the sleep command will allow you to slow down the test, thereby reducing any interference due to poor performance.

If you are interested in seeing additional information about a command, you can use the --enable_metadata command. This produces and displays internal metadata that may assist you in debugging commands for a complex test. Similarly, if you want to suppress the recording of the output, you can use --disable_result_log to turn off recording and --enable_result_log to turn it back on.

If you have commands that result in data that may change between runs (like date or time fields), you can tell the test suite to ignore those values by substituting another character string using the --replace_column column string command. For example, if your output produces the current time in the second column (column counting begins at 1, not 0), you can use the command --replace_column 2 CURTIME. This tells the test suite that the output from the next command is to have column 2 replaced with the string "CURTIME." While this does suppress the actual value in the output, it provides a way to ignore those values that cannot be predicted because they change between test runs.

Finally, if you need to include additional test commands within a test, you can use the --source include/filetoinclude.inc to include a file from the mysql-test/include directory. This practice is typical in tests that form a test suite with a set of commonly used commands.

Reporting Bugs

It is possible that you could find a bug as the result of running one of the tests or in the creation of your own test. MySQL AB welcomes feedback on the test suite and has provided a means of reporting bugs. However, before you fire up your e-mail and crank out an intensive report of the failure, be sure to confirm the bug thoroughly.

MySQL AB asks that you run the test on its own and discover the exact command and error codes behind the failure. You should first determine if the errors are the result of your environment (see the "Operating System-Specific Notes" section in the MySQL Reference Manual for potential issues—visit http://dev.mysql.com/doc/refman/5.1/en/operating-system-specific-notes.html for more details) by either running the test on a fresh installation or on another known-good installation. You should also run the commands in the test manually to confirm the error and error codes. Sometimes running the commands manually will reveal additional information you could not get otherwise. It may also help to run the server in debug mode. Lastly, if the test and error conditions can be repeated, you should include the test file, test results, test reject file, and any test data to MySQL when you submit your bug report.[6]

MySQL Benchmarking

MySQL AB has provided the community with a capable benchmarking facility called the MySQL Benchmarking Suite. The benchmarking suite is a collection of Perl modules and scripts designed to exercise the system saving the performance metrics. The benchmarking suite comes with

6. You have to earn that iPod!

most binary and source distributions and can be run on Windows.[7] When MySQL is installed, you will find the run-all-tests.pl Perl script in the sql-bench directory under the installation directory. The tests are designed in the regression test sense in that the tests are intended to be run to record the performance of the system under current conditions. The benchmarking suite is also available as a separate download for most operating systems from the MySQL developer web site (http://dev.mysql.com).

Like most benchmarking tools, the MySQL Benchmarking Suite is best used to determine the effects of changes to the system and the environment. The benchmarking suite differs somewhat from the testing suite in that the benchmarking suite has the ability to run benchmarks against other systems. It is possible to use the benchmarking suite to run the same benchmarks against your MySQL, Oracle, and Microsoft SQL Server installations. As you can imagine, doing so can be helpful in determining how much better MySQL performs in your environment than your existing database system. To run the benchmarks against the other servers, you can use the --server='server' command-line switch. Values for this parameter include MySQL, Oracle, Informix, and MS-SQL.

A host of command-line parameters are available for you to choose from to control the benchmarking suite. Table 4-2 lists a few popular ones and an explanation of each. See the README file in the sql-bench directory for more information about the command-line parameters.

Table 4-2. *Command-Line Parameters for the MySQL Benchmarking Suite*

Command-Line Parameter	Explanation
--log	Saves the results of the benchmarks to a file. Use with the --dir option to specify a directory to store the results in. Result files are named using the same output of the Unix command uname -a.
--user	Specifies the user to log into the server.
--password	Specifies the password of the user for logging into the server.
--host	Specifies the hostname of the server.
--small-test	Specifies running the minimal benchmarking tests. Omitting this parameter executes the entire benchmarking suite of tests. For most uses, the small tests are adequate for determining the more common performance metrics.

To run the benchmarking suite of tests, simply navigate to the sql-bench directory under your installation and run the command perl run-all-tests. You'll notice one important characteristic of the benchmarking suite: all tests are run serially. Thus, the tests are run one at a time. To test the performance of multiple processes, or threads, you'll need to use a third-party benchmarking suite such as Super Smack or mybench.

Another limitation of the benchmarking suite is that it is not currently extensible. That is, there is no facility to create your own tests for your own application. However, the source code is freely distributed, so those of you well versed in Perl can have at it. If you do create your own tests, be sure to share them with the global community of developers. You never know—someone might need the test you create.

---

7. Requires ActivePerl, the official Perl distribution for Windows. See www.activestate.org for details and to download the latest version.

SUPER SMACK AND MYBENCH

Super Smack is a benchmarking, stress testing, and load generation tool for MySQL. It is similar to the Apache bench tool. It is currently available for a limited set of Linux and Unix platforms. Super Smack can be found at http://vegan.net/tony/supersmack/. mybench is a simple customizable benchmarking framework for MySQL. It is written in Perl and can be found at http://jeremy.zawodny.com/mysql/mybench/.

Tip For best results, you should disable the MySQL query cache before running benchmarks. You can turn off the query cache by issuing the command SET GLOBALS query_cache_size = 0; in the MySQL client interface. This will allow your benchmarks to record the actual time of the queries rather than the time the system takes to retrieve the query from the cache. You'll get a more accurate reading of the performance of your system.

If the base set of benchmarks is all that you need, you can run the command perl run-all-tests --small-test and generate the results for the basic set of tests. While running all of the tests ensures a more thorough measurement of the performance, it can also take a long time to complete. If on the other hand you identify a particular portion of the system you want to measure, you can run an individual test by executing the test independently. For example, to test the connection to the server, you can run the command perl test-connect. Table 4-3 lists a few of the independent tests available for you to run.

Table 4-3. *Partial List of Benchmarking Tests*

Test	Description
test-ATIS.sh	Creates 29 tables and several selects on them
test-connect.sh	Tests the connection speed to the server
test-create.sh	Tests how fast a table is created
test-insert.sh	Tests create and fill operations of a table
test-wisconsin.sh	Runs a port of the PostgreSQL version of this benchmark

Note The benchmarking suite runs the tests in a single thread. MySQL AB has plans to add multithreaded tests to the benchmark suite in the future.

For more information about other forms of benchmarking available for MySQL, see
Michael Kruckenberg and Jay Pipes's *Pro MySQL*.[8] It is an excellent reference for all things MySQL.

Running the Small Tests

Let's examine what you can expect when you run the benchmarking tools on your system.
In this example, I ran the benchmarking suite using the small tests on my Windows system.
Listing 4-5 shows the top portion of the output file generated.

Listing 4-5. *Excerpt of Small Tests Benchmark*

```
D:\source\C++\mysql-5.1.9-beta\sql-bench>perl run-all-tests --small-test


Benchmark DBD suite: 2.15
Date of test:        2006-05-21 23:12:16
Running tests on:    Windows NT 5.1 x86
Arguments:           --small-test
Comments:
Limits from:
Server version:      MySQL 5.1.9 beta/
Optimization:        None
Hardware:

alter-table: Total time:  4 wallclock secs ( 0.05 usr  0.01 sys +
0.00 cusr  0.00 csys =  0.06 CPU)
ATIS: Total time:  6 wallclock secs ( 1.33 usr  0.28 sys +
0.00 cusr  0.00 csys =  1.61 CPU)
big-tables: Total time:  0 wallclock secs ( 0.14 usr  0.01 sys +
0.00 cusr  0.00 csys =  0.15 CPU)
connect: Total time:  4 wallclock secs ( 0.69 usr  0.39 sys +
0.00 cusr  0.00 csys =  1.08 CPU)
create: Total time:  1 wallclock secs ( 0.02 usr  0.00 sys +
0.00 cusr  0.00 csys =  0.02 CPU)
insert: Total time: 11 wallclock secs ( 2.59 usr  0.67 sys +
0.00 cusr  0.00 csys =  3.27 CPU)
select: Total time: 16 wallclock secs ( 4.06 usr  0.45 sys +
0.00 cusr  0.00 csys =  4.52 CPU)
transactions: Test skipped because the database doesn't support transactions
wisconsin: Total time: 15 wallclock secs ( 2.66 usr  0.44 sys +  0.00 cusr  0.00
 csys =  3.10 CPU)

All 9 test executed successfully
```

---

8. M. Kruckenberg and J. Pipes. *Pro MySQL* (Berkeley, CA: Apress, 2005).

At the top of the listing the benchmarking suite gives the metadata describing the tests run including the date the tests were run, the version of the operating system, the version of the server, and any special optimization or hardware installed (in this case, none). Take a look at what follows the metadata. You see the results of each of the tests run reporting the wallclock elapsed seconds. The times indicated in the parentheses are the times recorded during the execution of the benchmark suite itself and should be deducted from the actual wallclock seconds for accurate times. Don't be too concerned about this as this section is mostly used for a brief look at the tests in groups. The next section is the most interesting of all as it contains the actual data collected during each test. The results of the example benchmark tests are shown in Table 4-4. I have omitted some of the rows to save space.

Table 4-4. *Specific Test Result Data of the Small Tests Run (Totals per Operation)*

Operation	Total Seconds	usr	sys	cpu	Number of Tests
alter_table_add	3.00	0.01	0.00	0.01	92
alter_table_drop	1.00	0.02	0.01	0.03	46
connect	0.00	0.08	0.11	0.19	100
connect+select_1_row	1.00	0.09	0.09	0.19	100
connect+select_simple	1.00	0.08	0.03	0.11	100
count	1.00	0.02	0.00	0.02	100
count_distinct	1.00	0.05	0.00	0.05	100
count_distinct_2	0.00	0.00	0.00	0.00	100
select_range	1.00	0.08	0.03	0.11	41
select_range_key2	1.00	0.11	0.00	0.11	505
select_range_prefix	0.00	0.11	0.02	0.12	505
select_simple	0.00	0.05	0.00	0.05	1000
select_simple_cache	0.00	0.06	0.03	0.09	1000
select_simple_join	0.00	0.05	0.00	0.05	50
update_big	0.00	0.00	0.00	0.00	10
update_of_key	0.00	0.02	0.02	0.03	500
update_of_key_big	0.00	0.00	0.00	0.00	13
update_of_primary_key_many_keys	0.00	0.00	0.00	0.00	256
update_with_key	1.00	0.16	0.02	0.17	3000
update_with_key_prefix	1.00	0.09	0.02	0.11	1000
wisc_benchmark	2.00	0.97	0.14	1.11	34
TOTALS	56.00	11.45	2.19	13.58	78237

When performing benchmarks, I like to convert the latter part of the listing to a spreadsheet so that I can perform statistical analysis on the results. This also allows me to perform calculations using the expected, before, and after results. Table 4-4 shows the time spent for each operation in total seconds, the time spent in the benchmarking tools (usr, sys, cpu), and the number of tests run for each operation.

Notice at the bottom of Table 4-4 the columns are summed, giving you the total time spent executing the benchmark tests. This information, combined with that in Listing 4-1, forms the current baseline of the performance of my Windows system. I encourage you to create and archive your own benchmarks for your database servers.

Running a Single Test

Suppose you are interested in running the benchmark for creating tables. As shown in Table 4-3 the test is named test-create. To run this command, I navigated to the sql-bench directory and entered the command perl test-create. Listing 4-6 shows the results of running this command on my Windows system.

Listing 4-6. *Output of test-create Benchmark Test*

```
D:\source\C++\mysql-5.1.9-beta\sql-bench>perl test-create
```

```
Testing server 'MySQL 5.1.9 beta/' at 2006-05-22 21:47:51

Testing the speed of creating and dropping tables
Testing with 10000 tables and 10000 loop count

Testing create of tables
Time for create_MANY_tables (10000): 154 wallclock secs ( 2.22 usr
0.34 sys + 0.00 cusr  0.00 csys =  2.56 CPU)

Accessing tables
Time to select_group_when_MANY_tables (10000): 41 wallclock secs ( 0.91 usr
0.16 sys +  0.00 cusr  0.00 csys =  1.06 CPU)

Testing drop
Time for drop_table_when_MANY_tables (10000): 46 wallclock secs ( 1.19 usr
0.25 sys +  0.00 cusr  0.00 csys =  1.44 CPU)

Testing create+drop
Time for create+drop (10000): 130 wallclock secs ( 3.28 usr  0.47 sys +
0.00 cusr  0.00 csys =  3.75 CPU)
Time for create_key+drop (10000): 132 wallclock secs ( 3.08 usr  0.66 sys +
0.00 cusr  0.00 csys =  3.73 CPU)
Total time: 503 wallclock secs (10.69 usr  1.88 sys +
0.00 cusr  0.00 csys = 12.56 CPU)

D:\source\C++\mysql-5.1.9-beta\sql-bench>
```

In Listing 4-6 you see the typical parameters captured for each test run. Notice that the test is designed to run many iterations of the same test. This is necessary to ensure the timings aren't dependent on any single event and have more meaning when used as a set.

I chose this example so that you can consider another use of benchmarking. Suppose you want to create a new CREATE SQL command. In this case, you can modify the test-create script to include tests of your new command. Then later run the benchmark tests to establish the baseline performance of your new command. This is a powerful tool for you to use in your extension of the MySQL system. I encourage you to explore this option if you have any performance or even scalability requirements or concerns for your extensions.

Applied Benchmarking

I wanted to return to this topic before moving on as it is important to understand and appreciate the benefits of benchmarking. The only way benchmarking will be useful to you is if you archive your results. I find the best solution is to tuck the results away in individual directories named by the date the benchmarks were taken. I recommend placing the output files (from the --log parameter) along with a short description of the current configuration of the system and the environment (use your favorite system inspection software to do this) into a separate directory for each set of benchmarking tests.

If I need to compare the performance of the system to a known state, for example, whenever I change a server variable and want to see its effect on performance I can run the benchmarking tools before and after I make the change. Then I can look back through the history of the benchmarks and compare these results with the most stable state. This approach also allows me to track changes in system performance over time.

Benchmarking used in this way will enable you to manage your systems on a level few have achieved otherwise.

MySQL Profiling

Although no formal profiling tool or suite is included in the MySQL server suite of tools (or the source distribution), a number of diagnostic utilities are available that can be used as a simple set of profiling techniques. For example, you can check the status of thread execution, examine the server logs, and even examine how the optimizer will execute a query.

To see a list of the current threads, you can use the MySQL SHOW FULL PROCESSLIST command. This command shows all the current processes, or threads, running; the user running them; the host the connection was issued from; the database being used; current command; execution time; state parameters; and additional information provided by the thread. For example, if I ran the command on my system, the results would be something like what is shown in Listing 4-7.

Listing 4-7. *Output of the SHOW FULL PROCESSLIST Command*

```
mysql> SHOW FULL PROCESSLIST \G
```

```
*************************** 1. row ***************************
     Id: 7
   User: root
   Host: localhost:1175
     db: test
Command: Query
   Time: 0
  State: NULL
   Info: SHOW FULL PROCESSLIST
1 row in set (0.00 sec)
```

This example shows that I am the only user connected (root) running from the local host executing a query with an execution time of 0 and the command I am currently executing. The downside to this command is that it is a snapshot in time and must be run many times to detect patterns of performance bottlenecks. Fortunately, there is a way to do this. You can use a tool called mytop that repeatedly calls the command and displays several useful views of the data. For more information or to download mytop, see Jeremy Zawodny's web site (http://jeremy. zawodny.com/mysql/mytop).

■**Note** The mytop application has had limited success on the Windows platform.

Another useful command for displaying server information is the SHOW STATUS command. This command displays all the server and status variables. As you can imagine, that is a very long list. Fortunately, you can limit the display by passing the command a LIKE clause. For example, to see the thread information, enter the command SHOW STATUS LIKE "thread%";. Listing 4-8 shows the results of this command.

Listing 4-8. *The SHOW STATUS Command*

```
mysql> SHOW STATUS LIKE "threads%";
```

```
+-------------------+-------+
| Variable_name     | Value |
+-------------------+-------+
| Threads_cached    | 0     |
| Threads_connected | 1     |
| Threads_created   | 6     |
| Threads_running   | 1     |
+-------------------+-------+
4 rows in set (0.00 sec)
```

To examine the slow query log, you can set the log-slow-queries variable and set the query timeout using the long_query_time variable. Typical values for the long query timeout vary, but should be set to your own concept of what constitutes a long query. To display the slow queries, you can use the mysqldumpslow command to display the slow queries. This command groups the slow queries by similarity (also called buckets). Additional metadata provided include information on locks, expected rows and actual rows generated, and the timing data.

The general query log can be examined using the MySQL Administrator software. You can view all of the logs provided you are connected to the server locally. If you have never used the MySQLAdminstrator software, I encourage you to download it from http://dev.mysql.com/downloads and give it a try.

Tip You can use the MySQL Administrator software to control almost every aspect of the server, including startup settings, logging, and variables.

The last profiling technique included in the MySQL system is the ability to examine how the optimizer performs queries. While not strictly a performance-measuring device, it can be used to diagnose tricky queries that show up in the slow query log. As a simple example, let's see what the optimizer predicts about how the following query will be executed:

```
select * from customer where phone like "%575%"
```

This query is not very interesting and using the LIKE clause with %s surrounding the value is not efficient and almost sure to result in an index-less access method. If you run the command preceded by the EXPLAIN keyword, you see the results of the proposed query optimization. Listing 4-9 shows the results of using the EXPLAIN command.

Listing 4-9. *Output of EXPLAIN Command*

```
mysql> explain select * from customer where phone like "%575%" \G

*************************** 1. row ***************************
          id: 1
 select_type: SIMPLE
       table: customer
        type: ALL
possible_keys: NULL
         key: NULL
     key_len: NULL
         ref: NULL
        rows: 599
       Extra: Using where
1 row in set (0.00 sec)
```

The output shows that the command is a simple select on the customer table, there are no possible keys to use, there are 599 rows in the table, and the optimizer is using the WHERE clause. In this case, it is telling us that the execution will be a simple table scan without indexes—perhaps one of the slowest possible select statements.

Summary

In this chapter, I've presented a number of software testing techniques and strategies. You learned about the benefits of software testing and how to leverage test-driven development in your software projects. I also presented the testing facilities available to you for testing MySQL. I showed you the MySQL test and benchmark suites and introduced you to the profiling scripts for MySQL.

The knowledge of these testing facilities will prepare you to ensure your modifications to the MySQL source code are of the highest quality possible. With this knowledge, you are now ready to begin creating extensions and enhancements of the MySQL system that will meet the same high-quality standards that MySQL AB adheres to.[9] Now that you have this information, you can begin to design your solution and include testing early in your design phase.

The next chapter, which begins the second part of this book, introduces you to the most important tool in a developer's toolbox: debugging!

---

9. Why else would they have created and made available to you testing, benchmarking, and profiling tools?

PART 2

■■■

Extending MySQL

Using a hands-on approach, this section provides you with the tools you need to explore and extend the MySQL system. It introduces you to how the MySQL code can be modified and explains how you can use the system as an embedded database system. Chapter 5 reviews debugging skills and techniques to help make development easy and less prone to failure. Several debugging techniques are presented, along with the pros and cons of each. Chapter 6 contains a tutorial on how to embed the MySQL system in enterprise applications. Chapter 7 examines the MySQL pluggable storage engine capability, complete with examples and projects that permit you to build a sample storage engine. Chapter 8 presents the most popular modification to the MySQL code. You'll learn how to modify SQL commands to add new parameters and functions, and how to add new SQL commands.

CHAPTER 5

■■■

Debugging

This chapter discusses one of the most powerful tools any developer can wield: debugging. Good debugging skills help ensure that your software projects are easy to develop and less prone to failure. I'll also explore the most common techniques for debugging the MySQL system. If you have already developed solid debugging skills, feel free to skim the following sections and move on to the section "Debugging MySQL."

Debugging Explained

Anyone who has written anything more substantial than a Hello world program has encountered defects (bugs) in their software. Though most defects are easily found, others can be difficult to locate and correct.

If you wanted to explain the concept of debugging to a novice developer, you'd probably tell them it's largely a process of troubleshooting in an effort to discover what went wrong. You might also note that developing good debugging skills comes by way of mastering the appropriate debugging techniques and tools. While this may be an adequate introductory definition, you should take the time to gain a better understanding of debugging nuances.

For starters, it's important that you properly frame the sort of defect you're trying to locate and correct. There are two basic types of defects: *syntax errors* and *logic errors*. Syntax errors are naturally found during the code compilation process and although they too may be difficult to correct, we are forced to correct them in order to build the software. However, logic errors are those types of errors not found during compilation and thus they are usually manifested as defects during the execution of the software. Debugging therefore is the act of finding and fixing errors in your program.

■Note Tools are available that you can run at compile time (or earlier). These tools help minimize the risk of logic errors. They range from simple flow control analyzers that detect dead code to more sophisticated range and type checkers that walk your code to locate possible data mismatches. There are also tools designed to check for proper error handling using best practices for code hardening.

When a logic error is found, the system usually does something odd or produces erroneous data. In the more extreme cases, the system may actually crash. Well-structured systems that include code hardening best practices tend to be more robust than others because they are designed to capture and handle errors as they occur. Even then, some errors are so severe that the system crashes (or the operating system terminates it) in order to protect the data and the system state.

The art of debugging software is the ability to quickly locate the error, either by observing the system as its state changes or by direct inspection of the code and its data. We call the tools that we use to debug *system debuggers*. In the following sections, I'll examine some common debugging techniques and related debuggers.

THE ORIGINS OF DEBUGGING

You have no doubt heard stories about how the term *computer bug* was coined, and I'd like to tell my favorite one. I have the pleasure of working near the location where Admiral Grace Hopper discovered the first computer bug. Legend has it that Rear Admiral Hopper was working with a large computational computer called a Mark II Aiken Relay Calculator in 1945. To call it a large computer today would be a stretch, but it was the size of a semi back then. When a troublesome electronic problem was traced to a failed relay that had a moth trapped in it, Admiral Hopper noted that the source of the error was a "bug" and that the system had been "debugged" and was now operational. To this day we refer to the removal of defective code as *debugging*.

Debugging Techniques

There are almost as many debugging techniques as there are developers. It seems everyone debugs their code in a slightly different way. However, these approaches can generally be grouped into several categories.

The most basic of these approaches are included in the source code and become part of the executable. These include inline debugging statements (statements that print messages or values of variables during execution, e.g., `printf("Code is at line 199. my_var = %d\n", my_var);`) and error handlers. Most developers use these techniques either as a last resort (when a defect cannot be found easily) or during the development phase (to test the code as it is being written). While you may think that error handlers have more to do with robustness and hardening than debugging, they can also be powerful debugging tools. Since this approach embeds the debugging code into the program, you can use conditional compilation directives to omit the code when debugging is complete. Most developers leave the debugging statements in the code and thus they become part of the program. You should take care when using this technique to ensure the added debugging code does not adversely affect the program.

The debugging technique most of you know best is the use of external debuggers. *External debuggers* are tools designed to either monitor the system in real time or permit you to watch the execution of the code with the ability to stop and start the code at any point. These techniques are described in detail in the following sections. But first, let's take a look at the basic process for debugging.

Basic Process

Every debugging session is going to be unique, but the process should always follow the same basic steps. Being consistent in your debugging process can help make the experience more effective and more rewarding. There's no better feeling than crushing a particularly nasty bug after chasing it for hours. While you may have long established a preferred debugging method, chances are it consists of at least the following steps:

1. Identify the defect (bug reporting, testing).

2. Reproduce the defect.

3. Create a test to confirm the defect.

4. Isolate the cause of the defect.

5. Create a corrective patch and apply it.

6. Run a test to confirm the defect was repaired: Yes – continue, No – Go back to 4.

7. Run regression tests to confirm the patch does not affect other parts of your system.

Identifying the defect can sometimes be hard to do. When faced with a defect report, be it an official bug report or failed system test, you may be tempted to dismiss the defect as spurious, especially when the defect is not obvious. Those defects that cause the system to crash or damage data naturally get your attention right away. But what about those that happen once in a while or only under certain conditions? For those, you have to first assume the defect exists.

If you are fortunate enough to have a complete bug report that contains a description of how to re-create the defect, you can create a test from the defect and run it to confirm the presence of the defect. If you don't have a complete description of how to reproduce the defect, it can take some effort to get to that point.

Once you are able to re-create the defect, you should create a test that encompasses all of the steps in reproducing the problem. This test will be important later when you need to confirm that you've fixed the problem.

The next step is where the real debugging begins: isolating the defect. This is the point where you must employ one or more of the techniques discussed in this chapter to isolate and diagnose the cause of the defect. This is the most important and most challenging aspect of debugging software.

Creating a *patch* (sometimes called a *fix*) for the defect is usually an iterative process much like coding itself. You should apply your corrections one step at a time. Make one change at a time and test its effects on the defect and the rest of the system. When you think you have a viable patch, you can rerun your defect test to confirm it. If you have corrected the problem, the test will fail. As a reminder, a test designed to find defects that doesn't find the defect is considered a failed test—but that's exactly what you want! If the test passes, you should return to inspection and repair, repeating the iteration until your defect test fails.

CREATING AND USING A PATCH

A little-known software development technique is called a patch. A patch is simply a file that contains the differences between an original file and its modified form. When you create a patch, you run a GNU program called `diff`, and save the output to a file. (You can find `diff` at `www.gnu.org/software/diffutils/diffutils.html`. Unfortunately, the code is only available for Linux and Unix but can be run on Windows using Cygwin.) For example, if you were modifying the `mysqld.cc` file and added a line of code to change the version number, you could create a patch for the code change by running the command `diff -Naur mysqld.cc.old mysqld.cc > mysqld.patch`. This would create a file that looks like this:

```
--- mysqld.cc.old  2006-08-19 15:41:09.000000000 -0400
+++ mysqld.cc  2006-08-19 15:41:30.000000000 -0400
@@ -7906,6 +7906,11 @@
 #endif
   if (opt_log || opt_update_log || opt_slow_log || opt_bin_log)
     strmov(end, "-log");                          // This may slow down system
+/* BEGIN DBXP MODIFICATION */
+/* Reason for Modification: */
+/* This section adds the DBXP version number to the MySQL version number. */
+  strmov(end, "-DBXP 1.0");
+/* END DBXP MODIFICATION */
 }
```

You can also use `diff` when you want to create a difference file for an entire list of files or an entire directory. You can then use the resulting file to patch another installation of the files somewhere else.

When you use the patch, you use the GNU program called `patch`. (You can find `patch` at `www.gnu.org/software/patch/`. Unfortunately, once again the code is only available for Linux and Unix, but can be run on Windows using Cygwin.) The `patch` program reads the patch file from the `diff` program and applies it to the file as specified in the top of the patch. For example, to patch a `mysqld.cc` file that doesn't have the change you created with `diff`, you can run the command `patch < mysqld.patch`. The `patch` program applies the changes to the `mysqld.cc` file and merges the changes into the file.

Creating patches and applying patches is a handy way of distributing small changes to files—like those encountered when fixing defects. Whenever you fix a bug, you can create a patch and use the patch to track and apply the same changes to older files.

Many open source projects use the patch concept as a means of communicating changes. In fact, patches are the primary way in which the global community of developers makes changes to the MySQL source code. Instead of uploading whole files, they can send a patch to MySQL AB. From there, MySQL AB can examine the patch for correctness and either accept the changes (and apply the patch) or reject those changes. If you have never used the `diff` and `patch` programs, feel free to download them and experiment with them as you work through the examples.

Lastly, when the defect has been repaired, you should perform a regression testing step to confirm that no other defects have been introduced. If you are fortunate to be working on a system that is built using a component or modular architecture and the system is documented well, you may be able to easily identify the related components or modules by examining the requirements matrix. A *requirements matrix* tracks the requirements from use case, class, and sequence diagrams and identifies the tests created for each. Thus, when one part of a class (module) changes, you can easily find the set of tests you need to run for your regression testing. If you do not have a requirements matrix, you can either create one using a simple document or spreadsheet or annotate the source code files with the requirements they satisfy.

Inline Debugging Statements

Most novice developers start out placing print statements in their code. It is a common form of testing variables that permits them to learn the art of programming. You may think any debugging technique that uses inline debugging statements to be rudimentary or cumbersome, and you'd be partially correct. Inline debugging statements are cumbersome, but can also be a powerful tool. Inline debugging statements are any code that is used to document or present the data or state of the system at a point in time.

Before I present an example of inline debugging statements, let's consider the impact of using inline debugging statements. The first thing that comes to mind is that the debugging statements are code! Therefore, if the debugging statement does anything other than writing to the standard error stream (window), it could result in further unintended consequences. It should also be noted that inline debugging statements are usually stripped out or ignored (using conditional compilation) prior to building the system. If you are a tried-and-true validation and verification proponent, you'd argue that this process introduces additional unwarranted risk. That is, the system being compiled for use is different than the one used to debug.

However, inline debugging statements can be helpful in situations where either you cannot use an external debugger or the defect seems to occur at random intervals.[1] Examples of when these situations could occur include real-time systems, multiprocess and multithreaded systems, and large systems operating on large amounts of data.

INSTRUMENTATION

Inline debugging statements are considered by many to be a form of instrumentation. This includes code designed to track performance, data, user, client, and execution metrics. Instrumentation is usually implemented by placing statements in the code to display data values, warnings, errors, and so forth but may also be implemented using wrapper code that monitors the execution in a sandbox-like environment. One example of a software instrumentation suite is Pin by Intel. For more information about software instrumentation and Pin, see http://rogue.colorado.edu/Pin/docs/tutorials/AsplosTutorial.htm.

There are two types of inline debugging statements. The first is concerned with inspection. Lines of code are added to present the state of memory or the value of variables. This type of debugging statement is used during development and is typically commented out or ignored using conditional compilation. The second concerns tracing the path of the system as it executes. This type of debugging statement can be used at any time and is usually enabled or disabled by a switch at runtime. Since the first type is familiar to most developers (most of us learned debugging this way), I'll discuss the second with an example.

---

1. Personally, I don't believe in random intervals. Until computers can think for themselves, they are just machines following the instructions humans gave them.

Suppose you have a large system that is running in a multithreaded model and you're trying to determine what is causing a defect. Using inline debugging statements that present memory and variable values may help, but defects are rarely that easy to find. In this case, you may need to discover the state of the system leading up to the defect. If you had code in your system that simply wrote a log entry whenever it entered a function and another when it left (perhaps with some additional information about the data), it would be possible to determine what state the system was in by examining the log. Listing 5-1 depicts an excerpt from the MySQL source code that includes inline debugging statements. I've highlighted the debugging code in bold. In this case, each of the inline debugging statements writes an entry in a trace file that can be examined after the system executes (or crashes).

Listing 5-1. *Example of Inline Debugging Statements*

```
/**************************************************************************
** List all Authors.
** If you can update it, you get to be in it :)
**************************************************************************/

bool mysqld_show_authors(THD *thd)
{
  List<Item> field_list;
  Protocol *protocol= thd->protocol;
  DBUG_ENTER("mysqld_show_authors");

  field_list.push_back(new Item_empty_string("Name",40));
  field_list.push_back(new Item_empty_string("Location",40));
  field_list.push_back(new Item_empty_string("Comment",80));

  if (protocol->send_fields(&field_list,
                            Protocol::SEND_NUM_ROWS | Protocol::SEND_EOF))
    DBUG_RETURN(TRUE);

  show_table_authors_st *authors;
  for (authors= show_table_authors; authors->name; authors++)
  {
    protocol->prepare_for_resend();
    protocol->store(authors->name, system_charset_info);
    protocol->store(authors->location, system_charset_info);
    protocol->store(authors->comment, system_charset_info);
    if (protocol->write())
      DBUG_RETURN(TRUE);
  }
  send_eof(thd);
  DBUG_RETURN(FALSE);
}
```

Notice in Listing 5-1 that the first inline debugging statements code documents the arrival of the system at this function, or its state, by indicating the name of the function. Notice also that each exit point of the function is documented along with the return value of the function. An excerpt from a trace file running the SHOW AUTHORS command is shown in Listing 5-2. I've omitted a large section of the listing in order to show you how the trace file works for a successful execution of the SHOW AUTHORS command.

Listing 5-2. *Sample Trace File*

```
T@6    : | | | >mysqld_show_authors

...

T@6    : | | | | | >send_eof
T@6    : | | | | | | packet_header: Memory: 0x9b6ead8  Bytes: (4)
05 00 00 50
T@6    : | | | | | | >net_flush
T@6    : | | | | | | >vio_is_blocking
T@6    : | | | | | | | exit: 1
T@6    : | | | | | | <vio_is_blocking
T@6    : | | | | | | >net_real_write
T@6    : | | | | | | | >vio_write
T@6    : | | | | | | | | enter: sd: 17776, buf: 0x0734D278, size: 5029
T@6    : | | | | | | | | exit: 5029
T@6    : | | | | | | | <vio_write
T@6    : | | | | | | <net_real_write
T@6    : | | | | | <net_flush
T@6    : | | | | | info: EOF sent, so no more error sending allowed
T@6    : | | | | <send_eof
T@6    : | | | <mysqld_show_authors
```

Note These inline debug statements are turned off by default. You can turn them on by compiling the server with debug and running the server in debug mode using the --debug command-line switch. This creates a trace file with all of the debug statements. On Linux, the trace file is stored in /tmp/mysqld.trace and on Windows, the file is stored in c:\mysqld.trace. These files can become quite large as all of the functions in MySQL are written using inline debugging statements.

This technique, while simple, is a versatile tool. When you examine the flow of the system by inspecting the trace file, you can easily discover a starting point for further investigation. Sometimes just knowing where to look can be the greatest challenge.

Error Handlers

Have you ever encountered an error message while using software? Whether you're using something created in the Pacific Northwest or created by the global community of developers, chances are you've seen the end result of an error handler.

You may be wondering why I would include error handlers as a debugging technique. That's because a good error handler presents the cause of the problem along with any possible corrective options. Good error handlers provide developers with enough information to understand what went wrong and how they might overcome the problem, and in some cases, include additional information that can assist them in diagnosing the problem. That last bit can sometimes go too far. Too many of us have seen dialog boxes containing terse error messages with confusing resolution options like the one shown in Figure 5-1.

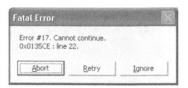

Figure 5-1. *Poor error handler example*

As humorous as this example may be, messages like it are seen by users every day. Developers who write error messages like this are not making themselves clear. Statements that may be perfectly understandable for developers of a system could be gibberish for its users. The best policy is to create error messages that explain what has gone wrong and offer the user a resolution if one exists or at least a means to report the problem. It is also a good idea to provide a way to record the information a developer needs to diagnose the problem. This could be done via logging, a system state dump, or an auto-generated report. Figure 5-2 depicts a better example of how to present errors to the user.

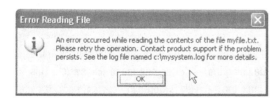

Figure 5-2. *Better error handler example*

Error handlers aren't just for reporting errors. There is another construct that is also called an error handler. This construct is simply the code used to trap and process (handle) errors. Perhaps you are familiar with the C++ try...catch block. This is an excellent example of an error handler as the language has been modified to include the construct in its syntax. Listing 5-3 depicts a typical try...catch block. The example shows the basic syntax for the C++ error handler (also called an exception handler).

Listing 5-3. *Example C++ Error Handler try...catch Block*

```
try
{
  //attempt file operation here
}
catch (CFileException* e)
{
  //handle the exception here
}
```

While Listing 5-3 is less sophisticated than the C++ construct, you can create error handlers in just about any language that supports conditional statements. For example, Listing 5-4 shows an example from the C language. Here, we see the return code is checked and, depending on the failure, the code handles the problem. Take care when creating error handlers from scratch. You want to be sure to cover all possible conditions so that you can successfully recover or at least process the error in a way that does not affect the performance of the system and (more importantly) loss or corruption of data.

Listing 5-4. *Example C Error Handler*

```
if ((archive= gzopen(share->data_file_name, "rb")) == NULL)
{
  if (errno == EROFS || errno == EACCES)
    DBUG_RETURN(my_errno= errno);
  DBUG_RETURN(HA_ERR_CRASHED_ON_USAGE);
}
```

Error handlers cover more than simply reporting errors. They are also a front line of defense for debugging. Good error handlers are written to not only trap and process the error but also to store or display diagnostic information.

Take another look at Listing 5-4. This code was taken from the ha_archive.cc file of the MySQL source code. Notice the line of code that I highlighted. This line is one of the numerous inline debugging statements found throughout the code, but its use in this error handler shows how you can record the diagnostic information necessary to troubleshoot a problem with this part of the system. If I were debugging a session about this code, I could run the server in debug mode and look to the trace file to read the diagnostic information recorded by this error handler.

I encourage you to consider writing all of your error-handling code in this manner. You can always display an appropriate error message to the user, but you should also always trap the error codes (return values) and record them and any other pertinent diagnostic information. Using error handlers in this manner will greatly enhance your debugging skills and make your system much easier to diagnose. I have found that sometimes I don't even need to run a debugger at all. A study of the trace files containing the diagnostic information can be enough to lead me directly to the source of the problem.

External Debuggers

A debugger is a software tool designed to analyze a set of executing code and trace the flow of the system as it executes. Most tools that we consider debuggers are actually executed in conjunction with the software being debugged, hence the name *external debugger*. However, for brevity and conformity, I'll refer to all the tools discussed in this section as simply debuggers.

There are several types of debuggers, but most fit into one of three categories. The debuggers you may be most familiar with are those that run as a separate tool that you can attach to a running process and control the system. There are also debuggers designed to run as an interactive process combining control with inspection capabilities. Others include specialized debuggers offering more advanced control of the system. I'll examine each of these types in the following sections.

Stand-alone

The most common debugger is called a stand-alone debugger. These debuggers run as a separate process and permit you to attach to a system that has been compiled to include the appropriate debug information (for mapping to source code, especially linking to the symbols in the code). Unless you're debugging code that contains the source files (like some forms of interpreted languages), you usually must have the source code files available and use those to complete the connection to the running process.

Once you've attached to the system (or process) you want to debug, stand-alone debuggers permit you to stop, start, and step through the execution. Stepping through refers to three basic operations:

1. Execute the current line of code and step into the next line of code.

2. Skip over the next line of code (execute function calls and return to the next line).

3. Execute until a particular line of code comes into focus.

The last operation usually refers to lines of code that have been tagged as the line to stop on (called a *breakpoint*) or the line that is currently highlighted (called run to cursor).

Stand-alone debuggers provide tools for inspecting memory, the call stack, and even sometimes the heap. The ability to inspect variables is perhaps the most important diagnostic tool debuggers can provide. After all, almost everything you will want to inspect is stored somewhere.

Note A *heap* is a structure that stores available memory addresses in a tree structure for fast allocation and deallocation of memory blocks. A *stack* is a structure that allows developers to place items on the stack in a first-in, last-out method (much like a stack of plates at a buffet).

Another characteristic of stand-alone debuggers is that they are not typically integrated with the development environment. That is, they are not part of the compiler suite of tools. Thus, many operate outside the development environment. The advantage of using stand-alone debuggers is that there are many to choose from, each with a slightly different feature set. This allows you to choose the stand-alone debugger that best meets your debugging needs.

A popular example of this type of debugger is the GNU Debugger (gdb). (For more information, visit www.gnu.org/software/gdb/documentation.) The gdb debugger runs on Linux and provides a way to control and inspect a system that has been compiled in debug mode. Listing 5-5 shows a sample program I wrote to calculate factorials. Those of you with a keen eye will spot the logic error, but let's assume the program was run as written. When I enter a value of 3, I should get the value 6 returned. Instead, I get 18.

Listing 5-5. *Sample Program (sample.c)*

```c
#include <stdio.h>
#include <stdlib.h>

static int factorial(int num)
{
  int i;
  int fact = num;

  for (i = 1; i < num; i++)
  {
    fact += fact * i;
  }
  return fact;
}

int main(int argc, char *argv[])
{
  int num;
  int fact = 0;

  num = atoi(argv[1]);
  fact = factorial(num);
  printf("%d! = %d\n", num, fact);
  return 0;
}
```

If I want to debug this program using gdb, I first have to compile the program in debug mode using the following command:

```
gcc -g -o sample sample.c
```

Once the program is compiled, I launch gdb using the following command:

```
gdb sample
```

When the gdb debugger issues its command prompt, I issue breakpoints using the break command (supplying the source file and line number for the break) and run the program, providing the necessary data. I can also print out any variables using the print command. If I want to continue the execution, I can issue the continue command. Finally, when done I can exit gdb with the quit command. Listing 5-6 shows a sample debug session using these commands.

Listing 5-6. *Sample gdb Session*

```
# gdb sample
```

```
GNU gdb 6.3
Copyright 2004 Free Software Foundation, Inc.
GDB is free software, covered by the GNU General Public License, and you are
welcome to change it and/or distribute copies of it under certain
conditions.
Type "show copying" to see the conditions.
There is absolutely no warranty for GDB.  Type "show warranty" for details.
This GDB was configured as "i586-suse-linux"...Using host libthread_db
library "/lib/tls/libthread_db.so.1".

(gdb) break sample.c:10
Breakpoint 1 at 0x804841d: file sample.c, line 10.
(gdb) run 3
Starting program: /home/Chuck/source/testddd/sample 3

Breakpoint 1, factorial (num=3) at sample.c:11
11            fact += fact * i;
(gdb) print i
$1 = 1
(gdb) print num
$2 = 3
(gdb) print fact
$3 = 3
(gdb) continue
Continuing.

Breakpoint 1, factorial (num=3) at sample.c:11
11            fact += fact * i;
(gdb) continue
Continuing.
3! = 18

Program exited normally.
(gdb) quit
#
```

Do you see the logic error? I'll give you a hint. What should the first value be for calculating the factorial of the number 3? Take a look at the variable declarations for the factorial method. Something smells with that int fact = num; declaration.

■**Note** Some folks may want to call debuggers like gdb interactive debuggers because they interact with the system while it is running, thus allowing the user to observe the execution. While this is true, keep in mind that gdb is controlling the system externally and you cannot see or interact with the source code other than through very simplistic methods (e.g., the list command, list, lists the source code). If gdb provided a graphical user interface that presented the source code and allowed you to see the data and interact with the source code, it would be an interactive debugger. But wait, that's what the ddd debugger does.

Interactive Debuggers

There are debuggers that are part of the development environment either as part of the compile-link-run tools or as an integrated part of the interactive development environment. Unlike stand-alone debuggers, interactive debuggers use the same or a very similar interface as the development tools. An excellent example of a well-integrated interactive debugger is the debugging facilities in Microsoft Visual Studio .NET. In Visual Studio, the interactive debugger is simply a different mode of the rapid application development process. You dress up a form, write a bit of code, and then run it in debug mode.

Figure 5-3 depicts a sample Visual Studio .NET 2005 debug session using a Windows variant of the sample program shown earlier.

Interactive debuggers have all of the same features as a stand-alone debugger. You can stop, start, step into, step over, and run to breakpoints or cursor. What makes using an interactive debugger most useful is when you detect the cause of a defect; you can stop the execution, make any necessary changes, and run the system again. Table 5-1 provides a brief description of these commands. While most debuggers have all of these commands and more, some use different names. Consult the documentation for your debugger for the precise names of the commands.

Table 5-1. *Basic Debugger Control Commands*

Command	Description
Start (Run)	Executes the system.
Stop (Break)	Temporarily halts execution of the code.
Step Into	Runs the next code statement, changing focus to the following statement. If the statement being executed is a function, this command will change focus to the first executable statement in the function being called.
Step Over	Runs the next code statement changing focus to the following statement. If the statement being executed is a function, this command will execute the function and change focus to the next executable statement following the function call.
Breakpoint	The debugger stops when code execution reaches the statement where the breakpoint has been issued. Many debuggers allow the use of conditional breakpoints where you can set the breakpoint to occur based on an expression.
Run to Cursor	The debugger resumes execution but halts the execution when control reaches the code statement where the cursor is placed. This is a form of a one-use breakpoint.

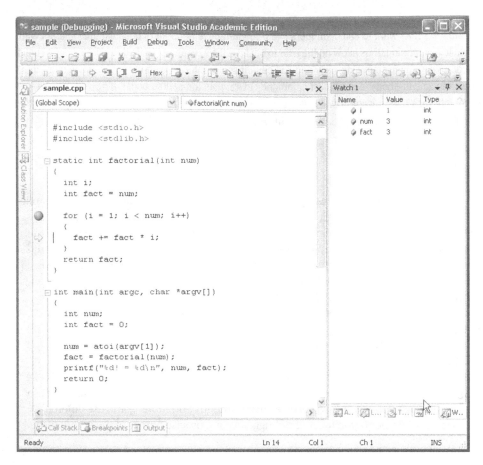

Figure 5-3. *Sample Visual Studio debugging (sample.c)*

The compilation and linking in this scenario happens in the background and often takes no longer than a moment to complete and you're back in the debugger. As you can imagine, interactive debuggers are real time savers. If you have never used a stand-alone debugger, you may be dismayed at the apparent lack of integration stand-alone debuggers have with the source code projects. What may seem like "old school" is really the state of most development. It is only through the relatively recent development of rapid application development tools that interactive debuggers have become the preferred tool for debugging.

GNU Data Display Debugger

Another example of an interactive debugger is the GNU Data Display Debugger (ddd), which is available at http://www.gnu.org/software/ddd. The ddd debugger permits you to run your program and see the code while it is running. It is similar in concept to the rapid application development debuggers like Visual Studio. Figure 5-4 shows our sample program run in ddd.

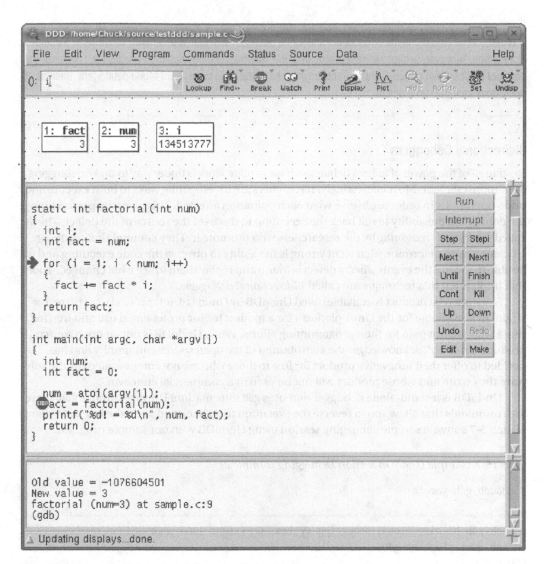

Figure 5-4. *Sample ddd session debugging "sample.c"*

Notice that the same variables are displayed in the upper portion of the window. With ddd, I can set breakpoints in the code by pointing and clicking on the line of code rather than having to remember the line number in the file I want to break on. I can also view the contents of any variable by double-clicking on the variable. I can even change values in a similar fashion. This allows me to experiment with how the code would perform with different values. This is a powerful feature that can allow the discovery of "off by one" errors (e.g., starting a list iterator index at 1 instead of 0).

■**Note** Some would call the ddd tool a stand-alone debugger because it essentially operates in a stand-alone mode. However, because of its sophisticated user interface and development-like layout, I consider the ddd tool a hybrid that matches the interactive type a bit better than most stand-alone debuggers. Besides, it really does kick gdb up a notch!

Bidirectional Debuggers

Despite all of the power of today's debuggers have to offer, work is under way to make debugging even more efficient. Most interestingly, researchers are investigating ways to both execute and undo operations in order to observe what each operation affected. This gives the person doing the debugging the ability to roll back the execution to discover the source of the defect. This is called *backwards reasoning* by the researchers who promote it. They contend that the most efficient way to determine what went wrong is the ability to observe the code executing and to be able to rewind the events when a defect is found and replay them to see what changed. Tools that implement this technique are called *bidirectional debuggers.*

A commercial product is available called UndoDB by Undo Ltd. (http://undo-software.com). UndoDB is available for the Linux platform for a modest fee for professional use and free for those who are not paid for their programming efforts. While UndoDB is not an open source product, Undo Ltd. acknowledges the contribution of the open source community and has decided to offer their innovative product for free to those who are not compensated for the software they write and whose product will not be used in a commercial endeavor.

UndoDB is a stand-alone debugger that uses gdb information. However, unlike gdb, there are commands that allow you to reverse the execution to go back and undo the last statement. Listing 5-7 shows a sample debugging session using UndoDB with our sample program.

Listing 5-7. *Sample UndoDB Session Debugging (sample.c)*

```
# undodb-gdb sample
```

```
Undodb-gdb bi-directional debugging system. Copyright 2006 Undo Ltd.
undodb-gdb: starting gdb...
GNU gdb 6.3
Copyright 2004 Free Software Foundation, Inc.
GDB is free software, covered by the GNU General Public License, and you are
welcome to change it and/or distribute copies of it under certain conditions.
Type "show copying" to see the conditions.
There is absolutely no warranty for GDB. Type "show warranty" for details.
This GDB was configured as "i586-suse-linux"...
Using host libthread_db library "/lib/tls/libthread_db.so.1".

(gdb) break sample.c:9
Breakpoint 1 at 0x8048414: file sample.c, line 9.
(gdb) run 3
Starting program: /home/Chuck/source/testddd/sample 3
```

```
Breakpoint 1, factorial (num=3) at sample.c:9
9 for (i = 1; i < num; i++)
(gdb) next
11 fact += fact * i;
(gdb) bnext

Program received signal SIGTRAP, Trace/breakpoint trap.
0x08048436 in factorial (num=3) at sample.c:9
9 for (i = 1; i < num; i++)
(gdb) next
11 fact += fact * i;
(gdb) break sample.c:13
Breakpoint 2 at 0x8048438: file sample.c, line 13.
(gdb) continue
Continuing.

Breakpoint 2, factorial (num=3) at sample.c:13
13 return fact;
(gdb) print fact
$1 = 18
(gdb) bnext

Program received signal SIGTRAP, Trace/breakpoint trap.
0x08048436 in factorial (num=3) at sample.c:9
9 for (i = 1; i < num; i++)
(gdb) print fact
$2 = 18
(gdb) bnext

Program received signal SIGTRAP, Trace/breakpoint trap.
0x08048429 in factorial (num=3) at sample.c:11
11 fact += fact * i;
(gdb) print fact
$3 = 6
(gdb) print i
$4 = 2
(gdb) next
9 for (i = 1; i < num; i++)
(gdb) print i
$5 = 2
(gdb) print fact
$6 = 18
(gdb) print num
$7 = 3
(gdb) next
```

```
Breakpoint 2, factorial (num=3) at sample.c:13
13 return fact;
(gdb) continue
Continuing.
3! = 18

(gdb) quit
The program is running. Exit anyway? (y or n) y
#
```

Notice the commands bnext in Listing 5-7. The bnext command is one of the unique UndoDB commands that allows for the back trace (bidirectional) of the execution. All of the UndoDB back trace commands are mirrors of the gdb commands. That makes this debugger very friendly to developers who use gdb.

THERE IS NO WRONG WAY

You may be wondering why I have included debugging methods that some may suggest are "old school" and not the latest vogue interactive development trend. I submit it is possible to argue that one debugging method is better than another in certain circumstances or even in the general case. However, it is true that any of the methods presented here, and potentially many others, can lead to successful results. Organizations should not force developers into a particular mold of "do it this way" (which applies to more than just debugging) because what works well for one instance or person may not work for others. My recommendation is to adopt whatever debugging tools or methods you feel best meet your needs and project. If that means using a trace-like method or an interactive method, it doesn't matter as long as you can efficiently and effectively debug your project. If you develop good troubleshooting skills and can get the information you need to discover the problem, how you get there shouldn't matter.

Debugging MySQL

You may have excellent debugging skills debugging your own applications, some of which may indeed be quite large. However, few have the opportunity to attempt to debug a large system like MySQL. While it isn't difficult, I have found many challenges during my work with the source code. I hope that the following sections give you the knowledge that I gained through my many trials. I encourage you to read through this section at least once and then follow my examples when you have time.

I'll begin by examining a debugging session with an example of debugging MySQL using inline debugging statements. I'll then move on to an error handler example followed by an in-depth look at debugging MySQL on both Linux and Windows. If you have been waiting for a chance to get your hands dirty with the MySQL source code, this section is for you. Roll up those sleeves and grab some of your favorite caffeine-laden beverage, because we're going in!

Inline Debugging Statements

MySQL AB has provided their customers with a robust inline debugging statements debugging tool based on the debugger originally created by Fred Fish and later modified by one of MySQL AB's founders, Michael "Monty" Widenius, for thread safety. This tool is actually a collection of C macros called DBUG.

Using DBUG is easy because the macros provided allow you to simply place a single code statement where you want to record something. The MySQL AB developers have many good examples throughout the code. They record a great many aspects of the execution of the server. The individual macros are referred to as debug tags (called DBUG tags in the MySQL documentation). The tags currently used in the MySQL source code include the following:

- DBUG_ENTER: Identify entry into a function using function specification.

- DBUG_EXIT: Record return results from function.

- DBUG_INFO: Record diagnostic information.

- DBUG_WARNING: Record an unusual event or unexpected event.

- DBUG_ERROR: Record error codes (used in error handlers mainly).

- DBUG_LOOP: Record entry or exit from a loop.

- DBUG_TRANS: Record transaction information.

- DBUG_QUIT: Record a failure resulting in premature system shutdown.

- DBUG_QUERY: Record query statement.

- DBUG_ASSERT: Record the error on a failed test of an expression.

Listing 5-8 shows how some of these tags are used in the mysqld_show_privileges() function. The highlighted code statements are some of the more commonly used DBUG tags.

Listing 5-8. *Example DBUG Tags*

```
bool mysqld_show_privileges(THD *thd)
{
  List<Item> field_list;
  Protocol *protocol= thd->protocol;
  DBUG_ENTER("mysqld_show_privileges");

  field_list.push_back(new Item_empty_string("Privilege",10));
  field_list.push_back(new Item_empty_string("Context",15));
  field_list.push_back(new Item_empty_string("Comment",NAME_LEN));
```

```
if (protocol->send_fields(&field_list,
                          Protocol::SEND_NUM_ROWS | Protocol::SEND_EOF))
  DBUG_RETURN(TRUE);

show_privileges_st *privilege= sys_privileges;
for (privilege= sys_privileges; privilege->privilege ; privilege++)
{
  protocol->prepare_for_resend();
  protocol->store(privilege->privilege, system_charset_info);
  protocol->store(privilege->context, system_charset_info);
  protocol->store(privilege->comment, system_charset_info);
  if (protocol->write())
    DBUG_RETURN(TRUE);
}
send_eof(thd);
DBUG_RETURN(FALSE);
}
```

The list of debug tags is quite comprehensive. The DBUG_ENTER and DBUG_RETURN tags are some of the most useful because they allow you to record a trace of the execution of the system throughout all of the functions called. It is especially important to point out that all the functions in the MySQL source code include these tags on entry and exit, respectively. Should you add your own functions, you should do the same and record the entry and exit(s) of your functions. These tags are written to a trace file stored in /tmp/mysqld.trace on Linux and c:\mysqld.trace on Windows.

It should be noted that the trace file created can become very large. Fortunately, you can control which tags are written to the trace file by supplying them on the command line. For example, to limit the trace file to display the more interesting debug tags, you can use a command like the following. The general format of the switches is a:b:c for turning on switches a, b, and c. Any switches that take parameters are separated by commas.

```
mysqld-debug --debug=d,info,error,query,general,where:t:L:g:O,
/tmp/mysqd.trace -u root
```

The previous command runs the MySQL server that is compiled with debug enabled (mysqld-debug). The command line parameter --debug=d,info,error,query,general, where:t:L:g:O,/tmp/mysqd.trace instructs the DBUG system to enable output from the DBUG_INFO, DBUG_ERROR, DBUG_QUERY, and DBUG_WHERE macros, turns on the trace lines for enter/exit of functions, includes the line number of the source code for the debug statement, enables profiling, and writes the file to /tmp/mysqld.trace. The -u root parameter passes the username root to the server for execution. Many more options are available; some common options are shown in Table 5-2.[2]

---

2. A complete list of the commonly used DBUG switches can be found in the MySQL reference manual in the appendix titled "Porting to Other Systems," under the subheading "The DBUG Package."

Table 5-2. *List of Commonly Used DBUG Switches*

Switch	Description
d	Turns on the output for the DBUG tags specified in the parameters. An empty list causes output for all tags.
D	Performs a delay after each output. The parameter specifies the number of tenths of seconds to delay. For example, D,40 will cause a delay of 4 seconds.
f	Limits the recording of debugging, tracing, and profiling to the list specified with d.
F	Outputs the name of the source file for every line of debug or trace recorded.
I	Outputs the process ID or thread ID for every line of debug or trace recorded.
g	Turns on profiling. The parameters specify the keywords for those items to be profiled. An empty list implies all keywords are profiled.
L	Outputs the source code line number for each line recorded.
n	Sets the nesting depth for each line of output. This can help make the output more readable.
N	Places sequential numbers on each line recorded.
o	Saves the output to the file specified in the parameter. The default is written to stderr.
O	Saves the output to the file specified in the parameter. The default is written to stderr. Flushes the file between each write.
P	Outputs the current process name for each line recorded.
t	Turns on function call/exit trace lines (represented as a vertical bar).

Listing 5-9 shows an excerpt of a trace run while executing the show authors; command. You can see the entire trace of the system as it runs the command and returns data (I have omitted many lines as this list was generated with the default debug switches). I've highlighted the most interesting lines. Notice also the trace lines that run down the lines of output. This allows you to follow the flow of the execution more easily.

If you write your own functions in MySQL, you can use the DBUG tags to record your own information to the trace file. This file can prove to be helpful in the event that your code causes unpredictable or unexpected behavior.

Listing 5-9. *Sample Trace of the Show Privileges Command*

```
338: | | | >mysqld_show_privileges
```

```
171: | | | | >alloc_root
220: | | | | <alloc_root
171: | | | | >alloc_root
220: | | | | <alloc_root
171: | | | | >alloc_root
220: | | | | <alloc_root
171: | | | | >alloc_root
```

```
220: | | | | <alloc_root
171: | | | | >alloc_root
220: | | | | <alloc_root
171: | | | | >alloc_root
220: | | | | <alloc_root
550: | | | | >send_fields
171: | | | | | >alloc_root
220: | | | | | <alloc_root
127: | | | | | >_mymalloc
202: | | | | | <_mymalloc
261: | | | | | >_myfree
315: | | | | | <_myfree
127: | | | | | >_mymalloc
202: | | | | | <_mymalloc
687: | | | | | >Protocol::write
688: | | | | | <Protocol::write
687: | | | | | >Protocol::write
688: | | | | | <Protocol::write
687: | | | | | >Protocol::write
688: | | | | | <Protocol::write
676: | | | | <send_fields
261: | | | | >_myfree
315: | | | | <_myfree
127: | | | | >_mymalloc
202: | | | | <_mymalloc
687: | | | | >Protocol::write
688: | | | | <Protocol::write
261: | | | | >_myfree
315: | | | | <_myfree
127: | | | | >_mymalloc
202: | | | | <_mymalloc
687: | | | | >Protocol::write
688: | | | | <Protocol::write
687: | | | | >Protocol::write
688: | | | | <Protocol::write
687: | | | | >Protocol::write
688: | | | | <Protocol::write
687: | | | | >Protocol::write
688: | | | | <Protocol::write
687: | | | | >Protocol::write
688: | | | | <Protocol::write
687: | | | | >Protocol::write
688: | | | | <Protocol::write
687: | | | | >Protocol::write
688: | | | | <Protocol::write
687: | | | | >Protocol::write
688: | | | | <Protocol::write
```

```
687: | | | | >Protocol::write
688: | | | | <Protocol::write
687: | | | | >Protocol::write
688: | | | | <Protocol::write
687: | | | | >Protocol::write
688: | | | | <Protocol::write
261: | | | | >_myfree
315: | | | | <_myfree
127: | | | | >_mymalloc
202: | | | | <_mymalloc
687: | | | | >Protocol::write
688: | | | | <Protocol::write
687: | | | | >Protocol::write
688: | | | | <Protocol::write
687: | | | | >Protocol::write
688: | | | | <Protocol::write
687: | | | | >Protocol::write
688: | | | | <Protocol::write
687: | | | | >Protocol::write
688: | | | | <Protocol::write
687: | | | | >Protocol::write
688: | | | | <Protocol::write
687: | | | | >Protocol::write
688: | | | | <Protocol::write
687: | | | | >Protocol::write
688: | | | | <Protocol::write
687: | | | | >Protocol::write
688: | | | | <Protocol::write
687: | | | | >Protocol::write
688: | | | | <Protocol::write
687: | | | | >Protocol::write
688: | | | | <Protocol::write
687: | | | | >Protocol::write
688: | | | | <Protocol::write
687: | | | | >Protocol::write
688: | | | | <Protocol::write
687: | | | | >Protocol::write
688: | | | | <Protocol::write
687: | | | | >Protocol::write
688: | | | | <Protocol::write
687: | | | | >Protocol::write
688: | | | | <Protocol::write
687: | | | | >Protocol::write
688: | | | | <Protocol::write
336: | | | | >send_eof
326: | | | | | >net_flush
186: | | | | | | >vio_is_blocking
```

```
189: | | | | | | <vio_is_blocking
549: | | | | | | >net_real_write
104: | | | | | | | >vio_write
118: | | | | | | | <vio_write
677: | | | | | | <net_real_write
336: | | | | | <net_flush
342: | | | | | info: EOF sent, so no more error sending allowed
344: | | | | <send_eof
359: | | | <mysqld_show_privileges
...
User time 0.34, System time 0.12
Maximum resident set size 0, Integral resident set size 0
Non-physical pagefaults 4734, Physical pagefaults 0, Swaps 0
Blocks in 0 out 0, Messages in 0 out 0, Signals 0
Voluntary context switches 152, Involuntary context switches 102
```

Take a look at the data provided at the end of the trace. This summary data can be useful when diagnosing defects associated with timing problems, page faults, blocking issues, and context switches. The old adage "When in doubt, check the code dump and trace file" holds true.

Error Handlers

There are no specific tools to demonstrate concerning error handlers in MySQL. You should strive to generate code that handles all possible errors. The best way to show you how to do this is with an example of an error handler that does not properly manage errors. Listing 5-10 shows an excerpt from the MySQL source code that has an issue with a particular type of error. This excerpt is from the Windows source code for version 5.0.15.

Listing 5-10. *Sample of Error Handler in MySQL*

```
int my_delete(const char *name, myf MyFlags)
{
  int err;
  DBUG_ENTER("my_delete");
  DBUG_PRINT("my",("name %s MyFlags %d", name, MyFlags));

  if ((err = unlink(name)) == -1)
  {
    my_errno=errno;
    if (MyFlags & (MY_FAE+MY_WME))
      my_error(EE_DELETE,MYF(ME_BELL+ME_WAITTANG+(MyFlags & ME_NOINPUT)),
        name,errno);
  }
  DBUG_RETURN(err);
} /* my_delete */
```

Can you see the defect? I'll give you a hint. The return value for the unlink() function in Windows has several important values that need to be checked. One of those is missing from the error handler shown in Listing 5-10. The defect resulted in the optimize() function improperly copying an intermediate file during its operation. Fortunately, this defect will have been fixed by the release of this book.

MySQL AB has provided a well-designed error message mechanism that can make your error handlers more robust. To add your own error messages, you can add them to the sql/errmsg.txt file. See the internals.pdf document for more details on adding your own error messages.

I cannot stress enough the importance of forming error handlers that handle all possible errors and take the appropriate actions to rectify and report the errors. Adding the DBUG macros to trace and record the error messages will ensure all of your debugging sessions are more efficient.

Debugging in Linux

One area where Linux excels is in the quality of its advanced development tools (primarily the GNU tools). These tools include excellent debuggers capable for handling not only single-threaded but also multithreaded systems.

Many debuggers are available for Linux. The most popular are gdb and ddd. The following sections present an example of each of the tools debugging the MySQL system. The scenario for these examples is to inspect what happens when the SHOW AUTHORS command is issued. I'll begin with the gdb debugger, and then show you the same scenario using ddd.

Using gdb

Let's begin by reexamining the show_authors() function. Refer back to Listing 5-1 for the complete code for the function. The first thing I need to do is make sure I have built my server with the debugger turned on. Do this by issuing the following commands from the root of the source folder:

```
./configure --with-debug
make
make install
```

These commands will cause the system to be compiled with the appropriate debugging information so that I can use the debugger. I can now launch the server in debug mode using the command mysqld-debug. Listing 5-11 shows the startup statements presented when the server starts.

■**Caution** You should ensure all installations of the MySQL server have been shut down prior to launching the server in debug mode. While not strictly necessary, this should allow you to avoid attempting to debug the wrong process.

Listing 5-11. *Starting MySQL Server in Debug Mode*

```
linux:~ # mysqld-debug -uroot
060530 20:42:07  InnoDB: Started; log sequence number 0 46403
060530 20:42:07 [Note] mysqld-debug: ready for connections.
Version: '5.1.9-beta-debug'  socket: '/var/lib/mysql/mysql.sock'  port: 3306
  MySQL Community Server - Debug (GPL)
```

Notice that in this case, I am using the socket specified as /var/lib/mysql/mysql.sock. This allows me to run a copy of the server in debug mode without affecting a running server. However, I need to tell the client to use the same socket. But first, I need to determine the process ID for my server. I can do this by issuing the ps -A command to list all of the running processes. Alternatively, I could issue the command ps -A | grep mysql and get the process IDs of all of the processes that include mysql in the name. The following demonstrates this command:

```
9740 pts/2    00:00:00 mysqld
```

Now that I have my process ID, I can launch gdb and attach to the correct process using the attach 10592 command. I also want to set a breakpoint in the show_authors() function. An examination of the source file shows that the first line that I'm interested in is line 207. I issue the command break /home/Chuck/MySQL/mysql-5.1.9-beta/sql/sql_show.cc:207. The format of this command is file:line#. Now that I have a breakpoint, I issue the command continue to tell the process to execute, and gdb will halt the program when the breakpoint is encountered. Listing 5-12 shows the complete debugging session.

Listing 5-12. *Running gdb*

```
# gdb
```

```
GNU gdb 6.3
Copyright 2004 Free Software Foundation, Inc.
GDB is free software, covered by the GNU General Public License, and you are
welcome to change it and/or distribute copies of it under certain
conditions.
Type "show copying" to see the conditions.
There is absolutely no warranty for GDB.  Type "show warranty" for details.
This GDB was configured as "i586-suse-linux".
(gdb) attach 10592
Attaching to process 10592
warning: could not load vsyscall page because no executable was specified
warning: try using the "file" command first
Reading symbols from /usr/sbin/mysqld-debug...done.
Using host libthread_db library "/lib/tls/libthread_db.so.1".
Reading symbols from /lib/tls/libpthread.so.0...done.
[Thread debugging using libthread_db enabled]
[New Thread 1075779264 (LWP 10592)]
[New Thread 1098349488 (LWP 10636)]
```

```
[New Thread 1098148784 (LWP 10601)]
[New Thread 1106926512 (LWP 10600)]
[New Thread 1104825264 (LWP 10599)]
[New Thread 1102724016 (LWP 10598)]
[New Thread 1095846832 (LWP 10596)]
[New Thread 1093745584 (LWP 10595)]
[New Thread 1091644336 (LWP 10594)]
[New Thread 1089543088 (LWP 10593)]
Loaded symbols for /lib/tls/libpthread.so.0
Reading symbols from /lib/tls/libc.so.6...done.
Loaded symbols for /lib/tls/libc.so.6
Reading symbols from /lib/libnss_files.so.2...done.
Loaded symbols for /lib/libnss_files.so.2
Reading symbols from /lib/libnss_dns.so.2...done.
Loaded symbols for /lib/libnss_dns.so.2
Reading symbols from /lib/libresolv.so.2...done.
Loaded symbols for /lib/libresolv.so.2
Reading symbols from /lib/libcrypt.so.1...done.
Loaded symbols for /lib/libcrypt.so.1
Reading symbols from /lib/libnsl.so.1...done.
Loaded symbols for /lib/libnsl.so.1
Reading symbols from /lib/tls/libm.so.6...done.
Loaded symbols for /lib/tls/libm.so.6
Reading symbols from /lib/ld-linux.so.2...done.
Loaded symbols for /lib/ld-linux.so.2
Reading symbols from /lib/libgcc_s.so.1...done.
Loaded symbols for /lib/libgcc_s.so.1
0xffffe410 in ?? ()
(gdb) break /home/Chuck/MySQL/mysql-5.1.9-beta/sql/sql_show.cc:207
Breakpoint 1 at 0x82e32bc: file sql_show.cc, line 207.
(gdb) continue
Continuing.
[Switching to Thread 1098349488 (LWP 10636)]

Breakpoint 1, mysqld_show_authors (thd=0x8f30100) at sql_show.cc:207
207        field_list.push_back(new Item_empty_string("Name",40));
(gdb) next
208        field_list.push_back(new Item_empty_string("Location",40));
(gdb) next
209        field_list.push_back(new Item_empty_string("Comment",80));
(gdb) next
212                                    Protocol::SEND_NUM_ROWS |
Protocol::SEND_EOF))
(gdb) next
216      for (authors= show_table_authors; authors->name; authors++)
(gdb) next
218        protocol->prepare_for_resend();
```

```
(gdb) print authors->name
$1 = 0x877ac9f "Brian (Krow) Aker"
(gdb) quit
```

To see the server in action, I need to launch a client to issue commands while I am running the debugger. I launch the MySQL command-line client using the following command:

```
mysql -u root -p -S /var/lib/mysql/mysql.sock
```

Listing 5-13 shows the initialization of the client specifying the desired socket on the command line. I then launch the SHOW AUTHORS command.

Listing 5-13. *Starting MySQL Client to Attach to Server*

```
Chuck@linux:~> mysql -u root -p -S /var/lib/mysql/mysql.sock
Enter password:
```

```
Welcome to the MySQL monitor.  Commands end with ; or \g.
Your MySQL connection id is 1 to server version: 5.1.9-beta-debug

Type 'help;' or '\h' for help. Type '\c' to clear the buffer.

mysql> show authors;
```

The first thing I notice when I enter the command is that the client stops. The reason is that the gdb debugger has encountered the breakpoint and has halted execution. When I switch back to the debugger, I can issue commands to step through the execution using the next command. I can also display the values of variables using the print command. (Listing 5-12 shows these commands in action.) Once I've finished my debugging session, I can shut down the server and exit the debugger.

The gdb debugger is a powerful tool, but it lacks the sophistication of debuggers found in most integrated development environments (IDEs). The ddd debugger makes up for this limitation by providing a robust graphical environment.

Using ddd

The GNU ddd debugger is an excellent example of an integrated debugger. Though not exclusively built around an IDE, the ddd debugger provides a similar experience. You can launch the program you wish to debug and view the source code. Using the integrated tools, you can set breakpoints, stop and start the program being debugged, set watches on variables, view the stack trace, and even edit variable values.

Several windows are associated with the debugger. The *data window* displays all of the data items you have set watches on. The *source window* (the main display area) displays the current source code for the program being debugged. The *debugger console* displays the host debugger (gdb) output. This window is handy for developers who use gdb because it permits you to enter your own gdb commands. Thus, you can use either the menu system to control the program or the debugger console to issue commands to the debugger directly.

The ddd debugger is actually a wrapper around the GNU gdb stand-alone debugger. In typical open source fashion, the developers of ddd reused what was already built (gdb) and instead of reinventing the wheel (the symbolic debugger code), they augmented it with a new set of functionality. Furthermore, ddd can support several stand-alone debuggers, making it very versatile. Indeed, it can support any language its host debugger can support. In many ways, ddd exemplifies what an integrated debugger should be. It has all of the tools you need to debug just about any program written in a host of languages.

One of the features I find most appealing about the ddd debugger is the ability to save a debugging session and recall it later. This gives you the advantage of not having to re-create a scenario to demonstrate or repeat a defect. I recommend that, to use it most effectively, you debug your program up to the point of defect discovery (say in the start of the function in question), set all of your watches and breakpoints, and then save the session. This will allow you to restart the debugging session again later should you need to retrace your steps. While not as efficient as a bidirectional debugger, saving a debugging session saves you a lot of time.

You can use the ddd debugger to examine core dumps. This allows you to examine the data in the core dump to determine the state of the program and the last few operations prior to the crash. That's really handy if the defect that caused the crash also causes the debugger to crash.[3] There is also support for remote debugging and examining memory directly. This allows you to debug a system running on another computer (typically a server) and manipulate the debugger on your development workstation. For more information about the ddd debugger, see the excellent documentation available at www.gnu.org/software/ddd/ddd.html#Doc.

Debugging MySQL using ddd can be accomplished using the following steps:

1. Stop any running MySQL servers. Use the command `mysqladmin -uroot -p shutdown` and enter your root password.

2. Change to the directory that contains your source code. If you are debugging the server (mysqld), then you want to change to the `sql` directory.

3. Launch the ddd debugger using the command `ddd mysqld-debug`.

4. Open the source code file you want to debug. In the following example I use `sql_show.cc`.

5. Set any breakpoints you want the code to stop at. In the following example I set a breakpoint at line 207 in the `show_authors()` function.

6. Use the Program ➤ Run menu to run the server, specifying the server is to run as the root user by supplying the parameters `-u root` in the dialog box.

7. Launch your MySQL client. In the following example, I use the normal MySQL command-line client.

8. Issue your commands in the client. The debugger will temporarily halt execution and stop on any breakpoints defined. From here, you can begin your debugging.

9. When you have finished debugging, exit the client and shut down the server using the command `mysqladmin -uroot -p shutdown` and enter your root password.

---

3. This is a most annoying situation that can be tricky to overcome. In these situations, I usually resort to inline debugging statements and core dumps for debugging.

■**Tip** You might need to extend the timeout duration for your test MySQL client. Debugging can take some time if you are stepping through a series of breakpoints or you are examining a lot of variables. The system is essentially in a zombie state while you are debugging. This may cause the server and the client to cease communication. Some clients are designed to terminate if they cannot communicate with the server after a period of time. If you are using the MySQL command-line client you will need to extend the timeout. You can do this by specifying the value on the command line using --connection-timeout=600. This gives you about 10 minutes to work with the debugger before the client drops the connection.

Listing 5-14 shows how you can use the ddd debugger to debug the MySQL server. I chose the same function from earlier, the show_authors() function in the sql_show.cc source file. In this scenario, I was interested in seeing how the server handled sending information to the client. You may recall from Chapter 3 that I mentioned having an example that showed the process of returning data to the client.

Listing 5-14. *The show_authors Function with Highlights*

```
/**************************************************************************
** List all Authors.
** If you can update it, you get to be in it :)
**************************************************************************/

bool mysqld_show_authors(THD *thd)
{
  List<Item> field_list;
  Protocol *protocol= thd->protocol;
  DBUG_ENTER("mysqld_show_authors");

  field_list.push_back(new Item_empty_string("Name",40));
  field_list.push_back(new Item_empty_string("Location",40));
  field_list.push_back(new Item_empty_string("Comment",80));

  if (protocol->send_fields(&field_list,
                            Protocol::SEND_NUM_ROWS | Protocol::SEND_EOF))
    DBUG_RETURN(TRUE);

  show_table_authors_st *authors;
  for (authors= show_table_authors; authors->name; authors++)
  {
    protocol->prepare_for_resend();
    protocol->store(authors->name, system_charset_info);
    protocol->store(authors->location, system_charset_info);
    protocol->store(authors->comment, system_charset_info);
```

```
    if (protocol->write())
      DBUG_RETURN(TRUE);
  }
  send_eof(thd);
  DBUG_RETURN(FALSE);
}
```

The statements in bold are the methods used to send data back to the client. The show_authors() function is perfect for demonstrating the process because it is the simplest of implementations (no complex operations—just sending data). The first highlighted statement shows the declaration of a pointer to the existing threads protocol class. The protocol class encapsulates all of the lower-level communication methods (such as networking and socket control). The next set of statements builds a field list. You always send a field list to the client first. Once the field list is built, you can send it to the client with the protocol->send_fields() method. In the loop, the code is looping through a list of authors defined in a linked list of show_table_authors_st. Inside the loop are the three principal methods used to send the data to the client. The first is protocol->prepare_for_resend(), which clears the appropriate buffers and variables for sending data. The next is protocol->store(), which places information in the send buffer. You should send each field as a separate call to this method. The protocol->write() method issues the appropriate action to send the data to the client. Finally, the send_eof() method instructs the communication mechanism to send the end-of-file marker to mark the end of the data. At this point, the client displays the data.

Let's see how this function works using the ddd debugger. I have built my server using the debug switches by issuing the following commands:

```
./configure --with-debug
make
make install
```

These commands will cause the system to be compiled with the debugging information so that I can use the debugger. Once I confirm no other servers are running, I launch the ddd debugger, load my source file (sql_show.cc), set a breakpoint in the show_authors() function at line 207, and then run the program. At that point, I launch my MySQL client program, setting the connection timeout to 10 minutes, and issue the SHOW AUTHORS command. Refer back to Listing 5-12 to see the server startup sequence; Listing 5-15 shows the client startup sequence.

Listing 5-15. *Starting the MySQL Client for Use with the ddd Debugger*

```
Chuck@linux:~> mysql -u root -p --connection-timeout=600
Enter password:
```

```
Welcome to the MySQL monitor.  Commands end with ; or \g.
Your MySQL connection id is 1 to server version: 5.1.9-beta-debug

Type 'help;' or '\h' for help. Type '\c' to clear the buffer.

mysql> show authors;
```

When execution reaches the breakpoint in the debugger, the server will stop and the ddd debugger will display the code with an arrow pointing to the breakpoint. You'll also notice that the client has stopped. If you take too long debugging, the client may time out. This is why I used the connection timeout override.

Once the debugger has halted execution, you can begin to explore the code and examine the values of any variable, the stack, or memory. I have set the debugger to examine the authors structure to see the data as it is being written to the client. Figure 5-5 depicts the ddd debugger with the authors structure displayed in the data window.

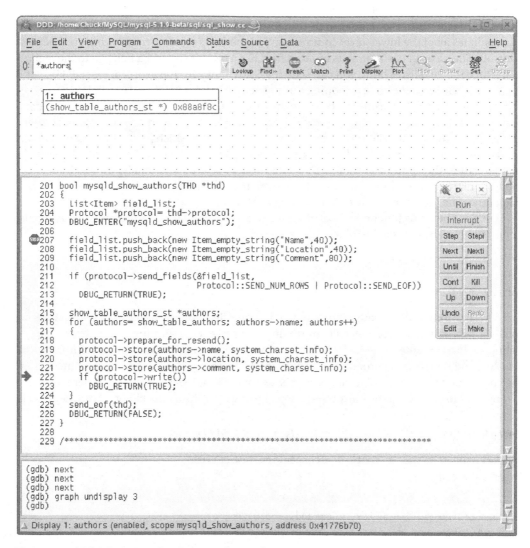

Figure 5-5. *ddd debugging the show_authors() function*

I can also expand the authors structure and see the current contents. Figure 5-6 shows the contents of the authors structure displayed in the data window.

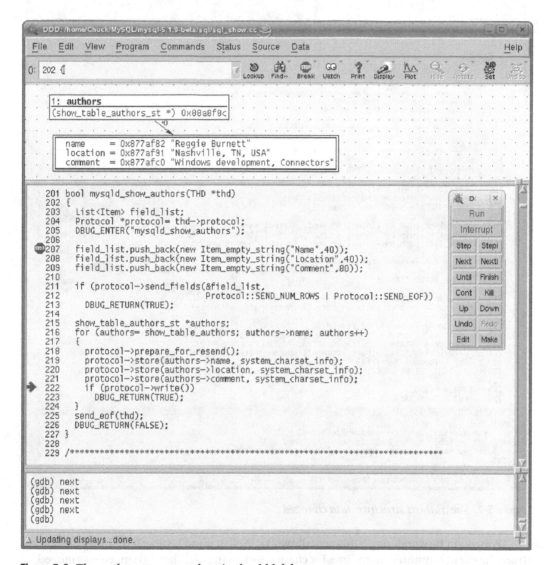

Figure 5-6. *The authors structure data in the ddd debugger*

Notice that the values and the addresses are displayed in the data window. The ddd debugger also allows you to modify the contents of memory. Let's say I am debugging this method and I want to change the values in the authors structure. I could do that simply by right-clicking on each of the items in the authors structure, choosing Set Value from the right-click menu, and then changing the value. Figure 5-7 shows that I've changed the contents of the authors structure.

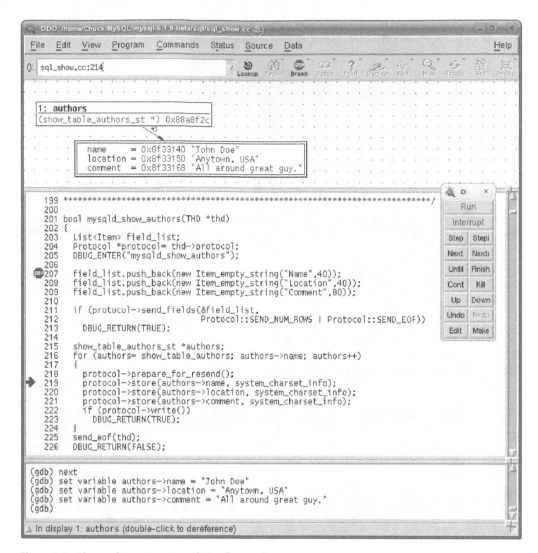

Figure 5-7. *The authors structure data changed*

You might be wondering if this actually works. Well, it does! Listing 5-16 shows the output from the client (I omitted many lines for clarity). Notice that the data I changed was indeed sent to the client.

Listing 5-16. *Resulting Output from Data Modifications*

```
+----------------+------------------+-----------------------------------------+
| Name           | Location         |Comment                                  |
+----------------+------------------+-----------------------------------------+
| John Doe       | Anytown, USA     | All around nice guy.                    |
...
+----------------+------------------+-----------------------------------------+
74 rows in set (48.35 sec)

mysql>
```

Once I've finished my debugging session, I issue the command to shut down the server and then exit ddd:

```
mysqladmin -uroot -p shutdown
```

As you can see from this simple example, debugging with ddd can be a useful experience and allows you to see the code as it executes. The power of being able to see the data as it is associated with the current execution is an effective means of discovering and correcting defects. I encourage you to try the example and play around with ddd until you are comfortable using it.

Debugging in Windows

The main method of debugging in Windows is using Microsoft Visual Studio .NET. Some developers have had success using other tools, such as external debuggers, but most will use the debugger that is integrated with Visual Studio .NET. Using an integrated debugger is convenient because you can compile and debug from the same interface.

■Note Older versions of the Windows source code for the MySQL system included project and solution files for Microsoft Visual Studio 6 and Visual Studio .NET 2003, respectively. You can convert these project and solution files to Visual Studio .NET 2005. The examples that follow use Visual Studio .NET 2005 Academic Version. The academic version is a full-featured release. It is branded as *academic* because it's sold to students and faculty at a reduced cost. A great number of vendors offer reduced pricing for academics.

I will use the same scenario as the ddd example earlier. While the steps are similar, you'll see some differences. Specifically, I begin my debugging session by launching Visual Studio and opening the mysql.sln solution file in the root of the source code directory. I make sure my session is set to compile the program in debug for the win32 platform. This will ensure that the proper debug information is compiled into the executable. Once Visual Studio is launched and the correct compilation mode is set, I can set my breakpoint (again, on line 207 in the show_authors() function). Figure 5-8 shows Visual Studio properly configured with the breakpoint set.

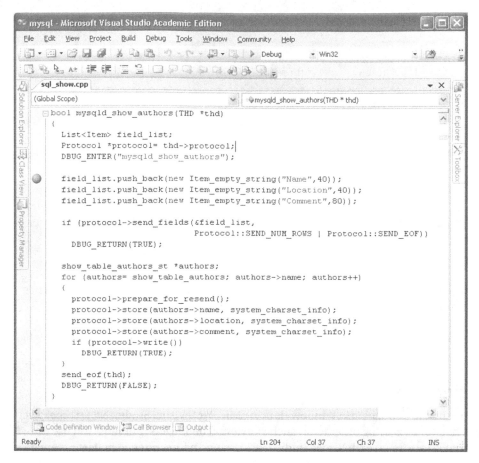

```cpp
bool mysqld_show_authors(THD *thd)
{
    List<Item> field_list;
    Protocol *protocol= thd->protocol;
    DBUG_ENTER("mysqld_show_authors");

    field_list.push_back(new Item_empty_string("Name",40));
    field_list.push_back(new Item_empty_string("Location",40));
    field_list.push_back(new Item_empty_string("Comment",80));

    if (protocol->send_fields(&field_list,
                              Protocol::SEND_NUM_ROWS | Protocol::SEND_EOF))
        DBUG_RETURN(TRUE);

    show_table_authors_st *authors;
    for (authors= show_table_authors; authors->name; authors++)
    {
        protocol->prepare_for_resend();
        protocol->store(authors->name, system_charset_info);
        protocol->store(authors->location, system_charset_info);
        protocol->store(authors->comment, system_charset_info);
        if (protocol->write())
            DBUG_RETURN(TRUE);
    }
    send_eof(thd);
    DBUG_RETURN(FALSE);
}
```

Figure 5-8. *Visual Studio debugger setup*

Caution You may encounter a large number of deprecation warnings when compiling the source code under Visual Studio .NET 2005. These warnings, number C4996, indicate that the older low-level methods have been replaced with newer implementations. Fortunately, the older methods are still available and the system will compile and run correctly. You can always turn off these warnings in the project settings.

To debug the server, I have to launch the server in debug mode. On Windows, you should use the switch to run the server stand-alone so that it doesn't run as a service. While this isn't strictly necessary, it allows you to see any messages from the server in the command window that would otherwise be suppressed. You can issue the following command to accomplish this:

```
mysqld-debug --debug --standalone
```

Once the server is running, I can attach to the process from Visual Studio using the Debug ➤ Attach to Process menu selection. Figure 5-9 shows the Attach to Process dialog box. I choose to run and attach to the `mysqld-debug` process so that I can also generate a trace file during the debugging session.

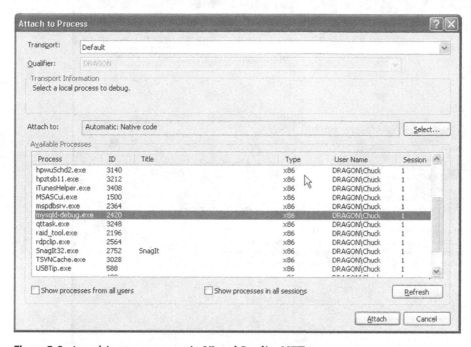

Figure 5-9. *Attaching to a process in Visual Studio .NET*

The next thing I need to do is launch the client. I once again use the `connect-timeout` parameter to set the timeout to a longer delay. The command I use to launch the client from a command window is

```
mysql -uroot -p --connect-timeout=600
```

With the client running, I can issue the `show authors;` command, which Visual Studio will intercept when the breakpoint is encountered. I can then use the step over (F10) and step into (F11) commands to step through the code. I stop the code inside the loop, which sends data, and inspect the authors structure. Figure 5-10 shows the state of the debugger after I have stepped into the loop.

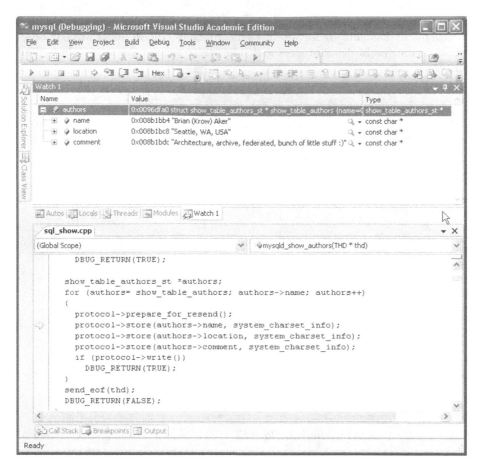

Figure 5-10. *Displaying variable values in Visual Studio .NET*

As with ddd, you can also change values of variables. However, doing so in Visual Studio is a bit more complicated. While there may be other options, the best way to change values in Visual Studio is to edit the values in the watch window. However, if the values in the watch window are pointers to memory locations, you have to change the memory location. Do this by opening the memory debug window and use the watch window to locate the memory location and edit it in place. Figure 5-11 shows the memory window open and the values edited.

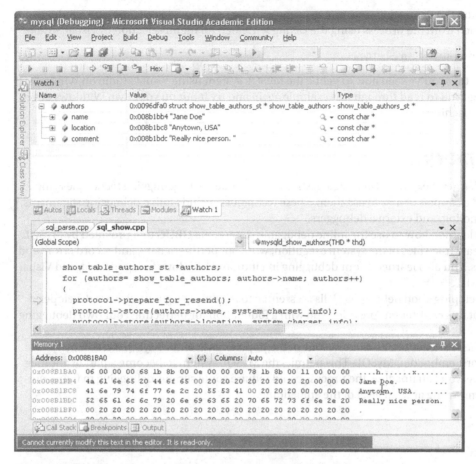

Figure 5-11. *Editing values in memory using Visual Studio .NET*

After the values in memory are edited, I can continue the execution and see the results in the client window. Listing 5-17 shows an excerpt of the sample output.

Listing 5-17. *Output of Debugging Session*

```
mysql> show authors;
```

```
+----------------+-----------------------+--------------------------------------+
| Name           | Location              | Comment                              |
+----------------+-----------------------+--------------------------------------+
| Jane Doe       | Anytown, USA          | Really nice person.                  |
...
+----------------+-----------------------+--------------------------------------+
74 rows in set (1 min 55.64 sec)

mysql>
```

To stop the debugging session, I issue the `shutdown` command in a command window and then detach from the process using the Debug ➤ Detach All menu selection in Visual Studio.

```
mysqladmin -uroot -p shutdown
```

Now that you've seen how to debug the MySQL system using Visual Studio on Windows, I encourage you to read through this example again and try it out on your own Windows development machine.

Summary

In this chapter, I explained debugging, showed you some basic debugging techniques, and provided examples of how to use them. These techniques include inline debugging statements, error handling, and external debuggers.

You learned how to use the inline debugging statements DBUG tool provided by MySQL AB to create trace files of the system execution, write out pertinent data, and record errors and warnings. You also learned about debugging in Linux and Windows using `gdb`, `ddd`, and Visual Studio .NET.

Developing good debugging skills is essential to becoming a good software developer. I hope that this chapter has provided you with a foundation for perfecting your own debugging skills.

In the next chapter, I'll examine one of the popular uses of the MySQL system by system integrators: embedded MySQL. This permits the MySQL system to become a part of another system. As you can imagine, the process could require some serious debugging to figure out what went wrong at what level of the embedding.

CHAPTER 6

■ ■ ■

Embedded MySQL

The MySQL server is well known for its lightweight and high-performance features, but did you know it can also be used as an embedded database for your enterprise applications? This chapter explains the concepts of embedded applications and how to use the MySQL C API for creating your own embedded MySQL applications. I'll introduce you to the techniques for compiling the embedded server and writing applications for both Linux and Windows.

Building Embedded Applications

Numerous applications have been built using lightweight database systems as internal data storage. If you use Microsoft Windows as your primary desktop operating system, the chances are you have seen or used at least one application that uses the Microsoft Access database engine. Even if the application doesn't advertise the use of Access, you can usually tell with just a cursory peek at the installation directory.

Some embedded applications use existing database systems on the host computer (like Access) while others use dedicated installations of larger database systems. Less obvious are those applications that include database systems compiled into the software itself.

What Is an Embedded System?

An *embedded system* is a system that is contained within another system. Simply put, the embedded system is a slave to the host system. The purpose of the embedded system is to provide some functionality that the host system requires. This could be communication mechanisms, data storage and retrieval, or even graphical user displays.

Embedded systems have traditionally been thought of as dedicated hardware or electronics. For example, an automated teller machine (ATM) is an embedded system that contains dedicated hardware. Today, embedded systems include not only dedicated hardware but also dedicated software systems. Unlike embedded hardware that is difficult or impossible to modify, embedded software is often modified to work in the specific environment. Embedded hardware and software share the quality of being self-contained and providing some service to the host system.

Embedded software systems are not typically the same applications as you see and use on a daily basis. Some, like those that use the embedded MySQL library, are adaptations of existing functionality rebuilt in order to work more efficiently inside another software system. However, unlike its stand-alone server version, the embedded MySQL server is designed to operate at a programmatic level. That is, the calls to the server are done via a programming language and not as ad hoc queries. Methods are exposed in the embedded server to take ad hoc queries as parameters and to initiate the server to execute them.

This means that the embedded MySQL server can only be accessed via another application. However, as you will see in the next few sections, embedded software can exist in a number of applications ranging in their level of integration from a closed programmatic-only access to a fully functional system that is "hidden" by the host application. Let's first look at the most common types of embedded systems.

Types of Embedded Systems

There are many types of embedded systems. They can be difficult to classify because of the unique nature of their use. However, embedded systems generally fall into one (or more) of these categories:

Real-time: A system that is used in installations that require a response and action within a given threshold on the part of the host system. The feature most common to this set of systems is timing. The execution time of every command process must be minimized to achieve the goals of the system. Often these systems are required to perform within events that occur externally rather than any internal processing speed. An example of a real-time system would be a router or a telecommunications switch.

Reactive: A system that responds solely to external events. These events tend to be recurring and cyclic in nature, but may also be in the form of user input (interactive systems are reactive systems). Reactive systems are designed to always be available for operation. Timing is usually secondary and limited only by the frequency of the cyclic operations. An example of a reactive system would be a safety monitoring system designed to page or alert service personnel when certain events or thresholds occur.

Process control: A system designed to control other systems. These systems tend to be those designed to monitor and control hardware devices such as robots and processing machinery. These systems are typically programmed to repeat a series of actions and generally do not vary from their intended programming or respond to external events or the threshold of status variables or conditions. An example of a process control system is the robot used on an automotive assembly line that assembles a specific component of the automobile.

Critical: A system that is used in installations that have a high cost factor such as safety, medical, or aviation. These systems are designed so that they cannot fail (or should never fail). Often these systems include variants of the embedded systems described earlier. An example of a critical system would include medical systems such as a respirator or artificial circulatory system.

Embedded Database Systems

An *embedded database system* is a system designed to provide data to a host application or environment. This data is usually requested in-process and therefore the database must respond to the request and return any information without delay. Embedded database systems are considered vital to the host application and the system as a whole. Thus, embedded database systems must also meet the timing requirements of the user. These requirements mean embedded database systems are generally classified as reactive systems.

All but the most trivial applications that individuals and businesses use produce, consume, and store data. Many applications have data that is well structured and has intrinsic value to the customer. Indeed, in many cases the data is persisted automatically and the customer expects the data to be available whenever she needs it. Such applications have as a subsystem either access methods or connectivity to external file or data-handling systems such as database servers.

Embedded systems that use files to access the data are faced with a number of problems, not the least of which is whether the data is accessible outside of the host application. In this case, the access restrictions may have to be created from scratch or added as yet another layer in the system. File systems often have very good performance and offer faster access times but are not as flexible as database systems. Database systems offer more flexibility in the form of the data being stored (as tables versus structured files) but usually incur slower access speeds.

While the reasons for protecting the data may be many and varied, the fundamental requirement is to store and retrieve the data in the most efficient manner possible without exposing the data to others. Many times this is simply a need for a database system. For example, an application like Adobe Bridge manages a lot of data about the files, projects, photos, and so forth that are used in the Adobe Production suite of tools. These files need to be organized in a way to make them easy to search for and retrieve. Adobe uses an embedded database (MySQL) to manage the metadata about the files stored by Adobe Bridge. In this case, the application uses the database system to handle the more difficult job of storing, searching, and retrieving the metadata about the objects it manages.

Since the data must be protected, the options to use an external database system become limiting because it is not always easy or possible to fully protect (or hide) the data. An embedded database system allows applications to use the full power of a database system while hiding the mechanisms and data from external sources.

Embedding MySQL

MySQL AB recognized early in the development of MySQL that many of its customers are systems integrators with a need for a robust, efficient, and programmatically accessible database system. They responded with not just an embedded library, but also a fully functional client library. The client library allows you to create your own MySQL clients. For example, you could create your own version of the MySQL command-line client. The client library is named libmysql. If you would like to see how a typical MySQL client uses this library, check out the mysql project source files.

The MySQL embedded library is named libmysqld after the name of the server executable. You may see the library referred to as the embedded server or simply the C API. This chapter is dedicated to the embedded library (libmysqld); however, much of the access and connectivity is similar between the client and embedded server libraries.

The embedded library provides numerous functions for accessing the database system via an application programming interface (API). The API provides a number of features that permit systems to take advantage of the MySQL server (programmatically). These features include the following:

- Connecting to and establishing a server instance

- Disconnecting from the server

- Shutting down the server using a controlled (safe) mechanism

- Manipulating server startup options

- Handling errors

- Generating DBUG trace files

- Issuing queries and retrieving the results

- Managing data

- Accessing the (near) full feature set of the MySQL server

This last point is one of the most significant differences between the stand-alone server and the embedded server. The embedded server does not use the full authentication mechanism and is disabled by default. This is one of the reasons an embedded MySQL system could be challenging to secure (see the later section "Security Concerns" for more details). However, you can turn on the authentication using the configuration option --with-embedded-privilege-control and recompile the embedded server. Other than that, the server behaves nearly identically to the stand-alone server with respect to features and capabilities.

What is really cool is that since the embedded library uses the same access methods as the stand-alone server, all of the databases and tables you create using the stand-alone server can be used with the embedded server. This allows you to create the tables and test them using the stand-alone server, then move them to the embedded system later. Although it is possible to have both access the same data directory, it is strictly discouraged and can result in loss of data and unpredictable behavior (you should never "share" data directories among MySQL server instances).

Does this mean you can have a stand-alone server executing on the same machine as an embedded server? Not only yes, but how many embedded servers would you like? As long as the embedded server instances aren't using the same data directory, you can have several running at the same time. It should be noted that the data each manages is separate from the data the others manage—no data is shared. I tried this out on my own system and it works. I've a 5.0.22 (Generally Available) GA embedded application running right alongside my 5.1.9-beta stand-alone server. I didn't have to stop or even interrupt the stand-alone to interact with the embedded server. How cool is that?

Note MySQL AB acknowledged at the 2006 MySQL Users' Conference that the embedded server included in version 5.1 was not working properly. However, the 5.0 source code has working embedded server code. All of the examples in this chapter are based on the 5.0.22 GA release of the server source code. I suspect by the time you read this, MySQL AB will have fixed the problems with 5.1. The examples in this chapter should be compatible with future releases of the 5.1 source code.

Methods of Embedding MySQL

There are many types of embedded applications. Embedded database applications typically fall into one of three categories. They are either partially hidden behind another interface (server embedding), part of a dedicated set of hardware and software isolated from the network (platform embedding), or a system that wraps or contains the database server (deep embedding). The following sections describe each of these types with respect to embedding the MySQL system.

Server Embedding

Server embedding is a system that is built with a stand-alone installation of the MySQL server. Instead of making MySQL available to anyone on the system or network, the server-level embedded system hides the MySQL server by turning off external (network) access. Thus, this form of an embedded MySQL system is simply a stand-alone server that has had its network access (TCP/IP) turned off.

However, this type of embedded MySQL system has the advantage that the server can be maintained using locally installed (and properly configured) client applications. So rather than having to load data using external applications, the system integrators, administrators, and developers can use the normal set of administration and development tools to maintain the embedded MySQL server.

One example of a server-level embedded MySQL system is the LeapTrack software produced by LeapFrog (www.leapfrogschoolhouse.com/do/findsolution?detailPage=overview&name=ReadingPro). MySQL reports that LeapFrog chose MySQL for its cross-platform support, allowing them to offer their product on a variety of platforms without changing the core database capabilities. Until then, LeapFrog had been using different proprietary database solutions for their various platforms.

Platform Embedding

Platform embedding is a bit more restrictive than the server-level embedding. This type of embedded system also uses a stand-alone installation of the MySQL system, but in this case the MySQL system is locked down. The only way to access the server is through the client interface. Applications typically communicate directly with the server using an API provided by the client as a gateway to the MySQL server.

The embedded system is responsible for providing mechanisms to perform maintenance on the database system. Fortunately, many of the dedicated offline administration tools like those for repairing InnoDB tables are still available and will work correctly. Only the client-level access to the server is disabled (except through the API).

One example of a platform-level embedded MySQL system is the NetIntercept solution from Sandstorm (www.sandstorm.net/products/netintercept). The NetIntercept product is designed as a stand-alone network system residing on typical rack-mounted servers and designed to have high-speed network access. The NetIntercept system is delivered to the customer as a single 2U or 4U computer system that can be plugged into the network and used as a component. Using MySQL as an embedded platform allows Sandstorm to take advantage of the MySQL system without having to burden their customers with a separate MySQL system. Instead, Sandstorm encapsulates (or hides) the MySQL database system within their own system. End users may never know that MySQL is a subcomponent of the NetIntercept product.

■**Note** The U in 2U refers to the number of vertical slots a piece of equipment needs for installation in a 19-inch rack. Thus, a 2U needs two spaces and a 4U needs four.

Deep Embedding (libmysqld)

Deep embedding is even more restrictive than platform embedding. This type of embedded system uses the MySQL system as an integral component. That means that not only is the MySQL system inaccessible from the network, but it is also inaccessible from the normal set of client applications. Rather, the system is built using the special embedded library provided by MySQL AB called `libmysqld`. Most embedded MySQL systems will fall into this category.

Since this type of embedded system still uses a MySQL mechanism for data access, it provides the same set of database functionality with only a few limitations (which I'll discuss in a moment). Developers gain the ability to use the deeply embedded MySQL system on a wide variety of platforms through a broad spectrum of development languages (as I explained earlier). Furthermore, it provides developers with a code-level solution that few if any relational database systems provide.

The biggest advantage of using a deeply embedded MySQL system is that it provides an almost completely isolated MySQL system that serves the purpose of the embedded application alone.

One example of a deeply embedded MySQL application is Adobe Bridge by Adobe (`www.adobe.com/creativesuite/bridge.html`). Adobe Bridge is part of the larger Adobe Creative Suite and is used for managing aspects of the data supported by the Creative Suite all while the end user is blissfully unaware they are running a dedicated MySQL system.[1] Most deeply embedded systems are desktop applications that users install on their local computers.

Resource Requirements

The requirements for running an embedded server depend on the type of embedding. If you are using server or platform embedding, the requirements are the same as a stand-alone installation. However, a deeply embedded MySQL system is different. A deeply embedded system should require approximately 2MB of memory to run in addition to the needs of the application. The compiled embedded server adds quite a bit more space to the executable memory size, but it isn't onerous or unmanageable.

Disk space is the most unpredictable resource to consider. This is true because it really depends on how much data the embedded system is using. Disk space and time are also concerns for high-throughput systems or systems that process a large number of changes to the data. Processing large numbers of changes to the data can often impact response time more than the space that is used. In these cases, the maintenance of the database may require special access to the server or special interfaces to allow administrator access to the data. This is an excellent case where having access to the database server in the server or platform embedding forms would be easier than that of one using deep embedding.

---

1. Well, until now it seems.

Security Concerns

Security is another area that depends on the type of embedding performed. If the system is built using server embedding, addressing security concerns can be quite challenging. This is true because the MySQL system is still accessible from the local server using the normal set of tools. It may be very difficult to lock this type of embedded system down completely.

Platform embedding is a lot easier because the embedded stand-alone MySQL system is only accessible through the embedded application. Unless the embedded application developers have a maladjusted ethical compass, they will have taken steps to ensure proper credentials are necessary to access the administration capabilities.

Deeply embedded systems present the most difficult case for protecting the data. The embedded MySQL system may not have any password set for it (they typically do not), because like platform embedding they require the user to use the interface provided to access the data. Unfortunately, it isn't that simple. In many cases, the data is placed in directories that are accessible by the user. Indeed, the data needs to be accessible to the user; otherwise, how would she be able to read the data?

That's the problem. The data files are unprotected and could be copied and accessed using another MySQL installation. This isn't limited to just the embedded server, but it is also a problem for the stand-alone server. Is that shocking? It could be if your organization has a limitation of tight control on the use of open source software. Imagine the look on your information assurance officer's face when he finds out. OK, so you might want to break it to him gently. Therefore, it may require additional security features included in the embedded application to protect the embedded MySQL system and its data appropriately.

Advantages of MySQL Embedding

The MySQL embedded API enables developers to use a full-featured MySQL server inside another application. The most important benefits are increased speed of data access (since the server is either part of or runs on the same hardware as the application), built-in database management tools, and a very flexible storage and retrieval mechanism. These benefits allow developers the opportunity to incorporate all of the benefits of using MySQL while hiding its implementation from the users. This means developers can increase the capabilities of their own products by leveraging the features of MySQL.

Limitations of MySQL Embedding

There are some limitations of using the embedded MySQL server. Fortunately, it is a short list. Most of the limitations make sense and are not normally an issue for system integrators. Table 6-1 lists the known limitations of using an embedded MySQL system. Included with each is a brief description.

Table 6-1. *Limitations of Using Embedded MySQL*

Limitation	Description
Security	Access control is turned off by default. The privilege system is inactive.
Replication	No replication or logging facilities.
External Access	No external network communications permitted (unless you build them).
Installation	Deeply embedded applications (such as `libmysqld`) may require additional libraries for deployment.
Data	The embedded server stores data just like the stand-alone server using a folder for each database and set of files for each table.
Version	The embedded server does not work with 5.1.9 beta but may work in later releases.
UDF	No user-defined functions are permitted.
Debug/Trace	No stack trace is generated with the core dump.
Connectivity	You cannot connect to an embedded server from network protocols. Note that you can provide this connectivity via your embedded application.
Resources	May be heavy if using a server or platform and supporting large amounts of data and/or many simultaneous connections.

The MySQL C API

A first glance at the MySQL C API documentation (a chapter entitled "APIs and Libraries" in the MySQL Reference Manual) may seem intimidating. Well, it is. The C API is designed to encapsulate all of the functionality of the stand-alone server. That's not a simple or easy task. Fortunately, MySQL AB provides ready access to the MySQL documentation online at http://dev.mysql.com/doc.

Note The documentation available online is usually the most up-to-date version available. If you have downloaded a copy for convenience, you may want to check the online documentation periodically. I've found answers to several stumbling blocks by reexamining the documentation online.

Ironically, perhaps the most intimidating aspect of the C API is the documentation itself. Simply stated, it is a bit terse and requires reading through several times before the concepts become clear. It is my goal to provide you a look into the C API in the form of a short tutorial and a couple of examples to help jumpstart your embedded application project.

Getting Started

The first recommendation I make to developers who want to learn how to build embedded applications is to read the documentation. Present text and chapter notwithstanding, it is always a good idea to read through the product documentation before you begin using an API even if you don't take to the information right away. I often find tidbits of information in the MySQL documentation that on the surface seem insignificant but later turn out to be the missing key between a successful compilation and a frustrating search for the source of the error.

I also recommend logging on to the MySQL AB web site and looking through the Forum (there is a dedicated embedded forum at http://forums.mysql.com) and Mailing List (http://lists.mysql.com) repositories. You don't have to read everything, but chances are some of your questions can be answered by reading the entries in these repositories. I also sometimes check out the MySQL blogs (www.planetmysql.org). Various authors have posted information about the embedded server and many other items of interest. There is so much interesting information out there that sometimes I find myself reading for over an hour at a time. Many MySQL experts consider this tactic the key to becoming a MySQL guru. Information is power.

The online documentation and the various lists and blogs are definitely the best source of the very latest about MySQL. The most important reading you should do is contained in the following sections. I'll present the major C API functions and walk through a simple example of an embedded application. Later, I'll demonstrate a more complex embedded application complete with an abstracted data access class and written in .NET.

The best way to learn how to create an embedded application is by coding one yourself. Feel free to open your favorite source code editor and follow along with me as I demonstrate a couple of examples. I'll first walk through each of the functions you need to call in the order they need to be called, then in a later section I'll show you how to build the library and write your first embedded server application.

Most Commonly Used Functions

A quick glance at the documentation shows the C API supports over 65 functions. Some of the functions have been deprecated, but MySQL AB is very good at pointing this out in the documentation (another good reason to read it). However, there are only a few functions that are used frequently.

Most of the functions in the library provide connection and server manipulation functions. Some are dedicated to gathering information about the server and the data while others are designed to provide calls to perform queries and other manipulations of the data. There are also functions for retrieving error information.

Table 6-2 lists the most commonly used functions. Included in the table are the names of the functions and a brief description of each. The functions are listed in roughly the order they would be called in a simple embedded server example.

■**Note** I encourage you to take some time after you have read through this chapter and understand the examples to read through the list of functions in the C API portion of the MySQL reference manual. You may find some interesting functions that meet your special database needs.

Table 6-2. *Most Commonly Used C API (libmysqld) Functions*

Function	Description
mysql_server_init()	Initializes the embedded server library.
mysql_init()	Starts the server.
mysql_options()	Allows you to change or set the server options.
mysql_debug()	Turns the debugging trace file on (DBUG).
mysql_real_connect()	Establishes connection to the embedded server.
mysql_query()	Issues a query statement (SQL). Statement is passed as a null terminated string.
mysql_store_results()	Retrieves the results from the last query.
mysql_fetch_row()	Returns a single row from the result set.
mysql_num_fields()	Returns the number of fields in the result set.
mysql_num_rows()	Returns the number of rows (records) in the result set.
mysql_error()	Returns a formatted error message (string) describing the last error.
mysql_errno()	Returns the error number of the last error.
mysql_free_result()	Frees the memory allocated to the result set. Note: don't forget to use this function often. It will not generate an error to call this on an empty result set.
mysql_close()	Closes the connection to the server.
mysql_server_end()	Finalizes the embedded server library and shuts down the server.

For a complete description of these functions including the return values and usage, see the MySQL reference manual.

Creating an Embedded Server

The embedded server is established as an instance during the initialization function calls. Most of the functions require a pointer to the instance of the server as a required parameter. When you create an embedded MySQL application, you need to create a pointer to the MYSQL object. You also need to create instances for a result set and a row from the result set (known as a record). Fortunately, the definition of the server and the major structures are defined in the MySQL header files. The two header files you need to use (and the only two for most applications) are

```
#include <my_global.h>
#include <mysql.h>
```

Creating pointer variables to the embedded server and the result set and record structure can be done by using the following statements:

```
MYSQL *mysql;                          // the embedded server class
MYSQL_RES *results;                    // stores results from queries
MYSQL_ROW record;                      // a single row in a result set
```

These statements allow you to have access to the embedded server (MYSQL), a result structure (MYSQL_RES), and a record (MYSQL_ROW). You can use global variables to define these pointers. Some of you may not like to use global variables and there's no reason you have to. The result set and record can be created and destroyed however you like. Just be sure to keep the MYSQL pointer variable the same instance throughout your application.

We're not done with the setup. We still need to establish some strings to use during connection. I've seen many different ways to accomplish this, but the most popular method is to create an array of character strings. At a minimum, you need to create character strings for the location of the my.cnf (my.ini in Windows) file and the location of the data. A typical set of initialization character strings is

```
static char *server_options[] = {"mysql_test",
  "--defaults-file=c:\\mysql_embedded\\my.ini",
  "--datadir=c:\\mysql_embedded\\data" };
```

The examples in this chapter depict the server options for a Windows compilation. If you use Linux, you will need to use the appropriate paths and change the my.ini to my.cnf. In this example, I use the label "mysql_test" (which is ignored by mysql_server_init()), the location of my.cnf (my.ini) file to the normal installation directory, and the data directory to the normal MySQL installation. If you want to establish both a stand-alone and an embedded server, you should use a different data location for each server. You would also want to use a different configuration file just to keep things tidy.

To help keep errors to a minimum, I also use an integer variable to identify the number of elements in my array of strings (I'll discuss this in a moment). This allows me to write bounds-checking code without having to remember how many elements are permitted. I can allow the number of elements to change at runtime, thereby allowing the bounds-checking code to adapt to changes as necessary.

```
int num_elements=sizeof(server_options) / sizeof(char *);
```

The last setup step is to create another array of character strings that identify the server groups that contain any additional server options in my configuration file (my.cnf). This defines the sections that will be read when the server is started.

```
static char *server_groups[] = {"libmysqld_server", "libmysqld_client" };
```

Initializing the Server

The embedded server must be initialized, or started, before you can connect to it. This usually involves two initialization calls followed by any number of calls to set additional options. The first initialization function you need to call to start an embedded server is mysql_server_init(). This function is defined as

```
int mysql_server_init(int argc, char **argv, char **groups)
```

The function is called only once before calling any other function. It takes as parameters argc and argv much the same as the normal arguments for a program (the same as the main function). In addition, the group labels from the configuration are passed to allow the server to read runtime server options. The return values are either a 0 for success or 1 for failure. This allows you to call the function inside a conditional statement and act if a failure occurs. Here's an example call of this function using the declarations from the startup section:

```
mysql_server_init(num_elements, server_options, server_groups);
```

Note In order to keep the example short and easily understood, I'll refrain from using error handling in the example source code. I'll revisit error handling in a later example.

The second initialization function you need to call is mysql_init(). This function allocates the MYSQL object for you in connecting to the server. This function is defined as

```
MYSQL *mysql_init(MYSQL *mysql)
```

Here is an example call of this function using the global variable defined earlier:

```
mysql = mysql_init(NULL);
```

Notice I use NULL to pass into the function. This is because it is the first call of the function requesting a new instance of the MYSQL object. In this case, a new object is allocated and initialized. If you called the function passing in an existing instance of the object, the function just initializes the object.

The function returns NULL if there was an error or the address of the object if successful. This means you can place this call in a conditional statement to process errors on failure or simply interrogate the MYSQL pointer variable to detect NULL.

Tip Almost all of the mysql_XXX functions return 0 for success and non-zero for failure. Only those that return pointers return non-zero for success and 0 (NULL) for failure.

Setting Options

The embedded server allows you to set additional connection options prior to connecting to the server. The function you use to set connection options is defined as

```
int mysql_options(MYSQL *mysql, enum mysql_option, const char *arg)
```

The first parameter is the instance of the embedded server object. The second parameter is an enumerated value from the possible options, and the last parameter is used to pass in a parameter value for the option selected using an optional character string. There is a long list of possible values for the option list. Some of the more commonly used options and their values are shown in Table 6-3. The complete set of options is listed in the MySQL reference manual.

Table 6-3. *Partial List of Connection Options*

Option	Value	Description
MYSQL_OPT_USE_REMOTE_CONNECTION	N/A	Forces the connection to use a remote server to connect to
MYSQL_OPT_USE_EMBEDDED_CONNECTION	N/A	Forces the connection to the embedded server
MYSQL_READ_DEFAULT_GROUP	Group	Instructs the server to read server configuration options from the specified group in the configuration file
MYSQL_SET_CLIENT_IP	IP address	Provides the IP address for embedded servers configured to use authentication

The following example calls to this function instruct the server to read configuration options from the [libmysqld_client] section of the configuration file and tell the server to use an embedded connection:

```
mysql_options(mysql, MYSQL_READ_DEFAULT_GROUP, "libmysqld_client");
mysql_options(mysql, MYSQL_OPT_USE_EMBEDDED_CONNECTION, NULL);
```

The return values are 0 for success and non-zero for any option that is invalid or has an invalid value.

Connecting to the Server

Now that the server is initialized and all of the options are set, you can connect to the server. The function you use to do this is called mysql_real_connect(). It has a large number of parameters that allow for fine-tuning of the connection. The function is declared as

```
MYSQL *mysql_real_connect(MYSQL *mysql, const char *host, const char *user, const
char *passwd, const char *db, unsigned int port, const char *unix_socket,
unsigned long client_flag)
```

This function must complete without errors. If it fails (in fact, if any of the previous functions fail), you cannot use the server and should either reattempt to connect to the server or gracefully abort the operation.

The parameters for the function include the MYSQL instance, a character string that defines the hostname (either an IP address or fully qualified name), a username, a password, the name of the initial database to use, the port number you want to use, the Unix socket number you want to use, and finally a flag to enable special client behavior. See the MySQL reference manual for more details on the client flags. Any parameter value specified as NULL will signal the function to use the default value for that parameter. Here is an example call to this function that connects using all defaults except the database:

```
mysql_real_connect(mysql, NULL, NULL, NULL, "information_schema", 0, NULL, 0);
```

The function returns a connection handle if successful and NULL if there is a failure. Most applications do not trap the connection handle. Rather, they check the return value for NULL. Notice that I do not use any of the authentication parameters. This is because the authentication is turned off by default. If I had compiled the embedded server with the authentication switch on, these parameters would have to be provided. Lastly, the fourth parameter is the name of the default database you want to connect to. This database must exist or you may encounter errors.

At this point, you should have all of the code necessary to set up variables to call the embedded server, initialize, set options, and connect to the embedded server. The following shows these operations as represented by the previous code samples:

```
#include "my_global.h"
#include "mysql.h"

MYSQL *mysql;                        //the embedded server class
MYSQL_RES *results;                  //stores results from queries
MYSQL_ROW record;                    //a single row in a result set

static char *server_options[] = {"mysql_test",
  "--defaults-file=c:\\mysql_embedded\\my.ini",
  "--datadir=c:\\mysql_embedded\\data" };
int num_elements=sizeof(server_options) / sizeof(char *);
static char *server_groups[] = {"libmyswld_server", "libmysqld_client" };

int main(void)
{
  mysql_server_init(num_elements, server_options, server_groups);
  mysql = mysql_init(NULL);
  mysql_options(mysql, MYSQL_READ_DEFAULT_GROUP, "libmysqld_client");
  mysql_options(mysql, MYSQL_OPT_USE_EMBEDDED_CONNECTION, NULL);
  mysql_real_connect(mysql, NULL, NULL, NULL, "information_schema",
    0, NULL, 0);

...

  return 0;
}
```

Running Queries

At last, we get to the good stuff—the meat of what makes a database system a database system: the processing of ad hoc queries. The function that permits you to issue a query is the mysql_query() function. The function is declared as

```
int mysql_query(MYSQL *mysql, const char *query)
```

The parameters for the function are the MYSQL object instance and a character string containing the SQL statement (null terminated). The SQL statement can be any valid query, including data manipulation statements (SELECT, INSERT, UPDATE, DELETE, DROP, etc.). If the query produces results, the results can be bound to a pointer variable for access by using the methods mysql_store_result() and mysql_fetch_row(). If no results are returned, the result set will be NULL.

An example call to this function to retrieve the list of databases on the server is shown here:

```
mysql_query(mysql, "SHOW DATABASES;");
```

The return value for this function is 0 if successful and non-zero if there is a failure.

Retrieving Results

Once you have issued a query, the next steps are to fetch the result set and store a reference to it in the result pointers' variable. You can then fetch the next row (record) and store it in the record structure (which happens to be a named array). The functions to accomplish this process are mysql_store_result() and mysql_fetch_row(), which are defined as

```
MYSQL_RES *mysql_store_result(MYSQL *mysql)
MYSQL_ROW mysql_fetch_row(MYSQL_RES *result)
```

The mysql_store_result() function accepts the MYSQL object as its parameter and returns an instance of the result set for the most recently run query. The function returns NULL if either an error has occurred or the last query did not return any results. You have to take care at this point to check for errors by calling the mysql_errno() function. If there was an error, you will have to call the error functions and compare the result to the list of known errors. The known error values generated from this function are CR_OUT_OF_MEMORY (no memory available to store the results), CR_SERVER_GONE_ERROR or CR_SERVER_LOST (the connection was lost to the server), and CR_UNKNOWN_ERR (a catchall error indicating the server is in an unpredictable state).

Note There are a number of possible conditions for using the mysql_store_results() function. The most common uses are described here. To explore the function usage in more detail or if you have problems diagnosing a problem with using the function, see the MySQL reference manual for more details.

The mysql_fetch_row() function accepts the result set as the only parameter. The function returns NULL if there are no more rows in the result set. This is handy because it allows you to use this feature in your loops or iterators. If this function fails, the return value of NULL is still set. It is up to you to check the mysql_errno() function to see if any of the defined errors have occurred. These errors include CR_SERVER_LOST, which indicates the connection has failed, and CR_UNKOWN_ERROR, which is a ubiquitous "something is wrong" error indicator.

Examples of these calls used together to query a table and print the results to the console are shown here:

```
mysql_query(mysql, "SELECT ItemNum, Description FROM tblTest");
results = mysql_store_result(mysql);
while(record=mysql_fetch_row(results))
{
  printf("%s\t%s\n", record[0], record[1]);
}
```

Notice that after the query is run, I call the mysql_store_result() function to get the results; then I placed the mysql_fetch_row() function inside my loop evaluation. Since mysql_fetch_row() returns NULL when no more rows are available (at the end of the record set), the loop will terminate at that point. While there are rows, I access each of the columns in the row using the array subscripts (starting at 0).

This example demonstrates the basic structure for all queries made to the embedded server. You can wrap this process and include it inside a class or abstracted set of functions. I demonstrate this in the second example embedded application.

Cleanup

The data returned from the query and placed into the result set required the allocation of resources. Since we are good programmers, we strive to free up the memory no longer needed to avoid memory leaks.[2] MySQL AB provides the mysql_free_result() function to help free those resources. This function is defined as

```
void mysql_free_result(MYSQL_RES *result)
```

This function is call-safe, meaning that you can call it using a result set that has already been freed without producing an error. That's just in case you get happy and start flinging "free" code everywhere. Don't laugh—I've seen programs with more "free" than "new" calls. Most of the time this isn't a problem, but if the free calls are not used properly, having too many of them could result in freeing something you don't want freed. As with the new operation, you should use the free operation with deliberate purpose and caution.

Here is an example call to this function to free a result set:

```
mysql_free_result(results);
```

Disconnecting from and Finalizing the Server

When you are finished with the embedded server, you need to disconnect and shut it down. This can be accomplished by using the mysql_close() and mysql_server_end() functions. The close function closes the connection and the other finalizes the server and deallocates memory. These functions are defined as

```
void mysql_close(MYSQL *mysql);
void mysql_server_end();
```

---

2. It isn't actually leaking so much as it is no longer referenced but still allocated, making that portion of memory unusable.

Example calls for these functions are shown here. Note that these are the last function calls you need to make and are normally called when shutting down your application.

```
mysql_close(mysql);
mysql_server_end();
```

Putting It All Together

Now, let's see all of this code together. Listing 6-1 shows a completed embedded server that lists the databases accessible from the given data directory. I'll go through the process of building and running this example in a later section.

■**Note** The following example is written for Windows. A Linux example is discussed in a later section.

Listing 6-1. *An Example Embedded Server Application*

```
#include "my_global.h"
#include "mysql.h"

MYSQL *mysql;                          //the embedded server class
MYSQL_RES *results;                    //stores results from queries
MYSQL_ROW record;                      //a single row in a result set

static char *server_options[] = {"mysql_test",
  "--defaults-file=c:\\mysql_embedded\\my.ini",
  "--datadir=c:\\mysql_embedded\\data" };
int num_elements=sizeof(server_options) / sizeof(char *);
static char *server_groups[] = {"libmyswld_server", "libmysqld_client" };

int main(void)
{
  mysql_server_init(num_elements, server_options, server_groups);
  mysql = mysql_init(NULL);
  mysql_options(mysql, MYSQL_READ_DEFAULT_GROUP, "libmysqld_client");
  mysql_options(mysql, MYSQL_OPT_USE_EMBEDDED_CONNECTION, NULL);
  mysql_real_connect(mysql, NULL, NULL, NULL, "information_schema",
    0, NULL, 0);
  mysql_query(mysql, "SHOW DATABASES;");                    // issue query
  results = mysql_store_result(mysql);                      // get results
  printf("The following are the databases supported:\n");
  while(record=mysql_fetch_row(results))                    // fetch row
  {
    printf("%s\n", record[0]);                              // process row
  }
```

```
mysql_query(mysql, "CREATE DATABASE testdb1;");
mysql_query(mysql, "SHOW DATABASES;");                    // issue query
results = mysql_store_result(mysql);                       // get results
printf("The following are the databases supported:\n");
while(record=mysql_fetch_row(results))                     // fetch row
{
  printf("%s\n", record[0]);                               // process row
}
mysql_free_result(results);
mysql_query(mysql, "DROP DATABASE testdb1;");              // issue query
mysql_close(mysql);
mysql_server_end();
return 0;
}
```

Error Handling

You may be wondering what happened to all of the error handling that you read about in a previous chapter. Well, the facilities are there in the C API. MySQL AB has provided for error handling using two functions. The first, `msyql_errno()`, retrieves the error number from the most recent error. The second, `mysql_error()`, retrieves the associated error message for the most recent error. These functions are defined as

```
unsigned int mysql_errno(MYSQL *mysql)
const char *mysql_error(MYSQL *mysql)
```

The parameter passed for both functions is the `MYSQL` object. Since these methods are error handlers, they are not expected to fail. However, if they are called when no error has occurred, `mysql_errno()` returns 0 and `mysql_error()` returns an empty character string.

Here are some example calls to these functions:

```
if(somethinggoeshinkyhere)
{
  printf("There was an error! Error number : %d = $s\n",
    mysql_errno(&mysql), mysql_error(&mysql));
}
```

Whew! That's all there is to it. I hope that my explanations clear the fog from the reference manual. I wrote this section primarily because I feel there aren't any decent examples out there that help you learn how to use the embedded server—at least none that capture what is needed in a few short pages.

Building Embedded MySQL Applications

The previous sections walked you through the basic functions used in an embedded MySQL application. This section will show you how to actually build an embedded MySQL application. I'll begin by showing you how to compile the application and move on to discuss methods of constructing the embedded library calls. I'll also present two example applications for you to use to experiment with your own system.

I've also included a brief foray into modifying the core MySQL source code. Yes, I know that may be a bit scary but I'll show you all of the details in a step-by-step fashion. Fortunately, it is an easy modification requiring changing only two files.

I encourage you to read the source code that I've included. I know there is a lot of it but I've trimmed it down to what I think is a manageable hunk. I've learned a lot of interesting things about the MySQL source code simply from reading through it. It is my goal that you gain additional insight into building your own embedded MySQL applications by studying the source code for these examples.

Compiling the Library (libmysqld)

The first thing you need to do before you can work with the embedded library (libmysqld) is to compile it. Distributions of the MySQL binaries do not include a precompiled embedded library. The embedded library is included in most source code distributions and can be found in the /libmysqld directory off the root of the source tree. The library is usually built without debug information. You will want to have a debug-enabled version for your development.

Compiling libmysqld on Linux

To compile the library under Linux, you need to set the configuration using the configure script and then perform a normal make and make install step. The configuration parameters that you will need are --with-debug and --with-embedded-server. The following shows the complete process. You will want to run this from the root of your source code directory. The compilation process can take a while so feel free to start that now while you read ahead. You can expect the compilation to take anywhere from a few minutes to about an hour depending on the speed of your machine and whether you have built the system previously with debug information.

Note The following commands build the server and install it into the default location. These operations require root privileges.

```
./configure --with-debug --with-embedded-server
make
make install
```

Tip To get a complete listing of all of the available configuration options, enter ./configure --help.

Compiling libmysqld on Windows

To compile the library under Windows, launch Visual Studio and open the main solution file in the root source code directory (mysql.sln). Turning debug on is simply a matter of selecting the libmysqld project and setting the build configuration to Embedded_debug win32. You can compile the library in the usual manner by selecting Build ➤ Build libmysqld or by building the complete solution. Any dependent projects will be built as needed. The compilation process can take a while so feel free to start that now while you read ahead. You can expect the compilation to take anywhere from a few minutes to about an hour depending on the speed of your machine and whether you have built the system previously with debug information.

What About Debugging?

You may be wondering if debugging in the embedded library works the same as the stand-alone server. Well, it does! In fact, you can use the same debugging methods. Debugging the embedded server at runtime is a bit of a challenge, but since the server is supposed to be embedded, you are not likely to need to debug down to that level. However, you may need to create a trace file in order to help debug your application.

I explained several debugging techniques in the last chapter. One of the most powerful and simple to use is the DBUG package. While the embedded server has all of that plumbing hooked up and indeed follows the same debugging practice of marking all entries and exits of functions, the DBUG package is not exposed via the embedded library.

You could create your own instance of the DBUG package and use that to write your own trace file. You may opt to do this for large applications using the embedded server. Most applications are small enough where the added work isn't helpful. In this case, it would be really cool if the embedded library offered a debugging option.

The DBUG package can be turned on either via the configuration file or through a direct call to the embedded library. This assumes, of course, that your embedded library was compiled with debug enabled.

Turning on the trace file at runtime requires a call to the embedded library. The method is mysql_debug() and takes one character string parameter that specifies the debug options. The following example turns the trace file on at runtime, specifying the more popular options and directing the library to write the trace file to the root directory. This method should be called before you have connected to the server.

```
mysql_debug("debug=d:t:i:O,\\mysqld_embedded.trace");
```

■**Tip** Use a different filename for your embedded server trace. This will help distinguish the embedded server trace from any other stand-alone server you may have running.

You can also turn debugging on using the configuration file. Simply place the string from the previous example into the my.cnf (my.ini) file that your source code specifies at startup (more on that in a moment).

What if you want to use the DBUG package from your embedded application but don't want to include the DBUG package in your own code? Are you simply out of luck? The embedded library doesn't expose the DBUG methods, but it could! The following paragraphs explain the procedure to modify the embedded server to include a simple DBUG method. I'm using a simple example as I do not want to throw you into the deep end just yet.

The first thing you need to do is to make a backup of the original source code. If you downloaded a tarred or zipped file, then you're fine. If you do find yourself struggling with getting the server to compile after you've added some code, returning to the original copy can have profound effects on your stress level (and sanity). This is especially true if you've removed your changes and it still doesn't compile!

Adding a new method is really easy. Edit the mysql.h file in the /include directory and add the definition. I chose to create a method that exposes the DBUG_PRINT function. I named it simply mysql_dbug_print(). Listing 6-2 shows the function definition for this method. Note that the function accepts a single character pointer. I use this to pass in a string I've defined in my embedded application. This allows me to write a string to the trace file as sort of a marker for where my embedded application synchronizes with the trace from the embedded server.

Listing 6-2. *Modifications to mysql.h*

```
/* BEGIN CAB MODIFICATION */
/* Reason for Modification: */
/* Adds a method to permit embedded applications to call DBUG_PRINT */
void STDCALL mysql_dbug_print(const char *a);
/* END CAB MODIFICATION */
```

To create the function, edit the /libmysqld/libmysqld.c file (/libmysqld/libmysqld.cc in Windows) and add the function to the rest of the source code. The location doesn't matter, just as long as it is in the main body of the source code somewhere. I chose to locate it near the other exposed library functions (near line number 91). Listing 6-3 shows the code for this method. Notice that the code simply echoes the string to the DBUG_PRINT method. Notice I also add a string to the end of the string passed. This helps me locate all of the trace lines that came from my application regardless of what I pass in to be printed.

Listing 6-3. *Modifications to libmysqld.c*

```
/* BEGIN CAB MODIFICATION */
/* Reason for Modification: */
/* Adds a method to permit embedded applications to call DBUG_PRINT */
void STDCALL mysql_dbug_print(const char *a)
{
  DBUG_PRINT(a, (" -- Embedded application."));
}
/* END CAB MODIFICATION */
```

To add a method to the embedded library in Windows you will also have to modify the libmysqld.def file to include the new method. Listing 6-4 shows an abbreviated listing as an example. Here I've added the mysql_dbug_print() statement to the file. Note that the file is maintained in alphabetical order.

Listing 6-4. *Modifications to libmysqld.def*

```
LIBRARY    LIBMYSQLD
DESCRIPTION  'MySQL 5.0 Embedded Server Library'
VERSION    5.0
EXPORTS
  _dig_vec_upper
  _dig_vec_lower
...
mysql_dbug_print
  mysql_debug
  mysql_dump_debug_info
  mysql_eof
...
```

That's it! Now just recompile the embedded server and your new method can be used in your application. I've done this to my installation of the embedded server. The examples that follow use this method to write a string to the trace file. This helps me greatly in finding the synchronization points in the trace file with my source code.

Tip In the previous listings I use the same commenting strategy that I presented in Chapter 3. This will help you identify any differences with the source code whenever you need to migrate to a newer version.

What About the Data?

Before you launch into creating and running your first embedded MySQL application, you should consider the data that you want to use. If you plan to create an embedded application that provides an administration interface that allows you to create tables and populate them, then you're all set. However, if you have not planned such an interface or similar facilities, you will need to get the database configured using other tools.

Fortunately, as long as you use the simpler table types (like MyISAM), you can use a stand-alone server and your favorite utilities to create the database and tables and populate them. Once the data has been created, you can copy the directories from the data directory of the stand-alone server installation to another location. Remember, it is important that you separate the embedded server data locations from that of the stand-alone server. Take note of where you place the data as you will need that for your embedded application.

I use this technique with all of my examples and my own embedded applications. It gives me the ability to shape and populate the data I want to use first without having to worry about creating an administration interface. Most embedded MySQL applications are built this way.

Creating a Basic Embedded Server

The previous sections showed you all of the necessary functions needed to use the embedded library. I'll show you a simple example using all of the functions I've described. I've included both a Linux and Windows example. While they are nearly identical, there are some minor differences in the source code. The biggest difference is how the programs are compiled. The examples in this chapter assume you are using an embedded library that has been compiled with debug information.

The example program reads the list of databases in the data directory for the embedded server printing the list to the console, creates a new database called testdb1, reads the list of databases again printing the list to the console, and finally deletes the database testdb1. While not very complicated, all of the example function calls are exercised. I've also included the calls to turn the trace file on (DBUG) and to print information to the trace file using the new mysql_dbug_print() function in the embedded library.

Linux Example

The first file you need to create is the configuration file (my.cnf). You can use an existing config-uration file, but I recommend copying it to the location of your embedded server. For example, if you created a directory named /var/lib/mysql_embedded, you would place the configuration file there and copy all of your data directories (the database files and folders) to that directory as well. Those are the only files that need to be in that directory. The only exception is if you wanted to use a different language for your embedded server. In this case, I recommend copying the appropriate files from a stand-alone installation to your embedded server directory and referencing them from the configuration file. Listing 6-5 shows the configuration file for the example program.

Listing 6-5. *Sample my.cnf File for Linux*

```
[mysqld]
basedir=/var/lib/mysql_embedded
datadir=/var/lib/mysql_embedded
#slow query log#=
#tmpdir#=
#port=3306
#set-variable=key_buffer=16M

[libmysqld_client]
#debug=d:t:i:O,\\mysqld_embedded.trace
```

Notice that I've disabled most of the options (by using the # symbol at the start of the line). I usually do this so that I can easily and quickly turn them on should I need to. Debugging is turned off so that I can show you how to turn it on programmatically.

The next file you need to create is the source code for the application. If you have followed along with the tutorial on the C API from earlier, it should look very familiar. Listing 6-6 shows the complete source code for a simple embedded MySQL application.

Listing 6-6. *Embedded Example 1 (Linux: example1_linux.c)*

```c
#include <my_global.h>
#include <mysql.h>

MYSQL *mysql;                       //the embedded server class
MYSQL_RES *results;                 //stores results from queries
MYSQL_ROW record;                   //a single row in a result set

/*
  These variables set the location of the ini file and data stores.
*/
static char *server_options[] = {"mysql_test",
  "--defaults-file=/var/lib/mysql_embedded/my.cnf",
  "--datadir=/var/lib/mysql_embedded" };
int num_elements=sizeof(server_options) / sizeof(char *);
static char *server_groups[] = {"libmysqld_server", "libmysqld_client" };

int main(void)
{
  /*
    This section initializes the server and sets server options.
  */
  mysql_server_init(num_elements, server_options, server_groups);
  mysql = mysql_init(NULL);
  mysql_options(mysql, MYSQL_READ_DEFAULT_GROUP, "libmysqld_client");
  mysql_options(mysql, MYSQL_OPT_USE_EMBEDDED_CONNECTION, NULL);
  /*
    The following call turns debugging on programmatically.
    Comment out to turn off debugging.
  */
  //mysql_debug("d:t:i:O,\\mysqld_embedded.trace");
  /*
    Connect to embedded server.
  */
  mysql_real_connect(mysql, NULL, NULL, NULL, "information_schema",
    0, NULL, 0);
  /*
    This section executes the following commands and demonstrates
    how to retrieve results from a query.

    SHOW DATABASES;
    CREATE DATABASE testdb1;
    SHOW DATABASES;
    DROP DATABASE testdb1;
  */
```

```
mysql_dbug_print("Showing databases.");                    //record trace
mysql_query(mysql, "SHOW DATABASES;");                     //issue query
results = mysql_store_result(mysql);                       //get results
printf("The following are the databases supported:\n");
while(record=mysql_fetch_row(results))                     //fetch row
{
  printf("%s\n", record[0]);                               //process row
}
mysql_dbug_print("Creating the database testdb1.");        //record trace
mysql_query(mysql, "CREATE DATABASE testdb1;");
mysql_dbug_print("Showing databases.");
mysql_query(mysql, "SHOW DATABASES;");                     //issue query
results = mysql_store_result(mysql);                       //get results
printf("The following are the databases supported:\n");
while(record=mysql_fetch_row(results))                     //fetch row
{
  printf("%s\n", record[0]);                               //process row
}
mysql_free_result(results);
mysql_dbug_print("Dropping database testdb1.");            //record trace
mysql_query(mysql, "DROP DATABASE testdb1;");              //issue query
/*
  Now close the server connection and tell server we're done (shutdown).
*/
mysql_close(mysql);
mysql_server_end();

  return 0;
}
```

I've added comments (some would say overkill) to help you follow along in the code. The first thing I do is create my global variables and set up my initialization arrays. I then initialize the server with the array options, set a few more options, and connect to the server. The body of the example application reads data from the database and prints it out. The last portion of the example closes and finalizes the server.

Compiling the example requires that I use the mysql_config script to identify the location of the libraries. The script returns to the command line the actual path each of the options passed to it. You can also run the script from a command line and see all of the options and their values. A sample command to compile the example is shown here:

```
gcc example1_linux.c -g -o example1_linux
  '/usr/local/mysql/bin/mysql_config --include --libmysqld-libs'
```

This command should work for most Linux systems. However, there are some cases where this could be a problem. If your MySQL installation is at another location, you may need to alter the phrase with the mysql_config script. If you have multiple installations of MySQL on your system or you have installed the embedded library in another location, you may not be able to use the mysql_config script because it will return the wrong library paths. This is also true for cases where you have multiple versions of the MySQL source code installed. You certainly want to avoid the case of using the include files from one version of the server to compile an embedded library from another. You could also run into problems if you do not have the earlier glibc libraries.

To correct these problems, you should first run the mysql_config script from the command line and note the paths for the libraries. You should also locate the correct paths to the libraries and header files you want to use. An example of how I overcame these problems is shown here (I have all of these situations on my SUSE machine):

```
g++ example1_linux.c -g -o example1_linux -lz -I/usr/include/mysql
-L/usr/lib/mysql -lmysqld -lz -lpthread -lcrypt -lnsl -lm -lpthread -lc
-lnss_files -lnss_dns -lresolv -lc -lnss_files -lnss_dns -lresolv -lrt
```

Notice I used the newer g++ compiler instead of the normal gcc. This is because my system has the latest GNU libraries and does not have the older ones. I could, of course, have loaded the older libraries and fixed this problem but typing g++ is much easier. OK, so we programmers are lazy.

Listing 6-7 shows the sample output of running this example under a typical installation of MySQL. In this case, I copied all of the data from the stand-alone server directory to my embedded server directory.

Listing 6-7. *Sample Output*

```
linux:/home/Chuck/source/Embedded # ./example1_linux
The following are the databases supported:
information_schema
mysql
test
The following are the databases supported:
information_schema
mysql
test
testdb1
linux:/home/Chuck/source/Embedded #
```

Please take some time and explore this example application on your own machine. I recommend you experiment with the body of the application and run a few queries of your own to get a feel for how you might write your own embedded MySQL application. If you implemented the mysql_dbug_print() function in your embedded library, try it out with the example by either removing the comments on the mysql_debug() function call or by removing the comments for the debug option in the configuration file.

The next example will show you how to encapsulate the embedded library calls and demonstrate their use in a more realistic application.

Windows Example

The first file you need to create is the configuration file (my.ini). You can use an existing config-uration file, but I recommend copying it to the location of your embedded server. For example, if you created a directory named c:/mysql_embedded, you would place the configuration file there and copy all of your data directories to that directory as well. Those are the only files that need to be in that directory. The only exception is if you wanted to use a different language for your embedded server. In this case, I suggest copying the appropriate files from a stand-alone installation to your embedded server directory and referencing them from the configuration file. Listing 6-8 shows the configuration file for the example program. I comment out most of the options because I use the defaults, but I left the options in the file so that you can see the most commonly used options and where they are specified in the file.

Listing 6-8. *Sample my.ini File for Windows*

```
[mysqld]
basedir=C:/mysql_embedded
datadir=C:/mysql_embedded/data
language=C:/mysql_embedded/share/english
#slow query log#=
#tmpdir#=
#port=3306
#set-variable=key_buffer=16M

[libmysqld_client]
#debug=d:t:i:O,\\mysqld_embedded.trace
```

Creating the project file is a little trickier. To get the most out of using Visual Studio, I recommend opening the master solution file from the root of the source code directory and adding your new application as a new project to that solution. You do not have to store your source code in the same source tree, but you should store it in such a way as to know what version of the source code it applies to.

You can create the project using the project wizard. You should select the C++ ➤ Win32 Console project template and name the project. This creates a new folder under the root of the folder specified in the wizard with the same name as the project. You should create an empty project and add your own source files.

Creating a project file as a subproject of the solution gives you some really cool advan-tages. To take advantage of the automated build process (no make files—yippee!), you need to add the libmysqld project to your projects dependencies. You can open the project dependencies tool from the Project ➤ Project Dependencies menu. You should also set the build configuration to Active(Debug) by using the solution's Configuration drop-down box and setting the platform to Active(Win32) using the solution's Platform drop-down box on the standard toolbar.

You also need to set some switches in the project properties. Open the project properties dialog box by selecting Project ➤ Properties or by right-clicking on the project and choosing Properties. The first item you will want to check is the runtime library generation. Set this switch to Multi-threaded Debug DLL (/MDd) by expanding the C/C++ label in the tree and clicking on the Code Generation label in the tree and selecting it from the Runtime Library drop-down list. This option causes your application to use the debug multithread- and DLL-specific version of the runtime library. Figure 6-1 shows the project properties dialog box and the location of this option.

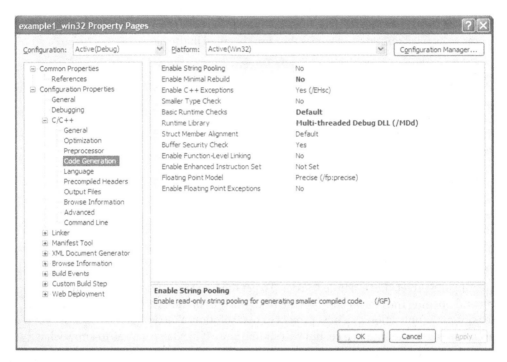

Figure 6-1. *Project properties dialog box, with the Code Generation page displayed*

The next property you need to change is to add the MySQL include directory to your project properties. The easiest way to do this is to expand the C/C++ label and click on the Command Line label. This will display the command-line parameters. To add a new parameter, type it in the Additional Options text box. In this case, you need to add something like /I ../include. If you located your project somewhere other than under the MySQL source tree, you may need to alter the parameter accordingly. Figure 6-2 shows the project properties dialog box and the location of this option.

You can also remove the precompiled header option if you do not want (or need) to use precompiled headers. This option is on the C/C++ Precompile Headers page in the project properties dialog box.

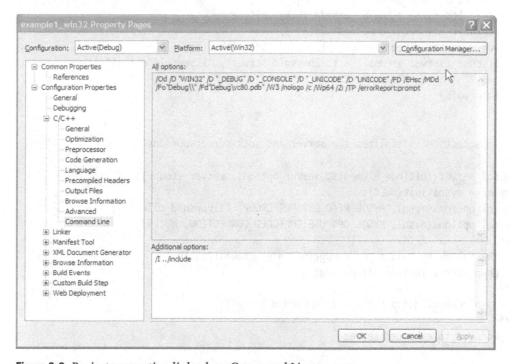

Figure 6-2. *Project properties dialog box: Command Line page*

Now that you have the project configured correctly, all you need to do is add your source file or paste in the example code if you chose to create the base project files when you created the project. Listing 6-9 shows the complete Windows version.

Listing 6-9. *Embedded Example 1 (Windows: example1_win32.cpp)*

```
#include "my_global.h"
#include "mysql.h"

MYSQL *mysql;                   //the embedded server class
MYSQL_RES *results;             //stores results from queries
MYSQL_ROW record;               //a single row in a result set
```

```
/*
  These variables set the location of the ini file and data stores.
*/
static char *server_options[] = {"mysql_test",
  "--defaults-file=c:\\mysql_embedded\\my.ini",
  "--datadir=c:\\mysql_embedded\\data" };
int num_elements=sizeof(server_options) / sizeof(char *);
static char *server_groups[] = {"libmysqld_server", "libmysqld_client" };

int main(void)
{
  /*
    This section initializes the server and sets server options.
  */
  mysql_server_init(num_elements, server_options, server_groups);
  mysql = mysql_init(NULL);
  mysql_options(mysql, MYSQL_READ_DEFAULT_GROUP, "libmysqld_client");
  mysql_options(mysql, MYSQL_OPT_USE_EMBEDDED_CONNECTION, NULL);
  /*
    The following call turns debugging on programmatically.
    Comment out to turn off debugging.
  */
  //mysql_debug("d:t:i:O,\\mysqld_embedded.trace");
  /*
    Connect to embedded server.
  */
  mysql_real_connect(mysql, NULL, NULL, NULL, "information_schema",
    0, NULL, 0);
  /*
    This section executes the following commands and demonstrates
    how to retrieve results from a query.

    SHOW DATABASES;
    CREATE DATABASE testdb1;
    SHOW DATABASES;
    DROP DATABASE testdb1;
  */
  mysql_dbug_print("Showing databases.");              //record trace
  mysql_query(mysql, "SHOW DATABASES;");               //issue query
  results = mysql_store_result(mysql);                 //get results
  printf("The following are the databases supported:\n");
  while(record=mysql_fetch_row(results))               //fetch row
  {
    printf("%s\n", record[0]);                         //process row
  }
  mysql_dbug_print("Creating the database testdb1.");  //record trace
  mysql_query(mysql, "CREATE DATABASE testdb1;");
```

```
mysql_dbug_print("Showing databases.");
mysql_query(mysql, "SHOW DATABASES;");                  //issue query
results = mysql_store_result(mysql);                    //get results
printf("The following are the databases supported:\n");
while(record=mysql_fetch_row(results))                  //fetch row
{
  printf("%s\n", record[0]);                            //process row
}
mysql_free_result(results);
mysql_dbug_print("Dropping database testdb1.");         //record trace
mysql_query(mysql, "DROP DATABASE testdb1;");           //issue query
/*
  Now close the server connection and tell server we're done (shutdown).
*/
mysql_close(mysql);
mysql_server_end();

  return 0;
}
```

I've added comments (some would say overkill) to help you follow along in the code. The first thing I do is create my global variables and set up my initialization arrays. I then initialize the server with the array options, set a few more options if necessary, and connect to the server. The body of the example application reads data from the database and prints it out. The last portion of the example closes and finalizes the server.

Compiling the example is really easy. Just select Build ➤ Build example1_win32. If you have already compiled the libmysqld project, all you should see is the compilation of the example. If for some reason the object files are out of date for libmysqld or any of its dependencies, Visual Studio will compile those as well.

Caution You may encounter some really strange errors found in the mysql_com.h or similar header files. The most likely cause of this may be an optimization strategy. Microsoft automatically includes the #define WIN32_LEAN_AND_MEAN statement in the stdafx.h file. If you have that turned on, it tells the compiler to ignore a host of includes and links that are not needed (normally). You will want to delete that line altogether (or comment it out). Your program should now compile without errors. If you opted to not use the stdafx files, you should not encounter this problem.

When the compilation is complete, you can either run the program from the debug menu commands or open a command window and run it from the command line. If this is your first time, you should see an error message like the following:

```
This application has failed to start because LIBMYSQLD.dll was not found.
Re-installing the application may fix this problem.
```

The reason for this error has nothing to do with the second sentence in the error message. It means the embedded library isn't in the search path. If you have worked with .NET or COM applications and never used C libraries, then you may have never encountered the error. Unlike .NET and COM, C libraries are not registered in a Global Assembly Cache (GAC) or registry. These libraries (DLLs) should be collocated with applications that call them or at least on an execution path. Most developers place a copy of the DLL in the execution directory.

To fix this problem, you'll need to copy the libmysqld.dll file from the lib_debug directory to the directory where the example1_win32.exe file resides (or add lib_debug to the execution path). Once you get past that hurdle, you should see an output like that shown in Listing 6-10.

Listing 6-10. *Example Output*

```
D:\source\C++\mysql-5.0.22\example1_win32\Debug>example1_win32
The following are the databases supported:
information_schema
cluster
mysql
test
The following are the databases supported:
information_schema
cluster
mysql
test
testdb1
```

Please take some time and explore this example application on your own machine. I recommend you experiment with the body of the application and run a few queries of your own to get a feel for how you might write your own embedded MySQL application. If you implemented the mysql_dbug_print() function in your embedded library, try it out with the example by either removing the comments on the mysql_debug() function call or by removing the comments for the debug option in the configuration file.

What About Error Handling?

Some of you may be wondering about error handling. Specifically, how can you detect problems with the embedded server and handle them gracefully? A number of the embedded library calls have error codes that you can interrogate and act on. The previous sections described the return values for the functions I'll be using. Although I didn't include much error handling in the first embedded MySQL examples, I will in the next example. Take note of how I capture the errors and handle sending the errors to the client.

Embedded Server Application

The previous examples showed you how to create a basic embedded MySQL application. While the examples showed how to connect and read data from a dedicated MySQL installation, they aren't good models for building your own embedded application because they lack enough coverage for all but the most trivial requirements. Oh, and they don't have any error handling! The example in this chapter, while fictional, is all about providing you with the tools you need to build a real embedded application.

This application, called the Book Vending Machine (BVM), is an embedded system designed to run on a dedicated Microsoft Windows–based PC with a touch screen. The system and its other input devices are housed in a specialized mechanical vending machine designed to dispense books. The idea behind the BVM is to allow publishers to offer their most popular titles in a semi-mobile package that the vendor can configure and replenish as needed. The BVM would allow publishers to install their vending machine in areas where space is at a premium. Examples include trade shows, airports, and shopping malls. These areas usually have high traffic consisting of customers interested in purchasing printed books. The BVM saves publishers money by reducing the need for a storefront and personnel to staff it.

Note I've often found myself wondering if this idea has ever been given consideration. I've read several articles predicting the continued rise of print-on-demand, but seldom have I seen anything written about how a book vending machine would work. I understand there are a few prototype installations by some publishers, but these trials have not generated much enthusiasm. I chose to use this example as a means to add some realism. I too read technical books and often find myself bored with unrealistic or trivial examples. Here is an example that I hope you agree is at least plausible.

The Interface

This application has a need for a dual interface; one for the normal vending machine activity and one to allow vendors to restock the vending machine adjusting the information as needed. The vending machine interface is designed to provide the customer with an array of buttons providing a thumbnail of books for specific slots in the vending machine. Since most modern vending machines use product buttons that are illuminated when the product is available and dimmed or turned off when the product is depleted, the BVM interface enables the button when the product in that slot is available and disables it when the product is depleted.

When the customer clicks a product button, the screen changes to a short, detailed display that describes the book and its price. If the customer wants to purchase the book, she can click Purchase and is prompted for payment. This application is written to simulate those activities. A real implementation would call the appropriate hardware control library to receive payment, validate the payment, and engage the mechanical part of the vending machine to disperse the product from the indicated slot. Figure 6-3 shows the main interface for the book vending machine. Figure 6-4 shows the effect of low quantity for some of the books.

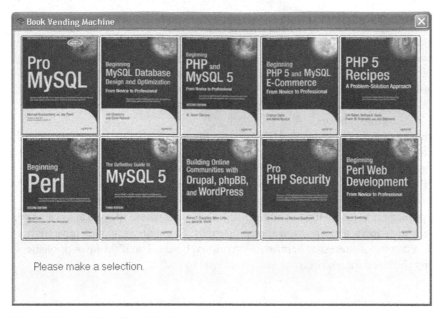

Figure 6-3. *Book Vending Machine customer interface*

Figure 6-4. *Resulting "Product Depleted" view of the customer interface*

Figure 6-5 shows a sample of the details for one of the books.

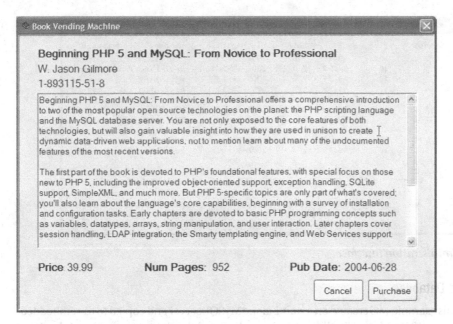

Figure 6-5. *Book details interface*

A vending machine wouldn't be very useful if there wasn't any way of replenishing the product. The BVM provides this via an administration interface. When the vendor needs to replenish the books or change the details to match a different set of books, the vendor opens the machine and closes the embedded application (this feature would have to be added to the example). The vendor would then restart the application providing the administrator switch on the command line like the one shown here:

```
C:\>Books BookVendingMachine -admin
```

The administration interface allows the vendor to enter an ad hoc query and execute it. Figure 6-6 shows the administration interface. The example shows a typical update operation to reset the quantity of the products. This interface allows the vendor to enter any query she needs to reset the data for the embedded application.

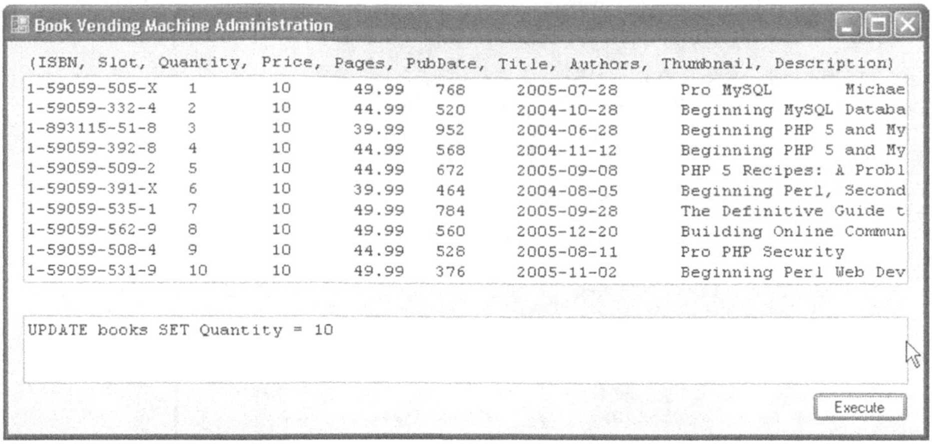

Figure 6-6. *Administration interface*

The Data and Database

The data for this example was created on a stand-alone MySQL server and copied to the embedded MySQL directory. When I created this application, I designed the data structures and the database to hold the data first. This is always a good idea.

Note Some developers may disagree, believing it is better to start with the user interface design and allow the data requirements to evolve. Neither practice is better than the other. The important point is the data must be a focus of your design.

Most of your projects will come with either requirements for the data or actual data in existing repositories. For new applications like this example, you should always design the database by designing the tables in such a way to represent the items and the relationships between them. This is usually a single step in a small project, but may be an iterative process where you use the initial tables and relationships as input to the design and planning of the user interfaces using UML drawings and modeling techniques. Changes to the database (the organization of the data) are often discovered during the later steps, which you then use as the starting point for going through the process again.

The data for this example consists of a short list of descriptive fields about the books in the machine. This includes the title, author, price, and description. I added the ISBN to use as a key for the table (since it is unique by definition and used by the publishing industry as a primary means of identifying the book). I also added some other fields that I would want to see before I decide to purchase a book. These include publication date and number of pages. I also needed to store a thumbnail image. (I chose an external method where I stored the path and filename to the file and read it from the file system. I could have used a binary large object (BLOB) to store the thumbnail, but this is easier—although admittedly error prone.) Lastly, I projected what I would need to run the user interface and decided to add a field to record the slot number where the book is located and dispensed and a field to measure the quantity on hand. I named the table books and placed it in a database named bvm. The CREATE SQL statement for the table is shown here. Listing 6-11 shows the layout of the table using the EXPLAIN command.

```
CREATE DATABASE BVM;
CREATE TABLE Books (ISBN varchar(15) NOT NULL,
Title varchar(125) NOT NULL, Authors varchar(100) NOT NULL,
Price float NOT NULL, Pages int NOT NULL, PubDate date NOT NULL,
Quantity int DEFAULT 0, Slot int NOT NULL, Thumbnail varchar(100) NOT NULL,
Description text NOT NULL);
```

Listing 6-11. *Table Structure*

```
mysql> explain Books;
```

Field	Type	Null	Key	Default	Extra
ISBN	varchar(15)	NO			
Title	varchar(125)	NO			
Authors	varchar(100)	NO			
Price	float	NO			
Pages	int(11)	NO			
PubDate	date	NO			
Quantity	int(11)	YES		0	
Slot	int(11)	NO			
Thumbnail	varchar(100)	NO			
Description	text	NO			

```
10 rows in set (0.08 sec)
```

To manage the thumbnail images, I chose to store the thumbnail filename in the thumbnail field and use a system-level option for the path. One way to do this is to create a command-line switch. Another is to place it in the MySQL configuration file and read it from there. You can also read it from the database. I chose to use a database table named settings that contains only two fields; FieldName, which stores the name of the option (e.g., "ImagePath"), and Value, which store its value (e.g., "c:\images\mypic.tif"). This method allows me to create any number of system options and control them externally. The CREATE SQL command for the settings table is shown here, followed by a sample INSERT command to set the ImagePath option for the example application:

```
CREATE TABLE settings (FieldName varchar(20), Value varchar(255));
INSERT INTO settings VALUES ("ImagePath", "c:\\mysql_embedded\\images\\");
```

Creating the Project

The best way to create the project is to use the wizard to create a new Windows project. I recommend opening the master solution file from the root of the source code directory and adding your new application as a new project to that solution. You don't have to store your source code in the same source tree, but you should store it in such a way as to know what version of the source code it applies to.

You can create the project using the project wizard. You should select the CLR Windows Forms Application project template and name the project. This creates a new folder under the root of the folder specified in the wizard with the same name as the project.

Creating a project file as a subproject of the solution gives you some really cool advantages. To take advantage of the automated build process (no make files—yippee!), you need to add the `libmysqld` project to your projects dependencies. You can open the project dependencies tool from the Project ➤ Project Dependencies menu. You should also set the build configuration to Active(Debug) by using the solution's Configuration drop-down box and set the platform to Active(Win32) using the solution's Platform drop-down box on the standard toolbar.

You also need to set some switches in the project properties. Open the project properties dialog box by selecting Project ➤ Properties or by right-clicking on the project and choosing Properties. The first item you will want to check is the runtime library generation. Set this switch to Multi-threaded Debug DLL (/MDd) by expanding the C/C++ label in the tree and clicking on the Code Generation label in the tree and selecting it from the Runtime Library drop-down list. Figure 6-1 earlier in this chapter shows the project properties dialog box and the location of this option.

The next property you need to change is to add the MySQL include directory to your project properties. The easiest way to do this is to expand the C/C++ label and click on the Command Line label. This will display the command-line parameters. To add a new parameter, type it in the Additional Options text box. In this case, you need to add something like `/I ../include`. If you located your project somewhere other than under the MySQL source tree, you may need to alter the parameter accordingly. Figure 6-2 earlier in this chapter shows the project properties dialog box and the location of this option.

You can also remove the precompiled header option if you do not want (or need) to use precompiled headers. This option is on the C/C++ Precompile Headers page in the project properties dialog box.

Lastly, you should set the common language runtime setting to `/clr`. You can set this in the project properties dialog box by clicking on General in the tree and selecting Common Language Runtime Support (/clr) from the Common Language Runtime support option. Figure 6-7 shows the project dialog box and the location of this option.

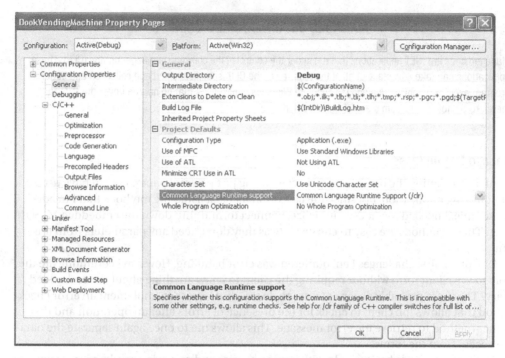

Figure 6-7. *Project properties dialog box: General page*

Design

Designing the application required that I meet two important requirements. Not only did I need to design a user interface that is easy to use and free from errors, I also needed to be able to call a C API from a .NET application. If you do some searching in the MySQL forums and lists you will see where several poor souls have struggled with getting this to work. If you follow along with my example, you should not encounter those problems. The main cause of the problems seems to be the inability to call the C API functions in the embedded library. I get around this by writing my application in C++ using managed C++ code. Yes, it is true that you cannot use C API calls in a managed application, but C++ allows you to temporarily turn that off and back on by using the #pragma unmanaged and #pragma managed directives.

The need to call unmanaged code is also a great motivator for encapsulation of the library calls. Unmanaged code enables the developer to write a DLL that can be used in programs that are not written in .NET. For this example, I am using a C++ class to encapsulate the C API calls wrapped in the #pragma unmanaged directive. This allows me to show you an example of using a .NET application that calls the embedded library C API directly. Cool, eh?

I also wanted to keep the user interface completely separate from anything to do with the embedded library. I wanted to do this so that I can provide you with an encapsulated database access class that you can reuse as the basis for your own applications. It also permits me to present to you one example (Windows) of a realistic application without long lists of source code for you to read through. The data access design for this example is therefore a single unmanaged C++ class that encapsulates the embedded library C API calls. The design also includes two forms: one for each of the user interfaces (Customer and Administrator).

MANAGED VS. UNMANAGED CODE

Managed code are .NET applications that run under the control of the common language runtime (CLR). These applications can take advantage of all of the features of the CLR, specifically garbage collection and better program execution control. Unmanaged code are Windows applications that do not run under the CLR and therefore do not benefit from the .NET enhancements.

Database Engine Class

I began by designing the database engine class using just pen and paper. I could have used a UML drawing application, but since the class is small I just listed the methods that I needed. For example, I needed methods to initialize, connect to, and shut down the embedded MySQL server. These methods are easy to encapsulate as they don't need any parameters from the form.

One of the first challenges I encountered was error handling. How can I communicate the errors to the client form without requiring the client to know anything about the embedded library? There are probably dozens of ways to do this, but I chose to implement an error check method that allows the client to check for the presence of errors after an operation and then another method to retrieve the error message. This allows me to once again separate the database access from the forms.

The class methods having to do with issuing queries and retrieving results are a design from a choice of implementations. I chose to implement an access iterator that permits the client to issue the query and then iterate through the results. I also needed a method that tells the database that a book has been vended so that the database can reduce the quantity on hand value for that book.

Data retrieval is accomplished using three methods that return a character string, an integer, or a large text field. I also added helper methods for getting a setting from the settings table, getting a field from the database (for the administrator interface), and a quick method to retrieve the quantity on hand.

Listing 6-12 shows the complete source code for the database class header. I named the class DBEngine. Table 6-4 includes a description and use for each method in the class.

Listing 6-12. *Database Engine Class Header (DBEngine.h)*

```
#pragma once
#pragma unmanaged
#include <stdio.h>

class DBEngine
{
private:
  bool mysqlError;
public:
  DBEngine(void);
  const char *GetError();
  int Error();
```

```
    void Initialize();
    void Shutdown();
    char *GetSetting(char *Field);
    char *GetBookFieldStr(int Slot, char *Field);
    char *GetBookFieldText(int Slot, char *Field);
    int GetBookFieldInt(int Slot, char *Field);
    int GetQty(int Slot);
    void VendBook(char *ISBN);
    void StartQuery(char *QueryStatement);
    void RunQuery(char *QueryStatement);
    int GetNext();
    char *GetField(int fldNum);
    ~DBEngine(void);
};
#pragma managed
```

Table 6-4. *Database Engine Class Methods*

Method	Return	Description
GetError()	char *	Returns the error message for the last error generated.
Error()	int	Returns 1 if the server has detected an error condition.
Initialize()	void	Encapsulates the embedded server initialization and connection operations.
Shutdown()	void	Encapsulates the embedded server finalization and shutdown operations.
GetSetting()	char *	Returns the value for the setting named. Looks up information in the settings table.
GetBookFieldStr()	char *	Returns a character string value from the books table for the field passed in the specified slot.
GetBookFieldText()	char *	Returns a character string value from the books table for the field passed in the specified slot.
GetBookFieldInt()	int	Returns an integer value from the books table for the field passed in the specified slot.
GetQty()	int	Returns the quantity on hand for the book in the specified slot.
VendBook()	void	Reduces the quantity on hand for the book in the specified slot.
StartQuery()	void	Initializes the query iterator by executing the query and retrieving the result set.
RunQuery()	void	A helper method designed to run a query that does not return results.
GetNext()	int	Retrieves the next record in the result set. Returns 0 if there are no more records in result set or non-zero for success.
GetField	char *	Returns the field name for the field number passed.

Defining the class was the easy part. Completing the code for all of these methods is a little harder. Instead of starting from scratch, I used the code from the first example and changed it into the database class source code. Listing 6-13 shows the complete source code for the database class. Notice that I've used the same global (well, local to this source) variables and arrays of characters for the initialization and startup options. This part should look very familiar to you. Take some time to read through this code. When you are done, I'll explain some of the grittier details.

Listing 6-13. *Database Engine Class (DBEngine.cpp)*

```
#pragma unmanaged

#include "DBEngine.h"
#include <stdlib.h>
#include <stdio.h>
#include "my_global.h"
#include "mysql.h"

MYSQL *mysql;                        //the embedded server class
MYSQL_RES *results;                  //stores results from queries
MYSQL_ROW record;                    //a single row in a result set
bool IteratorStarted;                //used to control iterator
MYSQL_RES *ExecQuery(char *Query);

/*
  These variables set the location of the ini file and data stores.
*/
static char *server_options[] = {"mysql_test",
  "--defaults-file=c:\\mysql_embedded\\my.ini",
  "--datadir=c:\\mysql_embedded\\data" };
int num_elements=sizeof(server_options) / sizeof(char *);
static char *server_groups[] = {"libmyswld_server", "libmysqld_client" };

DBEngine::DBEngine(void)
{
  mysqlError = false;
}

DBEngine::~DBEngine(void)
{
}

const char *DBEngine::GetError()
{
  return (mysql_error(mysql));
  mysqlError = false;
}
```

```cpp
bool DBEngine::Error()
{
  return(mysqlError);
}

char *DBEngine::GetBookFieldStr(int Slot, char *Field)
{
  char *istr = new char[10];
  char *str = new char[128];

  _itoa_s(Slot, istr, 10, 10);
  strcpy_s(str, 128, "SELECT ");
  strcat_s(str, 128, Field);
  strcat_s(str, 128, " FROM books WHERE Slot = ");
  strcat_s(str, 128, istr);
  mysqlError = false;
  results=ExecQuery(str);
  strcpy_s(str, 128, "");
  if (results)
  {
    mysqlError = false;
    record=mysql_fetch_row(results);
    if(record)
    {
      strcpy_s(str, 128, record[0]);
    }
    else
    {
      mysqlError = true;
    }
  }
  return (str);
}

char *DBEngine::GetBookFieldText(int Slot, char *Field)
{
  char *istr = new char[10];
  char *str = new char[128];

  _itoa_s(Slot, istr, 10, 10);
  strcpy_s(str, 128, "SELECT ");
  strcat_s(str, 128, Field);
  strcat_s(str, 128, " FROM books WHERE Slot = ");
  strcat_s(str, 128, istr);
  mysqlError = false;
  results=ExecQuery(str);
  delete str;
```

```
  if (results)
  {
    mysqlError = false;
    record=mysql_fetch_row(results);
    if(record)
    {
      return (record[0]);
    }
    else
    {
      mysqlError = true;
    }
  }
  return ("");
}


int DBEngine::GetBookFieldInt(int Slot, char *Field)
{
  char *istr = new char[10];
  char *str = new char[128];
  int qty = 0;

  _itoa_s(Slot, istr, 10, 10);
  strcpy_s(str, 128, "SELECT ");
  strcat_s(str, 128, Field);
  strcat_s(str, 128, " FROM books WHERE Slot = ");
  strcat_s(str, 128, istr);
  results=ExecQuery(str);
  if (results)
  {
    record=mysql_fetch_row(results);
    if(record)
    {
      qty = atoi(record[0]);
    }
    else
    {
      mysqlError = true;
    }
  }
  delete str;
  return (qty);
}


void DBEngine::VendBook(char *ISBN)
{
  char *str = new char[128];
```

```
  char *istr = new char[10];
  int qty = 0;

  strcpy_s(str, 128, "SELECT Quantity FROM books WHERE ISBN = '");
  strcat_s(str, 128, ISBN);
  strcat_s(str, 128, "'");
  results=ExecQuery(str);
  record=mysql_fetch_row(results);
  if (record)
  {
    qty = atoi(record[0]);
    if (qty >= 1)
    {
      _itoa_s(qty - 1, istr, 10, 10);
      strcpy_s(str, 128, "UPDATE books SET Quantity = ");
      strcat_s(str, 128, istr);
      strcat_s(str, 128, " WHERE ISBN = '");
      strcat_s(str, 128, ISBN);
      strcat_s(str, 128, "'");
      results=ExecQuery(str);
    }
  }
  else
  {
    mysqlError = true;
  }
}

void DBEngine::Initialize()
{
  /*
    This section initializes the server and sets server options.
  */
  mysql_server_init(num_elements, server_options, server_groups);
  mysql = mysql_init(NULL);
  if (mysql)
  {
    mysql_options(mysql, MYSQL_READ_DEFAULT_GROUP, "libmysqld_client");
    mysql_options(mysql, MYSQL_OPT_USE_EMBEDDED_CONNECTION, NULL);
    /*
      The following call turns debugging on programmatically.
      Comment out to turn off debugging.
    */
    //mysql_debug("d:t:i:O,\\mysqld_embedded.trace");
    /*
      Connect to embedded server.
    */
```

```
    if(mysql_real_connect(mysql, NULL, NULL, NULL, "information_schema",
      0, NULL, 0) == NULL)
    {
      mysqlError = true;
    }
    else
    {
      mysql_query(mysql, "use BVM;");
    }
  }
  else
  {
    mysqlError = true;
  }
  IteratorStarted = false;
}

void DBEngine::Shutdown()
{
  /*
    Now close the server connection and tell server we're done (shutdown).
  */
  mysql_close(mysql);
  mysql_server_end();
}

char *DBEngine::GetSetting(char *Field)
{
  char *str = new char[128];
  strcpy_s(str, 128, "SELECT * FROM settings WHERE FieldName = '");
  strcat_s(str, 128, Field);
  strcat_s(str, 128, "'");
  results=ExecQuery(str);
  strcpy_s(str, 128, "");
  if (results)
  {
    record=mysql_fetch_row(results);
    if (record)
    {
      strcpy_s(str, 128, record[1]);
    }
  }
  else
  {
    mysqlError = true;
  }
  return (str);
}
```

```
void DBEngine::StartQuery(char *QueryStatement)
{
  if (!IteratorStarted)
  {
    results=ExecQuery(QueryStatement);
    if (results)
    {
      record=mysql_fetch_row(results);
    }
  }
  IteratorStarted=true;
}

void DBEngine::RunQuery(char *QueryStatement)
{
  results=ExecQuery(QueryStatement);
  if (results)
  {
    record=mysql_fetch_row(results);
    if(!record)
    {
      mysqlError = true;
    }
  }
}

int DBEngine::GetNext()
{
  //if EOF then no more records
  IteratorStarted=false;
  record=mysql_fetch_row(results);
  if (record)
  {
    return (1);
  }
  else
  {
    return (0);
  }
}

char *DBEngine::GetField(int fldNum)
{
  if (record)
  {
    return (record[fldNum]);
  }
```

```
    else
    {
      return ("");
    }
}

MYSQL_RES *ExecQuery(char *Query)
{
  mysql_dbug_print("ExecQuery.");
  mysql_free_result(results);
  mysql_query(mysql, Query);
  return (mysql_store_result(mysql));
}
#pragma managed
```

One thing you should notice about this code is all of the error handling that I've added to make the code more robust, or hardened. While I do not have all of the possible error handlers implemented, the most important ones are.

The get methods are all implemented using the same process. I first generate the appropriate query (and thereby hide the SQL statement from the client), execute the query, retrieve the result set and then the record from the query, and return the value.

One method that is of interest is VendBook(). Take a moment and look through that one again. You'll see that I've followed a similar method of generating the query, but this time I don't get the results because there aren't any. Actually, there is a result—it is the number of records affected. This could be handy if you wanted to do some additional process or rule checking in your application.

The rest of the methods should look familiar to you as they are all copies of the original example I showed you except this time they have error handling included. Now, let's take a look at how the user interface code calls the database class.

Customer Interface (Main Form)

The source code for the customer interface is very large. This is due to the auto-generated code that Microsoft places in the form.h file. I'm including only those portions that I wrote. I've included this section to show you how you can write your own .NET (or other) user interfaces. Aside from the code in the button events, I am using only four additional methods that I need to complete the user interface. The first method, DisplayError(), is defined as

```
void DisplayError()
```

I use this function as a means to detect errors in the database class and to present the error message to the user. The implementation of the method is a typical call to the MessageBox::Show() function.

The second method is a helper method that completes the detail view of the book selected. The function is named LoadDetails(). I abstracted this method because I realized I would be repeating the code for all ten buttons.[3] Abstracting in this manner minimizes the code and permits easier debugging. This method is defined as

---

3. There was only one feature of Visual Basic I found really cool: control arrays. Alas, they are a thing of the past.

```
void LoadDetails(int Slot)
```

The method takes as a parameter the slot number (which corresponds to the button number). It queries the database using the database class methods and populates the detail interface elements. This is where most of the heavy lifting of communicating with the database engine class occurs.

■ **Note** You may be wondering what all that gnarly code is surrounding the character strings. It turns out the .NET string class is not compatible with the C-style character strings. The extra code I included is designed to marshal the strings between these formats.

The third method is a helper method named Delay() and is defined as

```
void Delay(int secs)
```

The function causes a delay in processing for the number of seconds passed as a parameter. While not something you would want to include in your own application, I added it to simulate the vending process. This is an excellent example of how you can use stubbed functionality to demonstrate an application. This can be especially helpful in prototyping a new interface.

The fourth method, CheckAvailability(), is used to turn the buttons on the interface on or off depending on whether there is sufficient quantity of the product available. This method is defined as

```
void CheckAvailability()
```

The function makes a series of calls to the database engine to check the quantity for each slot. If the slot is empty (quantity == 0), then the button is disabled.

Listing 6-14 shows an excerpt of the source code for the customer interface. I've omitted a great deal of the auto-generated code (represented as ...). Notice at the top of the file I reference the database engine header using the #include "DBEngine.h" directive. Also notice that I've defined a variable of type DBEngine. I use this object throughout the code. Since it is local to the form, I can use it in any event or method. I use the ... to indicate portions of the auto-generated code and comments omitted from the listing.

Listing 6-14. *Main Form Source Code (MainForm.h)*

```
#pragma once
#include "DBEngine.h"
#include <stdio.h>
#include <stdlib.h>
#include <string>
#include "vcclr.h"
#include <time.h>
```

```
namespace BookVendingMachine {

  const char GREETING[] = "Please make a selection.";

  DBEngine  *Database = new DBEngine();

...

#pragma endregion
  void DisplayError()
  {
    String ^str = gcnew String("There was an error with the database system.\n" \
                               "Please contact product support.\nError = ");
    str = str + gcnew String(Database->GetError());
    MessageBox::Show(str, "Internal System Error", MessageBoxButtons::OK,
                     MessageBoxIcon::Information);
  }

  void LoadDetails(int Slot)
  {
    int Qty = Database->GetBookFieldInt(Slot, "Quantity");
    if (Database->Error()) DisplayError();
    pnlButtons->Visible = false;
    pnlDetail->Visible = true;
    lblStatus->Visible = false;
    lblTitle->Text = gcnew String(Database->GetBookFieldStr(Slot, "Title"));
    if (Database->Error()) DisplayError();
    lblAuthors->Text =
      gcnew String(Database->GetBookFieldStr(Slot, "Authors"));
    if (Database->Error()) DisplayError();
    lblISBN->Text = gcnew String(Database->GetBookFieldStr(Slot, "ISBN"));
    if (Database->Error()) DisplayError();
    txtDescription->Text =
      gcnew String(Database->GetBookFieldText(Slot, "Description"));
    if (Database->Error()) DisplayError();
    lblPrice->Text = gcnew String(Database->GetBookFieldStr(Slot, "Price"));
    if (Database->Error()) DisplayError();
    lblNumPages->Text =
      gcnew String(Database->GetBookFieldStr(Slot, "Pages"));
    if (Database->Error()) DisplayError();
    lblPubDate->Text =
      gcnew String(Database->GetBookFieldStr(Slot, "PubDate"));
    if (Database->Error()) DisplayError();
    if(Qty < 1)
    {
      btnPurchase->Enabled = false;
    }
  }
```

```
  void CheckAvailability()
  {
    btnBook1->Enabled = (Database->GetBookFieldInt(1, "Quantity") >= 1);
    if (Database->Error()) DisplayError();
    btnBook2->Enabled = (Database->GetBookFieldInt(2, "Quantity") >= 1);
    if (Database->Error()) DisplayError();
    btnBook3->Enabled = (Database->GetBookFieldInt(3, "Quantity") >= 1);
    if (Database->Error()) DisplayError();
    btnBook4->Enabled = (Database->GetBookFieldInt(4, "Quantity") >= 1);
    if (Database->Error()) DisplayError();
    btnBook5->Enabled = (Database->GetBookFieldInt(5, "Quantity") >= 1);
    if (Database->Error()) DisplayError();
    btnBook6->Enabled = (Database->GetBookFieldInt(6, "Quantity") >= 1);
    if (Database->Error()) DisplayError();
    btnBook7->Enabled = (Database->GetBookFieldInt(7, "Quantity") >= 1);
    if (Database->Error()) DisplayError();
    btnBook8->Enabled = (Database->GetBookFieldInt(8, "Quantity") >= 1);
    if (Database->Error()) DisplayError();
    btnBook9->Enabled = (Database->GetBookFieldInt(9, "Quantity") >= 1);
    if (Database->Error()) DisplayError();
    btnBook10->Enabled = (Database->GetBookFieldInt(10, "Quantity") >= 1);
    if (Database->Error()) DisplayError();
  }

  void Delay(int secs)
  {
    time_t start;
    time_t current;

    time(&start);
    do
    {
      time(&current);
    } while(difftime(current,start) < secs);
  }

private: System::Void btnCancel_Click(System::Object^ sender,
                                      System::EventArgs^ e)
  {
    lblStatus->Visible = true;
    pnlDetail->Visible = false;
    pnlButtons->Visible = true;
    btnPurchase->Enabled = true;
    lblStatus->Text = gcnew String(GREETING);
  }
```

```cpp
private: System::Void btnPurchase_Click(System::Object^  sender,
                                        System::EventArgs^  e)
  {
    String ^orig = gcnew String(lblISBN->Text->ToString());
    pin_ptr<const wchar_t> wch = PtrToStringChars(orig);

    // Convert to a char*
    size_t origsize = wcslen(wch) + 1;
    const size_t newsize = 100;
    size_t convertedChars = 0;
    char nstring[newsize];
    wcstombs_s(&convertedChars, nstring, origsize, wch, _TRUNCATE);

    lblStatus->Visible = true;
    pnlDetail->Visible = false;
    pnlButtons->Visible = true;
    btnPurchase->Enabled = true;
    Database->VendBook(nstring);
    //
    // Simulate buying the book.
    //
    lblStatus->Text = "Please Insert your credit card.";
    this->Refresh();
    Delay(3);
    lblStatus->Text = "Thank you. Processing card number ending in 4-1234.";
    this->Refresh();
    Delay(3);
    lblStatus->Text = "Vending....";
    this->Refresh();
    Delay(5);
    this->Refresh();
    CheckAvailability();
    lblStatus->Text = gcnew String(GREETING);
  }

private: System::Void MainForm_Load(System::Object^  sender,
                                    System::EventArgs^  e)
  {
    String ^imageName;
    String ^imagePath;

    Database->Initialize();
    if (Database->Error()) DisplayError();
    //
    //For each button, check to see if there are sufficient qty and load
    //the thumbnail for each.
    //
```

```
    imagePath = gcnew String(Database->GetSetting("ImagePath"));

    imageName = imagePath +
      gcnew String(Database->GetBookFieldStr(1, "Thumbnail"));
    if (Database->Error()) DisplayError();
    btnBook1->Image = btnBook1->Image->FromFile(imageName);
    imageName = imagePath +
      gcnew String(Database->GetBookFieldStr(2, "Thumbnail"));
    if (Database->Error()) DisplayError();
    btnBook2->Image = btnBook2->Image->FromFile(imageName);
    imageName = imagePath +
      gcnew String(Database->GetBookFieldStr(3, "Thumbnail"));
    if (Database->Error()) DisplayError();
    btnBook3->Image = btnBook3->Image->FromFile(imageName);
    imageName = imagePath +
      gcnew String(Database->GetBookFieldStr(4, "Thumbnail"));
    if (Database->Error()) DisplayError();
    btnBook4->Image = btnBook4->Image->FromFile(imageName);
    imageName = imagePath +
      gcnew String(Database->GetBookFieldStr(5, "Thumbnail"));
    if (Database->Error()) DisplayError();
    btnBook5->Image = btnBook5->Image->FromFile(imageName);
    imageName = imagePath +
      gcnew String(Database->GetBookFieldStr(6, "Thumbnail"));
    if (Database->Error()) DisplayError();
    btnBook6->Image = btnBook6->Image->FromFile(imageName);
    imageName = imagePath +
      gcnew String(Database->GetBookFieldStr(7, "Thumbnail"));
    if (Database->Error()) DisplayError();
    btnBook7->Image = btnBook7->Image->FromFile(imageName);
    imageName = imagePath +
      gcnew String(Database->GetBookFieldStr(8, "Thumbnail"));
    if (Database->Error()) DisplayError();
    btnBook8->Image = btnBook8->Image->FromFile(imageName);
    imageName = imagePath +
      gcnew String(Database->GetBookFieldStr(9, "Thumbnail"));
    if (Database->Error()) DisplayError();
    btnBook9->Image = btnBook9->Image->FromFile(imageName);
    imageName = imagePath +
      gcnew String(Database->GetBookFieldStr(10, "Thumbnail"));
    if (Database->Error()) DisplayError();
    btnBook10->Image = btnBook10->Image->FromFile(imageName);

    CheckAvailability();
}
```

```
private: System::Void btnBook1_Click(System::Object^  sender,
                                     System::EventArgs^  e)
{
  LoadDetails(1);
}


private: System::Void btnBook2_Click(System::Object^  sender,
                                     System::EventArgs^  e)
{
  LoadDetails(2);
}


private: System::Void btnBook3_Click(System::Object^  sender,
                                     System::EventArgs^  e)
{
  LoadDetails(3);
}


private: System::Void btnBook4_Click(System::Object^  sender,
                                     System::EventArgs^  e)
{
  LoadDetails(4);
}


private: System::Void btnBook5_Click(System::Object^  sender,
                                     System::EventArgs^  e)
{
  LoadDetails(5);
}


private: System::Void btnBook6_Click(System::Object^  sender,
                                     System::EventArgs^  e)
{
  LoadDetails(6);
}


private: System::Void btnBook7_Click(System::Object^  sender,
                                     System::EventArgs^  e)
{
  LoadDetails(7);
}


private: System::Void btnBook8_Click(System::Object^  sender,
                                     System::EventArgs^  e)
{
  LoadDetails(8);
}
```

```
private: System::Void btnBook9_Click(System::Object^ sender,
                                     System::EventArgs^ e)
  {
    LoadDetails(9);
  }

private: System::Void btnBook10_Click(System::Object^ sender,
                                      System::EventArgs^ e)
  {
    LoadDetails(10);
  }

private: System::Void MainForm_FormClosing(System::Object^ sender,
    System::Windows::Forms::FormClosingEventArgs^ e)
  {
    Database->Shutdown();
  }

};
}
```

The MainForm_Load() event is where the database engine is initialized and the buttons are loaded with the appropriate thumbnails. I follow each call to the database with the statement

```
if (Database->Error()) DisplayError();
```

This statement allows me to detect when an error occurs and inform the user. Although I don't act on the error in this event, I could and do act on it in other events. If a severe database error occurs here, the worst case is the buttons will not be populated with the thumbnails. I use this concept throughout the source code.

The btnBook1_Click() through btnBook10_Click() events are implemented to call the LoadDetails() method and populate the details interface components with the proper data. As you can see, abstracting the loading of the details has saved me lots of code!

On the detail portion of the interface are two buttons. The btnCancel_Click() event returns the interface to the initial vending machine view. The btnPurchase_Click() event is a bit more interesting. It is here where the vending part occurs. Notice I first call the VendBook() method and then run the simulation for the vending process and return the interface to the vending view.

That's it! The customer interface is very straightforward—as most vending machines are. Just a row of buttons and a mechanism for taking in the money (in this case I assume the machine accepts credit cards as payment but a real vending machine would probably take several forms of payment).

Administration Interface (Administration Form)

The customer interface is uncomplicated and easy to use. But what about maintaining the data? How can a vendor replenish the stock of the vending machine or even change the list of books offered? One way to do that is to use an administration interface that is separate from the customer interface. You could also create another separate embedded application to handle this or possibly create the data on another machine and copy to the vending machine. I've chosen to build a simple administration form, as shown in Figure 6-8.

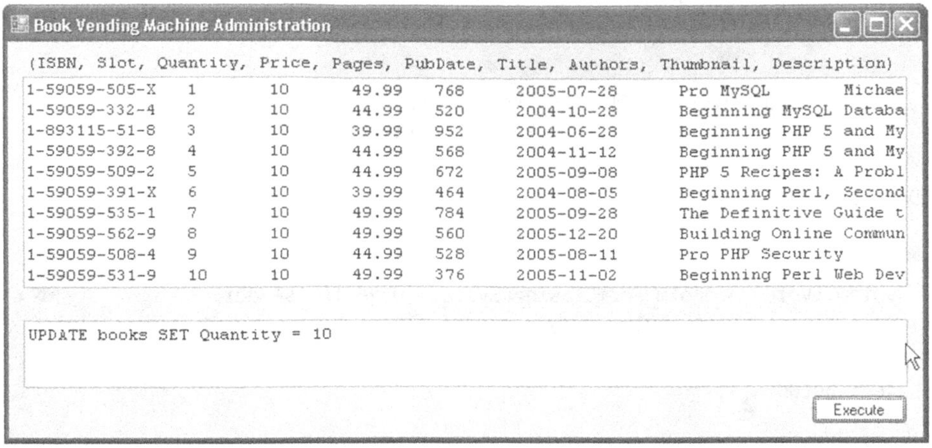

Book Vending Machine Administration

(ISBN,	Slot,	Quantity,	Price,	Pages,	PubDate,	Title, Authors, Thumbnail, Description)
1-59059-505-X	1	10	49.99	768	2005-07-28	Pro MySQL Michae
1-59059-332-4	2	10	44.99	520	2004-10-28	Beginning MySQL Databa
1-893115-51-8	3	10	39.99	952	2004-06-28	Beginning PHP 5 and My
1-59059-392-8	4	10	44.99	568	2004-11-12	Beginning PHP 5 and My
1-59059-509-2	5	10	44.99	672	2005-09-08	PHP 5 Recipes: A Probl
1-59059-391-X	6	10	39.99	464	2004-08-05	Beginning Perl, Second
1-59059-535-1	7	10	49.99	784	2005-09-28	The Definitive Guide t
1-59059-562-9	8	10	49.99	560	2005-12-20	Building Online Commun
1-59059-508-4	9	10	44.99	528	2005-08-11	Pro PHP Security
1-59059-531-9	10	10	49.99	376	2005-11-02	Beginning Perl Web Dev

```
UPDATE books SET Quantity = 10
```

Execute

Figure 6-8. *Example administration form*

Like with the customer interface, I need to create a helper function. This function is called LoadList() and is used to populate a list that displays all of the data in the books table. This is handy because it allows the vendor to see what the database contains.

Listing 6-15 shows an excerpt of the administration form source code. I've omitted the auto-generated Windows form code (represented as . . .). One item of interest at the top of the source code is that I've defined the pointer variable as AdminDatabase instead of Database. This is mainly for clarity and isn't meant to distract you from the usage of the database engine class. I use the . . . to indicate portions of the auto-generated code and comments omitted from the listing.

Listing 6-15. *Administration Form Source Code (AdminForm.h)*

```
#pragma once
#include "DBEngine.h"

using namespace System;
using namespace System::ComponentModel;
using namespace System::Collections;
using namespace System::Windows::Forms;
using namespace System::Data;
using namespace System::Drawing;


namespace BookVendingMachine {

  DBEngine  *AdminDatabase = new DBEngine();


...
```

```
#pragma endregion
  void LoadList()
  {
    int i = 0;
    int j = 0;
    String^ str;

    lstData->Items->Clear();
    AdminDatabase->StartQuery("SELECT ISBN, Slot, Quantity, Price," \
      " Pages, PubDate, Title, Authors, Thumbnail," \
      " Description FROM books");
    do
    {
      str = gcnew String("");
      for (i = 0; i < 10; i++)
      {
        if (i != 0)
        {
          str = str + "\t";
        }
        str = str + gcnew String(AdminDatabase->GetField(i));
      }
      lstData->Items->Add(str);
      j++;
    }while(AdminDatabase->GetNext());
  }

private: System::Void btnExecute_Click(System::Object^  sender,
                                       System::EventArgs^  e)
  {
    String ^orig = gcnew String(txtQuery->Text->ToString());
    pin_ptr<const wchar_t> wch = PtrToStringChars(orig);

    // Convert to a char*
    size_t origsize = wcslen(wch) + 1;
    const size_t newsize = 100;
    size_t convertedChars = 0;
    char nstring[newsize];
    wcstombs_s(&convertedChars, nstring, origsize, wch, _TRUNCATE);
    AdminDatabase->RunQuery(nstring);
    LoadList();
  }
```

```
private: System::Void Admin_Load(System::Object^  sender,
                                 System::EventArgs^  e)
  {
    AdminDatabase->Initialize();
    LoadList();
  }

private: System::Void AdminForm_FormClosing(System::Object^  sender,
    System::Windows::Forms::FormClosingEventArgs^  e)
  {
    AdminDatabase->Shutdown();
  }
};
}
```

Notice I've included the usual initialize and shutdown method calls to the database engine in the form load and closing events.

This interface is designed to accept an ad hoc query and execute it when the Execute button is clicked. Thus, the btnExecute_Click() is the only other method in this source code. The method calls the database engine and requests that the query be run but it is not checking for any results. That is because this interface is used to adjust things in the database, not select data. The last call in this method is the LoadList() helper method that repopulates the list.

Detecting Interface Requests

You might be wondering how I plan to detect which interface to execute. The answer is I use a command-line parameter to tell the code which interface to run. The switch is implemented in the main() function in the BookVendingMachine.cpp source file. The source code for processing command-line parameters is self-explanatory. Listing 6-16 contains the entire source code for the main() function for the embedded application.

Listing 6-16. *The BookVendingMachine Main Function (BookVendingMachine.cpp)*

```
// BookVendingMachine.cpp : main project file.

#include "MainForm.h"
#include "AdminForm.h"

using namespace BookVendingMachine;

[STAThreadAttribute]
int main(array<System::String ^> ^args)
{
  // Enabling Windows XP visual effects before any controls are created
  Application::EnableVisualStyles();
  Application::SetCompatibleTextRenderingDefault(false);
```

```
// Create the main window and run it
if ((args->Length == 1) && (args[0] == "-admin"))
{
  Application::Run(gcnew AdminForm());
}
else
{
  Application::Run(gcnew MainForm());
}
  return 0;
}
```

You should now be able to re-create this example from this text or by downloading the information from the book web site. I encourage you to become comfortable with the client source code (the forms) so that you can see and understand how the database engine is used. When you're ready, you can compile and run the example.

Compiling and Running

Compiling this example is just a matter of clicking on Build ➤ Build BookVendingMachine. If you have already compiled the libmysqld project, all you should see is the compilation of the example. If for some reason the object files are out of date for libmysqld or any of its dependencies, Visual Studio will compile those as well.

When the compilation is complete, you can either run the program from the debug menu commands or open a command window and run it from the command line by entering the command debug\BookVendingMachine from the project directory. If this is your first time, you should see an error message like the following:

```
This application has failed to start because LIBMYSQLD.dll was not found.
Re-installing the application may fix this problem.
```

The reason for this error has nothing to do with the second sentence in the error message. It means the embedded library isn't in the search path. If you have worked with .NET or COM applications and never used C libraries, then you may have never encountered the error. Unlike .NET and COM, C libraries are not registered in a GAC or registry. These libraries (DLLs) should be collocated with application that calls them or at least on an execution path. Most developers place a copy of the DLL in the execution directory.

To fix this problem, you will need to copy the libmysqld.dll file from the lib_debug directory to the directory where the bookvendingmachine.exe file resides (or add lib_debug to the execution path). Once you have copied the library to the execution directory, you should see the application run as shown in Figures 6-3, 6-4, and 6-5.

Take some time and play around with the interface. If the time delay is too annoying for you, you can reduce the number of seconds in the delay or comment out the delay method calls.

If you want to access the administration interface, you need to run the program using the -admin command-line switch. If you are running the example from the command line, you can enter the following command:

```
BookVendingMarchine -admin
```

If you want to run the example from Visual Studio using the debugger, you have to set the command-line switch in the project properties. Open the dialog box by selecting Project ➤ Project Properties and click on the Debugging label in the tree. You can add any number of command-line parameters by typing them into the Command Arguments option. Figure 6-9 shows the location of this option in the project properties.

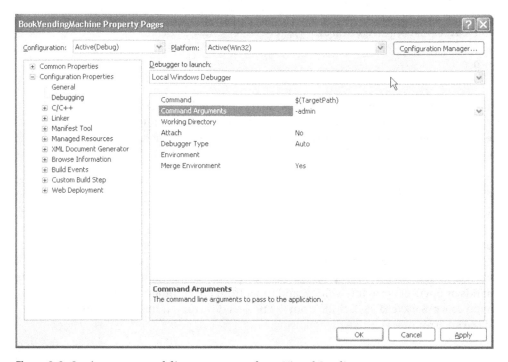

Figure 6-9. *Setting command-line arguments from Visual Studio*

I encourage you to try out the example. If you are not running Windows, you can still use the database engine class and provide your own interface for the application. This shouldn't be difficult now that you have seen one example of how that interface works with the abstracted libmysqld system calls. If you find yourself building unique vending machines using an embedded MySQL system, send me a photo!

Summary

In this chapter, you have learned how to create embedded MySQL applications. The MySQL embedded library is often overlooked, but has been highly successful in permitting systems integrators to add robust data management facilities to their enterprise applications and products.
Perhaps the most intriguing aspect of this chapter is your guided tour of the MySQL embedded library C API. I hope that by following the examples in this chapter you can appreciate the power of embedded MySQL applications. I also hope that you haven't tossed the book down in frustration if you've encountered issues with compiling the source code. Much of what makes a good open source developer is her ability to systematically diagnose and adapt

her environment to the needs of the current project. Do not despair if you had issues come up. Solving issues is a natural part of the learning cycle.

You also explored the concepts of turning on debug tracing for your embedded applications. I also took you on a brief journey into modifying the MySQL server source code by exposing a DBUG method through the embedded library that allows you to add your own strings to the DBUG trace output. You saw some of the interesting error-handling situations and how to handle them. Finally, I showed you an encapsulated database access class that you can use in your own embedded applications.

The next chapter will show you how to create your own storage engine. You should be impressed with the ease of extending the MySQL system to meet your needs. Just the embedded server library alone opens up a broad realm of possibilities. Add to that the ability to create your own storage engines and even (later) your own functions in MySQL, it is easy to see why MySQL is the "world's most popular open source database."

CHAPTER 7

■ ■ ■

Building Your Own Storage Engine

The pluggable storage engine is one of the most important features of the MySQL system. Database professionals have never had the ability to tune the physical storage of relational database systems to meet the needs of the data. MySQL provides this unique capability via the pluggable storage engine. With MySQL, database professionals can also tune the physical layer of their database systems by using the pluggable storage engine to choose the storage method that best optimizes the access methods for the database. That is a huge advantage over other relational database systems that use only a single storage mechanism.[1]

This chapter guides you through the process of creating your own storage engine. It is the first of the chapters in this book dedicated to demonstrating how to modify and extend the MySQL system. I begin by explaining the pluggable storage engine in some detail, then describe the process for building a storage engine and walk you through a tutorial for building a sample storage engine. If you've been itching to get your hands on the MySQL source code, now is the time to roll up your sleeves and refill that beverage. If you're a little wary of making these kinds of modifications, feel free to read through the chapter and follow the examples until you are comfortable with the process.

MySQL Pluggable Storage Engine Overview

A pluggable storage engine is a software layer in the architecture of the MySQL server. It is responsible for abstracting the physical data layer from the logical layers of the server, and provides the low-level input/output (I/O) operations for the server. When a system is developed in a layered architecture, it provides a mechanism for streamlining and standardizing the interfaces between the layers. It is this quality that is used to measure the success of a layered architecture. A powerful feature of layered architectures is the ability to modify one layer and, provided the interfaces do not change, not alter the adjacent layers.

MySQL AB has reworked the architecture of MySQL (starting in version 5.0) to incorporate this layered architecture approach. The pluggable storage engine was added in version 5.1 and is the most visible form of that endeavor. The pluggable storage engine empowers systems integrators and developers to use MySQL in environments where the data requires special

---

1. The use of clustered indexes and other data file optimizations notwithstanding.

processing to read and write. Furthermore, the pluggable storage engine architecture allows you to create your own storage engine.

■**Note** The current release of MySQL (5.1.9-beta) does not fully support the pluggable mechanism. A number of modifications are necessary to some of the MySQL source files in order to add and recognize a new storage engine (via the "handlerton," which I discuss in a moment). MySQL AB reports that these modifications will be unnecessary in future releases of the MySQL system.

One reason you would want to do this rather than convert the data to a format that can be ingested by MySQL is the cost of doing that conversion. For example, suppose you have a legacy application that your organization has been using for a long time. The data that the application has used is valuable to your organization and cannot be duplicated. Furthermore, you may need to use the old application. Rather than converting the data to a new format, you can create a storage engine that can read and write the data in the old format. Other examples include cases where the data and its access methods are such that you require special data handling to ensure the most efficient means of reading and writing the data. Furthermore, and perhaps most importantly, the pluggable storage engine can be used to connect data that is not normally connected to database systems. That is, you can create storage engines to read streaming data (e.g., RSS) or other nontraditional, nondisk stored data. Whatever your needs, MySQL can meet them by allowing you to create your own storage engines that will enable you to create an efficient specialize relational database system for your environment.

You can use the MySQL server as your relational database processing engine and wire it directly to your legacy data by providing a special storage engine that plugs directly into the server. This may not sound like an easy thing to do, but it really is.

The most important architectural element is the use of an array of single objects to access the storage engines (one object per storage engine). The control of these single objects is in the form of a complex structure called a *handlerton* (as in singleton—see the sidebar on singletons). A special class called a *handler* is a base class that uses the handlerton to complete the interface and provide the basic connectivity to enable a storage engine.

All storage engines are derived from the base handler class, which acts as a police officer marshaling the common access methods and function calls to the storage engine and from the storage engine to the server. In other words, the handler and handlerton structure act as an intermediary (or black box) between the storage engine and the server. As long as your storage engine conforms to the handler interface, you can plug it in to the server. All of the connection, authentication, parsing, and optimization is still performed by the server in the usual way. The different storage engines merely pass the data to and from the server in a common format, translating it to and from the specialized storage medium.

MySQL AB has documented the process of creating a new storage engine fairly well. As of this writing, Chapter 16 of the MySQL reference manual contains a complete explanation of the storage engine and all of the functions supported and required by the handler interface. I recommend reading the MySQL reference manual after you have read this chapter and worked through building the example storage engine. The MySQL reference manual in this case is best used as just that—a reference.

WHAT IS A SINGLETON?

There are situations in object-oriented programming when you may need to limit object creation such that only one object instantiation is made for a given class. One reason for this may be that the class protects a shared set of operations or data. For example, if you had a manager class designed to be a gatekeeper for access to a specific resource or data, you might be tempted to create a static or global reference to this object and therefore permit only one instance in the entire application. However, the use of global instances and constant structures or access functions flies in the face of the object-oriented mantra. Instead of doing that, you can create a specialized form of the object that restricts creation to only one instance so that it can be shared by all areas (objects) in the application. These special one-time-creation objects are called singletons. (For more information on singletons, see the article "Creating Singleton Objects Using Visual C++" by T. Kulathu Sarma at www.codeproject.com/gen/design/singleton.asp.) There are a variety of ways to create singletons:

- Static variables

- Heap-registration

- Runtime type information (RTTI)

- Self-registering

- Smart singletons (like smart pointers)

Now that you know what a singleton is, you're probably thinking that you've been creating these your entire career but didn't know it!

■ **Note** The pluggable storage engine isn't the only pluggable mechanism in MySQL. MySQL permits you to use pluggable text parsers and even user-defined functions. Future releases on MySQL may include pluggable stored procedure language processors.

Basic Process

The basic process for adding a new storage engine can be described as a series of stages. After all, a storage engine does not merely consist of a few lines of code; therefore the most natural way to develop something of this size and complexity is through an iterative process, where a small part of the system is developed and tested prior to moving on to another more complicated portion. In the tutorial that follows, I start with the most basic of functions and gradually add functionality until a fully functional storage engine emerges.

The first few stages create and add the basic data read and write mechanisms. Later stages add indexing and transaction support. Depending on what features you want to add to your own storage engine, you may not need to complete all of the stages. A functional storage engine should support, at a minimum, the functions defined in the first four stages.[2] The following list describes each of the stages:

---

2. Some special storage engines may not need to write data at all. For example, the BLACKHOLE storage engine does not actually implement any write functions. Hey, it's a blackhole!

1. *Stubbing the engine*—The first step in the process is creating the basic storage engine that can be plugged into the server. The basic source code files are created, the storage engine is established as a derivative of the handler base class, and the storage engine itself is plugged into the server source code.

2. *Working with tables*—A storage engine would not be very interesting if it didn't have a means of creating, opening, closing, and deleting files. This stage is where you set up the basic file-handling routines and establish that the engine is working with the files correctly.

3. *Reading and writing data*—To complete the most basic of storage engines, you must implement the read and write methods to read and write data from and to the storage medium.[3] This stage is where you add those methods to read data in the storage medium format and translate them to the MySQL internal data format. Likewise, you write out the data from the MySQL internal data format to the storage medium.

4. *Updating and deleting data*—To make the storage engine something that can be used in applications, you must also implement those methods that allow for altering data in the storage engine. This stage is where the resolution of updates and deletion of data is implemented.

5. *Indexing the data*—A fully functional storage engine should also include the ability to permit fast random reads and range queries. This stage is where you implement the second-most complex operation of file access methods—indexing. I have provided an index class that should make this step easier for you to explore on your own.

6. *Adding transaction support*—The last stage of the process involves adding transaction support to the storage engine. It is at this stage that the storage engine becomes a truly relational database storage mechanism suitable for use in transactional environments. This is the most complex operation of file-access methods.

Throughout this process, you should be conducting testing and debugging at every stage. In the sections that follow, I'll show you examples of debugging a storage engine and writing tests to test the various stages. All of the normal debugging and trace mechanisms can be used in the storage engine. You can also use the interactive debuggers and get in to see the code in action!

Source Files Needed

The source files you will be working with are typically created as a single code (or class) file and a header file. These files are named ha_<engine name>.c (or .cpp) and ha_<engine name>.h, respectively.[4] For example, the archive storage engine files are named ha_archive.cpp and ha_archive.h. The storage engine source code is located in the storage directory off the main

---

3. It is more correct to refer to the data the storage engine is reading and writing as a storage medium because there is nothing that stipulates the data must reside on traditional data storage mechanisms.

4. The MyISAM, InnoDB, and BDB storage engines contain additional source files. These are the oldest of the storage engines and are the most complex.

source code tree. Inside that folder are the source code files for the various storage engines. Aside from those two files, that's all you need to get started!

Unexpected Help

The MySQL reference manual mentions several source code files that can be helpful in learning about the storage engines. Indeed, much of what I'm including here has come from studying those resources. MySQL AB provides an example storage engine (called example) that provides a great starting point for creating a storage engine at stage 1. In fact, I'll use it to get you started in the tutorial.

The archive engine is an example of a stage 3 engine that provides good examples of reading and writing data. If you want to see more examples of how to do the file reading, writing, and updating, the CSV engine is a good place to look. The CSV engine is an example of a stage 4 engine (CSV can read and write data as well as update and delete data). The CSV engine differs from the naming convention because it was one of the first to be implemented. The source files are named ha_tina.cc and ha_tina.h. Finally, to see examples of stage 5 and 6 storage engines, you can examine the MyISAM, BDB (Berkeley Database), and InnoDB storage engines.

Before moving on to creating your own storage engine, I encourage you to take time to examine these storage engines in particular because embedded in the source code are some golden nuggets of advice and instruction on how storage engines should work. Sometimes the best way to learn and extend or emulate a system is by examining its inner workings.

The Handlerton

As I mentioned earlier, the standard interface for all storage engines is the *handlerton* class. It is implemented in the handler.cc and handler.h files in the sql directory, and uses many other structures to provide organization of all of the elements needed to support the plug-in interface and the abstracted interface.

You might be wondering how concurrency is ensured in such a mechanism. The answer is another structure! Each storage engine is responsible for creating a shared structure that is referenced from each instance of the handler among all the threads. Naturally, this means that some code must be protected. The good news is not only are there mutual exclusion (mutex) protection methods available, but the handlerton source code has been designed to minimize the need for these protections.

The handlerton structure is a large structure with many data items and methods. Data items are represented as their normal data types defined in the structure, but methods are implemented using function pointers. The use of function pointers is one of those brilliantly constructed mechanisms that advanced developers use to permit runtime polymorphism. It is possible using function pointers to redirect execution to a different (but equivalent interface) function. This is one of the techniques that make the handlerton so successful.

Listing 7-1 includes an abbreviated listing of the handlerton structure definition, and Table 7-1 includes a description of the more important elements.

■**Note** I have omitted the comments from the code to save space. I have also skipped the lesser important items of the structure for brevity. Please see the handler.h file for additional information about the handlerton structure.

Listing 7-1. *The MySQL Handlerton Structure*

```
typedef struct
{
  const int interface_version;
  #define MYSQL_HANDLERTON_INTERFACE_VERSION 0x0001
  const char *name;
  SHOW_COMP_OPTION state;
  const char *comment;
  enum legacy_db_type db_type;
  bool (*init)();
  uint slot;
  uint savepoint_offset;
  int  (*close_connection)(THD *thd);
  int  (*savepoint_set)(THD *thd, void *sv);
  int  (*savepoint_rollback)(THD *thd, void *sv);
  int  (*savepoint_release)(THD *thd, void *sv);
  int  (*commit)(THD *thd, bool all);
  int  (*rollback)(THD *thd, bool all);
  int  (*prepare)(THD *thd, bool all);
  int  (*recover)(XID *xid_list, uint len);
  int  (*commit_by_xid)(XID *xid);
  int  (*rollback_by_xid)(XID *xid);
  void *(*create_cursor_read_view)();
  void (*set_cursor_read_view)(void *);
  void (*close_cursor_read_view)(void *);
  handler *(*create)(TABLE_SHARE *table);
  void (*drop_database)(char* path);
  int (*panic)(enum ha_panic_function flag);
  int (*start_consistent_snapshot)(THD *thd);
  bool (*flush_logs)();
  bool (*show_status)(THD *thd, stat_print_fn *print, enum ha_stat_type stat);
  uint (*partition_flags)();
  uint (*alter_table_flags)(uint flags);
  int (*alter_tablespace)(THD *thd, st_alter_tablespace *ts_info);
  int (*fill_files_table)(THD *thd,
                          struct st_table_list *tables,
                          class Item *cond);
  uint32 flags;                               /* global handler flags */
  int (*binlog_func)(THD *thd, enum_binlog_func fn, void *arg);
  void (*binlog_log_query)(THD *thd, enum_binlog_command binlog_command,
                           const char *query, uint query_length,
                           const char *db, const char *table_name);
  int (*release_temporary_latches)(THD *thd);
} handlerton;
```

■**Note** The values in the Type column are const = constant, var = variable, enum = enumeration, and fptr = function pointer.

Table 7-1. *The Handlerton Structure*

Element	Description
const char *name	Storage engine name as reported to the server and returned by SHOW STORAGE ENGINES;.
SHOW_COMP_OPTION state	Determines whether the storage engine is available.
const char *comment	A comment that describes the storage engine and also returned by the SHOW command.
enum legacy_db_type db_type	An enumerated value saved in the .frm file that indicates which storage engine created the file. This value is used to determine the handler class associated with the table.
bool (*init)()	The method to initialize the storage engine (handler). Used to set up the internal memory for the handler.
uint slot	The position in the array of handlers that refers to this handlerton.
uint savepoint_offset	The size of memory needed to create savepoints for the storage engine.
int (*close_connection)(...)	The method used to close the connection.
int (*savepoint_set)(...)	The method that sets the savepoint to the savepoint offset specified in the savepoint_offset element.
int (*savepoint_rollback)(...)	The method to roll back (undo) a savepoint.
int(*savepoint_release)(...)	The method to release (ignore) a savepoint.
int(*commit)(...)	The commit method that commits pending transactions.
int(*rollback)(...)	The rollback method that rolls back pending transactions.
int(*prepare)(...)	The prepare method for preparing a transaction for commit.
int(*recover)(...)	The method to return a list of transactions being prepared.
int(*commit_by_xid)(...)	The method that commits a transaction by transaction ID.
int(*rollback_by_xid)(...)	The method that rolls back a transaction by transaction ID.
void *(*create_cursor_read_view)()	The method used to create a cursor.

Table 7-1. *The Handlerton Structure (Continued)*

Element	Description
void (*set_cursor_read_view)(void *)	The method used to switch to a specific cursor view.
void (*close_cursor_read_view)(void *)	The method used to close a specific cursor view.
handler *(*create)(TABLE_SHARE *table)	The method used to create the handler instance of this storage engine.
int (*panic)(enum ha_panic_function flag)	The method that is called during server shutdown and crashes.
int (*start_consistent_snapshot)(...)	The method called to begin a consistent read (concurrency).
bool (*flush_logs)()	The method used to flush logs to disk.
bool (*show_status)(...)	The method that returns status information for the storage engine.
uint (*partition_flags)()	The method used to return the flag used for partitioning.
uint (*alter_table_flags)(...)	The method used to return flag set for the ALTER TABLE command.
int (*alter_tablespace)(...)	The method used to return flag set for the ALTER TABLESPACE command.
int (*fill_files_table)(...)	The method used by the cluster server mechanisms to fill tables (see the documentation for the NDB engine).
uint32 flags	Flags that indicate what features the handler supports.
int (*binlog_func)(...)	The method to call back to the binary log function.
void (*binlog_log_query)(...)	The method used to query the binary log.
int (*release_temporary_latches)(...)	InnoDB specific use (see the documentation for the InnoDB engine).

The Handler Class

The other part of the equation for understanding the pluggable storage engine interface is the handler class. The handler class is derived from Sql_alloc, which means that all of the memory allocation routines are provided through inheritance. The handler class is designed to be the implementation of the storage handler. It provides a consistent set of methods for interfacing with the server via the handlerton structure. The handlerton and handler instances work as a unit to achieve the abstraction layer for the storage engine architecture. Figure 7-1 depicts these classes and how they are derived to form a new storage engine. The drawing shows the handlerton structure as an interface between the handler and the new storage engine.

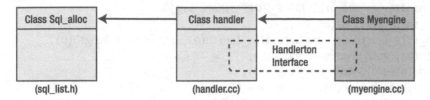

Figure 7-1. *Pluggable storage engine class derivation*

A complete detailed investigation of the handler class is beyond the scope of this book. Instead, I'll demonstrate the most important and most frequently used methods of the handler class implementing the stages of the sample storage engine. I'll explain each of the methods implemented and called in a more narrative format later in this chapter.

As a means of introduction to the handler class, I've provided an excerpt of the handler class definition in Listing 7-2. Take a few moments now to skim through the class. Notice the many methods available for a wide variety of tasks, such as creating, deleting, altering tables and methods to manipulate fields and indexes. There are even methods for crash protection, recovery, and backup.

Although the handler class is quite impressive and covers every possible situation for a storage engine, most storage engines do not use the complete list of methods. If you want to implement a storage engine with some of the advanced features provided, you should spend some time exploring the excellent coverage of the handler class in the MySQL reference manual. Once you become accustomed to creating storage engines, you can use the reference manual to take your storage engine to the next level of sophistication.

Listing 7-2. *The Handler Class Definition*

```
class handler :public Sql_alloc
{
...
  const handlerton *ht;              /* storage engine of this handler */
  byte *ref;                         /* Pointer to current row */
  byte *dupp_ref;                    /* Pointer to dupp row */
  ulonglong data_file_length;        /* Length of data file */
  ulonglong max_data_file_length;    /* Length of data file */
  ulonglong index_file_length;
  ulonglong max_index_file_length;
  ulonglong delete_length;           /* Free bytes */
  ulonglong auto_increment_value;
  ha_rows records;                   /* Records in table */
  ha_rows deleted;                   /* Deleted records */
  ulong mean_rec_length;             /* physical reclength */
  time_t create_time;                /* When table was created */
  time_t check_time;
  time_t update_time;
...
```

```
    handler(const handlerton *ht_arg, TABLE_SHARE *share_arg)
      :table_share(share_arg), ht(ht_arg),
      ref(0), data_file_length(0), max_data_file_length(0), index_file_length(0),
      delete_length(0), auto_increment_value(0),
      records(0), deleted(0), mean_rec_length(0),
      create_time(0), check_time(0), update_time(0),
      key_used_on_scan(MAX_KEY), active_index(MAX_KEY),
      ref_length(sizeof(my_off_t)), block_size(0),
      ft_handler(0), inited(NONE), implicit_emptied(0),
      pushed_cond(NULL)
      {}
...
  int ha_index_init(uint idx, bool sorted)
...
  int ha_index_end()
...
  int ha_rnd_init(bool scan)
...
  int ha_rnd_end()
...
  int ha_reset()
...
...
  virtual int exec_bulk_update(uint *dup_key_found)
...
  virtual void end_bulk_update() { return; }
...
  virtual int end_bulk_delete()
...
  virtual int index_read(byte * buf, const byte * key,
      uint key_len, enum ha_rkey_function find_flag)
...
  virtual int index_read_idx(byte * buf, uint index, const byte * key,
          uint key_len, enum ha_rkey_function find_flag);
  virtual int index_next(byte * buf)
   { return  HA_ERR_WRONG_COMMAND; }
  virtual int index_prev(byte * buf)
   { return  HA_ERR_WRONG_COMMAND; }
  virtual int index_first(byte * buf)
   { return  HA_ERR_WRONG_COMMAND; }
  virtual int index_last(byte * buf)
   { return  HA_ERR_WRONG_COMMAND; }
  virtual int index_next_same(byte *buf, const byte *key, uint keylen);
  virtual int index_read_last(byte * buf, const byte * key, uint key_len)
...
```

```
  virtual int read_multi_range_first(KEY_MULTI_RANGE **found_range_p,
                             KEY_MULTI_RANGE *ranges, uint range_count,
                             bool sorted, HANDLER_BUFFER *buffer);
  virtual int read_multi_range_next(KEY_MULTI_RANGE **found_range_p);
  virtual int read_range_first(const key_range *start_key,
                           const key_range *end_key,
                           bool eq_range, bool sorted);
  virtual int read_range_next();
  int compare_key(key_range *range);
  virtual int ft_init() { return HA_ERR_WRONG_COMMAND; }
  void ft_end() { ft_handler=NULL; }
  virtual FT_INFO *ft_init_ext(uint flags, uint inx,String *key)
    { return NULL; }
  virtual int ft_read(byte *buf) { return HA_ERR_WRONG_COMMAND; }
  virtual int rnd_next(byte *buf)=0;
  virtual int rnd_pos(byte * buf, byte *pos)=0;
  virtual int read_first_row(byte *buf, uint primary_key);
...
  virtual int restart_rnd_next(byte *buf, byte *pos)
    { return HA_ERR_WRONG_COMMAND; }
  virtual int rnd_same(byte *buf, uint inx)
    { return HA_ERR_WRONG_COMMAND; }
  virtual ha_rows records_in_range(uint inx, key_range *min_key,
                                key_range *max_key)
    { return (ha_rows) 10; }
  virtual void position(const byte *record)=0;
  virtual void info(uint)=0; // see my_base.h for full description
  virtual void get_dynamic_partition_info(PARTITION_INFO *stat_info,
                                   uint part_id);
  virtual int extra(enum ha_extra_function operation)
  { return 0; }
  virtual int extra_opt(enum ha_extra_function operation, ulong cache_size)
  { return extra(operation); }
...
  virtual int delete_all_rows()
...
  virtual ulonglong get_auto_increment();
  virtual void restore_auto_increment();
...
  virtual int reset_auto_increment(ulonglong value)
...
  virtual void update_create_info(HA_CREATE_INFO *create_info) {}
...
  int ha_repair(THD* thd, HA_CHECK_OPT* check_opt);
...
```

```
  virtual bool check_and_repair(THD *thd) { return HA_ERR_WRONG_COMMAND; }
  virtual int dump(THD* thd, int fd = -1) { return HA_ERR_WRONG_COMMAND; }
  virtual int disable_indexes(uint mode) { return HA_ERR_WRONG_COMMAND; }
  virtual int enable_indexes(uint mode) { return HA_ERR_WRONG_COMMAND; }
  virtual int indexes_are_disabled(void) {return 0;}
  virtual void start_bulk_insert(ha_rows rows) {}
  virtual int end_bulk_insert() {return 0; }
  virtual int discard_or_import_tablespace(my_bool discard)
...
  virtual uint referenced_by_foreign_key() { return 0;}
  virtual void init_table_handle_for_HANDLER()
...
  virtual void free_foreign_key_create_info(char* str) {}
...
  virtual const char *table_type() const =0;
  virtual const char **bas_ext() const =0;
  virtual ulong table_flags(void) const =0;
...
  virtual uint max_supported_record_length() const { return HA_MAX_REC_LENGTH; }
  virtual uint max_supported_keys() const { return 0; }
  virtual uint max_supported_key_parts() const { return MAX_REF_PARTS; }
  virtual uint max_supported_key_length() const { return MAX_KEY_LENGTH; }
  virtual uint max_supported_key_part_length() const { return 255; }
  virtual uint min_record_length(uint options) const { return 1; }
...
  virtual bool is_crashed() const  { return 0; }
...
  virtual int rename_table(const char *from, const char *to);
  virtual int delete_table(const char *name);
  virtual void drop_table(const char *name);

  virtual int create(const char *name, TABLE *form, HA_CREATE_INFO *info)=0;
...
  virtual int external_lock(THD *thd __attribute__((unused)),
                            int lock_type __attribute__((unused)))
...
  virtual int write_row(byte *buf __attribute__((unused)))
...
  virtual int update_row(const byte *old_data __attribute__((unused)),
                         byte *new_data __attribute__((unused)))
...
  virtual int delete_row(const byte *buf __attribute__((unused)))
...
};
```

A Brief Tour of a MySQL Storage Engine

The best way to see the handler work is to watch it in action. Therefore, let's examine a real storage engine in use before we start building one. You can follow along by compiling your server with debug if you haven't already. Go ahead and start your server and debugger, and then attach your debugging tool to the running server as described in Chapter 5.

I want to show you a simple storage engine in action. In this case, I'll use the archive storage engine. With the debugger open and the server running, open the ha_archive.cc file and place a breakpoint on the first executable line for the following methods:

- int ha_archive::create(...)

- static ARCHIVE_SHARE *ha_archive::get_share(...)

- int ha_archive::write_row(...)int ha_tina::rnd_next(...)

- int ha_archive::rnd_next(...)

Once the breakpoints are set, launch the command-line MySQL client, change to the test database, and issue this command:

```
CREATE TABLE testarc (a int, b varchar(20), c int) ENGINE=ARCHIVE;
```

You should immediately see the debugger halt in the create() method. This method is where the base data table is created. Indeed, it is one of the first things to execute. The my_create() method is called to create the file. Notice in this method that the field iterator loops through all of the fields in the table. This is important because it shows that the fields are already created. They are stored in the testarc.frm file in the data folder. Notice that the code is looking for a field with the AUTO_INCREMENT_FLAG set (at the top of the method); if the field is found, the code sets an error and exits. This is because the archive storage engine doesn't support auto-increment fields. You can also see that the method is creating a meta file and checking to see that the compression routines are working properly.

Take a moment and step through the code and watch the iterator. You can continue the execution at any time or, if you're really curious, continue to step through the return to the calling function.

Now, let's see what happens when we insert data. Go back to your MySQL client and enter this command:

```
INSERT INTO testarc VALUES (10, "test", -1);
```

This time, the code halts in the get_share() method. This method is responsible for creating the shared structure for all instances of the archive handler. As you step through this method, you can see where the code is setting the global variables and other initialization type tasks. Go ahead and let the debugger continue execution.

The next place the code halts is in the write_row() method. This method is where the data that is passed through the buf parameter is written to disk. The record buffer (byte *buf) is the mechanism that MySQL uses to pass rows through the system. It is a binary buffer containing the data for the row and other metadata. It is what the MySQL documentation refers to as the "internal format." As you step through this code, you will see the engine set some statistics, do some more error checking, and eventually write the data using the method real_write_row() at the end of the method. Go ahead and step through that method as well.

In the `real_write_row()` method you can see another field iterator. This iterator is iterating through the binary large objects (BLOB) fields and writing those to disk using the compression method. If you need to support BLOB fields, this is an excellent example of how to do so—just substitute your low-level IO call for the compression method. Go ahead and let the code continue; then return to your MySQL client and enter the following command:

```
SELECT * FROM testarc;
```

The next place the code halts is in the `rnd_next()` method. This is where the handler reads the data file and returns the data in the record buffer (`byte *buf`). Notice again that the code sets some statistics, does error checking, and then reads the data using the `get_row()` method. Step through this code a bit and then let it continue.

What a surprise! The code halts again at the `rnd_next()` method. This is because the `rnd_next()` method is one of a series of calls for a table scan. The method is responsible not only for reading the data but also for detecting the end of the file. Thus, in the example you're working through there should be two calls to the method. The first retrieves the first row of data and the second detects the end of the file (you inserted only one row). The following lists the typical sequence of calls for a table scan using the example you've been working through:

```
ha_spartan::info
ha_spartan::rnd_init
ha_spartan::extra
ha_spartan::rnd_next
ha_spartan::rnd_next
ha_spartan::extra
```

```
+------+------+------+
| a    | b    | c    |
+------+------+------+
| 10   | test | -1   |
+------+------+------+
1 row in set (26.25 sec)
```

Note The time returned from the query is actual elapsed time as recorded by the server and not execution time. Thus, the time spent in debugging counts.

Take some time and place breakpoints on other methods that may interest you. You can also spend some time reading the comments in this storage engine as they provide excellent clues to how some of the handler methods are used.

The Spartan Storage Engine

I chose for the tutorial on storage engines the concept of a basic storage engine that has all the features that a normal storage engine would have. This includes reading and writing data with index support. That is to say, it is a stage 5 engine. I call this sample storage engine the Spartan storage engine because in many ways it implements only the basic necessities for a viable database storage mechanism.

I'll guide you through the process of building the Spartan storage using the example (ha_example) MySQL storage engine. I'll refer you to the other storage engines for additional information as I progress through the tutorial. While you may find areas that you think could be improved upon (and indeed there are several), you should refrain from making any enhancements to the Spartan engine until you have it successfully implemented to the stage 5 level.

Let's begin by examining the supporting class files for the Spartan storage engine.

Low-Level I/O Classes

A storage engine is designed to read and write data using a specialized mechanism that provides some unique benefits to the user. This means that the storage engines, by nature, are not going to support the same features. Some of the storage engines in MySQL have the lower-level I/O functions embedded in the source files for the storage engine.

Most either use C functions defined in other source files or C++ classes defined in class header and source files. For the Spartan engine, I elected to use the latter method. I created a data file class as well as an index file class. Holding true to the intent of this chapter and the Spartan engine project, neither of the classes is optimized for performance. Rather, they provide a means to create a working storage engine and demonstrate most of the things you will need to do to create your own storage engine.

This section describes each of the classes in a general overview. You can follow along with the code and see how the classes work. Although the low-level classes are just the basics and could probably use a bit of fine-tuning, I think you'll find these classes beneficial to use and perhaps you'll even base your own storage engine I/O on them.

The Spartan_data Class

The primary low-level I/O class for the Spartan storage engine is the Spartan_data class. This class is responsible for encapsulating the data for the Spartan storage engine. Listing 7-3 includes the complete header file for the class. As you can see from the header, the methods for this class are simplistic. I implement just the basic open, close, read, and write operations.

Listing 7-3. *Spartan_data Class Header*

```
/*
  spartan_data.h

  This header defines a simple data file class for reading raw data to and
  from disk. The data written is in byte format so it can be anything you
  want it to be. The write_row and read_row accept the length of the data
  item to be read.
*/
#pragma once
#pragma unmanaged
#include "my_global.h"
#include "my_sys.h"
```

```cpp
class Spartan_data
{
public:
  Spartan_data(void);
  ~Spartan_data(void);
  int create_table(char *path);
  int open_table(char *path);
  long long write_row(byte *buf, int length);
  long long update_row(byte *old_rec, byte *new_rec,
                       int length, long long position);
  int read_row(byte *buf, int length, long long position);
  int delete_row(byte *old_rec, int length, long long position);
  int close_table();
  long long cur_position();
  int records();
  int del_records();
  int trunc_table();
  int row_size(int length);
private:
  File data_file;
  int header_size;
  int record_header_size;
  bool crashed;
  int number_records;
  int number_del_records;
  int read_header();
  int write_header();
};
```

Listing 7-4 includes the complete source code for the Spartan storage engine data class. Notice in the code I have included the appropriate DBUG calls to ensure my source code can write to the trace file should I wish to debug the system using the --with-debug switch. Notice also that the read and write methods used are the my_xxx platform-safe utility methods provided by MySQL AB.

Listing 7-4. *Spartan_data Class Source Code*

```cpp
/*
  Spartan_data.cpp

  This class implements a simple data file reader/writer. It
  is designed to allow the caller to specify the size of the
  data to read or write. This allows for variable length records
  and the inclusion of extra fields (like BLOBs). The data is
  stored in an uncompressed, unoptimized fashion.
*/
```

```
#include "spartan_data.h"
#include <my_dir.h>
#include <string.h>

Spartan_data::Spartan_data(void)
{
  data_file = -1;
  number_records = -1;
  number_del_records = -1;
  header_size = sizeof(bool) + sizeof(int) + sizeof(int);
  record_header_size = sizeof(byte) + sizeof(int);
}

Spartan_data::~Spartan_data(void)
{
}

/* create the data file */
int Spartan_data::create_table(char *path)
{
  DBUG_ENTER("Spartan_data::create_table");
  open_table(path);
  number_records = 0;
  number_del_records = 0;
  crashed = false;
  write_header();
  DBUG_RETURN(0);
}

/* open table at location "path" = path + filename */
int Spartan_data::open_table(char *path)
{
  DBUG_ENTER("Spartan_data::open_table");
  /*
    Open the file with read/write mode,
    create the file if not found,
    treat file as binary, and use default flags.
  */
  data_file = my_open(path, O_RDWR | O_CREAT | O_BINARY | O_SHARE, MYF(0));
  if(data_file == -1)
    DBUG_RETURN(errno);
  read_header();
  DBUG_RETURN(0);
}
```

```
/* write a row of length bytes to file and return position */
long long Spartan_data::write_row(byte *buf, int length)
{
  long long pos;
  int i;
  int len;
  byte deleted = 0;

  DBUG_ENTER("Spartan_data::write_row");
  /*
    Write the deleted status byte and the length of the record.
    Note: my_write() returns the bytes written or -1 on error
  */
  pos = my_seek(data_file, 0L, MY_SEEK_END, MYF(0));
  /*
    Note: my_malloc takes a size of memory to be allocated,
    MySQL flags (set to zero fill and with extra error checking).
    Returns number of bytes allocated -- <= 0 indicates an error.
  */
  i = my_write(data_file, &deleted, sizeof(byte), MYF(0));
  memcpy(&len, &length, sizeof(int));
  i = my_write(data_file, (byte *)&len, sizeof(int), MYF(0));
  /*
    Write the row data to the file. Return new file pointer or
    return -1 if error from my_write().
  */
  i = my_write(data_file, buf, length, MYF(0));
  if (i == -1)
    pos = i;
  else
    number_records++;
  DBUG_RETURN(pos);
}

/* update a record in place */
long long Spartan_data::update_row(byte *old_rec, byte *new_rec,
                                   int length, long long position)
{
  long long pos;
  long long cur_pos;
  byte *cmp_rec;
  int len;
  byte deleted = 0;
  int i = -1;
```

```
DBUG_ENTER("Spartan_data::update_row");
if (position == 0)
  position = header_size; //move past header
pos = position;
/*
  If position unknown, scan for the record by reading a row
  at a time until found.
*/
if (position == -1) //don't know where it is...scan for it
{
  cmp_rec = (byte *)my_malloc(length, MYF(MY_ZEROFILL | MY_WME));
  pos = 0;
  /*
    Note: my_seek() returns pos if no errors or -1 if error.
  */
  cur_pos = my_seek(data_file, header_size, MY_SEEK_SET, MYF(0));
  /*
    Note: read_row() returns current file pointer if no error or
    -1 if error.
  */
  while ((cur_pos != -1) && (pos != -1))
  {
    pos = read_row(cmp_rec, length, cur_pos);
    if (memcmp(old_rec, cmp_rec, length) == 0)
    {
      pos = cur_pos;      //found it!
      cur_pos = -1;       //stop loop gracefully
    }
    else if (pos != -1)   //move ahead to next rec
      cur_pos = cur_pos + length + record_header_size;
  }
  my_free((gptr)cmp_rec, MYF(0));
}
/*
  If position found or provided, write the row.
*/
if (pos != -1)
{
  /*
    Write the deleted byte, the length of the row, and the data
    at the current file pointer.
    Note: my_write() returns the bytes written or -1 on error
  */
```

```
    my_seek(data_file, pos, MY_SEEK_SET, MYF(0));
    i = my_write(data_file, &deleted, sizeof(byte), MYF(0));
    memcpy(&len, &length, sizeof(int));
    i = my_write(data_file, (byte *)&len, sizeof(int), MYF(0));
    pos = i;
    i = my_write(data_file, new_rec, length, MYF(0));
  }
  DBUG_RETURN(pos);
}

/* delete a record in place */
int Spartan_data::delete_row(byte *old_rec, int length,
                             long long position)
{
  int i = -1;
  long long pos;
  long long cur_pos;
  byte *cmp_rec;
  byte deleted = 1;

  DBUG_ENTER("Spartan_data::delete_row");
  if (position == 0)
    position = header_size; //move past header
  pos = position;
  /*
    If position unknown, scan for the record by reading a row
    at a time until found.
  */
  if (position == -1) //don't know where it is...scan for it
  {
    cmp_rec = (byte *)my_malloc(length, MYF(MY_ZEROFILL | MY_WME));
    pos = 0;
    /*
      Note: my_seek() returns pos if no errors or -1 if error.
    */
    cur_pos = my_seek(data_file, header_size, MY_SEEK_SET, MYF(0));
    /*
      Note: read_row() returns current file pointer if no error or
      -1 if error.
    */
    while ((cur_pos != -1) && (pos != -1))
    {
      pos = read_row(cmp_rec, length, cur_pos);
```

```
      if (memcmp(old_rec, cmp_rec, length) == 0)
      {
        number_records--;
        number_del_records++;
        pos = cur_pos;
        cur_pos = -1;
      }
      else if (pos != -1)   //move ahead to next rec
        cur_pos = cur_pos + length + record_header_size;
    }
    my_free((gptr)cmp_rec, MYF(0));
  }
  /*
    If position found or provided, write the row.
  */
  if (pos != -1)            //mark as deleted
  {
    /*
      Write the deleted byte set to 1 which marks row as deleted
      at the current file pointer.
      Note: my_write() returns the bytes written or -1 on error
    */
    pos = my_seek(data_file, pos, MY_SEEK_SET, MYF(0));
    i = my_write(data_file, &deleted, sizeof(byte), MYF(0));
    i = (i > 1) ? 0 : i;
  }
  DBUG_RETURN(i);
}

/* read a row of length bytes from file at position */
int Spartan_data::read_row(byte *buf, int length, long long position)
{
  int i;
  int rec_len;
  long long pos;
  byte deleted = 2;

  DBUG_ENTER("Spartan_data::read_row");
  if (position <= 0)
    position = header_size; //move past header
  pos = my_seek(data_file, position, MY_SEEK_SET, MYF(0));
  /*
    If my_seek found the position, read the deleted byte.
    Note: my_read() returns bytes read or -1 on error
  */
```

```
      if (pos != -1L)
      {
        i = my_read(data_file, &deleted, sizeof(byte), MYF(0));
        /*
          If not deleted (deleted == 0), read the record length then
          read the row.
        */
        if (deleted == 0) /* 0 = not deleted, 1 = deleted */
        {
          i = my_read(data_file, (byte *)&rec_len, sizeof(int), MYF(0));
          i = my_read(data_file, buf,
                      (length < rec_len) ? length : rec_len, MYF(0));
        }
        else if (i == 0)
          DBUG_RETURN(-1);
        else
          DBUG_RETURN(read_row(buf, length, cur_position() +
                               length + (record_header_size - sizeof(byte))));
      }
      else
        DBUG_RETURN(-1);
      DBUG_RETURN(0);
    }

    /* close file */
    int Spartan_data::close_table()
    {
      DBUG_ENTER("Spartan_data::close_table");
      if (data_file != -1)
      {
        my_close(data_file, MYF(0));
        data_file = -1;
      }
      DBUG_RETURN(0);
    }

    /* return number of records */
    int Spartan_data::records()
    {
      DBUG_ENTER("Spartan_data::num_records");
      DBUG_RETURN(number_records);
    }
```

```
/* return number of deleted records */
int Spartan_data::del_records()
{
  DBUG_ENTER("Spartan_data::num_records");
  DBUG_RETURN(number_del_records);
}


/* read header from file */
int Spartan_data::read_header()
{
  int i;
  int len;

  DBUG_ENTER("Spartan_data::read_header");
  if (number_records == -1)
  {
    my_seek(data_file, 0l, MY_SEEK_SET, MYF(0));
    i = my_read(data_file, (byte *)&crashed, sizeof(bool), MYF(0));
    i = my_read(data_file, (byte *)&len, sizeof(int), MYF(0));
    memcpy(&number_records, &len, sizeof(int));
    i = my_read(data_file, (byte *)&len, sizeof(int), MYF(0));
    memcpy(&number_del_records, &len, sizeof(int));
  }
  else
    my_seek(data_file, header_size, MY_SEEK_SET, MYF(0));
  DBUG_RETURN(0);
}


/* write header to file */
int Spartan_data::write_header()
{
  int i;

  DBUG_ENTER("Spartan_data::write_header");
  if (number_records != -1)
  {
    my_seek(data_file, 0l, MY_SEEK_SET, MYF(0));
    i = my_write(data_file, (byte *)&crashed, sizeof(bool), MYF(0));
    i = my_write(data_file, (byte *)&number_records, sizeof(int), MYF(0));
    i = my_write(data_file, (byte *)&number_del_records, sizeof(int), MYF(0));
  }
  DBUG_RETURN(0);
}
```

```
/* get position of the data file */
long long Spartan_data::cur_position()
{
  long long pos;

  DBUG_ENTER("Spartan_data::cur_position");
  pos = my_seek(data_file, 0L, MY_SEEK_CUR, MYF(0));
  if (pos == 0)
    DBUG_RETURN(header_size);
  DBUG_RETURN(pos);
}

/* truncate the data file */
int Spartan_data::trunc_table()
{
  DBUG_ENTER("Spartan_data::trunc_table");
  if (data_file != -1 )
  {
    my_chsize(data_file, 0, 0, MYF(MY_WME));
    write_header();
  }
  DBUG_RETURN(0);
}

/* determine the row size of the data file */
int Spartan_data::row_size(int length)
{
  DBUG_ENTER("Spartan_data::row_size");
  DBUG_RETURN(length + record_header_size);
}
```

Note the format I use to store the data. The class is designed to support reading data from disk and writing the data in memory to disk. I use a byte pointer to allocate a block of memory for storing the rows. What makes this really useful is that it provides the ability to write the rows in the table to disk using the internal MySQL row format. Likewise, I can read the data from disk and write it to a memory buffer and simply point the handler class to the block of memory to be returned to the optimizer.

However, I may not be able to predict the exact amount of memory needed to store a row. Some uses of the storage engine may have tables that have variable fields or even binary large objects (BLOBs). To overcome this problem, I chose to store a single integer length field at the start of each row. This allows me to scan a file and read variable-length rows by first reading the length field and then reading the number of bytes specified into the memory buffer.

■Tip Whenever coding an extension for the MySQL server, you should always use the my_xxx utility methods. The my_xxx utility methods are encapsulations of many of the base operating systems functions and provide a better level of cross-platform support.

The data class is rather straightforward and can be used to implement the basic read and write operations needed for a storage engine. However, I want to make the storage engine more efficient. To achieve good performance from my data file, I need to add an index mechanism. This is where things get a lot more complicated.

The Spartan_index Class

To solve the problem of indexing the data file, I implement a separate index class called Spartan_index. The index class is responsible for permitting the execution of point queries (query by index for a specific record), range queries (a series of keys either ascending or descending), as well as the ability to cache the index for fast searching. Listing 7-5 includes the complete header file for the Spartan_index class.

Listing 7-5. *Spartan_index Class Header*

```
/*
  spartan_index.h

  This header file defines a simple index class that can
  be used to store file pointer indexes (long long). The
  class keeps the entire index in memory for fast access.
  The internal memory structure is a linked list. While
  not as efficient as a B-tree, it should be usable for
  most testing environments. The constructor accepts the
  max key length. This is used for all nodes in the index.

  File Layout:
    SOF                            max_key_len (int)
    SOF + sizeof(int)              crashed (bool)
    SOF + sizeof(int) + sizeof(bool) DATA BEGINS HERE
*/
#include "my_global.h"
#include "my_sys.h"

const long METADATA_SIZE = sizeof(int) + sizeof(bool);
/*
  This is the node that stores the key and the file
  position for the data row.
*/
struct SDE_INDEX
{
  byte *key;
  long long pos;
  int length;
};
```

```
/* defines (doubly) linked list for internal list */
struct SDE_NDX_NODE
{
  SDE_INDEX key_ndx;
  SDE_NDX_NODE *next;
  SDE_NDX_NODE *prev;
};

class Spartan_index
{
public:
  Spartan_index(int keylen);
  Spartan_index();
  ~Spartan_index(void);
  int open_index(char *path);
  int create_index(char *path, int keylen);
  int insert_key(SDE_INDEX *ndx, bool allow_dupes);
  int delete_key(byte *buf, long long pos, int key_len);
  long long get_index_pos(byte *buf, int key_len);
  long long get_first_pos();
  byte *get_first_key();
  byte *get_last_key();
  byte *get_next_key();
  byte *get_prev_key();
  int close_index();
  int load_index();
  int destroy_index();
  SDE_INDEX *seek_index(byte *key, int key_len);
  SDE_NDX_NODE *seek_index_pos(byte *key, int key_len);
  int save_index();
  int trunc_index();
private:
  File index_file;
  int max_key_len;
  SDE_NDX_NODE *root;
  SDE_NDX_NODE *range_ptr;
  int block_size;
  bool crashed;
  int read_header();
  int write_header();
  long long write_row(SDE_INDEX *ndx);
  SDE_INDEX *read_row(long long Position);
  long long curfpos();
};
```

Notice that the class implements the expected form of create, open, close, read, and write methods. The load_index() method reads an entire index file into memory, storing the index as a doubly linked list. All of the index scanning and reference methods access the linked list in memory rather than accessing the disk. This saves a great deal of time and provides a way to keep the entire index in memory for fast insert and deletion. A corresponding method, save_index(), permits you to write the index from memory back to disk. The way these methods should be used is to call load_index() when the table is opened and then save_index() when the table is closed.

You may be wondering if there could be size limitations with this approach. Depending on the size of the index, how many indexes are created, and how many entries there are, this implementation could have some limitations. However, for the purposes of this tutorial and for the foreseeable use of the Spartan storage engine, this isn't a problem.

Another area you may be concerned about is the use of the doubly linked list. This implementation isn't likely to be your first choice for high-speed index storage. You are more likely to use a B-tree or some variant of one to create an efficient index access method. However, the linked list is easy to use and makes the implementation of a rather large set of source code a bit easier to manage. The example demonstrates how to incorporate an index class into your engine—not how to code a B-tree structure. This keeps the code simpler because the linked list is easier to code. For the purposes of this tutorial, the linked list structure will perform very well. In fact, you may even want to use it to form your own storage engine until you get the rest of the storage engine working, and then turn your attention to a better index class.

Listing 7-6 shows the complete source code for the Spartan_index class implementation. The code is rather lengthy so please feel free to either take some time and examine the methods or save the code reading for later and skip ahead to the description of how to start building the Spartan storage engine.

Listing 7-6. *Spartan_index Class Source Code*

```
/*
  Spartan_index.cpp

  This class reads and writes an index file for use with the Spartan data
  class. The file format is a simple binary storage of the
  Spartan_index::SDE_INDEX structure. The size of the key can be set via
  the constructor.
*/
#include "spartan_index.h"
#include <my_dir.h>

/* constuctor takes the maximum key length for the keys */
Spartan_index::Spartan_index(int keylen)
{
  root = NULL;
  crashed = false;
  max_key_len = keylen;
  index_file = -1;
  block_size = max_key_len + sizeof(long long) + sizeof(int);
}
```

```
/* constuctor (overloaded) assumes existing file */
Spartan_index::Spartan_index()
{
  root = NULL;
  crashed = false;
  max_key_len = -1;
  index_file = -1;
  block_size = -1;
}

/* destructor */
Spartan_index::~Spartan_index(void)
{
}

/* create the index file */
int Spartan_index::create_index(char *path, int keylen)
{
  DBUG_ENTER("Spartan_index::create_index");
  open_index(path);
  max_key_len = keylen;
  /*
    Block size is the key length plus the size of the index
    length variable.
  */
  block_size = max_key_len + sizeof(long long);
  write_header();
  DBUG_RETURN(0);
}

/* open index specified as path (pat+filename) */
int Spartan_index::open_index(char *path)
{
  DBUG_ENTER("Spartan_index::open_index");
  /*
    Open the file with read/write mode,
    create the file if not found,
    treat file as binary, and use default flags.
  */
  index_file = my_open(path, O_RDWR | O_CREAT | O_BINARY | O_SHARE, MYF(0));
  if(index_file == -1)
    DBUG_RETURN(errno);
  read_header();
  DBUG_RETURN(0);
}
```

```
/* read header from file */
int Spartan_index::read_header()
{
  int i;
  byte len;

  DBUG_ENTER("Spartan_index::read_header");
  if (block_size == -1)
  {
    /*
      Seek the start of the file.
      Read the maximum key length value.
    */
    my_seek(index_file, 0l, MY_SEEK_SET, MYF(0));
    i = my_read(index_file, &len, sizeof(int), MYF(0));
    memcpy(&max_key_len, &len, sizeof(int));
    /*
      Calculate block size as maximum key length plus
      the size of the key plus the crashed status byte.
    */
    block_size = max_key_len + sizeof(long long) + sizeof(int);
    i = my_read(index_file, &len, sizeof(bool), MYF(0));
    memcpy(&crashed, &len, sizeof(bool));
  }
  else
  {
    i = (int)my_seek(index_file, sizeof(int) + sizeof(bool), MY_SEEK_SET, MYF(0));
  }
  DBUG_RETURN(0);
}

/* write header to file */
int Spartan_index::write_header()
{
  int i;
  byte len;

  DBUG_ENTER("Spartan_index::write_header");
  if (block_size != -1)
  {
    /*
      Seek the start of the file and write the maximum key length
      then write the crashed status byte.
    */
```

```
      my_seek(index_file, 0l, MY_SEEK_SET, MYF(0));
      memcpy(&len, &max_key_len, sizeof(int));
      i = my_write(index_file, &len, sizeof(int), MYF(0));
      memcpy(&len, &crashed, sizeof(bool));
      i = my_write(index_file, &len, sizeof(bool), MYF(0));
    }
  DBUG_RETURN(0);
}

/* write a row (SDE_INDEX struct) to the index file */
long long Spartan_index::write_row(SDE_INDEX *ndx)
{
  long long pos;
  int i;
  int len;

  DBUG_ENTER("Spartan_index::write_row");
  /*
     Seek the end of the file (always append)
  */
  pos = my_seek(index_file, 0l, MY_SEEK_END, MYF(0));
  /*
    Write the key value.
  */
  i = my_write(index_file, ndx->key, max_key_len, MYF(0));
  memcpy(&pos, &ndx->pos, sizeof(long long));
  /*
    Write the file position for the key value.
  */
  i = i + my_write(index_file, (byte *)&pos, sizeof(long long), MYF(0));
  memcpy(&len, &ndx->length, sizeof(int));
  /*
    Write the length of the key.
  */
  i = i + my_write(index_file, (byte *)&len, sizeof(int), MYF(0));
  if (i == -1)
    pos = i;
  DBUG_RETURN(pos);
}

/* read a row (SDE_INDEX struct) from the index file */
SDE_INDEX *Spartan_index::read_row(long long Position)
{
  int i;
  long long pos;
  SDE_INDEX *ndx = NULL;

  DBUG_ENTER("Spartan_index::read_row");
```

```
  /*
    Seek the position in the file (Position).
  */
  pos = my_seek(index_file,(ulong) Position, MY_SEEK_SET, MYF(0));
  if (pos != -1L)
  {
    ndx = new SDE_INDEX();
    /*
      Read the key value.
    */
    i = my_read(index_file, ndx->key, max_key_len, MYF(0));
    /*
      Read the key value. If error, return NULL.
    */
    i = my_read(index_file, (byte *)&ndx->pos, sizeof(long long), MYF(0));
    if (i == -1)
    {
        delete ndx;
        ndx = NULL;
    }
  }
  DBUG_RETURN(ndx);
}

/* insert a key into the index in memory */
int Spartan_index::insert_key(SDE_INDEX *ndx, bool allow_dupes)
{
  SDE_NDX_NODE *p = NULL;
  SDE_NDX_NODE *n = NULL;
  SDE_NDX_NODE *o = NULL;
  int i = -1;
  int icmp;
  bool dupe = false;
  bool done = false;

  DBUG_ENTER("Spartan_index::insert_key");
  /*
    If this is a new index, insert first key as the root node.
  */
  if (root == NULL)
  {
    root = new SDE_NDX_NODE();
    root->next = NULL;
    root->prev = NULL;
    memcpy(root->key_ndx.key, ndx->key, max_key_len);
    root->key_ndx.pos = ndx->pos;
    root->key_ndx.length = ndx->length;
  }
```

```
        else //set pointer to root
          p = root;
        /*
          Loop through the linked list until a value greater than the
          key to be inserted, then insert new key before that one.
        */
        while ((p != NULL) && !done)
        {
          icmp = memcmp(ndx->key, p->key_ndx.key,
                        (ndx->length > p->key_ndx.length) ?
                        ndx->length : p->key_ndx.length);
          if (icmp > 0) // key is greater than current key in list
          {
            n = p;
            p = p->next;
          }
          /*
            If dupes not allowed, stop and return NULL
          */
          else if (!allow_dupes && (icmp == 0))
          {
            p = NULL;
            dupe = true;
          }
          else
          {
            n = p->prev; //stop, insert at n->prev
            done = true;
          }
        }
        /*
          If position found (n != NULL) and dupes permitted,
          insert key. If p is NULL insert at end else insert in middle
          of list.
        */
        if ((n != NULL) && !dupe)
        {
          if (p == NULL) //insert at end
          {
            p = new SDE_NDX_NODE();
            n->next = p;
            p->prev = n;
            memcpy(p->key_ndx.key, ndx->key, max_key_len);
            p->key_ndx.pos = ndx->pos;
            p->key_ndx.length = ndx->length;
          }
```

```
    else
    {
      o = new SDE_NDX_NODE();
      memcpy(o->key_ndx.key, ndx->key, max_key_len);
      o->key_ndx.pos = ndx->pos;
      o->key_ndx.length = ndx->length;
      o->next = p;
      o->prev = n;
      n->next = o;
      p->prev = o;
    }
    i = 1;
  }
  DBUG_RETURN(i);
}

/* delete a key from the index in memory. Note:
   position is included for indexes that allow dupes */
int Spartan_index::delete_key(byte *buf, long long pos, int key_len)
{
  SDE_NDX_NODE *p;
  int icmp;
  int buf_len;
  bool done = false;

  DBUG_ENTER("Spartan_index::delete_key");
  p = root;
  /*
    Search for the key in the list. If found, delete it!
  */
  while ((p != NULL) && !done)
  {
    buf_len = p->key_ndx.length;
    icmp = memcmp(buf, p->key_ndx.key,
                  (buf_len > key_len) ? buf_len : key_len);
    if (icmp == 0)
    {
      if (pos != -1)
        if (pos == p->key_ndx.pos)
          done = true;
      else
        done = true;
    }
    else
      p = p->next;
  }
```

```
  if (p != NULL)
  {
    /*
      Reset pointers for deleted node in list.
    */
    if (p->next != NULL)
      p->next->prev = p->prev;
    if (p->prev != NULL)
      p->prev->next = p->next;
    else
      root = p->next;
    delete p;
  }
  DBUG_RETURN(0);
}

/* update key in place (so if key changes!) */
int Spartan_index::update_key(byte *buf, long long pos, int key_len)
{
  SDE_NDX_NODE *p;
  bool done = false;

  DBUG_ENTER("Spartan_index::update_key");
  p = root;
  /*
    Search for the key.
  */
  while ((p != NULL) && !done)
  {
    if (p->key_ndx.pos == pos)
      done = true;
    else
      p = p->next;
  }
  /*
    If key found, overwrite key value in node.
  */
  if (p != NULL)
  {
    memcpy(p->key_ndx.key, buf, key_len);
  }
  DBUG_RETURN(0);
}
```

```
/* get the current position of the key in the index file */
long long Spartan_index::get_index_pos(byte *buf, int key_len)
{
  long long pos = -1;

  DBUG_ENTER("Spartan_index::get_index_pos");
  SDE_INDEX *ndx;
  ndx = seek_index(buf, key_len);
  if (ndx != NULL)
    pos = ndx->pos;
  DBUG_RETURN(pos);
}

/* get next key in list */
byte *Spartan_index::get_next_key()
{
  byte *key = 0;

  DBUG_ENTER("Spartan_index::get_next_key");
  if (range_ptr != NULL)
  {
    key = (byte *)my_malloc(max_key_len, MYF(MY_ZEROFILL | MY_WME));
    memcpy(key, range_ptr->key_ndx.key, range_ptr->key_ndx.length);
    range_ptr = range_ptr->next;
  }
  DBUG_RETURN(key);
}

/* get prev key in list */
byte *Spartan_index::get_prev_key()
{
  byte *key = 0;

  DBUG_ENTER("Spartan_index::get_prev_key");
  if (range_ptr != NULL)
  {
    key = (byte *)my_malloc(max_key_len, MYF(MY_ZEROFILL | MY_WME));
    memcpy(key, range_ptr->key_ndx.key, range_ptr->key_ndx.length);
    range_ptr = range_ptr->prev;
  }
  DBUG_RETURN(key);
}
```

```c
/* get first key in list */
byte *Spartan_index::get_first_key()
{
  SDE_NDX_NODE *n = root;
  byte *key = 0;

  DBUG_ENTER("Spartan_index::get_first_key");
  if (root != NULL)
  {
    key = (byte *)my_malloc(max_key_len, MYF(MY_ZEROFILL | MY_WME));
    memcpy(key, n->key_ndx.key, n->key_ndx.length);
  }
  DBUG_RETURN(key);
}

/* get last key in list */
byte *Spartan_index::get_last_key()
{
  SDE_NDX_NODE *n = root;
  byte *key = 0;

  DBUG_ENTER("Spartan_index::get_last_key");
  while (n->next != NULL)
    n = n->next;
  if (n != NULL)
  {
    key = (byte *)my_malloc(max_key_len, MYF(MY_ZEROFILL | MY_WME));
    memcpy(key, n->key_ndx.key, n->key_ndx.length);
  }
  DBUG_RETURN(key);
}

/* just close the index */
int Spartan_index::close_index()
{
  SDE_NDX_NODE *p;

  DBUG_ENTER("Spartan_index::close_index");
  if (index_file != -1)
  {
    my_close(index_file, MYF(0));
    index_file = -1;
  }
```

```
   while (root != NULL)
   {
     p = root;
     root = root->next;
     delete p;
   }
   DBUG_RETURN(0);
}

/* find a key in the index */
SDE_INDEX *Spartan_index::seek_index(byte *key, int key_len)
{
  SDE_INDEX *ndx = NULL;
  SDE_NDX_NODE *n = root;
  int buf_len;
  bool done = false;

  DBUG_ENTER("Spartan_index::seek_index");
  if (n != NULL)
  {
    while((n != NULL) && !done)
    {
      buf_len = n->key_ndx.length;
      if (memcmp(n->key_ndx.key, key,
          (buf_len > key_len) ? buf_len : key_len) == 0)
        done = true;
      else
        n = n->next;
    }
  }
  if (n != NULL)
  {
    ndx = &n->key_ndx;
    range_ptr = n;
  }
  DBUG_RETURN(ndx);
}

/* find a key in the index and return position too */
SDE_NDX_NODE *Spartan_index::seek_index_pos(byte *key, int key_len)
{
  SDE_NDX_NODE *n = root;
  int buf_len;
  bool done = false;
```

```
    DBUG_ENTER("Spartan_index::seek_index_pos");
    if (n != NULL)
    {
      while((n->next != NULL) && !done)
      {
        buf_len = n->key_ndx.length;
        if (memcmp(n->key_ndx.key, key,
            (buf_len > key_len) ? buf_len : key_len) == 0)
          done = true;
        else if (n->next != NULL)
          n = n->next;
      }
    }
    DBUG_RETURN(n);
  }

  /* read the index file from disk and store in memory */
  int Spartan_index::load_index()
  {
    SDE_INDEX *ndx;
    int i = 0;

    DBUG_ENTER("Spartan_index::load_index");
    if (root != NULL)
      destroy_index();
    /*
      First, read the metadata at the front of the index.
    */
    read_header();
    while(!eof(index_file))
    {
      ndx = new SDE_INDEX();
      i = my_read(index_file, (byte *)&ndx->key, max_key_len, MYF(0));
      i = my_read(index_file, (byte *)&ndx->pos, sizeof(long long), MYF(0));
      i = my_read(index_file, (byte *)&ndx->length, sizeof(int), MYF(0));
      insert_key(ndx, false);
    }
    DBUG_RETURN(0);
  }

  /* get current position of index file */
  long long Spartan_index::curfpos()
  {
    long long pos = 0;
```

```
  DBUG_ENTER("Spartan_index::curfpos");
  pos = my_seek(index_file, 0l, MY_SEEK_CUR, MYF(0));
  DBUG_RETURN(pos);
}

/* write the index back to disk */
int Spartan_index::save_index()
{
  SDE_NDX_NODE *n = root;
  int i;

  DBUG_ENTER("Spartan_index::save_index");
  i = chsize(index_file, 0L);
  write_header();
  while (n != NULL)
  {
    write_row(&n->key_ndx);
    n = n->next;
  }
  DBUG_RETURN(0);
}

int Spartan_index::destroy_index()
{
  SDE_NDX_NODE *n = root;

  DBUG_ENTER("Spartan_index::destroy_index");
  while (root != NULL)
  {
    n = root;
    root = n->next;
    delete n;
  }
  root = NULL;
  DBUG_RETURN(0);
}

/* ket the file position of the first key in index */
long long Spartan_index::get_first_pos()
{
  long long pos = -1;

  DBUG_ENTER("Spartan_index::get_first_pos");
  if (root != NULL)
    pos = root->key_ndx.pos;
  DBUG_RETURN(pos);
}
```

```
/* truncate the index file */
int Spartan_index::trunc_index()
{
  DBUG_ENTER("Spartan_index::trunc_table");
  if (index_file != -1)
  {
    my_chsize(index_file, 0, 0, MYF(MY_WME));
    write_header();
  }
  DBUG_RETURN(0);
}
```

Notice that, as with the Spartan_data class, I use the DBUG routines to set the trace elements for debugging. I also use the my_xxx platform-safe utility methods.

■ **Tip** These methods can be found in the mysys directory under the root of the source tree. They are normally implemented as C functions stored in a file of the same name (e.g., the my_write.c file contains the my_write() method).

The index works by storing a key using a byte pointer to a block of memory, a position value (long long) that stores a offset location on disk used in the Spartan_data class to position the file pointer, and a length field that stores the length of the key. The length variable is used in the memory compare method to set the comparison length. These data items are stored in a structure named SDE_INDEX. The doubly linked list node is another structure that contains an SDE_INDEX structure. The list node structure, named SDE_NDX_NODE, also provides the next and prev pointers for the list.

When using the index to store the location of data in the Spartan_data class file, you can call the insert_index() method, passing in the key and the offset of the data item in the file. This offset is returned on the my_write() method calls. This technique allows you to store the index pointers to data on disk and reuse that information without transforming it to position the file pointer to the correct location on disk.

The index is stored on disk in consecutive blocks of data that correspond to the size of the SDE_INDEX structure. The file has a header, which is used to store a crashed status variable and a variable that stores the maximum key length. The crashed status variable is helpful to identify the rare case when a file has become corrupted or errors have occurred during reading or writing that compromise the integrity of the file or its metadata. Rather than use a variable-length field like the data class, I chose to use a fixed-length memory block to simplify the read and write methods for disk access. In this case, I have made a conscious decision to sacrifice space for simplicity.

Now that you've had an introduction to the dirty work of building a storage engine—the low-level I/O functions—let's see how we can build a basic storage engine. I'll return to the Spartan_data and Spartan_index classes in later sections discussing stages 1 and 5, respectively.

Getting Started

The following tutorial assumes you have your development environment configured and you have compiled the server with the debug switch turned on (see Chapter 5). I'll examine each of the stages of building the Spartan storage engine. Before you get started, there's one very important step that you need to do: create a test file to test the storage engine so we can drive the development toward a specific goal. Chapter 4 examined the MySQL test suite and how to create and run tests. Feel free to refer to that chapter for additional details or a refresher.

Tip If you are using Windows, you cannot use the MySQL test suite. However, you can still create the test file and just copy and paste the statements into a MySQL client program and run the tests that way.

The first thing you should do is create a new test to test the Spartan storage engine. Even though the engine doesn't exist yet, in the spirit of test-driven development you should create the test before writing the code. Let's do that now.

The test file should begin as a simple test to create the table and retrieve rows from it. You can create a complete test file that includes all of the operations that I'll show you, but it may be best to start out with a simple test and extend it as you progress through the stages of building the Spartan storage engine. This has the added benefit that your test will only test the current stage and not generate errors for operations not yet implemented. Listing 7-7 shows a sample basic test to test a stage 1 Spartan storage engine.

As you go through this tutorial, you'll be adding statements to this test, effectively building the complete test for the completed Spartan storage engine as you go.

Listing 7-7. *Spartan Storage Engine Test File (spartandb.test)*

```
#
# Simple test for the Spartan storage engine
#
--disable_warnings
drop table if exists t1;
--enable_warnings

CREATE TABLE t1 (
  col_a int,
  col_b varchar(20),
  col_c int
) ENGINE=SPARTAN;

DROP TABLE t1;
```

You can create this file in the /mysql-test/t directory off the root of the source tree. When you execute it the first time, it's OK to have errors. In fact, you should execute the test before beginning stage 1. That way, you know the test works (it doesn't bomb out). If you recall from Chapter 4, you can execute the test by using the commands from the /mysql-test directory:

```
%> touch r/spartandb.result
%> ./mysql-test-run.pl spartanddb
%> cp r/cab.reject r/spartandb.result
%> ./mysql-test-run.pl spartandb
```

Did you try it? Did it produce errors? The test suite returned [failed], but if you examine the log file generated, you won't see any errors, but you will see warnings. Why didn't it fail? Well, it turns out that MySQL will use a default storage engine if the storage engine you specify on your create statement doesn't exist. In this case, my MySQL server installation issued the warning that the system was using the default MyISAM storage engine because the Spartan storage engine was not found. Listing 7-8 shows an example of the /mysql-test/r/spartandb.log file.

Listing 7-8. *Example Log File from Test Run*

```
drop table if exists t1;
CREATE TABLE t1 (
col_a int,
col_b varchar(20),
col_c int
) ENGINE=SPARTAN;
Warnings:
Warning 1266 Using storage engine MyISAM for table 't1'
DROP TABLE t1;
```

Stage 1: Stubbing the Engine

The goal of this stage is to produce a stubbed storage engine. The stubbed engine will have the most basic operation of being able to choose the engine on the CREATE statement and creating the base table meta file (.frm). I know that doesn't sound like much and while it doesn't actually store anything,[5] creating a stage 1 engine allows you to ensure you have all of the initial code changes necessary to register the storage engine with the server. I mentioned previously that some of these changes may not be necessary in future releases of the MySQL system. It is always a good idea to check the online reference manual for the latest changes prior to working with the MySQL source code.

Creating the Spartan Source Files

The first thing you will need to do is create a directory named spartan under the /storage directory off the main source code tree. I'll use the example storage engine to get us started. The MySQL reference manual suggests using the source files for the example storage engine as your basis. The example storage engine contains all of the necessary methods implemented with the correct code statements. This makes it easy to create the base source files for the Spartan storage engine.

---

5. The inspiration for this chapter was the lack of coverage available for those seeking to develop their own storage engine. Very few references go beyond creating a stage 1 engine in their examples.

> **Tip** Most source files named (.cc) referenced in Linux are named (.cpp) in Windows.

Copy the *.cc and *.h files from the /storage/example directory to the /storage/spartan directory. You should now have two files in the spartan directory: ha_example.cc (.cpp in Windows) and ha_example.h. The ha_ prefix indicates that the files are derived from the handler class and represent a table handler. Rename the files ha_spartan.cc (.cpp in Windows) and ha_spartan.h.

> **Note** The phrase *table handler* has been replaced with the more recent phrase *storage engine*. You may encounter bits of the documentation that talk about table handlers. They are synonymous with storage engines and apply accordingly.

The next step in creating the source files is to change all occurrences of the words example and EXAMPLE to spartan and SPARTAN, respectively. You can use your favorite code editor or text processor to effect the changes. The resulting files should have all the example identifiers changed to spartan (e.g., st_example_share should become st_spartan_share). Be sure to do the changes using case sensitivity. Your storage engine won't work if you don't do this correctly.

Edit the ha_spartan.cc file and change the comments on the handlerton declaration. An example of this change is

```
handlerton spartan_hton= {
  MYSQL_HANDLERTON_INTERFACE_VERSION,
  "SPARTAN",
  SHOW_OPTION_YES,
  "Spartan storage engine",
  DB_TYPE_SPARTAN_DB,
...
```

Lastly, edit the ha_spartan.h file and add the include directive to include the spartan_data.h file as shown here:

```
#include "spartan_data.h"
```

Adding the Source Files to the Project Files in Linux

If you use Linux, you need to create a makefile and include file and modify the configure script in the root of the source code tree. Copy the Makefile.am file from the /storage/example directory to the /storage/spartan directory. Open the Makefile.am file and replace all occurrences of example with spartan. While you have the Makefile.am file open, edit the noinst_HEADERS and libspartan_a_SOURCES lines and add the spartan_data files as shown here:

```
noinst_HEADERS  = ha_spartan.h spartan_data.h
libspartan_a_SOURCES  = ha_spartan.cc spartan_data.cc
```

Likewise, copy the Makefile.in file from the /storage/example directory to the /storage/ spartan directory. Open the Makefile.in file and replace all occurrences of example with spartan. While you have the Makefile.in file open, edit the noinst_HEADERS and libspartan_a_SOURCES lines and add the spartan_data files as shown here:

```
noinst_HEADERS   = ha_spartan.h spartan_data.h
libspartan_a_SOURCES  = ha_spartan.cc spartan_data.cc
am_libspartan_a_OBJECTS = ha_spartan.$(OBJEXT) spartan_data.$(OBJEXT)
```

The next step is to modify the configure script in the root of the source tree. Open this file and search for the word csv. The first occurrence should be in the Optional Packages: section. You need to add the option statement --with-spartan-storage-engine as shown here:

```
  --with-csv-storage-engine
                          enable csv storage engine (default is "yes")
  --with-spartan-storage-engine
                          enable spartan storage engine (default is "yes")
  --with-blackhole-storage-engine
                          enable blackhole storage engine (default is no)
```

The best way to add these statements is to copy the ones for the CSV storage engine and then replace all occurrences of csv and tina with spartan. The next section you need to create is the one that processes the makefiles. Find the one for the CSV storage engine and then copy the entire section and make the statement replacements. The resulting section should look like this:

```
# Check whether --with-spartan-storage-engine or
# --without-spartan-storage-engine was given.
if test "${with_spartan_storage_engine+set}" = set; then
  withval="$with_spartan_storage_engine"

else
   with_spartan_storage_engine='"yes"'
fi;
echo "$as_me:$LINENO: checking whether to use Spartan storage engine" >&5
echo $ECHO_N "checking whether to use Spartan storage engine... $ECHO_C" >&6
if test "${mysql_cv_use_spartan_storage_engine+set}" = set; then
  echo $ECHO_N "(cached) $ECHO_C" >&6
else
  mysql_cv_use_spartan_storage_engine=$with_spartan_storage_engine
fi
echo "$as_me:$LINENO: result: $mysql_cv_use_spartan_storage_engine" >&5
echo "${ECHO_T}$mysql_cv_use_spartan_storage_engine" >&6


if test "$mysql_cv_use_spartan_storage_engine" != no; then
if test "sparton_hton" != "no"
```

```
then
  cat >>confdefs.h <<\_ACEOF
#define WITH_spartan_storage_ENGINE 1
_ACEOF

  mysql_se_decls="${mysql_se_decls},spartan_hton"
  mysql_se_htons="${mysql_se_htons},&spartan_hton"
  if test "no" != "no"
  then
    mysql_se_objs="$mysql_se_objs no"
  fi
  mysql_se_dirs="$mysql_se_dirs storage/spartan"
  mysql_se_libs="$mysql_se_libs \$(top_builddir)/storage/spartan/libspartan.a"
else
  mysql_se_plugins="$mysql_se_plugins storage/spartan"
fi


          ac_config_files="$ac_config_files storage/spartan/Makefile"


fi
```

The next section you will change is the ac_config_target section. Once again, search for csv, copy the block, and make the statement replacements. The resulting section should look like this:

```
"storage/spartan/Makefile" ) CONFIG_FILES=➡
  "$CONFIG_FILES storage/spartan/Makefile" ;;
```

Similarly, you must also add #undef in the config.h.in file. Open the file and enter the following:

```
/* Build Spartan storage engine */
#undef WITH_SPARTAN_STORAGE_ENGINE
```

The configure.in include file for the configure script must have the creation statements added. Open that file and enter the following near the bottom of the file (copy and paste from an existing one and then replace the name):

```
MYSQL_STORAGE_ENGINE(spartan,,,"yes",,spartan_hton,storage/spartan,no,
  \$(top_builddir)/storage/spartan/libspartan.a,[
  AC_CONFIG_FILES(storage/spartan/Makefile)
])
```

■Tip MySQL AB may change this process slightly in future releases. Be sure to run the command ./configure --help to ensure the version of the code you are using still relies on the --with arguments. Changes may affect the code you need to change in the configure and configure.in files.

Create a directory named .deps in the /storage/spartan directory. Create a file named ha_example.Po in the /storage/spartan/.deps directory. Set the contents of the file to #dummy. When you compile the code, the make tools will overwrite the file with the proper Spartan storage engine parameters.

All that remains now is to make a small set of changes to a few server files and run the configure script before compiling. You should wait to compile after you've finished adding the Spartan storage engine to the server.

Adding the Source Files to the Project Files in Windows

If you use Windows, you need to create a new project, add the source files to it, and configure the project file settings. Open the main solution file in the root of the source tree. Add a new project to the solution and name it spartan. Place the project file in the /storage/spartan directory. Be sure to create a C++ Win32 | Win32 Project and not a console or .NET project. In the Win32 Application Wizard, click Next and then set the application type to static library and turn off precompiled headers. Once the project is created, add the Spartan_data and spartan_index source files to the project.

In order for the spartan project to find the appropriate include files, you need to open the Spartan Property Pages dialog box, select C/C++ and then General on the left, and select the Additional Include Directories option. The easiest way to do this is to open the Example Property Pages dialog box and copy the string from that project to the spartan project. Figure 7-2 shows the Spartan Property Pages dialog box with the correct include string added.

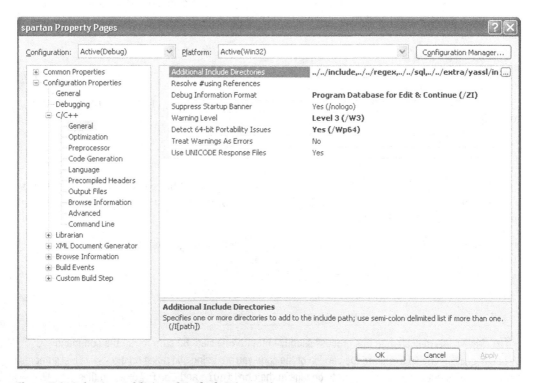

Figure 7-2. *Selecting Additional Include Directories*

While you have the properties dialog box open, select C/C++ and then Code Generation on the left, and then change the Runtime Library option to Multi-threaded debug (/MTd). Figure 7-3 depicts the Spartan Property Pages dialog box with the correct setting. Close this dialog box when you are done.

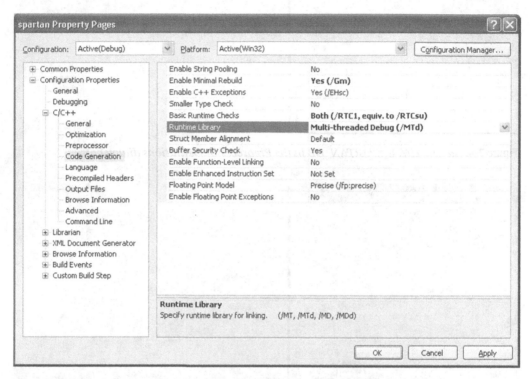

Figure 7-3. *Change the Runtime Library option to Multi-threaded debug (/MTd).*

You also have to add the spartan project to the mysqld project dependencies from the Project ➤ Project Dependencies menu. Be sure to set the configuration to compile in debug mode. The last step is to modify the project settings for the mysqld project. You need to add the HAVE_SPARTAN_DB and WITH_SPARTAN_STORAGE_ENGINE preprocessor directives. Open the mysqld project properties, click on C/C++ and then Preprocessor on the left, and then click the ellipsis button (...) next to the Preprocessor Definitions option. Figures 7-4 and 7-5 depict these modifications (keep in mind that order does not matter).

Tip If you discover that some of the source code that you want to edit is grayed out, it may be because the preprocessor definitions are either missing or misspelled.

All that remains now is to make a small set of changes to a few server files and compile the server. You should wait to compile after you've finished adding the Spartan storage engine to the server.

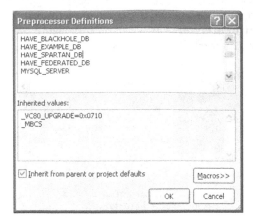

Figure 7-4. *Adding HAVE_SPARTAN_DB in the Preprocessor Definitions dialog box*

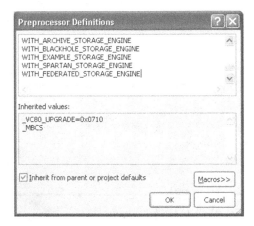

Figure 7-5. *Adding WITH_SPARTAN_STORAGE_ENGINE in the Preprocessor Definitions dialog box*

Adding the Spartan Storage Engine to the Server

Several files that must be modified in order to add the storage engine to the server. Table 7-2 lists the files that need to be changed and a summary of the changes necessary. Specific instructions for making these modifications follow, with excerpts of the source code for emphasis and clarification.

Table 7-2. *Summary of Changes to the MySQL Source Files*

Source File	Description of Changes
/include/my_config.h	Add #define statements for the Spartan storage engine.
/sql/handler.h	Add another entry to the legacy_db_type enumeration. This allows the handler to identify the spartan table type.

Table 7-2. *Summary of Changes to the MySQL Source Files*

Source File	Description of Changes
/sql/handler.cc	Add another entry to the show_table_alias_st structure. This allows MySQL to alias the spartan string with the table type identifier in the handler.h file.
/sql/handlerton-win.cpp (Windows only)	Add the #ifdef conditional compilation statements to work with the preprocessor directives.
/sql/mysql_priv.h	Add the #ifdef conditional statements to work with the preprocessor directives.
/sql/set_var.cc	Add the sys_var_have_variable settings for the Spartan engine strings.
/sql/mysqld.cc	Add the #undef statement and the SHOW_COMP_OPTION for the HAVE_SPARTAN_DB definition.

Open the my_config.h file and search for example. You should find the #define statement for the example storage engine near the bottom of the file. Copy and paste the two statements, then make the replacement for the Spartan storage engine. The following shows the correct code statements:

```
/* Build Spartan storage engine */
#define WITH_SPARTAN_STORAGE_ENGINE 1
```

Open the handler.h file and modify the legacy_db_type enumeration. Add the DB_TYPE_SPARTAN_DB element to the bottom of the list, above the DEFAULT database type element. This ensures that the value assigned to the DB_TYPE_SPARTAN_DB element does not conflict with the default storage engine element (notice the assignment DB_TYPE_DEFAULT=127). The following shows the completed code statements:

```
enum legacy_db_type
{
  DB_TYPE_UNKNOWN=0,DB_TYPE_DIAB_ISAM=1,
  DB_TYPE_HASH,DB_TYPE_MISAM,DB_TYPE_PISAM,
  DB_TYPE_RMS_ISAM, DB_TYPE_HEAP, DB_TYPE_ISAM,
  DB_TYPE_MRG_ISAM, DB_TYPE_MYISAM, DB_TYPE_MRG_MYISAM,
  DB_TYPE_BERKELEY_DB, DB_TYPE_INNODB,
  DB_TYPE_GEMINI, DB_TYPE_NDBCLUSTER,
  DB_TYPE_EXAMPLE_DB, DB_TYPE_ARCHIVE_DB, DB_TYPE_CSV_DB,
  DB_TYPE_FEDERATED_DB,
  DB_TYPE_BLACKHOLE_DB,
  DB_TYPE_PARTITION_DB,
  DB_TYPE_BINLOG,
  DB_TYPE_SPARTAN_DB,
  DB_TYPE_DEFAULT=127 // Must be last
};
```

Open the handler.cc file and modify the show_table_alias_st array. Add the DB_TYPE_SPARTAN_DB element and string to the bottom of the list, above the UNKNOWN database type element. Order does not matter, but convention shows MySQL AB uses the last element as a sentinel so you should not make it the last element. The following shows the correct code statements:

```
struct show_table_alias_st sys_table_aliases[]=
{
  {"INNOBASE",   DB_TYPE_INNODB},
  {"NDB",        DB_TYPE_NDBCLUSTER},
  {"BDB",        DB_TYPE_BERKELEY_DB},
  {"HEAP",       DB_TYPE_HEAP},
  {"MERGE",      DB_TYPE_MRG_MYISAM},
  {"SPARTAN",    DB_TYPE_SPARTAN_DB},
  {NullS,        DB_TYPE_UNKNOWN}
};
```

Open the handler-win.cpp file and add the #ifdef and extern statements to the file (Windows only). Copy and paste the #ifdef statements for the example storage engine, then make the replacements. The following shows the correct code statements:

```
#ifdef WITH_SPARTAN_STORAGE_ENGINE
extern handlerton spartan_hton;
#endif
```

You also need to modify the sys_table_types structure and add the #ifdef for the Spartan engine (Windows only). Copy and paste the #ifdef statements for the example storage engine and then make the replacements. Here are the correct code statements:

```
handlerton *sys_table_types[]=
{
  &heap_hton,
  &myisam_hton,
...
#ifdef WITH_SPARTAN_STORAGE_ENGINE
  &spartan_hton,
#endif
```

Open the mysql_priv.h file and add the #ifdef for the Spartan engine. Copy and paste the #ifdef statements for the example storage engine and make the replacements. The following are the correct code statements:

```
#ifdef WITH_SPARTAN_STORAGE_ENGINE
extern handlerton spartan_hton;
#define have_spartan_db spartan_hton.state
#else
extern SHOW_COMP_OPTION have_spartan_db;
#endif
```

Open the set_var.cc file and add the sys_var_have_variable array for the Spartan engine. Copy and paste the statements for the example storage engine and then make the replacements. The correct code statements are as follows:

```
sys_var_have_variable sys_have_spartan_db("have_spartan_engine",
                                          &have_spartan_db);
```

You also need to add the sys_have_spartan_db.name definition to the init_vars array. Again, copy and paste the statements for the example storage engine and then make the replacements. The following shows the correct code statements:

```
SHOW_VAR init_vars[]= {
  {"auto_increment_increment", (char*) &sys_auto_increment_increment, SHOW_SYS},
  {"auto_increment_offset",    (char*) &sys_auto_increment_offset, SHOW_SYS},
...
  {sys_have_example_db.name,   (char*) &have_example_db,          SHOW_HAVE},
  {sys_have_spartan_db.name,   (char*) &have_spartan_db,          SHOW_HAVE},
  {sys_have_federated_db.name,(char*) &have_federated_db,         SHOW_HAVE},
...
```

The last file you need to modify is mysqld.cc. Open the file and add the #undef statement for the Spartan engine. You also need to set the SHOW_COMP_OPTION located below the #undef statements. Copy and paste the statements for the example storage engine, then make the replacements. Here are the correct code statements:

```
/*************************************************************************
  Instantiate have_xyx for missing storage engines
**************************************************************************/
#undef have_berkeley_db
#undef have_innodb
#undef have_ndbcluster
#undef have_example_db
#undef have_spartan_db
#undef have_archive_db
#undef have_csv_db
#undef have_federated_db
#undef have_partition_db
#undef have_blackhole_db

SHOW_COMP_OPTION have_berkeley_db= SHOW_OPTION_NO;
SHOW_COMP_OPTION have_innodb= SHOW_OPTION_NO;
SHOW_COMP_OPTION have_ndbcluster= SHOW_OPTION_NO;
SHOW_COMP_OPTION have_example_db= SHOW_OPTION_NO;
SHOW_COMP_OPTION have_spartan_db= SHOW_OPTION_NO;
SHOW_COMP_OPTION have_archive_db= SHOW_OPTION_NO;
SHOW_COMP_OPTION have_csv_db= SHOW_OPTION_NO;
SHOW_COMP_OPTION have_federated_db= SHOW_OPTION_NO;
SHOW_COMP_OPTION have_partition_db= SHOW_OPTION_NO;
SHOW_COMP_OPTION have_blackhole_db= SHOW_OPTION_NO;
```

There is one other change you need to make. At the bottom of the ha_spartan.cc file, you should see a mysq_declare_plugin section. This is the code that the plug-in interface uses for hot plug-in of the engine. Feel free to modify this section to indicate that it is the Spartan storage engine. You can add your own name and comments to the code. This section isn't used yet, but when the pluggable storage engine architecture is complete you'll need this section to enable the plug-in interface.

Note This structure is likely to change. Please refer to the online MySQL reference manual for the latest changes.

```
#ifdef MYSQL_PLUGIN
mysql_declare_plugin
{
  MYSQL_STORAGE_ENGINE_PLUGIN,
  &spartan_hton,
  spartan_hton.name,
  "Dr. Bell",
  "Spartan Storage Engine -- Expert MySQL",
  spartan_init_func, /* Plugin Init */
  spartan_done_func, /* Plugin Deinit */
  0x0001 /* 0.1 */,
}
mysql_declare_plugin_end;
#endif
```

If that seemed like a lot of work for a pluggable storage engine, you're right—it is. Fortunately, this situation will improve in future releases of the MySQL system.

Compiling the Spartan Engine

Now that all of these changes have been made, it is time to compile the server and test the new Spartan storage engine. The process is the same as with other compilations. You can compile the server in debug mode so that you can generate trace files and use an interactive debugger to explore the source code while the server is running.

Compiling on Linux

Compiling the server on Linux requires building the project using the configure, make, and make install commands. To set up the server to detect the Spartan storage engine and to compile in debug mode, run the following commands:

```
./configure --with-spartan-storage-engine --with-debug
make
make install
```

All of the dependent projects will be compiled automatically. Since some of the key header files have been changed and some new preprocessor definitions were added, the compilation may take a bit longer.

Compiling on Windows

Compiling the server on Windows requires building the `mysqld` project in Visual Studio. All of the dependent projects will be compiled automatically. Since some of the key header files have been changed and some new preprocessor definitions were added, the compilation may take a bit longer.

Testing Stage 1 of the Spartan Engine

Once the server is compiled, you can launch it and run it. You may be tempted to test the server using the interactive MySQL client. That's OK, and I did exactly that. Listing 7-9 shows the results from the MySQL client after running a number of SQL commands. In this example, I ran the SHOW STORAGE ENGINES, CREATE TABLE, SHOW CREATE TABLE, and DROP TABLE commands. The results show that these commands work and that the spartandb test should pass when I run it.

Listing 7-9. *Example Manual Test of the Stage 1 Spartan Storage Engine*

```
mysql> SHOW STORAGE ENGINES;
```

Engine	Support	Comment	Transactions	XA	Savepoints
EXAMPLE	YES	Example storage engine	NO	NO	NO
MEMORY	YES	Hash based, stored in me	NO	NO	NO
MRG_MYISAM	YES	Collection of identical	NO	NO	NO
MyISAM	DEFAULT	Default engine as of MyS	NO	NO	NO
BLACKHOLE	YES	/dev/null storage engine	NO	NO	NO
SPARTAN	YES	Spartan storage engine	NO	NO	NO
InnoDB	YES	Supports transactions, r	YES	YES	YES
ARCHIVE	YES	Archive storage engine	NO	NO	NO
FEDERATED	YES	Federated MySQL storage	YES	NO	NO

```
9 rows in set (0.02 sec)

mysql> USE test;

Database changed
```

```
mysql> CREATE TABLE t1 (col_a int, col_b varchar(20), col_c int) ENGINE=SPARTAN;
```

```
Query OK, 0 rows affected (0.02 sec)
```

```
mysql> SHOW CREATE TABLE t1 \G
```

```
Current database: test

*************************** 1. row ***************************
       Table: t1
Create Table: CREATE TABLE `t1` (
  `col_a` int(11) DEFAULT NULL,
  `col_b` varchar(20) DEFAULT NULL,
  `col_c` int(11) DEFAULT NULL
) ENGINE=SPARTAN DEFAULT CHARSET=latin1
1 row in set (0.20 sec)
```

```
mysql> DROP TABLE t1;
```

```
Query OK, 0 rows affected (1 min 19.14 sec)
```

```
mysql>
```

I know that the storage engine is working because it is listed in the SHOW command and in the SHOW CREATE TABLE statement. Had the engine failed to connect, it may or may not have shown in the SHOW command but the CREATE TABLE command would have specified the MyISAM storage engine instead of the Spartan storage engine.

You should also run the spartandb test you created earlier (if you're running Linux). When you run the test this time, the test passes. That's because the storage engine is now part of the server and can be recognized. Let's put the SELECT command in and rerun the test. It should once again pass. At this point, you could add the test results to the /r directory for automated test reporting. Listing 7-10 shows the updated test.

Listing 7-10. *Updated Spartan Storage Engine Test File (spartandb.test)*

```
#
# Simple test for the Spartan storage engine
#
--disable_warnings
drop table if exists t1;
--enable_warnings
```

```
CREATE TABLE t1 (
  col_a int,
  col_b varchar(20),
  col_c int
) ENGINE=SPARTAN;

SELECT * FROM t1;

DROP TABLE t1;
```

Well, that's it for a stage 1 engine. It is plugged in and ready for you to add the Spartan_data and spartan_index classes. In the next stage, we'll add the ability to create, open, close, and delete files. That may not sound like much, but in the spirit of incremental development, you can add that bit, then test and debug until everything works before you move on to the more challenging operations.

Stage 2: Working with Tables

The goal of this stage is to produce a stubbed storage engine that can create, open, close, and delete data files. This stage is where you set up the basic file-handling routines and establish that the engine is working with the files correctly. MySQL has provided a number of file I/O routines for you that encapsulate the lower-level functions, making them platform-safe. The following is a sample of some of the functions available. See the files in the /mysys directory for more details.

- my_create(...): Create files

- my_open(...): Open files

- my_read(...): Read data from files

- my_write(...): Write data to files

- my_delete(...): Delete file

- fn_format(...): Create a platform-safe path statement

In this stage, I'll show you how to incorporate the Spartan_data class for the low-level I/O. I'll walk you through each change and include the completed method source code for each change.

Updating the Spartan Source Files

The first thing you need to do is either download the compressed source files from the Apress web site and copy them into your /storage/spartan directory or use the spartan_data.cc and spartan_data.h files you created earlier in the chapter.

Since I'm using Spartan_data class to handle the low-level I/O, I need to create an object pointer to hold an instance of that class. However, I need to place it somewhere where it can be shared. The reason for this is so that there won't be two or more instances of the class trying to read the same file. While that may be OK, it is more complicated and would require a bit more work. Instead, I'll place an object reference in the Spartan handler's shared structure.

Tip After you make each of the changes, compile the spartan project to make sure there are no errors. Correct any errors before proceeding to the next change.

Updating the Header File

Open the ha_spartan.h file and add the #include to include the spartan_data.h header file, then add the object reference to the st_spartan_share structure. Listing 7-11 shows the completed code change (comments omitted for brevity). Once you have this change made, go ahead and recompile the spartan source files to make sure there aren't any errors.

Listing 7-11. *Changes to Share Structure in ha_spartan.h*

```
#include "spartan_data.h"

#ifdef USE_PRAGMA_INTERFACE
#pragma interface        /* gcc class implementation */
#endif

...
typedef struct st_spartan_share {
  char *table_name;
  uint table_name_length,use_count;
  pthread_mutex_t mutex;
  THR_LOCK lock;
  Spartan_data *data_class;
} SPARTAN_SHARE;
```

Updating the Class File

The next series of modifications are done in the ha_spartan.cc file. Open that file and locate the get_share() method. Since there is an object reference now in the share structure, we need to instantiate it when the share is created. Add the instantiation of the Spartan_data class to the method. Name the object reference data_class. Listing 7-12 shows an excerpt of the method with changes. Notice that I set the initial use count of the share to 0 when created and incremented the count on subsequent references. This ensures the share is always available when there are references to it. The count is decremented when the share is dereferenced. When the count reaches 0, the memory in the share is released. This is necessary since the share contains the data and index classes that all shares need.

Tip If you are using Windows and IntelliSense in Visual Studio does not recognize the new Spartan_data class, you need to repair the .ncb file. Exit Visual Studio, delete the .ncb file from the source root, and then rebuild mysqld. This may take a while but when it is done IntelliSense will work again.

Listing 7-12. *Changes to the get_share() Method in ha_spartan.cc*

```
static SPARTAN_SHARE *get_share(const char *table_name, TABLE *table)
{
  SPARTAN_SHARE *share;
  uint length;
  char *tmp_name;

  pthread_mutex_lock(&spartan_mutex);  //create a lock for single access
  length=(uint) strlen(table_name);

  if (!(share=(SPARTAN_SHARE*) hash_search(&spartan_open_tables,
                                    (byte*) table_name,
                                    length)))
  {
    /*
      Allocate several memory blocks at one time.
      Note: my_multi_malloc takes MySQL flags
      (set to zero fill and with extra error checking),
      one or more pairs of addresses and size of memory to allocate.
    */
    if (!my_multi_malloc(MYF(MY_WME | MY_ZEROFILL),
                      &share, sizeof(*share),
                      &tmp_name, length+1,
                      NullS))
    {
      pthread_mutex_unlock(&spartan_mutex);
      return NULL;
    }
    /*
      Set the initial variables to defaults.
    */
    share->use_count=0;
    share->table_name_length=length;
    share->table_name = (char *)my_malloc(length + 1, MYF(0));
    strcpy(share->table_name,table_name);
    /*
      Insert table name into hash for future reference.
    */
    if (my_hash_insert(&spartan_open_tables, (byte*) share))
      goto error;
    thr_lock_init(&share->lock);
    /*
      Create an instance of data class
    */
    share->data_class = new Spartan_data();
    pthread_mutex_init(&share->mutex,MY_MUTEX_INIT_FAST);
  }
```

```
  share->use_count++; // increment use count on reference
  pthread_mutex_unlock(&spartan_mutex); //release mutex lock
  return share;

error:
  pthread_mutex_destroy(&share->mutex);
  my_free((gptr) share, MYF(0));

  return NULL;
}
```

Naturally, you also need to destroy the object reference when the share structure is destroyed. Locate the free_share() method and add the code to destroy the data class object reference. Listing 7-13 shows an excerpt of the method with the changes.

Listing 7-13. *Changes to the free_share() Method in ha_spartan.cc*

```
static int free_share(SPARTAN_SHARE *share)
{
  DBUG_ENTER("ha_spartan::free_share");
  pthread_mutex_lock(&spartan_mutex);
  if (!--share->use_count)
  {
    if (share->data_class != NULL)
      delete share->data_class;
    share->data_class = NULL;
    /*
      Remove the share from the hash.
    */
    hash_delete(&spartan_open_tables, (byte*) share);
    thr_lock_delete(&share->lock);
    pthread_mutex_destroy(&share->mutex);
    my_free((gptr)share->table_name, MYF(0));
}
  pthread_mutex_unlock(&spartan_mutex);

  DBUG_RETURN(0);
}
```

The handler instance of the Spartan storage engine also must provide the file extensions for the data files. Since there is both a data and an index file, you need to create two file extensions. You define the file extensions and add them to the ha_spartan_exts array. Use .sde for the data file and .sdi for the index file. MySQL uses these extensions for deletes and other maintenance operations. Locate the ha_spartan_exts array, add the #defines above it, and add those definitions to the array. Listing 7-14 shows the changes to the array structure.

Listing 7-14. *Changes to the ha_spartan_exts Array in ha_spartan.cc*

```
#define SDE_EXT ".sde"
#define SDI_EXT ".sdi"
...
static const char *ha_spartan_exts[] = {
  SDE_EXT,
  SDI_EXT,
  NullS
};
```

The first operation you need to add is the create file operation. This will create the empty
file to contain the data for the table. Locate the create() method and add the code to get a copy
of the share structure, then call the data class create_table() method and close the table.
Listing 7-15 shows the updated create method. I'll show you how to add the index class in a
later stage.

Listing 7-15. *Changes to the create() Method in ha_spartan.cc*

```
int ha_spartan::create(const char *name, TABLE *table_arg,
                       HA_CREATE_INFO *create_info)
{
  DBUG_ENTER("ha_spartan::create");
  char name_buff[FN_REFLEN];

  if (!(share = get_share(name, table)))
    DBUG_RETURN(1);
  /*
    Call the data class create table method.
    Note: the fn_format() method correctly creates a file name from the
    name passed into the method.
  */
  if (share->data_class->create_table(fn_format(name_buff, name, "", SDE_EXT,
                                      MY_REPLACE_EXT|MY_UNPACK_FILENAME)))
    DBUG_RETURN(-1);
  share->data_class->close_table();
}
```

The next operation you need to add is the open file operation. This will open the file that
contains the data for the table. Locate the open() method and add the code to get a copy of the
share structure and open the table. Listing 7-16 shows the updated open method. I'll show you
how to add the index class in a later stage.

Listing 7-16. *Changes to the open() Method in ha_spartan.cc*

```
int ha_spartan::open(const char *name, int mode, uint test_if_locked)
{
  DBUG_ENTER("ha_spartan::open");
  char name_buff[FN_REFLEN];
```

```
  if (!(share = get_share(name, table)))
    DBUG_RETURN(1);
  /*
    Call the data class open table method.
    Note: the fn_format() method correctly creates a file name from the
    name passed into the method.
  */
  share->data_class->open_table(fn_format(name_buff, name, "", SDE_EXT,
                                MY_REPLACE_EXT|MY_UNPACK_FILENAME));
  thr_lock_data_init(&share->lock,&lock,NULL);
  DBUG_RETURN(0);
}
```

Notice that I placed the code in a critical section identified between the method calls of
pthread_mutex_lock(&spartan_mutex) and pthread_mutex_unlock(&spartan_mutex). I do this
because there is only one instance of the data class object and I want to restrict access to the
object when the code in the critical section is executed. Although not strictly necessary for all
cases (like reading data), it is a good practice.

The close operation is done for us in the free_share() method so you don't need to add
anything there.

The next operation you need to add is the delete file operation. This will delete the files
that contain the data for the table. Locate the delete_table() method and add the code to get
a copy of the share structure, close the table, and call the my_delete() function to delete the
table. Listing 7-17 shows the updated delete method. I'll show you how to add the index class
in a later stage.

Listing 7-17. *Changes to the delete_table() Method in ha_spartan.cc*

```
int ha_spartan::delete_table(const char *name)
{
  DBUG_ENTER("ha_spartan::delete_table");
  char name_buff[FN_REFLEN];

  /*
    Begin critical section by locking the spartan mutex variable.
  */
  pthread_mutex_lock(&spartan_mutex);
  if (!(share = get_share(name, table)))
    DBUG_RETURN(1);
  share->data_class->close_table();
  /*
    Call the mysql delete file method.
    Note: the fn_format() method correctly creates a file name from the
    name passed into the method.
  */
  my_delete(fn_format(name_buff, name, "", SDE_EXT,
            MY_REPLACE_EXT|MY_UNPACK_FILENAME), MYF(0));
  /*
```

```
    End section by unlocking the spartan mutex variable.
  */
  pthread_mutex_unlock(&spartan_mutex);
  DBUG_RETURN(0);
}
```

There is one last operation that many developers forget to include. The RENAME TABLE command allows users to rename tables. Your storage handler must also be able to copy the file to a new name and then delete the old one. While the MySQL server handles the rename of the .frm file, you need to perform the copy for the data file. Locate the rename_table() method and add the code to get a copy of the share structure, close the table, and call the my_copy() function to copy the table. Listing 7-18 shows the updated rename table method. I'll show you how to add the index class in a later stage.

Listing 7-18. *Changes to the rename_table() Method in ha_spartan.cc*

```
int ha_spartan::rename_table(const char * from, const char * to)
{
  DBUG_ENTER("ha_spartan::rename_table ");
  char data_from[FN_REFLEN];
  char data_to[FN_REFLEN];

  if (!(share = get_share(from, table)))
    DBUG_RETURN(1);
  /*
    Begin critical section by locking the spartan mutex variable.
  */
  pthread_mutex_lock(&spartan_mutex);
  /*
    Close the table then copy it then reopen new file.
  */
  share->data_class->close_table();
  my_copy(fn_format(data_from, from, "", SDE_EXT,
          MY_REPLACE_EXT|MY_UNPACK_FILENAME),
          fn_format(data_to, to, "", SDE_EXT,
          MY_REPLACE_EXT|MY_UNPACK_FILENAME), MYF(0));
  share->data_class->open_table(data_to);
  /*
    End section by unlocking the spartan mutex variable.
  */
  pthread_mutex_unlock(&spartan_mutex);
  /*
    Delete the file using MySQL's delete file method.
  */
  my_delete(data_from, MYF(0));
  DBUG_RETURN(0);
}
```

OK, you now have a completed stage 2 engine. All that is left to do is compile the server and run the tests.

Testing Stage 2 of the Spartan Engine

When you run the spartandb test again, you should see all of the statements complete successfully. However, there are two things the test doesn't verify for you. First, you need to make sure the .sde file was created and deleted. Second, you need to make sure the rename command works.

Testing the commands for creating and dropping the table is easy. Launch your server and then a MySQL client. Issue the CREATE statement from the test and then use your file browser to navigate to the /data/test folder. There you should see two files: t1.frm and t1.sde. Return to your MySQL client and issue the DROP statement. Then return to the /data/test folder and verify that the files are indeed deleted.

Testing the command that renames the table is also easy. Repeat the CREATE statement test and then issue the command

```
RENAME TABLE t1 TO t2;
```

Use your file browser to navigate to the /data/test folder. There you should see two files: t2.frm and t2.sde. Return to your MySQL client and issue the DROP statement. Then return to the /data/test folder and verify that the files are indeed deleted.

Now that you have verified the RENAME statement works, add that to the spartandb test file and rerun the test. The test should complete without errors. Listing 7-19 shows the updated spartandb.test file.

Listing 7-19. *Updated Spartan Storage Engine Test File (spartandb.test)*

```
#
# Simple test for the Spartan storage engine
#
--disable_warnings
drop table if exists t1;
--enable_warnings

CREATE TABLE t1 (
  col_a int,
  col_b varchar(20),
  col_c int
) ENGINE=SPARTAN;

SELECT * FROM t1;

RENAME TABLE t1 TO t2;

DROP TABLE t2;
```

Well, that's it for a stage 2 engine. It is plugged in and creates, deletes, and renames files. In the next stage, we'll add the ability to read and write data.

Stage 3: Reading and Writing Data

The goal of this stage is to produce a working storage engine that can read and write data. In this stage, I'll show you how to incorporate the Spartan_data class for reading and writing data. I'll walk you through each change and include the completed method source code for each change.

Updating the Spartan Source Files

Making a stage 3 engine requires updates to the basic reading process (described earlier). To implement the read operation, you'll be making changes to the rnd_init(), rnd_next(), position(), and rnd_pos() methods in the ha_spartan.cc file. The position() and rnd_pos() methods are used during large sorting operations and use an internal buffer to store the rows. The write operation requires changes to only the write_row() method.

Updating the Header File

The position methods require that you store a pointer—either a record offset position or a key value to be used in the sorting operations. MySQL AB provides a nifty way of doing this, as you'll see in the position methods in a moment. Open the ha_spartan.h file and add the current_position variable to the ha_spartan class. Listing 7-20 shows an excerpt with the changes.

Listing 7-20. *Changes to the ha_spartan Class in ha_spartan.h*

```
class ha_spartan: public handler
{
  THR_LOCK_DATA lock;       /* MySQL lock */
  SPARTAN_SHARE *share;     /* Shared lock info */
  off_t current_position;   /* Current position in the file during a file scan */
...
```

Updating the Source File

Return to the ha_spartan.cc file as that is where the rest of the changes need to be made. The first method you need to change is rnd_init(). Here is where you need to set the initial conditions for a table scan. In this case, you can set the current position to 0 (start of file) and the number of records to 0, and specify the length of the item you want to use for the sorting methods. In this case, use a long long since that is the data type for the current position in the file. Listing 7-21 shows the updated method with the changes.

Listing 7-21. *Changes to the rnd_init() Method in ha_spartan.cc*

```
int ha_spartan::rnd_init(bool scan)
{
  DBUG_ENTER("ha_spartan::rnd_init");
  current_position = 0;
  records = 0;
  ref_length = sizeof(long long);
  DBUG_RETURN(0);
}
```

■**Caution** This is the point at which we start adding functionality beyond that of the example engine. Be
sure to correctly specify your return codes. The example engine tells the optimizer a function is not supported
by issuing the return statement DBUG_RETURN(HA_ERR_WRONG_COMMAND);. Be sure to change these to
something other than the wrong command return code (e.g., 0).

The next method you need to change is rnd_next(), which is responsible for getting the
next record from the file and detecting the end of the file. In this method, you can call the data
class read_row() method, passing in the record buffer, the length of the buffer, and the current
position in the file. Notice the return for the end of the file and the setting of more statistics.
The method also records the current position so the next call to the method will advance the
file to the next record. Listing 7-22 shows the updated method with the changes.

Listing 7-22. *Changes to the rnd_next() Method in ha_spartan.cc*

```
int ha_spartan::rnd_next(byte *buf)
{
  int rc;

  DBUG_ENTER("ha_spartan::rnd_next");
  ha_statistic_increment(&SSV::ha_read_rnd_next_count);
  /*
    Read the row from the data file.
  */
  rc = share->data_class->read_row(buf, table->s->rec_buff_length,
                                   current_position);
  if (rc != -1)
    current_position = (off_t)share->data_class->cur_position();
  else
    DBUG_RETURN(HA_ERR_END_OF_FILE);
  records++;
  DBUG_RETURN(0);
}
```

The Spartan_data class is nice because it stores the records in the same format as the
MySQL internal buffer. In fact, it just writes a few bytes of a header for each record storing a
deleted flag and the record length (for use in scanning and repairing). If you were working on a
storage engine that stored the data in a different format, you would need to perform the translation at this point. A sample of how that translation could be accomplished is found in the
ha_tina.cc file. The process looks something like this:

```
for (Field **field=table->field ; *field ; field++)
{
  /* copy field data to your own storage type */
  my_value = (*field)->val_str();
  my_store_field(my_value);
}
```

In this example, you are iterating through the field array, writing out the data in your own format. Look for the ha_tina::find_current_row() method for an example.

The next method you need to change is position(), which records the current position of the file in the MySQL pointer storage mechanism. It is called after each call to rnd_next(). The methods for storing and retrieving these pointers are my_store_ptr() and my_get_ptr(). The store pointer method takes a reference variable (the place you want to store something), the length of what you want to store, and the thing you want to store as parameters. The get pointer method takes a reference variable and the length of what you are retrieving and returns the item stored. These methods are used in the case of an order by rows where the data will need to be sorted. Take a look at the changes for the position() method shown in Listing 7-23 to see how you can call the store pointer method.

Listing 7-23. *Changes to the position() Method in ha_spartan.cc*

```
void ha_spartan::position(const byte *record)
{
  DBUG_ENTER("ha_spartan::position");
  my_store_ptr(ref, ref_length, current_position);
  DBUG_VOID_RETURN;
}
```

The next method you need to change is rnd_pos(), which is where you'll retrieve the current position stored and then read in the row from that position. Notice in this method we also increment the read statistic ha_read_rnd_next_count. This provides the optimizer information about how many rows there are in the table and can be helpful in optimizing later queries. Listing 7-24 shows the updated method with the changes.

Listing 7-24. *Changes to the rnd_pos() Method in ha_spartan.cc*

```
int ha_spartan::rnd_pos(byte * buf, byte *pos)
{
  DBUG_ENTER("ha_spartan::rnd_pos");
  ha_statistic_increment(&SSV::ha_read_rnd_next_count);
  current_position = (off_t)my_get_ptr(pos,ref_length);
  share->data_class->read_row(buf, current_position, -1);
  DBUG_RETURN(0);
}
```

The next method you need to change is info(), which returns information to the optimizer to help choose an optimal execution path. This is an interesting method to implement, and when you read the comments in the source code it'll seem humorous. What you need to do in this method is to return the number of records. MySQL AB states that you should always return a value of 2 or more. This disengages portions of the optimizer that are wasteful for a record set of one row. Listing 7-25 shows the updated info() method.

Listing 7-25. *Changes to the info() Method in ha_spartan.cc*

```
void ha_spartan::info(uint flag)
{
  DBUG_ENTER("ha_spartan::info");
  /* This is a lie, but you don't want the optimizer to see zero or 1 */
  if (records < 2)
    records= 2;
  DBUG_VOID_RETURN;
}
```

The last method you need to change is write_row(). This is where you'll be writing the data to the data file using the Spartan_data class again. Like the read, the Spartan_data class need only write the record buffer to disk preceded by a delete status flag and the record length. Listing 7-26 shows the updated method with the changes.

Listing 7-26. *Changes to the write_row() Method in ha_spartan.cc*

```
int ha_spartan::write_row(byte * buf)
{
  DBUG_ENTER("ha_spartan::write_row");
  ha_statistic_increment(&SSV::ha_write_count);
  pthread_mutex_lock(&spartan_mutex);
  share->data_class->write_row(buf, table->s->rec_buff_length);
  pthread_mutex_unlock(&spartan_mutex);
  DBUG_RETURN(0);
}
```

Notice once again I have placed a mutex (for example, critical section) around the write so that no two threads can write at the same time. Now is a good time to compile the server and debug any errors. When that is done, you'll have a completed stage 3 engine. All that is left to do is compile the server and run the tests.

Testing Stage 3 of the Spartan Engine

When you run the spartandb test again, you should see all of the statements complete successfully. If you are wondering why I always begin with running the test from the last increment, that's because you want to make sure none of the new code broke anything that the old code was doing. In this case, you can see that you can still create, rename, and delete tables. Now let's move on to testing the read and write operations.

Testing these functions is easy. Launch your server and then a MySQL client. If you have deleted the test table, re-create it again and then issue the command:

```
INSERT INTO t1 VALUES(1, "first test", 24);
INSERT INTO t1 VALUES(4, "second test", 43);
INSERT INTO t1 VALUES(3, "third test", -2);
```

After each statement you should see the successful insertion of the records. If you encounter errors (which you shouldn't), you can launch your debugger, set breakpoints in all of the read and write methods in the ha_spartan.cc file, and then debug the problem. You should not look any further than the ha_spartan.cc file as that is the only file that could contain the source of the error.[6]

Now you can issue a SELECT statement and see what the server sends back to you. Enter the command

```
SELECT * FROM t1;
```

You should see all three rows returned. Listing 7-27 shows the results of running the query.

Listing 7-27. *Results of Running INSERT/SELECT Statements*

```
+-------+-------------+-------+
| col_a | col_b       | col_c |
+-------+-------------+-------+
| 1     | first test  | 24    |
| 4     | second test | 43    |
| 3     | third test  | -2    |
+-------+-------------+-------+
3 rows in set (0.00 sec)
```

Now that you have verified that the read and writes work, add tests for those operations to the spartandb test file and rerun the test. The test should complete without errors. Listing 7-28 shows the updated spartandb.test file.

Listing 7-28. *Updated Spartan Storage Engine Test File (spartandb.test)*

```
#
# Simple test for the Spartan storage engine
#
--disable_warnings
drop table if exists t1;
--enable_warnings

CREATE TABLE t1 (
  col_a int,
  col_b varchar(20),
  col_c int
) ENGINE=SPARTAN;
```

---

6. Well, maybe the low-level I/O source code. It's always possible I've missed something or something has changed in the server since I wrote that class.

```
SELECT * FROM t1;
INSERT INTO t1 VALUES(1, "first test", 24);
INSERT INTO t1 VALUES(4, "second test", 43);
INSERT INTO t1 VALUES(3, "third test", -2);
SELECT * FROM t1;
RENAME TABLE t1 TO t2;
SELECT * FROM t2;
DROP TABLE t2;
```

Well, that's it for a stage 3 engine. It is now a basic read/write storage engine that does all of the basic necessities for reading and writing data. In the next stage, we'll add the ability to update and delete data.

Stage 4: Updating and Deleting Data

The goal of this stage is to produce a working storage engine that can update and delete data. In this stage, I'll show you how to incorporate the Spartan_data class for updating and deleting data. I'll walk you through each change and include the completed method source code for each change.

The Spartan_data class performs updating in place. That is, the old data is overwritten with the new data. Deletion is performed by marking the data as deleted and skipping the deleted records on reads. The read_row() method in the Spartan_data class skips the deleted rows. This may seem as if it will waste a lot of space, and that could be true if the storage engine were used in a situation where there are lots of deletes and inserts. To mitigate that possibility, you can always dump and then drop the table, and reload the data from the dump. This will remove the empty records. Depending on how you plan to build your own storage engine, this concept may be something you need to reconsider.

Updating the Spartan Source Files

This stage requires you to update the update_row(), delete_row(), and delete_all_rows() methods. The delete_all_rows() method is a time-saving method used to empty a table all at once rather than a row at a time. The optimizer may call this method for truncation operations and when it detects a mass delete query.

Updating the Header File

There are no changes necessary to the ha_spartan.h file for a stage 4 storage engine.

Updating the Source File

Open the ha_spartan.cc file and locate the update_row() method. This method has the old record and the new record buffers passed as parameters. This is great because we don't have indexes and must do a table scan to locate the record! Fortunately, the Spartan_data class has the update_row() method that will do that work for you. Listing 7-29 shows the updated method with the changes.

Listing 7-29. *Changes to the update_row() Method in ha_spartan.cc*

```
int ha_spartan::update_row(const byte * old_data, byte * new_data)
{
  DBUG_ENTER("ha_spartan::update_row");
  pthread_mutex_lock(&spartan_mutex);
  share->data_class->update_row((byte *)old_data, new_data,
                table->s->rec_buff_length, current_position -
                share->data_class->row_size(table->s->rec_buff_length));
  pthread_mutex_unlock(&spartan_mutex);
  DBUG_RETURN(0);
}
```

The delete_row() method is similar to the update method. In this case, we call the delete_row() method in the Spartan_data class, passing in the buffer for the row to delete, the length of the record buffer, and -1 for the current position to force the table scan. Once again, the data class method does all of the heavy lifting for you. Listing 7-30 shows the updated method with the changes.

Listing 7-30. *Changes to the delete_row() Method in ha_spartan.cc*

```
int ha_spartan::delete_row(const byte * buf)
{
  long long pos;

  DBUG_ENTER("ha_spartan::delete_row");
  if (current_position > 0)
    pos = current_position -
      share->data_class->row_size(table->s->rec_buff_length);
  else
    pos = 0;
  pthread_mutex_lock(&spartan_mutex);
  share->data_class->delete_row((byte *)buf,
                        table->s->rec_buff_length, pos);
  pthread_mutex_unlock(&spartan_mutex);
  DBUG_RETURN(0);
}
```

The last method you need to update is delete_all_rows(). This method deletes all data in the table. The easiest way to do that is to delete the data file and re-create it. The Spartan_data class does this a little differently. The trunc_table() method resets the file pointer to the start of the file and truncates the file using the my_chsize() method. Listing 7-31 shows the updated method with the changes.

Listing 7-31. *Changes to the delete_all_rows() Method in ha_spartan.c*

```
int ha_spartan::delete_all_rows()
{
  DBUG_ENTER("ha_spartan::delete_all_rows");
  pthread_mutex_lock(&spartan_mutex);
  share->data_class->trunc_table();
  pthread_mutex_unlock(&spartan_mutex);
  DBUG_RETURN(0);
}
```

OK, now compile the server and debug any errors. When that is done, you'll have a completed stage 4 engine. All that is left to do is compile the server and run the tests.

Testing Stage 4 of the Spartan Engine

You should verify everything is working in the stage 3 engine first and then move on to testing the update and delete operations. When you run the spartandb test again, you should see all of the statements complete successfully.

The update and delete tests will require you to have a table created and have data in it. You can always add data using the normal INSERT statements as before. Feel free to add your own data and fill up the table with a few more rows.

When you have some data in the table, select one of the records and issue an update command for it using something like

```
UPDATE t1 SET col_b = "Updated!" WHERE col_a = 1;
```

When you run that command followed by a SELECT * command, you should see the row updated. You can then delete a row by issuing a delete command like

```
DELETE FROM t1 WHERE col_a = 3;
```

When you run that command followed by a SELECT * command, you should see that the row has been deleted. Have we missed something? Savvy software developers may notice that this test isn't comprehensive and does not cover all possibilities that the Spartan_data class has to consider. For example, deleting a row in the middle of the data isn't the same as deleting one at the beginning or at the end of the file. Updating the data is the same.

That's OK, because you can add that functionality to the spartandb test file. You can add more INSERT statements to add some more data and then update the first and last rows and one in the middle. You can also do the same for the delete operation. Listing 7-32 shows the updated spartandb.test file.

Listing 7-32. *Updated Spartan Storage Engine Test File (spartandb.test)*

```
#
# Simple test for the Spartan storage engine
#
--disable_warnings
drop table if exists t1;
--enable_warnings
```

```
CREATE TABLE t1 (
  col_a int,
  col_b varchar(20),
  col_c int
) ENGINE=SPARTAN;

SELECT * FROM t1;
INSERT INTO t1 VALUES(1, "first test", 24);
INSERT INTO t1 VALUES(4, "second test", 43);
INSERT INTO t1 VALUES(3, "fourth test", -2);
INSERT INTO t1 VALUES(4, "tenth test", 11);
INSERT INTO t1 VALUES(1, "seventh test", 20);
INSERT INTO t1 VALUES(5, "third test", 100);
SELECT * FROM t1;
UPDATE t1 SET col_b = "Updated!" WHERE col_a = 1;
SELECT * from t1;
UPDATE t1 SET col_b = "Updated!" WHERE col_a = 3;
SELECT * from t1;
UPDATE t1 SET col_b = "Updated!" WHERE col_a = 5;
SELECT * from t1;
DELETE FROM t1 WHERE col_a = 1;
SELECT * FROM t1;
DELETE FROM t1 WHERE col_a = 3;
SELECT * FROM t1;
DELETE FROM t1 WHERE col_a = 5;
SELECT * FROM t1;
RENAME TABLE t1 TO t2;
SELECT * FROM t2;
DROP TABLE t2;
```

Notice that I've added some rows that have duplicate values. You should expect the server to update and delete all matches for rows with duplicates. Go ahead and run that test and see what it does. Listing 7-33 shows an example of the expected results for this test. When you run the test under the test suite, it should complete without errors.

Listing 7-33. *Sample Results of Stage 4 Test*

```
mysql> CREATE TABLE t1 (
    ->    col_a int,
    ->    col_b varchar(20),
    ->    col_c int
    -> ) ENGINE=SPARTAN;
```

```
Query OK, 0 rows affected (0.22 sec)
```

```
mysql> SELECT * FROM t1;
```

```
Empty set (0.02 sec)
```

```
mysql> INSERT INTO t1 VALUES(1, "first test", 24);
```

```
Query OK, 1 row affected (0.00 sec)
```

```
mysql> INSERT INTO t1 VALUES(4, "second test", 43);
```

```
Query OK, 1 row affected (0.00 sec)
```

```
mysql> INSERT INTO t1 VALUES(3, "fourth test", -2);
```

```
Query OK, 1 row affected (0.00 sec)
```

```
mysql> INSERT INTO t1 VALUES(4, "tenth test", 11);
```

```
Query OK, 1 row affected (0.00 sec)
```

```
mysql> INSERT INTO t1 VALUES(1, "seventh test", 20);
```

```
Query OK, 1 row affected (0.00 sec)
```

```
mysql> INSERT INTO t1 VALUES(5, "third test", 100);
```

```
Query OK, 1 row affected (0.00 sec)
```

```
mysql> SELECT * FROM t1;
```

```
+-------+--------------+-------+
| col_a | col_b        | col_c |
+-------+--------------+-------+
| 1     | first test   | 24    |
| 4     | second test  | 43    |
| 3     | fourth test  | -2    |
| 4     | tenth test   | 11    |
| 1     | seventh test | 20    |
| 5     | third test   | 100   |
+-------+--------------+-------+
6 rows in set (0.01 sec)
```

```
mysql> UPDATE t1 SET col_b = "Updated!" WHERE col_a = 1;
```

```
Query OK, 2 rows affected (0.00 sec)
Rows matched: 2  Changed: 2  Warnings: 0
```

```
mysql> SELECT * from t1;
```

```
+-------+--------------+-------+
| col_a | col_b        | col_c |
+-------+--------------+-------+
| 1     | Updated!     | 24    |
| 4     | second test  | 43    |
| 3     | fourth test  | -2    |
| 4     | tenth test   | 11    |
| 1     | Updated!     | 20    |
| 5     | third test   | 100   |
+-------+--------------+-------+
6 rows in set (0.00 sec)
```

```
mysql> UPDATE t1 SET col_b = "Updated!" WHERE col_a = 3;
```

```
Query OK, 1 row affected (0.00 sec)
```

```
Rows matched: 1  Changed: 1  Warnings: 0
```

```
mysql> SELECT * from t1;
```

```
+-------+-------------+-------+
| col_a | col_b       | col_c |
+-------+-------------+-------+
| 1     | Updated!    | 24    |
| 4     | second test | 43    |
| 3     | Updated!    | -2    |
| 4     | tenth test  | 11    |
| 1     | Updated!    | 20    |
| 5     | third test  | 100   |
+-------+-------------+-------+
6 rows in set (0.00 sec)
```

```
mysql> UPDATE t1 SET col_b = "Updated!" WHERE col_a = 5;
```

```
Query OK, 1 row affected (0.00 sec)
```

```
Rows matched: 1  Changed: 1  Warnings: 0
```

```
mysql> SELECT * from t1;
```

```
+-------+-------------+-------+
| col_a | col_b       | col_c |
+-------+-------------+-------+
| 1     | Updated!    | 24    |
| 4     | second test | 43    |
| 3     | Updated!    | -2    |
| 4     | tenth test  | 11    |
| 1     | Updated!    | 20    |
| 5     | Updated!    | 100   |
+-------+-------------+-------+
6 rows in set (0.02 sec)
```

```
mysql> DELETE FROM t1 WHERE col_a = 1;
```

```
Query OK, 2 rows affected (0.00 sec)
```

```
mysql> SELECT * FROM t1;
```

```
+-------+-------------+-------+
| col_a | col_b       | col_c |
+-------+-------------+-------+
| 4     | second test | 43    |
| 3     | Updated!    | -2    |
| 4     | tenth test  | 11    |
| 5     | Updated!    | 100   |
+-------+-------------+-------+
4 rows in set (0.00 sec)
```

```
mysql> DELETE FROM t1 WHERE col_a = 3;
```

```
Query OK, 1 row affected (0.00 sec)
```

```
mysql> SELECT * FROM t1;
```

```
+-------+-------------+-------+
| col_a | col_b       | col_c |
+-------+-------------+-------+
| 4     | second test | 43    |
| 4     | tenth test  | 11    |
| 5     | Updated!    | 100   |
+-------+-------------+-------+
3 rows in set (0.00 sec)
```

```
mysql> DELETE FROM t1 WHERE col_a = 5;
```

```
Query OK, 1 row affected (0.00 sec)
```

```
mysql> SELECT * FROM t1;
```

```
+-------+-------------+-------+
| col_a | col_b       | col_c |
+-------+-------------+-------+
| 4     | second test | 43    |
| 4     | tenth test  | 11    |
+-------+-------------+-------+
2 rows in set (0.00 sec)
```

```
mysql> RENAME TABLE t1 TO t2;
```

```
Query OK, 0 rows affected (0.00 sec)
```

```
mysql> SELECT * FROM t2;
```

```
+-------+-------------+-------+
| col_a | col_b       | col_c |
+-------+-------------+-------+
| 4     | second test | 43    |
| 4     | tenth test  | 11    |
+-------+-------------+-------+
2 rows in set (0.00 sec)
```

```
mysql> DROP TABLE t2;
```

```
Query OK, 0 rows affected (1.69 sec)
```

Well, that's it for a stage 4 engine. It is now a basic read/write/update/delete storage engine. In the next stage, we'll add the index class to make queries more efficient.

Stage 5: Indexing the Data

The goal of this stage is to produce a working storage engine that includes support for a single index (with a little work you can make it have multiple indexes). In this stage, I'll show you how to incorporate the Spartan_index class for indexing the data. There are a lot of changes that need to be made. I recommend reading through this section before beginning to follow along with the changes.

Begin by adding the Spartan_index class files to the project files. If you use Linux, you must edit the Makefile.am and Makefile.in files as you did for stage 1, adding the spartan_index files to the commands like that shown here.

The Makefile.am file should contain (near line 377):

```
noinst_HEADERS       = ha_spartan.h spartan_data.h spartan_index.h
libspartan_a_SOURCES = ha_spartan.cc spartan_data.cc spartan_index.cc
```

The Makefile.in file should contain (near line 91):

```
noinst_HEADERS       = ha_spartan.h spartan_data.h spartan_index.h
libspartan_a_SOURCES = ha_spartan.cc spartan_data.cc spartan_index.cc
am_libspartan_a_OBJECTS = ha_spartan.$(OBJEXT) spartan_data.$(OBJEXT) \
  spartan_index.$(OBJEXT)
```

If you use Windows, add the files to the spartan project.

The Spartan_index class works by saving the record pointer to the corresponding row in the Spartan_data class. When the server searches for a record by the primary key, it can use the Spartan_index class to find the record pointer and then access the record directly by issuing a direct read call via the Spartan_data class. This makes the process of reading a random record much faster than performing a table scan.

The source code in this section is designed to work for the most basic of indexing operations. Depending on how complex your queries become, these changes should suffice for most situations. I'll walk you through each change and include the completed method source code for each change.

Updating the Spartan Source Files

The Spartan_index class simply saves the current position of the file along with the key. The methods in ha_spartan.cc you'll need to update include index_read(), index_read_idx(), index_next(), index_prev(), index_first(), and index_last(). These methods are used to read values from the index and iterate through the index, as well as go to the front and back (start, end) of the index. Fortunately, the Spartan_index class provides all of these operations.

Updating the Header File

To use the index class, we must first add a reference to the spartan_index.h file in the ha_spartan.h header file. Listing 7-34 shows the completed code change (I've omitted comments for brevity). Once you have this change made, go ahead and recompile the spartan source files to make sure there aren't any errors.

Listing 7-34. *Changes to Share Structure in ha_spartan.h*

```
typedef struct st_spartan_share {
  char *table_name;
  uint table_name_length,use_count;
  pthread_mutex_t mutex;
  THR_LOCK lock;
  Spartan_data *data_class;
  Spartan_index *index_class;
} SPARTAN_SHARE;
```

Open the ha_spartan.h file and add the #include directive to include the spartan_index.h header file, and then add the object reference to the st_spartan_share structure. Listing 7-35 shows the completed code change (again, with comments omitted for brevity). Once you have this change made, go ahead and recompile the spartan source files to make sure there aren't any errors.

Listing 7-35. *Changes to Share Structure in ha_spartan.h*

```
#include "spartan_data.h"
#include "spartan_index.h"
```

```
#ifdef USE_PRAGMA_INTERFACE
#pragma interface       /* gcc class implementation */
#endif
```

...

```
typedef struct st_spartan_share {
  char *table_name;
  uint table_name_length,use_count;
  pthread_mutex_t mutex;
  THR_LOCK lock;
  Spartan_data *data_class;
  Spartan_index *index_class;
} SPARTAN_SHARE;
```

While you have the header file open, there are a few other changes that need to be made. You have to add flags to tell the optimizer what index operations are supported. You also have to set the boundaries for the index parameters: the maximum number of keys supported, the maximum length of the keys, and the maximum key parts. For this stage, set the parameters as shown in Listing 7-36. I've included the entire set of changes you need to make to the file. Notice the table_flags() method. This is where you tell the optimizer what limitations the storage engine has. I have set the engine to disallow BLOBs and not permit auto-increment fields. A complete list of these flags can be found in handler.h.

Listing 7-36. *Changes to the ha_spartan Class Definition in ha_spartan.h*

```
  const char *index_type(uint inx) { return "Spartan_index class"; }
  const char **bas_ext() const;
...
  ulong table_flags() const
  {
    return (HA_NO_BLOBS | HA_NO_AUTO_INCREMENT);
  }
...
  ulong index_flags(uint inx, uint part, bool all_parts) const
  {
    return (HA_READ_NEXT | HA_READ_PREV | HA_READ_RANGE |
           HA_READ_ORDER | HA_KEYREAD_ONLY);
  }
...
  uint max_supported_keys()        const { return 1; }
  uint max_supported_key_parts()   const { return 1; }
  uint max_supported_key_length()  const { return 128; }
```

There is one last thing that needs to be added. Identifying the key in a record turns out to be easy but not very intuitive. To make things easier to work with, I've written two helper methods: get_key(), which finds the key field and returns its value or 0 if there are no keys, and get_key_len(), which returns the length of the key. Add their definitions to the class header file (ha_spartan.h) as shown here:

```
byte *get_key();
int get_key_len();
```

You will implement these methods in the ha_spartan.cc class file.

Updating the Class File

You are now ready to implement the index methods in the class source file. Open the
ha_spartan.cc file and locate the get_share() method. Add the instantiation of the index class.
Listing 7-37 shows the completed code change.

Listing 7-37. *Changes to the get_share() Method in ha_spartan.cc*

```
static SPARTAN_SHARE *get_share(const char *table_name, TABLE *table)
{
  SPARTAN_SHARE *share;
  uint length;
  char *tmp_name;

  pthread_mutex_lock(&spartan_mutex);  //create a lock for single access
  length=(uint) strlen(table_name);

  if (!(share=(SPARTAN_SHARE*) hash_search(&spartan_open_tables,
                                  (byte*) table_name,
                                  length)))
  {
    /*
      Allocate several memory blocks at one time.
      Note: my_multi_malloc takes MySQL flags
      (set to zero fill and with extra error checking),
      one or more pairs of addresses and size of memory to allocate.
    */
    if (!my_multi_malloc(MYF(MY_WME | MY_ZEROFILL),
                      &share, sizeof(*share),
                      &tmp_name, length+1,
                      NullS))
    {
      pthread_mutex_unlock(&spartan_mutex);
      return NULL;
    }
    /*
      Set the initial variables to defaults.
    */
    share->use_count=0;
    share->table_name_length=length;
    share->table_name = (char *)my_malloc(length + 1, MYF(0));
    strcpy(share->table_name,table_name);
    /*
```

```
      Insert table name into hash for future reference.
    */
    if (my_hash_insert(&spartan_open_tables, (byte*) share))
      goto error;
    thr_lock_init(&share->lock);
    /*
      Create an instance of data class
    */
    share->data_class = new Spartan_data();
    /*
      Create an instance of index class
    */
    share->index_class = new Spartan_index();
    pthread_mutex_init(&share->mutex,MY_MUTEX_INIT_FAST);
  }
  share->use_count++; // increment use count on reference
  pthread_mutex_unlock(&spartan_mutex); //release mutex lock
  return share;

error:
  pthread_mutex_destroy(&share->mutex);
  my_free((gptr) share, MYF(0));

  return NULL;
    pthread_mutex_init(&share->mutex,MY_MUTEX_INIT_FAST);
  }
}
```

Naturally, you also need to destroy the object reference when the share structure is destroyed. Locate the free_share() method and add the code to destroy the index class object reference. Listing 7-38 shows the method with the changes.

Listing 7-38. *Changes to the free_share() Method in ha_spartan.cc*

```
static int free_share(SPARTAN_SHARE *share)
{
  DBUG_ENTER("ha_spartan::free_share");
  pthread_mutex_lock(&spartan_mutex);
  if (!--share->use_count)
  {
    if (share->data_class != NULL)
      delete share->data_class;
    share->data_class = NULL;
    if (share->index_class != NULL)
      delete share->index_class;
    share->index_class = NULL;
    hash_delete(&spartan_open_tables, (byte*) share);
    thr_lock_delete(&share->lock);
```

```
    pthread_mutex_destroy(&share->mutex);
    my_free((gptr)share->table_name, MYF(0));
  }
  pthread_mutex_unlock(&spartan_mutex);
  DBUG_RETURN(0);
}
```

Now would be a good time to compile and check for errors. When you're done, you can begin on the modifications for the index methods.

The first thing that needs to be done is to go back through the open, create, close, write, update, delete, and rename methods and add the calls to the index class to maintain the index. The code to do this involves identifying the field that is the key and then saving the key and its position to the index for retrieval later.

The open method must open both the data and index files together. The only extra step is to load the index into memory. Locate the open() method in the class file and add the calls to the index class for opening the index and loading the index into memory. Listing 7-39 shows the method with the changes.

Listing 7-39. *Changes to the open() Method in ha_spartan.cc*

```
int ha_spartan::open(const char *name, int mode, uint test_if_locked)
{
  DBUG_ENTER("ha_spartan::open");
  char name_buff[FN_REFLEN];

  if (!(share = get_share(name, table)))
    DBUG_RETURN(1);
  share->data_class->open_table(fn_format(name_buff, name, "", SDE_EXT,
                                MY_REPLACE_EXT|MY_UNPACK_FILENAME));
  share->index_class->open_index(fn_format(name_buff, name, "", SDI_EXT,
                                MY_REPLACE_EXT|MY_UNPACK_FILENAME));
  share->index_class->load_index();
  current_position = 0;
  thr_lock_data_init(&share->lock,&lock,NULL);
  DBUG_RETURN(0);
}
```

The create method must create both the data and index files together. Locate the create() method in the class file and add the calls to the index class for creating the index. Listing 7-40 shows the method with the changes.

Listing 7-40. *Changes to the create() Method in ha_spartan.cc*

```
int ha_spartan::create(const char *name, TABLE *table_arg,
                       HA_CREATE_INFO *create_info)
{
  DBUG_ENTER("ha_spartan::create");
  char name_buff[FN_REFLEN];
```

```
  if (!(share = get_share(name, table)))
    DBUG_RETURN(1);
  if (share->data_class->create_table(fn_format(name_buff, name, "", SDE_EXT,
                                      MY_REPLACE_EXT|MY_UNPACK_FILENAME)))
    DBUG_RETURN(-1);
  if (share->index_class->create_index(fn_format(name_buff, name, "", SDI_EXT,
                                       MY_REPLACE_EXT|MY_UNPACK_FILENAME),
                                       128))
    DBUG_RETURN(-1);
  share->index_class->close_index();
  share->data_class->close_table();
  DBUG_RETURN(0);
}
```

The close method must close both the data and index files together. However, since the index class uses an in-memory structure to store all changes, it must be written back to disk. Locate the close() method in the class file and add the calls to the index class for saving, destroying the in-memory structure and closing the index. Listing 7-41 shows the method with the changes.

Listing 7-41. *Changes to the close() Method in ha_spartan.cc*

```
int ha_spartan::close(void)
{
  DBUG_ENTER("ha_spartan::close");
  share->data_class->close_table();
  share->index_class->save_index();
  share->index_class->destroy_index();
  share->index_class->close_index();
  DBUG_RETURN(free_share(share));
}
```

Now let's make the changes to the writing and reading methods. However, since it is possible that no keys will be used, the method must check that there is a key to be added. To make things easier to work with, I've written two helper methods: get_key(), which finds the key field and returns its value or 0 if there are no keys, and get_key_len(), which returns the length of the key. Listing 7-42 shows these two helper methods. Go ahead and add those methods now to the ha_spartan.cc file.

Listing 7-42. *Additional Helper Methods in ha_spartan.cc*

```
byte *ha_spartan::get_key()
{
  byte *key = 0;

  DBUG_ENTER("ha_spartan::get_key");
```

```
    /*
      For each field in the table, check to see if it is the key
      by checking the key_start variable. (1 = is a key).
    */
    for (Field **field=table->field ; *field ; field++)
    {
      if ((*field)->key_start.to_ulonglong() == 1)
      {
        /*
          Copy field value to key value (save key)
        */
        key = (byte *)my_malloc((*field)->field_length,
                                MYF(MY_ZEROFILL | MY_WME));
        memcpy(key, (*field)->ptr, (*field)->key_length());
      }
    }
    DBUG_RETURN(key);
}

int ha_spartan::get_key_len()
{
  int length = 0;

  DBUG_ENTER("ha_spartan::get_key");
  /*
    For each field in the table, check to see if it is the key
    by checking the key_start variable. (1 = is a key).
  */
  for (Field **field=table->field ; *field ; field++)
  {
    if ((*field)->key_start.to_ulonglong() == 1)
      /*
        Copy field length to key length
      */
      length = (*field)->key_length();
  }
  DBUG_RETURN(length);
}
```

The write method must both write the record to the data file and insert the key into the index file. Locate the write_row() method in the class file and add the calls to the index class to insert the key if one is found. Listing 7-43 shows the method with the changes.

Listing 7-43. *Changes to the write_row() Method in ha_spartan.cc*

```
int ha_spartan::write_row(byte * buf)
{
  long long pos;
  SDE_INDEX ndx;

  DBUG_ENTER("ha_spartan::write_row");
  ha_statistic_increment(&SSV::ha_write_count);
  ndx.length = get_key_len();
  memcpy(ndx.key, get_key(), get_key_len());
  pthread_mutex_lock(&spartan_mutex);
  pos = share->data_class->write_row(buf, table->s->rec_buff_length);
  ndx.pos = pos;
  if (ndx.key != 0)
    share->index_class->insert_key(&ndx, false);
  pthread_mutex_unlock(&spartan_mutex);
  DBUG_RETURN(0);
}
```

The update method is also a little different. It must change both the record in the data file and the key in the index. Since the index uses an in-memory structure, the index file must be changed, saved to disk, and reloaded.

Note Savvy programmers will note something in the code for the `Spartan_index` that could be made to prevent the reloading step. Do you know what it is? Here's a hint: what if the index class update method updated the key and then repositioned it in the memory structure? I'll leave that experiment up to you. Feel free to go into the index code and improve it.

Locate the `write_row()` method in the class file and add the calls to the index class to update the key if one is found. Listing 7-44 shows the method with the changes.

Listing 7-44. *Changes to the update_row() Method in ha_spartan.cc*

```
int ha_spartan::update_row(const byte * old_data, byte * new_data)
{
  DBUG_ENTER("ha_spartan::update_row");
  pthread_mutex_lock(&spartan_mutex);
  share->data_class->update_row((byte *)old_data, new_data,
                table->s->rec_buff_length, current_position -
                share->data_class->row_size(table->s->rec_buff_length));
```

```
  if (get_key() != 0)
  {
    share->index_class->update_key(get_key(), current_position -
                      share->data_class->row_size(table->s->rec_buff_length),
                      get_key_len());
    share->index_class->save_index();
    share->index_class->load_index();
  }
  pthread_mutex_unlock(&spartan_mutex);
  DBUG_RETURN(0);
}
```

The delete method isn't as complicated. In this case, the method just needs to delete the data row and remove the index from the in-memory structure if one is found. Locate the delete_row() method in the class file and add the calls to the index class to delete the key if one is found. Listing 7-45 shows the method with the changes.

Listing 7-45. *Changes to the delete_row() Method in ha_spartan.cc*

```
int ha_spartan::delete_row(const byte * buf)
{
  long long pos;

  DBUG_ENTER("ha_spartan::delete_row");
  if (current_position > 0)
    pos = current_position -
      share->data_class->row_size(table->s->rec_buff_length);
  else
    pos = 0;
  pthread_mutex_lock(&spartan_mutex);
  share->data_class->delete_row((byte *)buf,
                                table->s->rec_buff_length, pos);
  if (get_key() != 0)
    share->index_class->delete_key(get_key(), pos, get_key_len());
  pthread_mutex_unlock(&spartan_mutex);
  DBUG_RETURN(0);
}
```

Likewise, the method for deleting all rows is very easy. In this case, we want to delete all data from the data and index file. Locate the delete_all_rows() method in the class file and add the calls to the index class to destroy the index and truncate the index file. Listing 7-46 shows the method with the changes.

Listing 7-46. *Changes to the delete_all_rows() Method in ha_spartan.cc*

```
int ha_spartan::delete_all_rows()
{
  DBUG_ENTER("ha_spartan::delete_all_rows");
  pthread_mutex_lock(&spartan_mutex);
  share->data_class->trunc_table();
  share->index_class->destroy_index();
  share->index_class->trunc_index();
  pthread_mutex_unlock(&spartan_mutex);
  DBUG_RETURN(0);
 }
```

The delete_table() method must delete both the data and index files. Locate the delete_table() method and add the code to destroy the in-memory structure, close the index, and call the my_delete() function to delete the index. Listing 7-47 shows the method with the changes.

Listing 7-47. *Changes to the delete_table() Method in ha_spartan.cc*

```
int ha_spartan::delete_table(const char *name)
{
  DBUG_ENTER("ha_spartan::delete_table");
  char name_buff[FN_REFLEN];

  if (!(share = get_share(name, table)))
    DBUG_RETURN(1);
  pthread_mutex_lock(&spartan_mutex);
  share->data_class->close_table();
  /*
    Destroy the index in memory and close it.
  */
  share->index_class->destroy_index();
  share->index_class->close_index();
  /*
    Call the mysql delete file method.
    Note: the fn_format() method correctly creates a file name from the
    name passed into the method.
  */
  my_delete(fn_format(name_buff, name, "", SDE_EXT,
          MY_REPLACE_EXT|MY_UNPACK_FILENAME), MYF(0));
  /*
    Call the mysql delete file method.
    Note: the fn_format() method correctly creates a file name from the
    name passed into the method.
  */
```

CHAPTER 7 ■ BUILDING YOUR OWN STORAGE ENGINE 341

```
  my_delete(fn_format(name_buff, name, "", SDI_EXT,
            MY_REPLACE_EXT|MY_UNPACK_FILENAME), MYF(0));
  pthread_mutex_unlock(&spartan_mutex);
  DBUG_RETURN(0);
}
```

The last of the changes to the general read and write file operations is to the rename_table() method. The rename_table() method for the index follows the same pattern as the previous changes. Locate the rename_table() method in the class file and add the code to copy the index file. Listing 7-48 shows the method with the changes.

Listing 7-48. *Changes to the rename_table() Method in ha_spartan.cc*

```
int ha_spartan::rename_table(const char * from, const char * to)
{
  DBUG_ENTER("ha_spartan::rename_table ");
  char data_from[FN_REFLEN];
  char data_to[FN_REFLEN];
  char index_from[FN_REFLEN];
  char index_to[FN_REFLEN];

  if (!(share = get_share(from, table)))
    DBUG_RETURN(1);
  /*
    Begin critical section by locking the spartan mutex variable.
  */
  pthread_mutex_lock(&spartan_mutex);
  /*
    Close the table then copy it then reopen new file.
  */
  share->data_class->close_table();
  my_copy(fn_format(data_from, from, "", SDE_EXT,
          MY_REPLACE_EXT|MY_UNPACK_FILENAME),
          fn_format(data_to, to, "", SDE_EXT,
          MY_REPLACE_EXT|MY_UNPACK_FILENAME), MYF(0));
  share->data_class->open_table(data_to);
  share->index_class->close_index();
  my_copy(fn_format(index_from, from, "", SDI_EXT,
          MY_REPLACE_EXT|MY_UNPACK_FILENAME),
          fn_format(index_to, to, "", SDI_EXT,
          MY_REPLACE_EXT|MY_UNPACK_FILENAME), MYF(0));
  share->index_class->open_index(index_to);
  /*
    End critical section by unlocking the spartan mutex variable.
  */
  pthread_mutex_unlock(&spartan_mutex);
```

```
  /*
    Delete the file using MySQL's delete file method.
  */
  my_delete(data_from, MYF(0));
  my_delete(index_from, MYF(0));
  DBUG_RETURN(0);
}
```

Wow! That was a lot of changes. As you can see, supporting indexes has made the code much more complicated. I hope you now have a better appreciation for just how well the existing storage engines in MySQL are built. Now, let's move on to making the changes to the indexing methods.

There are six methods that must be implemented to complete the indexing mechanism for a stage 5 storage engine. Take note as you go through these methods that some return a row from the data file based on the index passed in whereas others return a key. The documentation isn't clear about this, and the name of the parameter doesn't give us much of a clue, but I'll show you how they are used. These methods must return either a key not found or end-of-file return code. Take care to code these return statements correctly or you could encounter some strange query results.

The first method is the index_read() method. This method sets the row buffer to the row in the file that matches the key passed in. If the key passed in is null, then the method should return the first key value in the file. Locate the index_read() method and add the code to get the file position from the index and read the corresponding row from the data file. Listing 7-49 shows the method with the changes.

Listing 7-49. *Changes to the index_read() Method in ha_spartan.cc*

```
int ha_spartan::index_read(byte * buf, const byte * key,
                           uint key_len __attribute__((unused)),
                           enum ha_rkey_function find_flag
                           __attribute__((unused)))
{
  long long pos;

  DBUG_ENTER("ha_spartan::index_read");
  if (key == NULL)
    pos = share->index_class->get_first_pos();
  else
    pos = share->index_class->get_index_pos((byte *)key, key_len);
  if (pos == -1)
    DBUG_RETURN(HA_ERR_KEY_NOT_FOUND);
  current_position =
    pos + share->data_class->row_size(table->s->rec_buff_length);
  share->data_class->read_row(buf, table->s->rec_buff_length, pos);
  share->index_class->get_next_key();
  DBUG_RETURN(0);
}
```

The next index method is `index_read_idx()`. It is similar to the `index_read()` method but is called from other portions of the optimizer (e.g., where there is at most one matching row—see `sql_select.cc` for details). This method sets the row buffer to the row in the file that matches the key. If the key passed in is null, then the method should return the first key value and the first row in the file. Locate the `index_read_idx()` method and add the code to get the file position from the index and read a row from the data file. Listing 7-50 shows the method with the changes.

Listing 7-50. *Changes to the index_read_idx() Method in ha_spartan.cc*

```
int ha_spartan::index_read_idx(byte * buf, uint index, const byte * key,
                               uint key_len __attribute__((unused)),
                               enum ha_rkey_function find_flag
                               __attribute__((unused)))
{
  long long pos;

  DBUG_ENTER("ha_spartan::index_read_idx");
  pos = share->index_class->get_index_pos((byte *)key, key_len);
  if (pos == -1)
    DBUG_RETURN(HA_ERR_KEY_NOT_FOUND);
  share->data_class->read_row(buf, table->s->rec_buff_length, pos);
  DBUG_RETURN(0);
}
```

The next index method is `index_next()`. This method gets the next key in the index and returns the matching row from the data file. It is called during range index scans. Locate the `index_next()` method and add the code to get the next key from the index and read a row from the data file. Listing 7-51 shows the method with the changes.

Listing 7-51. *Changes to the index_next() Method in ha_spartan.cc*

```
int ha_spartan::index_next(byte * buf)
{
  byte *key = 0;
  long long pos;

  DBUG_ENTER("ha_spartan::index_next");
  key = share->index_class->get_next_key();
  if (key == 0)
    DBUG_RETURN(HA_ERR_END_OF_FILE);
  pos = share->index_class->get_index_pos((byte *)key, get_key_len());
  share->index_class->seek_index(key, get_key_len());
  share->index_class->get_next_key();
  if (pos == -1)
    DBUG_RETURN(HA_ERR_KEY_NOT_FOUND);
  share->data_class->read_row(buf, table->s->rec_buff_length, pos);
  DBUG_RETURN(0);
}
```

The next index method is also one of the range queries. The index_prev() method gets the previous key in the index and returns the matching row from the data file. It is called during range index scans. Locate the index_prev() method and add the code to get the previous key from the index and read a row from the data file. Listing 7-52 shows the method with the changes.

Listing 7-52. *Changes to the index_prev() Method in ha_spartan.cc*

```
int ha_spartan::index_prev(byte * buf)
{
  byte *key = 0;
  long long pos;

  DBUG_ENTER("ha_spartan::index_prev");
  key = share->index_class->get_prev_key();
  if (key == 0)
    DBUG_RETURN(HA_ERR_END_OF_FILE);
  pos = share->index_class->get_index_pos((byte *)key, get_key_len());
  share->index_class->seek_index(key, get_key_len());
  share->index_class->get_prev_key();
  if (pos == -1)
    DBUG_RETURN(HA_ERR_KEY_NOT_FOUND);
  share->data_class->read_row(buf, table->s->rec_buff_length, pos);
  DBUG_RETURN(0);
}
```

Notice that I had to move the index pointers around a bit to get the code for the next and previous to work. Range queries generate two calls to the index class the first time it is used: the first one gets the first key (index_read), and then the second calls the next key (index_next). Subsequent index calls are made to index_next(). Therefore, I must call the Spartan_index class method get_prev_key() to reset the keys correctly. This would be another great opportunity to rework the index class to work better with range queries in MySQL.

The next index method is also one of the range queries. The index_first() method gets the first key in the index and returns it. Locate the index_first() method and add the code to get the first key from the index and return the key. Listing 7-53 shows the method with the changes.

Listing 7-53. *Changes to the index_first() Method in ha_spartan.cc*

```
int ha_spartan::index_first(byte * buf)
{
  byte *key = 0;

  DBUG_ENTER("ha_spartan::index_first");
  key = share->index_class->get_first_key();
  if (key == 0)
    DBUG_RETURN(HA_ERR_END_OF_FILE);
  memcpy(buf, key, get_key_len());
  DBUG_RETURN(0);
}
```

The last index method is one of the range queries as well. The index_last() method gets the last key in the index and returns it. Locate the index_last() method and add the code to get the last key from the index and return the key. Listing 7-54 shows the method with the changes.

Listing 7-54. *Changes to the index_last() Method in ha_spartan.cc*

```
int ha_spartan::index_last(byte * buf)
{
  byte *key = 0;

  DBUG_ENTER("ha_spartan::index_last");
  key = share->index_class->get_last_key();
  if (key == 0)
    DBUG_RETURN(HA_ERR_END_OF_FILE);
  memcpy(buf, key, get_key_len());
  DBUG_RETURN(0);
}
```

OK, now compile the server and debug any errors. When that is done, you will have a completed stage 5 engine. All that is left to do is compile the server and run the tests.

If you decide to debug the Spartan storage engine code, you may notice during debugging that some of the index methods may not get called. That is because the index methods are used in a variety of ways in the optimizer. The order of calls depends a lot on the choices that the optimizer makes. If you are curious (like me) and want to see each and every method fire, you'll need to create a much larger data set and perform more complex queries. You can also check the source code and the reference manual for more details about each of the methods supported in the handler class.

Testing Stage 5 of the Spartan Engine

When you run the spartandb test again, you should see all of the statements complete success-fully. You should verify everything is working in the stage 4 engine and then move on to testing the index operations.

The index tests will require you to have a table created and have data in it. You can always add data using the normal INSERT statements as before. Now you need to test the index. Enter a command that has a WHERE clause on the index column (col_a) like the following:

```
SELECT * FROM t1 WHERE col_a = 2;
```

When you run that command, you should see the row returned. That isn't very interesting, is it? You've done all that work and it just returns the row anyway. Well, the best way to know that the indexes are working is to have large data tables with a diverse range of index values. That would take a while to do, and I encourage you to do so.

There's another way. You can launch the server and attach breakpoints (using your debugger) in the source code and issue the index-based queries. That may sound like lots of work and you may not have time to run but a few examples. That's fine, because you can add that functionality to the spartandb test file. You can add the key column to the CREATE and add more SELECT statements with WHERE clauses to perform point and range queries. Listing 7-55 shows the updated spartandb.test file.

Listing 7-55. *Updated Spartan Storage Engine Test File (spartandb.test)*

```
#
# Simple test for the Spartan storage engine
#
--disable_warnings
drop table if exists t1;
--enable_warnings

CREATE TABLE t1 (
  col_a int KEY,
  col_b varchar(20),
  col_c int
) ENGINE=SPARTAN;

INSERT INTO t1 VALUES (1, "first test", 24);
INSERT INTO t1 VALUES (2, "second test", 43);
INSERT INTO t1 VALUES (9, "fourth test", -2);
INSERT INTO t1 VALUES (3, 'eighth test', -22);
INSERT INTO t1 VALUES (4, "tenth test", 11);
INSERT INTO t1 VALUES (8, "seventh test", 20);
INSERT INTO t1 VALUES (5, "third test", 100);
SELECT * FROM t1;
UPDATE t1 SET col_b = "Updated!" WHERE col_a = 1;
SELECT * from t1;
UPDATE t1 SET col_b = "Updated!" WHERE col_a = 3;
SELECT * from t1;
UPDATE t1 SET col_b = "Updated!" WHERE col_a = 5;
SELECT * from t1;
DELETE FROM t1 WHERE col_a = 1;
SELECT * FROM t1;
DELETE FROM t1 WHERE col_a = 3;
SELECT * FROM t1;
DELETE FROM t1 WHERE col_a = 5;
SELECT * FROM t1;
SELECT * FROM t1 WHERE col_a = 4;
SELECT * FROM t1 WHERE col_a >= 2 AND col_a <= 5;
SELECT * FROM t1 WHERE col_a = 22;
DELETE FROM t1 WHERE col_a = 5;
SELECT * FROM t1;
SELECT * FROM t1 WHERE col_a = 5;
UPDATE t1 SET col_a = 99 WHERE col_a = 8;
SELECT * FROM t1 WHERE col_a = 8;
SELECT * FROM t1 WHERE col_a = 99;
RENAME TABLE t1 TO t2;
SELECT * FROM t2;
DROP TABLE t2;
```

Notice that I've changed some of the INSERT statements to make the index methods work. Go ahead and run that test and see what it does. Listing 7-56 shows an example of the expected results for this test. When you run the test under the test suite, it should complete without errors.

Listing 7-56. *Sample Results of Stage 5 Test*

```
mysql> CREATE TABLE t1 (
    ->   col_a int KEY,
    ->   col_b varchar(20),
    ->   col_c int
    -> ) ENGINE=SPARTAN;
Query OK, 0 rows affected (0.02 sec)

mysql>
mysql> SELECT * FROM t1;
Empty set (0.02 sec)

mysql> INSERT INTO t1 VALUES(1, "first test", 24);
Query OK, 1 row affected (0.00 sec)

mysql> INSERT INTO t1 VALUES(2, "second test", 43);
Query OK, 1 row affected (0.00 sec)

mysql> INSERT INTO t1 VALUES(9, "fourth test", -2);
Query OK, 1 row affected (0.00 sec)

mysql> INSERT INTO t1 VALUES (3, 'eighth test', -22);
Query OK, 1 row affected (0.02 sec)

mysql> INSERT INTO t1 VALUES(4, "tenth test", 11);
Query OK, 1 row affected (0.00 sec)

mysql> INSERT INTO t1 VALUES(8, "seventh test", 20);
Query OK, 1 row affected (0.00 sec)

mysql> INSERT INTO t1 VALUES(5, "third test", 100);
Query OK, 1 row affected (0.00 sec)

mysql> SELECT * FROM t1;
+-------+--------------+-------+
| col_a | col_b        | col_c |
+-------+--------------+-------+
| 1     | first test   | 24    |
| 2     | second test  | 43    |
| 9     | fourth test  | -2    |
| 3     | eighth test  | -22   |
| 4     | tenth test   | 11    |
```

```
| 8       | seventh test | 20    |
| 5       | third test   | 100   |
+-------+--------------+-------+
7 rows in set (0.00 sec)

mysql> UPDATE t1 SET col_b = "Updated!" WHERE col_a = 1;
Query OK, 1 row affected (0.00 sec)
Rows matched: 1  Changed: 1  Warnings: 0

mysql> SELECT * from t1;
+-------+--------------+-------+
| col_a | col_b        | col_c |
+-------+--------------+-------+
| 1     | Updated!     | 24    |
| 2     | second test  | 43    |
| 9     | fourth test  | -2    |
| 3     | eighth test  | -22   |
| 4     | tenth test   | 11    |
| 8     | seventh test | 20    |
| 5     | third test   | 100   |
+-------+--------------+-------+
7 rows in set (0.00 sec)

mysql> UPDATE t1 SET col_b = "Updated!" WHERE col_a = 3;
Query OK, 1 row affected (0.00 sec)
Rows matched: 1  Changed: 1  Warnings: 0

mysql> SELECT * from t1;
+-------+--------------+-------+
| col_a | col_b        | col_c |
+-------+--------------+-------+
| 1     | Updated!     | 24    |
| 2     | second test  | 43    |
| 9     | fourth test  | -2    |
| 3     | Updated!     | -22   |
| 4     | tenth test   | 11    |
| 8     | seventh test | 20    |
| 5     | third test   | 100   |
+-------+--------------+-------+
7 rows in set (0.00 sec)

mysql> UPDATE t1 SET col_b = "Updated!" WHERE col_a = 5;
Query OK, 0 rows affected (0.00 sec)
Rows matched: 0  Changed: 0  Warnings: 0
```

```
mysql> SELECT * from t1;
+-------+--------------+-------+
| col_a | col_b        | col_c |
+-------+--------------+-------+
| 1     | Updated!     | 24    |
| 2     | second test  | 43    |
| 9     | fourth test  | -2    |
| 3     | Updated!     | -22   |
| 4     | tenth test   | 11    |
| 8     | seventh test | 20    |
| 5     | Updated!     | 100   |
+-------+--------------+-------+
7 rows in set (0.00 sec)

mysql> DELETE FROM t1 WHERE col_a = 1;
Query OK, 1 row affected (0.00 sec)

mysql> SELECT * FROM t1;
+-------+--------------+-------+
| col_a | col_b        | col_c |
+-------+--------------+-------+
| 2     | second test  | 43    |
| 9     | fourth test  | -2    |
| 3     | Updated!     | -22   |
| 4     | tenth test   | 11    |
| 8     | seventh test | 20    |
| 5     | Updated!     | 100   |
+-------+--------------+-------+
6 rows in set (0.00 sec)

mysql> DELETE FROM t1 WHERE col_a = 3;
Query OK, 0 rows affected (0.00 sec)

mysql> SELECT * FROM t1;
+-------+--------------+-------+
| col_a | col_b        | col_c |
+-------+--------------+-------+
| 2     | second test  | 43    |
| 9     | fourth test  | -2    |
| 4     | tenth test   | 11    |
| 8     | seventh test | 20    |
| 5     | Updated!     | 100   |
+-------+--------------+-------+
5 rows in set (0.00 sec)
```

```
mysql> DELETE FROM t1 WHERE col_a = 5;
Query OK, 0 rows affected (0.00 sec)

mysql> SELECT * FROM t1;
+-------+-------------+-------+
| col_a | col_b       | col_c |
+-------+-------------+-------+
| 2     | second test | 43    |
| 9     | fourth test | -2    |
| 4     | tenth test  | 11    |
| 8     | seventh test| 20    |
+-------+-------------+-------+
4 rows in set (0.00 sec)

mysql> SELECT * FROM t1 WHERE col_a = 4;
+-------+------------+-------+
| col_a | col_b      | col_c |
+-------+------------+-------+
| 4     | tenth test | 11    |
+-------+------------+-------+
1 row in set (0.00 sec)

mysql> SELECT * FROM t1 WHERE col_a >= 2 AND col_a <= 5;
+-------+-------------+-------+
| col_a | col_b       | col_c |
+-------+-------------+-------+
| 2     | second test | 43    |
| 4     | tenth test  | 11    |
+-------+-------------+-------+
2 rows in set (0.02 sec)

mysql> SELECT * FROM t1 WHERE col_a = 22;
Empty set (0.00 sec)

mysql> DELETE FROM t1 WHERE col_a = 5;
Query OK, 0 rows affected (0.00 sec)

mysql> SELECT * FROM t1;
+-------+-------------+-------+
| col_a | col_b       | col_c |
+-------+-------------+-------+
| 2     | second test | 43    |
| 9     | fourth test | -2    |
| 4     | tenth test  | 11    |
| 8     | seventh test| 20    |
+-------+-------------+-------+
4 rows in set (0.00 sec)
```

```
mysql> SELECT * FROM t1 WHERE col_a = 5;
Empty set (0.00 sec)

mysql> UPDATE t1 SET col_a = 99 WHERE col_a = 8;
Query OK, 1 row affected (0.00 sec)
Rows matched: 1  Changed: 1  Warnings: 0

mysql> SELECT * FROM t1 WHERE col_a = 8;
Empty set (0.00 sec)

mysql> SELECT * FROM t1 WHERE col_a = 99;
+-------+--------------+-------+
| col_a | col_b        | col_c |
+-------+--------------+-------+
| 99    | seventh test | 20    |
+-------+--------------+-------+
1 row in set (0.00 sec)

mysql> RENAME TABLE t1 TO t2;
Query OK, 0 rows affected (0.02 sec)

mysql> SELECT * FROM t2;
+-------+--------------+-------+
| col_a | col_b        | col_c |
+-------+--------------+-------+
| 2     | second test  | 43    |
| 9     | fourth test  | -2    |
| 4     | tenth test   | 11    |
| 99    | seventh test | 20    |
+-------+--------------+-------+
4 rows in set (0.00 sec)

mysql> DROP TABLE t2;
Query OK, 0 rows affected (0.02 sec)
```

Well, that's it for a stage 5 engine. It is now a basic read/write/update/delete storage engine with indexing, which is the stage where most of the storage engines in MySQL are implemented. Indeed, for all but transactional environments this should be sufficient for your storage needs. In the next stage, I'll discuss the much more complex topic of adding transaction support.

Stage 6: Adding Transaction Support

Currently, only two of the traditional storage engines in MySQL support transactions: BDB and InnoDB.[7] Transactions provide a mechanism that permits a set of operations to execute as a single atomic operation. For example, if a database was built for a banking institution, the

---

7. The cluster storage engine (NDB) also supports transactions.

macro operations of transferring money from one account to another (money removed from one account and placed in another) would preferably be executed completely without interruption. Transactions permit these operations to be encased in an atomic operation that will back out any changes should an error occur before all operations are complete, thus avoiding data being removed from one table and never making it to the next table. A sample set of operations in the form of SQL statements encased in transactional commands is shown in Listing 7-57.

Listing 7-57. *Sample Transaction SQL Commands*

```
START TRANSACTION;
UPDATE SavingsAccount SET Balance = Balance-100
WHERE AccountNum = 123;
UPDATE CheckingAccount SET Balance = Balance + 100
WHERE AccountNum = 345;
COMMIT;
```

In practice, most database professionals specify the MyISAM table type if they require faster access and InnoDB if they need transaction support. Fortunately, MySQL AB has provided the pluggable storage engine with the capability to support transactions.

The facilities for performing transactions in storage engines is supported by the start_stmt() and external_lock() methods. The start_stmt() method is called when a transaction is started. The external_lock() method is used to signal a specific lock for a table and is called when an explicit lock is issued. Your storage engine must implement the new transaction in the start_stmt() method by creating a savepoint and registering the transaction with the server using the trans_register_ha() method. This method takes as parameters the current thread, whether you want to set the transaction across all threads, and the address of your handlerton. Calling this causes the transaction to start. An example implementation of the start_stmt() method is shown in Listing 7-58.

Listing 7-58. *Example start_stmt() Method Implementation*

```
int my_handler::start_stmt(THD *thd, thr_lock_type lock_type)
{
  DBUG_ENTER("my_handler::index_last");
  int error= 0;
  /*
    Save the transaction data
  */
  my_txn *txn= (my_txn *) thd->ha_data[my_handler_hton.slot];
  /*
    If this is a new transaction, create it and save it to the
    handler's slot in the ha_data array.
  */
  if (txn == NULL)
    thd->ha_data[my_handler_hton.slot]= txn= new my_txn;
```

```
    /*
      Start the transaction and create a savepoint then register
      the transaction.
    */
    if (txn->stmt == NULL && !(error= txn->tx_begin()))
    {
      txn->stmt= txn->new_savepoint();
      trans_register_ha(thd, FALSE, &my_handler_hton);
    }
    DBUG_RETURN(error);
}
```

Starting a transaction from external_lock() is a bit more complicated. MySQL calls the external_lock() method for every table in use at the start of a transaction. Thus, you have some more work to do to detect the transaction and process it accordingly. This can be seen in the check of the trx->active_trans flag. The start transaction operation is also implied when the external_lock() method is called for the first table. Listing 7-59 shows an example implementation of the external_lock() method (some sections are omitted for brevity). See the ha_innodb.cc file for the complete code.

Listing 7-59. *Example external_lock() Method Implementation (from InnoDB)*

```
int ha_innobase::external_lock(THD*  thd, int lock_type)
{
  row_prebuilt_t* prebuilt = (row_prebuilt_t*) innobase_prebuilt;
  trx_t*    trx;

  DBUG_ENTER("ha_innobase::external_lock");
  DBUG_PRINT("enter",("lock_type: %d", lock_type));

  update_thd(thd);

  trx = prebuilt->trx;

  prebuilt->sql_stat_start = TRUE;
  prebuilt->hint_need_to_fetch_extra_cols = 0;

  prebuilt->read_just_key = 0;
  prebuilt->keep_other_fields_on_keyread = FALSE;

  if (lock_type == F_WRLCK) {

    /* If this is a SELECT, then it is in UPDATE TABLE ...
    or SELECT ... FOR UPDATE */
    prebuilt->select_lock_type = LOCK_X;
    prebuilt->stored_select_lock_type = LOCK_X;
  }
```

```
    if (lock_type != F_UNLCK)
        {
      /* MySQL is setting a new table lock */

      trx->detailed_error[0] = '\0';

      /* Set the MySQL flag to mark that there is an active
      transaction */
      if (trx->active_trans == 0) {

        innobase_register_trx_and_stmt(thd);
        trx->active_trans = 1;
      } else if (trx->n_mysql_tables_in_use == 0) {
        innobase_register_stmt(thd);
      }

      trx->n_mysql_tables_in_use++;
      prebuilt->mysql_has_locked = TRUE;

...

    DBUG_RETURN(0);
    }

  /* MySQL is releasing a table lock */

  trx->n_mysql_tables_in_use--;
  prebuilt->mysql_has_locked = FALSE;

  /* If the MySQL lock count drops to zero we know that the current SQL
  statement has ended */

  if (trx->n_mysql_tables_in_use == 0) {

...

  DBUG_RETURN(0);
}
```

Now that you've seen how to start transactions, let's see how they are stopped (also known as *committed* or *rolled back*). Committing a transaction just means writing the pending changes to disk, storing the appropriate keys, and cleaning up the transaction. MySQL AB provides a method in the handlerton (int (*commit)(THD *thd, bool all)) that can be implemented using the function description shown here. The parameters are the current thread and whether you want the entire set of commands committed.

```
int (*commit)(THD *thd, bool all);
```

Rolling back the transaction is more complicated. In this case, you have to undo everything that was done since the last start of the transaction. MySQL AB supports rollback using a callback in the handlerton (int (*rollback)(THD *thd, bool all)) that can be implemented using the function description shown here. The parameters are the current thread and whether the entire transaction should be rolled back.

```
int (*rollback)(THD *thd, bool all);
```

To implement transactions, the storage engine must provide some sort of buffer mechanism to hold the unsaved changes to the database. Some storage engines use heap-like structures; others use queues and similar internal memory structures. If you are going to implement transactions in your storage engine, you'll need to create an internal caching (also called versioning) mechanism. When a commit is issued, the data must be taken out of the buffer and written to disk. When a rollback occurs, the operations must be canceled and their changes reversed.

Savepoints are another transaction mechanism available to you for managing data during transactions. Savepoints are areas in memory that allow you to save information. You can use them to save information during a transaction. For example, you may want to save information about an internal buffer you implement to store the "dirty" or "uncommitted" changes. The savepoint concept was created for just such a use.

MySQL AB provides several savepoint operations that you can define in your handlerton. These appear in lines 13 through 15 in the handlerton structure shown in Listing 7-1. The method descriptions for the savepoint methods are shown here:

```
uint savepoint_offset;
int (*savepoint_set)(THD *thd, void *sv);
int (*savepoint_rollback)(THD *thd, void *sv);
int (*savepoint_release)(THD *thd, void *sv);
```

The savepoint_offset value is the size of the memory area you want to save. The savepoint_set() method allows you to set a value to the parameter sv and save it as a savepoint. The savepoint_rollback() method is called when a rollback operation is triggered. In this case, the server returns the information saved in sv to the method. Similarly, savepoint_release() is called when the server responds to a release savepoint event and also returns the data via the sv that was set as a savepoint. For more information about savepoints, see the MySQL source code and online reference manual.

Tip For excellent examples of how the transaction facilities work, see the ha_innodb.cc and ha_berkeley.cc source files. You can also find information in the online reference manual.

Simply adding transaction support using the MySQL mechanisms is not the end of the story. Storage engines that use indexes[8] must provide mechanisms to permit transactions. These operations must be capable of marking nodes that have been changed by operations in a transaction, saving the original values of the data that has changed until such time that the

---

8. For the record, it is possible to have a stage 6 engine that does not support indexes. Indexes are not required for transaction processing. However, uniqueness should be a concern and performance will suffer.

transaction is complete. At this point, all of the changes are committed to the physical store (for both the index and the data). This will require making changes to the Spartan_index class.

Clearly, implementing transactions in a pluggable storage engine requires a lot of careful thought and planning. I strongly suggest if you are going to implement transactional support in your storage engine that you spend some time studying the BDB and InnoDB storage engines as well as the online reference manual. You may even want to set up your debugger and watch the transactions execute. Whichever way you go with your implementation of transactions, rest assured that if you get it working you will have something special. There are few excellent storage engines that support transactions and none (so far) that exceed the capabilities of the native MySQL storage engines.

Summary

In this chapter, I've taken you on a tour of the pluggable storage engine source code and showed you how to create your own storage engine. Through the Spartan storage engine, you learned how to construct a storage engine that can read and write data and that supports concurrent access and indexing. Although I explain all of the stages of building this storage engine, I leave adding transactional support for you to experiment with.

I have also not implemented all of the possible functions of a storage handler. Rather, I implemented just the basics. Now that you've seen the basics in action and had a chance to experiment, I recommend studying the online documentation and the source code while you design your own storage engine.

If you found this chapter a challenge, it's OK. Creating a database physical storage mechanism is not a trivial task. I hope you will come away from this chapter with a better understanding of what it takes to build a storage engine and a proper respect for those MySQL storage engines that implement indexing and transaction support. Neither of these tasks are trivial endeavors.

Finally, I must tell you that I have seen several areas of improvement for the data and index classes I have provided. While the data class seems fine for most applications, the index class could be improved. If you plan to use these classes as a jumping-off point for your own storage engine, I suggest getting your storage engine working with the classes as they are now and then going back and either updating or replacing them.

There are several areas in particular I recommend updating in the index class. Perhaps the most important change I recommend is changing the internal buffer to a more efficient tree structure. There are many to choose from, like the ubiquitous B-tree or hash mechanism. I also suggest that you change the way the class handles range queries. Lastly, there are several changes that need to be made to handle transaction support. The class needs to support whatever buffer mechanism you use to handle commits and rollbacks.

In the next chapter, I'll examine one of the more popular extensions of the MySQL system. This includes adding your own user-defined functions (UDFs), extending an existing SQL command, and adding your own SQL commands to the server. These techniques permit the MySQL system to evolve even further to meet your specific needs for your environment.

CHAPTER 8

■ ■ ■

Adding Functions and Commands to MySQL

One of the greatest challenges facing systems integrators is overcoming the limitations of the systems being integrated. This is usually a result of the system having limitations with, or not having certain functions or commands that are needed for, the integration. Often this means getting around the problem by creating more "glue" programs to translate or augment existing functions and commands.

The MySQL AB developers have recognized this need and added flexible options in the MySQL server to add new functions and commands. For example, you may need to add functions to perform some calculations or data conversions, or you may need a new command to provide specific data for administration. This chapter introduces you to the options available for adding functions and shows you how to add your own SQL commands to the server. Much of the background material for this chapter has been covered in previous chapters. Feel free to refer back to those chapters as you follow along.

Adding User-Defined Functions

User-defined functions (UDF) have been supported by MySQL for some time. A UDF is a new function (calculation, conversion, etc.) that you can add to the server, thereby expanding the list of native functions. The best thing about UDFs is they can be dynamically loaded at runtime. Furthermore, you can create your own libraries of UDFs and use them in your enterprise or even give them away for free (as open source). This is perhaps the first place systems integrators look for extending the MySQL server. MySQL AB had another genius-level idea with the dynamic load/unload UDF mechanism.

The mechanism is similar to the plug-in interface and, in fact, predates it. The UDF interface utilizes external dynamically loadable object files to load and unload UDFs. The mechanism uses a CREATE FUNCTION command to establish a connection to the loadable object file on a per-function basis and a DROP FUNCTION command to remove the connection for a function. Let's take a look at the syntax for these commands.

CREATE FUNCTION Syntax

The CREATE FUNCTION command registers the function with the server, placing a row in the func table for the selected database. The syntax is as follows:

```
CREATE FUNCTION function_name RETURNS [STRING | INTEGER | REAL] SONAME "mylib.so";
```

function_name represents the name of the function you are creating. The return type can be one of STRING, INTEGER, or REAL and the SONAME refers to the name of the library (.so or .dll) that contains the function. These libraries contain the source code for the functions. They are normally written as C functions and then compiled as an object file. The CREATE FUNCTION command tells the MySQL server to create a mapping of the function name in the command (function_name) to the object file. When the function is invoked, the server calls the function in the library for execution.

DROP FUNCTION Syntax

The DROP FUNCTION command unregisters the function with the server by removing the associated row from the func table in the selected database. The syntax is shown here. function_name represents the name of the function you are creating.

```
DROP FUNCTION function_name;
```

User-defined functions can be used anywhere the SQL language permits an expression. For example, you can use UDFs in stored procedures and SELECT statements. They are an excellent way to expand your server without having to modify the server source code. In fact, you can define as many UDFs as you please and even group them together to form libraries of functions. Each library is a single file containing source code that is compiled as a binary executable (.so in Linux or .dll in Windows). Let's take a look at how you can create a UDF library and use it in your own MySQL server installations.

Creating a User-Defined Library

There are two types of user-defined functions:

- You can create functions that operate as a single call evaluating a set of parameters and returning a single result.

- You can create functions that operate as aggregates being called from within grouping functions. For instance, you can create a UDF that converts one data type into another, such as a function that changes a date field from one format to another, or you can create a function that performs advanced calculations for a group of records, such as a sum of squares function. UDFs can return only integers, strings, or real values.

The single-call UDF is the most common. They are used to perform an operation on one or more parameters. In some cases, no parameters are used. For example, you could create a UDF that returned a value for a global status or label like SERVER_STATUS(). This form of UDF is typically used in field lists of SELECT statements or in stored procedures as helper functions.

Aggregate UDF functions are used in GROUP BY clauses. When they are used, they are called once for each row in the table and again at the end of the group.

The process for creating a UDF library is to create a new project that exposes the UDF load/unload methods (xxx_init and xxx_deinit, where xxx is the name of the function) and the function itself. The xxx_init and xxx_deinit functions are called once per statement. If you are creating an aggregate function, you also need to implement the grouping functions xxx_clear and xxx_add. The xxx_clear function is called to reset the value (at the start of a group).

The xxx_add function is called for each row in the grouping, and the function itself is called at the end of the group processing. Thus, the aggregate is cleared, then data is added for each call to add. Finally, the function itself is called to return the value.

Once the functions are implemented, you compile the file and copy it to the bin directory of your server installation. You can load and use the functions using the CREATE FUNCTION command.

■Note Unless otherwise stated, files named .cc are named .cpp in the Windows release of the MySQL source code.

MySQL AB has provided an example UDF project that contains samples of all the types of functions you may want to create. This provides an excellent starting point for adding your own functions. The sample functions include the following:

- A metaphon function that produces a soundex-like operation on strings

- A sample function that returns a double value that is the sum of the character code values of the arguments divided by the sum of the length of all the arguments

- A sample function that returns an integer that is the sum of the lengths of the arguments

- A sequence function that returns the next value in a sequence based on the value passed

- An example aggregate function that returns the average cost from the list of integer arguments (quantity) and double arguments (cost)

Depending on your needs, you may find some of these examples useful.

Let's begin by copying the example UDF project. Create a new folder named expert_udf in the root of your source code directory. Locate the udf_example.cc file located in the /examples/udf_example directory off the root of your source code tree and copy the file to the expert_udf directory. Rename the file expert_udf.cc.

■Note Some distributions of the MySQL source code may place these files in the /sql directory. If that is the case, you may not need to modify the makefiles.

If you are using Linux, you should also copy the makefiles from the /examples/udf_example directory to the new /expert_udf directory. You will have to open these files and replace the appropriate path- and filenames (e.g., udf_example with expert_udf). Although the udf_example file is listed in some distributions of the MySQL source code, you typically want to keep this as a separate compile. Go ahead and compile the expert_udf file and copy it to your MySQL server installation. You can compile the file with these commands:

```
gcc -shared -o expert_udf.so expert_udf.cc -I/usr/local/mysql/include/mysql
```

Note To use UDFs on Linux, you must compile the server using dynamic libraries. Use the `-with-mysqld-ldflags=---rdynamic` switch for the `configure` command before you compile.

If you are using Windows, you also have to copy the udf_example Visual Studio project file and the udf_example.def file to the expert_udf directory. Rename these files to expert_udf.vcproj and expert_udf.def. Open the project file in Notepad (or WordPad) and replace the path- and filenames (e.g., udf_example with expert_udf). Some distributions of the MySQL source code have errors in the definition file. Listing 8-1 shows the correct contents of the expert_udf.def file. The best way to compile this file is to open the mysql.sln file from the root of the source code directory and add the expert_udf project to the solution. Open the project properties and be sure to verify that the include files are pointing to the appropriate locations. You can then compile the project and copy the expert_udf.dll file to the bin directory of your MySQL server installation.

Listing 8-1. *The expert_udf.def Source Code*

```
LIBRARY      MYUDF
DESCRIPTION  'MySQL Sample for UDF'
VERSION      1.0
EXPORTS
  metaphon_init
  metaphon_deinit
  metaphon
  myfunc_double_init
  myfunc_double
  myfunc_int
  myfunc_int_init
  sequence_init
  sequence_deinit
  sequence
  avgcost_init
  avgcost_deinit
  avgcost_reset
  avgcost_add
  avgcost_clear
  avgcost
```

Caution Windows users will have to remove the networking UDFs from the library. These are not supported directly on Windows. Comment out the functions if you encounter errors about missing header files or external functions.

If you encounter errors during the compilation, go back and correct them. The most likely cause is a missed filename replacement or incorrect path.

Now that the library is compiled, let's test the load and unload operations. This will ensure that the library has been properly compiled and is located in the correct location. Open a MySQL client window and issue the CREATE FUNCTION and DROP FUNCTION commands to load all of the functions in the library. Listing 8-2 shows the commands for loading and unloading the first five functions. The listing shows the commands for Windows; replace expert_udf.dll with expert_udf.so on Linux.

Listing 8-2. *Sample CREATE and DROP FUNCTION Commands*

```
CREATE FUNCTION metaphon RETURNS STRING SONAME "expert_udf.dll";
CREATE FUNCTION myfunc_double RETURNS REAL SONAME "expert_udf.dll";
CREATE FUNCTION myfunc_int RETURNS INTEGER SONAME "expert_udf.dll";
CREATE FUNCTION sequence RETURNS INTEGER SONAME "expert_udf.dll";
CREATE AGGREGATE FUNCTION avgcost RETURNS REAL SONAME "expert_udf.dll";

DROP FUNCTION metaphon;
DROP FUNCTION myfunc_double;
DROP FUNCTION myfunc_int;
DROP FUNCTION sequence;
DROP FUNCTION avgcost;
```

Listings 8-3 and 8-4 show the correct results when you run the CREATE FUNCTION and DROP FUNCTION commands shown earlier.

Listing 8-3. *Installing the Functions*

```
mysql> CREATE FUNCTION metaphon RETURNS STRING SONAME "expert_udf.dll";
```

```
Query OK, 0 rows affected (0.00 sec)
```

```
mysql> CREATE FUNCTION myfunc_double RETURNS REAL SONAME "expert_udf.dll";
```

```
Query OK, 0 rows affected (0.00 sec)
```

```
mysql> CREATE FUNCTION myfunc_int RETURNS INTEGER SONAME "expert_udf.dll";
```

```
Query OK, 0 rows affected (0.00 sec)
```

```
mysql> CREATE FUNCTION sequence RETURNS INTEGER SONAME "expert_udf.dll";
```

```
Query OK, 0 rows affected (0.00 sec)
```

```
mysql> CREATE AGGREGATE FUNCTION avgcost RETURNS REAL SONAME "expert_udf.dll";
```

```
Query OK, 0 rows affected (0.00 sec)
```

Listing 8-4. *Uninstalling the Functions*

```
mysql> DROP FUNCTION metaphon;
```

```
Query OK, 0 rows affected (0.00 sec)
```

```
mysql> DROP FUNCTION myfunc_double;
```

```
Query OK, 0 rows affected (0.00 sec)
```

```
mysql> DROP FUNCTION myfunc_int;
```

```
Query OK, 0 rows affected (0.00 sec)
```

```
mysql> DROP FUNCTION sequence;
```

```
Query OK, 0 rows affected (0.00 sec)
```

```
mysql> DROP FUNCTION avgcost;
```

```
Query OK, 0 rows affected (0.00 sec)
```

Now let's run the commands and see if they work. Go back to your MySQL client window and run the CREATE FUNCTION commands again to load the UDFs. Listing 8-5 shows sample execution of each of the first five UDFs in the library. Feel free to try out the commands as shown. Your results should be similar.

Listing 8-5. *Example Execution of UDF Commands*

```
mysql> SELECT metaphon("This is a test.");
```

```
+----------------------------+
| metaphon("This is a test.") |
+----------------------------+
| OSSTS                      |
+----------------------------+
1 row in set (0.00 sec)
```

```
mysql> SELECT myfunc_double(5.5, 6.1);
```

```
+------------------------+
| myfunc_double(5.5, 6.1) |
+------------------------+
| 50.17                  |
+------------------------+
1 row in set (0.01 sec)
```

```
mysql> SELECT myfunc_int(5, 6, 8);
```

```
+--------------------+
| myfunc_int(5, 6, 8) |
+--------------------+
| 19                 |
+--------------------+
1 row in set (0.00 sec)
```

```
mysql> SELECT sequence(8);
```

```
+-------------+
| sequence(8) |
+-------------+
| 9           |
+-------------+
1 row in set (0.00 sec)
```

```
mysql> CREATE TABLE testavg (order_num int key auto_increment, cost double,
mysql> qty int);
```

```
Query OK, 0 rows affected (0.02 sec)
```

```
mysql> INSERT INTO testavg (cost, qty) VALUES (25.5, 17);
```

```
Query OK, 1 row affected (0.00 sec)
```

```
mysql> INSERT INTO testavg (cost, qty) VALUES (0.23, 5);
```

```
Query OK, 1 row affected (0.00 sec)
```

```
mysql> INSERT INTO testavg (cost, qty) VALUES (47.50, 81);
```

```
Query OK, 1 row affected (0.00 sec)
```

```
mysql> SELECT avgcost(qty, cost) FROM testavg;
```

```
+--------------------+
| avgcost(qty, cost) |
+--------------------+
| 41.5743            |
+--------------------+
1 row in set (0.03 sec)
```

The last few commands show a very basic use of the avgcost() aggregate function. You would typically use aggregate functions when using the GROUP BY clause. However, these functions can also be used in place of columns for analysis of the values in the table.

Adding a New User-Defined Function

Let's now add a new UDF to the library. What if you are working on an integration project and the requirements call for expressing dates in the Julian format? The Julian conversion simply takes the day of the year (number of days elapsed since December 31 of the previous year) and adds the year to form a numeric value, like DDDYYYY. In this case, you need to add a function that takes a month, date, and year value and returns the date expressed as a Julian date. The function should be defined as

```
longlong julian(int month, int day, int year);
```

I kept the function simple and used three integers. The function could be implemented in any number of ways (e.g., accepting a date or string value). Now let's add the JULIAN function to the UDF library you just built.

This is what makes creating your own UDF library so valuable. Any time you encounter a need for a new function, you can just add it to the existing library without having to create a new project from scratch.

The process for adding a new UDF begins with adding the function declarations to the extern section of the UDF library source code and then implementing the functions. You can then recompile the library and deploy it to the bin directory of your MySQL server installation. Let's walk through that process with the JULIAN function.

Open the expert_udf.cc file and add the function declarations. Recall that you need definitions for the julian_init(), julian_deinit(), and julian() functions. The julian_init() function takes three arguments:

- UDF_INIT, a structure that the method can use to pass information among the UDF methods

- UDF_ARGS, a structure that contains the number of arguments, the type of arguments, and the arguments

- A string that the method should return if an error occurs

The julian() method takes four arguments:

- The UDF_INIT structure completed by the julian_init() function

- A UDF_ARGS structure that contains the number of arguments, the type of arguments, and the arguments

- A char pointer that is set to 1 if the result is null

- A message that is sent to the caller if an error occurs

The julian_deinit() function uses the UDF_INIT structure completed by the julian_init() function.

When a method is called from the server, a new UDF_INIT structure is created and passed to the function, the arguments are placed in the UDF_ARGS structure, and the julian_init() function is called. If that function returns without errors, the julian() function is called with the UDF_INIT structure from the julian_init() function. After the julian() function completes, the julian_deinit() function is called to clean up the values saved in the UDF_INIT structure. Listing 8-6 shows an excerpt of the extern section of the file with the JULIAN functions added.

Listing 8-6. *The extern Declarations for JULIAN (expert_udf.cc)*

```
extern "C" {
my_bool julian_init(UDF_INIT *initid, UDF_ARGS *args, char *message);
longlong julian(UDF_INIT *initid, UDF_ARGS *args, char *is_null, char *error);
void julian_deinit(UDF_INIT *initid);
...
```

You can now add the implementation for these functions. I find it helpful to copy the example functions that match my return types and then modify them to match my needs. The julian_init() function is responsible for initializing variables and checking correct usage. Since the JULIAN function requires three integer parameters, you need to add appropriate error handling to enforce this. Listing 8-7 shows the implementation of the julian_init() function.

Listing 8-7. *Implementation for the julian_init() Function (expert_udf.cc)*

```
my_bool julian_init(UDF_INIT *initid, UDF_ARGS *args, char *message)
{
  if (args->arg_count != 3) /* if there are not three arguments */
  {
    strcpy(message, "Wrong number of arguments: JULIAN() requires 3 arguments.");
    return 1;
  }
  if ((args->arg_type[0] != INT_RESULT) ||
      (args->arg_type[1] != INT_RESULT) ||
      (args->arg_type[2] != INT_RESULT))
  {
    strcpy(message, "Wrong type of arguments: JULIAN() requires 3 integers.");
    return 1;
  }
  return 0;
}
```

Notice in Listing 8-7 that the argument count is checked first followed by type checking of the three parameters. This ensures they are all integers. Savvy programmers will note that the code should also check for ranges of the values. Since the code does not check ranges of the parameters, this could lead to unusual or invalid return values. I leave this to you to complete should you decide to implement the function in your library. It is always a good practice to check range values when the domain and range of the parameter values is known.

The julian_deinit() function isn't really needed since there are no memory or variables to clean up. You can implement an empty function just to complete the process. It is always a good idea to code this function even if you don't need it. Listing 8-8 shows the implementation for this function. Since we didn't use any new variables or structures, the implementation is simply an empty function. If there had been variables or structures created, you would deallocate them in this function.

Listing 8-8. *Implementation for the julian_deinit() Function (expert_udf.cc)*

```
void julian_deinit(UDF_INIT *initid)
{
}
```

The real work of the JULIAN function occurs in the julian() implementation. Listing 8-9 shows the completed julian() function.

Note Some sophisticated Julian calendar methods calculate the value as elapsed days since a start date (usually in the 18th or 19th century). This method assumes the need is for a Julian day/year value.

Listing 8-9. *Implementation for the julian() Function (expert_udf.cc)*

```
longlong julian(UDF_INIT *initid, UDF_ARGS *args, char *is_null, char *error)
{
  longlong jdate = 0;
  static int DAYS_IN_MONTH[] = {31, 28, 31, 30, 31, 30, 31, 31, 30, 31, 30, 31};
  int month = 0;
  int day = 0;
  int year = 0;
  int i;

  /* copy memory from the arguments */
  memcpy(&month, args->args[0], args->lengths[0]);
  memcpy(&day, args->args[1], args->lengths[1]);
  memcpy(&year, args->args[2], args->lengths[2]);

  /* add the days in the month for each prior month */
  for (i = 0; i < month - 1; i++)
    jdate += DAYS_IN_MONTH[i];

  /* add the day of this month */
  jdate += day;

  /* find the year */
  if (((year % 100) != 0) && ((year % 4) == 0))
    jdate++;  /*leap year!*/

  /* shift day of year to left */
  jdate *= 10000;

  /* add the year */
  jdate += year;
  return jdate;
}
```

Notice the first few lines after the variable declarations. This is an example of how you can marshal the values from the args array to your own local variables. In this case, I converted the first three parameters to integer values. The rest of the source code is the calculation of the Julian date value that is returned to the caller.

If you are using Windows, you also need to modify the expert_udf.def file and add the methods for the JULIAN function. Listing 8-10 shows the updated expert_udf.def file.

Listing 8-10. *The expert_udf.def Source Code*

```
LIBRARY     MYUDF
DESCRIPTION  'MySQL Sample for UDF'
VERSION     1.0
EXPORTS
  metaphon_init
  metaphon_deinit
  metaphon
  myfunc_double_init
  myfunc_double
  myfunc_int
  myfunc_int_init
  sequence_init
  sequence_deinit
  sequence
  avgcost_init
  avgcost_deinit
  avgcost_reset
  avgcost_add
  avgcost_clear
  avgcost
  julian_init
  julian_deinit
  julian
```

Once the library is compiled, you can copy the library to the bin directory of your MySQL server installation. If you are running Linux, you will be copying the file expert_udf.so; if you are running Windows, you will be copying the file expert_udf.dll from the /expert_udf/debug directory.

I recommend stopping the server before you copy the file and restarting it after the copy is complete. This is because it is possible (depending on where you placed your new function) that the object file could be different from the previous compilation. It is always a good practice to do any time you make changes to the executable code.

Go ahead and perform the library installation, then enter the CREATE FUNCTION command and try out the new function. Listing 8-11 shows an example of installing and running the JULIAN function on Windows.

Listing 8-11. *Sample Execution of the julian() Function*

```
mysql> CREATE FUNCTION julian RETURNS INTEGER SONAME "expert_udf.dll";
```

```
Query OK, 0 rows affected (0.00 sec)
```

```
mysql> SELECT JULIAN(7, 4, 2006);
```

```
+--------------------+
| JULIAN(7, 4, 2006) |
+--------------------+
| 1852006            |
+--------------------+
1 row in set (0.00 sec)
```

You can use the expert_udf library as the start of your own library or follow the steps in this section to copy it and create your libraries. UDF libraries can help you expand the capabilities of your server to meet almost any computational need. The libraries are easy to create and require only a small number of functions for implementation. Except for the need to have the dynamically loaded version for Linux, UDFs work very well with little special configuration requirements.

Adding Native Functions

Native functions are those that are compiled as part of the MySQL server. They can be used without having to load them from a library and are therefore always available. There is a long list of available native functions ranging from ABS() to UCASE() and many more. For more information about the currently supported set of native functions, consult the online MySQL reference manual.

If the function that you want to use isn't available (it's not one of the built-in native functions), you can add your own native function by modifying the source code. Now that you have a JULIAN function, wouldn't it be best if there were an equivalent function to convert a Julian date back to a Gregorian date? I'll show you how to add a new native function in this section. The process for adding a new native function involves changing the mysqld source code files. The files that you need to change are summarized in Table 8-1.

Table 8-1. *Changes to mysqld Source Code Files for Adding a New Native Function*

File	Description of Changes
lex.h	Add the symbol for the native function to the lexical analyzer symbols.
item_create.h	Add a create_func_xxx function declaration.
item_create.cc	Add the implementation for the create_func_xxx function.
item_str_func.h	Add the class definition for the function.
item_str_func.cc	Add the class implementation for the function.
lex_hash.h	Regenerate the lexical hash for the symbols in the lexical analyzer and parser.

■**Note** Files are located in the /sql directory off the root of the source code tree.

The changes necessary for the lex.h header file involve adding the symbol for the function and defining the name of the create_func_xxx function. This function is used to instantiate an instance of the class for use in the processing of commands. Open the lex.h header file and add the following symbol definition to the symbols[] array. The items in the array are in alphabetical order so you should place the following in the same order:

```
{ "GREGORIAN",    F_SYM(FUNC_ARG1),0,CREATE_FUNC(create_func_gregorian)},
```

The values for the entry are the name of the function, a call to the F_SYM() function to associate the token in the parser, the length of the name (which is set in sql_lex.cc), and a reference to the create function for the new symbol. These entries are used to create a mapping of the symbols identified to locations in the code.

You may be wondering how this array is used to tell the parser what to do when the symbol is detected. The mechanism used is called a *lexical hash*. If you compile the code and try to run it, you will find that the new symbol isn't detected. This is because you must generate a new instance of the lexical hash. The lexical hash is an implementation of an advanced hashing lookup procedure from the works of Knuth.[1] It is generated using a command-line utility that implements the algorithm. The utility, gen_lex_hash, has one source code file named gen_lex_hash.cc. This program produces a file that you will use to replace the existing lexical hash header file (lex_hash.h). When modifying the MySQL source code, keep this rule of thumb in mind: whenever you change the code in lex.h and add symbols, you must generate the lex_hash.h file using gen_lex_hash. I provide instructions for both Windows and Linux later in this section.

Now that you've told the lexical analyzer there is a create function, you need to provide a function declaration. Open the item_create.h file and add the following function declaration. The Item* a argument is a pointer to the argument used by the function.

```
Item *create_func_gregorian(Item* a);
```

Now let's add the function implementation. This simply instantiates the class we'll define in a moment. Open the item_create.cc file and add the instantiation as shown in Listing 8-12.

Listing 8-12. *Modifications to the item_create.cc File*

```
Item *create_func_gregorian(Item* a)
{
  return new Item_func_gregorian(a);
}
```

Now that the create function is implemented, you need to create a new class to implement the code for the function. This is where most developers get very confused. MySQL AB has provided a number of the Item_xxx_func base (and derived) classes for you to use. For example, derive your class from Item_str_func for functions that return a string and Item_int_func for

---

1. Knuth, D. E., *The Art of Computer Programming. 2nd ed.* (Reading: Addison-Wesley, 1997).

those that return an integer. Similarly, there are other classes for functions that return other types. This is a departure from the dynamically loadable UDF interface and is the main reason you would choose to create a native function versus a dynamically loadable one. For more information about what Item_xxx_func classes there are, see the item.h file in the /sql directory off the root of the source code tree.

Since the Gregorian function will return a string, you need to derive from the Item_str_func class, define the class in item_str_func.h, and implement the class in item_str_func.cc. Open the item_str_func.h file and add the class definition to the header file as shown in Listing 8-13. Notice that this class has only four functions that must be declared. The minimal functions needed are the function that contains the code for the function (Item_func_gregorian), a value function (val_str), a function that returns the name (func_name), and a function to set the maximum length of the string argument (fix_length_and_dec). You can add any others that you might need, but these four are the ones required for functions that return strings. Other item base (and derived) classes may require additional functions such as val_int(), val_double(), and so on. Check the definition of the class you need to derive from in order to identify the methods that must be overridden; these are known as virtual functions.

Listing 8-13. *Modifications to the item_str_func.h File*

```
class Item_func_gregorian :public Item_str_func
{
public:
  Item_func_gregorian(Item *a) :Item_str_func(a) {}
  String *val_str(String *str);
  const char *func_name() const { return "gregorian"; }
  void fix_length_and_dec();
};
```

Let's add the class implementation. Open the item_strfunc.cc file and add the implementation of the Gregorian class functions as shown in Listing 8-14. You need to implement the main function, val_str(), which does the work of the Julian-to-Gregorian operation. You also need to implement the fix_length_and_dec() function to set the limit of the size of the string returned.

Listing 8-14. *Modifications to the item_strfunc.cc File*

```
String *Item_func_gregorian::val_str(String *str)
{
  static int DAYS_IN_MONTH[] = {31, 28, 31, 30, 31, 30, 31, 31, 30, 31, 30, 31};
  longlong jdate = args[0]->val_int();
  int year = 0;
  int month = 0;
  int day = 0;
  int i;
  char cstr[30];
```

```
      cstr[0] = 0;
      str->length(0);

      /* get date from value (right 4 digits */
      year = jdate - ((jdate / 10000) * 10000);

      /* get value for day of year and find current month*/
      day = (jdate - year) / 10000;
      for (i = 0; i < 12; i++)
        if (DAYS_IN_MONTH[i] < day)
          day = day - DAYS_IN_MONTH[i]; /* remainder is day of current month */
        else
        {
          month = i + 1;
          break;
        }

      /* format date string */
      sprintf(cstr, "%d", month);
      str->append(cstr);
      str->append("/");
      sprintf(cstr, "%d", day);
      str->append(cstr);
      str->append("/");
      sprintf(cstr, "%d", year);
      str->append(cstr);
      if (null_value)
        return 0;
      return str;
}

void Item_func_gregorian::fix_length_and_dec()
{
    max_length=30;
}
```

Now it's time to generate the lexical hash. Please read the section that applies to your operating system. Take note of the process and run through the process until you have a working gen_lex_hash command-line utility.

Generating the Lexical Hash on Windows

You must first open the main solution and add the gen_lex_hash project in the /sql directory. Add these to the project dependencies: dbug, libmysql, mysys, strings, taocrypt, yassl, and zlib. Then compile the project. The compiler will include any of the dependencies that haven't been processed. When the compilation is complete, open a command prompt and navigate to the /sql directory in the root of the source code tree. Generate the lexical hash by running the gen_lex_hash.exe utility as shown here:

```
gen_lex_hash > lex_hash.h
```

This will generate a new lex_hash.h file to use when compiling the server that will recognize the new symbols added to the lex.h file.

Generating the Lexical Hash on Linux

Linux users, this is your chance to smile. The build scripts for the MySQL server include the compilation of the gen_lex_hash utility. For some distributions of the MySQL source code (5.1 and later), the utility is located in the /sql directory and is compiled with the mysqld server. Other distributions (some Windows distributions) place the utility in a directory named gen_lex_hash and have their own makefile. Generate the lexical hash by running the gen_lex_hash utility as shown here:

```
gen_lex_hash > lex_hash.h
```

This will generate a new lex_hash.h file to use when compiling the server that will recognize the new symbols added to the lex.h file. However, you really don't need to do this step because the makefile included with the Linux source code distribution performs this step for you. The only reason you might want to run the command is if you want to ensure there are no errors.

Compiling and Testing the New Native Function

Recompile your server and reload it. If you encounter errors during compile, go back and check the statements you entered for errors. Once the errors are corrected and you have a new executable, stop your server and copy the new executable to the location of your MySQL installation and restart the server. You can now execute the native function Gregorian as shown in Listings 8-15 and 8-16. To test the Gregorian function for correctness, you can run the julian() command first and use that value as input to the gregorian() function.

Listing 8-15. *Running the julian() Function*

```
mysql> select julian(7,4,2006);
```

```
+------------------+
| julian(7,4,2006) |
+------------------+
| 1852006          |
+------------------+
1 row in set (0.00 sec)
```

Listing 8-16. *Running the gregorian() Function*

```
mysql> select gregorian(1852006);
```

```
+--------------------+
| gregorian(1852006) |
+--------------------+
| 7/4/2006           |
+--------------------+
1 row in set (2.44 sec)
```

Well, that's about it for adding native functions. Now that you have had an introduction to creating native functions, you can further plan your integration with MySQL to include customizations to the server source code.

Adding SQL Commands

If you find that the native SQL commands do not meet your needs and you cannot solve your problems with user-defined functions, you may have to add a new SQL command to the server. This section shows you how to add your own SQL commands to the server.

Adding new SQL commands is considered by many to be the most difficult extension of all to the MySQL server source code. As you will see, the process isn't as complicated as it is tedious. To add new SQL commands, you must modify the parser (in sql\sql_yacc.yy) and add the commands to the SQL command processing code (in sql\sql_parse.cc).

When a client issues a query, a new thread is created and the SQL statement is forwarded to the parser for syntactic validation (or rejection due to errors). The MySQL parser is implemented using a large Lex-YACC script that is compiled with Bison. The parser constructs a query structure used to represent the query statement (SQL) in memory as a data structure that can be used to execute the query. Thus, to add a new command to the parser, you will need a copy of GNU Bison. You can download Bison from the GNU web site[2] and install it.

WHAT IS LEX AND YACC AND WHO'S BISON?

Lex stands for "lexical analyzer generator" and is used as a parser to identify tokens and literals as well as syntax of a language. YACC stands for "yet another compiler compiler" and is used to identify and act on the semantic definitions of the language. The use of these tools together with Bison (a YACC-compatible parser generator that generates C source code from the Lex/YACC code) provides a rich mechanism of creating subsystems that can parse and process language commands. Indeed, that is exactly how MySQL uses these technologies.

---

2. Linux/Unix users can download it from the GNU web site (www.gnu.org/software/bison). Windows users can download a Win32 version from http://gnuwin32.sourceforge.net/packages/bison.htm.

Let's assume you want to add a command to the server to show the current disk usage of all of the databases in the server. Although there are external tools that can retrieve this information, you desire a SQL equivalent function that you can easily use in your own database-driven applications. Let's also assume you want to add this as a SHOW command. Specifically, you want to be able to execute the command SHOW DISK_USAGE and retrieve a result set that has each database listed as a row along with the total size of all of the files (tables) listed in kilobytes.

Adding a new SQL command involves adding symbols to the lexical analyzer and adding the SHOW DISK_USAGE command syntax to the YACC parser (sql_yacc.yy). The new parser must be compiled into a C program by Bison and then a new lexical hash created using the gen_lex_hash utility described earlier. The code for the parser to direct control to the new command is placed in the large case statement in sql_parse.cc with a case for the new command symbol.

Let's begin with adding the symbols to the lexical analyzer. Open the lex.h file and locate the static SYMBOL symbols[] array. You can make the symbol anything you want, but it should be something meaningful (like all good variable names). Be sure to choose a symbol that isn't already in use. In this case, use the symbol DISK_USAGE. This acts like a label to the parser identifying it as a token. Place a statement in the array to direct the lexical analyzer to generate the symbol and call it DISK_USAGE_SYM. The list is in (roughly) alphabetic order, so place it in the proper location. Listing 8-17 shows an excerpt of the array with the symbols added.

Listing 8-17. *Updates to the lex.h File for the SHOW DISK_USAGE Command*

```
static SYMBOL symbols[] = {
  { "&&",      SYM(AND_AND_SYM)},
...
  { "DISK",    SYM(DISK_SYM)},
/* BEGIN CAB MODIFICATION */
/* Reason for Modification: */
/* This section identifies the tokens for the SHOW DISK_USAGE command*/
  { "DISK_USAGE",          SYM(DISK_USAGE_SYM)},
/* END CAB MODIFICATION */
  { "DISTINCT",    SYM(DISTINCT)},
...
```

The next thing you need to do is add a mnemonic to identify the command. This mnemonic will be used in the parser to assign to the internal query structure and to control the flow of execution via a case in the large switch statement in the sql_parse.cc file. Open the sql_lex.h file and add the new command to the enum_sql_command enumeration. Listing 8-18 shows the modifications with the new command mnemonic.

Listing 8-18. *Changes to the sql_lex.h File for the SHOW DISK_USAGE Command*

```
enum enum_sql_command {
  SQLCOM_SELECT, SQLCOM_CREATE_TABLE, SQLCOM_CREATE_INDEX, SQLCOM_ALTER_TABLE,
  SQLCOM_UPDATE, SQLCOM_INSERT, SQLCOM_INSERT_SELECT,
  SQLCOM_DELETE, SQLCOM_TRUNCATE, SQLCOM_DROP_TABLE, SQLCOM_DROP_INDEX,
...
```

```
  SQLCOM_SHOW_COLUMN_TYPES, SQLCOM_SHOW_STORAGE_ENGINES, SQLCOM_SHOW_PRIVILEGES,
/* BEGIN CAB MODIFICATION */
/* Reason for Modification: */
/* This section captures the enumerations for the SHOW DISK_USAGE command tokens */
  SQLCOM_SHOW_DISK_USAGE,
/* END CAB MODIFICATION */
  SQLCOM_HELP, SQLCOM_CREATE_USER, SQLCOM_DROP_USER, SQLCOM_RENAME_USER,
...
```

Now that you have the new symbol and the command mnemonic, you now need to add code to the sql_yacc.yy file to define the new token that you used in the lex.h file and add the source code for the new SHOW DISK_USAGE SQL command. Open the sql_yacc.yy file and add the new token to the list of tokens (near the top). These are defined (roughly) in alphabetical order, so place the new token in the proper order. Listing 8-19 shows the modifications to the sql_yacc.yy file.

Listing 8-19. *Adding the Token to the sql_yacc.yy File*

```
...
%token  DISK_SYM
/* BEGIN CAB MODIFICATION */
/* Reason for Modification: */
/* This section defines the tokens for the SHOW DISK_USAGE command */
%token  DISK_USAGE_SYM
/* END CAB MODIFICATION */
%token  DISTINCT
...
```

Note If you use Windows, the sql_yacc.yy file is not included in the source code distribution. You must download one of the Linux source code distributions and retrieve the file from there. Make sure you use the same version of the Linux source code that matches your Windows source code.

You also need to add the command syntax to the parser YACC code (also in sql_yacc.yy). Locate the show: label and add the command as shown in Listing 8-20.

Listing 8-20. *Parser Syntax Source Code for the SHOW DISK_USAGE Command*

```
show:
/* BEGIN CAB MODIFICATION */
/* Reason for Modification: */
/* This section captures (parses) the SHOW ALV statement */
  SHOW DISK_USAGE_SYM
  {
      LEX *lex=Lex;
      lex->sql_command= SQLCOM_SHOW_DISK_USAGE;
```

```
}
/* END CAB MODIFICATION */
  | SHOW
```

■**Caution** Don't forget the | before the original SHOW statement.

You're probably wondering what this code does. It looks rather benign and yet it is important to get this part right. In fact, this is the stage where most developers give up and fail to add new commands.

The set of code identified by the show: label is executed whenever the SHOW token is identified by the parser. YACC code is almost always written this way.[3] The SHOW DISK_USAGE_SYM statement indicates the only valid syntax that has the SHOW and DISK_USAGE tokens appearing (in that order). If you look through the code, you'll find other similar syntactical arrangements. The code block following the syntax statement gets a pointer to the lex structure and sets the command attribute to the new command token SQLCOM_SHOW_DISK_USAGE. Notice how this code matches the SHOW and DISK_USAGE_SYM symbols to the SQLCOM_SHOW_DISK_USAGE command so that the SQL command switch in the sql_parse.cc file can correctly route the execution to the implementation of the SHOW DISK_USAGE command.

Notice also that I placed this code at the start of the show: definition and used the vertical bar symbol (|) in front of the previous SHOW syntax statement. The vertical bar is used as an "or" for the syntax switch. Thus, the statement is valid if and only if it meets one of the syntax statement definitions. Feel free to look around in this file and get a feel for how the code works. Don't sweat over learning every nuance. What I have shown you is the minimum of what you need to know to create a new command. If you decide to implement more complex commands, study the examples of similar commands to see how they handle tokens and variables.

Next, you need to add the source code to the large command statement switch in sql_parse.cc. Open the file and add a new case to the switch statement as shown in Listing 8-21.

Listing 8-21. *Adding a Case for the New Command*

```
...
  case SQLCOM_SHOW_AUTHORS:
    res= mysqld_show_authors(thd);
    break;
/* BEGIN CAB MODIFICATION */
/* Reason for Modification: */
/* This section adds the code to call the new SHOW DISK_USAGE command. */
  case SQLCOM_SHOW_DISK_USAGE:
    res = show_disk_usage_command(thd);
    break;
/* END CAB MODIFICATION */
```

---

3. To learn more about the YACC parser and how to write YACC code, see the following web site for more
   information: http://dinosaur.compilertools.net/.

```
case SQLCOM_SHOW_PRIVILEGES:
  res= mysqld_show_privileges(thd);
  break;
...
```

Notice I just added a call to a new function named show_disk_usage_command(). You will add this function to the sql_show.cc file. The name of this function matches the tokens in the lex.h file and the symbols identified in the sql_yacc.yy file and the command switch in the sql_parse.cc file. Not only does this make it clear what is going on, it also helps to keep the already large switch statement within limits. Feel free to look around in this file as it is the heart of the command statement flow of execution. You should be able to find all of the commands like SELECT, CREATE, and so on.

Now, let's add the code to execute the command. Open the mysql_priv.h file and add the function declaration for the new command as shown in Listing 8-22. I have placed the function declaration near the same functions as defined in the sql_parse.cc file. This isn't required, but it helps organize the code a bit.

Listing 8-22. *Function Declaration for the New Command*

```
...
bool mysqld_show_authors(THD *thd);
bool show_disk_usage_command(THD *thd);
bool mysqld_show_privileges(THD *thd);
...
```

The last modification is to add the implementation for the show_disk_usage_command() function (Listing 8-23). Open the sql_show.cc file and add the function implementation for the new command. The code in Listing 8-23 is stubbed out. I did this to ensure that the new command was working before I added any code. This practice is a great one to follow if you have to implement complex code. Implementing just the basics helps to establish that your code changes are working and that any errors encountered are not related to the stubbed code. This practice is especially important to follow whenever modifying or adding new SQL commands.

Listing 8-23. *The show_disk_usage_command() Implementation*

```
/* BEGIN CAB MODIFICATION */
/* Reason for Modification: */
/* This section adds the code to call the new SHOW DISK_USAGE command. */
bool show_disk_usage_command(THD *thd)
{
  List<Item> field_list;
  Protocol *protocol= thd->protocol;
  DBUG_ENTER("show_disk_usage");

  /* send fields */
  field_list.push_back(new Item_empty_string("Database",50));
  field_list.push_back(new Item_empty_string("Size (Kb)",30));
```

```
  if (protocol->send_fields(&field_list,
                      Protocol::SEND_NUM_ROWS | Protocol::SEND_EOF))
    DBUG_RETURN(TRUE);

  /* send test data */
  protocol->prepare_for_resend();
  protocol->store("test_row", system_charset_info);
  protocol->store("1024", system_charset_info);
  if (protocol->write())
    DBUG_RETURN(TRUE);

  send_eof(thd);
  DBUG_RETURN(FALSE);
}
/* END CAB MODIFICATION */
```

I want to call your attention to the source code for a moment. If you recall, in a previous chapter I mentioned there were low-level network functions that allowed you to build a result set and return it to the client. Look at the lines of code indicated by the /* send fields */ comment. This code creates the fields for the result set. In this case, I'm creating two fields (or columns) named Database and Size (Kb). These will appear as the column headings in the MySQL client utility when the command is executed.

Notice the protocol->XXX statements. This is where I use the Protocol class to send rows to the client. I first call prepare_for_resend() to clear the buffer, then make as many calls to the overloaded store() method setting the value for each field (in order). Finally, I call the write() method to write the buffer to the network. If anything goes wrong, I exit the function with a value of true (which means errors were generated). The last statement that ends the result set and finalizes communication to the client is the send_eof() function, which sends an end-of-file signal to the client. You can use these same classes, methods, and functions to send results from your commands.

If you want to compile the server, you can, but you'll encounter errors concerning the DISK_USAGE_SYM symbol. If you have other errors during this compile, please fix them before moving on.

Now let's get back to the lexical hash and parser code. If you've been studying the MySQL source code, you've probably noticed that there are sql_yacc.cc and sql_yacc.h files. These files are generated from the sql_yacc.yy file by Bison. Let's use Bison to generate these files. Open a command window and navigate to the /sql directory off the root of your source code tree. Run the following command:

```
bison -y -d sql_yacc.yy
```

This generates two new files: y.tab.c and y.tab.h. These files will replace the sql_yacc.cc and sql_yacc.h files, respectively. Before you copy them, make a backup of the original files. After you have made a backup of the files, copy y.tab.c to sql_yacc.cc (.cpp on Windows) and y.tab.h to sql_yacc.h.

Note If you're using Linux, you don't need to do this step because the makefile included with the Linux source code distribution performs this step for you. The only reason you might want to run the command is if you want to run the command to ensure there are no errors.

Windows users will encounter problems with some definitions missing from the compiled `sql_yacc.cpp` file. If you get errors about the yyerror missing or `MYSQLparse` missing, open the `sql_yacc.cpp` file, add the statements shown in Listing 8-24, and rerun the Bison command to generate the `y.tab.c` and `y.tab.h` files.

Listing 8-24. *Missing #define Statements*

```
/* If NAME_PREFIX is specified substitute the variables and functions
   names.  */
#define yyparse MYSQLparse
#define yylex   MYSQLlex
#define yyerror MYSQLerror
#define yylval  MYSQLlval
#define yychar  MYSQLchar
#define yydebug MYSQLdebug
#define yynerrs MYSQLnerrs
```

Once the `sql_yacc.cc` and `sql_yacc.h` files are correct, generate the lexical hash by running this command:

```
gen_lex_hash > lex_hash.h
```

Everything is now set for you to compile the server. Since you have modified a number of the key header files, you may encounter longer-than-normal compilation times. Should you encounter compilation errors, please correct them before you proceed.

Once the server is compiled and you have a new executable, stop your server and copy the new executable to the location of your MySQL installation and restart the server. You can now execute the new command in a MySQL client utility. Listing 8-25 shows an example of the SHOW DISK_USAGE command.

Listing 8-25. *Example Execution of the SHOW DISK_USAGE Command*

```
mysql> SHOW DISK_USAGE;
```

```
+----------+-----------+
| Database | Size (Kb) |
+----------+-----------+
| test_row | 1024      |
+----------+-----------+
1 row in set (0.00 sec)
```

OK, now that everything is working, open the `sql_show.cc` file and add the actual code for the SHOW DISK_USAGE command as shown in Listing 8-26.

Listing 8-26. *The Final show_disk_usage_command Source Code*

```
/* This section adds the code to call the new SHOW DISK_USAGE command. */
bool show_disk_usage_command(THD *thd)
{
  List<Item> field_list;
  List<char> dbs;
  char *db_name;
  char *path;
  MY_DIR *dirp;
  FILEINFO *file;
  longlong fsizes = 0;
  longlong lsizes = 0;
  Protocol *protocol= thd->protocol;
  DBUG_ENTER("show_disk_usage");

  /* send the fields "Database" and "Size" */
  field_list.push_back(new Item_empty_string("Database",50));
  field_list.push_back(new Item_int("Size (Kb)",(longlong) 1,21));
  if (protocol->send_fields(&field_list,
                       Protocol::SEND_NUM_ROWS | Protocol::SEND_EOF))
    DBUG_RETURN(TRUE);

  /* get database directories */
  mysql_find_files(thd, &dbs, 0, mysql_data_home, 0, 1);
  List_iterator_fast<char> it_dbs(dbs);
  path = (char *)my_malloc(PATH_MAX, MYF(MY_ZEROFILL));
  dirp = my_dir(mysql_data_home, MYF(MY_WANT_STAT));
  fsizes = 0;
  lsizes = 0;
  for (int i = 0; i < (int)dirp->number_off_files; i++)
  {
    file = dirp->dir_entry + i;
    if (strncasecmp (file->name, "ibdata", 6) == 0)
      fsizes = fsizes + file->mystat->st_size;
    else if (strncasecmp (file->name, "ib", 2) == 0)
      lsizes = lsizes + file->mystat->st_size;
  }

  /* send InnoDB data to client */
  protocol->prepare_for_resend();
  protocol->store("InnoDB TableSpace", system_charset_info);
  protocol->store((longlong)fsizes);
```

```
  if (protocol->write())
    DBUG_RETURN(TRUE);
  protocol->prepare_for_resend();
  protocol->store("InnoDB Logs", system_charset_info);
  protocol->store((longlong)lsizes);
  if (protocol->write())
    DBUG_RETURN(TRUE);

  /* now send database name and sizes of the databases */
  while (db_name = it_dbs++)
  {
    fsizes = 0;
    strcpy(path, mysql_data_home);
    strcat(path, "/");
    strcat(path, db_name);
    dirp = my_dir(path, MYF(MY_WANT_STAT));
    for (int i = 0; i < (int)dirp->number_off_files; i++)
    {
      file = dirp->dir_entry + i;
      fsizes = fsizes + file->mystat->st_size;
    }
    protocol->prepare_for_resend();
    protocol->store(db_name, system_charset_info);
    protocol->store((longlong)fsizes);
    if (protocol->write())
      DBUG_RETURN(TRUE);
  }
  send_eof(thd);

  /* free memory */
  my_free((gptr)path, MYF(0));
  DBUG_RETURN(FALSE);
}
/* END CAB MODIFICATION */
```

Note On Windows, substitute MAX_PATH for PATH_MAX in the my_malloc() calls and use strnicmp in place of the strncasecmp.

When you compile and load the server, then run the command, you should see something similar to the example shown in Listing 8-27.

Listing 8-27. *Example Execution of the new SHOW DISK_USAGE Command*

```
mysql> SHOW DISK_USAGE;
```

```
+--------------------+----------+
| Database           | Size (Kb) |
+--------------------+----------+
| InnoDB TableSpace  | 10485760 |
| InnoDB Logs        | 20971520 |
| cluster            | 9867     |
| mysql              | 617310   |
| test               | 9720     |
+--------------------+----------+
5 rows in set (0.65 sec)
```

The list shows you the cumulative size of each database on your server in the MySQL data directory. One thing you might want to do is add a row that returns the grand total of all disk space used (much like a WITH ROLLUP clause). I leave this modification for you to complete as you experiment with implementing the function.

I hope that this short section on creating new SQL commands has helped eliminate some of the confusion and difficulty surrounding the MySQL SQL command-processing source code. Now that you have this information, you can plan your own extensions to the MySQL commands to meet your own unique needs.

Adding to the Information Schema

The last area I want to cover in this chapter is adding information to the information schema. The *information schema* is an in-memory collection of logical tables that contain status and other pertinent data (also known as *metadata*) about the server and its environment. Introduced in version 5.0.2, the information schema has become an important tool for administration and debugging the MySQL server, its environment, and databases.[4] For example, the information schema makes it easy to display all the columns for all the tables in a database by using this SQL command:

```
SELECT table_name, column_name, data_type FROM information_schema.columns
WHERE table_schema = 'test';
```

The metadata is grouped into logical tables that permit you to issue SELECT commands against them. This provides a unique and useful way to get information about the server. Table 8-2 lists some of the logical tables and their uses.

---

4. For more information about the information schema, see the online MySQL reference manual.

Table 8-2. *Information Schema Logical Tables*

Name	Description
schemata	Provides information about databases.
tables	Provides information about the tables in all the databases.
columns	Provides information about the columns in all the tables.
statistics	Provides information about indexes for the tables.
user_privileges	Provides information about the database privileges. It encapsulates the mysql.db grant table.
table_privileges	Provides information about the table privileges. It encapsulates the mysql.tables_priv grant table.
column_privileges	Provides information about the column privileges. It encapsulates the mysql.columns_priv grant table.
collations	Provides information about the collations for the character sets.
key_column_usage	Provides information about the key columns.
routines	Provides information about the procedures and functions (does not include user-defined functions).
views	Provides information about the views from all the databases.
triggers	Provides information about the triggers from all the databases.

Since the disk usage command falls into the category of metadata, I'll show you how to add it to the information schema mechanism in the server. The process is actually pretty straightforward, with no changes to the sql_yacc.yy code or lexical hash. Instead, you add a mnemonic and a case for the switch statement in the function that creates the schema table for the disk usage function, define a structure to hold the columns for the table, and then add the source code to execute it.

Let's begin with modifying the header files for the new mnemonic. Open the table.h file and locate the enum_schema_tables enumeration. Add a new mnemonic named SCH_DISKUSAGE to the list. Listing 8-28 shows an excerpt of the enumerations with the new mnemonic added.

Listing 8-28. *Changes to the enum_schema_tables Enumeration*

```
enum enum_schema_tables
{
  SCH_CHARSETS= 0,
  SCH_COLLATIONS,
  SCH_COLLATION_CHARACTER_SET_APPLICABILITY,
  SCH_COLUMNS,
  SCH_COLUMN_PRIVILEGES,
  SCH_ENGINES,
/* BEGIN CAB MODIFICATION */
/* Reason for Modification: */
/* This section adds the code to call the new SHOW DISK_USAGE command. */
```

```
  SCH_DISKUSAGE,
/* END CAB MODIFICATION */
  SCH_EVENTS,
...
```

Now you need to add the case for the switch command in the `prepare_schema_tables()` function that creates the new schema table. Open the `sql_parse.cc` file and add the case statement shown in Listing 8-29. Notice that I just added the case without a break statement. This allows the code to fall through to code that satisfies all of the case. This is an elegant alternative to lengthy `if-then-else-if` statements that you see in most source code.

Listing 8-29. *Modifications to the prepare_schema_table Function*

```
int prepare_schema_table(THD *thd, LEX *lex, Table_ident *table_ident,
                         enum enum_schema_tables schema_table_idx)
{
  DBUG_ENTER("prepare_schema_table");
...
  case SCH_ENGINES:
/* BEGIN CAB MODIFICATION */
/* Reason for Modification: */
/* This section adds the code to call the new SHOW DISK_USAGE command. */
  case SCH_DISKUSAGE:
/* END CAB MODIFICATION */
  case SCH_COLLATIONS:
...
```

You may have noticed I refer to the disk usage schema table as DISKUSAGE. I do this because the DISK_USAGE token has already been defined in the parser and lexical hash. If I had used DISK_USAGE and issued the command SELECT * FROM DISK_USAGE, I'd have gotten an error. This is because the parser associates the DISK_USAGE token with the SHOW command and not with the SELECT command.

Now we're at the last set of code changes. You need to add a structure that the information schema functions can use to create the field list for the table. Open the `sql_show.cc` file and add a new array of type ST_FIELD_INFO as shown in Listing 8-30. Notice that the columns are named the same and have the same types as in the show_disk_usage_command().

Listing 8-30. *New Field Information Structure for the DISKUSAGE Schema Table*

```
/* BEGIN CAB MODIFICATION */
/* Reason for Modification: */
/* This section adds the code to call the new SHOW DISK_USAGE command. */
ST_FIELD_INFO disk_usage_fields_info[]=
{
  {"DATABASE", 40, MYSQL_TYPE_STRING, 0, 0, "Database"},
  {"SIZE (Kb)", 21 , MYSQL_TYPE_LONG, 0, 0, "Size (Kb)"},
  {0, 0, MYSQL_TYPE_STRING, 0, 0, 0}
};
/* END CAB MODIFICATION */
```

The next change you need to make is to add a row in the schema_tables array (also in sql_show.cc). Locate the array and add a statement like that shown in Listing 8-31. This statement tells the information schema functions to associate the table name DISKUSAGE with the field structure disk_usage_fields_info, to create the table by calling create_schema_table(), and to fill the rows of the table with the fill_disk_usage() function. The make_old_format tells the code to make sure the column names are shown. The last four parameters are a pointer to a function to do some additional processing on the table, two index fields, and a bool variable to indicate that it is a hidden table. In the example, I set the pointer to the function to NULL (0); –1 indicates the indexes aren't used, and 0 indicates the table is not hidden.

Listing 8-31. *Modifications to the schema_tables Array*

```
ST_SCHEMA_TABLE schema_tables[]=
{
...
  {"ENGINES", engines_fields_info, create_schema_table,
   fill_schema_engines, make_old_format, 0, -1, -1, 0},
/* BEGIN CAB MODIFICATION */
/* Reason for Modification: */
/* This section adds the code to call the new SHOW DISK_USAGE command. */
  {"DISKUSAGE", disk_usage_fields_info, create_schema_table,
   fill_disk_usage, make_old_format, 0, -1, -1, 0},
/* END CAB MODIFICATION */
  {"EVENTS", events_fields_info, create_schema_table,
   fill_schema_events, make_old_format, 0, -1, -1, 0},
...
```

OK, we're on the home stretch. All that is left is to implement the fill_disk_usage() function. Scroll up from the schema_tables array[5] and insert the implementation for the fill_disk_usage() function as shown in Listing 8-32.

Listing 8-32. *The fill_disk_usage Function Implementation*

```
/* BEGIN CAB MODIFICATION */
/* Reason for Modification: */
/* This section adds the code to call the new SHOW DISK_USAGE command. */
int fill_disk_usage(THD *thd, TABLE_LIST *tables, COND *cond)
{
  TABLE *table= tables->table;
  CHARSET_INFO *scs= system_charset_info;
  List<Item> field_list;
  List<char> dbs;
  char *db_name;
  char *path;
  MY_DIR *dirp;
```

---

5. Remember, if you do not use function declarations you must locate the code for functions in front of the code that references it.

```
FILEINFO *file;
longlong fsizes = 0;
longlong lsizes = 0;
Protocol *protocol= thd->protocol;
DBUG_ENTER("fill_disk_usage");

/* get database directories */
mysql_find_files(thd, &dbs, 0, mysql_data_home, 0, 1);
List_iterator_fast<char> it_dbs(dbs);
path = (char *)my_malloc(PATH_MAX, MYF(MY_ZEROFILL));
dirp = my_dir(mysql_data_home, MYF(MY_WANT_STAT));
fsizes = 0;
for (int i = 0; i < (int)dirp->number_off_files; i++)
{
  file = dirp->dir_entry + i;
  if (strncasecmp(file->name, "ibdata", 6) == 0)
    fsizes = fsizes + file->mystat->st_size;
  else if (strncasecmp(file->name, "ib", 2) == 0)
    lsizes = lsizes + file->mystat->st_size;
}

/* send InnoDB data to client */
table->field[0]->store("InnoDB TableSpace", strlen("InnoDB TableSpace"), scs);
table->field[1]->store((longlong)fsizes, TRUE);
if (schema_table_store_record(thd, table))
  DBUG_RETURN(1);
table->field[0]->store("InnoDB Logs", strlen("InnoDB Logs"), scs);
table->field[1]->store((longlong)lsizes, TRUE);
if (schema_table_store_record(thd, table))
  DBUG_RETURN(1);

/* now send database name and sizes of the databases */
while (db_name = it_dbs++)
{
  fsizes = 0;
  strcpy(path, mysql_data_home);
  strcat(path, "/");
  strcat(path, db_name);
  dirp = my_dir(path, MYF(MY_WANT_STAT));
  for (int i = 0; i < (int)dirp->number_off_files; i++)
  {
    file = dirp->dir_entry + i;
    fsizes = fsizes + file->mystat->st_size;
  }
  restore_record(table, s->default_values);
```

```
      table->field[0]->store(db_name, strlen(db_name), scs);
      table->field[1]->store((longlong)fsizes, TRUE);
      if (schema_table_store_record(thd, table))
        DBUG_RETURN(1);
  }

  /* free memory */
  my_free((gptr)path, MYF(0));
  DBUG_RETURN(0);
}
/* END CAB MODIFICATION */
```

Note On Windows, substitute `MAX_PATH` for `PATH_MAX` in the `my_malloc()` calls and use `strnicmp` in place of the `strncasecmp`.

I copied the code from the previous `DISK_USAGE` command, removing the calls for creating fields (that's handled via the `disk_usage_fields_info` array) and the code for sending rows to the client. Instead, I use an instance of the `TABLE` class/structure to store values in the `fields` array starting at zero for the first column. The call to the function `schema_table_store_record()` function dumps the values to the network protocols for me.

Everything is now set for you to compile the server. Since you have modified one of the key header files (`table.h`), you may encounter longer-than-normal compilation times as some of the dependencies for the `mysqld` project may have to be compiled. Should you encounter compilation errors, please correct them before you proceed.

Once the server is compiled and you have a new executable, stop your server and copy the new executable to the location of your MySQL installation and restart the server. You can now execute the new command in a MySQL client utility. Listing 8-33 shows an example of using the information schema, displaying all of the available schema tables, and dumping the contents of the new `DISKUSAGE` table.

Listing 8-33. *Example Information Schema Use with the new DISKUSAGE Schema Table*

```
mysql> USE INFORMATION_SCHEMA;
Database changed
mysql> SHOW TABLES;
```

```
+--------------------------------------+
| Tables_in_information_schema         |
+--------------------------------------+
| CHARACTER_SETS                       |
| COLLATIONS                           |
| COLLATION_CHARACTER_SET_APPLICABILITY |
| COLUMNS                              |
| COLUMN_PRIVILEGES                    |
```

```
| ENGINES                               |                              |
| DISKUSAGE                             |                              |
| EVENTS                                |                              |
| FILES                                 |                              |
| KEY_COLUMN_USAGE                      |                              |
| PARTITIONS                            |                              |
| PLUGINS                               |                              |
| PROCESSLIST                           |                              |
| ROUTINES                              |                              |
| SCHEMATA                              |                              |
| SCHEMA_PRIVILEGES                     |                              |
| STATISTICS                            |                              |
| TABLES                                |                              |
| TABLE_CONSTRAINTS                     |                              |
| TABLE_PRIVILEGES                      |                              |
| TRIGGERS                              |                              |
| USER_PRIVILEGES                       |                              |
| VIEWS                                 |                              |
+---------------------------------------+
23 rows in set (0.00 sec)
```

```
mysql> SELECT * FROM DISKUSAGE;
```

```
+--------------------+-----------+
| DATABASE           | SIZE (Kb) |
+--------------------+-----------+
| InnoDB TableSpace  | 10485760  |
| InnoDB Logs        | 20971520  |
| cluster            | 9867      |
| mysql              | 617310    |
| test               | 9720      |
+--------------------+-----------+
5 rows in set (0.31 sec)
```

Now that you know how to add to the information schema, the sky is the limit for what you can add to enable your database professionals to more closely monitor and tune your MySQL servers.

Summary

In this chapter, I've shown you how to extend the capabilities of the MySQL server by adding your own new functions and commands.

You learned how to build a UDF library that can be loaded and unloaded at runtime, how to add a native function to the server source code, and how to add a new SHOW command to the parser and query execution code. You also learned how to add schema tables to the information schema.

The ability to extend the server in this manner makes MySQL more flexible than any other database system. The UDF mechanism is one of the easiest to code and far surpasses the competition in sophistication and speed. The fact that the server is open source means you can also get right into the source code and add your own SQL commands for your specific environment. Regardless of whether you use these facilities, I'm sure you can appreciate knowing that you aren't limited by the "out of the box" functions and commands.

In the next chapter, I'll discuss some advanced topics in database server design and implementation. The next chapter will prepare you for using the MySQL server source code as an experimental platform for studying database system internals.

PART 3

■ ■ ■

Advanced Database Internals

Part 3 delves deeper into the MySQL system and gives you an insider's look at what makes the system work. Chapter 9 revisits the topic of query execution in the MySQL architecture and introduces how you can conduct experiments with the source code. Chapter 10 presents the MySQL internal query representation and provides an example alternative query representation. Chapter 11 introduces the MySQL internal query optimizer; it describes an example alternative query optimizer that uses the internal representation implementation from the previous chapter. The chapter also shows you how to alter the MySQL source code to implement the alternative query optimizer. Chapter 12 combines the techniques from the previous chapters to implement an alternative query processing engine.

■■■
Database System Internals

This chapter presents some database system internals concepts in preparation for studying database system internals at a deeper level. I'll present more in-depth coverage of how queries are represented internally within the server and how queries are executed. I'll explore these topics from a more general viewpoint and then close the chapter with a discussion of how you can use the MySQL system to conduct your own experiments with the MySQL system internals. Lastly, I'll introduce the database system's internals experiment project.

Query Execution

Most database systems use either an iterative or interpretative execution strategy. *Iterative* methods provide ways of producing a sequence of calls available for processing discrete operations (e.g., join, project, etc.), but are not designed to incorporate the features of the internal representation. Translation of queries into iterative methods uses techniques of functional programming and program transformation. There are several algorithms that generate iterative programs from relational algebra–based query specifications.

The implementation of the query execution mechanism creates a set of defined compiled functional primitives, formed using a high-level language, that are then linked together via a call stack or procedural call sequence. When a query execution plan is created and selected for execution, a compiler (usually the same one used to create the database system) is used to compile the procedural calls into a binary executable. Due to the high cost of the iterative method, compiled execution plans are typically stored for reuse for similar or identical queries.

Interpretative methods, on the other hand, perform query execution using existing compiled abstractions of basic operations. The query execution plan chosen is reconstructed as a queue of method calls that are each taken off the queue and processed; the results are then placed in memory for use with the next or subsequent calls. Implementation of this strategy is often called *lazy evaluation* because the available compiled methods are not optimized for best performance; rather, they are optimized for generality.

MySQL Query Execution Revisited

Query processing and execution in MySQL is interpretive. It is implemented using a threaded architecture whereby each query is given its own thread of execution. Figure 9-1 depicts a block diagram that describes the MySQL query processing methodology.

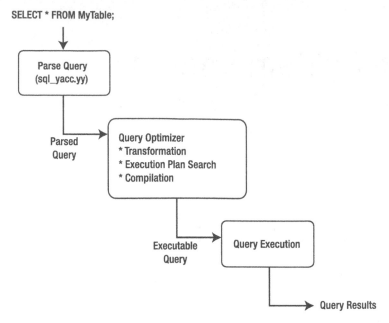

SELECT * FROM MyTable;

Figure 9-1. *MySQL query execution*

When a client issues a query, a new thread is created and the SQL statement is forwarded
to the parser for syntactic validation (or rejection due to errors). As you saw in the previous
chapter, the MySQL parser is implemented using a large Lex-YACC script that is compiled with
Bison. The parser constructs a data structure used to hold the query. This data structure, or
query structure, can be used to execute the query. Once the query structure is created, control
passes to the query processor, which performs checks such as verifying table integrity and
security access. Once the required access is granted and the tables are opened (and locked if
the query is an update), control is passed to individual methods that execute the basic query
operations such as select, restrict, and project. Optimization is applied to the data structure by
ordering the lists of tables and operations to form a more efficient query based on common
practices. This form of optimization is called a SELECT-PROJECT-JOIN query processor. The
results of the query operations are returned to the client using established communication
protocols and access methods.

What Is a Compiled Query?

One area that is often confusing is the concept of what "compiled" means. A compiled query is
an actual compilation of an iterative query execution plan, but some researchers (like C. J.
Date) consider a compiled query one that has been optimized and stored for future execution.
As a result, you must take care when considering using a compiled query. In this work, the use
of the word *compiled* is avoided because the query optimizer and execution engine do not
store the query execution plan for later reuse, nor does the query execution require any compilation or assembly to work.

■**Note** The concept of a stored procedure is a saved plan—it is compiled, or optimized, for execution at a later date and can be run many times on data that meets its input parameters.

Exploring MySQL Internals

How can you teach someone how an optimizer works without allowing them to get their hands dirty with a project? Furthermore, how can you be expected to know the internals of a database system without actually seeing them? I answer these questions in this section by discussing how MySQL can be used as an experimental test bed for professionals and academics alike.

Getting Started Using MySQL for Experiments

There are several ways to use MySQL to conduct experiments. For example, you could study the internal components using an interactive debugger or use the MySQL system as a host for your own implementation of internal database technologies.

If you are going to conduct experiments, consider using a dedicated server for the experiments. This is important if you plan to use MySQL to develop your own extensions. You don't want to risk contamination of your development server by the experiments.

Experimenting with the MySQL Source Code

The most invasive method of experimenting with MySQL is through modifications to the source code. This involves observing the system as it runs and then designing experiments to change portions by replacing an algorithm or section of code with another and observing the changes in behavior. Although this approach will enable you to investigate the internal workings of MySQL, making changes to the source code in this manner may result in the server becoming too unstable for use—especially if you push the envelope of the algorithms and data structures. However, there is no better way to learn the source code than to observe it in action. Tests conducted in this manner can then be used to gather data for other forms of experimentation.

Using MySQL As a Host for Experimental Technologies

A less invasive method of conducting experiments with MySQL is by using MySQL as a host for your own experimental code. This allows you to focus on the optimizer and execution engine without worrying about the other parts of the system. There are a great many parts to a database system. To name only a few, there are subcomponents in MySQL for network communication, data input, and access control, and even utilities for using and managing files and memory. Rather than create your own subcomponents, you can use MySQL's resources in your own code.

I've implemented the experiment project described in this book using this method. I'll show you how to connect to the MySQL parser and use the MySQL parser to read, test, and accept valid commands and redirect the code to the experimental project optimizer and execution routines.

The parser and lexical analyzer identify strings of alphanumeric characters (also known as tokens) that have been defined in the parser or lexical hash. The parser tags all of the tokens with location information (the order of appearance in the stream), and identifies literals and numbers using logic that recognizes specific patterns of the nontoken strings. Once the parser is done, control returns to the lexical analyzer. The lexical analyzer in MySQL is designed to recognize specific patterns of the tokens and nontokens. Once valid commands are identified, control is then passed to the execution code for each command. The MySQL parser and lexical analyzer can be modified to include the new tokens, or keywords, for the experiment. See Chapter 8 for more details on how to modify the parser and lexical analyzer. The commands can be designed to mimic those of SQL, representing the typical data manipulation commands such as select, update, insert, and delete as well as the typical data definition commands such as create and drop.

Once control is passed to the experimental optimization/execution engine, the experiments can be run using the MySQL internal query representation structures or converted to another structure. From there, experimental implementation for query optimization and execution can be run and the results returned to the client by using the MySQL system to send the result sets back to the client. This allows you to use the network communication and parsing subcomponents while implementing your own internal database components.

Running Multiple Instances of MySQL

One of the lesser-known facts about the MySQL server is that it is possible to run multiple instances of the server on a single machine. This allows you to run your modified MySQL system on the same machine as your development installation. You may want to do this if your resources are limited or you want to run your modified server on the same machine as another installation for comparison purposes. Running multiple instances of MySQL requires specifying certain parameters on the command line or in the configuration file.

At a minimum, you need to specify either a different TCP port or socket for the server to communicate on and specify different directories for the database files. An example of starting a second instance of MySQL on Windows is shown here:

```
mysqld-debug --port 3307 --datadir="c:/mysql/test_data" --console
```

In this example, I'm telling the server to use TCP port 3307 (the default is 3306) and to use a different data directory and run as a console application. To connect to the second instance of the server, I must tell the client to use the same port as the server. For example, to connect to my second instance I'd launch the MySQL client utility with

```
mysql -uroot --port 3307
```

The --port parameter can also be used with the mysqladmin utility. For example, to shut down the second instance running on port 3307, issue the following command:

```
mysqladmin -uroot --port 3307 shutdown
```

There is a potential for problems with this technique. It is easy to forget which server you're connected to. A safe way to prevent confusion or to avoid issuing a query (like a DELETE or DROP) to the wrong server is to change the prompt on your MySQL client utilities to indicate which server you are connected to. For example, issue the command prompt DBXP-> to set your prompt for the MySQL client connected to the experimental server and prompt Development-> for the MySQL client connected to the development server. This technique allows you to see at a glance which server you are about to issue a command. Examples of using the prompt command in the MySQL client are shown in Listing 9-1.

Listing 9-1. *Example of Changing the MySQL Client Prompt for the Experimental Server*

```
mysql> prompt DBXP->
PROMPT set to 'DBXP->'
DBXP->show databases;
```

```
+--------------------+
| Database           |
+--------------------+
| information_schema |
| mysql              |
| test               |
+--------------------+
3 rows in set (0.01 sec)

DBXP->
```

Tip You can also set the current database in the prompt by using the \d option. For example, to set the prompt in the client connected to the experimental server, issue the command prompt DBXP:\d->. This sets the prompt to indicate you are connected to the experimental server and the current database (specified by the last use command) separated by a colon (e.g., DBXP:Test->).

You can do the same on Linux or you can use a special script named mysqld_multi that allows you to use a single configuration script for multiple instances of the server (this script is not available on Windows). The script sets the correct parameters and then calls mysqld_safe or mysqld. To manage the multiple instances, you can use the MySQL Instance Manager tool (mysqlmanager, also available only on Linux) to monitor the servers and their status. You can use the tool to manage the servers either locally or remotely.

You can use this technique to restrict access to your modified server. If you change the port number or socket, then only those who know the correct parameters can connect to the server. This will enable you to minimize risk of exposure of the modifications to the user population. If your development environment is diverse with a lot of experimentation and research projects that share the same resources (which is often the case in academia), you may also want to take these steps to protect your own experiments from contamination of and by other projects. This isn't normally a problem but it helps to take the precaution.

■**Caution** If you use binary, query, or slow query logs, you must also specify an alternative location for the log files for each instance of the MySQL server. Failure to do so may result in corruption of your log files and/ or data.

Limitations and Concerns

Perhaps the most challenging aspect of using MySQL for experimentation is modifying the parser to recognize the new keyword for the SQL commands (see Chapter 8). Although not precisely a complex or new implementation language, modification of the YACC files requires careful attention to the original developers' intent. The solution involves placing copies of the SQL syntax definitions for the new commands at the top of each of the parser command definitions. This permits you to intercept the flow of the parser in order to redirect the query execution.

The most frequent and least trivial challenge of all is keeping up with the constant changes to the MySQL code base. Unfortunately, the frequency of upgrades is unpredictable. If you want to keep up to date with feature changes, the integration of the experimental technologies requires reinserting the modifications to the MySQL source files with each release of the source code. This is probably not a concern for anyone wanting to experiment with MySQL. If you find yourself wanting to keep up with the changes due to extensions you are writing, you should probably consider building a second server for experimentation and do your development on the original server.

■**Tip** The challenge that you are most likely to encounter is examining the MySQL code base and discovering the meaning, layout, and use of the various internal data representations. The only way to overcome this is through familiarity. I encourage you to visit and read the documentation (MySQL reference and system internals manuals) and articles on the MySQL web site, blogs, and message forums. They are a wealth of information. While some are difficult to absorb the concepts presented become clearer with each reading. Resist the temptation to become frustrated with the documentation. Give it a rest, then go back later and read it again. I find nuggets of useful information every time I (re)read the technical material.

The Database System Internals Experiment

I built the database experiment project (DBXP) to allow you to explore the MySQL internals and to let you explore some alternative database system internal implementations. You can use this experiment to learn more about how database systems are constructed and how they work under the hood.

Why an Experiment?

The DBXP is an experiment rather than a solution because it is incomplete. That is, the technologies are implemented with minimal error handling, a limited feature set, and low robustness.

This doesn't mean the DBXP technologies can't be modified for use as replacements for the MySQL system internals; rather, the DBXP is designed for exploration rather than production.

Overview of the Experiment Project

The DBXP project is a series of classes that implement alternative algorithms and mechanisms for internal query representation, query optimization, query execution, and file access. This not only gives you an opportunity to explore an advanced implementation of query optimization theory, but also enables the core of the DBXP technology to execute without modification of the MySQL internal operation. This provides the additional security that the native MySQL core executable code will not be affected by the addition of the DBXP technologies. This added benefit can help mitigate some of the risks of modifying an existing system.

The implementation of the MySQL parser (see sql_parse.cc) directs control to specific instances of the execution subprocesses by making calls to functions implemented for each SQL command. For example, the SHOW command is redirected to functions implemented in the sql_show.cc file. The MySQL parser code in sql_parse.cc needs to be modified to redirect processing to the DBXP query processor.

The first step in the DBXP query processor is to convert the MySQL internal query representation to the experimental internal representation. The internal representation chosen is called a *query tree*, where each node contains an atomic relational operation (select, project, join, etc.) and the links represent data flow. Figure 9-2 shows a conceptual example of a query tree. In the example, I use notation as follows; project/select (Π), restrict (Σ), and join (Φ). The arrows represent how data would flow from the tables up to the root. A join operation is represented as a node with two children. As data is presented from each child, the join operation is able to process that data and pass the results to the next node up in the tree (its parent). Each node can have zero, one, or two children and has exactly one parent.

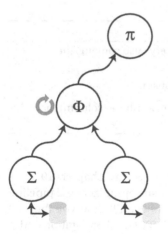

Figure 9-2. *Query tree concept*

The query tree was chosen because it permits the DBXP query optimizer to use tree manipulation algorithms. That is, optimization uses the tree structure and tree manipulation algorithms to arrange nodes in the tree in a more efficient execution order. Furthermore, execution of the optimized query is accomplished by traversing the tree to the leaf nodes, performing the operation as specified by the node, and passing information back up the links. This technique also made possible execution in a pipeline fashion where data is passed from the leaf nodes to the root node one data item at a time.

Traversing the tree down to a leaf for one data item and returning it back up the tree (a process known as *pulsing*) permits each node to process one data item, returning one row at a time in the result set. This pulsing, or polling, of the tree permits the execution of the pipeline. The result is a faster initial return of query results and a perceived faster transmission time of the query results to the client. Witnessing the query results returning more quickly—although not all at once—gives the user the perception of faster queries.

Using MySQL to host the DBXP implementation begins at the MySQL parser where the DBXP code takes over the optimization and execution of the query and then returns the results to the client one row at a time using the MySQL network communications utilities.

Components of the Experiment Project

The experiment project is designed to introduce you to alternatives to how database systems internals could be implemented and to allow you to explore the implementations by adding your own modifications to the project. DBXP is implemented using a set of simple C++ classes that represent objects in a database system.

There are classes for tuples, relations, indexes, and the query tree. Additional classes have been added to manage multiuser access to the tables. An example high-level architecture of the DBXP is shown in Figure 9-3.

A complete list of the classes in the project is shown in Table 9-1. The classes are stored in source files by the same name as the class (e.g., the Attribute class is defined and implemented in the files named attribute.h and attribute.cc, respectively).

Table 9-1. *Database Internals Experiment Project Classes*

Class	Description
Query_tree	Provides internal representation of the query. Also contains the query optimizer.
Expression	Provides an expression evaluation mechanism.
Attribute	Operations for storing and manipulating an attribute (column) for a tuple (row).

These classes represent the basic building blocks of a database system. Chapters 10 through 12 contain a complete explanation of the query tree, heuristic optimizer, and pipeline execution algorithms. The chapters also include overviews of the utility. I'll show you the implementation details of some parts (the most complex) of the DBXP implementation and leave the rest for you to implement as exercises.

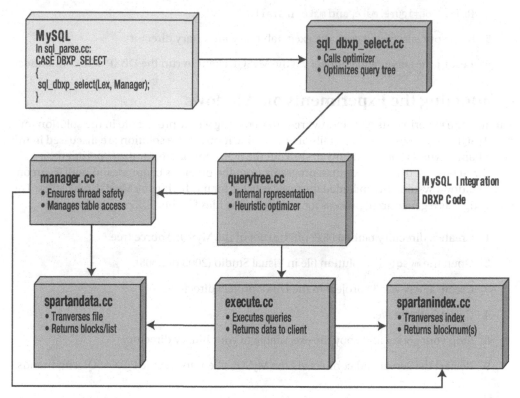

Figure 9-3. *High-level diagram of the experiment project*

■Note Suggestions on how to use the experiment project in a classroom setting are presented in the introduction section of this book.

Conducting the Experiments on Linux

Running the experiments on Linux requires creating make files for the new project and compiling them with the MySQL server. None of the project files requires any special compilation or libraries. Details of the modifications to the MySQL configuration and make files are discussed in the next chapter when I show you how to stub out the SQL commands for the experiment.

If you haven't tried the example programs from the previous chapters and built them on your Linux workstation, I've included the basic process for modifying the MySQL make files. The following lists a generalized process for modifying the files for the DBXP experiment:

1. Create a directory named DBXP off the root of the MySQL source tree.

2. Create a Makefile.am in the DBXP project directory.

3. Add the project to the configure and configure.in files.

4. Run ./configure, make, and make install.

5. Stop your server and copy the executable to your binary directory.

6. Restart the server and connect via the MySQL client to run the DBXP SQL commands.

Conducting the Experiments on Windows

Running the experiments on Windows requires creating a new project file in the solution for the MySQL server (mysql.sln). Details of the modifications to the solution are discussed in the next chapter when I show you how to stub out the SQL commands for the experiment.

If you haven't tried the example programs from the previous chapters and built them on your Windows system, I've included the basic process for modifying the MySQL make files. The following lists a generalized process for modifying the files for the DBXP experiment:

1. Create a directory named DBXP off the root of the MySQL source tree.

2. Open the mysql.sln solution file in Visual Studio (2003 or 2005).

3. Create a new Win32 project in the DBXP project directory.

4. Compile the server.

5. Stop your server and copy the executable to your binary directory.

6. Restart the server and connect via the MySQL client to run the DBXP SQL commands.

Summary

In this chapter, I have presented some of the more complex database internal technologies. You learned about how queries are represented internally within the server and how they are executed. More importantly, you discovered how MySQL can be used to conduct your own database internals experiments. The knowledge of these technologies should provide you with a greater understanding of why and how the MySQL system was built and how it executes.

In the next chapter, I'll show you more about internal query representation through an example implementation of a query tree structure. The next chapter begins a series of chapters designed as a baseline for you to implement your own query optimizer and execution engine. If you've ever wondered what it takes to build a database system, the next chapters will show you how to get started on your own query engine.

■ ■ ■

## CHAPTER 10

Internal Query Representation

This chapter presents the first part of the advanced database technologies for the database experiment project (DBXP). I begin by introducing the concept of the query tree structure used for storing a query in memory. Next I'll present the query tree structure used for the project and the first in a series of short projects for implementing the DBXP code. The chapter concludes with a set of exercises you can use to learn more about MySQL and query trees.

The Query Tree

A query tree is a tree structure that corresponds to a query, where leaf nodes of the tree contain nodes that access a relation and internal nodes with zero, one, or more children. The internal nodes contain the relational operators. These operators include project (depicted as π), restrict (depicted as σ), and join (depicted as either θ or $\bowtie$).[1] The edges of a tree represent data flow from bottom to top—that is, from the leaves, which correspond to data in the database, to the root, which is the final operator producing the query results. Figure 10-1 depicts an example of a query tree.

An evaluation of the query tree consists of evaluating an internal node operation whenever its operands are available and passing the results from evaluating the operation up the tree to the parent node. The evaluation terminates when the root node is evaluated and replaced by the tuples that form the result of the query. The following sections present a variant of the query tree structure for use in storing representations of queries in memory. The advantages of using this mechanism versus a relational calculus internal representation are shown in Table 10-1.

---

1. Strangely, few texts give explanations for the choice of symbol. Traditionally, θ represents a theta-join and $\bowtie$ represents a natural join, but most texts interchange these concepts, resulting in all joins represented using one or the other symbol (and sometimes both).

```
SELECT name
FROM faculty f, classes c
WHERE f.id = c.fac_id AND
f.department_id = 'CS' AND c.semester = 'F2001'
```

πname(σdepartment_id='CS'^semester='F2001'(f ⋈ id=fac_id c)

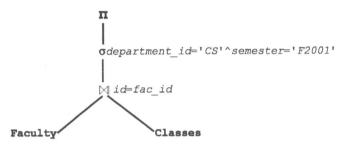

Figure 10-1. *An example query tree[2]*

Table 10-1. *Advantages of Using a Query Tree vs. Relational Calculus*

Operational Requirement	Query Tree	Relational Calculus
Can it be reduced?	Yes. It is possible to prune the query tree prior to evaluating query plans.	Only through application of algebraic operations.
Can it support execution?	Yes. The tree can be used to execute queries by passing data up the tree.	No. Requires translation to another form.
Can it support relational algebra expressions?	Yes. The tree lends itself well to relational algebra.	No. Requires conversion.
Can it be implemented in database systems?	Yes. Tree structures are a common data structure.	Only through designs that model the calculus.
Can it contain data?	Yes. The tree nodes can contain data, operations, and expressions.	No. Only the literals and variables that form the expression.

Clearly, the query tree internal representation is superior to the more traditional mechanism employed in modern database systems. For example, the internal representation in MySQL is that of a set of classes and structures designed to contain the query and its elements for easy (fast) traversal. It organizes data for the optimization and execution.[3]

---

2. Although similar drawings has appeared in several places in the literature, it contains a subtle nuance of database theory that is often overlooked. Can you spot the often misused trait? Hint: What is the domain of the semester attribute? Which rule has been violated by encoding data in a column?

3. Some would say it shouldn't have to as the MySQL internal structure is used to organize the data for the optimizer. Query trees, on the other hand, are designed to be optimized and executed in place.

There are some disadvantages to the query tree internal representation. Most optimizers are not designed to work within a tree structure. If you wanted to use the query tree with an optimizer, the optimizer would have to be altered. Similarly, query execution will be very different from most query processing implementations. In this case, the query execution engine will be running from the tree rather than as a separate step. These disadvantages are addressed in later chapters as I explore an alternative optimizer and execution engine.

The DBXP query tree is a tree data structure that uses a node structure that contains all of the parameters necessary to represent the following operations:

- *Restriction*: Allows you to include results that match an expression of the attributes

- *Projection*: Provides the ability to select attributes to include in the result set

- *Join*: Lets you combine two or more relations to form a composite set of attributes in the result set

- *Sort (order by)*: Allows you to order the result set

- *Distinct*: Provides the ability to reduce the result set to unique tuples

---

■Note Distinct is an operation that is added to accomplish a relational operation that isn't supported by most SQL implementations and is not an inherent property of relational algebra.

Projection, restriction, and join are the basic operations. Sort and distinct are provided as additional utility operations that assist in the formulation of a complete query tree (all possible operations are represented as nodes). Join operations can have join conditions (theta-joins) or no conditions (equi-joins). The join operation is subdivided into the following operations:

- *Inner*: The join of two relations returning tuples where there is a match.

- *Outer (left, right, full)*: Return all rows from at least one of the tables or views mentioned in the FROM clause, as long as those rows meet any WHERE search conditions. All rows are retrieved from the left table referenced with a left outer join, and all rows from the right table referenced in a right outer join. All rows from both tables are returned in a full outer join. Values for attributes of nonmatching rows are returned as null values.

  - *Leftouter*: The join of two relations returning tuples where there is a match plus all tuples from the relation specified to the left, leaving nonmatching attributes specified from the other relation empty (null)

  - *Rightouter*: The join of two relations returning tuples where there is a match plus all tuples from the relation specified to the right, leaving nonmatching attributes specified from the other relation empty (null)

  - *Fullouter*: The join of two relations returning all tuples from both relations, leaving nonmatching attributes specified from the other relation empty (null)

- *Crossproduct*: The join of two relations mapping each tuple from the first relation to all tuples from the other relation

The query tree also supports some set operations. The set operations supported include the following:

- *Union*: The set operation where only matches from two relations with the same schema are returned

- *Intersect*: The set operation where only the nonmatches from two relations with the same schema are returned

WHAT IS A THETA-JOIN?

You may be wondering why some joins are called equi-joins while others are called theta-joins. Equi-joins are joins where the join condition is an equality (=). A theta-join is a join where the join condition is an inequality (>, <, >=, <=, <>). Technically, all joins are theta-joins. Theta-joins are rare whereas equi-joins are common.

While the DBXP query trees provides the union and intersect operations, most database systems support unions in the form of a concatenation of result sets. However, although the MySQL parser does not currently support intersect operations, it does support unions. Further modification of the MySQL parser is necessary to implement the intersect operation. The following sections describe the major code implementations and classes created to transform MySQL query representation to a DBXP query tree.

Query Transformation

The MySQL parser must be modified to identify and parse the SQL commands. However, we need a way to tell the parser that we want to use the DBXP implementation and not the existing query engine. To make the changes easy, I simply added a keyword (e.g., DBXP) to the SQL commands that redirects the parsing to code that converts the MySQL internal representation into the DBXP internal representation. Although this process adds some execution time and requires a small amount of extra computational work, the implementation simplifies the modifications to the parser and provides a common mechanism to compare the DBXP data structure to that of the MySQL data structure. I refer to SQL commands with the DBXP keyword as simply DBXP SQL commands.

The process of transformation[4] begins in the MySQL parser, which identifies commands as being DBXP commands. The system then directs control to a class named `sql_dbxp_parse.cc` that manages the transformation of the parsed query from the MySQL form to the DBXP internal representation (query tree). This is accomplished by a method named `build_query_tree`. This method is called only for `SELECT` and `EXPLAIN SELECT` statements.

DBXP Query Tree

The heart of the DBXP query optimizer is the DBXP internal representation data structure. It is used to represent the query once the SQL command has been parsed and transformed.

---

4. Although many texts on the subject of query processing disagree about how each process is differentiated, they do agree that certain distinct process steps must occur.

This structure is implemented as a tree structure (hence the name *query tree*), where each node has zero, one, or two children. Nodes with zero children are the leaves of the tree, those with one child represent internal nodes that perform unary operations on data, and those with two children are either join or set operations. The actual node structure from the source code is shown in Listing 10-1.

Listing 10-1. *DBXP Query Tree Node*

```
struct query_node
{
  query_node();
  ~query_node();
  int               nodeid;
  int               parent_nodeid;
  bool              sub_query;
  bool              child;
  query_node_type   node_type;
  type_join         join_type;
  join_con_type     join_cond;
  COND              *where_expr;
  COND              *join_expr;
  TABLE_LIST        *relations[4];
  bool              preempt_pipeline;
  List<Item>        *fields;
  query_node        *left;
  query_node        *right;
};
```

Some of these variables are used to manage node organization and form the tree itself. Two of the most interesting are nodeid and parent_nodeid. These are used to establish parentage of the nodes in the tree. This is necessary as nodes can be moved up and down the tree as part of the optimization process. The use of a parent_nodeid variable avoids the need to maintain reverse pointers in the tree.[5]

The sub_query variable is used to indicate the starting node for a subquery. Thus, the data structure can support nested queries (subqueries) without additional modification of the structure. The only caveat is that the algorithms for optimization are designed to use the subquery indicator as a stop condition for tree traversal. That is, when a subquery node is detected, optimization considers the subquery a separate entity. Once detected, the query optimization routines are rerun using the subquery node as the start of the next optimization. Thus, any number of subqueries can be supported and represented as subtrees in the tree structure. This is an important feature of the query tree that overcomes the limitation found in many internal representations.

The where_expr variable is a pointer to the MySQL COND item tree that manages a typical general expression tree.

---

5. A practice strongly discouraged by Knuth and other algorithm gurus.

The relations array is used to contain pointers to relation classes that represent the abstraction of the internal record structures found in the MySQL storage engines. The relation class provides an access layer to the data stored on disk via the storage engine handler class. The array size is currently set at 4. The first two positions (0 and 1) correspond to the left and right child, respectively. The next two positions (2 and 3) represent temporary relations such as reordering (sorting) and the application of indexes.

Note The relations array size is set at 4, which means you can process queries with up to four tables. If you need to process queries with more than four tables, you will need to change the transformation code shown later in this chapter to accept more than four tables.

The fields attribute is afields is a pointer to the MySQL Item class that contains the fields for a table. It is useful in projection operations and maintaining attributes necessary for operations on relations (e.g., the propagation of attributes that satisfy expressions but are not part of the result set).

The last variable of interest is the preempt_pipeline variable, which is used by the DBXP Execute class to implement a loop in the processing of the data from child nodes. Loops are necessary anytime an operation requires iteration through the entire set of data (rows). For example, a join that joins two relations on a common attribute in the absence of indexes that permit ordering may require iteration through one or both child nodes in order to achieve the correct mapping (join) operation.

This class is also responsible for query optimization (described in Chapter 11). Since the query tree provides all of the operations for manipulating the tree and since query optimization is also a set of tree operations, optimization was accomplished using methods placed in a class that wraps the query tree structure (called the query tree class).

The optimizer methods implement a heuristic algorithm (described in Chapter 11). Execution of these methods results in the reorganization of the tree into a more optimal tree and the separation of some nodes into two or more others that can also be relocated to form a more optimal tree. An optimal tree permits a more efficient execution of the query.

Cost optimization is also supported in this class using an algorithm that walks the tree, applying available indexes to the access methods for each leaf node (nodes that access the relation stores directly).

This structure can support a wide variety of operations, including restrict, project, join, set, and ordering (sorting). The query node structure is designed to represent each of these operations as a single node and can store all pertinent and required information to execute the operation in place. Furthermore, the EXPLAIN command was implemented as a postorder traversal of the tree, printing out the contents of each node starting at the leaves (see the show_plan method later in this chapter). The MySQL equivalent of this operation requires much more computational time and is implemented with a complex set of methods.

Thus, the query tree is an internal representation that can represent any query and provide a mechanism to optimize the query by manipulating the tree. Indeed, the tree structure itself simplifies optimization and enables the implementation of a heuristic optimizer by providing a means to associate query operations as nodes in a tree. This query tree therefore is a viable mechanism for use in any relational database system and can be generalized for use in a production system.

Implementing DBXP Query Trees in MySQL

This section presents the addition of the DBXP query tree structure to the MySQL source code. This first step in creating a relational database research tool is designed to show you how the query tree works and how to transform the MySQL query structure into a base query tree (not optimized). Later chapters will describe the optimizer and execution engine. The following sections show you how to add the query tree and add stubs for executing SELECT and EXPLAIN SELECT commands.

Files Added and Changed

While following through the examples in this chapter, you will create several files and modify some of the MySQL source code files. Table 10-2 lists the files that will be added and changed.

Table 10-2. *Summary of Files Added and Changed*

File	Description
mysqld.cc	Added the DBXP version number label to the MySQL version number
lex.h	Added DBXP tokens to the lexical hash
query_tree.h	DBXP query tree header file (new file)
query_tree.cc	DBXP query tree class file (new file)
sql_dbxp_parse.cc	DBXP parser helper code file (new file)
sql_lex.h	Added SQL command to hash symbols
sql_yacc.yy	Added SQL command parsing to the parser
sql_parse.cc	Added the code to handle the new commands to the "big switch"

Creating the Tests

The following section explains the process of stubbing the SELECT DBXP command, the query tree class, and the EXPLAIN SELECT DBXP and SELECT DBXP commands. The goal is to permit the user to enter any valid SELECT command, process the query, and return the results.

■**Note** Since the DBXP engine is an experimental engine, it is limited to queries that represent the basic operations for retrieving data. Keeping the length of these chapters to a manageable size and complexity requires that the DBXP engine not process queries with aggregates, those containing a HAVING, GROUP BY, or ORDER BY clause. (There is nothing prohibiting this so you are free to implement these operations yourself.)

The following sections detail the steps necessary to create these three aspects of the DBXP code. Rather than create three small tests, I'll create a single test file and use that to test the functions. For those operations that are not implemented, you can either comment out the query statements by adding a pound sign (#) at the beginning of the command or run the test as shown and ignore the inevitable errors for commands not yet implemented (thereby keeping true to the test first development mantra). Listing 10-2 shows the ExpertMySQLCh10.test file.

Listing 10-2. *Chapter Tests (ExpertMySQLCh10.test)*

```
#
# Sample test to test the SELECT DBXP and EXPLAIN SELECT DBXP commands
#

# Test 1: Test stubbed SELECT DBXP command.
SELECT DBXP * FROM no_such_table;

# Test 2: Test stubbed Query Tree implementation.
SELECT DBXP * FROM customer;

# Test 3: Test stubbed EXPLAIN SELECT DBXP command.
EXPLAIN SELECT DBXP * FROM customer;
```

Of course, you can use this test as a guide and add your own commands to explore the new code. Please refer to Chapter 4 for more details on how to create and run this test using the MySQL Test Suite.

Stubbing the SELECT DBXP Command

In this section, you'll learn how to add a custom SELECT command to the MySQL parser. You'll see how the parser can be modified to accommodate a new command that mimics the traditional SELECT command in MySQL.

Identifying the Modifications

The first thing you should do is to identify a MySQL server that has the DBXP technologies. We can do this by adding a label to the MySQL version number to ensure we can always tell that we're connected to the modified server.

■**Tip** You can use the command SELECT VERSION() at any time to retrieve the version of the server. If you are using the MySQL command-line client, you can change the command prompt to indicate that the server you are connected to is the server with the DBXP code.

To append the version label, open the mysqld.cc file and locate the set_server_version method. Add a statement to append a label onto the MySQL version number string. Listing 10-3 shows the modified set_server_version method.

Listing 10-3. *Changes to the mysqld.cc File*

```
static void set_server_version(void)
{
  char *end= strxmov(server_version, MYSQL_SERVER_VERSION,
                     MYSQL_SERVER_SUFFIX_STR, NullS);
#ifdef EMBEDDED_LIBRARY
  end= strmov(end, "-embedded");
#endif
#ifndef DBUG_OFF
  if (!strstr(MYSQL_SERVER_SUFFIX_STR, "-debug"))
    end= strmov(end, "-debug");
#endif
  if (opt_log || opt_update_log || opt_slow_log || opt_bin_log)
    strmov(end, "-log");                       // This may slow down system
/* BEGIN DBXP MODIFICATION */
/* Reason for Modification: */
/* This section adds the DBXP version number to the MySQL version number. */
  strmov(end, "-DBXP-1.0");
/* END DBXP MODIFICATION */
}
```

Modifying the Lexical Structures

Now, let's add the tokens you'll need to identify the SELECT DBXP command. Open the lex.h file and add the code shown in bold in Listing 10-4 to the symbols array.

Listing 10-4. *Changes to the lex.h File*

```
static SYMBOL symbols[] = {
/* BEGIN DBXP MODIFICATION */
/* Reason for Modification: */
/* This section identifies the symbols and values for the DBXP tokens */
  { "WITH_DBXP_QUERYTREE", SYM(DBXP_SYM)},
  { "DBXP",                SYM(DBXP_SYM)},
/* END DBXP MODIFICATION */
```

Now it's time to generate the lexical hash. Read the section that follows for your operating system. Run through the process until you have a working gen_lex_hash command-line utility.

Generating the Lexical Hash on Windows

Open the main solution and add the gen_lex_hash project in the /sql directory. Add to the project dependencies the projects dbug, libmysql, mysys, strings, taocrypt, yassl, and zlib and then compile the project. The compiler will process the files that haven't been compiled. When the compilation is complete, open a command prompt and navigate to the /sql directory in the root of the source code tree. Generate the lexical hash by running the gen_lex_hash.exe utility as shown here:

```
gen_lex_hash > lex_hash.h
```

This will generate a new lex_hash.h file for use in compiling the server to recognize the new symbols added to the lex.h file.

Generating the Lexical Hash on Linux

Linux users, this is your opportunity to smile. The build scripts for the MySQL server include the compilation of the gen_lex_hash utility. The utility is located in a directory named gen_lex_hash and has its own makefile. Generate the lexical hash by running the gen_lex_hash utility as shown here:

```
gen_lex_hash > lex_hash.h
```

This will generate a new lex_hash.h file for use in compiling the server to recognize the new symbols added to the lex.h file. However, you don't need to do this step because the makefile included with the Linux source code distribution performs this step for you. The only reason you might want to run the command is to ensure there are no errors.

Adding the SQL Commands

This section explains how to add the new SELECT DBXP command to the parser. The modifications begin with adding a new case statement to the parser command switch in the sql_parse.cc file. The switch uses enumerated values for the cases. To add a new case, you must add a new enumerated value. These values are identified in the parser code and stored in the lex->sql_command member variable. To add a new enumerated value to the lexical parser, open the sql_lex.h file and add the code shown in bold in Listing 10-5 to the enum_sql_command enumeration.

Listing 10-5. *Adding the SELECT DBXP Command Enumeration*

```
enum enum_sql_command {
...
/* BEGIN DBXP MODIFICATION */
/* Reason for Modification: */
/* This section captures the enumerations for the DBXP command tokens */
  SQLCOM_DBXP_SELECT,
/* END DBXP MODIFICATION */
```

Adding the SELECT DBXP Command to the MySQL Parser

Once the new enumerated value for the case statement is added, you must also add code to the parser code (sql_yacc.yy) to identify the new SELECT DBXP statement. You'll add a new token to the parser so that the parser can distinguish a normal MySQL SELECT statement from one that you want to process with the DBXP code. One way to do this is to program the parser so that, when the token is present, it indicates the parser should set the sql_command variable to the SQLCOM_DBXP_SELECT value instead of the normal MySQL select enumerated value (SQLCOM_SELECT). This technique allows you to issue the same basic SELECT statement to both the normal MySQL code and the DBXP code. For example, the following SELECT statements both accomplish the same task; they just will be optimized differently. The first one will be directed to the SQLCOM_SELECT case statement whereas the second will be directed to the SQLCOM_DBXP_SELECT case statement.

```
SELECT * FROM customer;
SELECT DBXP * FROM customer;
```

The code to add the new token is shown in Listing 10-6. Locate the list of tokens in the sql_yacc.yy file and add the code (the list is in roughly alphabetical order).

Listing 10-6. *Adding the Command Symbol to the Parser*

```
%token  DAY_SYM
/* BEGIN DBXP MODIFICATION */
/* Reason for Modification: */
/* This section defines the tokens for the DBXP commands */
%token  DBXP_SYM
/* END DBXP MODIFICATION */
%token  DEALLOCATE_SYM
```

Listing 10-7 shows the parser code needed to identify the SELECT DBXP command and to process the normal parts of the select command. Notice the parser identifies the select and DBXP symbols then provides for other parsing of the select options, fields list, and FROM clause. Immediately after that line is the code that sets the sql_command. Notice the code also places a vertical bar (|) before the original select command parser code. This is the "or" operator that the parser syntax uses to process variations of a command. To add this change to the parser, open the sql_yacc.yy file and locate the select: label, then add the code as shown in Listing 10-7.

Listing 10-7. *Adding the Command Syntax Operations to the Parser*

```
select:
/* BEGIN DBXP MODIFICATION */
/* Reason for Modification: */
/* This section captures (parses) the SELECT DBXP statement */
  SELECT_SYM DBXP_SYM DBXP_select_options DBXP_select_item_list
                          DBXP_select_from
  {
    LEX *lex= Lex;
    lex->sql_command = SQLCOM_DBXP_SELECT;
  }

/* END DBXP MODIFICATION */
  | select_init
  {
    LEX *lex= Lex;
    lex->sql_command= SQLCOM_SELECT;
  }
  ;
```

Notice also that the code references several other labels. Listing 10-8 contains the code for these operations. The first is the DBXP_select_options, which identifies the valid options for the SELECT command. While this is very similar to the MySQL select options, it provides for only two options: DISTINCT and COUNT(*). The next operation is the DBXP_select_from code that identifies the tables in the FROM clause. It also calls the DBXP_where_clause operation to identify the WHERE clause. The next operation is the DBXP_select_item_list, which resembles the MySQL code. Lastly, the DBXP_where_clause operation identifies the parameters in the WHERE clause. Take some time to go through this code and follow the operations to their associated labels to see what each does. To add this code to the parser, locate the select_from: label and add the code above it. Although it doesn't matter where you place the code, this location seems more logical as it is in the same area with the MySQL select operations. Listing 10-8 shows the complete source code for the SELECT DBXP parser code.

Listing 10-8. *Additional Operations for the SELECT DBXP Command*

```
/* BEGIN DBXP MODIFICATION */
/* Reason for Modification: */
/* This section captures (parses) the sub parts of the SELECT DBXP statement */

DBXP_select_options:
  /* empty */
  |
    /* Allow the distinct command switch */
    DISTINCT { Select->options|= SELECT_DISTINCT; }
  |
    /* Enable the count(*) operation */
    COUNT_SYM '(' '*' ')'
    {
      /* Here we want to add the "count(*)" as an item field */
      THD *thd= YYTHD;
      if (add_item_to_list(thd,
        new Item_field(&thd->lex->current_select->context,
        NULL,NULL,"COUNT(*)")))
          YYABORT;
    }
  ;
/* The following sections define the rest of the SELECT command tokens */
DBXP_select_from:
  FROM join_table_list DBXP_where_clause;
/* parse the items in the select list (fields) */
DBXP_select_item_list:
  /* empty */
```

```
    | DBXP_select_item_list ',' select_item
    | select_item
    | '*'
      {
        THD *thd= YYTHD;
        if (add_item_to_list(thd,
            new Item_field(&thd->lex->current_select->context,NULL,NULL,"*")))

          YYABORT;
      };
/* process the where clause capturing the expressions */
DBXP_where_clause:
  /* empty */  { Select->where= 0; }
  | WHERE expr
    {
      Select->where= $2;
      if ($2)
        $2->top_level_item();
    }
    ;


/* END DBXP MODIFICATION */

select_from:
...
```

Now that you've made the changes to the lexical parser, you have to generate the equivalent C source code. You can use Bison to generate these files. Open a command window and navigate to the /sql directory off the root of your source code tree. Run the following command:

```
bison -y -d sql_yacc.yy
```

This generates two new files: y.tab.c and y.tab.h. These files replace the sql_yacc.cc and sql_yacc.h files, respectively. Before you copy them, make a backup of the original files. After you've done so, copy y.tab.c to sql_yacc.cc (.cpp on Windows) and y.taqb.h to sql_yacc.h.

Note If you are using Linux, you don't need to do this step because the makefile included with the Linux source code distribution performs this step for you. The only reason you might want to run the command is if you want to ensure there are no errors. Newer distributions of MySQL source code (e.g., 5.1) include this step as well.

WHAT IS LEX AND YACC AND WHO'S BISON?

Lex stands for "lexical analyzer generator" and is used as a parser to identify tokens and literals as well as syntax of a language. YACC stands for "yet another compiler compiler" and is used to identify and act on the semantic definitions of the language. The use of these tools together with Bison (a YACC-compatible parser generator that generates C source code from the Lex/YACC code) provides a rich mechanism of creating subsystems that can parse and process language commands. Indeed, that is exactly how MySQL uses these technologies.

Windows users may encounter problems if some definitions are missing from the compiled sql_yacc.cpp (.cc) file. If you get errors about the yyerror missing or MYSQLparse missing, open the sql_yacc.cpp (.cc) file and add the statements shown in Listing 10-9.

Listing 10-9. *Missing #define Statements*

```
/* If NAME_PREFIX is specified substitute the variables and function
   names.  */
#define yyparse MYSQLparse
#define yylex   MYSQLlex
#define yyerror MYSQLerror
#define yylval  MYSQLlval
#define yychar  MYSQLchar
#define yydebug MYSQLdebug
#define yynerrs MYSQLnerrs
```

Stubbing the SELECT DBXP Command

If you compile the server now, you can issue SELECT DBXP commands, but nothing will happen. That's because you need to add the case statement to the parser switch in sql_parse.cc. Since we do not yet have a complete DBXP engine, let's make the exercise a bit more interesting by stubbing out the case statement. Listing 10-10 shows a complete set of scaffold code you can use to implement the SELECT DBXP command. In this code, I use the MySQL utility classes to establish a record set. The first portion of the code sets up the field list for the fictional table. Following that are lines of code to write data values to the network stream and finally send an end-of-file marker to the client. Writing data to the output stream requires calls to protocol->prepare_for_resend(), storing the data to be sent using protocol->store(), and then writing the buffer to the stream with protocol->write().

Listing 10-10. *Modifications to the Parser Command Switch*

```
/* BEGIN DBXP MODIFICATION */
/* Reason for Modification: */
/* This section adds the code to call the new SELECT DBXP command. */
  case SQLCOM_DBXP_SELECT:
  {
    List<Item> field_list;
```

```
    /* The protocol class is used to write data to the client. */
    Protocol *protocol= thd->protocol;

    /* Build the field list and send the fields to the client */
    field_list.push_back(new Item_int("Id",(longlong) 1,21));
    field_list.push_back(new Item_empty_string("LastName",40));
    field_list.push_back(new Item_empty_string("FirstName",20));
    field_list.push_back(new Item_empty_string("Gender",2));
    if (protocol->send_fields(&field_list,
                              Protocol::SEND_NUM_ROWS | Protocol::SEND_EOF))
      DBUG_RETURN(TRUE);
    protocol->prepare_for_resend();

    /* Write some sample data to the buffer and send it with write() */
    protocol->store((longlong)3);
    protocol->store("Flintstone", system_charset_info);
    protocol->store("Fred", system_charset_info);
    protocol->store("M", system_charset_info);
    if (protocol->write())
      DBUG_RETURN(TRUE);

    protocol->prepare_for_resend();
    protocol->store((longlong)5);
    protocol->store("Rubble", system_charset_info);
    protocol->store("Barnie", system_charset_info);
    protocol->store("M", system_charset_info);
    if (protocol->write())
      DBUG_RETURN(TRUE);

    protocol->prepare_for_resend();
    protocol->store((longlong)7);
    protocol->store("Flintstone", system_charset_info);
    protocol->store("Wilma", system_charset_info);
    protocol->store("F", system_charset_info);
    if (protocol->write())
      DBUG_RETURN(TRUE);

    /*
      send_eof() tells the communication mechanism that we're finished
      sending data (end of file).
    */
    send_eof(thd);
    break;
  }
/* END DBXP MODIFICATION */
  case SQLCOM_PREPARE:
...
```

This stub code returns a simulated record set to the client whenever a SELECT DBXP command is detected. Go ahead and enter this code, then compile and run the test.

Testing the SELECT DBXP Command

The test we want to run is to issue a SELECT DBXP command and verify that the statement is parsed and processed by the new stubbed case statement. You can run the test you created earlier or simply enter a SQL statement like the following (make sure you type the DBXP part) in a MySQL command-line client:

```
SELECT DBXP * from no_such_table;
```

It doesn't matter what you type after the DBXP as long as it is a valid SQL SELECT statement. Listing 10-11 shows an example of the output you should expect.

Listing 10-11. *Results of Stub Test*

```
mysql> select DBXP * from no_such_table;
```

```
+----+------------+-----------+--------+
| Id | LastName   | FirstName | Gender |
+----+------------+-----------+--------+
| 3  | Flintstone | Fred      | M      |
| 5  | Rubble     | Barnie    | M      |
| 7  | Flintstone | Wilma     | F      |
+----+------------+-----------+--------+
3 rows in set (0.23 sec)

mysql>
```

Adding the Query Tree Class

Now that you have a stubbed SELECT DBXP command, you can begin to implement the DBXP-specific code to execute a SELECT command. In this section I'll show you how to add the basic query tree class and transform the MySQL internal structure to the query tree. I won't go all the way into the bowels of the query tree code until the next chapter.

Adding the Query Tree Header File

Adding the query tree class requires creating the query tree header file and referencing it in the MySQL code. The query tree header file is shown in Listing 10-12. Notice that I named the class Query_tree. This follows the MySQL coding guidelines by naming classes with an initial capital. Take a moment to scan through the header code. You will see there isn't a lot of code there—just the basics of the query tree node structure and the enumerations. Notice there are enumerations for node type, join condition type, join, and aggregate types. These enumerations are what permit the query tree nodes to take on unique roles in the execution of the query. I'll explain more about how these are used in the next chapter.

You can create the file any way you choose (or download it). Name it query_tree.h and place it in the /sql directory of your MySQL source tree. Don't worry about how to add it to the project; I'll show you how to do that in a later section.

Listing 10-12. *The Query Tree Header File*

```
/*
  Query_tree.h

  DESCRIPTION
    This file contains the Query_tree class. It is responsible for containing the
    internal representation of the query to be executed. It provides methods for
    optimizing and forming and inspecting the query tree. This class is the very
    heart of the DBXP query capability! It also provides the ability to store
    a binary "compiled" form of the query.

  NOTES
    The data structure is a binary tree that can have 0, 1, or 2 children. Only
    Join operations can have 2 children. All other operations have 0 or 1
    children. Each node in the tree is an operation and the links to children
    are the pipeline.

  SEE ALSO
    query_tree.cc
*/
#include "mysql_priv.h"

class Query_tree
{
public:
  /*
    This enumeration lists the available query node (operations)
  */
  enum query_node_type
  {
    qntUndefined = 0,
    qntRestrict = 1,
    qntProject = 2,
    qntJoin = 3,
    qntSort = 4,
    qntDistinct = 5
  };
```

```
/*
  This enumeration lists the available join operations
*/
enum join_con_type
{
  jcUN = 0,
  jcNA = 1,
  jcON = 2,
  jcUS = 3
};

/*
  This enumeration lists the available join types
*/
enum type_join
{
  jnUNKNOWN      = 0,          /* undefined */
  jnINNER        = 1,
  jnLEFTOUTER    = 2,
  jnRIGHTOUTER   = 3,
  jnFULLOUTER    = 4,
  jnCROSSPRODUCT = 5,
  jnUNION        = 6,
  jnINTERSECT    = 7
};

  enum AggregateType          /* used to add aggregate functions */
  {
      atNONE     = 0,
      atCOUNT    = 1
  };

/*
  STRUCTURE query_node

  DESCRIPTION
    This structure contains all of the data for a query node:

    NodeId -- the internal id number for a node
    ParentNodeId -- the internal id for the parent node (used for insert)
    SubQuery -- is this the start of a subquery?
    Child -- is this a Left or Right child of the parent?
    NodeType -- synonymous with operation type
    JoinType -- if a join, this is the join operation
    join_con_type -- if this is a join, this is the "on" condition
```

```
         Expressions -- the expressions from the "where" clause for this node
         Join Expressions -- the join expressions from the "join" clause(s)
         Relations[] -- the relations for this operation (at most 2)
         PreemptPipeline -- does the pipeline need to be halted for a sort?
         Fields -- the attributes for the result set of this operation
         Left -- a pointer to the left child node
         Right -- a pointer to the right child node
*/
  struct query_node
  {
    query_node();
    //query_node(const query_node &o);
    ~query_node();
    int               nodeid;
    int               parent_nodeid;
    bool              sub_query;
    bool              child;
    query_node_type   node_type;
    type_join         join_type;
    join_con_type     join_cond;
    COND              *where_expr;
    COND              *join_expr;
    TABLE_LIST        *relations[4];
    bool              preempt_pipeline;
    List<Item>        *fields;
    query_node        *left;
    query_node        *right;
  };

  query_node *root;              //The ROOT node of the tree

  ~Query_tree(void);
  void ShowPlan(query_node *QN, bool PrintOnRight);
};
```

With the query tree header file you also need the query tree source file. The source file must provide the code for the constructor and destructor methods of the query tree class. Listing 10-13 shows the completed constructor and destructor methods. Create the query_tree.cc file and enter this code (or download it). Place this file in the /sql directory of your MySQL source tree. I'll show you how to add it to the project in a later section.

Note If you use Windows, you should name the *.cc files *.cpp.

Listing 10-13. *The Query Tree Class*

```
/*
  Query_tree.cc

  DESCRIPTION
    This file contains the Query_tree class. It is responsible for containing the
    internal representation of the query to be executed. It provides methods for
    optimizing and forming and inspecting the query tree. This class is the very
    heart of the DBXP query capability! It also provides the ability to store
    a binary "compiled" form of the query.

  NOTES
    The data structure is a binary tree that can have 0, 1, or 2 children. Only
    Join operations can have 2 children. All other operations have 0 or 1
    children. Each node in the tree is an operation and the links to children
    are the pipeline.

  SEE ALSO
    query_tree.h
*/
#include "query_tree.h"

Query_tree::query_node::query_node()
{
  where_expr = NULL;
  join_expr = NULL;
  child = false;
  join_cond = Query_tree::jcUN;
  join_type = Query_tree::jnUNKNOWN;
  left = NULL;
  right = NULL;
  nodeid = -1;
  node_type = Query_tree::qntUndefined;
  sub_query = false;
  parent_nodeid = -1;
}

Query_tree::query_node::~query_node()
{
  if(left)
    delete left;
  if(right)
    delete right;
}
```

```
Query_tree::~Query_tree(void)
{
  if(root)
    delete root;
}
```

Building the Query Tree from the MySQL Structure

What we need next is the code to perform the transformation from the MySQL internal structure to the query tree. Let's use a helper source file rather than adding the code to the sql_parse.cc file. In fact, many of the commands represented by the case statements (in the sql_parse.cc file) are done this way. Create a new file named sql_dbxp_parse.cc. Create a new function in that file named build_query_tree as shown in Listing 10-14. The code is a basic transformation method. Take a moment to look through the code as you type it in (or download and copy and paste it into the file).

Listing 10-14. *The DBXP Parser Helper File*

```
/*
  sql_dbxp_parse.cc

  DESCRIPTION
    This file contains methods to execute the DBXP SELECT query statements.

  SEE ALSO
    query_tree.cc
*/
#include "query_tree.h"

/*
  Build Query Tree

  SYNOPSIS
    build_query_tree()
    THD *thd          IN the current thread
    LEX *lex          IN the pointer to the current parsed structure
    TABLE_LIST *tables  IN the list of tables identified in the query

  DESCRIPTION
    This method returns a converted MySQL internal representation (IR) of a
    query as a query_tree.

  RETURN VALUE
    Success = Query_tree * -- the root of the new query tree.
    Failed = NULL
*/
```

```
Query_tree *build_query_tree(THD *thd, LEX *lex, TABLE_LIST *tables)
{
  DBUG_ENTER("build_query_tree");
  Query_tree *qt = new Query_tree();
  Query_tree::query_node *qn =
    (Query_tree::query_node *)my_malloc(sizeof(Query_tree::query_node),
    MYF(MY_ZEROFILL | MY_WME));
  TABLE_LIST *table;
  int i = 0;
  int num_tables = 0;

  /* Create a new restrict node. */
  qn->parent_nodeid = -1;
  qn->child = false;
  /*
    Set the query type to unknown because we're creating a project node.
  */
  qn->join_type = (Query_tree::type_join) jnUNKNOWN;
  qn->nodeid = 0;
  qn->node_type = (Query_tree::query_node_type) qntProject;
  qn->left = 0;
  qn->right = 0;

  if(lex->select_lex.options & SELECT_DISTINCT)
  {
    //qt->set_distinct(true); /* placeholder for future modifications */
  }

  /* Get the tables (relations) */
  i = 0;
  for(table = tables; table; table = table->next_local)
  {
    num_tables++;
    qn->relations[i] = table;
    i++;
  }

  /* Populate attributes */
  qn->fields = &lex->select_lex.item_list;
  /* Process joins */
  if (num_tables > 0)  //indicates more than 1 table processed
    for(table = tables; table; table = table->next_local)
      if ((table->on_expr != 0) && (qn->join_expr == 0))
        qn->join_expr = table->on_expr;
  qn->where_expr = lex->select_lex.where;
  qt->root = qn;
  DBUG_RETURN(qt);
}
```

Notice that the build_query_tree code begins with creating a new query node, identifies the tables used in the query, populates the fields list, and captures the join and where expressions. These are all of the basic items needed to execute the most basic of queries.

Stubbing the Query Tree Execution

Now let's consider what it takes to create a query tree in code. Create a new function named DBXP_select_command and copy the code from Listing 10-15. Place this function in the sql_DBXP_parse.cc file. This function will be called from the case statement in sql_parse.cc.

Listing 10-15. *Handling the SELECT DBXP Command*

```
/*
  Perform Select Command

  SYNOPSIS
    DBXP_select_command()
    THD *thd            IN the current thread

  DESCRIPTION
    This method executes the command using the query tree and optimizer.

  RETURN VALUE
    Success = 0    /* Note: The use of 0 as success is a MySQL coding rule. */
    Failed = 1
*/
int DBXP_select_command(THD *thd)
{
  DBUG_ENTER("dbxp_select_command");
  Query_tree *qt = build_query_tree(thd, thd->lex,
                      (TABLE_LIST*) thd->lex->select_lex.table_list.first);
  List<Item> field_list;
  Protocol *protocol= thd->protocol;
  field_list.push_back(new
      Item_empty_string("Database Experiment Project (DBXP)",40));
  if (protocol->send_fields(&field_list,
                            Protocol::SEND_NUM_ROWS | Protocol::SEND_EOF))
    DBUG_RETURN(TRUE);
  protocol->prepare_for_resend();
  protocol->store("Query tree was built.", system_charset_info);
  if (protocol->write())
    DBUG_RETURN(TRUE);
  send_eof(thd);
  delete qt;
  DBUG_RETURN(0);
}
```

This code begins by calling the transformation function (build_query_tree) and then creates a stubbed result set. This time, I create a record set with only one column and one row that is used to pass a message to the client that the query tree transformation completed. Although this code isn't very interesting, it is a placeholder for you to conduct more experiments on the query tree (see exercises at the end of the chapter). Place the sql_DBXP_parse.cc file in the /sql directory of your MySQL source tree.

Stubbing the SELECT DBXP Command Revisited

Open the sql_parse.cc file and add a function declaration for the DBXP_select_command function, placing the declaration near the phrase mysql_execute_command. Listing 10-16 shows the complete function header for the DBXP_select_command function. Enter this code above the comment block as shown.

Listing 10-16. *Modifications to the Parser Command Code*

```
/* BEGIN DBXP MODIFICATION */
/* Reason for Modification: */
/* This section adds the code to call the new SELECT DBXP command. */
int DBXP_select_command(THD *thd);
/* END DBXP MODIFICATION */


/***************************************************************************
** mysql_execute_command
** Execute command saved in thd and current_lex->sql_command
***************************************************************************/
```

You can now change the code in the case statement (also called the parser command switch) to call the new DBXP_select_command function. Listing 10-17 shows the complete code for calling this function. Notice that the only parameter we need to pass in is the current thread (thd). The MySQL internal query structure and all other metadata for the query are referenced via the thread pointer. As you can see, this technique cleans up the case statement quite a bit. It also helps to modularize the DBXP code to make it easier to maintain and modify for your experiments.

Listing 10-17. *Modifications to the Parse Command Switch (sql_parse.cc)*

```
/* BEGIN DBXP MODIFICATION */
/* Reason for Modification: */
/* This section adds the code to call the new SELECT DBXP command. */
  case SQLCOM_DBXP_SELECT:
  {
    res = DBXP_select_command(thd);
    if (res)
      goto error;
    break;
  }
/* END DBXP MODIFICATION */
```

```
case SQLCOM_PREPARE:
{
...
```

Before you can compile the server, you need to add the new source code files (query_tree.h, query_tree.cc, and sql_DBXP_parse.cc) to the project (make) file.

Adding the Files to the Makefile on Linux

Adding the project files on Linux requires modifying the Makefile.am file in the /sql directory from the root of the source tree. Open the Makefile.am file and locate the mysqld_SOURCES label. Add source code files to the list of sources for compilation of the server project (mysqld). Listing 10-18 shows the start of the definition and the project files added.

Listing 10-18. *Modifications to the Makefile.am File*

```
mysqld_SOURCES = sql_lex.cc sql_handler.cc sql_partition.cc \
      item.cc item_sum.cc item_buff.cc item_func.cc \
      item_cmpfunc.cc item_strfunc.cc item_timefunc.cc \
      thr_malloc.cc item_create.cc item_subselect.cc \
      item_row.cc item_geofunc.cc item_xmlfunc.cc \
      field.cc strfunc.cc key.cc sql_class.cc sql_list.cc \
      net_serv.cc protocol.cc sql_state.c \
      lock.cc my_lock.c \
      sql_string.cc sql_manager.cc sql_map.cc \
      mysqld.cc password.c hash_filo.cc hostname.cc \
      set_var.cc sql_parse.cc sql_yacc.yy \
      sql_dbxp_parse.cc query_tree.cc \
...
```

■**Caution** Be sure to use spaces when formatting the lists when modifying the makefiles.

Adding the Files to the mysqld Project on Windows

Adding the project files in Windows is easy. Right-click on the mysqld project in Visual Studio and add the files (query_tree.h, query_tree.cc, and sql_DBXP_parse.cc) using the Add ➤ Existing Item menu option. When you compile the mysqld project, the new source code files will be compiled with the rest.

Testing the Query Tree

Once the server is compiled without errors, you can test it using a SQL statement. Unlike the last test, you should enter a valid SQL command that references objects that exist. You could either run the test (see Listing 10-19) as described in an earlier section or enter the following command in the MySQL command-line client:

```
SELECT DBXP * from customer;
```

Listing 10-19. *Results of SELECT DBXP Test*

```
mysql> SELECT DBXP * FROM customer;
```

```
+-----------------------------------+
| Database Experiment Project (DBXP) |
+-----------------------------------+
| Query tree was built.             |
+-----------------------------------+
1 row in set (0.00 sec)

mysql>
```

You've stubbed out the SELECT DBXP operation and built a query tree, but that isn't very interesting. What if we had a way to see what the query looks like? We'll create a function that works like the EXPLAIN command only instead of a list of information about the query we'll create a graphical representation[6] of the query in tree form.

Showing Details of the Query Tree

Adding a new command requires adding a new enumeration for a new case statement in the parser switch in sql_parse.cc and adding the parser code to identify the new command. You also have to add the code to execute the new command to the sql_DBXP_parse.cc file. While creating and adding an EXPLAIN command to the parser that explains query trees sounds complicated, the EXPLAIN SELECT command is available in MySQL, so we can copy a lot of that code and reuse much of it.

Adding the EXPLAIN SELECT DBXP Command to the MySQL Parser

To add the new enumeration to the parser, open the sql_lex.h file and add an enumeration named SQLCOM_DBXP_EXPLAIN_SELECT following the code for the SQLCOM_DBXP_SELECT enumeration. Listing 10-20 shows the completed code changes. Once the code is added, you can regenerate the lexical hash as described earlier.

Listing 10-20. *Adding the EXPLAIN Enumeration*

```
/* BEGIN DBXP MODIFICATION */
/* Reason for Modification: */
/* This section captures the enumerations for the DBXP command tokens */
  SQLCOM_DBXP_SELECT,
  SQLCOM_DBXP_EXPLAIN_SELECT,
/* END DBXP MODIFICATION */
```

Now let's add the code to the parser. Open the sql_yacc.yy file and locate the describe: label. Listing 10-21 shows the code for the new EXPLAIN command. Type this code in after the

---

6. As graphical as a command-line interface will allow, anyway.

describe: label and before the original MySQL code. Don't forget to add the vertical bar (|) before the original EXPLAIN code.

Listing 10-21. *Modifications to the Parser for the EXPLAIN Command*

```
describe:
/* BEGIN DBXP MODIFICATION */
/* Reason for Modification: */
/* This section captures (parses) the EXPLAIN (DESCRIBE) DBXP statements */
  describe_command SELECT_SYM DBXP_SYM DBXP_select_options
    DBXP_select_item_list DBXP_select_from
  {
    LEX *lex= Lex;
    lex->lock_option= TL_READ;
    lex->sql_command = SQLCOM_DBXP_EXPLAIN_SELECT;
    lex->select_lex.db= 0;
    lex->verbose= 0;
  }

/* END DBXP MODIFICATION */

  | describe_command table_ident
...
```

Notice in this code the parser identifies an EXPLAIN SELECT DBXP command. In fact, it calls many of the same operations as the SELECT DBXP parser code. The only differences are that this code sets the sql_command to the new enumeration (SQLCOM_DBXP_EXPLAIN_SELECT). Notice also the vertical bar | (or operator) added to the existing code.

The changes to the parser switch statement in sql_parse.cc require adding the function declaration for the code in sql_DBXP_parse.cc that will execute the EXPLAIN command. Open the sql_parse.cc file and add the function declaration for the EXPLAIN function. Name the function DBXP_explain_select_command (are you starting to see a pattern?). Add this at the same location as the DBXP_select_command function declaration. Listing 10-22 shows the complete code for both DBXP commands.

Listing 10-22. *Modifications to the Parser Command Code*

```
/* BEGIN DBXP MODIFICATION */
/* Reason for Modification: */
/* This section adds the code to call the new SELECT DBXP command. */
int DBXP_select_command(THD *thd);
int DBXP_explain_select_command(THD *thd);
/* END DBXP MODIFICATION */

/****************************************************************************
** mysql_execute_command
** Execute command saved in thd and current_lex->sql_command
****************************************************************************/
```

You also need to add the new case statement for the DBXP explain command. The statements are similar to the case statement for the SELECT DBXP command. Listing 10-23 shows the new case statement added.

Listing 10-23. *Modifications to the Parser Switch Statement*

```
/* BEGIN DBXP MODIFICATION */
/* Reason for Modification: */
/* This section adds the code to call the new SELECT DBXP command. */
  case SQLCOM_DBXP_SELECT:
  {
    res = DBXP_select_command(thd);
    if (res)
      goto error;
    break;
  }
  case SQLCOM_DBXP_EXPLAIN_SELECT:
  {
    res = DBXP_explain_select_command(thd);
    if (res)
      goto error;
    break;
  }
/* END DBXP MODIFICATION */
```

Creating a show_plan Function

The EXPLAIN SELECT DBXP command shows the query path as a tree printed out within the confines of character text. The EXPLAIN code is executed in a function named show_plan in the sql_DBXP_parse.cc file. A helper function named write_printf is used to make the show_plan code easier to read. Listings 10-24 and 10-25 show the completed code for both of these methods.

Listing 10-24. *Adding a Function to Capture the Protocol Store and Write Statements*

```
/*
  Write to vio with printf.

  SYNOPSIS
    write_printf()
    Protocol *p      IN the Protocol class
    char *first      IN the first string to write
    char *last       IN the last string to write

  DESCRIPTION
    This method writes to the vio routines printing the strings passed.
```

```
    RETURN VALUE
       Success = 0
       Failed = 1
*/
int write_printf(Protocol *p, char *first, char *last)
{
  char *str = (char *)my_malloc(256, MYF(MY_ZEROFILL | MY_WME));

  DBUG_ENTER("write_printf");
  strcpy(str, first);
  strcat(str, last);
  p->prepare_for_resend();
  p->store(str, system_charset_info);
  p->write();
  my_free((gptr)str, MYF(0));
  DBUG_RETURN(0);
}
```

Notice that the write_printf code calls the protocol->store and protocol->write functions to write a line of the drawing to the client. I'll let you explore the show_plan source code shown in Listing 10-25 to see how it works. I'll show you an example of the code executing in the next section. The code uses a postorder traversal to generate the query plan from the query tree starting at the root. Add these methods to the sql_DBXP_parse.cc file.

Listing 10-25. *The show_plan Source Code*

```
/*
  Show Query Plan

  SYNOPSIS
    show_plan()
    Protocol *p        IN the MySQL protocol class
    query_node *Root   IN the root node of the query tree
    query_node *qn     IN the starting node to be operated on.
    bool print_on_right IN indicates the printing should tab to the right
                          of the display.

  DESCRIPTION
    This method prints the execute plan to the client via the protocol class

  WARNING
    This is a RECURSIVE method!
    Uses postorder traversal to draw the query plan

  RETURN VALUE
    Success = 0  /* The use of 0 as success is a MySQL coding rule */
    Failed = 1
*/
```

```
int show_plan(Protocol *p, Query_tree::query_node *root,
              Query_tree::query_node *qn, bool print_on_right)
{
  DBUG_ENTER("show_plan");

  /* spacer is used to fill white space in the output */
  char *spacer = (char *)my_malloc(80, MYF(MY_ZEROFILL | MY_WME));
  char *tblname = (char *)my_malloc(256, MYF(MY_ZEROFILL | MY_WME));
  int i = 0;

  if(qn != 0)
  {
    show_plan(p, root, qn->left, print_on_right);
    show_plan(p, root, qn->right, true);

    /* Draw incoming arrows */
    if(print_on_right)
      strcpy(spacer, "             |                ");
    else
      strcpy(spacer, "      ");

    /* Write out the name of the database and table */
    if((qn->left == NULL) && (qn->right == NULL))
    {
      /*
         If this is a join, it has 2 children so we need to write
         the children nodes feeding the join node. Spaces are used
         to place the tables side-by-side.
      */
      if(qn->node_type == Query_tree::qntJoin)
      {
        strcpy(tblname, spacer);
        strcat(tblname, qn->relations[0]->db);
        strcat(tblname, ".");
        strcat(tblname, qn->relations[0]->table_name);
        if(strlen(tblname) < 15)
          strcat(tblname, "                ");
        else
          strcat(tblname, "           ");
        strcat(tblname, qn->relations[1]->db);
        strcat(tblname, ".");
        strcat(tblname, qn->relations[1]->table_name);
        write_printf(p, tblname, "");
        write_printf(p, spacer, "     |                                |");
        write_printf(p, spacer, "     |   ----------------------------");
        write_printf(p, spacer, "     |   |");
        write_printf(p, spacer, "     V   V");
      }
  }
```

```
   else
   {
     strcpy(tblname, spacer);
     strcat(tblname, qn->relations[0]->db);
     strcat(tblname, ".");
     strcat(tblname, qn->relations[0]->table_name);
     write_printf(p, tblname, "");
     write_printf(p, spacer, "       |");
     write_printf(p, spacer, "       |");
     write_printf(p, spacer, "       |");
     write_printf(p, spacer, "       V");
   }
 }
 else if((qn->left != 0) && (qn->right != 0))
 {
   write_printf(p, spacer, "      |                            |");
   write_printf(p, spacer, "      |     ----------------------------");
   write_printf(p, spacer, "      |    |");
   write_printf(p, spacer, "      V    V");
 }
 else if((qn->left != 0) && (qn->right == 0))
 {
   write_printf(p, spacer, "      |");
   write_printf(p, spacer, "      |");
   write_printf(p, spacer, "      |");
   write_printf(p, spacer, "      V");
 }
 else if(qn->right != 0)
 {
 }
 write_printf(p, spacer, "-------------------");

 /* Write out the node type */
 switch(qn->node_type)
 {
 case Query_tree::qntProject:
   {
     write_printf(p, spacer, "|     PROJECT    |");
     write_printf(p, spacer, "-------------------");
     break;
   }
 case Query_tree::qntRestrict:
   {
     write_printf(p, spacer, "|    RESTRICT    |");
     write_printf(p, spacer, "-------------------");
     break;
   }
```

```
      case Query_tree::qntJoin:
        {
          write_printf(p, spacer, "|      JOIN      |");
          write_printf(p, spacer, "------------------");
          break;
        }
      case Query_tree::qntDistinct:
        {
          write_printf(p, spacer, "|    DISTINCT    |");
          write_printf(p, spacer, "------------------");
          break;
        }
      default:
        {
          write_printf(p, spacer, "|     UNDEF      |");
          write_printf(p, spacer, "------------------");
          break;
        }
      }
      write_printf(p, spacer, "| Access Method: |");
      write_printf(p, spacer, "|    iterator    |");
      write_printf(p, spacer, "------------------");
      if(qn == root)
      {
        write_printf(p, spacer, "         |");
        write_printf(p, spacer, "         |");
        write_printf(p, spacer, "         V");
        write_printf(p, spacer, "    Result Set");
      }
    }
  my_free((gptr)spacer, MYF(0));
  my_free((gptr)tblname, MYF(0));
  DBUG_RETURN(0);
}
```

The last thing you need to add is the code to perform the DBXP EXPLAIN command, call the show_plan() method, and return a result to the client. Listing 10-26 shows the complete code for this function. Notice that in this function I build the query tree and then create a field list using a single-character string column named "Execution Path," then call show_plan to write the plan to the client.

Listing 10-26. *The DBXP EXPLAIN Command Source Code*

```
/*
  Perform EXPLAIN command.

  SYNOPSIS
    DBXP_explain_select_command()
    THD *thd              IN the current thread

  DESCRIPTION
    This method executes the EXPLAIN SELECT command.

  RETURN VALUE
    Success = 0
    Failed = 1
*/
int DBXP_explain_select_command(THD *thd)
{
  DBUG_ENTER("dbxp_explain_select_command");
  Query_tree *qt = build_query_tree(thd, thd->lex,
                    (TABLE_LIST*) thd->lex->select_lex.table_list.first);
  List<Item> field_list;
  Protocol *protocol= thd->protocol;
  field_list.push_back(new Item_empty_string("Execution Path",NAME_LEN));
  if (protocol->send_fields(&field_list,
                            Protocol::SEND_NUM_ROWS | Protocol::SEND_EOF))
    DBUG_RETURN(TRUE);
  protocol->prepare_for_resend();
  show_plan(protocol, qt->root, qt->root, false);
  send_eof(thd);
  delete qt;
  DBUG_RETURN(0);
}
```

Now, let's compile the server and give it a go with the test file.

Testing the DBXP EXPLAIN Command

As with the previous tests, you can either use the test described in an earlier section or enter a valid SQL command in the MySQL command-line client. Listing 10-27 shows an example of what the query execution path would look like. It should be stated at this point that the query is not optimized and will appear as a single node. Once you add the optimizer (see Chapter 11), the query execution path will reflect the appropriate execution for the query statement entered.

Listing 10-27. *Results of the DBXP EXPLAIN Test*

```
mysql> EXPLAIN SELECT DBXP * FROM customer;
```

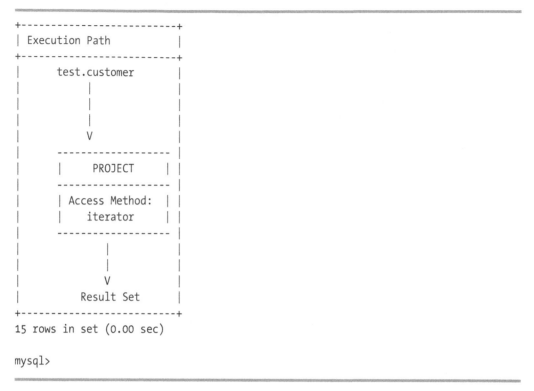

```
+------------------------+
| Execution Path         |
+------------------------+
|       test.customer    |
|          |             |
|          |             |
|          |             |
|          V             |
|     ------------------ |
|     |    PROJECT    | ||
|     ------------------ |
|     | Access Method: | ||
|     |    iterator   | ||
|     ------------------ |
|             |          |
|             |          |
|             V          |
|        Result Set      |
+------------------------+
15 rows in set (0.00 sec)

mysql>
```

This is much more interesting than a dull listing of facts. Adding the EXPLAIN command at this stage of the DBXP project allows you to witness and diagnose how the optimizer is forming the query tree. You'll find this very helpful when you begin your own experiments.

If you haven't been doing so thus far, you should run the complete test that tests all three portions of the code presented in this chapter.

Summary

I presented in this chapter some of the more complex database internal technologies. You learned how queries are represented internally within the MySQL server as they are parsed and processed via the "big switch." More importantly, you discovered how MySQL can be used to conduct your own database internals experiments with the query tree class. The knowledge of these technologies should provide you with a greater understanding of why and how the MySQL internal components are built.

In the next chapter, I'll show you more about internal query representation through an example implementation of a query tree optimization strategy. If you've ever wondered what it takes to build an optimizer for a relational database system, the next chapter will show you an example of a heuristic query optimizer using the query tree class.

Exercises

The following lists several areas for further exploration. They represent the types of activities you might want to conduct as experiments (or as a class assignment) to explore relational database technologies.

1. The query in Figure 10-1 exposes a design flaw in one of the tables. What is it? Does the flaw violate any of the normal forms? If so, which one?

2. Explore the TABLE structure and change the SELECT DBXP stub to return information about the table and its fields.

3. Change the EXPLAIN SELECT DBXP command to produce an output similar to the MySQL EXPLAIN SELECT command.

4. Modify the build_query_tree function to identify and process the LIMIT clause.

5. How can the query tree query_node structure be changed to accommodate HAVING, GROUP BY, and ORDER clauses?

CHAPTER 11

∎ ∎ ∎

Query Optimization

The query tree class shown in Chapter 10 forms the starting point for building the experimental query optimization and execution engine for DBXP. In this chapter, I'll show you how to add the optimizer to the query tree class. I'll begin by explaining the rationale for the heuristics (or rules) used in the optimizer, and then jump into writing the code. Because the code for some of the functions is quite lengthy, the code examples shown in this chapter are excerpts. If you are following along by coding the examples, I recommend you download the source code for this chapter instead of typing in the code from scratch.

Types of Query Optimizers

The first query optimizers were designed for use in early database systems such as System R[1] and INGRES.[2] These optimizers were developed for a particular implementation of the relational model and have stood the test of time as illustrations for how to implement optimizers. Many of the commercially available database systems are based on these works. Since then, optimizers have been created for extensions of the relational model to include object-oriented and distributed database systems.

One example is the Volcano optimizer, which uses a dynamic programming algorithm to generate query plans for cost-based optimization in object-oriented database systems. Another example is concerned with how to perform optimization in heterogeneous database systems (similar to distributed systems, but there is no commonly shared concept of organization). In these environments it is possible to use statistical methods for deriving optimization strategies.

Another area in which the requirements for query optimization generate unique needs is that of memory-resident database systems. Memory-resident database systems are designed to contain the entire system and all of the data in the computer's secondary memory (i.e., disk). While most of these applications are in the area of embedded systems, some larger distributed systems that consist of a collection of systems use memory-resident databases to expedite information flow. Optimization in memory-resident database systems requires faster algorithms

---

1. P. G. Selinger, M. M. Astraham, D. D. Chamberlin, R. A. Lories, and T. G. Price. 1979. Access Path Selection in a Relational Database Management System. *Proceedings of the ACM SIGMOD International Conference on the Management of Data*, Aberdeen, Scotland: 23–34. Considered by some to be the "Bible of Query Optimization."
2. M. Stonebraker, E. Wong, P. Kreps. 1976. The Design and Implementation of INGRES. *ACM Transactions on Database Systems* 1(3): 189–222.

because the need for optimizing retrieval is insignificant compared to the need for processing the query itself.[3]

All of the research into traditional and nontraditional optimization is based on the firmament of the System R optimizer. The System R optimizer is a cost-based optimizer that uses information gathered about the database and the data, or statistics, in the relations to form cost estimates for how the query would perform. Additionally, the concept of arranging the internal representation of the query into different but equivalent internal representations (they generate the same answer) provides a mechanism to store the alternative forms. Each of these alternative forms is called a *query plan*. The plan with the least cost is chosen as the most efficient way to execute the query.

One of the key features identified in the System R work was the concept of selectivity—the prediction of results based on the evaluation of an expression that contained references to attributes and their values. Selectivity is central to determining in what order the simple expressions in a conjunctive selection should be tested. The most selective expression (that is, the one with the smallest selectivity) will retrieve the smallest number of tuples (rows). Thus, that expression should be the basis for the first operation in a query. Conjunctive selections can be thought of as the "intersection" conditions. Conversely, disjunctive selections are the "union" conditions. Order has no effect among the disjunctive conditions.

Certain query optimizers, such as System R, do not process all possible join orders. Rather, they restrict the search to certain types of join orders that are known to produce more efficient execution. For example, multiway joins might be ordered so that the conditions that generate the least possible results are performed first. Similarly, the System R optimizer considers only those join orders where the right operand of each join is one of the initial relations. Such join orders are called left-deep join orders. Left-deep join orders are particularly convenient for pipeline execution, since the right operand is normally a relation (versus an intermediate relation), and thus only one input to each join is pipelined. The use of pipelining is a key element of the optimizer and execution engine for the database experiment project.

Cost-Based Optimizers

A cost-based optimizer generates a range of query-evaluation plans from the given query by using the equivalence rules, and chooses the one with the least cost based on the metrics (or statistics) gathered about the relations and operations needed to execute the query. For a complex query, many equivalent plans are possible.

The goal of cost-based optimization is to arrange the query execution and table access utilizing indexes and statistics gathered from past queries. Systems such as Microsoft SQL Server and Oracle use cost-based optimizers.

The portion of the database system responsible for acquiring and processing statistics (and many other utility functions) is called the *database catalog*. The catalog maintains statistics about the referenced relations and the access paths available on each of them. These will be used later in access path selection to select the most efficient plan (with the least cost). For example, System R maintains statistics on the following for each table:

---

3. Query execution in traditional systems includes not only processing the query but also accessing the data from physical media. However, memory-resident systems do not have the long access times associated with retrieval from physical media.

- The cardinality of each relation

- The number of pages in the segment that hold tuples of each relation

- The fraction of data pages in the segment that hold tuples of relation (blocking factor, or fill)

- For each index:

  - The number of distinct keys in each index

  - The number of pages in each index

These statistics come from several sources within the system. The statistics are created when a relation is loaded and when an index is created. They are then updated periodically by a user command,[4] which can be run by any user. System R does not update these statistics in real time because of the extra database operations and the locking bottleneck this would create at the system catalogs. Dynamic updating of statistics would tend to serialize accesses that modify the relation contents and thus limit the ability of the system to process simultaneous queries in a multiuser environment.

The use of statistics in cost-based optimization is not very complex. Most database professionals interviewed seem to think the gathering and application of statistics is a complex and vital element of query optimization. Although it is true that cost-based query optimization and even hybrid optimization schemes use statistics for cost and/or ranking, they are neither complex nor critical. Take, for instance, the concept of evenly distributed values among attributes. This concept alone is proof of the imprecise nature of the application of statistics. Statistical calculations are largely categorical in nature and not designed to generate a precise value. They merely assist in determining whether one query execution plan is generally more costly than another.

Frequency distribution of attribute values is a common method for predicting the size of query results. By forming a distribution of possible (or actual[5]) values of an attribute, the database system can use the distribution to calculate a cost for a given query plan by predicting the number of tuples (or rows) that the plan must process. Modern database systems, however, deal with frequency distributions of individual attributes only, because considering all possible combinations of attributes is very expensive. This essentially corresponds to what is known as the attribute value independence assumption, and although rarely true, it is adopted by almost all relational database systems.

Gathering the distribution data requires either constant updating of the statistics or predictive analysis of the data. Another tactic is the use of uniform distributions where the distribution of the attribute values is assumed to be equal for all distinct values. For example, given 5,000 tuples and a possible 50 values for a given attribute, the uniform distribution assumes each value is represented 100 times. This is rarely the case and is often incorrect. However, given the absence of any statistics, it is still a reasonable approximation of reality in many cases.

The memory requirements and running time of dynamic programming grow exponentially with query size (i.e., number of joins) in the worst case since all viable partial plans generated in each step must be stored to be used in the next one. In fact, many modern systems place a

4. This practice is still in use today by most commercial database systems.
5. The accumulation of statistics in real time is called piggyback statistic generation.

limit on the size of queries that can be submitted (usually around 15 joins), because for larger queries the optimizer crashes due to very high memory requirements. Nevertheless, most queries seen in practice involve fewer than ten joins, and the algorithm has proved to be effective in such contexts. It is considered the standard in query optimization search strategies. Some of the statistics gathered about rows (or tuples) in tables (or relations) for use in cost-based optimizers include the following:

- The number of tuples in the table

- The number of blocks containing rows (the block count)

- The size of the row in bytes

- The number of distinct values for each attribute (or column)

- The selection cardinality of each attribute (sometimes represented as evenly distributed)

- The fan-out of internal nodes of an index (the number of children resulting in subtrees)

- The height of the B-tree for an index

- The number of blocks at the leaf level of the index

The cost of writing the final result of an operation back to disk is ignored. Regardless of the query-evaluation plan used, this cost does not change; therefore, not including it in the calculations does not affect the choice of the plan.

Most database systems today use a form of dynamic programming to generate all possible query plans. While dynamic programming offers good performance for cost optimization, it is a complex algorithm that can require more resources for the more complex queries. While most database systems do not encounter these types of queries, researchers in the areas of distributed database systems and high-performance computing have explored alternatives and variants to dynamic programming techniques. The recent research by Kossmann and Stocker shows that we are beginning to see the limits of traditional approaches to query optimization.[6] What are needed are more efficient optimization techniques that generate execution plans that follow good practices rather than exhaustive exploration. In other words, we need optimizers that perform well in a variety of general environments as well as optimizers that perform well in unique database environments.

Heuristic Optimizers

The goal of heuristic optimization is to apply rules that ensure good practices for query execution. Systems that use heuristic optimizers include INGRES and various academic variants. Most systems typically use heuristic optimization as a means of avoiding the really bad plans rather than as a primary means of optimization.

Heuristic optimizers use rules on how to shape the query into the most optimal form prior to choosing alternative implementations. The application of heuristics, or rules, can eliminate queries that are likely to be inefficient. Using heuristics as a basis to form the query plan ensures

---

6. D. Kossman, and K. Stocker. 2000. Iterative Dynamic Programming: A New Class of Query Optimization Algorithms. *ACM Transactions on Database Systems* 25(1): 43–82.

that the query plan is most likely (but not always) optimized prior to evaluation. Such heuristics include

- Performing selection operations as early as possible. It is usually better to perform selections earlier than projections because they reduce the number of tuples to be sent up the tree.

- Performing projections early.

- Determining which selection operations and join operations produce the smallest result set and use those first (left-most-deep).

- Replacing Cartesian products with join operations.

- Moving projection attributes as far down as possible in the tree.

- Identifying subtrees whose operations can be pipelined.

Heuristic optimizers are not new technologies. Researchers have created rules-based optimizers for various specialized purposes. One example is the Prairie rule-based query optimizer. This rule-based optimizer permits the creation of rules based on a given language notation. Queries are processed using the rules to govern how the optimizer performs. In this case, the Prairie optimizer is primarily a cost-based optimizer that uses rules to tune the optimizer.

Aside from examples like Prairie and early primitives such as INGRES, no commercial database systems implement a purely heuristic optimizer. For those that do have a heuristic or rule-based optimization step, it is usually implemented as an addition to or as a preprocessor to a classic cost-based optimizer or as a preprocessing step in the optimization.

Semantic Optimizers

The goal of semantic optimization is to form query execution plans that use the semantics, or topography, of the database and the relationships and indexes within to form queries that ensure the best practice available for executing a query in the given database. Semantic query optimization uses knowledge of the schema (e.g., integrity constraints) for transforming a query into a form that may be answered more efficiently than the original version.

Although not yet implemented in commercial database systems as the primary optimization technique, semantic optimization is currently the focus of considerable research. Semantic optimization operates on the premise that the optimizer has a basic understanding of the actual database schema. When a query is submitted, the optimizer uses its knowledge of system constraints to simplify or to ignore a particular query if it is guaranteed to return an empty result set. This technique holds great promise for providing even more improvements to query processing efficiency in future relational database systems.

Parametric Optimizers

Ioannidis, in his work on parametric query optimization, describes a query optimization method that combines the application of heuristic methods with cost-based optimization. The resulting query optimizer provides a means to produce a smaller set of effective query plans from which cost can be estimated, and thus the lowest-cost plan of the set can be executed.[7] Query plan generation is created using a random algorithm, called sipR. This permits systems that utilize

---

7. Y. E. Ioannidis, R. T. Ng, K. Shim, and T. Sellis. 1997. Parametric Query Optimization. *VLDB Journal* 6:132–151.

parametric query optimization to choose query plans that can include the uncertainty of parameter changes (such as buffer sizes) to choose optimal plans either formed on the fly or from storage.

It is interesting to note that in his work, Ioannidis suggests that the use of dynamic programming algorithms may not be needed and thus the overhead in using these techniques avoided. Furthermore, he found that database systems that use heuristics to prune or shape the query prior to applying dynamic programming algorithms for query optimization are usually an enhanced version of the original algorithm of System R. Ioannidis showed that for small queries (approximately up to ten joins), dynamic programming is superior to randomized algorithms, whereas for large queries the opposite holds true.

Heuristic Optimization Revisited

The heuristic optimization process uses a set of rules that have been defined to guarantee good execution plans. Thus, the effectiveness of a heuristic optimizer to produce good plans is based solely on the effectiveness and completeness of its rules. The following paragraphs describe the rules used to create the DBXP query optimizer. Although these rules are very basic, when applied to typical queries the resulting execution is near optimal with fast performance and accurate results.

Some basic strategies were used to construct the query tree initially. Specifically, all executions take place in the query tree node. Restrictions and projections are processed on a branch and do not generate intermediate relations. Joins are always processed as an intersection of two paths. A multiway join would be formed using a series of two-way joins. The following rules represent the best practices for forming a set of heuristics to generate good execution plans. The DBXP optimizer is designed to apply these rules in order to transform the query tree into a form that ensures efficient execution.[8]

1. Split any nodes that contain a project and join or restrict and join. This step is necessary because some queries specify the join condition in the WHERE clause[9] and thus can "fool" the optimizer into forming join nodes that have portions of the expressions that are not part of the join condition.

2. Push all restrictions down the tree to leaves. Expressions are grouped according to their respective relations into individual query tree nodes. Although there are some complex expressions that cannot be reduced, most can be easily reduced to a single relation. By placing the restrictions at the leaves, the number of resulting tuples that must be passed up the tree is reduced.

3. Place all projections at the lowest point in the tree. Projections should be placed in a node above restrictions and will further reduce the amount of data passed through the tree by eliminating unneeded attributes from the resulting tuples. It should be noted that the projections may be modified to include attributes that are needed for operations such as joins that reside in the parentage of the projection query tree node.

8. In this case, efficient execution may not be the optimal solution.
9. A common technique practiced by novice database users.

4. Place all joins at intersections of projections or restrictions of the relations contained in the join clause.[10] This ensures that the least amount of tuples are evaluated for the most expensive operation—joins. Intermediate query tree nodes may be necessary that order the resulting tuples from the child nodes. These intermediate nodes, called utility operations, may sort or group the tuples depending on the type of join and can greatly increase the performance of the join.

Note Other heuristics can be used. The previous list contains those that generate the greatest gain in performance.

An interesting counterargument to the practice of pushing selections and restrictions down the tree is given by Lee, Shih, and Chen.[11] In their work, they suggest that under some conditions some selections and projections may be more costly than joins. Their argument presents a query optimizer based on graph theory that can more accurately predict query optimization for situations where complex selects and projections are present. Nevertheless, the general case is that "efficient" execution plans can be constructed for the majority of queries using the rules I've listed.

The DBXP Query Optimizer

Although these rules offer a complete set of operations for forming the optimal query tree, they do not address balancing multiway joins or applying indexes. These steps are considered cost-based optimizations. For this reason, most heuristic optimizers are implemented as a two-phase optimization, where the first pass generates an optimized query path and a second pass applies cost-optimization strategies.

Thus, the DBXP optimizer is implemented as a two-pass operation. The first operation rearranges the tree for execution using a heuristic algorithm. The second pass walks the tree, changing the access method for nodes that have relations with indexes available on the attributes being operated on. I leave the implementation of the cost-optimization pass as an exercise for the reader.

Designing the Tests

Creating comprehensive tests for a heuristic optimizer would require writing SQL statements that cover all possible paths through the optimizer. In essence, you would need to create a test that tests all possible queries, both valid and invalid. However, implementing the heuristic optimizer is only the second part of the DBXP engine. In the previous chapter, we created the basic query tree internal representation and stubbed the execution methods. In this chapter, we will create the optimizer but will not be able to execute the queries. You can continue to use the stubbed execution to test the optimizer but, rather than presenting the results of the

---

10. May disallow the use of indexes for the join operation.
11. C. Lee, C. Shih, and Y. Chen. 2001. A Graph-Theoretic Model for Optimizing Queries Involving Methods. *VLDB Journal* 9:327–343.

queries, you can reuse the code from the previous chapter to show the query plan instead of the query results.

With this in mind, let's design a few basic queries that exercise the optimizer to show it is processing the queries. We take care of query execution in the next chapter. Listing 11-1 shows a sample test that exercises the query optimizer.

Listing 11-1. *Sample DBXP Query Optimizer Test (ExpertMySQLCh11.test)*

```
#
# Sample test to test the SELECT DBXP optimizer
#

# Test 1:
SELECT DBXP * FROM staff;

# Test 2:
SELECT DBXP id FROM staff WHERE staff.id = '123456789';

# Test 3:
SELECT DBXP id, dir_name FROM staff, directorate
WHERE staff.dno = directorate.dnumber;

# Test 4:
SELECT DBXP * FROM staff JOIN tasking ON staff.id = tasking.id
WHERE staff.id = '123456789';
```

■**Tip** The database used in these examples is included in the Appendix.

Of course, you can use this test as a guide and add your own commands to explore the new code. Please refer to Chapter 4 for more details on how to create and run this test using the MySQL Test Suite.

Stubbing the SELECT DBXP Command

Since there is no query execution capability, the query commands can be optimized but not executed. The show plan mechanism (the EXPLAIN command) can serve as a means to demonstrate the optimizer. To add this functionality, you can open the sql_dbxp_parse.cc file and alter the DBXP_select_command() method as shown in Listing 11-2.

Listing 11-2. *Stubbing the Query Optimizer for Testing*

```
int DBXP_explain_select_command(THD *thd);

/*
  Perform SELECT DBXP Command
```

```
SYNOPSIS
  DBXP_select_command()
  THD *thd              IN the current thread

DESCRIPTION
  This method executes the SELECT command using the query tree and optimizer.

RETURN VALUE
  Success = 0
  Failed = 1
*/
int DBXP_select_command(THD *thd)
{
  DBUG_ENTER("DBXP_select_command");
  DBXP_explain_select_command(thd);
  DBUG_RETURN(0);
}
```

These changes alter the code to call the EXPLAIN command code rather than executing the query. This allows the tests to return a valid result set (the query plan) so that we can test the optimizer without the query execution portion.

Note I use a function declaration above the DBXP_select_command() method. This allows the code to call forward to the DBXP_explain_select_command() method without using a header file.

There is also a change necessary to the DBXP_explain_select_command() method. You need to add the call to the new optimize methods. This includes the heuristic_optimization() and cost_optimization() methods. I will discuss the heuristic optimization in more detail in the following sections. Listing 11-3 shows the modifications to the EXPLAIN code.

Listing 11-3. *Modifications to the EXPLAIN Command Code*

```
/*
  Perform EXPLAIN command.

SYNOPSIS
  DBXP_explain_select_command()
  THD *thd              IN the current thread

DESCRIPTION
  This method executes the EXPLAIN SELECT command.

RETURN VALUE
  Success = 0
  Failed = 1
```

```
*/
int DBXP_explain_select_command(THD *thd)
{
  bool res;
  select_result *result = thd->lex->result;

  DBUG_ENTER("DBXP_explain_select_command");

  /* Prepare the tables (check access, locks) */
  res = check_table_access(thd, SELECT_ACL, thd->lex->query_tables, 0);
  if (res)
    DBUG_RETURN(1);
  res = open_and_lock_tables(thd, thd->lex->query_tables);
  if (res)
    DBUG_RETURN(1);

  /* Create the query tree and optimize it */
  Query_tree *qt = build_query_tree(thd, thd->lex,
          (TABLE_LIST*) thd->lex->select_lex.table_list.first);
  qt->heuristic_optimization();
  qt->cost_optimization();

  /* create a field list for returning the query plan */
  List<Item> field_list;

  /* use the protocol class to communicate to client */
  Protocol *protocol= thd->protocol;

  /* write the field to the client */
  field_list.push_back(new Item_empty_string("Execution Path",NAME_LEN));
  if (protocol->send_fields(&field_list,
                            Protocol::SEND_NUM_ROWS | Protocol::SEND_EOF))
    DBUG_RETURN(TRUE);
  protocol->prepare_for_resend();

  /* generate the query plan and send it to client */
  show_plan(protocol, qt->root, qt->root, false);
  send_eof(thd); /* end of file tells client no more data is coming */

  /* unlock tables and cleanup memory */
  mysql_unlock_read_tables(thd, thd->lock);
  delete qt;
  DBUG_RETURN(0);
}
```

Important MySQL Structures and Classes

There are a number of key structures and classes in the MySQL source code. You have already seen many of them in the examples thus far. Some of the more important ones are documented in the MySQL Internals manual. Unfortunately, there is no document that lists them all. The following sections describe some of these structures and classes that you will encounter when working with the DBXP query optimizer (and later the query execution code). These include the TABLE structure, the Field class, and a few of the common Item iterators (the Item class is discussed in Chapter 3).

TABLE Structure

The most important MySQL structure that you will work with when writing the optimizer is the TABLE structure. This structure is defined in /sql/table.h called st_table. It is redefined in /sql/handler.h as TABLE. Most of the MySQL source code refers to the structure as TABLE.

This structure is important because it contains all of the pertinent data for a table. It contains everything from a pointer to the appropriate storage handler class to a list of the fields, keys, and temporary buffers for storing rows while executing the query. While the structure is immense (like most important structures in MySQL), there are a few key attributes that you will see over and over again. Table 11-1 lists some of the more important attributes for the TABLE structure. For a detailed examination of the TABLE structure, see the handler.h file.

Table 11-1. *TABLE Structure Overview*

Attribute	Description
file	A reference to the storage engine object.
field	An array of fields for the table.
fields	The number of fields in the field array.
table_name	The name of the table. This could be the alias or actual (real) name. Depends on how it was referenced in the query statement.
real_name	The actual name of the table (not the alias).
path	The location of the .frm file for the table.
record[]	Two buffers used to store rows from the table during query execution.
reclength	The total length of the record (in bytes).
rec_buff_length	The length of the record buffers.
keys	The number of keys specified for the table.
next	A pointer to the next table in a list of tables.
prev	A pointer to the previous table in a list of tables.

Note The path attribute was changed in version 5.1 to allow different filename and table names.

The Field Class

The Field class contains all of the attributes and methods for creating, assigning values to, and manipulating fields (or attributes) for the tables in the database. The Field class is defined in the /sql/field.h file and implemented in the /sql/field.cc file. The Field class is actually a base from which several types of fields are derived. These derived classes are named Field_XXX and can be found in several places within the MySQL source code.

Since it is only a base class,[12] there are many methods in the class that are intended to be overwritten by the derived class (they're defined as virtual). However, many of the derived classes have the same set of basic attributes and methods. Table 11-2 lists the attributes and methods that you will encounter in working with the DBXP source code. For a detailed examination of the Field class, see the field.h file.

Table 11-2. *The Field Class*

Attribute/Method	Description
ptr	A pointer to the field within the record buffer.
null_ptr	A pointer to a byte (or bytes) in the record buffer that indicates which attributes can contain NULL.
table_name	The table name associated with this field.
field_name	The attribute name for this field.
field_length	The length of the field. Indicates the number of bytes that can be stored.
is_null()	Checks to see if the field is NULL.
move_field()	Changes the pointer of the field in memory to point to a different location.
store()	A series of overloaded methods used to store values into the fields.
val_str()	Gets the value of the field as a string.
val_int()	Gets the value of the field as an integer.
result_type()	Gets the data type of the field.
cmp()	Returns the comparison result of the field with the value passed.

Iterators

There are three types of iterators in the MySQL source code. You have already seen these iterators while working with the code in Chapters 7 and 8. Iterators are special constructs that make it easy to create and navigate a list of objects and are typically presented as either linked lists or arrays. The iterators in MySQL are implemented as template classes, which take as a parameter the type of the data on which the list operates. The MySQL iterators are linked lists, but some

---

12. It isn't a true abstract class because it contains some methods that are defined in the source code. A true abstract class defines all methods as virtual and therefore are used as interfaces rather than base classes.

behave more like queues and stacks. The following sections describe some of the available iterator classes in MySQL. These iterators are defined in the /sql/sql_list.h header file.

template <> class List

The List template class is implemented as a queue or stack with methods for pushing items onto the back of the list using the push_back() method or on the front of the list using the push_front() method. Items can be retrieved using the pop() method or deleted by using the remove() method. You can loop through the list by using the next attribute of the data item, but the list is normally used to form a linked list of items (e.g., List<Item> item_list), then one of the List_iterator classes is used to loop through the list quickly. This class is derived from the base_list class (also defined in /sql/sql_list.h).

template <> class List_iterator

The List_iterator class is implemented as a linked list with methods for moving through the list using the overloaded ++ operator. Items can be retrieved using the ref() method or deleted by using the remove() method. The list can be restarted from the front by issuing the rewind() method. This class is derived from the base_list class (also defined in /sql/sql_list.h).

template <> class List_iterator_fast

The List_iterator_fast class is essentially the same as the List_iterator class, but optimized for fast-forward traversal. Implemented as a linked list with methods for moving through the list using the overloaded ++ operator. Items can be retrieved using the ref() method or deleted by using the remove() method. This class is derived from the base_list class (also defined in /sql/sql_list.h).

Examples

Using the iterators is easy. If you want to use a list to manipulate items, a simple list like the List<Item_field> would be the best choice. However, if you want to loop through a list of fields quickly, you can create a list iterator as either a List_iterator<Item_field> or a List_iterator_fast<Item_field>. Examples of loop structures are shown in Listing 11-4.

Listing 11-4. *Example Iterators*

```
/* create a list and populate with some items */
List<Item> item_list;
item_list.push_back(new Item_int((int32)
          join->select_lex->select_number));
item_list.push_back(new Item_string(join->select_lex->type,
  strlen(join->select_lex->type), cs));
item_list.push_back(new Item_string(message,strlen(message),cs));

../* start a basic list iterator to iterate through the item_list */
  List_iterator<Item_field> item_list_it(*item_list);
```

```
/* control the iteration using an offset */
while ((curr_item= item_list_it++))
{
  /* do something */
}

../* start a fast list iterator to iterate through the item_list */
List_iterator_fast<Item_field> li(item_equal->fields);

/* control the iteration using an offset */
while ((item= li++))
{
  /* do something */
}
```

The DBXP Helper Classes

I mentioned in Chapter 9 two additional classes used in the DBXP engine. These classes are designed to make the optimizer easier to code and easier to understand. They are encapsulations of the existing MySQL classes (and structures) and reuse many of the methods available in the MySQL code.

The first helper class is a class encapsulates the attributes used in a query. These attributes are represented in the MySQL code as Item and Item_field classes. The helper class, named Attribute, makes access to these classes easier by providing a common interface for accessing items. Listing 11-5 shows the header file for the Attribute class.

Listing 11-5. *The Attribute Class Header*

```
class Attribute
{
public:
  Attribute(void);
  int remove_attribute(int num);
  Item *get_attribute(int num);
  int add_attribute(bool append, Item *new_item);
  int num_attributes();
  int index_of(char *table, char *value);    /* find index of attr in list */
  int hide_attribute(Item *item, bool hide); /* remove from result set */
private:
  List<Item> attr_list;
  bool hidden[256];    /* used to indicate attributes not returned to client */
};
```

The second helper class is a class encapsulates the expressions used in a query. These attributes are represented in the MySQL code as COND classes. The helper class, named Expression, provides a common (and simplified) interface to the COND classes. Listing 11-6 shows the header file for the Expression class.

Listing 11-6. *The Expression Class Header*

```
struct expr_node
{
  COND       *left_op;
  COND       *operation;
  COND       *right_op;
  expr_node *next;
};

class Expression
{
public:
  Expression(void);
  int remove_expression(int num);
  expr_node *get_expression(int num);
  int add_expression(bool append, expr_node *new_item);
  int num_expressions();
  int index_of(char *table, char *value);
  int reduce_expressions(TABLE *table);
  bool has_table(char *table);
  int convert(COND *mysql_expr);
private:
  expr_node *root;
  int num_expr;
};
```

I use a structure to contain the expressions in the form of left operand, operator, right operand. This is a more simplified approach than the expression tree that the MySQL classes represent, making it easier to read the optimizer code. The simpler approach also makes it easier to evaluate the conditions in an interactive debugger.

Note I omit some of the details of these helper classes in the text as they are very simple abstractions of calling the MySQL methods for the TABLE structure and the Item and Field classes. However, the files are included in the online chapter source code. The source code for this book is available for download at http://www.apress.com in the Source Code section.

These helper class and header files should be placed in the /sql directory and added to your project file. I'll show you how to do that in the "Compiling and Testing the Code" section.

Modifications to the Existing Code

There is one other minor modification necessary to implement the optimizer: we need to add the code to use the new Attribute and Expression classes. Open the query_tree.h header file and make the changes shown in Listing 11-7. As you can see, I've changed the where_expr and join_expr attributes to use the new Expression class. Likewise, I changed the attributes attribute to use the new Attribute class.

Listing 11-7. *Changes to the Query Tree Class*

```
struct query_node
{
  query_node();
  //query_node(const query_node &o);
  ~query_node();
  int                nodeid;
  int                parent_nodeid;
  bool               sub_query;
  int                child;
  query_node_type    node_type;
  type_join          join_type;
  join_con_type      join_cond;
  Expression         *where_expr;
  Expression         *join_expr;
  TABLE_LIST         *relations[MAXNODETABLES];
  bool               preempt_pipeline;
  Attribute          *attributes;
  query_node         *left;
  query_node         *right;
};
```

A number of methods also need to be added to the query tree class. Instead of listing every method and its implementation, I have included the rest of the query tree definition in Listing 11-8. This code is also added to the query_tree.h file.

Listing 11-8. *New Methods for the Query Tree Class*

```
query_node *root;              //The ROOT node of the tree

Query_tree(void);
~Query_tree(void);
int heuristic_optimization();
int cost_optimization();
bool distinct;

private:
  bool h_opt;            //has query been optimized (rules)?
  bool c_opt;            //has query been optimized (cost)?

  int push_projections(query_node *QN, query_node *pNode);
  query_node *find_projection(query_node *QN);
  bool is_leaf(query_node *QN);
  bool has_relation(query_node *QN, char *Table);
```

```
    bool has_attribute(query_node *QN, Item *a);
    int del_attribute(query_node *QN, Item *a);
    int push_restrictions(query_node *QN, query_node *pNode);
    query_node *find_restriction(query_node *QN);
    query_node *find_join(query_node *QN);
    int push_joins(query_node *QN, query_node *pNode);
    int prune_tree(query_node *prev, query_node *cur_node);
    int balance_joins(query_node *QN);
    int split_restrict_with_project(query_node *QN);
    int split_restrict_with_join(query_node *QN);
    int split_project_with_join(query_node *QN);
    bool find_table_in_tree(query_node *QN, char *tbl);
    bool find_table_in_expr(Expression *expr, char *tbl);
    bool find_attr_in_expr(Expression *expr, char *tbl, char *value);
    int apply_indexes(query_node *QN);
};
```

Notice that there are only two public methods: heuristic_optimization() and cost_optimization(). I have also added a public attribute named distinct that you can use to assist in implementing the distinct operation (see the exercises at the end of the chapter). The rest of the methods are the helper methods for the optimization code. I'll explain some of the more interesting ones and leave the mundane for you to explore.

Now that we have some helper classes to make the optimizer easier to implement, we need to incorporate them into the translation code that translates the MySQL internal query representation to the DBXP query tree. Open the sql_dbxp_parse.cc file and locate the build_query_tree() method. Listing 11-9 shows the changes necessary to add the new Attribute and Expression classes.

Listing 11-9. *Changes to the Build Query Tree Method*

```
/*
  Build Query Tree

  SYNOPSIS
    build_query_tree()
    THD *thd            IN the current thread
    LEX *lex            IN the pointer to the current parsed structure
    TABLE_LIST *tables  IN the list of tables identified in the query

  DESCRIPTION
    This method returns a converted MySQL internal representation (IR) of a
    query as a query_tree.

  RETURN VALUE
    Success = Query_tree * -- the root of the new query tree.
    Failed = NULL
```

```
*/
Query_tree *build_query_tree(THD *thd, LEX *lex, TABLE_LIST *tables)
{
  DBUG_ENTER("build_query_tree");
  Query_tree *qt = new Query_tree();
  Query_tree::query_node *qn =
    (Query_tree::query_node *)my_malloc(sizeof(Query_tree::query_node),
    MYF(MY_ZEROFILL | MY_WME));
  TABLE_LIST *table;
  int i = 0;
  Item *w;
  int num_tables = 0;

  /* create a new restrict node */
  qn->parent_nodeid = -1;
  qn->child = false;
  qn->join_type = (Query_tree::type_join) 0;
  qn->nodeid = 0;
  qn->node_type = (Query_tree::query_node_type) 2;
  qn->left = NULL;
  qn->right = NULL;
  qn->attributes = new Attribute();
  qn->where_expr = new Expression();
  qn->join_expr = new Expression();

  if(lex->select_lex.options & SELECT_DISTINCT)
  {
    //qt->set_distinct(true); /* placeholder for exercise */
  }

  /* Get the tables (relations) */
  i = 0;
  for(table = tables; table; table = table->next_local)
  {
    num_tables++;
    qn->relations[i] = table;
    i++;
  }

  /* prepare the fields (find associated tables) for query */
  List <Item> all_fields;
  if (setup_wild(thd, tables, thd->lex->select_lex.item_list, &all_fields, 1))
    DBUG_RETURN(NULL);
  if (setup_fields(thd, lex->select_lex.ref_pointer_array,
    lex->select_lex.item_list, 1, &all_fields, 1))
    DBUG_RETURN(NULL);
  qt->result_fields = lex->select_lex.item_list;
```

```
/* get the attributes from the raw query */
w = lex->select_lex.item_list.pop();
while (w != 0)
{
  qn->attributes->add_attribute(true, w);
  w = lex->select_lex.item_list.pop();
}

/* get the joins from the raw query */
if (num_tables > 0)  //indicates more than 1 table processed
  for(table = tables; table; table = table->next_local)
  {
    if (table->on_expr != 0)
      qn->join_expr->convert(thd, table->on_expr);
  }

/* get the expressions for the where clause */
qn->where_expr->convert(thd, lex->select_lex.where);

/* get the join conditions for the joins */
qn->join_expr->get_join_expr(qn->where_expr);

/* if there is a where clause, set node to restrict */
if (qn->where_expr->num_expressions() > 0)
  qn->node_type = (Query_tree::query_node_type) 1;

qt->root = qn;
DBUG_RETURN(qt);
}
```

It is at this point that the include files need adjusting. Normally when you need to access a class header or some other definition in a header file, you simply add an #include statement at the top of the header file for the new class you are creating. This is a typical C++ method of including header files. Unfortunately, this isn't a coding standard in MySQL. Specifically, if header files include definitions and implementation, you run into problems treating them like C++ headers.

To solve this problem, you need to move the #include "mysql_priv.h" statements to your source files, placing them above the #include for your header file. For example, the following statements appear at the top of the query_tree.cc file:

```
#include "mysql_priv.h"
#include "query_tree.h"
```

The query_tree.h header file includes the attribute and expression header files using

```
#include "attribute.h"
#include "expression.h"
```

This allows the code to be compiled in the correct order without re-creating anything in the mysql_priv.h file.

Caution If you encounter strange errors while compiling, check to make sure you are not including the `attribute`, `expression`, and `query_tree` header files in your compilation. The compiler will automatically include these files by following the include directives.

Details of the Heuristic Optimizer

The heuristic optimizer is implemented using the model of the rules described earlier. The methods used in the heuristic optimizer each implement some or all the rules. These methods are listed in Table 11-3.

Table 11-3. *Heuristic Methods in the Heuristic Optimizer*

Method	Description
split_restrict_with_join()	Searches the tree for nodes that have a restriction (has expressions) and a join expression. It divides the node into two nodes: one for the restriction and one for the join.
split_project_with_join()	Searches the tree for nodes that have a projection (has attributes) and a join expression. It divides the node into two nodes: one for the projection and one for the join.
split_restrict_with_project()	Searches the tree for nodes that have a restriction (has expressions) and a projection (has attributes). It divides the node into two nodes: one for the restriction and one for the projection.
find_restriction()	Searches the tree for a restriction node that is not already at a leaf.
push_restrictions()	Pushes the restrictions down the tree to the lowest node possible. It looks for situations where the restriction can reside at a leaf. This method is used with find_restrictions() in a loop (the loop ends when no more restrictions are found that are not already at a leaf).
find_projection()	Searches the tree for a projection node that is not already at a leaf.
push_projections()	Pushes the projections down the tree to the lowest node possible. It looks for situations where the projection can reside at a leaf or as a parent of a restriction. This method is used with find_projections() in a loop (the loop ends when no more projections are found that are not already at a leaf or the parent of a leaf that is a restriction).
find_join()	Searches the tree for a join node.
push_joins()	Pushes the joins down the tree to the nodes as parents to qualifying restrictions and/or projections (those that operate on the tables in the join).
prune_tree()	Identifies nodes in the tree that have been optimized away and are no longer valid (no attributes or expressions and not a join or sort) and deletes them.

The implementation of the heuristic optimizer reads very easily. Listing 11-10 shows the source code implementation for the heuristic_optimization() method.

Listing 11-10. *The DBXP Heuristic Optimization Method*

```
/*
  Perform heuristic optimization

  SYNOPSIS
    heuristic_optimization()

  DESCRIPTION
    This method performs heuristic optimization on the query tree. The
    operation is destructive in that it rearranges the original tree.

  RETURN VALUE
    Success = 0
    Failed = 1
*/
int Query_tree::heuristic_optimization()
{
  DBUG_ENTER("heuristic_optimization");
  query_node        *pNode;
  query_node        *nNode;

  h_opt = true;
  /*
    First, we have to correct the situation where restrict and
    project are grouped together in the same node.
  */
  split_restrict_with_join(root);
  split_project_with_join(root);
  split_restrict_with_project(root);

  /*
    Find a node with restrictions and push down the tree using
    a recursive call. continue until you get the same node twice.
    This means that the node cannot be pushed down any further.
  */
  pNode = find_restriction(root);
  while(pNode != 0)
  {
    push_restrictions(root, pNode);
    nNode = find_restriction(root);
```

```
  /*
    If a node is found, save a reference to it unless it is
    either the same node as the last node found or
    it is a leaf node. This is done so that we can ensure we
    continue searching down the tree visiting each node once.
  */
  if(nNode != 0)
  {
    if(nNode->nodeid == pNode->nodeid)
      pNode = 0;
    else if(is_leaf(nNode))
      pNode = 0;
    else
      pNode = nNode;
  }
}


/*
  Find a node with projections and push down the tree using
  a recursive call. Continue until you get the same node twice.
  This means that the node cannot be pushed down any further.
*/
pNode = find_projection(root);
while(pNode != 0)
{
  push_projections(root, pNode);
  nNode = find_projection(root);
  /*
    If a node is found, save a reference to it unless it is
    either the same node as the last node found or
    it is a leaf node. This is done so that we can ensure we
    continue searching down the tree visiting each node once.
  */
  if(nNode != 0)
  {
    if(nNode->nodeid == pNode->nodeid)
      pNode = 0;
    else if(is_leaf(nNode))
      pNode = 0;
    else
      pNode = nNode;
  }
}

/*
  Find a join node and push it down the tree using
  a recursive call. Continue until you get the same node twice.
  This means that the node cannot be pushed down any further.
```

```
*/
pNode = find_join(root);
while(pNode != 0)
{
  push_joins(root, pNode);
  nNode = find_join(root);
  /*
    If a node is found, save a reference to it unless it is
    either the same node as the last node found or
    it is a leaf node. This is done so that we can ensure we
    continue searching down the tree visiting each node once.
  */
  if(nNode != 0)
  {
    if(nNode->nodeid == pNode->nodeid)
      pNode = 0;
    else if(is_leaf(nNode))
      pNode = 0;
    else
      pNode = nNode;
  }
  else
    pNode = nNode;
}

/*
  Prune the tree of "blank" nodes
  Blank Nodes are:
   1) projections without attributes that have at least 1 child
   2) restrictions without expressions
   BUT...Can't delete a node that has TWO children!
*/
prune_tree(0, root);

/*
  Lastly, check to see if this has the DISTINCT option.
  If so, create a new node that is a DISTINCT operation.
*/
if(distinct && (root->node_type != qntDistinct))
{
  int i;
  pNode = (query_node*)my_malloc(sizeof(query_node),
          MYF(MY_ZEROFILL | MY_WME));
  pNode->sub_query = 0;
  pNode->attributes = 0;
  pNode->join_cond = jcUN;  /* (join_con_type) 0; */
  pNode->join_type = jnUNKNOWN;  /* (type_join) 0; */
```

```
      pNode->left = root;
      pNode->right = 0;
      for(i = 0; i < MAXNODETABLES; i++)
        pNode->relations[i] = NULL;
      pNode->nodeid = 90125;
      pNode->child = LEFTCHILD;
      root->parent_nodeid = 90125;
      root->child = LEFTCHILD;
      pNode->parent_nodeid = -1;
      pNode->node_type = qntDistinct;
      pNode->attributes = new Attribute();
      pNode->where_expr = new Expression();
      pNode->join_expr = new Expression();
      root = pNode;
    }
  DBUG_RETURN(0);
}
```

Notice the loops for locating restrictions, projections, and joins. The code is designed to walk through the tree using a preorder traversal, applying the rules until there are no more conditions that violate the rules (i.e., no "bad" node placements).

The following listings show some of the source code for the major methods in the heuristic_optimization() method as described earlier. To save space, I have omitted listing the lesser helper methods as they are simple abstractions of the MySQL structure and class methods. You should download the source code for this chapter and examine the other helper methods to see how they work.

The split_restrict_with_join() method searches the tree for joins that have where expressions (thus are both joins and restrictions) and breaks them into two nodes: a join and a restrict node. Listing 11-11 shows the source code for this method.

Listing 11-11. *Split Restrict With Join*

```
/*
  Split restrictions that have joins.

  SYNOPSIS
    split_restrict_with_join()
    query_node *QN IN the node to operate on

  DESCRIPTION
    This method looks for joins that have where expressions (thus are both
    joins and restrictions) and breaks them into two nodes.

  NOTES
    This is a RECURSIVE method!

  RETURN VALUE
    Success = 0
    Failed = 1
```

```
*/
int Query_tree::split_restrict_with_join(query_node *QN)
{
  int j = 0;
  int i = 0;

  DBUG_ENTER("split_restrict_with_join");
  if(QN != 0)
  {
    if(((QN->join_expr->num_expressions() > 0) &&
       (QN->where_expr->num_expressions() > 0)) &&
        ((QN->node_type == qntJoin) || (QN->node_type == qntRestrict)))
    {
      bool isleft = true;
      /*
         Create a new node and:
           1) Move the where expressions to the new node.
           2) Set the new node's children = current node children
           3) Set the new node's relations = current node relations.
           4) Set current node's left or right child = new node;
           5) Set new node's id = current id + 200;
            6) set parent id, etc.
           7) determine which table needs to be used for the
              restrict node.
      */
      query_node *new_node = (query_node*)my_malloc(sizeof(query_node),
                          MYF(MY_ZEROFILL | MY_WME));
      new_node->node_type = qntRestrict;
      new_node->parent_nodeid = QN->nodeid;
      new_node->nodeid = QN->nodeid + 200;
      new_node->where_expr = QN->where_expr;
      new_node->join_expr = new Expression();
      QN->where_expr = new Expression();

      /*
        Loop through tables and move table that matches
        to the new node
      */
      for(i = 0; i < MAXNODETABLES; i++)
      {
        if (QN->relations[i] != NULL)
        {
          if (find_table_in_expr(new_node->where_expr,
                QN->relations[i]->table_name))
          {
            new_node->relations[j] = QN->relations[i];
            j++;
```

```
      if (i != 0)
        isleft = false;
      QN->relations[i] = NULL;
    }
  }
}

/* set children to point to balance of tree */
new_node->right = 0;
if (isleft)
{
  new_node->child = LEFTCHILD;
  new_node->left = QN->left;
  QN->left = new_node;
}
else
{
  new_node->child = RIGHTCHILD;
  new_node->left = QN->right;
  QN->right = new_node;
}
if (new_node->left)
  new_node->left->parent_nodeid = new_node->nodeid;
j = QN->attributes->num_attributes();
if ((QN->node_type == qntJoin) && (j > 0))
{
  Attribute *attribs = 0;
  Item * attr;
  int ii = 0;
  int jj = 0;
  if ((QN->attributes->num_attributes() == 1) &&
      (strcasecmp("*",
      ((Field *)QN->attributes->get_attribute(0))->field_name) == 0))
  {
    new_node->attributes = new Attribute();
    new_node->attributes->add_attribute(j,
      QN->attributes->get_attribute(0));
  }
  else
  {
    attribs = new Attribute();
    for (i = 0; i < (int)new_node->relations[0]->table->s->fields; i++)
    {
      Item *f = (Item *)new_node->relations[0]->table->field[i];
      attribs->add_attribute(true, (Item *)f);
    }
    j = attribs->num_attributes();
```

```
          new_node->attributes = new Attribute();
          for (i = 0; i < j; i++)
          {
            attr = attribs->get_attribute(i);
            jj = QN->attributes->index_of(
              (char *)((Field *)attr)->table->s->table_name.str,
              (char *)((Field *)attr)->field_name);
            if (jj > -1)
            {
              new_node->attributes->add_attribute(ii, attr);
              ii++;
              QN->attributes->remove_attribute(jj);
            }
            else if (find_attr_in_expr(QN->join_expr,
             (char *)((Field *)attr)->table->s->table_name.str,
             (char *)((Field *)attr)->field_name))
            {
              new_node->attributes->add_attribute(ii, attr);
              new_node->attributes->hide_attribute(attr, true);
              ii++;
            }
          }
        }
      }
      else
      {
        QN->node_type = qntJoin;
        new_node->attributes = new Attribute();
      }
    }
    split_restrict_with_join(QN->left);
    split_restrict_with_join(QN->right);
  }
  DBUG_RETURN(0);
}
```

The split_project_with_join() method searches the tree for joins that have attributes
(thus are both joins and projections) and breaks them into two nodes: a join and a project
node. Listing 11-12 shows the source code for this method.

Listing 11-12. *Split Project With Join*

```
/*
  Split projections that have joins.

  SYNOPSIS
    split_project_with_join()
    query_node *QN IN the node to operate on
```

```
    DESCRIPTION
      This method looks for joins that have attributes (thus are both
      joins and projections) and breaks them into two nodes.

    NOTES
      This is a RECURSIVE method!

    RETURN VALUE
      Success = 0
      Failed = 1
*/
int Query_tree::split_project_with_join(query_node *QN)
{
  int j = 0;
  int i;

  DBUG_ENTER("split_project_with_join");
  if(QN != 0)
  {
    if((QN->join_expr->num_expressions() > 0) &&
       ((QN->node_type == qntJoin) || (QN->node_type == qntProject)))
    {
      /*
        Create a new node and:
          1) Move the where expressions to the new node.
          2) Set the new node's children = current node children
          3) Set the new node's relations = current node relations.
          4) Set current node's left or right child = new node;
          5) Set new node's id = current id + 300;
          6) set parent id, etc.
      */
      QN->node_type = qntJoin;
      if (QN->left == 0)
      {
        query_node *new_node = (query_node*)my_malloc(sizeof(query_node),
                              MYF(MY_ZEROFILL | MY_WME));
        new_node->node_type = qntProject;
        new_node->parent_nodeid = QN->nodeid;
        new_node->nodeid = QN->nodeid + 300;
        for(i = 0; i < MAXNODETABLES; i++)
          new_node->relations[i] = 0;
        new_node->relations[0] = QN->relations[0];
        QN->relations[0] = 0;
        new_node->left = QN->left;
        QN->left = new_node;
        new_node->right = 0;
        new_node->child = LEFTCHILD;
```

```
if (new_node->left != 0)
  new_node->left->parent_nodeid = new_node->nodeid;
j = QN->attributes->num_attributes();
new_node->attributes = new Attribute();
new_node->where_expr = new Expression();
new_node->join_expr = new Expression();
if ((j == 1) &&
    (strcasecmp("*", QN->attributes->get_attribute(0)->name) == 0))
{
  new_node->attributes = new Attribute();
  new_node->attributes->add_attribute(j, QN->attributes->get_attribute(0));
  if (QN->right != 0)
    QN->attributes->remove_attribute(0);
}
else if (j > 0)
{
  Attribute *attribs = 0;
  Item * attr;
  int ii = 0;
  int jj = 0;
  attribs = new Attribute();
  for (i = 0; i < (int)new_node->relations[0]->table->s->fields; i++)
  {
    Field *f = new_node->relations[0]->table->field[i];
    attribs->add_attribute(true, (Item *)f);
  }
  j = attribs->num_attributes();
  for (i = 0; i < j; i++)
  {
    attr = attribs->get_attribute(i);
    jj = QN->attributes->index_of(
      (char *)((Field *)attr)->table->s->table_name.str,
      (char *)((Field *)attr)->field_name);
    if (jj > -1)
    {
      new_node->attributes->add_attribute(ii, attr);
      ii++;
      QN->attributes->remove_attribute(jj);
    }
    else if (find_attr_in_expr(QN->join_expr,
      (char *)((Field *)attr)->table->s->table_name.str,
      (char *)((Field *)attr)->field_name))
    {
      new_node->attributes->add_attribute(ii, attr);
      new_node->attributes->hide_attribute(attr, true);
      ii++;
    }
```

```
            }
          }
        }
        if (QN->right == 0)
        {
          query_node *new_node = (query_node*)my_malloc(sizeof(query_node),
                                  MYF(MY_ZEROFILL | MY_WME));
          new_node->node_type = qntProject;
          new_node->parent_nodeid = QN->nodeid;
          new_node->nodeid = QN->nodeid + 400;
          for(i = 0; i < MAXNODETABLES; i++)
            new_node->relations[0] = 0;
          new_node->relations[0] = QN->relations[1];
          QN->relations[1] = 0;
          new_node->left = QN->right;
          QN->right = new_node;
          new_node->right = 0;
          new_node->child = RIGHTCHILD;
          if (new_node->left != 0)
            new_node->left->parent_nodeid = new_node->nodeid;
          j = QN->attributes->num_attributes();
          new_node->attributes = new Attribute();
          new_node->where_expr = new Expression();
          new_node->join_expr = new Expression();
          if ((j == 1) &&
              (strcasecmp("*", (char *)QN->attributes->get_attribute(0)->name) == 0))
          {
            new_node->attributes = new Attribute();
            new_node->attributes->add_attribute(j, QN->attributes->get_attribute(0));
            QN->attributes->remove_attribute(0);
          }
          else if (j > 0)
          {
            Attribute *attribs = 0;
            Item * attr;
            int ii = 0;
            int jj = 0;
            attribs = new Attribute();
            for (i = 0; i < (int)new_node->relations[0]->table->s->fields; i++)
            {
              Field *f = new_node->relations[0]->table->field[i];
              attribs->add_attribute(true, (Item *)f);
            }
            j = attribs->num_attributes();
            new_node->attributes = new Attribute();
            for (i = 0; i < j; i++)
            {
```

```
            attr = attribs->get_attribute(i);
            jj = QN->attributes->index_of(
              (char *)((Field *)attr)->table->s->table_name.str,
              (char *)((Field *)attr)->field_name);
            if (jj > -1)
            {
              new_node->attributes->add_attribute(ii, attr);
              ii++;
              QN->attributes->remove_attribute(jj);
            }
            else if (find_attr_in_expr(QN->join_expr,
              (char *)((Field *)attr)->table->s->table_name.str,
              (char *)((Field *)attr)->field_name))
            {
              new_node->attributes->add_attribute(ii, attr);
              new_node->attributes->hide_attribute(attr, true);
              ii++;
            }
          }
        }
      }
    }
    split_project_with_join(QN->left);
    split_project_with_join(QN->right);
  }
  DBUG_RETURN(0);
}
```

The split_restrict_with_project() method searches the tree for restrictions that have attributes (thus are both projections and restrictions) and breaks them into two nodes: a restrict and a project node. Listing 11-13 shows the source code for this method.

Listing 11-13. *Split Restrict With Project*

```
/*
  Split restrictions that have attributes (projections).

  SYNOPSIS
    split_restrict_with_project()
    query_node *QN IN the node to operate on

  DESCRIPTION
    This method looks for restrictions that have attributes (thus are both
    projections and restrictions) and breaks them into two nodes.

  NOTES
    This is a RECURSIVE method!
```

```
      RETURN VALUE
        Success = 0
        Failed = 1
*/
int Query_tree::split_restrict_with_project(query_node *QN)
{
  DBUG_ENTER("split_restrict_with_project");
  if(QN != 0)
  {
    if(((QN->attributes->num_attributes() > 0) &&
      (QN->where_expr->num_expressions() > 0)) &&
      ((QN->node_type == qntProject) || (QN->node_type == qntRestrict)))
    {
      /*
        Create a new node and:
          1) Move the expressions to the new node.
          2) Set the new node's children = current node children
          3) Set the new node's relations = current node relations.
          4) Set current node's left child = new node;
          5) Set new node's id = current id + 1000;
          6) set parent id, etc.
      */
      query_node *new_node = (query_node*)my_malloc(sizeof(query_node),
                             MYF(MY_ZEROFILL | MY_WME));
      new_node->child = LEFTCHILD;
      new_node->node_type = qntRestrict;
      if(new_node->node_type == qntJoin)
      {
        new_node->join_cond = QN->join_cond;
        new_node->join_type = QN->join_type;
      }
      QN->node_type = qntProject;
      new_node->attributes = new Attribute();
      new_node->where_expr = QN->where_expr;
      new_node->join_expr = new Expression();
      QN->where_expr = new Expression();
      new_node->left = QN->left;
      new_node->right = QN->right;
      new_node->parent_nodeid = QN->nodeid;
      new_node->nodeid = QN->nodeid + 1000;
      if(new_node->left)
        new_node->left->parent_nodeid = new_node->nodeid;
      if(new_node->right)
        new_node->right->parent_nodeid = new_node->nodeid;
      for(int i = 0; i < MAXNODETABLES; i++)
      {
        new_node->relations[i] = QN->relations[i];
```

```
      QN->relations[i] = NULL;
    }
    QN->left = new_node;
    QN->right = 0;
  }
  split_restrict_with_project(QN->left);
  split_restrict_with_project(QN->right);
  }
  DBUG_RETURN(0);
}
```

The find_restriction() method searches the tree from the starting node (QN) for the next restriction in the tree. If a restriction is found, a pointer to the node is returned; otherwise, the method returns NULL. Listing 11-14 shows the source code for this method.

Listing 11-14. *Find Restriction*

```
/*
  Find a restriction in the subtree.

  SYNOPSIS
    find_restriction()
    query_node *QN IN the node to operate on

  DESCRIPTION
    This method looks for a node containing a restriction and returns the node
    pointer.

  NOTES
    This is a RECURSIVE method!
    This finds the first restriction and is biased to the left tree.

  RETURN VALUE
    Success = query_node * the node located
    Failed = NULL
*/
Query_tree::query_node *Query_tree::find_restriction(query_node *QN)
{
  DBUG_ENTER("find_restriction");
  query_node   *N;

  N = 0;
  if(QN != 0)
  {
    /*
      A restriction is a node marked as restrict and
      has at least one expression
    */
```

```
      if (QN->where_expr->num_expressions() > 0)
        N = QN;
      else
      {
        N = find_restriction(QN->left);
        if(N == 0)
          N = find_restriction(QN->right);
      }
    }
  }
  DBUG_RETURN(N);
}
```

The push_restriction() method searches the tree from the starting node (QN) and pushes the restriction node (pNode) down the tree to nodes that contain the relations specified in the restriction. Listing 11-15 shows the source code for this method.

Listing 11-15. *Push Restrictions*

```
/*
  Push restrictions down the tree.

  SYNOPSIS
    push_restrictions()
    query_node *QN IN the node to operate on
    query_node *pNode IN the node containing the restriction attributes

  DESCRIPTION
    This method looks for restrictions and pushes them down the tree to nodes
    that contain the relations specified.

  NOTES
    This is a RECURSIVE method!
    This finds the first restriction and is biased to the left tree.

  RETURN VALUE
    Success = 0
    Failed = 1
*/
int Query_tree::push_restrictions(query_node *QN, query_node *pNode)
{
  query_node      *NewQN;

  DBUG_ENTER("push_restrictions");
  if((QN != 0) && (pNode != 0) && (pNode->left != 0))
  {
    /*
```

```
Conditions:
   1) QN is a join node
   2) QN is a project node
   3) QN is a restrict node
   4) All other nodes types are ignored.

Methods:
   1) if join or project and the children are not already restrictions
      add a new node and put where clause in new node else
      see if you can combine the child node and this one
   2) if the node has the table and it is a join,
      create a new node below it and push the restriction
      to that node.
   4) if the node is a restriction and has the table,
      just add the expression to the node's expression list
*/


/* if projection, move node down tree */
if((QN->nodeid != pNode->nodeid) && (QN->node_type == qntProject))
{
  if (QN->left != 0)
  {
    QN->left = (query_node*)my_malloc(sizeof(query_node),
               MYF(MY_ZEROFILL | MY_WME));
    NewQN = QN->left;
    NewQN->left = 0;
  }
  else
  {
    NewQN = QN->left;
    QN->left = (query_node*)my_malloc(sizeof(query_node),
               MYF(MY_ZEROFILL | MY_WME));
    QN->left->left = NewQN;
    NewQN = QN->left;
  }
  NewQN->sub_query = 0;
  NewQN->join_cond = jcUN;  /* (join_con_type) 0; */
  NewQN->join_type = jnUNKNOWN;  /* (type_join) 0; */
  NewQN->right = 0;
  for(long i = 0; i < MAXNODETABLES; i++)
    NewQN->relations[i] = 0;
  NewQN->nodeid = QN->nodeid + 1;
  NewQN->parent_nodeid = QN->nodeid;
  NewQN->node_type = qntRestrict;
  NewQN->attributes = new Attribute();
  NewQN->where_expr = new Expression();
  NewQN->join_expr = new Expression();
```

```
      if (pNode->relations[0])
        NewQN->where_expr->reduce_expressions(pNode->relations[0]->table);
      if ((QN->relations[0] != NULL) && (QN->relations[0] == pNode->relations[0]))
        if (QN->relations[0])
          if (find_table_in_expr(pNode->where_expr, QN->relations[0]->table_name))
          {
            NewQN->relations[0] = QN->relations[0];
            QN->relations[0] = 0;
          }
      else
      {
        if (pNode->relations[0])
          if (find_table_in_tree(QN->left, pNode->relations[0]->table_name))
            NewQN->relations[0] = 0;
        pNode->where_expr = NULL;
        pNode->relations[0] = 0;
      }
    }
    /* if join, move restrict node down tree */
    else if((QN->nodeid != pNode->nodeid) &&
      ((QN->left == 0) || (QN->right == 0)) &&
      (QN->node_type == qntJoin))
    {
      if(QN->relations[0] != 0)
      {
        QN->left = (query_node*)my_malloc(sizeof(query_node),
                   MYF(MY_ZEROFILL | MY_WME));
        NewQN = QN->left;
        NewQN->sub_query = 0;
        NewQN->join_cond = jcUN;   /* (join_con_type) 0; */
        NewQN->join_type = jnUNKNOWN;   /* (type_join) 0; */
        NewQN->left = 0;
        NewQN->right = 0;
        for(long i = 0; i < MAXNODETABLES; i++)
          NewQN->relations[i] = 0;
        NewQN->nodeid = QN->nodeid + 1;
        NewQN->parent_nodeid = QN->nodeid;
        NewQN->node_type = qntRestrict;
        NewQN->attributes = new Attribute();
        NewQN->where_expr = new Expression();
        NewQN->join_expr = new Expression();
        NewQN->relations[0] = QN->relations[0];
        QN->relations[0] = 0;
        if (pNode->relations[0])
          NewQN->where_expr->reduce_expressions(pNode->relations[0]->table);
      }
```

```
      else if(QN->relations[1] != 0)
      {
        QN->right = (query_node*)my_malloc(sizeof(query_node),
                   MYF(MY_ZEROFILL | MY_WME));
        NewQN = QN->left;
        NewQN->sub_query = 0;
        NewQN->join_cond = jcUN;   /* (join_con_type) 0; */
        NewQN->join_type = jnUNKNOWN;   /* (type_join) 0; */
        NewQN->left = 0;
        NewQN->right = 0;
        for(long i = 0; i < MAXNODETABLES; i++)
          NewQN->relations[i] = 0;
      }
      NewQN->nodeid = QN->nodeid + 1;
      NewQN->parent_nodeid = QN->nodeid;
      NewQN->node_type = qntRestrict;
      NewQN->attributes = new Attribute();
      NewQN->where_expr = new Expression();
      NewQN->join_expr = new Expression();
      NewQN->relations[0] = QN->relations[1];
      QN->relations[1] = 0;
      NewQN->where_expr->reduce_expressions(pNode->relations[0]->table);
    }
    push_restrictions(QN->left, pNode);
    push_restrictions(QN->right, pNode);
  }
  DBUG_RETURN(0);
}
```

The find_projection() method searches the tree from the starting node (QN) for the next projection in the tree. If a projection is found, a pointer to the node is returned; otherwise, the method returns NULL. Listing 11-16 shows the source code for this method.

Listing 11-16. *Find Projection*

```
/*
  Find a projection in the tree

  SYNOPSIS
    find_projection()
    query_node *QN IN the node to operate on

  DESCRIPTION
    This method looks for a node containing a projection and returns the node
    pointer.
```

```
  NOTES
    This finds the first projection and is biased to the left tree.
    This is a RECURSIVE method!

  RETURN VALUE
    Success = query_node * the node located or NULL for not found
    Failed = NULL
*/
Query_tree::query_node *Query_tree::find_projection(query_node *QN)
{
  DBUG_ENTER("find_projection");
  query_node    *N;

  N = 0;
  if(QN != 0)
  {
    /*
      A projection is a node marked as project and
      has at least one attribute
    */
    if((QN->node_type == qntProject) &&
       (QN->attributes != 0))
      N = QN;
    else
    {
      N = find_projection(QN->left);
      if(N == 0)
        N = find_projection(QN->right);
    }
  }
  DBUG_RETURN(N);
}
```

The push_projection() method searches the tree from the starting node (QN) and pushes
the projection node (pNode) down the tree to nodes that contain the relations specified in the
projection. Listing 11-17 shows the source code for this method.

Listing 11-17. *Push Projections*

```
/*
  Push projections down the tree.

  SYNOPSIS
    push_projections()
    query_node *QN IN the node to operate on
    query_node *pNode IN the node containing the projection attributes
```

```
   DESCRIPTION
     This method looks for projections and pushes them down the tree to nodes
     that contain the relations specified.

   NOTES
     This is a RECURSIVE method!

   RETURN VALUE
     Success = 0
     Failed = 1
*/
int Query_tree::push_projections(query_node *QN, query_node *pNode)
{
  DBUG_ENTER("push_projections");
  Item *   a;
  int        i;
  int        j;

  if((QN != 0) && (pNode != 0))
  {
    if((QN->nodeid != pNode->nodeid) &&
       (QN->node_type == qntProject))
    {
      i = 0;
      j = QN->attributes->num_attributes();

      /* move attributes to new node */
      while(i < j)
      {
        a = QN->attributes->get_attribute(i);
        if(has_relation(QN,
          (char *)((Field *)a)->table->s->table_name.str))
        {
          if(!has_attribute(QN, a))
            insert_attribute(QN, a);
          del_attribute(pNode, a);
        }
        i++;
      }
    }
    if(pNode->attributes->num_attributes() != 0)
    {
      push_projections(QN->left, pNode);
      push_projections(QN->right, pNode);
    }
  }
  DBUG_RETURN(0);
}
```

The find_join () method searches the tree from the starting node (QN) for the next join in the tree. If a join is found, a pointer to the node is returned; otherwise, the method returns NULL. Listing 11-18 shows the source code for this method.

Listing 11-18. *Find Join*

```
/*
  Find a join in the subtree.

  SYNOPSIS
    find_restriction()
    query_node *QN IN the node to operate on

  DESCRIPTION
    This method looks for a node containing a join and returns the
    node pointer.

  NOTES
    This is a RECURSIVE method!
    This finds the first restriction and is biased to the left tree.

  RETURN VALUE
    Success = query_node * the node located
    Failed = NULL
*/
Query_tree::query_node *Query_tree::find_join(query_node *QN)
{
  DBUG_ENTER("find_join");
  query_node              *N;
  N = 0;

  if(QN != 0)
  {
    /*
      if this is a restrict node or a restrict node with
      at least one expression it could be an unprocessed join
      because the default node type is restrict
    */
    if(((QN->node_type == qntRestrict) ||
      (QN->node_type == qntRestrict)) && (QN->join_expr->num_expressions() > 0))
      N = QN;
    else
    {
      N = find_join(QN->left);
      if(N == 0)
        N = find_join(QN->right);
    }
```

```
    }
    DBUG_RETURN(N);
}
```

The push_joins() method searches the tree from the starting node (QN) and pushes the
join node (pNode) down the tree to a position where the join is the parent of two nodes that
contain the relations specified in the children of the join. Listing 11-19 shows the source code
for this method.

Listing 11-19. *Push Joins*

```
/*
  Push joins down the tree.

  SYNOPSIS
    push_restrictions()
    query_node *QN IN the node to operate on
    query_node *pNode IN the node containing the join

  DESCRIPTION
    This method looks for theta joins and pushes them down the tree to the
    parent of two nodes that contain the relations specified.

  NOTES
    This is a RECURSIVE method!

  RETURN VALUE
    Success = 0
    Failed = 1
*/
int Query_tree::push_joins(query_node *QN, query_node *pNode)
{
  DBUG_ENTER("push_joins");
  COND *lField;
  COND *rField;
  expr_node *node;

  if(!pNode->join_expr)
    DBUG_RETURN(0);
  node = pNode->join_expr->get_expression(0);
  if (!node)
    DBUG_RETURN(0);      .
  lField = node->left_op;
  rField = node->right_op;

  /* Node must have expressions and not be null */
  if((QN != NULL) && (pNode != NULL) &&
     (pNode->join_expr->num_expressions() > 0))
```

```
{
  /* check to see if tables in join condition exist */
  if((QN->nodeid != pNode->nodeid) &&
    (QN->node_type == qntJoin) &&
     QN->join_expr->num_expressions() == 0 &&
     ((has_relation(QN->left,
       (char *)((Field *)lField)->table->s->table_name.str) &&
      has_relation(QN->right,
        (char *)((Field *)rField)->table->s->table_name.str)) ||
     (has_relation(QN->left,
       (char *)((Field *)rField)->table->s->table_name.str) &&
      has_relation(QN->right,
        (char *)((Field *)lField)->table->s->table_name.str))))
  {
    /* move the expression */
    QN->join_expr = pNode->join_expr;
    pNode->join_expr = new Expression();
    QN->join_type = jnINNER;
    QN->join_cond = jcON;
  }
  push_joins(QN->left, pNode);
  push_joins(QN->right, pNode);
  }
  DBUG_RETURN(0);
}
```

The prune_tree() method searches the tree for blank nodes (nodes that have no longer have any operation or function) that are a result of performing heuristic optimization on the tree and deletes them. Listing 11-20 shows the source code for this method.

Listing 11-20. *Prune Tree*

```
/*
  Prune the tree of dead limbs.

  SYNOPSIS
    prune_tree()
    query_node *prev IN the previous node (parent)
    query_node *cur_node IN the current node pointer (used to delete).

  DESCRIPTION
    This method looks for blank nodes that are a result of performing
    heuristic optimization on the tree and deletes them.
```

```
  NOTES
    This is a RECURSIVE method!

  RETURN VALUE
    Success = 0
    Failed = 1
*/
int Query_tree::prune_tree(query_node *prev, query_node *cur_node)
{
  DBUG_ENTER("prune_tree");
  if(cur_node != 0)
  {
    /*
      Blank Nodes are 1) projections without attributes
      that have at least 1 child, or 2) restrictions
      without expressions
    */
    if((((cur_node->node_type == qntProject) &&
      (cur_node->attributes->num_attributes() == 0)) ||
      ((cur_node->node_type == qntRestrict) &&
      (cur_node->where_expr->num_expressions() == 0))) &&
      ((cur_node->left == 0) || (cur_node->right == 0)))
    {
      /*
        Redirect the pointers for the nodes above and
        below this node in the tree.
      */
      if(prev == 0)
      {
        if(cur_node->left == 0)
        {
          cur_node->right->parent_nodeid = -1;
          root = cur_node->right;
        }
        else
        {
          cur_node->left->parent_nodeid = -1;
          root = cur_node->left;
        }
        my_free((gptr)cur_node, MYF(0));
        cur_node = root;
      }
```

```
        else
        {
          if(prev->left == cur_node)
          {
            if(cur_node->left == 0)
            {
              prev->left = cur_node->right;
              if (cur_node->right != NULL)
                cur_node->right->parent_nodeid = prev->nodeid;
            }
            else
            {
              prev->left = cur_node->left;
              if (cur_node->left != NULL)
                cur_node->left->parent_nodeid = prev->nodeid;
            }
            my_free((gptr)cur_node, MYF(0));
            cur_node = prev->left;
          }
          else
          {
            if(cur_node->left == 0)
            {
              prev->right = cur_node->right;
              if (cur_node->right != NULL)
                cur_node->right->parent_nodeid = prev->nodeid;
            }
            else
            {
              prev->right = cur_node->left;
              if (cur_node->left != NULL)
                cur_node->left->parent_nodeid = prev->nodeid;
            }
            my_free((gptr)cur_node, MYF(0));
            cur_node = prev->right;
          }
        }
        prune_tree(prev, cur_node);
      }
      else
      {
        prune_tree(cur_node, cur_node->left);
        prune_tree(cur_node, cur_node->right);
      }
    }
  DBUG_RETURN(0);
}
```

Compiling and Testing the Code

If you haven't already done so, download the source code for this chapter and place the files in the /sql directory off the root of your source tree. Spend a few moments looking through the source code so that you are familiar with the methods. Taking the time to look through the code now will help should you need to debug the code to work with your configuration or if you want to add other enhancements or work the exercises. Once you have all of the source code files downloaded and have examined the code, you must add the files to your makefiles (in Linux) and project files (in Windows). See the sections "Adding the Files to the Makefile on Linux" and "Adding the Files to the mysqld Project on Windows" in Chapter 10 for the details on how to do this for your operating system. You will be adding the attribute and expression helper source files to your project. Once you have the files added to the project, compile the server and ensure there are no compilation errors.

Running the Tests

Once you have the new code installed and compiled, you can run the server and perform the tests. You can run the test you created earlier or you can enter the commands in a MySQL client utility. Listing 11-21 shows the expected output of running the commands listed in the test.

Listing 11-21. *Example Test Runs*

```
mysql> SELECT DBXP * FROM staff;
```

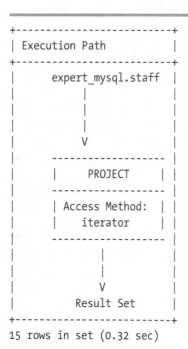

```
+--------------------------+
| Execution Path           |
+--------------------------+
|      expert_mysql.staff  |
|          |               |
|          |               |
|          |               |
|          V               |
|    ------------------     |
|    |    PROJECT    |  |   |
|    ------------------     |
|    | Access Method: |  |  |
|    |    iterator    |  |  |
|    ------------------     |
|          |               |
|          |               |
|          V               |
|       Result Set         |
+--------------------------+
15 rows in set (0.32 sec)
```

```
mysql> SELECT DBXP id FROM staff WHERE staff.id = '123456789';
```

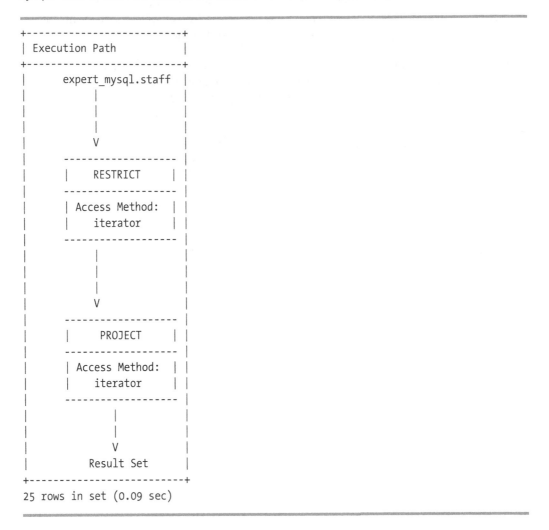

```
+-------------------------+
| Execution Path          |
+-------------------------+
|      expert_mysql.staff |
|            |            |
|            |            |
|            |            |
|            V            |
|      ------------------ |
|      |    RESTRICT    | |
|      ------------------ |
|      | Access Method: | |
|      |    iterator    | |
|      ------------------ |
|            |            |
|            |            |
|            |            |
|            V            |
|      ------------------ |
|      |    PROJECT     | |
|      ------------------ |
|      | Access Method: | |
|      |    iterator    | |
|      ------------------ |
|            |            |
|            |            |
|            V            |
|       Result Set        |
+-------------------------+
25 rows in set (0.09 sec)
```

```
mysql> SELECT DBXP id, dir_name FROM staff, directorate
mysql> WHERE staff.dno = directorate.dnumber;
```

```
+--------------------------------------------------+
| Execution Path                                   |
+--------------------------------------------------+
|        expert_mysql.staff                        |
|             |                                    |
|             |                                    |
|             |                                    |
|             V                                    |
```

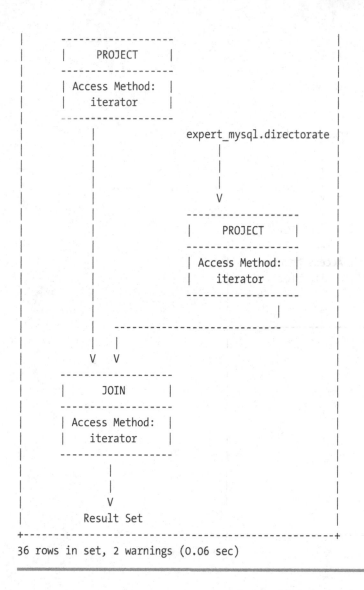

```
|        ------------------                                 |
|        |    PROJECT     |                                 |
|        ------------------                                 |
|        | Access Method: |                                 |
|        |    iterator    |                                 |
|        ------------------                                 |
|                |              expert_mysql.directorate |
|                |                          |              |
|                |                          |              |
|                |                          |              |
|                |                          V              |
|                |              ------------------         |
|                |              |    PROJECT     |         |
|                |              ------------------         |
|                |              | Access Method: |         |
|                |              |    iterator    |         |
|                |              ------------------         |
|                |                       |                 |
|                |      --------------------------         |
|                |      |                                  |
|                |      |                                  |
|                V      V                                  |
|        ------------------                                 |
|        |      JOIN      |                                 |
|        ------------------                                 |
|        | Access Method: |                                 |
|        |    iterator    |                                 |
|        ------------------                                 |
|                |                                          |
|                |                                          |
|                V                                          |
|          Result Set                                       |
+----------------------------------------------------------+
```

36 rows in set, 2 warnings (0.06 sec)

```
mysql> SELECT DBXP * FROM staff JOIN tasking ON staff.id = tasking.id
mysql> WHERE staff.id = '123456789';
```

```
+------------------------------------------------+
| Execution Path                                 |
+------------------------------------------------+
|        expert_mysql.staff                      |
|                |                               |
|                |                               |
|                |                               |
|                V                               |
```

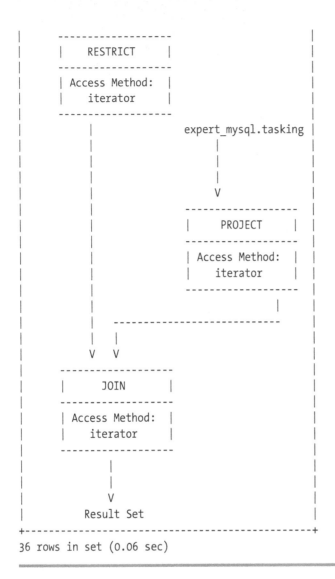

```
|    ------------------                                    |
|    |   RESTRICT    |                                     |
|    ------------------                                    |
|    | Access Method: |                                    |
|    |    iterator    |                                    |
|    ------------------          expert_mysql.tasking |
|            |                            |               |
|            |                            |               |
|            |                            |               |
|            |                            V               |
|            |                   ------------------        |
|            |                   |    PROJECT    |  |
|            |                   ------------------        |
|            |                   | Access Method: |  |
|            |                   |    iterator    |  |
|            |                   ------------------        |
|            |                            |     |  |
|            |      ---------------------------    |
|        |   |                                     |
|        V   V                                     |
|    ------------------                            |
|    |     JOIN      |                             |
|    ------------------                            |
|    | Access Method: |                            |
|    |    iterator    |                            |
|    ------------------                            |
|            |                                     |
|            |                                     |
|            V                                     |
|        Result Set                                |
+----------------------------------------------------+
36 rows in set (0.06 sec)
```

mysql>

   Notice how the query plans differ for each of the statements entered. Take some time to explore other query statements to see how the optimizer optimizes other forms of queries.

Summary

I presented in this chapter the most complex database internal technology—an optimizer. You learned how to expand the concept of the query tree to incorporate a query optimizer that uses the tree structure in the optimization process. More importantly, you discovered how to construct a heuristic query optimizer. The knowledge of heuristic optimizers should provide you with a greater understanding of the DBXP engine and how it can be used to study database technologies in more depth. It doesn't get any deeper than an optimizer!

In the next chapter, I will show you more about query execution through an example implementation of a query tree optimization strategy. The next chapter will complete the DBXP engine by linking the heuristic query optimizer using the query tree class to an execution process that—surprise—also uses the query tree structure.

Exercises

The following lists several areas for further exploration. They represent the types of activities you might want to conduct as experiments (or as a class assignment) to explore relational database technologies.

1. Complete the code for the `balance_joins()` method. Hint: You will need to create an algorithm that can move conjunctive joins around so that the join that is most restrictive is executed first (is lowest in the tree).

2. Complete the code for the `cost_optimization()` method. Hint: You will need to walk the tree and indicate nodes that can use indexes.

3. Examine the code for the heuristic optimizer. Does it cover all possible queries? If not, are there any other rules that can be used to complete the coverage?

4. Examine the code for the query tree and heuristic optimizer. How can you implement the distinct node type as listed in the query tree class? Hint: See the code that follows the `prune_tree()` method in the `heuristic_optimization()` method.

5. How can you change the code to recognize invalid queries? What are the conditions that determine a query is invalid and how would you test for them?

6. (advanced) MySQL does not currently support the intersect operation (as defined by Date). Change the MySQL parser to recognize the new keyword and process queries like `SELECT * FROM A INTERSECT B`. Are there any limitations of this operation and are they reflected in the optimizer?

7. (advanced) How would you implement the `GROUP BY`, `ORDER BY`, and `HAVING` clauses? Make the changes to the optimizer to enable these clauses.

CHAPTER 12

■ ■ ■

Query Execution

The query tree class shown in Chapter 10 and the heuristic optimizer shown in Chapter 11 form the first two of the three components that make up the DBXP query execution engine. In this chapter, I'll show you how to expand the query tree class to process project, restrict, and join operations. This will give you a glimpse into the world of database query execution. I'll begin by briefly explaining the basic principles of the query execution algorithms and then jump into writing the code. Because the code for some of the methods is quite lengthy, not all of the code examples shown in this chapter include the complete source code. If you are following along by coding the examples, consider loading the source code for this chapter and using it rather than typing in the code from scratch.

Query Execution Revisited

The query execution process is the implementation of the various relational theory operations. These operations include project, restrict, join, cross-product, union, and intersect. Few database systems implement union and intersect.

Note Union and intersect are not the same as the UNION operator in SQL. The union and intersect relational operations are set operations whereas the UNION operator in SQL simply combines the results of two or more SELECT statements that have compatible result columns.

Writing algorithms to implement these operations is very straightforward and often omitted from relational theory and database systems texts. It is unfortunate that the algorithms are omitted because the join operation is nontrivial. The following sections describe the basic algorithms for the relational operations.

Project

The project (or projection) operation is one where the result set contains a subset of the attributes (columns) in the original relation (table).[1] Thus, the result set can contain fewer

---

1. For simplicity, I'll use the attribute/column, tuple/row, and relation/table terms interchangeably.

attributes than the original relation. Users specify projections in a SQL SELECT command by listing the desired columns in the column list immediately following the SELECT keyword. For example, the following command projects the first_name and last_name columns from the staff table.

```
SELECT first_name, last_name FROM staff
```

The project algorithm to implement this operation is shown in Listing 12-1.

Listing 12-1. *Project Algorithm*

```
begin
  do
    get next tuple from relation
    for each attribute in tuple
      if attribute.name found in column_list
        write attribute data to client
      fi
  while not end_of_relation
end
```

As you can see from the listing, the code to implement this algorithm limits sending data to the client to the data specified in the column list.

Restrict

The restrict (or restriction) operation is one where the result set contains a subset of the tuples (rows) in the original relation (table). Thus, the result set can contain fewer tuples than the original relation. Users specify restrictions in a SQL SELECT command by listing the desired conditions in the WHERE clause immediately following the FROM clause. For example, the following command restricts the result set from the staff table to those employees who make more than $65,000.00 annually.

```
SELECT first_name, last_name FROM staff WHERE salary > 65000.00
```

The restrict algorithm to implement this operation is shown in Listing 12-2.

Listing 12-2. *Restrict Algorithm*

```
begin
  do
    get next tuple from relation
    if tuple attribute values match conditions
      write attribute data to client
    fi
  while not end_of_relation
end
```

As you can see from the listing, the code to implement this algorithm is where the data values in the tuple match the conditions in the WHERE clause. This algorithm is often implemented with an additional optimization step to reduce the expressions to a minimal set (e.g., omitting always true conditions).

Join

The join operation is one where the result set contains the tuples (rows) that match a specified combination of two relations (tables). Three or more tables are joined using n-1 joins where n is the number of tables. In the case of three tables joined (A, B, C), the join is a combination of two of the tables and the result of that join joined with the remaining table. The combinations of how the joins are linked—as a left-deep or right-deep tree or even as a bushy tree—are one of order of execution of the intermediate joins. Examples of these types of tree arrangements are shown in Figure 12-1.

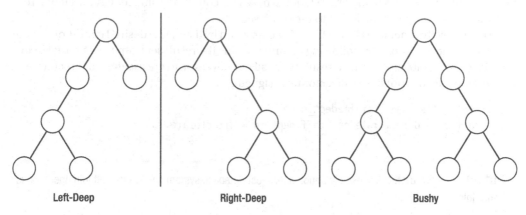

Figure 12-1. *Example tree arrangements*

Joins are most often used in a master/detail relationship where one table (the base or master table) references one or more subtables (detail tables) where one record in the base table matches one or more records in the detail tables. For example, you could create a customer table that contains information about customers and an orders table that contains data about the customers' orders. The customer table is the base table and the orders table is the subtable.

```
SELECT customer.name, orders.number
FROM customer JOIN orders on customer.id = orders.customerid
```

Users specify joins in a SQL SELECT command by listing the desired tables and join conditions in the FROM clause. For example, the following command joins the records from the customer table with those records in the orders table. Note that in this case, the join condition is a simple equal relationship with a common column that the tables share.

The algorithm for a join operation is not as straightforward as those described earlier. This is because the join operation can be represented in several forms. You can choose to join using a simple column from table A = column from table B expression as in the previous example, or elect to control the output by choosing to include only matching rows (inner), matching and nonmatching rows (outer) from the left, right, or both tables. The join operations therefore include inner join (sometimes called natural or equi-joins[2]), left outer join, right outer join, full outer join, cross-product, union, and intersect. The following sections describe each of these operations in detail.

---

2. Natural joins are equi-joins where the superfluous (duplicate) condition attribute values are removed.

■**Note** Some database texts treat the cross-product, union, and intersect as discrete operations. However, I consider them specialized forms of the join operation.

Inner Join

The inner join operation is one where the result set contains a subset of the tuples (rows) in the original relations (tables) where there is a match on the join condition. It is called an inner join because only those rows in the first relation whose join condition value matches that of a row in the second relation are included in the result set.

Users specify inner joins in a SQL SELECT command by listing the desired conditions in the FROM clause. For example, the following command joins the result set from the staff table to the directorate table, returning a result set of all employees who are assigned a directorate (one employee does not have a directorate assigned).

```
SELECT staff.last_name, staff.dept_name
FROM staff JOIN directorate on staff.dept_id = directorate.id
```

■**Note** The keyword INNER is usually optional for most database systems as the default join operation is an inner join.

The inner join algorithm to implement this operation is shown in Listing 12-3. This algorithm is but one of several forms of join algorithms. The algorithm shown is a variant of a merge-join. Thus, it is possible to implement this algorithm using another equally capable join algorithm, such as a nested loop join algorithm.

Listing 12-3. *Join Algorithm*

```
begin
  sort relation a as rel_a on join column(s)
  sort relation b as rel_b on join column(s)
  do
    get next tuple from rel_a
    get next tuple from rel_b
    if join column values match join conditions
      write attribute data to client
    fi
    check rewind conditions
  while not end_of_rel_a and not end_of_rel_b
end
```

Users can also specify an inner join by including the join condition in the WHERE clause as shown here. Some database professionals discourage this variant because it can be mistaken for a normal SELECT command. However, most agree that the variant is functionally equivalent and most database optimizers are written to accommodate it.

```
SELECT staff.last_name, directorate.dept_name
FROM staff, directorate WHERE staff.dept_id = directorate.id
```

As you can see from the listing, the code to implement this algorithm requires the use of a sort. A sort is needed to order the rows in the tables on the join columns so that the algorithm can correctly identify all of the matches should there be any duplicate condition values among the rows. To illustrate this point, consider the tables shown in Listing 12-4.

Listing 12-4. *Example Join Tables (Unordered)*

staff table

```
+------------+-----------+-----------+---------+
| first_name | last_name | id        | dept_id |
+------------+-----------+-----------+---------+
| Bill       | Smith     | 123456789 | 5       |
| Aaron      | Hill      | 987987987 | 4       |
| Alicia     | Wallace   | 330506781 | 4       |
| Howard     | Bell      | 333445555 | 5       |
| William    | Wallace   | 220059009 | <null>  |
| Steven     | Marrow    | 401550022 | 5       |
| Tamra      | English   | 453453453 | 5       |
| Chad       | Borg      | 990441234 | 1       |
| Lillian    | Wallace   | 987654321 | 4       |
+------------+-----------+-----------+---------+
```

directorate table

```
+----+----------------+
| id | dept_name      |
+----+----------------+
| 5  | Research       |
| 4  | Administration |
| 6  | Marketing      |
| 1  | Headquarters   |
+----+----------------+
```

■**Note** Some database systems (such as MySQL) return the rows in the original, unordered sequence. The examples shown are included in order of the internal sort for emphasis.

Notice the tables are not ordered. If you were to run the example join shown using the algorithm without ordering the rows, you'd have to read all of the rows from one of the tables for each row read from the other. For example, if the staff table were read in the order shown, you would read one row from the directorate table for the first join, two rows from the directorate table for the next row from staff, followed by two, one, one, one, four, two rows, with a total of 14 reads from the directorate table to complete the operation. However, if the tables were ordered as shown in Listing 12-5, you would be able to avoid rereading the rows from the directorate table.

Listing 12-5. *Example Join Tables (Ordered by Join Column)*

staff table

first_name	last_name	id	dept_id
William	Wallace	220059009	<null>
Chad	Borg	990441234	1
Aaron	Hill	987987987	4
Alicia	Wallace	330506781	4
Lillian	Wallace	987654321	4
Howard	Bell	333445555	5
Steven	Marrow	401550022	5
Tamra	English	453453453	5
Bill	Smith	123456789	5

directorate table

id	dept_name
1	Headquarters
4	Administration
5	Research
6	Marketing

But this creates another problem. How do you know not to read another row from either table? Notice the last step in the inner join algorithm. This is where the implementation can get a bit tricky. What you need to do here is be able to reuse a row that has already been read so that you can compare one row from one table to many rows in another. This gets tricky when you consider that you may have to advance (go forward one row) or rewind (go back one row) from either table.

If you follow the algorithm by hand with the ordered example tables (reading from the staff table as rel_a first), you'll see that the algorithm would require the "reuse" of the directorate row with an id of 4 twice and the row with and id of 5 three times. The caching of the rows is sometimes called "rewinding" the table read pointers. The result set of this example is shown in Listing 12-6.

Listing 12-6. *Example Inner Join Result Set*

```
+-----------+----------------+
| last_name | dept_name      |
+-----------+----------------+
| Borg      | Headquarters   |
| Hill      | Administration |
| Wallace   | Administration |
| Wallace   | Administration |
| Bell      | Research       |
| Marrow    | Research       |
| English   | Research       |
| Smith     | Research       |
+-----------+----------------+
```

Outer Join

Outer joins are similar to inner joins but in this case, we are interested in obtaining all of the rows from the left, right, or both tables. That is, we include the rows from the table indicated (left, right, or both—also called full) regardless of whether there is a matching row in the other table. Each of these operations can be represented by a slight variance of the general outer join algorithm.

Users specify outer joins in a SQL SELECT command by listing the desired conditions in the FROM clause and invoking one of the options (left, right, full). Some database systems default to using left if the option is omitted. For example, the following command joins the result set from the staff table to the directorate table, returning a result set of all employees and the directorate:

```
SELECT staff.last_name, directorate.dept_name
FROM staff LEFT OUTER JOIN directorate on staff.dept_id = directorate.id
```

Note that this differs from the inner join as no rows from the left table are omitted. Listing 12-7 shows the basic outer join algorithm. The following sections describe how the algorithm implements each of the three types of outer joins.

Listing 12-7. *The Outer Join Algorithm*

```
begin
  sort relation a as rel_a on join column(s)
  sort relation b as rel_b on join column(s)
  do
    get next tuple from rel_a
    get next tuple from rel_b
    if type is FULL
      if join column values match join conditions
        write attribute data from both tuples to client
      else
        if rel_a has data
          write NULLS for rel_b
```

```
        else if rel_b has data
          write NULLS for rel_a
        fi
    else if type is LEFT
      if join column values match join conditions
        write attribute data from rel_a to client
      else
        if rel_a has data
          write NULLS for rel_a
      fi
    else if type is RIGHT
      if join column values match join conditions
        write attribute data from rel_b to client
      else
        if rel_b has data
          write NULLS for rel_a
      fi
    fi
    check rewind conditions
  while not end_of_rel_a and not end_of_rel_b
end
```

Next, we discuss examples of each of the types of outer joins.

Left Outer Join

Left outer joins are those that include all rows from the left table concatenated with rows from the right table. For those rows that do not match the join condition, null values are returned for the columns from the right table.

```
SELECT staff.last_name, directorate.dept_name
FROM staff LEFT OUTER JOIN directorate on staff.dept_id = directorate.id
```

Listing 12-8 shows the result set for the left outer join of the sample tables.

Listing 12-8. *Example Left Outer Join Result Set*

```
+-----------+-----------------+
| last_name | dept_name       |
+-----------+-----------------+
| Wallace   | <null>          |
| Borg      | Headquarters    |
| Hill      | Administration  |
| Wallace   | Administration  |
| Wallace   | Administration  |
| Bell      | Research        |
| Marrow    | Research        |
| English   | Research        |
| Smith     | Research        |
+-----------+-----------------+
```

Right Outer Join

Right outer joins are those that include all rows from the right table concatenated with rows from the left table. For those rows that do not match the join condition, null values are returned for the columns from the left table.

```
SELECT staff.last_name, directorate.dept_name
FROM staff RIGHT OUTER JOIN directorate on staff.dept_id = directorate.id
```

Listing 12-9 shows the result set for the left outer join of the sample tables.

Listing 12-9. *Example Left Outer Join Result Set*

```
+-----------+----------------+
| last_name | dept_name      |
+-----------+----------------+
| Borg      | Headquarters   |
| Hill      | Administration |
| Wallace   | Administration |
| Wallace   | Administration |
| Smith     | Research       |
| Bell      | Research       |
| Marrow    | Research       |
| English   | Research       |
| <null>    | Marketing      |
+-----------+----------------+
```

Full Outer Join

Full outer joins are those that include all rows from both tables concatenated together. For those rows that do not match the join condition, null values are returned for the columns from the non-matching table.

```
SELECT staff.last_name, directorate.dept_name
FROM staff FULL OUTER JOIN directorate on staff.dept_id = directorate.id
```

Listing 12-10 shows the result set for the full outer join of the sample tables.

Listing 12-10. *Example Full Outer Join Result Set*

```
+-----------+----------------+
| last_name | dept_name      |
+-----------+----------------+
| Wallace   | <null>         |
| Borg      | Headquarters   |
| Hill      | Administration |
| Wallace   | Administration |
| Wallace   | Administration |
| Bell      | Research       |
| Marrow    | Research       |
```

```
| English   | Research        |
| Smith     | Research        |
| <null>    | Marketing       |
+-----------+-----------------+
```

Cross-Product

The cross-product operation is where the result set contains each row of the left table combined with every row from the right table. Thus, the result set contains n x m rows, where n represents the number of rows in the left table and m represents the number of rows in the right table. While simple in concept, not all database systems support the cross-product operation.

Note It is possible in some database systems to represent a cross-product query using a query like `SELECT * FROM table1, table2`. In this case, there are no join conditions, so all rows from `table1` are matched with all of the rows from `table2`. Try it out yourself on MySQL. You'll see that MySQL supports cross-product operations using this method.

Users specify the cross-product operation by including the keyword CROSS in place of JOIN in the FROM clause. You may be thinking that this operation has limited applicability, but you'd be surprised at its usefulness. Suppose you were modeling possible outcomes for an artificial intelligence algorithm. You may have tables that store possible next moves (outcomes) and other tables that store stimuli. If you wanted to find all of the possible combinations given a list of stimuli selected from one table and the possible effects on the moves selected from another, you can produce a result set that shows all of the combinations. Listing 12-11 presents an example of such a scenario.

Listing 12-11. *Sample Cross-Product Scenario*

```
CREATE TABLE next_stim
SELECT source, stimuli_id FROM stimuli WHERE likelihood >= 0.75
+------------+------------+
| source     | stimuli_id |
+------------+------------+
| obstacle   | 13         |
| other_bot  | 14         |
| projectile | 15         |
| chasm      | 23         |
+------------+------------+

CREATE TABLE next_moves
SELECT move_name, next_move_id, likelihood FROM moves WHERE likelihood >= 0.90
```

```
+------------+--------------+------------+
| move_name  | next_move_id | likelihood |
+------------+--------------+------------+
| turn left  | 21           | 0.25       |
| reverse    | 18           | 0.40       |
| turn right | 22           | 0.45       |
+------------+--------------+------------+
```

SELECT * FROM next_stim CROSS next_moves

```
+------------+------------+------------+--------------+------------+
| source     | stimuli_id | move_name  | next_move_id | likelihood |
+------------+------------+------------+--------------+------------+
| obstacle   | 13         | turn left  | 21           | 0.25       |
| obstacle   | 13         | reverse    | 18           | 0.40       |
| obstacle   | 13         | turn right | 22           | 0.45       |
| other_bot  | 14         | turn left  | 21           | 0.25       |
| other_bot  | 14         | reverse    | 18           | 0.40       |
| other_bot  | 14         | turn right | 22           | 0.45       |
| projectile | 15         | turn left  | 21           | 0.25       |
| projectile | 15         | reverse    | 18           | 0.40       |
| projectile | 15         | turn right | 22           | 0.45       |
| chasm      | 23         | turn left  | 21           | 0.25       |
| chasm      | 23         | reverse    | 18           | 0.40       |
| chasm      | 23         | turn right | 22           | 0.45       |
+------------+------------+------------+--------------+------------+
```

Listing 12-12 shows the cross-product algorithm. Notice that this sample is written using two steps: one to combine the rows and one to remove the duplicates.

Listing 12-12. *The Cross-Product Algorithm*

```
begin
  do
    get next tuple from rel_a
    do
      get next tuple from rel_b
      write tuple from rel_a concat tuple from rel_b to client
    while not end_of_rel_b
  while not end_of_rel_a
  remove duplicates from temp_table
  return data from temp_table to client
end
```

As you can see from the listing, the code to implement this algorithm is really one of two loops where the rows from the left table are concatenated with the rows from the right table (i.e., a nested loop algorithm).

Union

The union operation is the same as the set operation. In this case, the join is the union of all of the rows in both tables with duplicate rows removed. Naturally, the tables must be of the same design for this operation to work. This differs from the SQL union in that the SQL union includes rows from all SELECT commands (with compatible column lists) regardless of duplicates. Unlike the other joins, the implementation of the union operation is sometimes implemented in two steps: one to combine the tables and another to remove the duplicates.

Users specify the union command by including the keyword UNION in place of JOIN in the FROM clause. Let's say you wanted to combine two employee tables (one that includes all employees who work in the United States and another that includes employees who work in Canada) and ensure you get a result set that has all of the employees listed once. You could union the two using a command like the following:

```
SELECT * from us_employees UNION ca_employees
```

Let's look at this one a little closer. Listing 12-13 shows examples of the tables mentioned. A quick glance will show that there are two employees who work both in the United States and Canada. If you used the SQL UNION command, you'd get the contents of both tables and with those two employees counted twice. Listing 12-14 shows the results of the union operation using the sample tables.

Listing 12-13. *Sample Employee Tables*

US employees table

```
+------------+-----------+-----------+---------+
| first_name | last_name | id        | dept_id |
+------------+-----------+-----------+---------+
| Chad       | Borg      | 990441234 | 1       |
| Alicia     | Wallace   | 330506781 | 4       |
| Howard     | Bell      | 333445555 | 5       |
| Tamra      | English   | 453453453 | 5       |
| Bill       | Smith     | 123456789 | 5       |
+------------+-----------+-----------+---------+
```

Canada employees table

```
+------------+-----------+-----------+---------+
| first_name | last_name | id        | dept_id |
+------------+-----------+-----------+---------+
| William    | Wallace   | 220059009 | <null>  |
| Aaron      | Hill      | 987987987 | 4       |
| Lillian    | Wallace   | 987654321 | 4       |
| Howard     | Bell      | 333445555 | 5       |
| Bill       | Smith     | 123456789 | 5       |
+------------+-----------+-----------+---------+
```

Listing 12-14. *Example Union Result Set*

```
+------------+-----------+-----------+---------+
| first_name | last_name | id        | dept_id |
+------------+-----------+-----------+---------+
| Chad       | Borg      | 990441234 | 1       |
| Alicia     | Wallace   | 330506781 | 4       |
| Howard     | Bell      | 333445555 | 5       |
| Tamra      | English   | 453453453 | 5       |
| Bill       | Smith     | 123456789 | 5       |
| William    | Wallace   | 220059009 | <null>  |
| Aaron      | Hill      | 987987987 | 4       |
| Lillian    | Wallace   | 987654321 | 4       |
+------------+-----------+-----------+---------+
```

Listing 12-15 shows the union algorithm. Notice that this sample is written using two steps to combine and then remove duplicates.

Listing 12-15. *The Union Algorithm*

```
begin
  do
    get next tuple from rel_a
    write tuple from rel_a to temp_table
    get next tuple from rel_b
    write tuple from rel_b to temp_table
  while not end_of_rel_a or end_of_rel_b
  remove duplicates from temp_table
  return data from temp_table to client
end
```

Intersect

The intersect operation is the same as the set operation. In this case, the join is the intersection of the rows that are in both tables, with duplicate rows removed. Naturally, the tables must be of the same design for this operation to work.

Users specify the intersect operation by including the keyword INTERSECT in place of JOIN in the FROM clause. Let's say you wanted to combine two employee tables (one that includes all employees who work in the United States and another that includes employees who work in Canada) and ensure you get a result set that has all of the employees who work in both the United States and Canada. You could intersect the two using a command like this:

```
SELECT * from us_employees INTERSECT ca_employees
```

Let's look at this one a little closer. Using the example tables from Listing 12-13, you will see that there are two employees who work both in the United States and Canada. Listing 12-16 shows the results of the intersect operation using the sample tables. Listing 12-17 shows the intersect algorithm.

Listing 12-16. *Example Intersect Result Set*

```
+------------+-----------+-----------+---------+
| first_name | last_name | id        | dept_id |
+------------+-----------+-----------+---------+
| Howard     | Bell      | 333445555 | 5       |
| Bill       | Smith     | 123456789 | 5       |
+------------+-----------+-----------+---------+
```

Listing 12-17. *The Intersect Algorithm*

```
begin
  do
    get next tuple from rel_a
    get next tuple from rel_b
    if join column values match intersection conditions
      write tuple from rel_a to client
  while not end_of_rel_a or end_of_rel_b
end
```

DBXP Query Execution

Query execution in DBXP is accomplished using the optimized query tree. The tree structure itself is used as a pipeline for processing the query. When a query is executed, a get_next() method is issued on each of the children of the root node. Another get_next() method call is made to each of their children. This process continues as the tree is traversed to the lowest level of the tree containing a reference to a single table. Consider the following query:

```
SELECT col1, col2 FROM table_a JOIN
(SELECT col2, col8 FROM table_b WHERE col6 = 7)
ON col8 WHERE table_a.col7 > 14
```

The query is retrieving data from table_a that matches a subset of the data in table_b. Notice that I wrote the subset as a subquery. The query tree execution easily accommodates a subquery mechanism in which a subquery would be represented as a subtree. Figure 12-2 shows a high-level view of the concept.

The operation for each node is executed for one row in the relation. Upon completion, the result of that operation passes up the result to the next operation in the tree. If no result is produced, control remains in the current node until a result is produced. As the tree is being climbed back to the root, the results are passed to each parent in turn until the root node is reached. Once the operation in the root node is complete, the resulting tuple is passed to the client. In this way, execution of the query appears to produce results faster because data (results) are shown to the client much earlier than if the query were to be executed for the entire set of operations before any results are given to the client.

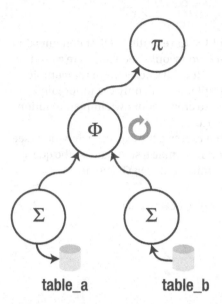

table_a   table_b

Figure 12-2. *Query tree execution*

The Query_tree class is designed to include the operations necessary to execute the query. Operations are included for project, restrict, and join. A prepare() method is called at the start of query execution. The prepare() method walks the query tree, initializing all of the nodes for execution. Execution is accomplished by using a while loop that iterates through the result set, issuing a pulse to the tree starting at the root node. A pulse is a call to the get_next() method that is propagated down the tree. Each node that is pulsed issues a pulse to each of its children, starting with the left child. A separate parameterized method is provided for each of the following operations: do_restrict(), do_project(), and do_join().[3] These methods operate using one or two tuples as input and return either a null or a tuple. A null return indicates the tuple or tuples do not satisfy the current operation. For example, a do_restrict() operation accepting a tuple operates using the expression class to evaluate the values in the tuple. If the expression evaluates to false, a null result is returned. If the expression evaluates to true, the same tuple is returned.[4]

This process is repeated throughout the tree, passing a single tuple up the tree to the root. The resulting tuple from the root is then processed by the external while loop and presented to the client via the existing MySQL client communication protocols. This form of execution is called a pipeline because of the way nodes are traversed, passing a single node through the tree and thus through all of the operations in the query.

---

3. Set operations (intersect, union) and sorting are implemented as specialized forms of join operations.
4. Actually, all tuples are passed by reference so the item returned is the same pointer.

Designing the Tests

Creating comprehensive tests for a query execution would require writing SQL statements that cover all possible paths through the optimizer. In essence, you would need to create a test that tests all possible queries, both valid and invalid. However, the DBXP execution is incomplete. Although the project and restrict operations are fully implemented, only the inner join is implemented in the do_join() method. This permits you to create your own implementations for the remaining join operations in the stable DBXP environment.

With this in mind, let's design a few basic queries that exercise the execution engine to see how the DBXP engine processes queries. Listing 12-18 shows a sample test to exercise the query optimizer. Feel free to add your own queries to test the limits of the DBXP engine.

Listing 12-18. *Sample DBXP Query Execution Test (ExpertMySQLCh12.test)*

```
#
# Sample test to test the SELECT DBXP execution
#

# Test 1:
SELECT DBXP first_name, last_name, sex, id FROM staff;

# Test 2:
SELECT DBXP id FROM staff;

# Test 3:
SELECT DBXP dir_name FROM directorate;

# Test 4:
SELECT DBXP id, dir_name FROM staff
JOIN directorate ON staff.mgr_id = directorate.dir_head_id;

# Test 5:
SELECT DBXP * FROM staff WHERE staff.id = '123456789';

# Test 6:
SELECT DBXP first_name, last_name FROM staff JOIN directorate
WHERE staff.mgr_id = directorate.dir_head_id and directorate.dir_code = 'N41';

# Test 7:
SELECT DBXP * FROM directorate
JOIN building ON directorate.dir_code = building.dir_code;

# Test 8:
SELECT DBXP directorate.dir_code, dir_name, building, dir_head_id
FROM directorate JOIN building ON directorate.dir_code = building.dir_code;
```

Tip The database used in these examples is included in the Appendix.

Please refer to Chapter 4 for more details on how to create and run the test in Listing 12-18 using the MySQL Test Suite.

Updating the SELECT DBXP Command

Since we now have a means to execute queries, we can replace the code in the DBXP_select_command() method with code that runs the SELECT commands. This method will check table access, open and lock the tables, execute the query, send results to the client, and unlock the tables. Listing 12-19 shows the completed DBXP_select_command().

Listing 12-19. *Completed SELECT DBXP Command*

```
/*
  Perform Select Command

  SYNOPSIS
    DBXP_select_command()
    THD *thd              IN the current thread

  DESCRIPTION
    This method executes the SELECT command using the query tree and optimizer.

  RETURN VALUE
    Success = 0
    Failed = 1
*/
int DBXP_select_command(THD *thd)
{
  bool res;
  READ_RECORD *record;
  select_result *result = thd->lex->result;

  DBUG_ENTER("DBXP_select_command");

  /* Prepare the tables (check access, locks) */
  res = check_table_access(thd, SELECT_ACL, thd->lex->query_tables, 0);
  if (res)
    DBUG_RETURN(1);
  res = open_and_lock_tables(thd, thd->lex->query_tables);
  if (res)
    DBUG_RETURN(1);
```

```
/* Create the query tree and optimize it */
Query_tree *qt = build_query_tree(thd, thd->lex,
                    (TABLE_LIST*) thd->lex->select_lex.table_list.first);
qt->heuristic_optimization();
qt->cost_optimization();
qt->prepare(qt->root);
if (!(result= new select_send()))
  DBUG_RETURN(1);

/* use the protocol class to communicate to client */
Protocol *protocol= thd->protocol;

/* write the field list for returning the query results */
if (protocol->send_fields(&qt->result_fields,
                          Protocol::SEND_NUM_ROWS | Protocol::SEND_EOF))
  DBUG_RETURN(1);

/* pulse the execution engine to get a row from the result set */
while (!qt->Eof(qt->root))
{
  record = qt->get_next(qt->root);
  if (record != NULL)

    /* send the data to the client */
    send_data(protocol, qt->result_fields, thd);
}
send_eof(thd);

/* unlock tables and cleanup memory */
qt->cleanup(qt->root);
mysql_unlock_read_tables(thd, thd->lock);
delete qt;
DBUG_RETURN(0);
}
```

This implementation now has all of the elements necessary to execute queries. It begins with checking table access and opening the tables. Assuming these steps complete successfully, the DBXP query engine calls are next, beginning with building the query tree and then optimizing, and finally the executing the query in a loop. Notice the loop is a simple while not end of file loop that calls the get_next() method on the root node. If a tuple (record) is returned, the code writes the row to the client; otherwise, it calls the get_next() method until the end of the file is detected. When all tuples have been processed, the code frees all used memory and unlocks the tables. Since I placed the code that sends data to the client in one place outside the query tree methods, the implementation for all of the relational operations is simplified a bit. As you will see in the following section, the query tree methods resemble those of the theoretical algorithms.

The DBXP Algorithms

Now that the code to operate the DBXP query engine is complete, let's turn our attention to how the DBXP Query_tree class implements the relational operations.

Project

The DBXP project operation is implemented in a method called do_project() of the Query_tree class. This method is easy to implement because the MySQL base classes provide a fast way to do the projection. Instead of looping through the attributes in the row, we can use the MySQL base classes to send the data to the client.

The do_project() method can be simplified to just store the current row in the buffer and return the row to the next node in the tree. When control returns to the DBXP_select_command() method, a helper method named send_data() is used to send the data to the client. Listing 12-20 shows the code for the do_project() method.

Listing 12-20. *DBXP Project Method*

```
/*
  Perform project operation.

  SYNOPSIS
    do_project()
    query_node *qn IN the operational node in the query tree.
    READ_RECORD *t -- the tuple to apply the operation to.

  DESCRIPTION
    This method performs the relational model operation entitled
    "project". This operation is a narrowing of the result set
    vertically by restricting the set of attributes in the
    output tuple.

  NOTES
    Returns 0 (null) if no tuple satisfies child operation
    (does NOT indicate the end of the file or end of query
    operation. Use Eof() to verify.

  RETURN VALUE
    Success = new tuple with correct attributes
    Failed = NULL
*/
READ_RECORD *Query_tree::do_project(query_node *qn, READ_RECORD *t)
{
  DBUG_ENTER("do_project");
  if (t != NULL)
  {
    if (qn == root)
```

```
    /*
        If the left table isn't NULL, copy the record buffer from
        the table into the record buffer of the relations class.
        This completes the read from the storage engine and now
        provides the data for the projection which is accomplished
        in send_data().
    */
    if (qn->relations[0] != NULL)
      memcpy((byte *)qn->relations[0]->table->record[0],
        (byte *)t->rec_buf,
        qn->relations[0]->table->s->rec_buff_length);
  }
  DBUG_RETURN(t);
}
```

Notice that in this code, all that must be done is copying the data read from the storage engine into the record buffer of the table object. I accomplish this by copying the memory from the READ_RECORD read from the storage engine into the table's first READ_RECORD buffer, copying in the number of bytes specified in the rec_buff_length attribute of the table.

Restrict

The DBXP restrict operation is implemented in a method called do_restrict() of the Query_tree class. The code uses the where_expr member variable of the Query_tree class that contains an instantiation of the Expression helper class. The implementation of the restrict operation is therefore simplified to calling the evaluate() method of the Expression class. Listing 12-21 shows the code for the do_restrict() method.

Listing 12-21. *DBXP Restrict Method*

```
/*
  Perform restrict operation.

  SYNOPSIS
    do_restrict()
    query_node *qn IN the operational node in the query tree.
    READ_RECORD *t -- the tuple to apply the operation to.

  DESCRIPTION
    This method performs the relational model operation entitled
    "restrict". This operation is a narrowing of the result set
    horizontally by satisfying the expressions listed in the
    where clause of the SQL statement being executed.
```

```
   RETURN VALUE
     Success = true
     Failed = false
*/
bool Query_tree::do_restrict(query_node *qn, READ_RECORD *t)
{
  bool found = false;

  DBUG_ENTER("do_restrict");
  if (qn != NULL)
  {
    /*
       If the left table isn't NULL, copy the record buffer from
       the table into the record buffer of the relations class.
       This completes the read from the storage engine and now
       provides the data for the projection which is accomplished
       in send_data().

       Lastly, evaluate the where clause. If the where clause
       evaluates to true, we keep the record else we discard it.
    */
    if (qn->relations[0] != NULL)
      memcpy((byte *)qn->relations[0]->table->record[0],
        (byte *)t->rec_buf,
        qn->relations[0]->table->s->rec_buff_length);
    if (qn->where_expr != NULL)
      found = qn->where_expr->evaluate(qn->relations[0]->table);
  }
  DBUG_RETURN(found);
}
```

When a match is found, the data is copied to the record buffer of the table. This associates the data in the current record buffer with the table. It also allows the use of the many MySQL methods to manipulate fields and send data to the client.

Join

The DBXP join operation is implemented in a method called do_join() of the Query_tree class. The code uses the join_expr member variable of the Query_tree class that contains an instantiation of the Expression helper class. The implementation of the evaluation of the join conditions is therefore simplified to calling the evaluate() method of the Expression class.

This method is the most complex of all of the DBXP code. The reason for the complexity is due in part to the many conditions under which a join must be evaluated. The theoretical join algorithm described previously and the examples shown illustrate the complexity. I will expand on that a bit here in preparation for your examination of the do_join() source code. Listing 12-22 presents the simplified pseudocode for the do_join() method.

Listing 12-22. *The DBXP Join Algorithm*

```
begin
  if preempt_pipeline
    do
      if no left child
        get next tuple from left relation
      else
        get next tuple from left child
      fi
      insert tuple in left buffer in order by join column for left relation
    until eof
    do
      if no right child
        get next tuple from right relation
      else
        get next tuple from right child
      fi
      insert tuple in right buffer in order by join column for right relation
    until eof
  fi
  if left record pointer is NULL
    get next tuple from left buffer
  fi
  if right record pointer is NULL
    get next tuple from right buffer
  fi
  if there are tuples to process
    write attribute data of both tuples to table record buffers
    if join column values match join conditions
      check rewind conditions
      clear record pointers
      check for end of file
      set return record to left record pointer (indicates a match)
   else if left join value < right tuple join value
      set return record to NULL (no match)
      set left record pointer to NULL
    else if left join value > right tuple join value
      set return record to NULL (no match)
      set right record pointer to NULL
    fi
  else
    set return record to NULL (no match)
  fi
end
```

Since the join method is called repeatedly from the get_next() method, the algorithm has been altered to use the preempt_pipeline member variable from the query_node. This variable is set to TRUE during the prepare() method prior to executing the query tree. This allows the join method to detect when the first call is made so that the temporary buffers can be created. In this way, the traversal of the tree is preempted until the join operation completes for the first match (or the end of the file if no matches).

Notice that the algorithm uses two buffers to store the ordered rows from the incoming tables. These buffers are used to read records for the join operation and are represented using a record pointer for each buffer. If a match is found, both record pointers are set to NULL, which forces the code to read the next record. If the evaluation of the join condition indicates that the join value from the left table is less than the right, the left record pointer is set to NULL so that on the next call to the do_join() method, the next record is read from the left record buffer. Similarly, if the left join value is greater than the right, the right record pointer is set to NULL and on the next call a new record is read from the right record buffer.

Now that the basics of the do_join() method have been explained, take a look at the source code. Listing 12-23 shows the code for the do_join() method.

Note I chose to not use a helper function to create the temporary buffers for the first step of the join operation so that I could keep the code together for easier debugging. Thus, the decision was purely for convenience. You can save a bit of code if you want by making this part of the code a helper function.

Listing 12-23. *DBXP Join Method*

```
/*
  Perform join operation.

  SYNOPSIS
    do_join()
    query_node *qn IN the operational node in the query tree.
    READ_RECORD *t -- the tuple to apply the operation to.

  DESCRIPTION
    This method performs the relational model operation entitled
    "join". This operation is the combination of two relations to
    form a composite view. This algorithm implements ALL variants
    of the join operation.

  NOTES
    Returns 0 (null) if no tuple satisfies child operation (does
    NOT indicate the end of the file or end of query operation.
    Use Eof() to verify.

  RETURN VALUE
    Success = new tuple with correct attributes
    Failed = NULL
*/
```

```
READ_RECORD *Query_tree::do_join(query_node *qn)
{
  READ_RECORD *next_tup;
  int i;
  TABLE *ltable = NULL;
  TABLE *rtable = NULL;
  Field *fright = NULL;
  Field *fleft = NULL;
  record_buff *lprev;
  record_buff *rprev;
  expr_node *expr;

  DBUG_ENTER("do_join");
  if (qn == NULL)
    DBUG_RETURN(NULL);

  /* check join type because some joins require other processing */
  switch (qn->join_type)
  {
    case (jnINNER) :
    case (jnLEFTOUTER) :
    case (jnRIGHTOUTER) :
    case (jnFULLOUTER) :
    {

      /*
        preempt_pipeline == true means we need to stop the pipeline
        and sort the incoming rows. We do that by making an in-memory
        copy of the record buffers stored in left_record_buff and
        right_record_buff
      */
      if (qn->preempt_pipeline)
      {
        left_record_buff = NULL;
        right_record_buff = NULL;
        next_tup = NULL;

        /* Build buffer for tuples from left child. */
        do
        {
          /* if left child exists, get row from it */
          if (qn->left != NULL)
            lbuff = get_next(qn->left);

          /* else, read the row from the table (the storage handler */
          else
          {
```

```
    /*
       Create space for the record buffer and
       store pointer in lbuff
    */
    lbuff = (READ_RECORD *) my_malloc(sizeof(READ_RECORD),
                          MYF(MY_ZEROFILL | MY_WME));
    lbuff->rec_buf =
      (byte *) my_malloc(qn->relations[0]->table->s->rec_buff_length,
                          MYF(MY_ZEROFILL | MY_WME));

    /* check for end of file. Store result in eof array */
    qn->eof[0] =
      qn->relations[0]->table->file->rnd_next(lbuff->rec_buf);
    if (qn->eof[0] != HA_ERR_END_OF_FILE)
      qn->eof[0] = false;
    else
    {
      lbuff = NULL;
      qn->eof[0] = true;
    }
  }
  /* if the left buffer is not null, get a new row from table */
  if (lbuff != NULL)
  {
    /* we need the table information for processing fields */
    if (qn->left == NULL)
      ltable = qn->relations[0]->table;
    else
      ltable = get_table(qn->left);
    if (ltable != NULL)
      memcpy((byte *)ltable->record[0], (byte *)lbuff->rec_buf,
        ltable->s->rec_buff_length);

    /* get the join expression */
    expr = qn->join_expr->get_expression(0);
    Field *cur_field = (Field *)expr->left_op;
    for (Field **field = ltable->field; *field; field++)
      if (strcasecmp((*field)->field_name, cur_field->field_name)==0)
        fleft = (*field);

    /*
       If field was found, add the row to the in-memory buffer
       ordered by the join column.
    */
    if ((fleft != NULL) && (!fleft->is_null()))
      insertion_sort(true, fleft, lbuff);
  }
```

```
    } while (lbuff != NULL);
    /* Build buffer for tuples from right child. */
    do
    {
      /* if right child exists, get row from it */
      if (qn->right != NULL)
        rbuff = get_next(qn->right);

      /* else, read the row from the table (the storage handler */
      else
      {
        /*
           Create space for the record buffer and
           store pointer in rbuff
        */
        rbuff = (READ_RECORD *) my_malloc(sizeof(READ_RECORD),
                            MYF(MY_ZEROFILL | MY_WME));
        rbuff->rec_buf =
          (byte *) my_malloc(qn->relations[0]->table->s->rec_buff_length,
                            MYF(MY_ZEROFILL | MY_WME));

        /* check for end of file. Store result in eof array */
        qn->eof[1] =
          qn->relations[1]->table->file->rnd_next(rbuff->rec_buf);
        if (qn->eof[1] != HA_ERR_END_OF_FILE)
          qn->eof[1] = false;
        else
        {
          rbuff = NULL;
          qn->eof[1] = true;
        }
      }
      /* if the right buffer is not null, get a new row from table */
      if (rbuff != NULL)
      {
        /* we need the table information for processing fields */
        if (qn->right == NULL)
          rtable = qn->relations[1]->table;
        else
          rtable = get_table(qn->right);
        if (rtable != NULL)
          memcpy((byte *)rtable->record[0], (byte *)rbuff->rec_buf,
            rtable->s->rec_buff_length);

        /* get the join expression */
        expr = qn->join_expr->get_expression(0);
        Field *cur_field = (Field *)expr->right_op;
```

```
      for (Field **field = rtable->field; *field; field++)
        if (strcasecmp((*field)->field_name, cur_field->field_name)==0)
          fright = (*field);

    /*
       If field was found, add the row to the in-memory buffer
       ordered by the join column.
    */
    if ((fright != NULL) && (!fright->is_null()))
      insertion_sort(false, fright, rbuff);
  }
} while (rbuff != NULL);
left_record_buffer_ptr = left_record_buff;
right_record_buffer_ptr = right_record_buff;
qn->preempt_pipeline = false;
}
/*
  This is where the actual join code begins.
  We get a tuple from each table and start the compare.
*/

/*
   if lbuff is null and the left record buffer has data
   get the row from the buffer
*/
if ((lbuff == NULL) && (left_record_buffer_ptr != NULL))
{
  lbuff = left_record_buffer_ptr->record;
  lprev = left_record_buffer_ptr;
  left_record_buffer_ptr = left_record_buffer_ptr->next;
}

/*
   if rbuff is null and the right record buffer has data
   get the row from the buffer
*/
if ((rbuff == NULL) && (right_record_buffer_ptr != NULL))
{
  rbuff = right_record_buffer_ptr->record;
  rprev = right_record_buffer_ptr;
  right_record_buffer_ptr = right_record_buffer_ptr->next;
}

/*
  if the left buffer was null, check to see if a row is
  available from left child.
*/
```

```
    if (ltable == NULL)
      if (qn->left == NULL)
        ltable = qn->relations[0]->table;
      else
        ltable = get_table(qn->left);

    /*
      if the right buffer was null, check to see if a row is
      available from right child.
    */
    if (rtable == NULL)
      if (qn->right == NULL)
        rtable = qn->relations[1]->table;
      else
        rtable = get_table(qn->right);

    /*
      If there are two rows to compare, copy the record buffers
      to the table record buffers. This transfers the data
      from the internal buffer to the record buffer. It enables
      us to reuse the MySQL code for manipulating fields.
    */
    if ((lbuff != NULL) && (rbuff != NULL))
    {
      memcpy((byte *)ltable->record[0], (byte *)lbuff->rec_buf,
        ltable->s->rec_buff_length);
      memcpy((byte *)rtable->record[0], (byte *)rbuff->rec_buf,
        rtable->s->rec_buff_length);

      /* evaluate the join condition */
      i = qn->join_expr->compare_join(qn->join_expr->get_expression(0),
        ltable, rtable);

      /* if there is a match...*/
      if (i == 0)
      {
        /* return the row in the next_tup pointer */
        next_tup = lbuff;

        /* store next rows from buffer (already advanced 1 row) */
        record_buff *left = left_record_buffer_ptr;
        record_buff *right = right_record_buffer_ptr;

        /*
          Check to see if either buffer needs to be rewound to
          allow us to process many rows on one side to one row
          on the other
        */
```

```
      check_rewind(left_record_buffer_ptr, lprev,
        right_record_buffer_ptr, rprev);

      /* set pointer to null to force read on next loop */
      lbuff = NULL;
      rbuff = NULL;

      /*
        If the left buffer has been changed and if the
        buffer is not at the end, set the buffer to the next row.
      */
      if (left != left_record_buffer_ptr)
      {
        if (left_record_buffer_ptr != NULL)
        {
          lbuff = left_record_buffer_ptr->record;
        }
      }

      /*
        If the right buffer has been changed and if the
        buffer is not at the end, set the buffer to the next row.
      */
      if (right != right_record_buffer_ptr)
      {
        if (right_record_buffer_ptr != NULL)
        {
          rbuff = right_record_buffer_ptr->record;
        }
      }

      /* Now check for end of file and save results in eof array */
      if (left_record_buffer_ptr == NULL)
        qn->eof[2] = true;
      else
        qn->eof[2] = false;
      if (right_record_buffer_ptr == NULL)
        qn->eof[3] = true;
      else
        qn->eof[3] = false;
    }

    /* if the rows didn't match...*/
    else
    {
      /* get next rows from buffers (already advanced) */
      record_buff *left = left_record_buffer_ptr;
      record_buff *right = right_record_buffer_ptr;
```

```
/*
   Check to see if either buffer needs to be rewound to
   allow us to process many rows on one side to one row
   on the other. The results of this rewind must be
   saved because there was no match and we may have to
   reuse one or more of the rows.
*/
check_rewind(left_record_buffer_ptr, lprev,
   right_record_buffer_ptr, rprev);

/*
  If the left buffer has been changed and if the
  buffer is not at the end, set the buffer to the next row
  and copy the data into the record buffer/
*/
if (left != left_record_buffer_ptr)
{
  if (left_record_buffer_ptr != NULL)
  {
    memcpy((byte *)ltable->record[0],
      (byte *)left_record_buffer_ptr->record->rec_buf,
      ltable->s->rec_buff_length);
    lbuff = left_record_buffer_ptr->record;
  }
}

/*
  If the right buffer has been changed and if the
  buffer is not at the end, set the buffer to the next row
  and copy the data into the record buffer/
*/
if (right_record_buffer_ptr != NULL)
  if ((right_record_buffer_ptr->next == NULL) &&
    (right_record_buffer_ptr->prev == NULL))
    lbuff = NULL;
if (right != right_record_buffer_ptr)
{
  if (right_record_buffer_ptr != NULL)
  {
    memcpy((byte *)rtable->record[0],
      (byte *)right_record_buffer_ptr->record->rec_buf,
      rtable->s->rec_buff_length);
    rbuff = right_record_buffer_ptr->record;
  }
}
```

```
      /* Now check for end of file and save results in eof array */
      if (left_record_buffer_ptr == NULL)
        qn->eof[2] = true;
      else
        qn->eof[2] = false;
      if (right_record_buffer_ptr == NULL)
        qn->eof[3] = true;
      else
        qn->eof[3] = false;
  }
 }
 else
   next_tup = NULL; /* at end, return null */
 break;
}

/* placeholder for exercise... */
case (jnCROSSPRODUCT) :
{
  break;
}
/*
  placeholder for exercises...
  Union and intersect are mirrors of each other -- same code will
  work for both except the dupe elimination/inclusion part (see below)
*/
case (jnUNION) :
case (jnINTERSECT) :
{
  break;
}
}
DBUG_RETURN(next_tup);
}
```

Notice in the code that under any condition other than a match, the record returned from the code is set to NULL. This allows the loop in the get_next() method to repeatedly call the do_join() method until a match is returned. This is similar to the way the do_restrict() method call is made.

You may note that I have not implemented the code for any of the other join operations. The main reason is that it allows you to experiment with the code (see the exercises at end of this chapter). Fortunately, you should find that the code can be modified with a few simple alterations to allow the processing of the outer joins. Adding code for the cross-product, union, and intersect operations can be accomplished by implementing the theoretical algorithm described in the first part of this chapter.

After you have studied the pseudocode for the method, you should find reading the code easier. The most complex part of this code is the check_rewind() method. This is implemented as a function in the class to make the code less complex and easier to read. There are several other helper methods, which are described in more detail in the following section.

Other Methods

Several helper methods make up the DBXP execution engine. Table 12-1 lists the new methods and their uses. The more complex methods are described in more detail in the text that follows.

Table 12-1. *The DBXP Execution Engine Helper Methods*

Class::Method	Description
Query_tree::get_next()	Retrieves next tuple from child node.
Query_tree::insertion_sort()	Creates an ordered buffer of READ_RECORD pointers. Used in the join operations for ordering the incoming tuples.
Query_tree::Eof()	Checks for the end-of-file condition for the storage engine or temporary buffers.
Query_tree::check_rewind()	Checks to see if the record buffers need to be adjusted to reread tuples for multiple matches.
send_data()	Sends data to the client. See sql_dbxp_parse.cc.
Expression::evaluate()	Evaluates the WHERE clause for a restrict operation.
Expression::compare_join()	Evaluates the join condition for a join operation.
Handler::rnd_init()	Initializes read from storage engine (see Chapter 7).
Handler::rnd_next()	Reads the next tuple from storage engine (see Chapter 7).

The get_next() Method

The get_next() method is the heart of the query execution flow in DBXP. It is responsible for calling the do_... methods that implement the query operations. It is called once from the while loop in the DBXP_select_command() method. Once this method is initiated the first time, it performs the operation for the current node, calling the children nodes to get their result. The process is repeated in a recursive fashion until all the children in the current node have returned a single tuple. Listing 12-24 shows the code for the get_next() method.

Listing 12-24. *The get_next() Method*

```
/*
  Get the next tuple (row) in the result set.

  SYNOPSIS
    Eof()
    query_node *qn IN the operational node in the query tree.
```

```
  DESCRIPTION
    This method is used to get the next READ_RECORD from the pipeline.
    The idea is to call prepare() after you've validated the query then call
    get_next to get the first tuple in the pipeline.

  RETURN VALUE
    Success = next tuple in the result set
    Failed = NULL
*/
READ_RECORD *Query_tree::get_next(query_node *qn)
{
  READ_RECORD *next_tup = NULL;
  int         i = 0;
  DBUG_ENTER("get_next");

  /*
    For each of the possible node types, perform the query operation
    by calling the method for the operation. These implement a very
    high-level abstraction of the operation. The real work is left
    to the methods.
  */
  switch (qn->node_type)
  {
    /* placeholder for exercises... */
    case Query_tree::qntDistinct :
      break;

    /* placeholder for exercises... */
    case Query_tree::qntUndefined :
      break;

    /* placeholder for exercises... */
    case Query_tree::qntSort :
      if (qn->preempt_pipeline)
        qn->preempt_pipeline = false;
      break;

    /*
      For restrict, get a row (tuple) from the table and
      call the do_restrict method looping until a row is returned
      (data matches conditions), then return result to main loop
      in DBXP_select_command.
    */
```

```
case Query_tree::qntRestrict :
  do
  {
    /* if there is a child, get row from child */
    if (qn->left != NULL)
      next_tup = get_next(qn->left);

    /* else get the row from the table stored in this node */
    else
    {
      /* create space for the record buffer */
      if (next_tup == NULL)
        next_tup = (READ_RECORD *) my_malloc(sizeof(READ_RECORD),
                                    MYF(MY_ZEROFILL | MY_WME));
      next_tup->rec_buf =
        (byte *) my_malloc(qn->relations[0]->table->s->rec_buff_length,
                                  MYF(MY_ZEROFILL | MY_WME));

      /* read row from table (storage handler */
      qn->eof[0] = qn->relations[0]->table->file->rnd_next(next_tup->rec_buf);

      /* check for end of file */
      if (qn->eof[0] != HA_ERR_END_OF_FILE)
        qn->eof[0] = false;
      else
      {
        qn->eof[0] = true;
        next_tup = NULL;
      }
    }

    /* if there is a row, call the do_restrict method */
    if (next_tup)
      if(!do_restrict(qn, next_tup))
      {
        /* if no row to return, free memory used */
        my_free((gptr)next_tup->rec_buf, MYF(0));
        my_free((gptr)next_tup, MYF(0));
        next_tup = NULL;
      }
  } while ((next_tup == NULL) && !Eof(qn));
  break;

/*
  For project, get a row (tuple) from the table and
  call the do_project method. If successful,
  return result to main loop in DBXP_select_command.
*/
```

```
case Query_tree::qntProject :

  /* if there is a child, get row from child */
  if (qn->left != NULL)
  {
    next_tup = get_next(qn->left);
    if (next_tup)
      if (!do_project(qn, next_tup))
      {
        /* if no row to return, free memory used */
        my_free((gptr)next_tup->rec_buf, MYF(0));
        my_free((gptr)next_tup, MYF(0));
        next_tup = NULL;
      }
  }

  /* else get the row from the table stored in this node */
  else
  {
    /* create space for the record buffer */
    if (next_tup == NULL)
      next_tup = (READ_RECORD *) my_malloc(sizeof(READ_RECORD),
                                MYF(MY_ZEROFILL | MY_WME));
    next_tup->rec_buf =
      (byte *)my_malloc(qn->relations[0]->table->s->rec_buff_length + 20,
                                MYF(MY_ZEROFILL | MY_WME));

    /* read row from table (storage handler */
    qn->eof[0] = qn->relations[0]->table->file->rnd_next(next_tup->rec_buf);

    /* check for end of file */
    if (qn->eof[0] != HA_ERR_END_OF_FILE)
      qn->eof[0] = false;
    else
    {
      qn->eof[0] = true;
      next_tup = NULL;
    }

    /* if there is a row, call the do_project method */
    if (next_tup)
      if (!do_project(qn, next_tup))
      {
        /* no row to return, free memory used */
        my_free((gptr)next_tup->rec_buf, MYF(0));
        my_free((gptr)next_tup, MYF(0));
```

```
          next_tup = NULL;
        }
      }
      break;

    /*
      For join, loop until either a row is returned from the
      do_join method or we are at end of file for both tables.
      If successful (data matches conditions),
      return result to main loop in DBXP_select_command.
    */
    case Query_tree::qntJoin :
      do
      {
        if (next_tup)
        {
          /* if no row to return, free memory used */
          my_free((gptr)next_tup->rec_buf, MYF(0));
          my_free((gptr)next_tup, MYF(0));
          next_tup = NULL;
        }
        next_tup = do_join(qn);
      }
      while ((next_tup == NULL) && !Eof(qn));
      break;
  }
  DBUG_RETURN(next_tup);
}
```

The send_data() Method

The send_data() method is a helper router that writes data to the client using the MySQL
Protocol class to handle the communication chores. This method was borrowed from the MySQL
source code and rewritten slightly to accommodate the (relative) simplistic execution of the
DBXP execution engine. In this case, the Item superclass is used to send the field values to the
client using the item->send() method. Listing 12-25 shows the code for the send_data() method.

Listing 12-25. *The send_data() Method*

```
/*
  Send data

  SYNOPSIS
    send_data()
    Protocol *p        IN the Protocol class
    THD *thd           IN the current thread
    List<Item> *items  IN the list of fields identified in the row
```

```
    DESCRIPTION
      This method sends the data to the client using the protocol class.

    RETURN VALUE
      Success = 0
      Failed = 1
*/
bool send_data(Protocol *protocol, List<Item> &items, THD *thd)
{
  DBUG_ENTER("send_data");

  /* use a list iterator to loop through items */
  List_iterator_fast<Item> li(items);

  char buff[MAX_FIELD_WIDTH];
  String buffer(buff, sizeof(buff), &my_charset_bin);

  /* this call resets the transmission buffers */
  protocol->prepare_for_resend();

  /* for each item in the list (a field), send data to the client */
  Item *item;
  while ((item=li++))
  {
    /*
      Use the MySQL send method for the item class to write to network.
      If unsuccessful, free memory and send error message to client.
    */
    if (item->send(protocol, &buffer))
    {
      protocol->free();        /* Free used buffer */
      my_message(ER_OUT_OF_RESOURCES, ER(ER_OUT_OF_RESOURCES), MYF(0));
      break;
    }
  }
  /* increment row count */
  thd->sent_row_count++;

  /* if network write was ok, return */
  if (!thd->vio_ok())
    DBUG_RETURN(0);
  /* write failed, return error code to client */
  if (!thd->net.report_error)
    DBUG_RETURN(protocol->write());
```

```
  /* remove last row from buffer for error processing */
  protocol->remove_last_row();
  DBUG_RETURN(1);
}
```

The method uses the item class, calling the send() method and passing in a pointer to an instance of the protocol class. This is how data for a field item is written to the client. The send_data() method is where the projection and join column lists are processed to complete the operations. This is one of the nicest touches in the MySQL source code. But how do the MySQL classes know what columns to send? Take a look back at the build_query_tree() method. Recall that there is a list identified in the select_lex class. The DBXP code captures these fields in the line of code shown here. This list is directly from the columns list in the SELECT command and populated by the parser code.

```
qt->result_fields = lex->select_lex.item_list;
```

These fields are captured in the thread extended structure. The MySQL code simply writes out any data that is present in this list of fields.

The check_rewind() Method

This method is the part of the join algorithms that is most often omitted in database texts. The method adjusts the buffers for rows coming from the tables to allow the algorithm to reuse processed rows. This is necessary because one row from one table may match more than one row from another. While the concept of the method is relatively straightforward, it can be a challenge to write the code yourself. Fortunately, I've saved you the trouble.

The code works by examining the rows in the record buffers. It takes as input pointers to the record buffers along with the previous record pointer in the buffer. The record buffer is implemented as a doubly linked list to allow movement forward and back through the buffers.

There are several conditions that this code must process in order to keep the flow of data to the do_join() method. These conditions are the result of the evaluation of the join condition(s) after a match has been detected. The result of a failed match is handled in the do_join() method.

- If the next record in the left buffer is a match to the right buffer, rewind the right buffer until the join condition of the right buffer is less than the left.

- If the next record in the left buffer is not a match to the right buffer, set the right buffer to the previous right record pointer.

- If the left record buffer is at the end and there are still records in the right buffer, and if the join value of the previous left record pointer is a match to the right record pointer, set the left record pointer to the previous left record pointer.

The method is implemented with a bias to the left record buffer. In other words, the code keeps the right buffer synchronized with the left buffer (also called a left-deep join execution). Listing 12-26 shows the code for the check_rewind() method.

Listing 12-26. *The check_rewind() Method*

```
/*
  Adjusts pointers to record buffers for join.

  SYNOPSIS
    check_rewind()
    record_buff *cur_left IN the left record buffer
    record_buff *cur_left_prev IN the left record buffer previous
    record_buff *cur_right IN the left record buffer
    record_buff *cur_right_prev IN the left record buffer previous

  DESCRIPTION
    This method is used to push a tuple back into the buffer
    during a join operation that preempts the pipeline.

  NOTES
    Now, here's where we have to check the next tuple in each
    relation to see if they are the same. If one of them is the
    same and the other isn't, push one of them back.

    We need to rewind if one of the following is true:
    1. The next record in R2 has the same join value as R1
    2. The next record in R1 has the same join value as R2
    3. The next record in R1 has the same join value and R2 is
       different (or EOF)
    4. The next record in R2 has the same join value and R1 is
       different (or EOF)

  RETURN VALUE
    Success = int index number
    Failed = -1
*/
int Query_tree::check_rewind(record_buff *cur_left,
                             record_buff *curr_left_prev,
                             record_buff *cur_right,
                             record_buff *curr_right_prev)
{
  record_buff *left_rcd_ptr = cur_left;
  record_buff *right_rcd_ptr = cur_right;
  int i;
  DBUG_ENTER("check_rewind");

  /*
    If the next tuple in right record is the same as the present tuple
      AND the next tuple in right record is different, rewind until
      it is the same
```

```
      else
        Push left record back.
  */


  /* if both buffers are at EOF, return -- nothing to do */
  if ((left_rcd_ptr == NULL) && (right_rcd_ptr == NULL))
    DBUG_RETURN(0);


  /* if the currently processed record is null, get the one before it */
  if (cur_right == NULL)
    right_rcd_ptr = curr_right_prev;


  /*
    if left buffer is not at end, check to see
    if we need to rewind right buffer
  */
  if (left_rcd_ptr != NULL)
  {
    /* compare the join conditions to check order */
    i = memcmp(left_rcd_ptr->field_ptr, right_rcd_ptr->field_ptr,
      left_rcd_ptr->field_length < right_rcd_ptr->field_length ?
      left_rcd_ptr->field_length : right_rcd_ptr->field_length);

    /*
      i == 0 means the rows are the same. In this case, we need to
      check to see if we need to advance or rewind the right buffer.
    */
    if (i == 0)
    {
      /*
        If there is a next row in the right buffer, check to see
        if it matches the left row. If the right row is greater
        than the left row, rewind the right buffer to one previous
        to the current row or until we hit the start.
      */
      if (right_rcd_ptr->next != NULL)
      {
        right_rcd_ptr = right_rcd_ptr->next;
        i = memcmp(left_rcd_ptr->field_ptr, right_rcd_ptr->field_ptr,
          left_rcd_ptr->field_length < right_rcd_ptr->field_length ?
          left_rcd_ptr->field_length : right_rcd_ptr->field_length);
        if (i > 0)
        {
          do
          {
```

```
            if (right_rcd_ptr->prev != NULL)
            {
              right_rcd_ptr = right_rcd_ptr->prev;
              i = memcmp(left_rcd_ptr->field_ptr, right_rcd_ptr->field_ptr,
                left_rcd_ptr->field_length < right_rcd_ptr->field_length ?
                left_rcd_ptr->field_length : right_rcd_ptr->field_length);
            }
          }
          while ((i == 0) && (right_rcd_ptr->prev != NULL));

          /* now advance one more to set pointer to correct location */
          if (right_rcd_ptr->next != NULL)
            right_rcd_ptr = right_rcd_ptr->next;
        }
        /* if no next right row, rewind to previous row */
        else
          right_rcd_ptr = right_rcd_ptr->prev;
      }
      /*
        If there is a next row in the left buffer, check to see
        if it matches the right row. If there is a match and the right
        buffer is not at start, rewind the right buffer to one previous
        to the current row.
      */
      else if (left_rcd_ptr->next != NULL)
      {
        if (right_rcd_ptr->prev != NULL)
        {
          i = memcmp(left_rcd_ptr->field_ptr, right_rcd_ptr->prev->field_ptr,
            left_rcd_ptr->field_length < right_rcd_ptr->prev->field_length ?
            left_rcd_ptr->field_length : right_rcd_ptr->prev->field_length);
        }
        if ((i == 0) && (right_rcd_ptr->prev != NULL))
          right_rcd_ptr = right_rcd_ptr->prev;
      }
    }
    /* if the left row is less than right row, rewind right buffer */
    else if (i < 0)
    {
      if (right_rcd_ptr->prev != NULL)
        right_rcd_ptr = right_rcd_ptr->prev;
    }
    /* if the right row is less than the left row, advance right row */
```

```
      else
      {
        if (right_rcd_ptr->next != NULL)
          right_rcd_ptr = right_rcd_ptr->next;
      }
    }
    /*
      Rows don't match so advance the right buffer and check match again.
      if they still match, rewind left buffer.
    */
    else
    {
      if (right_rcd_ptr->next != NULL)
      {
        i = memcmp(curr_left_prev->field_ptr, right_rcd_ptr->field_ptr,
          curr_left_prev->field_length < right_rcd_ptr->field_length ?
          curr_left_prev->field_length : right_rcd_ptr->field_length);
        if (i == 0)
          left_rcd_ptr = curr_left_prev;
      }
    }
    /* set buffer pointers to adjusted rows from buffers */
    left_record_buffer_ptr = left_rcd_ptr;
    right_record_buffer_ptr = right_rcd_ptr;
    DBUG_RETURN(0);
}
```

Now that you've had a close look at the source code for the DBXP query execution, it's time to compile the code and take it for a test ride.

Compiling and Testing the Code

If you haven't already done so, download the source code for this chapter and place the files in the /sql directory off the root of your source tree. Take a few moments to look through the source code so that you can be familiar with the methods. Taking the time to look through the code now will help should you need to debug the code to work with your configuration or if you want to add other enhancements or work the exercises. Once you have all of the source code files downloaded and have examined the code, you must add the files to your makefiles (in Linux) and project files (in Windows).

Tip See Chapter 11 for details on how to add the source files to the projects and compile.

Once you have the new code installed and compiled, you can run the server and perform the tests. You can run the test you created earlier, or you can enter the commands in a MySQL client utility. Listing 12-27 shows the expected output of running the commands listed in the test.

Listing 12-27. *Example Test Runs*

```
mysql> SELECT DBXP first_name, last_name, sex, id FROM staff;
```

```
+------------+------------+------+-----------+
| first_name | last_name  | sex  | id        |
+------------+------------+------+-----------+
| Bill       | Smith      | M    | 333445555 |
| William    | Walters    | M    | 123763153 |
| Alicia     | St.Cruz    | F    | 333444444 |
| Goy        | Hong       | F    | 921312388 |
| Rajesh     | Kardakarna | M    | 800122337 |
| Monty      | Smythe     | M    | 820123637 |
| Richard    | Jones      | M    | 830132335 |
| Edward     | Engles     | M    | 333445665 |
| Beware     | Borg       | F    | 123654321 |
| Wilma      | Maxima     | F    | 123456789 |
+------------+------------+------+-----------+
10 rows in set (0.01 sec)
```

```
mysql> SELECT DBXP id FROM staff;
```

```
+-----------+
| id        |
+-----------+
| 333445555 |
| 123763153 |
| 333444444 |
| 921312388 |
| 800122337 |
| 820123637 |
| 830132335 |
| 333445665 |
| 123654321 |
| 123456789 |
+-----------+
10 rows in set (0.00 sec)
```

```
mysql> SELECT DBXP dir_name FROM directorate;
```

```
+-----------------+
| dir_name        |
+-----------------+
| Development     |
| Human Resources |
| Management      |
+-----------------+
3 rows in set (0.00 sec)
```

```
mysql> SELECT DBXP id, dir_name FROM staff
mysql> JOIN directorate ON staff.mgr_id = directorate.dir_head_id;
```

```
+-----------+-----------------+
| id        | dir_name        |
+-----------+-----------------+
| 123763153 | Human Resources |
| 921312388 | Human Resources |
| 333445555 | Management      |
| 123654321 | Management      |
| 800122337 | Development     |
| 820123637 | Development     |
| 830132335 | Development     |
| 333445665 | Development     |
| 123456789 | Development     |
+-----------+-----------------+
9 rows in set (0.01 sec)
```

```
mysql> SELECT DBXP * FROM staff WHERE staff.id = '123456789';
```

```
+-----------+------------+----------+-----------+------+--------+-----------+
| id        | first_name | mid_name | last_name | sex  | salary | mgr_id    |
+-----------+------------+----------+-----------+------+--------+-----------+
| 123456789 | Wilma      | N        | Maxima    | F    | 43000  | 333445555 |
+-----------+------------+----------+-----------+------+--------+-----------+
1 row in set (0.00 sec)
```

```
mysql> SELECT DBXP first_name, last_name FROM staff JOIN directorate
WHERE staff.mgr_id = directorate.dir_head_id and directorate.dir_code = 'N41';
```

```
+------------+-------------+
| first_name | last_name   |
+------------+-------------+
| Rajesh     | Kardakarna  |
| Monty      | Smythe      |
| Richard    | Jones       |
| Edward     | Engles      |
| Wilma      | Maxima      |
+------------+-------------+
5 rows in set (0.01 sec)
```

```
mysql> SELECT DBXP * FROM directorate
mysql> JOIN building ON directorate.dir_code = building.dir_code;
```

```
+----------+-----------------+-------------+----------+----------+
| dir_code | dir_name        | dir_head_id | dir_code | building |
+----------+-----------------+-------------+----------+----------+
| M00      | Management      | 333444444   | M00      | 1000     |
| N01      | Human Resources | 123654321   | N01      | 1453     |
| N41      | Development     | 333445555   | N41      | 1300     |
| N41      | Development     | 333445555   | N41      | 1301     |
| N41      | Development     | 333445555   | N41      | 1305     |
+----------+-----------------+-------------+----------+----------+
5 rows in set (0.01 sec)
```

```
mysql> SELECT DBXP directorate.dir_code, dir_name, building, dir_head_id
mysql> FROM directorate JOIN building
mysql> ON directorate.dir_code = building.dir_code;
```

```
+----------+-----------------+----------+-------------+
| dir_code | dir_name        | building | dir_head_id |
+----------+-----------------+----------+-------------+
| M00      | Management      | 1000     | 333444444   |
| N01      | Human Resources | 1453     | 123654321   |
| N41      | Development     | 1300     | 333445555   |
| N41      | Development     | 1301     | 333445555   |
| N41      | Development     | 1305     | 333445555   |
+----------+-----------------+----------+-------------+
5 rows in set (0.01 sec)
```

```
mysql>
```

Summary

I presented in this chapter the internal database query execution operations. You learned how to expand the concept of the query tree to incorporate a query execution engine that uses the tree structure in the execution process. The knowledge of these technologies should provide you with a greater understanding of the DBXP engine and how it can be used to study database technologies in more depth.

You've reached the end of the book and may be wondering what else there is to do. This part of the book has provided you with an experimental engine based in MySQL that will allow you to explore your own implementation of the internal database technologies. Best of all, you can tweak the DBXP code any way you wish. Perhaps you just want to experiment, but you may also want to implement the union and intersect operations, or just expand the DBXP engine to implement the full set of query features in MySQL. Whatever you choose to do with what you have learned from this section of the book, you can always amaze your friends and coworkers by implementing an alternative query engine for MySQL!

Exercises

The following lists several areas for further exploration. They represent the types of activities you might want to conduct as experiments (or as a class assignment) to explore relational database technologies.

1. Complete the code for the `do_join()` method to support all of the join types supported in MySQL. Hint: You need to be able to identify the type of join before you begin optimization. Look to the parser for details.

2. Examine the code for the `check_rewind()` method in the `Query_tree` class. Change the implementation to use temporary tables to avoid high memory usage when joining large tables.

3. Evaluate the performance of the DBXP query engine. Run multiple test runs and record execution times. Compare these results to the same queries using the native MySQL query engine. How does the DBXP engine compare to MySQL?

4. Why is the remove duplicates operation not necessary for the intersect operation? Are there any conditions where this is false? If so, what are they?

5. (advanced) MySQL does not currently support a cross-product or intersect operation (as defined by Date). Change the MySQL parser to recognize these new keywords and process queries like `SELECT * FROM A CROSS B` and `SELECT * FROM A INTERSECT B` and add these functions to the execution engine. Hint: See the `do_join()` method.

6. (advanced) Form a more complete list of test queries and examine the limitations of the DBXP engine. What modifications are necessary to broaden the capabilities of the DBXP engine?

Appendix

This appendix contains a consolidated list of the references used in this book, along with a description of the sample database used in the examples and some helpful hints on how to solve the chapter exercises for Chapters 10–12.

Bibliography

The following bibliography contains additional sources of interesting articles and papers. The bibliography is arranged by topic.

Database Theory

Belussi, A. , E. Bertino, and B. Catania. 1998. An Extended Algebra for Constraint Databases. *IEEE Transactions on Knowledge and Data Engineering* 10(5): 686–705.

Date, C. J. and H. Darwen. 2000. *Foundation for Future Database Systems: The Third Manifesto.* Reading, MA: Addison-Wesley.

Date, C. J. 2001. *The Database Relational Model: A Retrospective Review and Analysis.* Reading, MA: Addison-Wesley.

Elmasri, R. and S. B. Navathe. 2003. *Fundamentals of Database Systems*, 4th ed. Boston: Addison-Wesley.

Franklin, M. J. , B. T. Jonsson, and D. Kossmann. 1996. Performance Tradeoffs for Client-Server Query Processing. *Proceedings of the 1996 ACM SIGMOD International Conference on Management of Data*, Montreal, Canada, 149–160.

Gassner, P., G. M. Lohman, K. B. Schiefer, and Y. Wang. 1993. Query Optimization in the IBM DB2 Family. *Bulletin of the Technical Committee on Data Engineering* 16(4): 4–17.

Ioannidis, Y. E., R. T. Ng, K. Shim, and T. Sellis. 1997. Parametric Query Optimization. *VLDB Journal* 6:132–151.

Kossman, D. and K. Stocker. 2000. Iterative Dynamic Programming: A New Class of Query Optimization Algorithms. *ACM Transactions on Database Systems* 25(1): 43–82.

Lee, C., C. Shih, and Y. Chen. 2001. A Graph-Theoretic Model for Optimizing Queries Involving Methods. *VLDB Journal* 9: 327–343.

Selinger, P. G., M. M. Astraham, D. D. Chamberlin, R. A. Lories, and T. G. Price. 1979. Access Path Selection in a Relational Database Management System. *Proceedings of the ACM SIGMOD International Conference on the Management of Data*, Aberdeen, Scotland, 23–34.

Stonebraker, M., E. Wong, P. Kreps. 1976. The Design and Implementation of INGRES. *ACM Transactions on Database Systems* 1(3): 189–222.

Stonebraker, M. and J. L. Hellerstein. 1998. *Readings in Database Systems*, 3rd ed. San Mateo, CA: Morgan Kaufmann Publishers.

Tucker, A. B. 2004. *Computer Science Handbook*, 2nd ed. Boca Raton, FL: CRC Press.

Werne, B. 2001. *Inside the SQL Query Optimizer*. Progress Worldwide Exchange 2001, Washington, DC: www.peg.com/techpapers/2001Conf/.

General

Rosenberg, D., M. Stephens, and M. Collins-Cope. 2005. *Agile Development with ICONIX Process*. Berkeley, CA: Apress.

MySQL

Burgelman, R.A., A. S. Grove, and P. E. Meza. 2006. *Strategic Dynamics*. New York: McGraw-Hill.

Kruckenberg, M. and J. Pipes. 2005. *Pro MySQL*. Berkeley, CA: Apress.

Open Source

Paulson, J. W. 2004. An Empirical Study of Open-Source and Closed-Source Software Products. *IEEE Transactions on Software Engineering*, 30(5): 246–256.

Web Sites

www.opensource.org—Open Source Initiative (OSI)

http://dev.mysql.com—MySQL's Developer Zone

www.mysql.com/company/legal/licensing/opensource-license.html—MySQL Open Source License

www.gnu.org/licenses/gpl.html—The GNU General Public License

www.mysql.com/support/community_support.html—MySQL support options

www.bitkeeper.com—BitKeeper

www.activestate.com—ActivePerl for Windows

http://jeremy.zawodny.com/mysql/mytop—mytop for MySQL

www.gnu.org/software/diffutils/diffutils.html—Diffutils for Linux

www.gnu.org/software/patch/—patch (GNU Project)

www.gnu.org/software/gdb/documentation—GDB: The GNU Project Debugger

ftp://www.gnu.org/software/ddd—GNU Data Display Debugger

http://undo-software.com—Undo Software

http://forums.mysql.com—MySQL Forums

http://lists.mysql.com—MySQL Lists

http://gnuwin32.sourceforge.net/packages/bison.htm—Bison

www.dinosaur.compilertools.net—Lex and YACC

www.postgresql.org/—PostgreSQL

Sample Database

The following sample database is used in the later chapters of this text. Listing A-1 shows the SQL dump of the database.

Listing A-1. *Sample Database Create Statements*

```
-- MySQL dump 10.10
--
-- Host: localhost    Database: expert_mysql
-- ----------------------------------------------------------
-- Server version          5.1.9-beta-debug-DBXP 1.0

/*!40101 SET @OLD_CHARACTER_SET_CLIENT=@@CHARACTER_SET_CLIENT */;
/*!40101 SET @OLD_CHARACTER_SET_RESULTS=@@CHARACTER_SET_RESULTS */;
/*!40101 SET @OLD_COLLATION_CONNECTION=@@COLLATION_CONNECTION */;
/*!40101 SET NAMES utf8 */;
/*!40103 SET @OLD_TIME_ZONE=@@TIME_ZONE */;
/*!40103 SET TIME_ZONE='+00:00' */;
/*!40014 SET @OLD_UNIQUE_CHECKS=@@UNIQUE_CHECKS, UNIQUE_CHECKS=0 */;
/*!40014 SET @OLD_FOREIGN_KEY_CHECKS=@@FOREIGN_KEY_CHECKS, FOREIGN_KEY_CHECKS=0
*/;
/*!40101 SET @OLD_SQL_MODE=@@SQL_MODE, SQL_MODE='NO_AUTO_VALUE_ON_ZERO' */;
/*!40111 SET @OLD_SQL_NOTES=@@SQL_NOTES, SQL_NOTES=0 */;

CREATE DATABASE IF NOT EXISTS expert_mysql;

--
-- Table structure for table `expert_mysql`.`building`
--

DROP TABLE IF EXISTS `expert_mysql`.`building`;
CREATE TABLE `expert_mysql`.`building` (
  `dir_code` char(4) NOT NULL,
  `building` char(6) NOT NULL
) ENGINE=MyISAM DEFAULT CHARSET=latin1;

--
-- Dumping data for table `expert_mysql`.`building`
--


/*!40000 ALTER TABLE `expert_mysql`.`building` DISABLE KEYS */;
LOCK TABLES `expert_mysql`.`building` WRITE;
INSERT INTO `expert_mysql`.`building` VALUES
('N41','1300'),
('N01','1453'),
```

```
('M00','1000'),
('N41','1301'),
('N41','1305');
UNLOCK TABLES;
/*!40000 ALTER TABLE `expert_mysql`.`building` ENABLE KEYS */;


--
-- Table structure for table `expert_mysql`.`directorate`
--

DROP TABLE IF EXISTS `expert_mysql`.`directorate`;
CREATE TABLE `expert_mysql`.`directorate` (
  `dir_code` char(4) NOT NULL,
  `dir_name` char(30) DEFAULT NULL,
  `dir_head_id` char(9) DEFAULT NULL,
  PRIMARY KEY (`dir_code`)
) ENGINE=MyISAM DEFAULT CHARSET=latin1;


--
-- Dumping data for table `expert_mysql`.`directorate`
--


/*!40000 ALTER TABLE `expert_mysql`.`directorate` DISABLE KEYS */;
LOCK TABLES `expert_mysql`.`directorate` WRITE;
INSERT INTO `expert_mysql`.`directorate` VALUES
('N41','Development','333445555'),
('N01','Human Resources','123654321'),
('M00','Management','333444444');
UNLOCK TABLES;
/*!40000 ALTER TABLE `directorate` ENABLE KEYS */;


--
-- Table structure for table `expert_mysql`.`staff`
--

DROP TABLE IF EXISTS `expert_mysql`.`staff`;
CREATE TABLE `expert_mysql`.`staff` (
  `id` char(9) NOT NULL,
  `first_name` char(20) DEFAULT NULL,
  `mid_name` char(20) DEFAULT NULL,
  `last_name` char(30) DEFAULT NULL,
  `sex` char(1) DEFAULT NULL,
  `salary` int(11) DEFAULT NULL,
  `mgr_id` char(9) DEFAULT NULL,
  PRIMARY KEY (`id`)
) ENGINE=MyISAM DEFAULT CHARSET=latin1;
```

```
--
-- Dumping data for table `expert_mysql`.`staff`
--


/*!40000 ALTER TABLE `expert_mysql`.`staff` DISABLE KEYS */;
LOCK TABLES `expert_mysql`.`staff` WRITE;
INSERT INTO `expert_mysql`.`staff` VALUES
('333445555','John','Q','Smith','M',30000,'333444444'),
('123763153','William','E','Walters','M',25000,'123654321'),
('333444444','Alicia','F','St.Cruz','F',25000,NULL),
('921312388','Goy','X','Hong','F',40000,'123654321'),
('800122337','Rajesh','G','Kardakarna','M',38000,'333445555'),
('820123637','Monty','C','Smythe','M',38000,'333445555'),
('830132335','Richard','E','Jones','M',38000,'333445555'),
('333445665','Edward','E','Engles','M',25000,'333445555'),
('123654321','Beware','D','Borg','F',55000,'333444444'),
('123456789','Wilma','N','Maxima','F',43000,'333445555');
UNLOCK TABLES;
/*!40000 ALTER TABLE `expert_mysql`.`staff` ENABLE KEYS */;


--
-- Table structure for table `tasking`
--

DROP TABLE IF EXISTS `expert_mysql`.`tasking`;
CREATE TABLE `expert_mysql`.`tasking` (
  `id` char(9) NOT NULL,
  `project_number` char(9) NOT NULL,
  `hours_worked` double DEFAULT NULL
) ENGINE=MyISAM DEFAULT CHARSET=latin1;


--
-- Dumping data for table `tasking`
--


/*!40000 ALTER TABLE `tasking` DISABLE KEYS */;
LOCK TABLES `expert_mysql`.`tasking` WRITE;
INSERT INTO `expert_mysql`.`tasking` VALUES
('333445555','405',23),
('123763153','405',33.5),
('921312388','601',44),
('800122337','300',13),
('820123637','300',9.5),
('830132335','401',8.5),
('333445555','300',11),
```

```
('921312388','500',13),
('800122337','300',44),
('820123637','401',500.5),
('830132335','400',12),
('333445665','600',300.25),
('123654321','607',444.75),
('123456789','300',1000);
UNLOCK TABLES;
/*!40000 ALTER TABLE `expert_mysql`.`tasking` ENABLE KEYS */;
/*!40103 SET TIME_ZONE=@OLD_TIME_ZONE */;

/*!40101 SET SQL_MODE=@OLD_SQL_MODE */;
/*!40014 SET FOREIGN_KEY_CHECKS=@OLD_FOREIGN_KEY_CHECKS */;
/*!40014 SET UNIQUE_CHECKS=@OLD_UNIQUE_CHECKS */;
/*!40101 SET CHARACTER_SET_CLIENT=@OLD_CHARACTER_SET_CLIENT */;
/*!40101 SET CHARACTER_SET_RESULTS=@OLD_CHARACTER_SET_RESULTS */;
/*!40101 SET COLLATION_CONNECTION=@OLD_COLLATION_CONNECTION */;
/*!40111 SET SQL_NOTES=@OLD_SQL_NOTES */;
```

Chapter Exercise Notes

This section contains some hints and helpful direction for the exercises included in Chapters 10, 11, and 12. Some of the exercises are practical exercises whose solutions would be too long to include in an appendix. For those exercises that require programming to solve, I include some hints as to how to write the code for the solution. In other cases, I include additional information that should assist you in completing the exercise.

Chapter 10

The following questions are from Chapter 10.

Question 1. The query in Figure 10-1 exposes a design flaw in one of the tables. What is it? Does the flaw violate any of the normal forms? If so, which one?

Look at the semester attribute. How many values does the data represent? Packing data like this makes for some poor-performing queries if you need to access part of the attribute (or field). For example, to query for all of the semesters in 2001, you would have to use a WHERE clause and use the LIKE operator: WHERE semester LIKE '%2001'. This practice of packing fields (also called multivalued fields) violates first normal form.

Question 2. Explore the TABLE structure and change the SELECT DBXP stub to return information about the table and its fields.

Change the code to return information like we did in Chapter 8 when we explored the show_disk_usage_command() method. This time, however, include the metadata about the table. Hint: See the table class.

Question 3. Change the EXPLAIN SELECT DBXP command to produce an output similar to the MySQL EXPLAIN SELECT command.

Change the code to produce the information in a table like that of the MySQL EXPLAIN command. Note that you will need additional methods in the Query_tree class to gather information about the optimized query.

Question 4. Modify the build_query_tree function to identify and process the LIMIT clause.

The changes to the code require you to identify when a query has the LIMIT clause and to abbreviate the results accordingly. Hint: Here is the code to capture the value of the LIMIT clause. You'll need to modify the code in the DBXP_select_command() method to handle the rest of the operation.

```
SELECT_LEX_UNIT *unit= &lex->unit;
unit->set_limit(unit->global_parameters);
```

Question 5. How can the query tree query_node structure be changed to accommodate HAVING, GROUP BY, and ORDER clauses?

The best design is one that stays true to the query tree concept. That is, consider a design where each of these clauses is a separate node in the tree. Consider also if there are any heuristics that may apply to these operations. Hint: Would it not be more efficient to process the HAVING clause nearest the leaf nodes? Lastly, consider rules that govern how many of each of these nodes can exist in the tree.

Chapter 11

The following questions are from Chapter 11.

Question 1. Complete the code for the balance_joins() method. Hint: You will need to create an algorithm that can move conjunctive joins around so that the join that is most restrictive is executed first (is lowest in the tree).

This exercise is all about how to move joins around in the tree to push the most restrictive joins down. The tricky part is using the statistics of the tables to determine which joins will produce the fewest results. Look to the handler and table classes for information about accessing this data. Beyond that, you will need helper methods to traverse the tree and get information about the tables. This is necessary because it is possible (and likely) that the joins will be higher in the tree and may not contain direct reference to the table.

Question 2. Complete the code for the cost_optimization() method. Hint: You will need to walk the tree and indicate nodes that can use indexes.

This exercise requires you to interrogate the handler and table classes to determine which tables have indexes and what those columns are.

Question 3. Examine the code for the heuristic optimizer. Does it cover all possible queries? If not, are there any other rules that can be used to complete the coverage?

You should discover that there are many such heuristics and that this optimizer covers only the most effective of the heuristics. For example, you could implement heuristics that take into account the GROUP BY and HAVING operations, creating methods similar to how I implemented the heuristics for project and restrict.

Question 4. Examine the code for the query tree and heuristic optimizer. How can you implement the distinct node type as listed in the query tree class? Hint: See the code that follows the prune_tree() method in the heuristic_optimization() method.

Most of the hints for this exercise are in the sample code. The excerpt that follows shows how you can identify when a DISTINCT option is specified on the query.

Question 5. How can you change the code to recognize invalid queries? What are the conditions that determine a query is invalid and how would you test for them?

Part of the solution for this exercise is done for you. For example, a query statement that is syntactically incorrect will be detected by the parser and an appropriate error displayed. However, for those queries that are syntactically correct but semantically meaningless, you will need to add additional error handling code to detect any anomalies. For example, try a query that is syntactically correct but references the wrong fields for the table. Create tests of this nature and trace (or debug) the code. You should see places in the code where additional error handling can be placed. Lastly, you could also create a method in the Query_tree class that validates the query tree itself. This could be particularly handy if you attempt to create additional node types or implement other heuristic methods.

Question 6. (advanced) MySQL does not currently support the intersect operation (as defined by Date). Change the MySQL parser to recognize the new keyword and process queries like SELECT * FROM A INTERSECT B. Are there any limitations of this operation and are they reflected in the optimizer?

What sounds like a very difficult problem has a very straightforward solution. Consider adding a new node type named intersect that has two children. The operation merely returns those rows that are in both tables. Hint: Use one of the many merge sort variants to accomplish this.

Question 7. (advanced) How would you implement the GROUP BY, ORDER BY, and HAVING clauses? Make the changes to the optimizer to enable these clauses.

There are many ways to accomplish this. In keeping with the design of the Query_tree class, each of these operations can be represented as another node type. You can build a method to handle each of these, just as we did with restrict, project, and join. Note, however, that the HAVING clause is used with the GROUP BY clause and the ORDER BY clause is usually processed last.

Chapter 12

The following questions are from Chapter 12.

Question 1. Complete the code for the do_join() method to support all of the join types supported in MySQL. Hint: You need to be able to identify the type of join before you begin optimization. Look to the parser for details.

To complete this exercise, you may want to restructure the code in the do_join() method. The example I used keeps all of the code together, but a more elegant solution would be one where the select-case statement in the do_join() method called helper methods for each type of join and possibly other helper methods for common operations (i.e., see the preempt_pipeline code). The code for the other forms of joins is going to be very similar to the join implemented in the example code.

Question 2. Examine the code for the check_rewind() method in the Query_tree class. Change the implementation to use temporary tables to avoid high memory usage when joining large tables.

This exercise also has a straightforward solution. See the MySQL code in the sql_select.cc file for details on how to create a temporary table. Hint: It's very much the same as create table and insert. You could also use the base Spartan classes and create a temporary table that stores the record buffers.

Question 3. Evaluate the performance of the DBXP query engine. Run multiple test runs and record execution times. Compare these results to the same queries using the native MySQL query engine. How does the DBXP engine compare to MySQL?

There are many ways to record execution time. You could use a simple stopwatch and record the time based on observation or you could add code that captures the system time. This latter method is perhaps the quickest and most reliable way to determine relative speed. I use the term *relative* because many factors concerning the environment and what is running at the time of the execution could affect performance. When you conduct your test runs, be sure to use multiple test runs and perform statistical analysis on the results. This will give you a normalized set of data to compare.

Question 4. Why is the remove duplicates operation not necessary for the intersect operation? Are there any conditions where this is false? If so, what are they?

Let's consider what an intersect operation is. It is simply the rows that appear in each of the tables involved (you can intersect on more than two tables). Duplicates in this case are not possible if the tables themselves do not have duplicates. However, if the tables are the result of operations performed in the tree below and have not had the duplicates removed and the distinct operation is included in the query, you will need to remove duplicates. Basically, this is an "it depends" answer.

Question 5. (advanced) MySQL does not currently support a cross-product or intersect operation (as defined by Date). Change the MySQL parser to recognize these new keywords and process queries like SELECT * FROM A CROSS B and SELECT * FROM A INTERSECT B and add these functions to the execution engine. Hint: See the do_join() method.

The files you need to change are the same files we changed when adding the DBXP keyword. These include lex.h and sql_yacc.yy. You may need to extend the sql_lex structure to include provisions for recording the operation type.

Question 6. (advanced) Form a more complete list of test queries and examine the limitations of the DBXP engine. What modifications are necessary to broaden the capabilities of the DBXP engine?

First, the query tree should be expanded to include the HAVING, GROUP BY, and ORDER BY clauses. You should also consider adding the capabilities for processing aggregate functions. These aggregate functions (e.g., max(), min(), etc.) could be fit into the Expression class and new methods created to parse and evaluate the aggregate functions.

Index

Printed in the United States
By Bookmasters

Printed in the United States
By Bookmasters